Android Apps for Absolute Beginners

Covering Android 7

Fourth Edition

Wallace Jackson

Apress®

Android Apps for Absolute Beginners: Covering Android 7

Wallace Jackson
Lompoc, California, USA

ISBN-13 (pbk): 978-1-4842-2267-6   ISBN-13 (electronic): 978-1-4842-2268-3
DOI 10.1007/978-1-4842-2268-3

Library of Congress Control Number: 2017934892

Managing Director: Welmoed Spahr
Editorial Director: Todd Green
Acquisitions Editor: Steve Anglin
Development Editor: Matthew Moodie
Technical Reviewer: Chaim Krause
Coordinating Editor: Mark Powers
Copy Editor: Karen Jameson
Compositor: SPi Global
Indexer: SPi Global
Artist: SPi Global

Distributed to the book trade worldwide by Springer Science+Business Media New York, 233 Spring Street, 6th Floor, New York, NY 10013. Phone 1-800-SPRINGER, fax (201) 348-4505, e-mail orders-ny@springer-sbm.com, or visit www.springeronline.com. Apress Media, LLC is a California LLC and the sole member (owner) is Springer Science + Business Media Finance Inc (SSBM Finance Inc). SSBM Finance Inc is a **Delaware** corporation.

For information on translations, please e-mail rights@apress.com, or visit http://www.apress.com/rights-permissions.

Apress titles may be purchased in bulk for academic, corporate, or promotional use. eBook versions and licenses are also available for most titles. For more information, reference our Print and eBook Bulk Sales web page at http://www.apress.com/bulk-sales.

Any source code or other supplementary material referenced by the author in this book is available to readers on GitHub via the book's product page, located at www.apress.com/9781484222676. For more detailed information, please visit www.apress.com/source-code.

Printed on acid-free paper

This Android Apps for Absolute Beginners book is dedicated to everyone in the open source community who is working so diligently to make professional application development software and media content development tools freely available to multimedia application developers to utilize to achieve creative dreams and financial goals. Last, but not least, I dedicate this book to my father, Parker Jackson, my family, my life-long friends, and content production ranch neighbors, for their constant help, assistance, and those stimulating, late night BBQs.

Contents at a Glance

Contents

About the Author

Wallace Jackson has been writing for leading multimedia publications about his work process for interactive new media content development since the advent of *Multimedia Producer Magazine* nearly two decades ago, when he wrote about advanced computer processor architecture for a special issue centerfold (removable "mini-issue" insert) distributed at the SIGGRAPH trade show. Since then, Wallace has written for a significant number of other popular publications about his work in interactive 3D and new media advertising campaign design, including *3D Artist Magazine*, *Desktop Publishers Journal*, *Cross Media Magazine*, *AV Video and Multimedia Producer Magazine*, *Digital Signage Magazine,* and *Kiosk Magazine*.

Wallace Jackson has authored more than half a dozen Android Development book titles for Apress, including several titles in the popular *Pro Android* series. This particular *Android Apps for Absolute Beginners* title has been rewritten entirely from scratch four times, and this fourth edition is one of the most thorough and comprehensive Absolute Beginner Android titles to be found in the market.

Wallace is currently the CEO of **Mind Taffy Design**, a new media content production and digital campaign design and development agency located in North Santa Barbara County, halfway between clientele in Silicon Valley to the north and in Hollywood, "The OC," and San Diego to the south. Mind Taffy also produces interactive 3D content for major brands around the world from their content production studio on Point Concepcion Peninsula in the California Central Coast area. Mind Taffy Design has created open source technology (HTML5, Java, and Android) and digital new media content deliverables for more than a quarter century (since 1991) for a large number of the top-branded manufacturers in the world, including Sony, Samsung, IBM, Epson, Nokia, TEAC, Sun, SGI, Dell, Compaq, ViewSonic, Western Digital, CTX International, KDS USA, KFC, ADI, and Mitsubishi.

Wallace received his undergraduate degree in Business Economics from the University of California at Los Angeles (UCLA) and his graduate degree in MIS Design and Implementation from the University of Southern California (USC). His postgraduate degree from USC is in Marketing Strategy. He also completed the USC Graduate Entrepreneurship Program at USC's popular Marshall School of Business MBA program. You can connect with Wallace at: `http://www.linkedin.com/wallacejackson` and follow him on Twitter `@wallacejackson` if you like, or visit the iTVset.com or iTVclock.com websites to see his i3D HD and UHD work.

About the Technical Reviewer

Chaim Krause presently lives in Leavenworth, Kansas, where the U.S. Army employs him as a Simulation Specialist. In his spare time he likes to play PC games and occasionally develops his own. He has recently taken up the sport of golf to spend more time with his significant other, Ivana. Although he holds a BA in Political Science from the University of Chicago, Chaim is an autodidact when it comes to computers, programming, and electronics. He wrote his first computer game in BASIC on a Tandy Model I Level I and stored the program on a cassette tape. Amateur radio introduced him to electronics while the Arduino and the Raspberry Pi provided a medium to combine computing, programming, and electronics into one hobby.

Acknowledgments

I would like to acknowledge all my fantastic editors and the support staff at Apress who worked long hours and toiled so very hard on this book to make it the ultimate *Absolute Beginner* Android title.

Matthew Moodie, for his work as the Lead Editor on the book, and for his experience and guidance in the process of making this book one of the great Android Absolute Beginner development titles.

Mark Powers, for his work as the Coordinating Editor on the book, and for his constant diligence in making sure I hit or surpassed my deadlines.

Chaim Krause, for his work as the Technical Reviewer on the book, and for making sure I didn't make any programming mistakes. Java code with mistakes does not run properly, if at all, unless they are very lucky mistakes, which is quite rare in computer programming these days.

Frank Serafine, my close friend, the world's finest and most respected sound designer, and popular rock musician, for contributing the background audio sample used in this book. This audio sample is from his stellar (no pun intended) work on some of the world's most popular science fiction as well as action adventure movies and television shows, including but not limited to *Star Trek* and *Hunt for Red October*.

Finally, I'd like to acknowledge **Oracle** for acquiring Sun Microsystems, and for continuing to enhance Java so that it remains the premiere open source programming language; and **Google**, for making Android the premiere open source operating system, and for acquiring ON2's VP8 and VP9 video codecs (WebM) and making these available to multimedia producers on the Android OS and HTML5 platforms, allowing open source video encoding performance similar to HEVC (H.265).

Introduction

The Android OS is currently the most popular operating system in the world. The Android OS runs on everything from smartwatches to HD or UHD smartphones to touchscreen tablets to e-book readers to game consoles to smartglasses to smartwatches to auto dashboards to new ultra-high definition interactive television sets (or iTV sets). If you want your apps to run everywhere, Android is the optimal solution.

There are even more types of consumer electronics devices, such as those found in the automotive, home appliance, security, robotics, drones, photography, industrial, and home automation markets, which are adopting the open source Android OS as their platform as time goes on. This book will show you how to develop applications for these new device-type verticals as they emerge into the market.

Since there are literally billions of Android consumer electronics devices owned by billions of people all over the world, it stands to reason that developing great Android applications for all these people might be an extremely lucrative undertaking, assuming that you have the right concept and design.

This book will help you go a long way toward learning how to develop Android applications that will run across the plethora of Android-compatible consumer electronics devices; and across all popular versions of the Android OS, including 32-bit Android 4.4 OS and the 64-bit Android 5, 6, and 7 OSes.

Developing an Android application that works well across all of these types of consumer electronics devices requires a very specific work process if you are an Absolute Beginner, involving leveraging all the Android Studio helper features, which I cover during this book. I had to write *Android Apps for Absolute Beginners, Fourth Edition*, from scratch because most of Android Studio 2.3's new features are targeted at Absolute Beginners. This book is intended for readers who are Absolute Beginners to Android development. Of course you must be technically savvy, but this book is for readers who are not yet familiar with computer programming concepts and techniques.

The book will be more advanced than previous editions of *Android Apps for Absolute Beginners*. The first edition of this book was a mere 300 pages, as Android 1.5 was the first version to appear on Android hardware devices (smartphones), and a second edition of this book was 33% longer, at 400 pages. I've expanded this version of the book even more.

I designed this book to be a more comprehensive overview of the Android application development work process than most beginning Android application development books, because, at this point, there is really no way to sugarcoat the Android application development process. The new Android Studio IDE is however attempting to help beginners code and design applications using some helper features and drag-and-drop visual design editors that we will cover in detail in the book.

To become the leading Android 7 application developer that you seek to become, you will have to understand, as well as master, XML markup, user interface design, Java 8 programming, as well as new media content creation. Once you have done this, hopefully by the end of this book, you will be able to create the vanguard user experience required to create popular, best-selling Android 7 apps.

Android apps used to be developed for 32-bit Android 1.x through 4.x using Eclipse ADT's IDE. Starting with 64-bit Android 5, Eclipse ADT IDE was replaced with Android Studio. Android applications are not developed via Android Studio alone (currently at version 2.3), but are also developed in conjunction with several key genres (2D, SVG, i3D, audio, video, imaging, SFX, etc.) of new media content development software packages.

For this reason, this book covers a wide variety of popular open source software packages, including GIMP 2.8.18, Planetside Terragen 4, Sorenson Squeeze Pro 11, and Audacity 2.1. These professional new media content production tools should be utilized in conjunction with developing your Android 7 applications. This book will show you exactly how to accomplish this, as well as how to download, install, update, configure, and actually use a number of the popular open source software packages.

This comprehensive Android 4/7 application development work process will allow you to experience exactly how the use of all of these multimedia content development software packages needs to fit into your overall Android application development work process. This 100% comprehensive "soup to nuts" multimedia-centric Android app development approach sets this 32-bit Android 4.4 and 64-bit Android 5/6/7 book title distinctly apart from all of the other Android application development titles that are currently on the market. This book covers an Android development process at a broad level while at the same time showing the Absolute Beginner Android application developer how to use an Android Studio handholding approach, by leveraging Android Studio's ability to code bootstrap application projects allowing you to simply add your application specifics, use pop-up Java and XML code helper dialogs, use code completion, utilize a new Visual Design Editor, and implement backward compatibility features.

Chapter 1 starts at the absolute ground level, explaining what Android is, where it came from, what it is used for, where it is going, what its benefits include, what is covered in this book, as well as what is not covered in this book, as well as what some of the new features in Android 7.1.1 (called Nougat) include.

Chapter 2 covers how to assemble your Android Studio 2.3 application development workstation from scratch. This starts by covering hardware requirements and considerations, and then downloading and installing the current Java SE 8 JDK and Android Studio 2.3, along with more than half a dozen powerful open source content development applications, including Fusion, Audacity, Inkscape, Blender, GIMP, Lightscape, Open Office, and more.

Chapter 3 gives you an overview of how the Android Studio IDE, Java 8, XML, multimedia assets, and Android hardware devices are used together to create Android applications. You will be exploring the Android Studio 2.3 IDE, and learn how to have Android Studio create an application Java code and XML markup infrastructure for you to use to create your Android 7.1.1 application with. You will examine an Android Project structure and hierarchy, to see how everything comes together, and will learn about the project resource folder hierarchy and new media formats and genres that are supported in Android, of which there are many. You will learn about Android Drawables, Animation, and Menu capabilities, and how to pre-define data, constants, user interface design, and multimedia assets for your applications by using XML markup. You will learn how to update your Android Studio 2.3 IDE, so you can keep your Android development workstation current, as new versions are released.

Chapter 4 teaches you all about the XML markup language, including how to use the new Android Studio Visual Design Editor to generate entire XML markup code listings that define complex user interface design. We will dissect what XML parent and child tags are used for in UI layout containers and how to create functional UI elements in a UI design using widgets. You will also look at how XML can be used to define your application constants (fixed settings, UI designs, themes, and assets that will not change during your application's usage). We will do all of this while expanding on the Hello World application that you created in Chapter 3, by adding 2D graphics and a user interface design to make the application more professional, and show you how to add appeal to your bootstrap Android 7.1.1 app.

Chapter 5 serves as a Java 8 primer for those not yet exposed to Java 8, and as a review for those who have been exposed to Java 8 before. You learn all about the Java 8 SE programming language, including packages, classes, methods, constants, variables, interfaces, modifiers, keywords, versions, objects, and OOP concepts and techniques. All of this is additionally demonstrated using a sample Java code project and its structures. Thus, the first third of this Android 7.1.1 book is foundational material, which explains how the Android 7 OS works together as a whole, as well as how each of these components works in and of itself. You will build on this learning material throughout the remainder of the book.

Chapters 6 explores user interface design concepts, techniques, and workflows for Android Studio 2.3 – specifically your Visual Design Editor usage, and the Android `View`, `ViewGroup`, and `Activity` classes, which user interface design code, UI layout containers, and UI elements (called widgets) come from. You learn how `View` and `ViewGroup` subclasses are used to create UI layout containers filled with UI widgets, and how an `Activity` screen hosts and displays these, and all about the `Activity` class life cycle, and how these organize the application Java 8 code into logical phases (create, start, pause, resume, stop, destroy). You create a user interface design from scratch, for the project you created in Chapters 3 and 4, including graphics (`Drawable` objects) assets, UI design elements, and Android 7 OS themes.

Chapter 7 takes your static application, and makes it interactive, by using Android 7 `Intent` objects and coding Java event handling and event listening constructs for user interface elements defined using XML. This is where the book starts to get more complicated, both conceptually, with real-time event queue processing and application component communication using Intent objects, as well as Java 8 code-wise, with deeply nested event processing structures, explicit Intent objects, and implicit Intent Filter concepts. You will learn about the Android `Intent` class and objects and about what operating system events do to allow applications to know what is going on in the operating environment and what users are doing with the hardware and with user interface designs (covered during Chapter 6).

Chapter 8 examines Pure Android UI design patterns. These are guidelines for making your Android applications look and feel like they belong on the popular Android platform. This chapter covers the new Material Design paradigm, introduced in 64-bit Android 5, and advanced concepts such as i3D UI design, real-time automated shadowing, and animated user interface design concepts. We cover different types of hardware devices that run Android OS, and the different types of Android APIs, such as the core API for smartphones and tablets; the Wear 2.0 API, for smartwatches; the Glass API, for smartglasses; the Auto API, for automobile dashboards; and the Android TV API, for iTV Sets. I show you how to have Android Studio create one of these design paradigms, the sliding drawer UI design, for you, and how to examine the XML and Java code to understand how it works under the hood. We then test and configure this application using an AVD emulator and an Android manifest XML definition file.

Chapters 9 delves into the concepts and work process of Digital Imaging for Android, including how to create NinePatch drawables; how to use GIMP 2.8.18 to create image assets; Android `Drawable` classes; supported digital image formats; and digital image concepts such as pixels, resolution, alpha channels, aspect ratio, color depth, dithering, compositing, blending modes, anti-aliasing, and similar concepts that are supported across Android's advanced digital image compositing, rendering, and Porter-Duff blending and transfer (compositing) algorithms. I show you how to have Android Studio 2.3 create a navigation drawer UI design pattern for you, and how to create multi-state image buttons.

Chapter 10 brings your application into the fourth dimension using 2D animation engines in Android such as the frame (bitmap) `AnimationDrawable` class and the tween (vector) `Animation` class. This chapter outlines the necessary animation concepts, data formats, and classes, and shows you how to create frame (or bitmap) animation, tween (vector, or procedural) animation, and a hybrid (frame and procedural combined) animation. We also add these animation assets to the `NavDrawerPattern` project that you created in Chapter 9, to show how different animation approaches will work inside of one of the five different pure Android design patterns you'll create during the course of this book.

Chapter 11 shows you how to stream Digital Video content to your Android application by using the `Uri`, `MediaPlayer`, and `MediaController` classes. This chapter goes into detail regarding digital video concepts, formats, and data footprint optimization, and also shows you how to create a 3D digital video asset from scratch, using Planetside Software's Terragen 4 and Sorenson Squeeze Desktop Pro 11. You'll code a `DigitalVideoMedia` project using yet another Android design pattern (`FullscreenActivity`) and address how to code a captive (part of the APK) video, and a streaming (from an external server) video asset.

Chapter 12 gets your Android hardware device's speakers involved by adding digital audio assets to your application, using the powerful Android SoundPool class. This chapter goes into detail regarding digital audio concepts, formats, and data footprint optimization, and also shows you how to optimize a digital audio asset from scratch, using open source Audacity 2.1.2. You'll code a fourth, DigitalAudioSequencer project, using yet another pure Android design pattern (ScrollingActivity) and you'll code a children's educational application that teaches kids the sounds that different animals make.

Chapter 13 offloads processing-intensive tasks to Android OS for background processing. You'll learn about advanced operating system processing concepts like threads, processes, and services, which are used to perform background processing using the Android Service or Thread class. We'll add this capability to the DigitalAudioSequencer application you created in Chapter 12 so it can play ambient background audio as a Service process, using the Android MediaPlayer operated by the Service class.

Chapter 14 looks into the Android SQLite database management system, as well as Android ContentProvider, ContentResolver, and ContentValues classes. You will learn about RDBMS database theory and how to use Android content providers to access databases.

Whereas the first five chapters of the book are foundational information, in the final five chapters of this book, you will learn about some of the more advanced development topics that normally would not be included in an Absolute Beginner title. I included these so that the important topics regarding leading-edge Android application development are all in this one, single, unified book. The included advanced topics include 2D animation, digital video, digital audio, threads, processes, and SQLite databases.

This book attempts to be the most comprehensive Absolute Beginners book for Android application development out there, by covering most, if not all of, the significant Android Studio 2.3 application development assistance features, and those core Android classes that will always need to be used to create leading-edge, 32-bit Android 4.4.4, or 64-bit Android 5.0 through 7.1.1, software applications.

It is the intention of this book to take you from being an "Absolute Beginner" in Android application development, to having a comprehensive, solid, intermediate knowledge of both 32-bit Android 4.4 and 64-bit Android 7.1.1 application development.

You should be advised that this book contains a significant amount of technical knowledge and work processes that may take more than one read-through to assimilate into your application development knowledge base (your current Android knowledge "quiver of arrows," so to speak). This vast journey developing backwardly compatible applications for 32-bit Android 4.0 (API Level 15) through the 64-bit Android 7.1.1 (API Level 25, and later versions) will be well worth your time, however; rest assured.

An Introduction to Android 7.0 Nougat

These days, you will see Android OS powered devices of every size and shape everywhere you look. They can be worn on your person, thanks to Android WEAR; used in an appliance, thanks to Android TV; and they are a part of your car, thanks to Android AUTO. Android devices will provide you entertainment in your living room taking the form of your iTV set; help you learn at school using a tablet; inform you in bed using an e-book reader; or excite you on the couch using an Android game console, such as the OUYA, the Razer Forge, or the nVidia Shield.

In this chapter, we will explore some basic history regarding Google's Android operating system (OS), to give you a high-level overview of the history of Android. We will look at the benefits of learning Android application development, and which open source programming languages and OSs Android is based upon. We will look at the percentage distribution amongst the different Android versions, and the new features in Android 7.0 Nougat.

The History of the Android OS: An Impressive Growth

The Android OS was originally created by **Andy Rubin** to be an OS for mobile phones. This happened around the dawn of the 21st century. In July of 2005, Google acquired Android and made Andy Rubin the Senior Vice President of Mobile Platforms for Google, where he remained until November of 2014. Many feel this acquisition of Android OS by Google was largely in response to the appearance of Apple's iPhone around that same time. However, there were enough other large players, such as RIM Blackberry, Nokia Symbian, and Microsoft Windows Mobile, that it was deemed to be a savvy business decision for Google to purchase the engineering talent of Android Incorporated along with its Android OS intellectual property. This allowed Google to insert their Internet search engine company into the emerging mobile market, which many now refer to as **Internet 2.0**.

© Wallace Jackson 2017

W. Jackson, *Android Apps for Absolute Beginners*, DOI 10.1007/978-1-4842-2268-3_1

Internet 2.0, or the **Mobile Internet**, allows users of consumer electronic products to access content via widely varied data networks, using portable consumer electronic devices. These currently include tablets, smartphones, phablets (a phone-tablet hybrid), game consoles, smartwatches, smartglasses, personal robots, drones, cameras, and e-book e-readers. These days, Android OS–based devices will also include those not-so-portable consumer electronics devices such as iTV sets, home media centers, automobile dashboards, automobile stereos, music players, home appliances, home control installations, and digital signage system set-top boxes.

This ever-growing Android phenomenon puts new media content such as games, 3D animation, interactive television, digital video, digital audio, e-books, and high-definition imagery into our lives at every turn. Android is one of those popular open source vehicles (others being HTML5 and JavaFX) that digital artists will increasingly leverage in order to be able to develop new media creations that their end users have never before experienced. Over the past decade, Android has matured and evolved, to become a stable, exceptionally reliable, embedded open source OS. An Android OS that started out with its initial version just a decade ago, once acquired by Google, has released stable OS versions 1.5, 1.6, 2.0, 2.1, 2.2, 2.37, 3.0, 3.1, 3.2, 3.3, 4.0, 4.1, 4.2, 4.3, 4.4, 5.0, 5.1, and 6.0.

As of the writing of this book, Android 7.1.1 is in beta, with a projected release in Q1 of 2017. Android 7.1.1 should show up in 64-bit Android devices in 2017 and 2018. If you want to see the latest statistics regarding each of the previous Android OS revisions, directly from the Android developer website, you should visit this URL:

`http://developer.android.com/about/dashboards/index.html`

Table 1-1 shows this progression of all the popular versions of Android OS that have been installed on popular embedded OS consumer electronics products over the past decade. I wanted to collect all of this Android OS information together into one single infographic for you, so that you could get a "bird's eye view" of the current historic progression of the Android OS. As you can see, there are certain Android market share "sweet spots." In case you're wondering what an **embedded OS** is, it's like having an entire personal computer on a motherboard that's small enough to fit in a handheld device, and which is powerful enough to run applications, or "apps."

Table 1-1. Released Android OS Versions, Their Internal OS Names, API Levels, and Current Market Share

VERSION	CODENAME	API LEVEL	MARKET SHARE
1.5	Cupcake	3	Less than 0.1%
1.6	Donut	4	Less than 0.1%
2.0, 2.1	Eclair	5, 6, 7	Less than 0.1%
2.2	Froyo	8	Less than 0.1%
2.3.7	Gingerbread	9, 10	2.0% (Kindle Fire)
3.0, 3.1, 3.2	Honeycomb	11, 12, 13	Less than 0.1%
4.0, 4.0.4	Ice Cream Sandwich	14, 15	1.0%
4.1.2	Jelly Bean	16	6.8%
4.2.2	Jelly Bean Plus	17	9.4%
4.3.1	Jelly Bean Plus	18	2.7%
4.4.4, 4.4W	Kit Kat	19, 20	31.6%
5.0	Lollipop	21	15.4%
5.1	Lollipop	22	20.0%
6.0	Marshmallow	23	10.1%
7.0 and 7.1.1	Nougat	24 and 25	Less than 0.1% (so far)

Just like today's personal computers and laptops, the Internet 2.0 devices, such as smartphones, tablets, e-readers, smartwatches, and iTV sets, now feature quad-core (4 CPU) and even octa-core (8 CPU) computer processing power, as well as two gigabytes of system memory. This is approaching the power of a modern-day PC, such as the workstation you are going to set up during the next chapter of this book, which you can get for $500 at Walmart. Mini-tower PCs feature octa-core 64-bit processors along with 6GB or 8GB of system memory, and a 750GB (or larger) hard disk drive with Windows 10, Fedora 24, or Ubuntu Mate 17.04.

The Android OS contains the power of a complete computer OS. It is based on the **Linux Kernel** open source platform, and Oracle (formerly Sun Microsystems) **Java 8 Standard Edition**, one of the world's most popular programming languages. Android 5 and 6 also use a 64-bit Linux Kernel, along with the Java 7 Standard Edition.

> **Note**   This term **open source** refers to software that has been developed collaboratively, usually by an **open community** of individuals, and is **freely available** for **commercial use** (or non-commercial use). Open source software also comes with all the **source code**, so that it can be further modified, if necessary. The Android OS is open source, though Google develops it internally before releasing the source code. From that point on, the source code is freely available for commercial use by software developers.

It's not uncommon for an Android device to have a 2.4GHz processor and 2GB of fast, computer-grade DDR3 memory. This rivals desktop computers of just a few years ago, and notebooks that are still currently available. You will continue to see this convergence of Internet 2.0 (mobile device) OSs with desktop OSs, such as we are seeing with Windows 10 and Windows Mobile, and with Chrome OS and Opera OS currently, as time goes on.

Once it became evident that Java, the Android OS, and open source software platforms were vanguard forces to be reckoned with, a bunch of the popular consumer electronics manufacturers, including Philips, Sony, HTC, Samsung, LG Electronics, and others, formed and then joined the **Open Handset Alliance** (**OHA**). This was all done in order to put the momentum behind Google's open source Android platform, and it worked! Today, hundreds of leading branded consumer electronics manufacturers leverage Android as an OS on their consumer electronic devices. In fact, Android OS is used more than any other OS that has ever existed on the planet.

This development of the OHA is a significant benefit to Android developers. Android allows developers to create their applications using a single IDE, or integrated development environment, and now this support by the OHA enables developers to deliver their content across dozens of major branded manufacturers' hardware products, as well as across several different types of consumer electronic devices, including smartphones, iTV sets, e-book readers, smartwatches, game consoles, home media centers, set-top boxes, and touchscreen tablets. The Android OS affords developers a plethora of powerful content delivery tools and device playback possibilities, to say the least! You have realized this, as you are reading this book right now, so you can get in on all this power!

In summary, Android is a seasoned OS that has become one of the biggest players in computing today, and with Google behind it. Android uses freely available open source technologies, such as the Linux Kernel, Java SE 8, and open standards such as XML, CSS3, MPEG-4, JPEG, PNG, MP3, OGG Vorbis, FLAC, SVG, WebM, WebP, OpenGL 3.2, WebKit, Vulkan, and HTML5. Android incorporates all of these open source resources, so that it can provide the free new media content and application delivery platform to Android developers, and an OS platform to consumer electronics manufacturers. Can you spell OPPORTUNITY? I sure can! It's spelled: **A-N-D-R-O-I-D**!

Advantage Android 7.0: How Can Android Benefit Me?

There are simply too many benefits for the Android OS development platform to ignore your Android applications development workflow, and environment, for even one minute longer. We are going to get you set up with all of the latest IDE's, new media apps, programming languages, and Android OS SDKs and components during the next chapter, so that you will have an extremely valuable Android 7.1.1 multimedia content development workstation.

That's great, but how can Android benefit me, you might be thinking? First of all, Android is based upon open source technology, and it's free for commercial development use, with no up-front costs and no on-going royalties. Android, at its inception, was not as refined as expensive paid technologies from Apple, Adobe, and Microsoft.

During the past several decades, open source software technology has become equally as sophisticated as conventional paid software technologies. You will see this during this book as you work with your professional-level Android Studio 2.3 (IntelliJ) IDEA and the new media content software that you'll be acquiring (for free) during the next chapter, when we put together an Android Studio content development workstation, 100% from scratch.

The increasing adoption of open source technology over paid software is clearly evident with Internet 2.0, as the majority of the consumer electronics manufacturers have chosen Android and HTML5, based on a Linux Kernel and using Java, JavaFX, and JavaScript, over Windows 10, Windows Mobile, iOS, and Macintosh OS/X OSes.

For this key reason, Android developers can develop applications not only for their smartphones, but also for new and emerging consumer electronics device ecosystems, which include never-before-seen products such as smartglasses and smartwatches, or UHD (4K, or IMAX) iTV sets, which are network compatible and available to connect to the Google Android (Play) Marketplace. The Android App Marketplace was rebranded by Google as Google Play, due to legal action brought by Apple Computer over what Google calls their Android application storefront.

The free nature of open source translates directly to more sales of more consumer electronics devices in more areas of your potential customer's lives, and this offers steadily increasing Android market share, and an ever-increasing incentive to develop for the Android 7.1.1 OS over "closed" technologies such as Windows or iOS, and over less popular and less prolific PC OSes, such as OS/X, Open Solaris, and Linux distributions.

In addition to being free for commercial use, the Android OS has one of the largest, wealthiest, and most innovative companies in modern-day computing currently behind it: Google. Add in the OHA, and you have more than a trillion dollars of mega-brand companies behind you, supporting your app development efforts. It certainly seems too good to be true; however, it's a fact: if you're an Android developer (which you are about to be, in about a dozen or so chapters), then you now have a supreme hardware and software sales and support team behind your new media content development business.

Finally, and most important, it's much easier to get your Android applications **published** than it is with those other platforms that are similar to Android 7.1.1 (I won't mention names here, to protect the not-so-innocent). We all know we would rather spend our time on applications development than on trying to get our Android apps approved for sale!

We've all heard those horror stories regarding major development companies waiting months, and sometimes years, for their apps to be approved for other app marketplaces. These problems are nearly non-existent on the open source Android platform. Publishing an app in the Google Play store is as easy as paying $50, uploading your Android .apk file, and specifying whether you are offering a free or a paid download. Let's take a look at what we are going to cover during this book, and at what we are not going to be covering. Finally, we'll look at the new Android 7.0 "Nougat" operating system features, before we finish up with this first chapter.

The Scope of This Book

This book is an introduction to the core features and attributes of Android, and to the work process for developing applications for Android. The book is intended for absolute beginners; that is, people who have never created an application on the Android platform for a consumer electronic device. If you are already familiar with Android, then this book is not appropriate for you. I do not assume that readers know what Java is; or how XML works; or what styles or themes are; or what a codec, alpha channel, color depth, dithering, or a blending mode algorithm is.

All I know is that by the end of this book, you're going to appear as if you are speaking a foreign language when you start talking about new media Android application development in front of friends, family, and clientele, which ultimately will get you hired, and hopefully, well paid. Be advised that it will take far more than one book to learn the "ins and outs" of Android, so be sure to check out all of the other Android and Pro Android titles at http://www.apress.com.

What Is Covered in This Book

This book covers the basic and essential elements of Android application development, including but not limited to the following areas:

- The open source software development tools required to develop for the Android 7.x platform

- Where to get this free software development environment, as well as professional new media content creation tools that can be used in conjunction with the Android Studio 2.3 IDE

- How to properly install and configure the necessary tools for Android 7 application development, as well as for new media content creation tools that can be used with Android Studio 2.3

- Which third-party tools are useful to use in conjunction with the Android Studio 2.3 IDE

- Which OSs and platforms currently support development for Android using these tools

- The concepts and programming constructs for Java and XML, and their practical applications in creating Android applications

- How Android Studio 2.3 goes about setting up an Android application

- How Android OS defines Android application user interface (UI) components using the View class

- How Android OS controls UI component layout on the display screen using the ViewGroup class

- How Android can communicate with other Android applications using the Intent class

- How Android apps interface with content providers, datastores, resources, networks, and the Internet

- How Android alerts users to events that may be taking place, inside or outside of an Android app

- How Android applications are defined for publishing using the app's Android manifest XML file

- How Android applications can use threads for background processing using the Service class

It is important to know that Android OS has more than 250 Java packages, and that one book cannot introduce you to everything that is available to you in the Android 7.1.1 OS development environment. This Android development environment contains functionality that allows you to do just about anything imaginable, from putting a button on the display screen; to synthesizing speech; creating virtual reality or smart watch faces; leveraging interactive television set or auto dashboard features; or accessing advanced smartphone features, such as the high-resolution camera, Bluetooth communication, NFC, GPS, gyroscope, compass, or accelerometer. If you would like to review each of these Android packages for yourself, you can find them at the following URL for the Android developer website:

https://developer.android.com/reference/**packages.html**

> **Note**   A package in Java is a collection of programming utilities, or functions, that all have related (and interconnected) functionality. For example, the java.io package contains the utilities that deal with input and output (IO) to your program, such as reading the contents of a file, or saving data to a file. A later Java primer chapter describes how to organize your Java code into your own custom Android application packages.

Unlike this book, most Android books will specialize in a specific area of Android programming. For instance, my *Pro Android Wearables* (Apress, 2015) title focuses on SmartWatch application development, and my *Pro Android Graphics* (Apress, 2014) focuses on Android graphics pipeline design. We will be learning about APIs, or Application Programming Interfaces, in the chapter on Java. There is plenty of complexity in each Android API, which ultimately, from the developer's perspective, translates into incredible creative power. What is the price of this power, you might ask? Your valuable time spent mastering each API is the only price you will pay, as Android 7.x OS is otherwise free for commercial use.

What Is Not Covered in This Book

So then what is not covered in this book? What cool powerful capabilities do you have to look forward to in the next level book on Android programming? In a nutshell, anything that's not a core class or feature that Android apps are built upon. On the hardware side, we will not be looking at how to control the camera, access GPS data from the smartphone, or access the accelerometer, or the gyroscope, which allows the user to turn the smartphone around, or have the application react to the smartphone position. We will not be delving into advanced touchscreen concepts, such as gestures; accessing other device hardware, such as a microphone, Bluetooth, NFC, and Wi-Fi connections; or image compositing, which is covered in *Pro Android Graphics* (Apress, 2013).

On the software side, we will not be diving into creating your own Android MySQLite database structure, or real-time 3D rendering system (OpenGL ES 3.2 and Vulkan), although we will take a closer look at these areas in later chapters, so that you know how to utilize them, and how they fit into the overall Android 7.1.1 infrastructure. We will not be exploring speech synthesis and speech recognition, nor the universal language support that allows developers to create applications that display characters correctly in dozens of international languages and foreign character sets. We will not be getting into advanced programming such as game development, artificial intelligence, image compositing pipelines, blending modes, and physics simulations. We won't get into advanced user interface design concepts and techniques, such as the topics covered in my *Pro Android UI* (Apress, 2014) title or my *Learn Android App Development* (Apress, 2013) title that I wrote previously.

What's New in Android Nougat: Powerful New Features

In this section, I will go over some of the new features that will make Android 7 (Nougat) more attractive to both end users and developers alike. Even new end-user features can be considered "wins" for Android developers, because these new features serve to expand the majority market share currently enjoyed by Android OS. One of these new features even allows Android apps to run on Google Chrome OS, which runs on millions of ChromeBook, ChromePhone, and ChromeCast (iTV) products, greatly expanding the market for Android 7.x Nougat applications.

> **Note**   Android Version 7.1.1 Nougat is currently in beta development during the writing of this book, and should be released on devices at about the same time that this book is released to the public.

Since it expands Android onto netbooks, notebooks, laptops, and PCs, let's take a look at the **Custom Pointer API** first. This new API allows pointing devices (mice and cursors) to be used with Android devices such as iTV sets or personal computers, making Android more like a desktop operating system with context-sensitive cursor graphics for the pointer.

Android Apps for the Google Chrome OS: Custom Pointer API

Recent versions of the Google Chrome OS have a placeholder for an entry point into the Google Play store, which indicates that Google is going to make Android applications run under the Google Chrome OS. Part of this on the Android application development side is the Custom Pointer API, which will allow keyboard and mouse support for Google Chrome OS users, and could also help Android TV users to interface with their iTV Sets as well. Until iTV Set and PC Android support came into view recently, Android OS was primarily a touchscreen environment. However, Android has had some basic support for mice and keyboards for several years now. Mice will become more common with new Android devices such as iTV sets emerging, and Android 7.1.1 moves to support these with the addition of a new Custom Pointer API, which is available as of the developer previews (betas). The cursor can actually change to indicate different user interactions, just like a mouse pointer (cursor) does on your desktop PC or laptop.

The Custom Pointer API allows developers to customize the cursor (also called the pointer) visibility, appearance (icon used), and behavior. The capability of controlling the cursor appearance and visibility is especially useful when your users are using their mouse (or trackball or touchpad) to interact with objects in your application such as user interface components or game players or game pieces. The default pointer for the API will use the standard pointer icon for its appearance. The Custom Pointer API includes advanced functions that allow developers to change the pointer icon's appearance in real time based upon your user's mouse (or touchpad or trackball) movement. The Custom Pointer API allows your Android application cursor to function more like a traditional desktop computing cursor, which will change depending on what the application user is doing. For example, when you hover a cursor over a text field, the pointer icon will become an "insertion bar" text cursor. If you move the cursor over a link, the pointer will change to a pointing finger. If you drag objects the cursor will show an open hand pointer. If you hover over a resizable window border, the cursor will show the appropriate resize direction arrow. Developers can change pointer behavior in their apps by using this API, which is detailed on the Android developer website, which is located at:

https://**developer.android.com**/reference/android/view/**PointerIcon.html**

The implication of this Chrome OS to Android OS "bridge" is also important to Android developers, as it allows both of these rapidly growing platforms to fuel each other's growth. Chrome OS gives Android applications a new platform, with ChromeBook (laptops); ChromeCast (iTV sets); and possibly a Chrome PC, Chrome Phone, and Chrome SmartWatch in the future. In the other direction, Android applications will give Chrome OS a massive digital library of software that will eventually match up with the number of applications available for desktop OS leader Microsoft and their Windows 10 OS. What this may signify is that now that Google has won the mobile OS market, they're now going to go after the desktop OS market. Chrome OS is impressive, like most Linux distros, and brand-new ChromeBooks are priced to sell rapidly (in the United States they are $120 to $180, with quad-core CPUs).

Power and CPU Optimization: Sustained Performance Mode API

Google started focusing on Android device power consumption optimization via CPU and memory performance optimization back in Android 5.0, which I covered in my *Android Apps for Absolute Beginners Third Edition* (Apress, 2014). An even more advanced API dedicated to power saving and battery life optimization is in Android 7 Nougat. It is called the Sustained Performance Mode API, and gives developers a way to define when their app uses CPU, display and memory resources, which are the things that can potentially drain the device battery life.

The power optimization objective of the Sustained Performance Mode API in Android 7.x is to allow developers to identify their applications that need to use memory and processor cycles high rates of speed for long durations. This would include multimedia applications such as virtual reality (VR), augmented reality (AR), or interactive 3D (i3D) real-time rendered games. Using the Sustained Performance Mode API allows developers to specify the performance level that is sustainable for the duration of the application execution without monopolizing the device CPU, memory, and display (and therefore the battery life). According to Google, this new API should allow "OEMs to provide hints about device-performance capabilities for long-running apps. Application developers can use these hints to tune apps, for a predictable, consistent level of device performance, over long periods of time."

Seamless Updates: Background Installation to Secondary Partition

Android 7 now features a seamless download, install, and update system for your Android OS. Instead of users being prompted and then required to download Android OS updates, then install them, and finally reboot, starting with Android 7.0, the OS will **automatically** download and install its next revision on a **secondary disk storage partition**. When users subsequently reboot an Android device, the OS will switch partitions once a newer version is completely installed on the second (other) partition, and then you will have the latest Android OS revision. This saves users from having to spend device-use time going through a time-consuming Android OS update process.

The idea of automatically downloading Android versions in the background is not new, but with Android 7, it also installs the OS. That means users do not have to reboot their devices and waste device-usage time witnessing a lengthy installing-update dialog screen. With Seamless Update, once everything has been installed and users reboot, things will be ready to use on the next startup. It is important to note that this is the same approach to OS updates that Google Chromebook OS utilizes, so the fusion of Android OS and Chrome OS continues to happen.

When an Android update is released by Google, the update is installed to a secondary partition. Once the device is restarted, the secondary partition becomes the primary partition, and the primary partition becomes the secondary. This approach will be supported by Android 7.0 and later hardware devices. This does not require consumer electronics device manufacturers to release updates any faster, unfortunately; it just means Android 7 will install an update in the background while Android end users are doing more important things with the device!

Multiple Concurrent Windows: Run Two Android Apps at Once

The first Android 7 feature to be officially confirmed was a multiple concurrent window mode, which is another feature addition that makes Android come closer to being used as a desktop computing and iTV set operating system. This is because desktop PCs now use HDTVs and UHDTVs as displays and because interactive TV set devices are one of these HD or UHD screens with a quad-core or octa-core computer inside of it.

Android 7.1.1 developers will need to add support for multiple concurrent window modes to their apps. Compatible apps will be able to be opened up side by side in Android 7 or later. Windows can be resized using slider UI elements. Users will be able to drag and drop content between multiple concurrent windows, and windows can be toggled into full-screen mode by dragging a UI slider to the edge of the window. Developers will also be able to specify a minimum initial window size for the app window.

Picture in a Picture: Watch Video or TV in an Android TV HD iTV Set

There is a new picture-in-a-picture (PIP) mode for Android TV that is similar to this same feature in Apple iOS 9. This works like a minimized video in YouTube, which is not surprising, as Google owns both Android TV and YouTube. The Android 7 picture-in-a-picture mode essentially allows an app to be positioned over the rest of the Android iTV OS user interface using an overlaid window, with no chrome (border). In an Android 7 overview, Google used an example of a video player app to show the picture-in-a-picture mode.

This picture-in-a-picture capability is clearly targeted at HD and UHD iTV sets running Android TV; however, Google did indicate support for larger devices as well, so this could mean large tablets with HD and UHD (iTV set) capable resolutions should be able to leverage this new feature. It is interesting to see hardware devices conforming their screen resolutions with 16:9 and 16:10 widescreen aspect ratios, to support Blu-ray (1280 by 720), True HD (1920 by 1080) and Ultra HD (4096 or 3840 by 2160) video, television, and film content. The reason for this is to prevent CPU and memory usage for pixel scaling, and most device (smartphone, tablet, iTV set, e-reader, game console and auto dashboard) screens will be one of these three pixel resolutions, going out into the future. Samsung has enabled PIP in the video player on their smartphones already, and Apple has done the same on the iPhone, so there's no reason for Google to limit this PIP feature only to larger Android device hardware.

Change Display Density: Adjusting Pixel Per Inch (PPI) via Slider

Android 7 includes an ability to set different display densities, which will serve to zoom all elements on the screen in or out. This helps to help improve device accessibility for users with impaired vision. To access the new feature, go to Settings ➤ Display ➤ Display Size. Android 7.x allows you to change the display size on your device, also known as changing your display's DPI (dots per inch) or PPI (pixels per inch) setting. Simply go to Settings ➤ Display ➤ Display Size and slide a slider, and this will change the perceived size of the onscreen content.

Google claims this feature will not require developers to make changes to the code in their apps; however, in user interface design developers need to select a DPI level (LDPI, MDPI, HDPI, XHDPI, etc.). To make sure there is enough resolution for Android to leverage for this new feature, Android developers should create higher DPI designs (HDPI, XHDPI, or XXHDPI) so that there is more data available to sample for scaling algorithms. This will allow Android OS to "render" the density-altered text and graphics, whether content is zoomed in (large), or zoomed out (small). Developers should test this feature to make sure it works properly within their application.

Keyboard Themes: Customize Onscreen Keyboard Using Skins

One of the most popular things to do since MP3 players were released decades ago is to "skin" or provide a custom user experience (background graphics and edge detail) for the user interface for a given application. The 5.1 version of Google Keyboard comes with theme (skins) customization features that developers (and users) that custom skin their apps are going to utilize. Now you can have thoroughly customizable keyboards and a selection of preconfigured themes to choose from.

After installing Google Keyboard 5.1, if it is not preinstalled already, users are presented with a menu option called "Themes." Users can choose from several included layouts, but the real advantage here is that Google Keyboard 5.1 puts the pixels in the user's control, to allow users to "skin" whatever style of keyboard they desire. This includes adding custom images to the background of the keyboard, and developers can access this feature as well to customize the keyboard look and feel to their application look and feel, or UX (User eXperience).

Enhanced Doze Mode: Control Android 7.0 Device Resting States

Just like developers can manage power using the Sustained Performance API, so to can Android Users using the Enhanced Doze Mode. One of the favorite Android 6 features (Doze Mode) is vastly improved in Android 7. Android Doze features two levels for its power optimization system. The first level kicks in when the screen has been dark (off) for a while, whether your Android device is motionless (stationary) or not. This means users can enjoy the benefit of Enhanced Doze Mode anytime that the device is not in use, even when it is in your pocket, purse, briefcase, or backpack. Once the device screen has been off for a while, Enhanced Doze Mode will also shut down all network access, except for during certain occasional periods of activity, and will also schedule any processing during those brief windows of time. Note that this behavior will only go into effect if the device is on battery power, and will not kick in if the device is attached to an AC power charging source.

The second layer of Android 7.0 Enhanced Doze Mode works like the Android 6 Doze Mode, but with significant improvements. When the device is laying still, the OS will enter a deep hibernation mode, deferring all network and other activity, except for during some wide (spaced-out) maintenance windows before slipping back to sleep. If the device remains stationary, after a while Android OS will place it into a deeper state Enhanced Doze Mode, which has no wake locks, defers alarms as well as data synchronization and processing jobs, and shuts down GPS services and Wi-Fi connection scanning. The deeper the doze mode, the further these windows of intermittent activity will be spaced out, allowing for more battery savings the less you move your device. If you are worried about the device dozing off too much, this is also not a problem, as once you activate the device screen, or plug the device in, the device will exit Enhanced Doze Mode altogether, until its criteria are met again.

OpenJDK: Moving Android Java from Oracle Java to OpenJDK

Google and Oracle have been in legal contention for several years regarding the use of Java in Android, since Oracle purchased Sun Microsystems to obtain Java (and the Solaris OS) and Google purchased Android, as you learned earlier in this chapter. Java 6 was utilized up until Android 6, which uses Java 7, while Android 7.x will use Java 8. To settle these legal contentions, Google plans to officially make the switch to **OpenJDK** in Android 7. OpenJDK code still belongs to Oracle, but OpenJDK is, as the name suggests, part of an open source JDK (Java Development Kit). Anticipation of an open source Java 8 development programming language move have been percolating for a quite a while now, as snippets of open source Java code have recently shown up as far back as Android 6.

Google confirmed all of these speculations in 2016 with the following statement: *"As an open-source platform, Android is built upon the collaboration of the open-source community. In our upcoming release of Android, we plan to move Android's Java language libraries to an OpenJDK-based approach, creating a common code base for developers to build apps and services. Google has long worked with and contributed to the OpenJDK community, and we look forward to making even more contributions to the OpenJDK project in the future."*
– A Google Corporate Spokesperson

Note that in the next chapter you will still download and install the Oracle Java 8 SE JDK to be able to run IntelliJ IDEA and Android Studio with, but the Android packages we will be learning about in this book will be based upon the OpenJDK. What is the difference in the package code, you may wonder. From the end user's standpoint, there will likely be little to no noticeable change in the Android OS user experience. It is developers who will likely have to adapt to the new Java standard. Fortunately you will have never coded Android before, so you will start with the OpenJDK Android API and thus you will not be affected by any slight Java 8 API code changes.

The Data Plan Saver: Sync Only When Connected to a Wi-Fi Portal

Since networks charge you per unit of data transferred, it is important to optimize the data usage for your cellular data plan. Android 7 has a new **Data Plan Saver** feature that can help users take control of their data usage. When the data saver setting is enabled, it stops background data syncs from occurring, except when connected to Wi-Fi networks. Not only will this Data Plan Saver block data-expensive background activities from using up your data plan allowance, it will limit the amount of data that applications use in the foreground as well.

Users can create an "exception list" that highlights specific apps that users want to sync as usual, so that they can still make use of the Data Plan Saver feature. Android users have been able to specify cellular network data limits using their settings menu in previous OS revision, and now in Android 7, there is this additional feature that will let users take their data saving specifications even one step further.

The Future of Android: 3D, VR, AR, OpenGL, and Vulkan

Interactive 3D, or i3D, has been growing in popularity for over a decade now, due to the advent of 3D gaming consoles like the Nintendo Wii, Sony PlayStation, and Microsoft xBox. **Vulkan** is an i3D rendering API that manages multi-core GPUs in an efficient, highly optimized fashion, and will eventually replace **OpenGL ES 3.2**.

Khronos Vulkan: i3D Rendering Engine That Replaces OpenGL ES

Vulkan is a leading-edge i3D programming API being developed by industry experts for use in Android games and other i3D applications on other platforms such as HTML5 and Linux. Vulkan is being created (coded) by i3D experts from across the gaming and effects industry by working together through Khronos.org, which you can find at http://www.khronos.org, as you may have surmised. The Vulkan API is at: http://www.khronos.org/vulkan/ and was released a year ago, on February 16, 2016. Vulkan will be included in the Android 7.1.1 OS release later this year, and will be powered by the nVidia Tegra Parker chipset.

What the Vulkan API does is to provide common, low-level (direct) access to i3D processing (GPU) hardware on a wide range of operating systems and platforms. If you want to explore how to leverage the Vulkan API on Android 7 (and later), and learn all the latest Vulkan techniques, you can research NVIDIA developer information, as well as NVIDIA's main Vulkan developer hub, at https://developer.nvidia.com/vulkan-android Do this because nVidia manufactures the powerful Tegra 3D processors, including the latest "Parker" chipset, used in more and more i3D and VR capable Android devices such as iTV sets and game consoles.

Vulkan for Android: Leading-Edge i3D Performance for Android 7.0

Vulkan for Android is unlike current Android graphics APIs, such as OpenGL ES 3.x, in that its processing engine does not perform certain application optimizations, such as graphics processing pipeline reuse, for instance. Android applications that use Vulkan must implement pipeline optimizations themselves. If they don't, it is possible that they could even implement worse performance than apps running OpenGL ES 3.2. For this reason, I am using OpenGL ES 3.x, and optimizing the assets that the engine renders to achieve a similar result to Vulkan.

When apps implement scheduling optimizations themselves, they have the potential to do so more successfully than the rendering engine can, because they have access to contextual usage information for any given rendering scenario. As a result, skillfully optimizing an app that uses Vulkan could potentially yield better performance than if the app were using OpenGL ES. It is important to note that properly creating and optimizing the geometry and shader assets that are being rendered can often provide even greater performance enhancements. I cover this in my *Android Studio New Media Fundamentals* (Apress, 2015) title in greater detail.

For instance, one of the key rendering engine optimizations is to minimize the number of rendering "passes" or calls to the rendering engine on each frame of the game (i3D) or animation (3D). In general, the less calls, the less processing overhead is incurred. Additionally, for embedded device GPU architectures starting and ending a rendering pass is a processor intensive undertaking. Android apps improve performance by organizing rendering operations into as few render passes as possible using well-formed Java 8 classes and methods, which we will be learning about in Chapter 5.

OpenGL ES for Android: Desktop i3D Performance for Android 7.0

OpenGL ES 3.2 was released around the same time as Vulkan and promises to bring more advanced in mobile graphics capabilities and quality by incorporating the Android Extension Pack (AEP) functionality into the core of OpenGL ES. The AEP was announced with the launch of Android 5, and added a set of i3D rendering technologies to Android OS using "extensions" to OpenGL ES 3.1. These have now been added "natively" to Android 7 OpenGL ES 3.2 API.

The introduction of OpenGL ES 3.2 builds on a previous release, to add 3D graphics functionality making full use of mobile, iTV set, and automotive dashboard hardware. OpenGL ES 3.2 has a number of improvements over OpenGL ES 3.1. OpenGL ES 3.2 compliant hardware supports Tessellation, which adds 3D geometry detail. It includes new geometry shaders, ASTC texture compression for an optimized memory footprint, floating-point rendering for high-accuracy compute processing, and enhanced debugging features. These high-end features are already found in Khronos Group's OpenGL 4.0 specification. High-quality special effects are also a part of OpenGL ES 3.2, including deferred rendering, physically based shaders, HDR tone mapping, Global Illumination, and reflections. These features will bring desktop-quality graphics to Android 7 devices running OpenGL ES 3.2.

Summary

In this first chapter, you learned about Android 7, including its history, advantages to developers, and its major new features. I outlined what we will, and will not, be covering during over the course of this absolute beginners title. In the next chapter, you'll learn exactly how to download, install, and set up an Android 7.1.1 application development workstation, and how to configure it for use for Android 7.x application and content development.

Chapter 2

Setting Up an Android Studio Development System

These days, you see Android operating system powered devices of every size and shape, everywhere you look. These can be worn on your person; used in home appliances; as a part of your car; or providing entertainment in your living room, taking the form of your iTV set, or a tablet, an e-book reader, or even an Android game console.

During this chapter, you'll learn how to assemble a 64-bit workstation that will allow you to develop applications for the Android 7 (and previous versions) operating system (OS). This will give you a high-level overview of the software requirements, the workstation hardware requirements, which open source programming language software development kits (SDK) and integrated development environment (IDE) you will need to download and install, where to download these and how to properly install them, and how to configure and update them as well.

You will get all of the tedious Google searches and downloads out of the way regarding how to go about obtaining all of these professional open source software and content development packages, SDKs, IDEs, and related plug-in components, which together will form your comprehensive **Android Studio 2.3 production workstation**.

Even though this is an "Absolute Beginners" Android title, I want to teach you how to put together a pro Android development workstation, so that you are all ready to get into the various *Pro Android* series of books from Apress (after you finish mastering this book, of course). So that everyone experiences this book equally, this chapter will outline all of the steps needed to obtain a completely decked-out Android 7.1.1 development workstation.

Assembling Your Android 7 Development Workstation

In this chapter, I will outline a detailed overview of what will be needed to put together a complete Android Studio development workstation, which you'll be able to utilize throughout this book, and others, to create Android apps.

© Wallace Jackson 2017
W. Jackson, *Android Apps for Absolute Beginners*, DOI 10.1007/978-1-4842-2268-3_2

The first thing that you will do is to download the entire Java SE 8 software development kit (SDK), which Oracle calls the **JavaSE 8 JDK** (Java Development Kit). Android Studio uses Java Standard Edition (SE) Version 8 update 121, as of Android Studio 2.3, as well as the IntelliJ 2016.3 IDEA.

> **Note**   Java 9 also exists, and is under a beta release, at Java 9 Build 156. In the third quarter of 2017, there will be a Java Version 9 released, which will include powerful JavaFX 8.0 APIs that turn the Java programming language into a powerful new media engine. JavaFX 8.0 will also work in the 64-bit Android OS.

The second thing that we will download and install is the Android Studio Development Toolset, which we will get from Google's **tools.android.com** website. Android Studio is currently at Version 2.3 (Android 7.1.1), and Android 6 used Android Studio Version 2.1. Android Studio currently consists of the **IntelliJ 2016.3 IDEA** along with the **Android 25 APIs.** These Application Programming Interfaces (APIs) bridge the **Android 7.1.1 SDK** with the IntelliJ IDEA, making them into one seamless Android 7 software development environment. It is important to note that IntelliJ can also be used for other types of non-Android application development as well, including HTML5, Java, JavaFX, and C++, among others.

After your core Android development environment software is downloaded, you'll then download and install external **new media asset development** tools, which you will utilize in conjunction with Android 7.1.1 to do things such as UI wireframing (Pencil), digital image editing (GIMP), digital audio editing (Audacity), digital video editing (Lightworks or DaVinci Resolve), 3D modeling and animation (Blender), digital illustration (Inkscape), visual effects (Fusion), and even running your Android development business (OpenOffice). Professional Android applications use more than just Android code, they use what I call "new media assets," such as digital audio, digital images, digital video, 3D, and SVG, all of which you will learn to reference from Android using XML (eXtensible Markup Language).

All of these software development tools, which you will be downloading and installing, will come close to matching all of the primary feature sets of the expensive paid software packages, such as those from Microsoft (Office and Visual Studio), Apple (Logic, Avid, Final Cut Pro), Autodesk (Maya, Flint, Smoke, Flame and 3D Studio Max), and Adobe (Photoshop CS, Premeire and After Effects).

Each of these paid software packages would cost a couple thousand dollars each to purchase and maintain, so plan on paying ten thousand (your local currency unit here) to put together a similar paid software workstation to develop for the proprietary (closed) iOS or the Windows consumer electronics device platforms.

Open source software is free to download, install, and even to upgrade, and is continually adding features and becoming more and more professional, each and every day. You'll be completely amazed at how professional open source software packages have become over the last decade or so; if you have not experienced this already, you are about to, in a very significant way. I also have *Digital New Media Fundamentals* books on each of these new media software genres, in case you need to get up to speed on the basics of each genre of new media, and I also wrote an *Android Studio New Media Fundamentals* (Apress, 2015) title, covering all of them. You can even run your workstation on Ubuntu Linux 17.04 if you like!

Android Development Workstation: Hardware Foundation

Since during the chapter you will put together what will be the foundation for your Android applications development system for the duration of this book, let's take a moment to discuss the Android development workstation's hardware configuration, as that's an important factor for your performance (speed of development), which is as important as the software itself.

This section will therefore cover a plethora of important systems hardware considerations that you should consider when assembling your workstation.

I recommend using at a bare minimum an **Intel i7 hexa-core** processor, or an **AMD 64-bit octa-core** processor, with at least **16GB** of **DDR3-1600** memory. I'm using the Octa-core AMD 8350 with 16GB of DDR3-2000, but I recently got an Octacore Intel i7 workstation for Android Studio 2.3 development. Intel also now has a deca-core i7 processor. This would be the equivalent of having 20 AMD cores, as each Intel core can host two threads, so even an i7 quad-core looks like 8 AMD cores to an OS thread-scheduler algorithm.

AMD has a 16-core processor as well, which is usually deployed inside of server architectures, but this CPU can be used in a client-side Android development workstation, which would greatly speed video compression or 3D rendering for your Android applications development.

There are also high-speed DDR3 1866, and DDR4 2400 clockspeed memory module components available. A high number signifies faster memory access speed. To calculate the actual megahertz speed at which memory is cycling, divide the number by 4 (1333=333Mhz, 1600=400Mhz, 1866=466Mhz, 2400=600Mhz clock rate). Memory access speed is the key workstation performance factor because your processor is usually "bottle-necked" by the speed at which the processor cores can access the data (in memory) that they need to process.

With all this high-speed processing and memory access going on inside your workstation while it is operating, it is also important to keep everything cool so that you do not experience "thermal problems." I recommend using a wide **full-tower** enclosure, with **120mm** or **230mm** cooling fans (one or two at least), as well as a captive liquid induction cooling fan on the CPU. This type of CPU cooler has cooling tubes filled with water that touch the CPU and draw away heat, turning the water into steam, which rises up the tubes to the cooling fan, which cools this steam, condensing it back into water, which runs back down the pipe to cool the CPU. It's important to note that the cooler your system runs, the longer it lasts, and the faster it runs, which is important for Android 7 application development.

If you really want the maximum performance, especially while emulating Android Virtual Devices (AVDs), which are used for app prototyping or testing, which you will learn about in the next chapter, you'll want to make sure that your Android development workstation has a solid state disk (**SSD**) hard drive as its primary (C:\ "boot" drive) disk drive, from which your applications and OS software will launch.

You can always use more affordable hard disk drive (**HDD**) hardware for your D:\ (secondary) hard disk drive, for your data storage, which does not need the speed of operation as it is just used for long-term storage.

For my OS, I'm using **64-bit Windows 10** OS, which is not very memory efficient, for this book since it is very commonly found on computers. Linux 64-bit OSes are also extremely memory efficient; a good example of this is Ubuntu Mate 17.04 which uses around 350MB of system memory. It's important to note that Windows 10 comes on most quad-core workstations in retail stores such as Walmart and Staples, and with an OS price of several hundred dollars if purchased separately, you could look at the hardware as essentially being free. That said, Ubuntu 17.04 running on Intel i7 will be an order of magnitude faster for development, especially emulation of Android devices.

Android Development Workstation: Software Foundation

To create a well-rounded Android applications development workstation, you will be installing content development open source software, after you install Java SE 8u121, IntelliJ IDEA 2016.3, and the Android Studio 2.3 application development environment. These are all open source programming packages, and therefore we will be assembling a 100% open source workstation for your company, with the exception of the Windows 10 OS. If you use Ubuntu 17.04 your workstation would be 100% open source and free.

For those readers who have just purchased their new Android workstations, and who are going to put their Android development software suite together completely from scratch, I'll go through an entire work process throughout the rest of this chapter, starting with Java SE 8u121, as it is the foundation for IntelliJ IDEA 2016 as well as for Android Studio. After that, you will acquire the Android Studio 2.3 (Android 7.1.1 and IntelliJ 2016 Bundle). Finally, we'll search for, and download, your new media content development software, including digital imaging, digital audio, digital video, 3D animation, and visual effects, all of which will be used with Android Studio. We will even acquire a complete business software suite called Open Office 4.2, originally created by Sun Microsystems, and acquired, and made open source, by Oracle, who also owns the OpenJDK and Java 8 programming language.

Java 8: Download and Install a Foundation for Android

Before you run a Java SE installation, you should remove any older versions of Java SE using your Windows **Control Panel**, via the **Add or Remove Programs** (XP or Vista), or **Programs and Features** (Windows 7, 8 or 10) utility. To remove an older version of the Java JDK or Java Runtime Environment (JRE) select them and right-click on the selected entry and use the "Uninstall/Remove" option to uninstall.

This will be necessary especially if your workstation is not brand new, so that only your latest Java SE 8u121 and JRE 8u121 are the sole Java versions that are currently installed on your new Android development workstation.

To install a new JDK:

1. The first thing that you will want to do is to visit **Oracle's Java Archive** website, and download and install the latest **Java 8 JDK** environment, which at the time of writing this book was **Java SE 8u121**. Note that Java8u91 is shown in Figure 2-1, as that was what I was using in 2016 to develop this book.

Figure 2-1. *Oracle TechNetwork web site Java SE 8u91 Archive; scroll down to the middle, and accept the license agreement*

The URL is in the address bar of Figure 2-1, or you can simply Google **Java SE 8 JDK Archive Download**, which will also give you the latest link to this web page, which I'll include here, in case you want to cut and paste:

```
http://www.oracle.com/technetwork/java/javase/downloads/jdk8-downloads-2133151.html
```

You can pull the scrollbar on the right side of the web page down the page, until you see the **Java SE Development Kit 8u121 Windows x64** download link, which you can see at the very bottom of Figure 2-1. This last link in the long list of version links is the latest revision of the Java SE 8 JDK Development Kit, and since you want to get the latest, bug-free, Java 8 version for 64-bit Windows 10 OS, then this is the download you'll want.

Make sure that you use this **Java SE Development Kit 8u121** download link, and do not use a JRE download link. The JRE is part of the JDK 8u121, so you do not have to worry about getting the Java Runtime separately. In case you're wondering, you will indeed use the JRE to launch and run your IntelliJ IDEA, and you will also use the JDK inside of IntelliJ, to provide your Java 8 programming language foundation for the Android 7.x OpenJDK API used by the Android 7.x classes.

> **Note**   The JRE is the executable (platform) that runs the Java 8 or JavaFX 8 software, once it has been compiled into an application, and thus a JRE will be needed to run IntelliJ IDEA 2016.3. This is because IntelliJ IDEA 2016.3 (dot three means version three) was originally coded using Java SE.

Make sure **not** to download a JDK 7u79 from the Java 7 download page, because Android 7 uses JavaSE 8u121 and the IntelliJ 2016.3 IDEA, **not** Java 7 and the NetBeans 7.4 IDE with its ADT plug-ins, so **be very careful** regarding this foundational installation step.

I actually use a completely different workstation for Android development, which has Java SE 8u121 and IntelliJ 2016.3 IDEA under Android Studio 2.3, and I have another HTML5 and JavaFX 8 development workstation that has Java SE 8u91 and NetBeans 8.1 installed on it.

2. Once you click on the **Accept License Agreement** radio button, you will activate the Java SE 8 Development Kit 8u121 Download section of this page, shown in Figure 2-1, where you will be able to select the OS you want to use. Once you click on this Accept License Agreement radio button on the top left of this download links table, the links will become bolded, and you will be able to click on the link for the OS version that you need to use for your 64-bit workstation.

3. Click on the "**Windows x64**" link. This is the 64-bit version of Java for Windows, which I am using on my Windows 10 workstation. If you are using Linux, then click on "Linux x64" instead.

    If you're on Windows and your OS is 64-bit, you would use the **Windows x64** link; otherwise, you would use the **Windows x86** link. To find out what level of bit-depth your Windows OS is running at, open the **Start** menu, right-click on the **Computer** option, and select the **Properties** menu option. For Windows 10, right-click the start menu (Windows) icon and then choose System. This will tell you all about your computer's hardware, including if it is using a 32-bit or 64-bit CPU and OS. Optimally, your workstation should match the bit-depth of the CPU with the bit-depth of the OS, and I highly recommend using a 64-bit OS for Android application development, as much older 32-bit software has been outdated for almost a full decade now.

4. Once the installation executable has downloaded, locate the file on your workstation's hard disk, and install Oracle's Java SE 8u121 JDK on your system, by double-clicking on the **EXE** file.

5. Accept the default setting in the second dialog, seen on the top-middle in Figure 2-2, and click on the **Next** buttons in the first two dialogs, which will extract the installation.

6. Accept the default Java installation folder value, which is shown in the dialog on the bottom left in Figure 2-2, entitled **Destination Folder**.

7. After Java installs, as shown in the center bottom dialog in Figure 2-2, use the **Close** button to finish the installation, and use your **Control Panel ➤ Programs and Features** utility to confirm the successful JDK 8 installation on your Android 7.x development workstation.

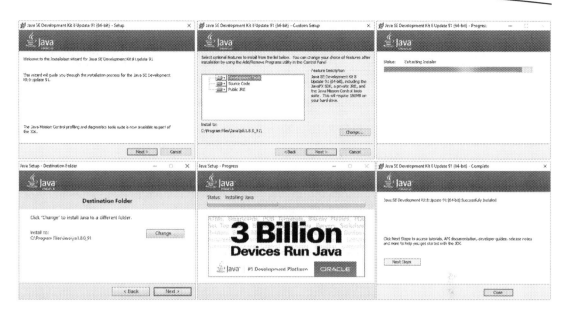

Figure 2-2. The six dialogs which install the Java 8 SE JDK onto your Android Studio 2.3 software development workstation

Once Java 8u121 (or later) JDK is installed on your workstation, you can then download and install the **Android Studio Installer** from the **tools.android.com** website. You can also use that same Add or Remove Programs utility in your Control Panel (that you just used for Java) to remove older Android Studio versions, and to confirm the success of the new Android Studio 2.3 installation, just like you did for your Java SE 8 JDK installation.

Android Studio: Download and Install Android Studio 2

Now we need to visit the **tools.android.com** website, and download and install the Android development environment Android Studio 2.3 zip file from the /download/studio/ folder of the site, located at the following URL:

`http://tools.android.com/download/studio/`

1. Click on the **Android Studio Stable Channel** link, found on the bottom right of the Android Studio Project website's home page. There is also a **Canary** (latest untested build) Channel, a **Developer** Channel (latest internally tested build), and a **Beta** Channel (latest beta or externally tested build). I do not recommend that Absolute Beginners use these channels until they're more advanced users.

2. This will take you to a page with "**Android Studio Stable Channel**" at the top. Click the topmost link to download the most recent version of Android Studio 2.3.x and then right-click on the file once it is on your system and select the Run as Administrator option from the context-sensitive menu. You will see the **Welcome to Android Studio** dialog shown on the left side of Figure 2-3.

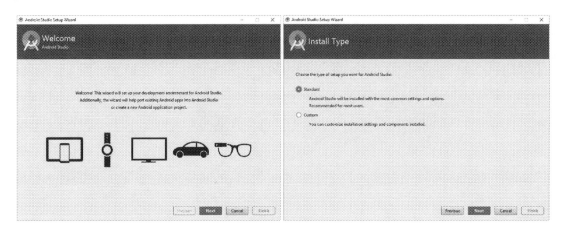

Figure 2-3. Launch the Android Studio installer, click the Next button, and select a Standard install and click the Next button

3.   Click the **Next** button and select the **Standard** install option from the **Install Type** dialog shown on the right side of Figure 2-3, and then again click on the **Next** button, and advance to the Android Studio **Verify Settings** dialog screen.

4.   If you want to review or change installation settings, click the **Previous** button; otherwise click on the **Finish** button to begin the Installation of Android Studio, as shown on the left in Figure 2-4.

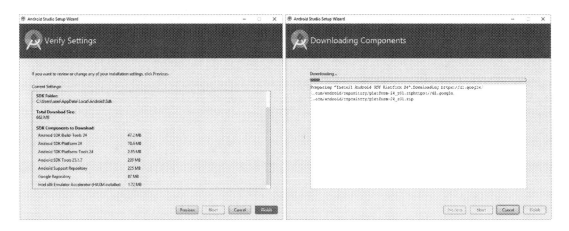

Figure 2-4. In Verify Settings, review the SDK components to install, and click Finish to begin Downloading SDK components

5.   Once you click Finish, the **Downloading Components** dialog, shown on the right side in Figure 2-4, will appear, and you will see a **Downloading...** progress bar with a data field area showing you what components are being downloaded and installed.

6. If there are any components that cannot install or which fail for some reason, you will see red colored text, as is shown on the left-hand side in Figure 2-5. In my case, I have an AMD OctaCore CPU and so the Intel HAXM component will not install as it requires an Intel CPU architecture. I then clicked the **Finish** button, and launched Android Studio 2.3. Since I am writing this book to release at the same time as Android 7.1.1 (Android 2.3), I am using Preview (beta) versions of the IDE in order to be able to write this book to coincide with the stable version release.

7. **At the bottom of the Welcome to Android Studio launch screen you will see a tool gear icon and a Configure drop-down menu,** as is shown in the middle of Figure 2-5. Select the **Check for Update,** to force Android Studio to check its repository (Android component software server database), so that you can make sure that you have all the latest Android SDK component versions installed.

8. To see what components make up the Android Studio installation, drop-down this Configure menu a second time, as shown on the top-right corner of Figure 2-5, and select the **SDK Manager** option.

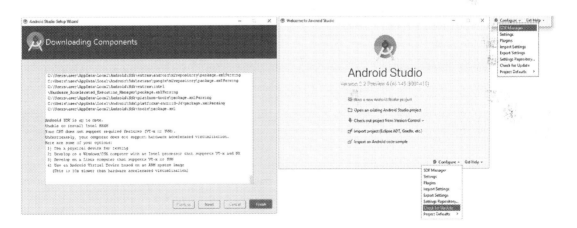

Figure 2-5. *Finish downloading components, and use the Configure menu to check for updates, and then manage the SDK*

9. In the **Default Settings** dialog, under the **Appearance & Behavior ➤ System Settings ➤ Android SDK** section, in the **SDK Platforms** tab, make sure that Android 7.1.1 is installed. This is shown on the left side of Figure 2-6.

10. Click the **SDK Tools** tab, to review what Android Studio 2.3 has installed. This is shown on the right side of Figure 2-6. Select the **Google USB Driver**, which you'll need to work with hardware devices.

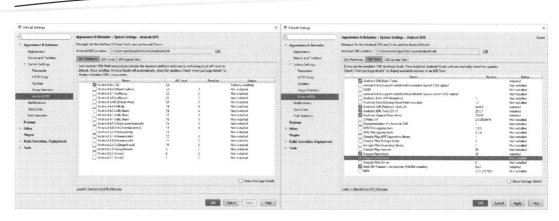

Figure 2-6. SDK Manager

11. Next, click on the **SDK Update Sites** tab, as seen on the left side of Figure 2-7, to make sure all of the repositories are in place, and click on the **OK** button (shown as number 1 in Figure 2-7).

12. Click on the **OK** button in the **Confirm Change** dialog, shown as number 2 in Figure 2-7, which appears because you selected Google's USB Driver to be added as a component of Android Studio.

13. In the **License Agreement** dialog, shown on the right side of Figure 2-7, click on the **Accept** radio button, shown as number 3, to accept the Google USB Driver licensing agreement.

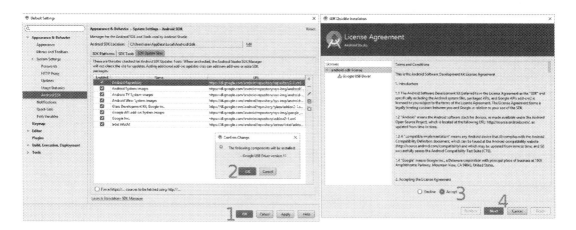

Figure 2-7. Install the Google USB Driver (latest version) so that you can test your apps on real Android hardware devices

14. After the USB Driver download and install, shown in Figure 2-8, is complete, click the **Finish** button.

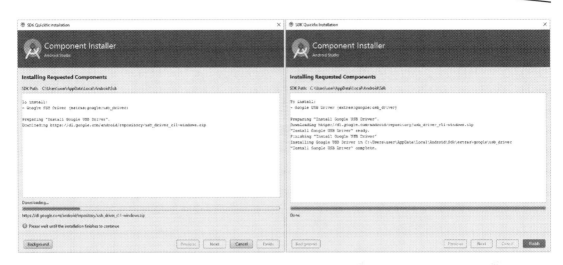

Figure 2-8. *Google USB Driver; installing the requested components in the Component Installer dialog in Android Studio 2.3*

15.   Next, let's go back into the **SDK Tools** tab, as is shown in Figure 2-9, and make sure that the **Google USB Driver** is showing as being installed. This is the equivalent of using your Programs and Features utility in Windows. Now, you can plug your Android devices into your Android Studio workstation, and test your applications on a real Android device, instead of using a slow and cumbersome AVD (Android Virtual Device) emulator. Next, click the **OK** button, and exit the Default Settings dialog.

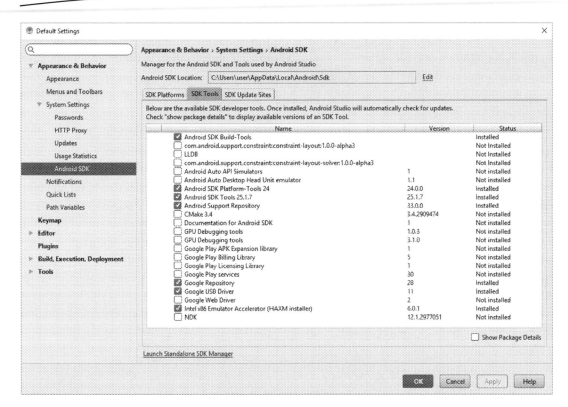

Figure 2-9. *The minimum Android 7.1.1 development tools needed for absolute beginners are now confirmed to be installed*

Now that we have Android Studio working on your workstation, I'm going to give you a bonus in this chapter, and tell you how to obtain some other professional-level software packages that will help your Android development business to create "front-end" multimedia assets that will set your products apart from the rest of the marketplace because you will add audio, video, imagery, 3D, and 2D SVG Illustration to enhance your user experience (UX) and User Interface (UI) design. These are also free for commercial use, making your workstation more valuable.

Open Source New Media Content Software: UI and UX

As you can see in Table 2-1, there are professional software tools for each of the new media asset genres that are supported in Android 7.x. Each of these has been under development for well over a decade, and match all the primary features found in paid multimedia software packages, costing in some cases thousands of dollars each.

Table 2-1. *New Media Genres supported by Android 7 asset data formats, along with open source software and their URLs*

New Media Asset Genre	Open Source Software Package Name	URL for Download
Digital Image Compositing	GIMP 2.8.18 (Version 3 due out in 2017)	`http://www.gimp.org/`
Digital Audio Editing	Audacity 2.1.2	`http://www.teamaudacity.org/`
Digital Illustration or Painting	Inkscape 0.91	`http://www.inkscape.org/`
Visual Effects (VFX) Compositing	Blackmagic Design Fusion 8.2	`http://www.blackmagicdesign/fusion/`
Digital Video Editing and Effects	Editshare Lightworks or DaVinci Resolve	`http://www.lwks.com/`
3D Modeling and Animation	Blender 2.78b (Version 2.8 due in 2017)	`http://blender.org/`
Office Productivity Suite	Apache (formerly Oracle) Open Office 4.1.2	`http://www.openoffice.org/`

I recommend that you go to each of these URLs and download these impressive free multimedia production software packages, because there are no strings attached, and because they give you the capability to make your Android 7.1.1 applications an order of magnitude more desirable, by making them visually (and aurally) superior.

New Media Software: Download and Installation Work Process

I'm not going to spend a lot of time going through how to download and install the new media packages because the work process is so similar to what you did during this chapter. Find the download link, find the installer file on your workstation, right-click and run the installer as **Administrator**, and create a short-cut launch icon on your taskbar. Also, make sure to remove any older versions before you do this, by using the **Programs and Features** utility.

Finally, let's take a look at powerful new media content production software packages that are almost free, in case you're intending to create Android new media applications (games, iTV shows, wallpaper, watchfaces, etc.) specifically.

Other Affordable New Media Software Readers Should Know About

There are also some extremely affordable (less than $100 up to $200) new media software packages, which you should take a look at as well, if you are serious about creating impressive new media assets for use in your Android 7.x application development. In the area of 3D, these include:

- NeverCenter SILO 2.3.1 (Quads 3D Modeling)
- Hash Animation Master 18 (Character Animation)

▓   Moment of Inspiration 3D 3 (NURBs 3D Modeling)

▓   TerraGen 4 Pro (3D virtual worlds generation)

▓   Hexagon 2.5 (Polygon 3D Modeling)

▓   Auto-Des-Sys Bonzai (3D Modeling, with all 3D modeling paradigms being supported)

In the area of digital imaging, digital video editing, digital illustration. and digital painting, Corel Corporation in Canada offers a large number of software packages under or around $100 that offer an amazing value. Many of these (other than CorelDRAW) were acquired from other software companies, are covered in my *Digital Painting Fundamentals and Digital Video Editing Fundamentals* (Apress, 2016) titles, and include:

▓   Corel Painter 2016 (formerly Fractal Design Painter)

▓   Corel PaintShop Pro (like Photoshop or GIMP 3)

▓   Corel VideoStudio Ultimate

▓   CorelCAD 2016

▓   A number of different versions of CorelDRAW (Graphics X8, Home/ Student X7, and Technical X7)

Corel has a number of affordable DVD Authoring and Office Suite solutions as well.

There are also other open source packages in the 3D software genre and include:

▓   SketchUp (architectural rendering)

▓   TerraGen 4 Free Version (virtual world creation)

▓   Microsoft TrueSpace 8 (3D Animation)

▓   Wings 3D (3D Modeling)

▓   Bishop 3D (3D Modeling)

▓   POV Ray 3.7 (3D Rendering)

▓   DAZ Studio 4.9 (Character Modeling)

For audio composition, production, and engineering areas, impressive packages include:

▓   Rosegarden (Music Composition, MIDI, Score Publishing) for Linux and Windows

▓   Qtractor (Sound Design) for Linux

The list of amazing open source software just goes on and on, which is why I took a page or two out of this book to expose you to all of it, as it can make your Android software development workstation at least ten times (known as an "order of magnitude") more impressive than it would be using only the Android Studio 2.3 IDE, Java SE 8, IntelliJ 2016.3.3 and the OpenJDK.

Summary

In this second chapter, you learned about Android Studio and its hardware requirements, and acquired the software that you will need to be able to create your comprehensive Android 7.1.1 application development workstation. I also showed you how to install Android Studio; configure Android Studio; upgrade Android Studio; examine what SDK packages were active in Android Studio; and how to enhance Android Studio with additional Android software development features, such as the ability to test Android applications on a real-world Android device, by connecting it using a USB cable (USB to Micro-USB) in conjunction with Google's latest USB driver software.

From Java SE 8, to Android Studio (IntelliJ), to new media content production software, to business productivity tools, you downloaded and then installed the most impressive open source software packages that can be found anywhere on this planet, adding incredible value to your Android 7.1.1 development workstation with zero monetary outlay. You did this in order to create a foundation for the Android application development work process that we will be undertaking throughout this book; and rather than install these software packages as we go along, I made the decision to get all of our *Absolute Beginners* readers 100% set up with this amazing software right off the bat!

I did this in case you wanted to explore some of the many features of these powerful, exciting new media content production software packages before you actually use them during this book. I think that's only fair.

The best thing about the process was that we accomplished it by using open source, 100% free for commercial usage and professional-level application software packages, which is pretty darned amazing, if you think about it.

We started by downloading and installing Oracle's **Java SE 8u121 JDK** or **Java Development Kit**, which is the Java 8 programming language's SDK. This Java JDK is required to use IntelliJ 2016.3 and Android Studio 2.3, so you can develop application software for Android 7.1.1 OS (and all previous Android versions) for consumer electronic devices.

We then visited the **Android Developer Tools** website, and downloaded and installed **Android Studio 2.3**, which offers the **IntelliJ 2016 IDEA** and seamlessly integrates **Android 7.1.1 SDK Development Tools** on top of IntelliJ and the Java SE 8 JDK and JRE. I also showed you how to get all of the professional new media content development tools that you will want to leverage to create the new media assets used in your Android application, especially if you are targeted graphics-centric HD or UHD iTV set, smartphone, tablet or e-reader device hardware. Lower SD resolution smartwatches will also need to leverage new media visuals to "skin" your users' smartwatches to make them visually impressive to their friends and family.

In the next chapter on how Android and Android Studio works, you will see how these new media assets integrate into Android using XML, and how to create an Android Project using the Android Studio 2.3 software that you just installed during this chapter. This is getting exciting already! Hang on, you're in for a wild and fun ride!

Chapter 3

An Introduction to the Android Studio Integrated Development Environment

During this chapter, we will take a look at how the Android Studio 2.3 development environment and Android platform works. Android OS has moved away from using the Eclipse Integrated Development Environment (IDE) with Android Development Tools (ADT), and as of 64-bit Android 5.0 and later, has adopted the IntelliJ IDEA (Integrated Development Environment Application). We installed IntelliJ as part of Android Studio 2.3 in the previous chapter, and have already used some of its configuration tools and dialogs, such as the SDK Manager, to configure it for basic Android application development usage.

To cover this overview of Android Studio 2.3 and IntelliJ IDEA properly, and still make steady progress toward actual hands-on Android application development at the same time, in this chapter I will show you the work process for creating an empty Android application "bootstrap." This is the foundation that you will always use when you start creating your Android applications. This bootstrap application structure provides you with the basic foundation of an Android 7.1.1 application, which also makes it perfect for Absolute Beginners to learn the minimum code structure that Android applications are built on. This includes an Android Activity Java class, an Android Manifest application definition XML file, a PNG32 Android application icon, a basic menu system XML definition, and a basic user interface (UI) layout container XML definition.

We will take a closer look at all of the basic Android application components during this chapter, by looking at the Android application resource folder structure in IntelliJ IDEA, which the **Start a New Android Project** series of dialogs will also automatically create for you. As you have seen already in Chapter 2, this is inside of the Android Studio start menu, which you saw in red as the first item in the middle section of the screenshot in Figure 2-5.

© Wallace Jackson 2017
W. Jackson, *Android Apps for Absolute Beginners*, DOI 10.1007/978-1-4842-2268-3_3

We will do a detailed examination of the bootstrap (empty) Android application file and folder structure in IntelliJ. This will tell you how Android Studio 2.3 (and Android 7 OS) wants to see your application components and assets structured and organized. We will also take a detailed look at some other **resource** folders that are not auto-created in the bootstrap Android application project folder structure, so that you know what you can optionally create yourself. You will be creating some of these specialized resource folders during the book, such as the **/res/anim/** folder, which holds XML animation definitions. Custom resource folders usually hold new media assets such as animation, video, audio, user interface designs, and other assets that will enhance the Android application user experience.

As you progress in your knowledge of Android, you will enhance the application foundation that you will put into place in this chapter into something that is truly impressive, and learn more about the Android 7.x OS as well as Android Studio 2.3 and IntelliJ IDEA in the process. After you get some high-level overview regarding how everything fits together inside Android Studio, we can then start "drilling down" into XML for asset definition and Java 8 for application logic programming during Chapters 4 and 5.

Android Application Structure: Java, XML, and Assets

Android 7 components are built on the solid foundation of the 64-bit Linux OS Kernel. Android 6 runs on Linux Kernel 3.18.10, and Android 7 runs on Linux Kernel 4.4.1 or later. Later Linux Kernels have more features and fewer bugs, as you might expect.

On top of the are a massive number (thousands) of high-level Java functions, or Java methods, that are logically arranged by using Java classes. These classes are stored by what tasks they accomplish using around one hundred Java packages. These packages are further organized into Java libraries, or APIs, which simplify your task of communicating with Android and its Linux Kernel as well as with device hardware.

This is inherently complex, as you might well imagine, so don't expect to cover all of Android 7's functionality in one book (or even a dozen, for that matter). I'll cover Java 8 concepts of libraries and packages, as well as what Java objects, constants, classes, and methods are, during Chapter 5.

On top of this complex Java code libraries layer, you can define app assets using a high-level (and less complex) layer of XML markup. XML markup allows you to more easily define your application's Java object structures, as well as any data constants that will be used in your Java 8 programming logic. Additionally, XML markup can define your application UI design, style, theme, and new media assets. These design-oriented assets allow you to control how your Android application looks, sounds, and functions, and ultimately will define the user experience.

Since XML is easier to create Android application content in, I will be using it in the middle five chapters of this book, to show you how to define various application components, assets, looks, and feels. I will be covering XML-based UI, graphics, and animation design in Chapters 6 through 10. Figure 3-1 shows the hierarchy of an Android application structure starting with the foundation of the Linux OS Kernel, hidden from the developer; and Java 8, XML, and new media assets that developers create, code, design, define, and construct, eventually marrying these layers together into an Android application. These layers tend to reduce in complexity from bottom to top, especially if your new media assets already exist.

Figure 3-1. *The Android OS foundation: from Linux Kernel, to Java Libraries, to XML Definitions, to Application Media Assets*

Creating new media assets from scratch can be as complex as Java programming can be, so if your assets do not already exist, these levels of decreasing complexity do not necessarily hold true. If you want to start on the road to mastering new media content production, I have a series of six books on mastering new media fundamentals (search for this author's name, at: http://www.Apress.com), as well as an *Android Studio New Media Fundamentals* (Apress, 2015) title, which contains information and work processes regarding 3D, digital audio, digital video, digital image compositing, and digital illustration (SVG) new media content creation.

Android 7 Platform Structure: A Collection of Open Technologies

As you have learned, the foundation on which Android is built is the carefully coded, and painstakingly tested, Linux Kernel. Linux and its core services manage physical hardware for smartphones, tablets, e-book readers, smartwatches, and iTV sets, and give Android applications complete access to the features of each consumer electronics device, including GPS, touchscreen, memory, data storage, camera, flash, gyroscope, compass, accelerometer, barometric sensor, biometric (e-Health) sensors, Bluetooth, Wi-Fi, NFC, 4G LTE, USB, and much more.

Linux doesn't do it all alone, however. Android has a wide array of Java API libraries, that provide higher-level customized functions and services for things like SQLite database management, 2D image compositing, image blending, SVG rendering, 3D rendering, web page (HTML5, CSS3 and JS) rendering, digital audio playback, digital video streaming, frame-based and procedural animation, Bluetooth, and more. The majority of these are based on open technologies, such as SQL, GIF, SVG, WebKit, OpenGL, Vulkan, PNG, FLAC, Ogg Vorbis, Ogg Theora, VP8, and VP9. Some "almost" open source (these patents expire in a few years) have been licensed for Android by Google, such as MPEG-4, MP3, WAVE, BMP, JPEG, Bluetooth, and similar new media technologies.

The higher-level Java functional libraries are the ones that Android app developers use to create their applications. This is so that developers do not have to "talk" directly to the low-level operating system functions. This is done so that application development becomes an order of magnitude more easily! You will be learning about some of the core Java 8 functional libraries that are used to develop Android 7.1.1 applications during the course of this book, starting with this chapter when we look at the basic (empty) Android application bootstrap Java code.

The Android OS on the user side of the equation (versus the developer side, which we will be focusing on during this book) also includes a large number of "end-user utility" applications, which Android device users have come to expect on their Android device. Examples of these include a phone call management utility, an e-mail client, various social media platform clients, a contact manager, a web browser, an alarm clock, a calendar, Google Maps, Google Search, a media player, and possibly some basic casual games, to name a few.

Android OS supports all of the popular open source new media formats that developers will want to use in their applications, including the powerful ON2 VP9 video codec, added in Android 5. ON2 was acquired by Google, and VP8 and VP9 were released in an open source video codec called WebM, which you can find in Android as well as in browsers such as Firefox, Opera, and Chrome. Both the WebM and the MPEG-4 H.264 AVC digital video codec's "Quality to File Size Ratio," and therefore their playback performance, are fairly impressive for open source video codecs. Also added in Android 5.0 was the ability to play back MPEG-H H.265 HEVC content.

For more information regarding the two dozen new media formats that are supported in Android 7.1.1 you can visit:

`http://developer.android.com/guide/appendix/`**`media-formats.html`**

The next section of this chapter introduces Java's **Dalvik Virtual Machine** (VM), which optimizes your Java code, so that it will execute effectively in low-power, embedded (portable and iTV set) consumer electronics devices.

> **Note**   In this book you will build apps using a combination of XML and Java. These sit in layers on top of the operating system, as shown in Figure 3-1. However, you could, if you were advanced in Android development, access the operating system and its services directly, using the lower-level language C++, by utilizing the **Android Native Development Kit (NDK)**, rather than using higher-level **Software Development Kit** (**Android SDK**), which we will be using for this book. You might consider this "under-the-hood" approach for an application that needs the utmost speed, such as a game, or real-time heart-monitoring workout program. This Android NDK is currently beyond the scope of this book.

Now let's take a look at the runtime, or **compiled** version, of your Android application, and how it uses Java bytecode with the **Android Run-Time (ART)** to optimize the runtime (end user) performance of an Android app.

Android 7 Executable Structure: Compiled Runtime Java Bytecode

Everything in the Android Studio 2.3 development environment, as well as all of the included applications, is created by using a combination of Java code and XML markup. This is compiled by IntelliJ and Gradle into a Java "bytecode" version of your app that will be "executed" (run) using the Android Run-Time (ART) utility, which is a part of Android OS. IntelliJ creates this bytecode, and puts it into the .DEX file format (similar to an .EXE file).

This .DEX file extension and data format essentially amounts to being a compact, low-level executable file format that the Android operating system, and therefore Android devices that run Android OS, will be able to understand and run. A DEX is not specifically encrypted, but if you look at the contents of one of these compiled files, it will not be readily decipherable. The flow of XML, to Java code, to bytecode, to executable data would be as follows:

```
XML (.XML) → Java (.CLASS) → ByteCode (.DEX) → App (.APK) → Runtime (ART) → Device
Display
```

The Android runtime environments before Android 4.4 used only Dalvik Virtual Machine (DVM); and in Android 4.4, you could choose between DVM and ART. Android 5.0 and later use only ART. These runtimes give your apps access to hardware device features, as well as the low-level Android and Linux Kernel functions, so that you don't have to do all of that low-level programming yourself.

The good news is that an an Android Absolute Beginner, you don't need to understand much about ART, other than what this .DEX file is, the place it provides in the chain of code to runtime, and that it will do a good job optimizing your application for your users. To use the Java programming language, you'll simply **include** the appropriate components from the Java libraries you need in your program, using something in Java called an **import statement**. After you do this, your app's code can employ that built-in Java library's capabilities. You will learn how to put a number of these powerful Java libraries to work later on in this chapter, and in all the chapters, for that matter, during the remainder of the book. We will also cover this in detail in the Java Primer in Chapter 5.

Next, I show you how to create your first Android application, so that you can see how to organize your Android 7 application assets in a highly structured Android project hierarchy, which must be followed for Android apps to work properly. In this way we can get right to some hands-on use of the Android Studio application development environment, to see how you create a new, empty Android bootstrap application infrastructure; and start learning about Android Development, Android Studio, Java, XML, Gradle, application resources, and new media assets.

Creating Android 7 Apps: Android Studio's New Project

By now you are probably quite eager to fire up Android Studio and IntelliJ 2016, and to create your first Android 7 application. We need to do this so that you can observe how Java code, XML markup, and new media assets, called "resources" in Android, work together when it comes to creating your own custom Android 7.0 application.

A time-honored tradition across every programming language is for new users to create a "Hello World" application. Let's create our own Absolute Beginner Hello World Android application, right here and now. Just so that we do things as "out-of-the-box" as possible, we will eventually turn this application into a "Hello Universe" application during the book so that we can expand (no pun intended) on the bootstrap (empty) application that Android Studio creates for us as we learn more and more about Android graphics, user interface design, and so forth. We'll add all sorts of impressive features that you'll find around our universe.

First, we will launch Android Studio, and create the new application. Then we will take a look at all of the files that Android Studio creates for us, as well as the Java and XML code that Android Studio generates to get your app up and running. We will then examine in detail the resource folder hierarchy for the project structure and see how Android Studio wants you to structure your Android 7.0 project assets (resources).

Finally, we will take a look at how to upgrade to later versions of Android Studio when you already have Android Studio installed. A later version of Android Studio 2.3 was released when I was working on this chapter, so I took some screenshots that show what you will see when a new version of Android Studio is released and how to handle the download, upgrade, and installation process from inside of Android Studio itself.

The Android Studio Welcome Menu: Creating a New Android 7 App

The first step is to launch Android Studio 2.3. From there, using the **Welcome to Android Studio** menu that you saw in Figure 2-5 in Chapter 2, you will create your new Android 7.1.1 application project. The application infrastructure we are about to create (or Android Studio is about to create for us) will contain your application's Java programming logic, XML markup, new media assets, and your other application resources.

1. To launch Android Studio, find and click the Android Studio quick launch icon, located on your workstation taskbar. If you didn't create one of these, find **Studio64.exe** on your hard drive (you can use Search in your File Management Utility), and double-click it.

2. You will see the **Welcome to Android Studio** launch dialog, and you will click the first option, **Start a New Android Studio Project**. If you want to see a screenshot of this aforementioned dialog, see Figure 2-5, from Chapter 2.

3. Once you select this option you will get the **New Project** dialog, as is shown in Figure 3-2. This is the first in a series of five dialogs you will be using to create a blank Android Studio project. These dialogs will step you through the process of creating a new Android application project infrastructure. Accept the default **My Application** name for your app and **user.example.com Company Domain**. Since this is the Absolute Beginners title, you will not need to select your **Include C++ Support** option check box. Click the **Next** button to advance to the **Target Android Devices** dialog, where you will accept the default **Phone and Tablet** application type option.

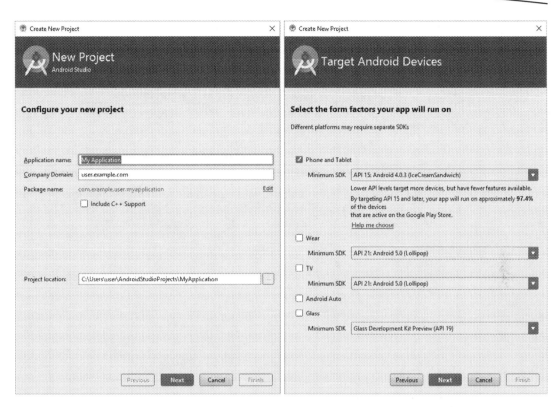

Figure 3-2. Accept the default My Application name, user.example.com Company Name, Phone and Tablet, and click Next

4. After you click a second **Next** button in the Target Android Devices dialog, there is a possibility that Android Studio might launch the **Installing Android SDK** repository updater progress bar, which can be seen in Figure 3-3. What Android Studio is doing is that it is checking the Android APIs that you have specified for the use of the core Android OS (phone and tablet), as well as Android Wear 2, Android TV, Android Auto, or Glass. If any of these need installing or updates, this Installing Android SDK update function will kick in automatically and make Android Studio compliant with the application types that you wish to develop your Android application for.

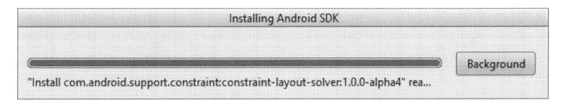

Figure 3-3. Android Studio will install any components needed for those target Android devices that you want to utilize

5. Once Android Studio has downloaded all of the new updates and APIs that you will need to develop the Android application you have specified in the Target Android Devices dialog, you will get the **Installing Requested Components** dialog shown in Figure 3-4. This will show you what is being added to your Android Studio. Once you see **Done** at the bottom left of this dialog, click the **Next** button to advance to the next dialog and continue creating a new blank Android application bootstrap software infrastructure.

Figure 3-4. The Installing Requested Components dialog will tell you what APIs Android Studio has installed for you

6. The next dialog you will encounter is the **Add an Activity to Mobile** dialog, which can be seen in Figure 3-5. The default option is the creation of an **Empty Activity** (shown selected in blue in the top middle of this figure). This is the best option for an Absolute Beginner title, as we will need to examine what the minimum XML markup and Java code is required to create Android applications. We will then build up from that knowledge, and learn about what comprises the basic Android application infrastructure.

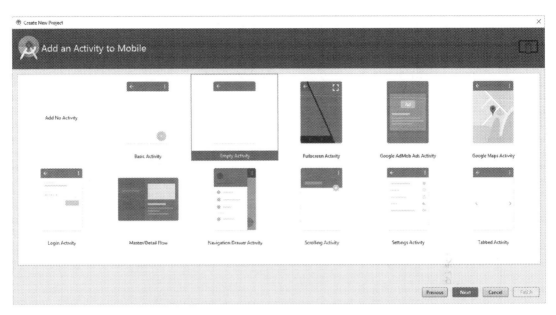

Figure 3-5. *In the Add an Activity to Mobile dialog, accept the default Empty Activity option, shown in blue, and click Next*

7. Take a look at some of the other options in the **Add an Activity to Mobile** dialog to see what Android Studio is able to create for you. This is a pretty cool feature, because Android Studio will do a lot of the core application Java coding and XML markup for you automatically, allowing you to get to that application development stage where you can drop in your new media assets, and define your software functionality much more rapidly. You can create a Fullscreen Activity for iTV sets or tablets; Google AdMob and Maps Activities; Navigation Drawer Activity; a Scrolling Activity; a Tabbed Activity; a Basic Android Activity; and various utility-based Activities, such as login screens, settings collections, master-detail data display utilities and more. In case you may be wondering what this "Activity" is, it is a functional user interface display screen or collection of functionality in Android.

8. After you click the **Next** button, you will advance to the **Customize the Activity** dialog, which is shown on the left-hand side in Figure 3-6. Accept the default **MainActivity** Java class name and the **activity_ main.xml** user interface layout container name, as we will be learning about these Android application component naming conventions as well during this chapter. Leave both the **Generate Layout File** (so Android Studio writes XML markup for you), as well as the **Backwards Compatibility (AppCompat)** options selected. The AppCompat API inclusion allows you to code apps for Android 7.0, which also work

on Android 4.0.3, 5.0, and 6.0, as you already specified in the Target Android Devices dialog, shown on the right-hand side, back in Figure 3-2.

9. Once you click on the **Finish** button, Android Studio will start building the Gradle files for your application, as can be seen (numbered as 2) in Figure 3-6. Gradle is an open source build tool that was adopted in Android 5.0 and which manages the compilation (building) of your Android application. Prior to Android 5 Eclipse used the Apache Ant and Apache Maven build tools. Since this is an Absolute Beginner title, we will not be delving deeply into the complexities of Gradle build tools and configurations, other than to utilize them to create your Android applications.

10. If at some time your Windows Firewall blocks the OpenJDK Platform binary using the Windows Alert dialog, like the one shown in the right-middle of Figure 3-6, click the **Allow Access** button (numbered as 3), to allow the OpenJDK Platform binary to communicate with your own private network. You can also select public networks as well, if you know for a fact that they are safe. After you do this, the Gradle build tool will continue to create Android 7 application build files, and a progress bar dialog will tell you precisely which files are being generated for you. We will take a look at these files a bit later on, so you know what, and where, they are in your project.

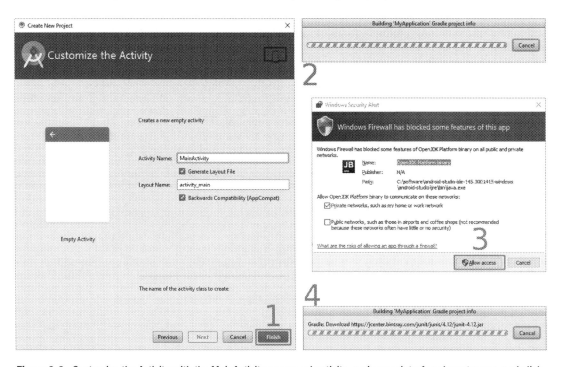

Figure 3-6. *Customize the Activity with the MainActivity name and activity_main user interface layout name, and click Finish*

11.   Once this Gradle build process has been completed, Android Studio will launch. You will see your **MyApplication** project name in the title bar, as well as the location of your project files and the Android Studio version, as can be seen on the top left in Figure 3-7. In my case, the project files are located in the **C:\Users** folder, under **C:\Users\user\AndroidStudioProjects\MyApplication**.

12.   In the **Tip of the Day** dialog that comes up in the middle of the screen (I moved it to show you what was behind it in a virgin launch), look through some or all of the tips, and then use the **Close** button to close that educational feature of Android Studio 2.3. You can leave the **Show Tips on Startup** checked, if you want to avail yourself of this feature later on, which I will recommend that you do as an Absolute Beginner, until you are familiar with Android Studio. I numbered this first step as number 1 in Figure 3-7.

13.   After you close the Tip of the Day dialog, Android Studio will open a pop-up dialog, numbered as 2 in Figure 3-7, that asks if you want to share your usage statistics with Google so that they can make user interface and user experience improvements to Android Studio 2.3. If this is acceptable to you, click the **I agree** link, and if not, click the **I don't agree** link.

14.   Android Studio and the Gradle build system will continue to build and index the project, as seen at the bottom right in Figure 3-7, using a progress bar and a text update as to what is being done.

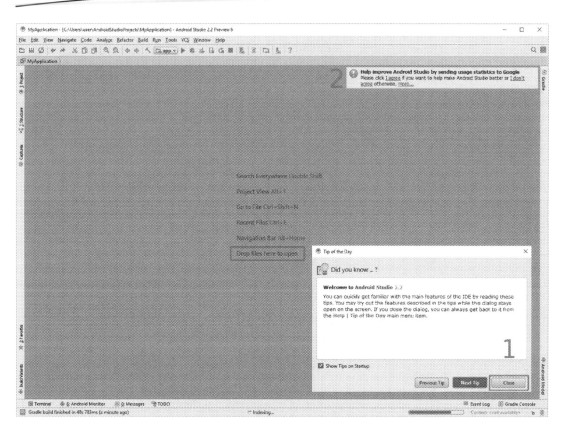

Figure 3-7. Close the Tip of the Day dialog, agree (or disagree) to help improve Android Studio, finish indexing your project

15. Also notice in the center of the Android Studio screen there are some
     shortcuts that you can use to speed up your Android 7 applications
     development (this is why I have moved the Tip of the Day dialog
     out of the way). At the bottom of the list, notice the "Drop files
     here to open," which lets you know you can drag existing Android
     Studio files into Android Studio 2.3 to open them. You can also use
     Double Shift to Search Everywhere, **Alt+1** to get a Project View,
     Ctrl+Shift+N to Go to a File, **Ctrl+E** to open Recent Files, and
     Alt+Home to access the navigation bar.

Once your new project build has finished building, indexing, generating Java code and XML
markup, and all of the other steps needed to create your Android application, the blank
screen in Android Studio will be replaced with the project navigation and development
panes that we will use during the remainder of the book to develop (and learn) Android
applications.

These various panes let you navigate your project structure as well as edit your Java code
and XML markup structure, as well as more complex files such as the Gradle build files that
use the Groovy programming language. Let's explore Android Studio 2.3 next, and see what

we can learn about Android applications, and how they need to be put together, in order to compile (build) into a usable Android package (.APK) file that you can use in Google's Play Store, to publish applications.

Exploring Your Android Studio Project: The Android App Structure

Once Android Studio opens, use the right-facing arrows to open the primary application folders, so you get what is seen on the left half of the screen in Figure 3-8. The right-facing arrows are called expand arrows, which turn into downward-facing arrows, called collapse arrows. These arrow heads toggle folder directories open or closed, as you'll see, once you get familiar with them. As you can see, Android has a top-level **app** folder, which contains three primary subfolders: **manifests**, **java**, and **res** (resources). java and res subfolders have subfolders as well.

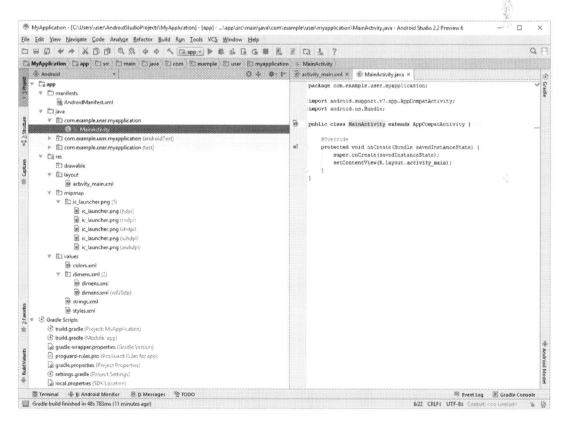

Figure 3-8. Open the Android Project pane folder hierarchy, and see what folders need to be used for Android Development

Your application Java code is in an app\java\com.example.user.myapplication folder that takes its name from the Application Name and Company Domain fields, which you saw in Figure 3-2. Inside of that folder is the Java code file MainActivity.java, which when compiled into Java bytecode, will become MainActivity.class after a build.

Your application resources (I like to call these your application's "assets") on the other hand are contained in the app\res\drawable (images and illustration), app\res\layout (user interface design), app\res\mipmap (app icons), and the app\res\values folder and its subfolders, which contain XML definitions and constant values for the app.

We will be getting into what the Java code in the **MainActivity.java** tab in the Android Studio central editing pane does in Chapter 5, so in this chapter, let's focus on the contents of the Android project management pane, and learn what all of the components are that make up an Android project structure. As we do this during this chapter, we will take a look at the various subfolders and what components of our Android application need to be stored in certain subfolders. One of the things you need to do to become an Android developer is to learn how Android projects need to be organized. It's really too bad there is not "forced organization" in more areas of our lives, because as you will soon see, Android is organized in such a way that it forces your application development work process to be surgically precise!

Let's take a quick look at the **activity_main.xml** tab, which is shown selected in the center of Figure 3-9. You will be learning about XML in Chapter 4, but I wanted to make sure you knew how to click on tabs in the editing section of Android Studio, so you can go back and forth easily between editing your app's XML markup and Java code.

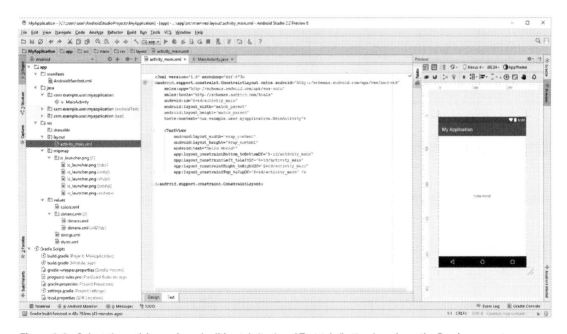

Figure 3-9. *Select the activity_main.xml editing tab (top) and Text tab (bottom), and use the Preview pane to see your app*

As you can see, Java files go in the /app/java folder hierarchy, and the rest of the folders contain XML files and (or) new media assets. There are a large number of different types of resource folders, which start with specific names, such as **drawable** (image, animation, or shape assets), **layout** (UI Design XML definition assets), **mipmap** (app icon imagery), and **values** (value constants defining colors, dimensions, styles, and text strings).

You can also add other types of Android application project asset folders to this project folder hierarchy, which we will be doing during the course of this book, when we add advanced assets like digital video and animation. Since these folders also require specific names, which indicate the type of assets, as well as their functionality, I will outline what Android asset folder types (indicated by their folder names) and naming conventions are. I will provide them in a tabular format in Table 3-1, just so you have an overview of Android's project folder hierarchy.

Table 3-1. Android Project Directory (Folder) Hierarchy, showing key subfolders that you will be using during this book

Android Project Subfolder Name	Type of application assets that this subfolder must contain
/manifest	Android Manifest XML files (your application permissions and specifications)
/java	Java source code files (your Java programming language application logic)
/res	Project resources (your new media assets, UI, menus, and XML markup definitions)
/res/drawable	Digital imaging and digital illustration assets (these are called "drawables" in Android)
/res/layout	UI design layout XML definitions (UI elements are "Views" or "ViewGroups" in Android)
/res/mipmap	Application icons (resolution/density-specific [DPI] PNG32 digital image graphics assets)
/res/menu	Application menu item XML definitions (we will be creating these from scratch later on)
/res/anim	2D image/illustration animation (procedural, frame, or tween animation XML definition)
/res/animator	Android widget (UI elements) property animation (also XML definitions)
/res/xml	Custom XML definitions (other than UI, menu, style, theme, animation, constants, etc.)
/res/raw	Digital video or digital audio assets (which have already been data footprint optimized)
/res/values	Data values that remain fixed for the application duration (these are called constants)
/res/values/colors	Application color value constants
/res/values/dimens	Application dimension (width and height) constants
/res/values/strings	Application text string (labels, titles, messages, fixed text phrases) constants
/res/values/styles	Application styles and themes
/res/values/bool	Application Boolean (true or false data value) constants
/res/values/array	Application data array (lists or collections of data values) constants
/res/values/integer	Application integer constants

Let's spend the rest of the chapter taking a look at the types of resource folders and what they contain, as this will show you what an Android application can contain, where you will need to place assets in order for them to be utilized properly, and show you capabilities and design factors that you'll need to be aware of to make Android apps work on different Android hardware device types with various sizes, shapes, orientations, and resolutions.

Android Resource: Project Folder Hierarchy for Assets

If you want to add custom animation, custom menus, digital video, or digital audio to your Android project, you will have to create new folders under your project resource folder hierarchy. You will be learning how to do this during the course of this book, as you learn about how to add these types of assets to your Android application. I want to expand on Table 3-1 for you to give you a deeper understanding regarding the different folder types that are available for use in your Android applications. This is so that you have a high-level view of what is possible in Android development and the types of Android assets you are going to learn how to incorporate during this book.

Your "external" new media assets, that is, those which are created outside of Android Studio using software like GIMP, Fusion, Lightscape, Blender, Audacity, and Inkscape are kept in the resources folder, shown in Figure 3-9 opened up to show all subfolders, and referenced as app/res/.

Other "internal" resource assets, which are ultimately referenced by your Java code, or in other XML definitions, are created using XML markup in what I call "definition files," because they define application assets using XML markup. XML definitions can include things such as number, text and Boolean constants, styles, themes, menus, animation, and user interface layouts, and these are also kept in the resources (app/res) folder hierarchy.

There are many different resource types in Android, and they either have their own subfolders under the app/res/ project folder, or their own filenames, under the /res/values/ folder. We'll go over the majority of these in detail in the next eight sections of this chapter.

You can also provide **alternate resources** in this application project resource folder hierarchy. The **alternate resource folders** provide support for a wide array of device types or physical hardware specifications, by grouping new media assets, user interface designs, and style and theme definitions into specifically named alternate resource folders. The \res\ values-sw600dp folder is an example of an alternate resource folder name that would hold assets that are specific to an application design for 600-pixel or larger screen dimensions. The sw signifies "smallest width" and thus anything larger than 600 DIP (Device Independent Pixels) would qualify.

At runtime, Android 7 will use the appropriate resource based on the device hardware specification.

> **Note**   Runtime is the stage when your code runs as an application. This is after the compilation process when Android Studio turns your code into bytecode. The ART uses this bytecode to run the application at runtime.

As an example, if you want to provide different UI design layouts that morph, or change, based on the physical screen size, shape, or orientation (portrait or landscape), you can define different UI layout designs using different layout folder names, such as app\res\ layout-land for a landscape-specific UI layout design, or app\res\layout-port for a portrait-specific UI layout design.

As another example, you could define different string (a collection or array of text characters) values, which would be evaluated at runtime based on the language setting on the end user's Android device. As you can see, there is a reason for the way Android organizes resources, and one of the major reasons is so that developers can create alternate resources (alternate resource folders) that can be accessed at runtime based on Android device characteristics. As this book progresses, I will show you how to reference and access external resources from within your Java code and XML markup. We will look into how to set up alternate resource folders in the chapters covering user interface design, themes, and styles. Let's look at Android drawable assets next, as most apps will use digital image (PNG) and digital illustration (SVG) assets.

Android Drawables: Images or Illustration That Draws on the Screen

A "drawable" in Android is aptly named, as it is anything that can be drawn onto the display screen. As you can see in Figure 3-9, Android Studio created five different application icon drawable-dpi versions for your PNG32 app icon. The app icon is named ic_launcher. png and is in the app/res/mipmap folder in the five most common pixel density **drawable-mdpi**, **drawable-hdpi**, **drawable-xhdpi**, **drawable-xxhdpi**, and **xxxhdpi** DPI resolutions. The latest XXXHDPI resolution density was added in Android 4.2 to accommodate Ultra-High Definition (UHD) displays, such as those found on 4K TVs, which have a 4096 by 2160 resolution; or the screen on the Samsung Galaxy S7, which has a 2560 by 1440 pixel resolution screen. From smartwatch (ldpi) to 4K TV (xxxhdpi), Android has a density constant to fit any consumer electronics hardware device.

You will be learning all about pixels and resolutions during Chapter 9 when we cover graphic design, but to give you an overview here of what the different DPI levels are for Android screen resolution density constants, I have put all of the density constants and their specifics in Table 3-2, for those of you who are already "pixel savvy."

Table 3-2. Android Device DPI: Seven levels of Pixel Density constants specifically supported in Android 7 and previous APIs

Android DPI Constant (and its Density Level)	Constant Name	Pixel Density	Pixel Multiplier	Minimum Display	Icon Size (in pixels)	Action Bar Icon Size	Notify Icon Size
LDPI (Low Density)	small	120	0.75	426x320	36x36	24x24	18x18
MDPI (Medium Density)	normal	160	1.0	470x320	48x48	32x32	24x24
TVDPI (HDTV 1280x720)	tv	213	1.33	640x360	64x64	48x48	32x32
HDPI (High Density)	large	240	1.5	640x480	72x72	48x48	36x36
XHDPI (Extra-High Density)	xlarge	320	2.0	960x720	96x96	64x64	48x48
XXHDPI (Super-High Density)	xxlarge	480	3.0	1280x960	144x144	96x96	72x72
XXXHDPI (Ultra-High Density)	xxxlarge	640	4.0	1920x1080	192x192	128x128	96x96

As you can see in Figure 3-9, I opened the `drawable` folder for you to show the `ic_launcher` graphic file that Android Studio created for you in five different resolution density versions. If you are wondering what the pixel dimensions are for these ic_launcher files, take a look at the sixth column in Table 3-2.

There are about a dozen different types of drawable objects in Android, each of which has their very own class. Some of the more important drawable types include `BitmapDrawable`, `ShapeDrawable`, `NinePatchDrawable`, `AnimationDrawable`, `LayerDrawable`, `TransitionDrawable`, and `StateListDrawable`, to name a few. I will try and implement as many different types of drawables as I can during this book, so you will be well rounded when it comes to using drawables in Android application development.

There are several types of drawable assets that will need to be placed in the drawable folders for these assets to be visible to, and accessible to, the Android application. The primary one is **bitmaps**, which we will be covering in Chapter 9, as well as media assets that are based upon (created with) bitmaps, such as **frame animation**, which we will be covering in Chapter 10. Assets that reference Bitmaps or Frame Animation in an XML definition file format would also be kept in this folder, as would any XML definitions creating **shapes** (2D vector graphics).

Android User Interface Design Layout: Asset to Design UI Layout

A "layout" in Android is also aptly named, as it is a definition of how your user interface elements and drawable assets are going to be "laid out" relative to each other on the Android device display screen. Once we get you up to speed on Java, in Chapter 5, you will be learning more about UI layout design throughout the rest of this book! Chances are, if you want your Android app to have a custom design for each type of device (iTV, smartphone, tablet, smartwatch, and iTV set), you're going to have a number of custom /res/layout folders, not just /res/layout-land or /res/layout-port folders as I gave as an example earlier. You can have complex alternate resource folders as well, such as /res/layout-sw800dp-land for tablet, and /res/layout-sw480dp-port for phone or smartwatch.

The /res/layout/ folder and any custom layout alternate resource folders that you create will generally contain UI layout definition XML files. As you will see during Chapters 6 and 8, and over the rest of the book, UI layouts in Android are defined using XML layout definitions. These are handcrafted using XML markup, and stored in filename.xml files in the /res/layout folder or one of the alternate layout resource folders that you create.

Since we are going to look at the XML for the UI layout that Android Studio created for us in Chapter 4, and because we have a couple of chapters coming up specifically covering UI layout design, I am going to leave the /res/layout/ folder coverage at that, and move on to look at some of the other resource folder types next. Although Android applications tend to use Activity screens filled with UI widgets for navigation, Android does support menus as well, so let's take a look at that next, as it is often integrated with the Activity user interface design layout.

Android Menu Design: Asset to Define Menu Structure and Options

A "menu" in Android is exactly what it says it is, and what you would expect it to be: a menu, or a list full of options, for your end users to select from in order to navigate around your Android application infrastructure. In previous versions of Android. menu use was not as much as a priority as it is going to be as iTV set devices and integration with Chrome OS (and Android laptops and PC sticks) become popular with billions of consumers.

There are several types of menus in Android, including pop-up menus, context-sensitive menus, and options menus. We will get more into menu design as we progress through this book, adding menu items to your application's menu. Technically, the Android menu that your application uses, via a hardware MENU button on the Android device or via those three vertical dots on the **Action Bar** at the top of an Android device if there is no hardware MENU button, is called the **Options Menu**. The **Status Bar** is always above the Action Bar, at the very top of every Android device, and holds the battery power indicator, network mode indicator (3G, 4G, 4G LTE, and so forth), signal strength indicator, wireless connection indicator, and other device operation indicators.

In addition to the options menu, the Action Bar contains your application icon; application title; and if you code it correctly, either icons or text tabs that can access areas of your app, each of which is generally an Activity with its own UI design layout scheme.

The app/res/menu/ folder will contain XML definitions outlining the menu structure that you want to create for your application. Notice in Figure 3-9 that Android Studio follows file naming conventions for Java and XML files, so you would want to follow those and name the file containing your menu definition menu_main.xml. Notice the file naming convention; a menu_main.xml menu XML definition, a MainActivity.java and an activity_main.xml layout XML definition file. These all logically match up (type+function), so you know they are all functionally related to each other. This is because each Activity will have a UI layout and a menu, so this keeps things organized so that you know what code works together as an Android application complexity increases over time.

Android Data Values: Assets to Define Fixed Application Constants

A "value" in the Android project folder hierarchy is what is known in Java programming as a "constant." Values in Java code are different than Java constants, as they are meant to change, whereas constants are meant to stay the same (that's why they're called constants). We will be getting into this distinction as far as Java goes soon, in Chapter 5, when we look at the Java programming language specifically. You will, of course, be required to understand exactly how Java works before we get much further into the book, as things will get more and more complicated with each successive chapter.

Android values (constants) are a bit more flexible than Java constants, because once your Java code places these initial constant values into memory, the application code may change them if needed.

Let's examine the `app/res/values/` folder from the current application bootstrap project in more detail. This is where you (or Android Studio, in the case of the New Android Application Project series of dialogs) will place any predefined application values. These exist in the form of XML files. These XML files contain constant definitions that define constant names and their data values.

The value constants that are defined inside of these XML files will later be referenced inside of your Java code, or via your XML markup. For example, these values might be **strings** (a collection of text characters), **styles** (how you want a UI design to be formatted throughout your app), **dimensions** (numeric size specifications), or other constants that need to be "hard-coded" values that your Java code or XML markup uses in your program logic or UI design that you do not want to change.

The logic behind having an `app/res/values/` folder involves holding all of your constant values for your application in one place. This is a similar concept to the repository we used in Chapter 2 to update Android Studio, only the `/res/values/` is a resource repository for value constants that are used in your Android application. The `/res/values/` folder is therefore your application constants repository data (folder) structure, and its usage allows you to make your application constant changes in one single location. In this way, if you need to adjust your constant values during application development or testing, you can do this using XML files.

Figure 3-9 shows four examples of the types of constant value XML files that Android Studio has already created for you and placed into the `app/res/values/` folder in your bootstrap Android application IntelliJ project hierarchy:

- **colors.xml:** An XML file that will define the **color constant values** to be used in your application. These allow you to standardize the UI. For example, you could define your app's background color as a constant. Then, if you decide to tweak it later, you need to do the tweak in only one place and the change is implemented across your entire application.

We cover color theory and hexadecimal color values in detail in Chapter 9, which will cover Android graphic design concepts and principles.

▓ **dimens.xml:** An XML file that defines **dimension constant values** like standard screen dimensions, or font sizes for your UI. You can then use these values across your app, to ensure it is consistent.

▓ **strings.xml:** An XML file that defines **text** (known as "strings" in Java) **values** that are used in your application. For example, you can place your screen titles, menu options, or your app name, here, and reference these text constants in your code. If you need to change or refine these items in the future, you simply do it in this one central location, rather than in your Java code or XML markup.

▓ **styles.xml:** An XML file that defines **UI design styles** that you'll use across your application. These styles constants will be applied to the UI elements, which will then reference these styles constant definitions, allowing you to separate the look and feel of your app from the physical layout and UI functionality. This makes your app easier to refine, change, and enhance stylistically over time.

Some of the other types of value constant XML definition files that you could later create, and locate, in your Android project's `app/res/values/` folder would include the following data value constant types:

▓ **arrays.xml:** An XML file that defines any **series of data value constants** that are intended to be utilized together (known in Java as an array) in your application. For example, this could be a list of icon files, a list of graphic layers, a list of menu items, or a list of options to display to the user.

▓ **integers.xml:** An XML file that defines **numeric integer constant** values that will be used in your Java programming logic for your Android application. We will be covering this topic in Chapter 5.

▓ **bool.xml:** An XML file that defines **Boolean constant** values (true or false) that will be used for the default (initial) setting for logic states (like switches) in your application. Examples of these might include states such as on or off, yes or no, visible or hidden, minimized or maximized, and so forth.

Notice that Android uses certain file name conventions for the different types of XML files in the `app/res/values/` folder, adding another level of complexity. It is important to note that you can also create your own customized XML files and file names in this folder, so you are not limited to the constant types that are discussed here. Next, let's cover the folder names that Android Studio (IntelliJ) did not automatically create for you, and that you can optionally utilize to contain other asset types, such as animation, digital video, digital audio, or custom XML data.

Android Anim Folder: Assets Defining Vector or Tween Animation

Besides frame animation, also known as bitmap animation, or raster animation, Android 7 also supports **vector animation**, which it terms **tween animation**. This type of animation is also known in the industry as **procedural animation**, and is created using Java code or XML markup parameter definitions, rather than by "flipbooking" through a series or collection of bitmap images (like frames of video) to create the illusion of motion.

Whereas bitmap animation in Android uses the BitmapAnimation class, tween animation in Android uses just the Animation class, and thus the proper folder to contain resources or assets related to procedural animation is not the app/res/drawable/ folder, but instead the app/res/anim/ folder, which you will have to create in order to utilize this type of animation in Android. Fortunately, we will be covering this during Chapter 10, so you will create this Android animation resource folder at that time.

Android Animator: Assets for User Interface Property Animation

There is a third type of animation in Android, called **property animation**, used to animate "properties" also known as "attributes" or "parameters," for any of your UI widgets, called "Views" in Android, and this can even be done across your entire UI design. You can use this to obtain impressive special effects, especially transitional effects, which will entice your end users and increase your app professionalism. Property animation XML definition files are held in the app/res/animator/ folder, and reference the UI elements that you want to animate, as well as To and From data values that are interpolated between to create a smooth property animation. The reason the folder is called the animator folder is because the Android Java class is called ViewPropertyAnimator.

Android Raw Folder: Pre-Optimized Video and Audio Asset Files

The app/res/raw/ folder in Android OS holds your application's "raw data." Raw data in Android is not optimized (touched) in any way by the Android OS, it is simply played back (usually streamed) from this folder "as-is." This is the folder that you want to contain your new media assets for which you have taken the time to optimize the data footprint (file size) to quality ratio. This would be done outside of Android Studio, using new media software packages like Audacity, GIMP, Inkscape, or Lightworks, all of which you downloaded and installed in Chapter 2.

We'll be looking at how to create and leverage the app/res/raw/ folder a bit later on in this book during Chapters 11 and 12, where I will cover the Android MediaPlayer and MediaController classes, as well as how to play back digital audio and digital video new media asset resources using this particular raw asset resource folder.

Android XML: Arbitrary XML and Configurations

The last resource folder that you should know about is the app/res/xml/ folder, which is used to contain non-Android XML files that specify data structures or configuration parameters that are for use in your application but which are external to (outside of) the scope of Android-specified XML structures. As you will see during Chapter 4 and the rest of the book, Android defines a great many application components and characteristics using XML, and this (the XML markup) must be done (written or structured) in exactly the correct way or format. This folder usually contains XML files that have nothing to do with the Android app creation process, but that are "parsed" (read) by an Android application using a Resources.getXML() method. We cover Java method calls in Chapter 5.

Updating Android Studio: Upgrading an SDK over Time

When I fired up Android Studio to create the figures for this chapter, there was an **update available** link on the startup screen. I clicked it and got a **Default Settings** dialog, seen in Figure 3-10, showing an Android 7 update.

1. Select the **Update Available SDK Version** (on the upper right, highlighted in blue, in Figure 3-10), in this case this is **24.0.1**, or Android 7.0.1, if you prefer, and then click on the OK button.

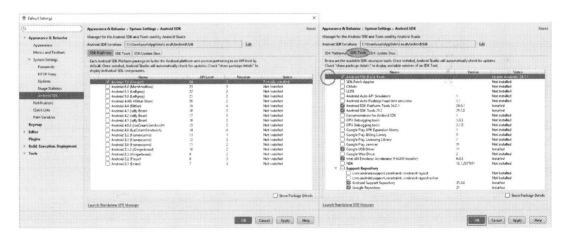

Figure 3-10. *If you see an update link on the Android Studio startup screen, click it and see what new SDK has been released*

2. Click the **SDK Tools** tab and select **the Show Package Details** and make sure **24.0.1** is selected, seen as step number 1 in Figure 3-11; and click the **OK** button, seen as step number 2 in Figure 3-11.

3. Click the **OK** in the **Confirm Change** dialog, seen as step number
    3 in Figure 3-11, and wait until the installation finishes, seen as step
    number 4. Click **Finish** when the update is installed, seen as step
    number 5 in Figure 3-11.

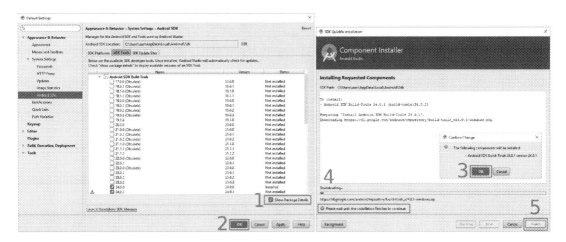

Figure 3-11. Create a New Layer dialog

4. Deselect the **Show Package Details** option, and make sure that the
    24.0.1 update, or whatever more recent update you are probably
    looking at, is showing as being installed. For my installation this was
    24.0.1, and is shown in Figure 3-12. Once everything is updated,
    click the OK button to exit, and when Android Studio launches it will
    then be the most recent version. Note that in the future this could be
    API 25 or 26, as API revisions come out quarterly.

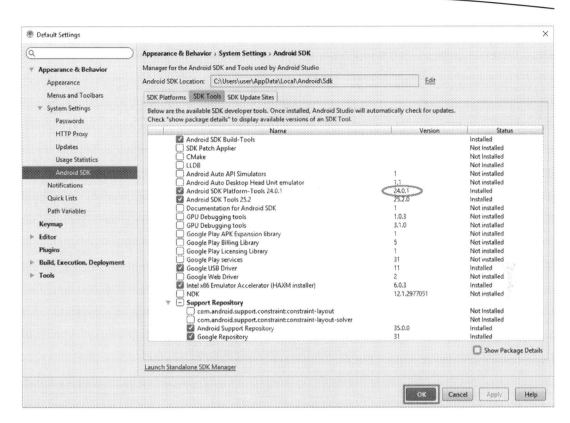

Figure 3-12. Use a Select ➤ Invert menu sequence to invert the selection so it selects the logo instead of white areas

Make sure to update Android Studio whenever it informs you that an update is available, as it is connected in real time to the Android Studio server. Now we're ready for XML markup!

Summary

In this third chapter, you learned about how the Android platform is structured, and about how it deals with the application at runtime, when one of your end users launches it on one of their many Android hardware devices. You learned about Dalvik Virtual Machine (DVM) and Android RunTime (ART) virtual machines (VM). You learned how to create an Android Studio 2.3 application bootstrap and Android project folder foundation, by using the New Android Application Project series of dialogs in Android Studio. You took a closer look at the folders that comprise an Android 7 application, most of which (besides the Java source app/java/ folder) are application resource folders. We looked at the various types of resource folders that you can have in an Android application.

In the next chapter, you will learn all about the XML markup language by taking an in-depth look at the Android application that you created during this chapter, including the XML files in the app/res/values/ folder as well as the app/res/layout/ folder and the AndroidManifest.xml file from your app/manifests/ project folder.

Introduction to XML: Defining Android Apps, UI Design, and Constants

During this chapter, we will take a closer look at how Android's XML capabilities allow application developers, and more importantly, application designers, to define their Android 7 application user interface (UI) design, styles, themes, constants, permissions, icons, activities, services, and how they function within the Google Play e-storefront, all without having any knowledge of Java programming. Of course, I am going to teach you Java programming in this book, starting with the next chapter, but you could hire people to do just Android 7 design, and all they would have to know is how to use the XML and Visual Design Editor features that we are going to learn about during this chapter. It is important to note that these same XML concepts that you will be learning in this chapter apply to both the 32-bit Android 4.4.4 OS as well as to the 64-bit Android 5.0, 5.1, 6.0, 7.0, and to the new Android 7.1.1 OS.

In the previous chapter, you created the foundation for your Hello World bootstrap Android application using the Android Studio 2.3 (IntelliJ 2016) New Android Application series of dialogs. As part of this new application creation process, more than half a dozen XML definition files were created. We are going to review all of these XML files during this chapter, as well as show you how to add features to them and refine them. We will do this so that you can learn the basics of XML implementation, and also to show you how to visually design user interfaces, add text constant values, create styles using Android themes (high-level Android OS user interface element styles), set your screen layout dimensions, request your Android application permissions, and define your Java 8 code module configuration. These last two are done using the Android Manifest XML definition. All this can easily be implemented using only XML, or eXtensible Markup Language, once you know the rules of the XML game in Android 7.x.

© Wallace Jackson 2017
W. Jackson, *Android Apps for Absolute Beginners*, DOI 10.1007/978-1-4842-2268-3_4

We will again take a closer look at all of the basic Android application components that are defined using XML in your bootstrap project during this chapter; but this time, instead of doing this by looking at the Android Studio application (app) resource (res) folder structure, we will do this by looking at the XML files themselves. We will be learning about the Android Manifest XML definition file and its functions, structure, and its role in defining and controlling how your application will work within the Android OS. It is important to note that the AndroidManifest.xml application characteristics definition file works in exactly the same way, whether you are developing for 32-bit Android 4.4.4 OS devices, or for 64-bit Android 5.0 through 7.1.1 OS devices. We'll also look at the Android Studio Visual Design Editor.

As you progress in your knowledge of Android – in this chapter, this will be your knowledge of XML – you will continue to enhance the application foundation that you put into place in Chapter 3, and will continue to do so during each chapter in the book, learning the fundamental capabilities of Android OS, as well as the Android Studio 2.3 IDE in the process.

Extensible Markup Language: XML Overview

XML stands for **eXtensible Markup Language**. Extensible means that you can use it for whatever you like (think "customizable"). You could in fact create your own set of XML tags for any purpose that you wish. It is a markup language, because it uses simple "tags" to define what you wish to do. Most of you will be familiar with another markup language called HTML5, or Hypertext Markup Language V5, which is used for creating HTML5 websites, and more recently, for creating HTML5 applications.

Markup languages differ from programming languages, in that they use **tags**, **parameters** (also called attributes or characteristics) within these tags, and **nesting structures** to accomplish tasks that high-level programming languages, such as Java 8, will implement using complex programming structures like data arrays, logic loops, and method calls. We will be getting into Java 8 and these types of Java constructs in Chapter 5's Java primer. You're really learning two programming languages: one that uses code, and the other that uses markup, and how they work together in Android Studio, during this book.

The reason for this approach, that is, using XML for everything that could possibly be construed as being design oriented, is that using XML frees the members of your application development team who are designing your application's usability, feature access, user interface, user experience, styles, theme, graphics, and the like, from having to learn (that is, understand) how Java 8 programming works.

As you will soon see, when you compare this chapter to the next one on Java, XML markup is an order of magnitude easier to learn and implement than Java 8 programming structures and concepts are. For this reason, during this Absolute Beginners book, I'm going to implement everything that I possibly can using XML markup, including using the parts of Android Studio where you can "drag and drop" components into the Visual Design Editor, and have Android Studio write your XML markup for you, which is a great way to learn XML markup as you design user interfaces. I will do this so that I can quickly get you to an intermediate level of 32-bit Android 4.4.4 and 64-bit Android 5.0 through 7.1.1 application development in this book in less than 600 (dense) pages of learning material.

Although I'd like to take all the credit for this book being able to take you so very far from being an Absolute Beginner (zero Android app development experience) to an Android developer, the primary reason this is possible is because Google Android OS developers made sure the advanced, "front-facing" features, which allow you to ratchet up the "wow-factor" for your applications, can be designed and implemented almost entirely using XML, often using only a few lines of Java programming logic!

Some examples of advanced Android design-related features that you can implement primarily using XML markup "definitions" include multi-state graphics, skinned UI elements (custom graphic design User Interface elements), frame or bitmap image animation, vector or "tween" (procedural) animation, user interface layout design animation (UI property animator), options menus, pop-up menus, and context-sensitive menus, dialog boxes, alert dialogs, styles, themes, and your application's manifest.

You can also implement less advanced, strategic design features using XML, including string (text) constant values for your app, integer (numeric) value constants, state or status (Boolean) value constants (such as on or off, visible or hidden, true or false), and screen spacing (dimension) values for your UI designs. Arrays, which are collections of data used in your app (like a simple database), can also be created, and loaded with their data values, by using XML files. Again, remember that all of this holds true for XML in 32-bit Android 4.4.4 devices and for 64-bit Android 5.0 through 7.1.1 devices.

XML markup is contained in **simple text format** files identified using the **.xml** file extension. You can create XML files in a text editor, such as Windows Notepad; however, most programmers usually use a software editing tool with programming and markup design features, such as Eclipse, IntelliJ, and NetBeans. These XML files can then be read or "**parsed**" by the Android OS, or your application Java code, and turned into Java object structures using an XML "data or object definition" in each XML file.

XML Naming Schema: Tag and Parameter Repository

XML is comprised of "**tags**" and their "**parameters**." Parameters are part of the tags, and are used to **configure** and fine-tune what each of these tags accomplishes, as well as to **reference** any new media assets, or text fonts, or color values, or styles, or themes, or other XML definitions, and similar Android application assets that might be required to "skin," or otherwise define how that application user interface element will appear, or "render," relative to your users' Android device display screen.

XML tags and parameters that you can use in any particular design framework, such as in Android 7.1.1 development, are specified by using an XML "**naming schema.**" This definition of the XML tags and their parameters are stored in a **centralized repository**, similar to the one Android Studio accessed in Chapter 2, when you did a Check for Updates function; or Chapter 3, when I updated Android 7 to API 24.0.1, or when you update the Android 7.1.1 API 25 to the next version coming in late 2017.

The SDK repository hosts the latest Android SDK versions and code base, whereas the Android XML repository is located at a different URL location (a different folder) on Google's Android OS servers. The reason XML needs to have a naming schema is because this language is inherently designed to be "**extensible**." This means there is no "standard" version of XML; each version is customized for some required implementation (end use) by whatever person or organization needs to use it. The process of making sure that XML tags and their attributes or parameters are correct, or valid and in conformance with their XML definition, is called **XML validation**.

Android XML has been specifically customized for, and implemented for, the development of Android applications. For example, Android OS developers created the XML tag named <ConstraintLayout> for UI design using Constraint Layouts. The ConstraintLayout Java class was introduced in Android 7, as an improvement to the Android RelativeLayout Java class, which was covered in my previous three editions of this book (and still exists in the SDK), and was specifically designed to work hand-in-hand (code-in-code) with the drag and drop **Layout Editor** in Android Studio 2.3. Since this is an Absolute Beginner title, we will be showing you how to use the Layout Editor and ConstraintLayout class together, so that you can use Android Studio 2.3 for visual design rather than writing XML markup.

The XML naming schema is referenced inside of each of your XML definition files, at the very top, as you'll see in Figure 4-1, in the first two lines of XML markup in the central editing pane of Android Studio. This is done so that the XML markup inside of your XML file can reference its XML naming schema.

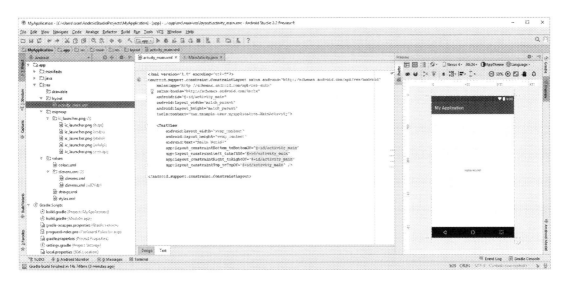

Figure 4-1. The contents of the activity_main.xml file in the app/res/layout folder in the Android Studio middle editing pane

Android Studio does not need to validate the XML file in "real time", so you do not need an active Internet connection to be able to develop the XML markup.

In any custom extensible markup language, such as the one that has been created by Google for Android, the XML version is declared on the first line, and the naming schema URL reference needs to be contained in the **first** outermost **parent** tag, which is most always the second line of XML markup. The following lines of XML markup from Figure 4-1 declare XML and the XML naming schema, abbreviated as XMLNS, as well as configuring the `ConstraintLayout` Java class characteristics using attributes or parameters inside of the parent `<ConstraintLayout>` tag:

```
<?xml version="1.0" encoding="utf-8" ?>
<   android.support.constraint.ConstraintLayout
    xmlns:android="http://schemas.android.com/apk/res/android"
    xmlns:app="http://schemas.android.com/apk/res-auto"
    xmlns:tools="http://schemas.android.com/tools"
    android:id="@+id/activity_main"
    android:layout_width="match_parent"
    android:layout_height="match_parent"
    tools:context="com.example.user.myapplication.MainActivity" >
```

This parent layout container tag will usually contain other child tags, which are nested inside of, and underneath, the opening parent tag. This nesting of child tags, as well as nesting parameters inside of the tag, can more easily seen if the XML programmer uses **indenting** to show which tags are inside of other higher-level (parent) tags, as I have done in the above markup, and which Android Studio has done as seen in Figure 4-1 in the `activity_main.xml` editor tab in the middle of the screen.

Let's take a look at the Constraint Layout UI design in the `activity_main.xml` file, which Android Studio created for you as the UI layout foundation to start building your UI design upon for the `MyApplication` Hello World Android application. As seen in Figure 4-1, the first line of the parent `<ConstraintLayout>` UI layout container tag has `xmlns:android="http://schemas.android.com/apk/res/android"` as its first parameter. This parameter defines the XML naming schema repository for Android 7 as being in the `schemas` virtual server, on an `android.com` HTTP address, in an `/apk` folder, in a `/res` subfolder, and finally in an `/android` sub-subfolder.

In this case the `<ConstraintLayout>` container is the parent tag and the `xmlns:android` is one of the parameters that configures this tag. This parameter will allow this UI layout tag to reference the XML naming scheme repository, and defines the prefix `android` as a **markup shortcut** to reference this repository. Note that just because it references the proper XML definition repository does not mean that it is connecting in real time to check this repository, as I pointed out earlier (it is used as a unique identifier). As you can see inside of the `<ConstraintLayout>` tag, there are a significant number (three) of parameters that start with `android:` and what this `android:` reference equates to, as it is defined by that first `xmlns:android` parameter. Essentially, what is happening here, is that this `xmlns:android` parameter is defining a shortcut for all the other parameters that start with `android:` to be able to check themselves against the XML naming schema repository. Thus, because of the `xmlns:android` URL definition parameter, the `android:width="match_parent"` parameter is actually shorthand for an `http://schemas.android.com/apk/res/android:width="match_parent"` parameter.

The same code-replacement logic would apply to the `xmlns:tools` parameter in conjunction with your `tools:context="com.example.user.myapplication.MainActivity"` `<ConstraintLayout>` parameter, also seen in Figure 4-1. An XML tools parameter sets the **context** for the `ConstraintLayout` definition as the `MainActivity` class, which Android Studio created for you, using the New Android Application dialogs.

As you can see here, Android OS really has three XML naming schemas (language definitions), in three different software repositories, as there is also one that defines an `app:` shortcut that you can see is used inside of the `<TextView>` child tag inside of the `<ConstraintLayout>` parent tag. This is set to `xmlns:app="http://schemas.android.com/apk/res-auto"` and is used in four `app:layout_constraint` parameters. The Android Package APK naming schema was designed for high-level, design-oriented XML and is at `schemas.android.com/apk`. It is also the XML naming schema you will be using 99% of the time in your Android application development, and the one I will be covering throughout this book.

The Android Tools (`tools`) naming schema was created to provide low-level (OS-related usage) XML, and is at `schemas.android.com/tools`. You can use it to do things such as declare the `Context` object using XML. You'll learn more about `Context` objects during Chapter 14, when I cover Android Service class concepts and structures, as well as when we encounter `Context` objects. This `Context` object here defines the context for the `ConstraintLayout` class UI design as your `MainActivity` activity class, which is obvious as context is set to the `MainActivity` class in your `com.example.user.myapplication` Android project, as can be seen in Figure 4-1, and in the previous XML markup example.

XML Syntax: Containers, Brackets, and Nesting

There are two ways to code (or to mark up, to be more precise) any XML tag, and which markup approach you use depends upon whether that tag is going to have any children (nested tags) or not. Attributes, also known as parameters, are inside of each tag and configure the tag and what it will do. Parameters would not be considered children of the tag, but are attributes specifying values or references customizing the tag. Parameters will use quotation marks to do this, such as the `android:text="data value"` parameter, which we'll be changing shortly to more closely follow Android design conventions.

If an XML tag is a parent tag (which it is if it has "nested" or child tags inside of it), it can be said to be a **container**, just like the XML file itself is the container for that entire XML construct, which Android uses for data or Java object **definition** of one type or another, as you will see throughout this chapter, as well as throughout the rest of this book.

Fortunately the bootstrap UI layout design seen in Figure 4-1 shows both of these types of bracketing treatments, so I can simply describe the usage here, and you can observe it in Figure 4-1 or in Android Studio if you have it running on your computer workstation, which I am hoping you do.

Since the `<TextView>` UI element that defines a Text User Interface element on the screen (as you might have guessed) stands alone; has zero children; and has parameters configuring width, height, and text content, this tag is opened using the `<TextView` portion of the tag, and is closed using the `/>` character sequence. Tags that contain other tags are closed using only the right-chevron `>` bracket.

So, with `android` and `app` parameters inside of this `TextView` tag, your tag structure will look like this:

```
<TextView  android:parameter="value"  app:parameter="value"  />
```

The XML for this child tag, which is shown in Figure 4-1 and below in full, uses **indentation** for easy parameter views, as well as setting Android Text class constants that you will learn about in the next chapter covering Java. The android:text parameter references a Java String directly setting a text data value in quotes. I will be showing you how to use a text String constant in your strings.xml file a bit later on during this chapter, which is really how things should have been set up initially by Android Studio.

For now, we are just going to look at the syntax of XML—that is, how it needs to be constructed or structured (written on the screen). We will look at how it all works together in the next section of this chapter. Since your <ConstraintLayout> tag does indeed have a child <TextView> tag nested inside it, it will use a different (parent) bracket configuration. Using high-level pseudo-code, it looks like this:

```
<android.support.constraint.ConstraintLayout xmlns:parameter="value"
android:parameter="value" >
    <TextView  android:parameter="value"  app:parameter="value"  />
</ConstraintLayout>
```

Once you put parameters inside of the parent and child tags, and indent everything, so that you know what level each of these tags and its parameters are supposed to be at, it will look exactly like what you see in Figure 4-1, which I will replicate below. We will be going over what all of this XML markup is doing during this chapter, as well as using the Visual Design Editor to add User Interface elements to it. Since an entire book could be written on XML (and has, such as my 2014 *Pro Android UI* title from Apress), this will be one of the longer chapters in the book, as a significant percentage of what your application looks like, and what it is allowed to do via the Android OS, will ultimately be defined using XML markup definitions.

```
<?xml version="1.0" encoding="utf-8" ?>
<android.support.constraint.ConstraintLayout
    xmlns:android="http://schemas.android.com/apk/res/android"
    xmlns:app="http://schemas.android.com/apk/res-auto"
    xmlns:tools="http://schemas.android.com/tools"
    android:id="@+id/activity_main"
    android:layout_width="match_parent"
    android:layout_height="match_parent"
    tools:context="com.example.user.myapplication.MainActivity" >
    <TextView
        android:layout_width="match_parent"
        android:layout_height="match_parent"
        android:text="Hello World!"
        app:layout_constraintBottom_toBottomOf="@+id/activity_main"
        app:layout_constraintBottom_toLeftOf="@+id/activity_main"
        app:layout_constraintBottom_toRightOf="@+id/activity_main"
        app:layout_constraintBottom_toTopOf="@+id/activity_main" />
</android.support.constraint.ConstraintLayout>
```

In summary, any tag that you will use as a parent tag will have an **opening tag**; in this case that is the <ConstraintLayout> tag, and its paired **closing tag** </ConstraintLayout> with the tag name in both the opening and the closing tag. The closing tag will have a slash in front of the tag name to signify to the XML parsing engine (the code that is interpreting the XML markup and turning it into something else; in this case, Java objects, data constants, and data variables) that this is the closing tag.

Alternatively, the child tag that has no children of its own will have the closing slash at the end of the opening tag, like this: `<TextView android:parameters app:parameters />` which allows a much more compact way of writing a child tag. You might think of this as an **implicit** closing tag, so a tag with no child tags nested inside of it, will not have an **explicit** closing tag, or a backslash in front of the tag name inside of `< >` chevron bracketing like the `</ConstraintLayout>` UI layout container has. Since a layout container will always inherently be a container it will always have child tags, and therefore UI layout container tags will always have an explicit closing tag at the bottom of the XML definition. It is important to note, **nesting** can be more than one level deep, so you can have the following structure:

```
<ConstraintLayout>
    <LinearLayout>
        <TextView  android:parameter="data value" />
        <ImageView android:parameter="data value" />
        <TextView  android:parameter="data value" />
    </LinearLayout>
</ConstraintLayout>
```

As you can see, the explicit closing tags must be in the reverse order from the opening tag order, so that the XML tag structure exhibits the proper nesting for the parsing engine within its level hierarchy.

XML Referencing: Chain XML Constructs Together

XML files can also reference other XML files, so that you can create a chain where XML definitions can be modular, since they can be blocks of code that can be used by more than one XML construct. XML file referencing is somewhat akin to XML tag nesting, but it spans across files. XML referencing in Android is done by using an @ symbol, which is specific to Android XML file referencing syntax.

Android uses the @ character to signify that another XML file is being referenced, as you will see over the rest of the chapter, as we look at how to use XML markup, to define values, dimensions, strings, styles, themes, and your Android Manifest, which defines everything regarding your application.

Without this referencing capability XML markup would end up being all lumped together in one or two massive files. Referencing allows an XML structure to be created, such as the XML structure for your Hello World bootstrap application, which the Android Studio IDE put into place for you using the New Android Application Project series of dialogs.

We'll be looking at your application's current XML structure, and all of the files within it, as well as how these XML files reference each other. We will also be looking at how to change tag parameter values within these XML files in order to customize an Android application during the remainder of this book.

Once we're all finished looking at each of the XML files that are currently in your bootstrap project, I'll include a visual of how all of these go together to for the foundational XML structure for your Android application that Android Studio created for you in Chapter 3. If you want to cheat and look ahead in this chapter, you can go ahead and take a quick peek; the visual is in Figure 4-11.

Let's take a closer look at the `strings.xml` file located in the `app/res/values` folder first, as this is one of the most often used XML files in Android application development, and one we'll be adding to soon.

Open the `app/res/values` folder by clicking the right-facing arrow next to it. Find and right-click on the `strings.xml` file, and select the **Jump to Source** option from the context-sensitive menu. This is how you open an editing tab for a file you want to view or edit in the Android Studio 2.3 central editing pane, so if you are used to a File Open, or a File Edit, context menu sequence, then pay close attention to this!

As you can see in Figure 4-2, the `strings.xml` file does not need to reference the XML repository URL, as it just contains resource constant definitions, using the parent `<resources>` tag, and, in this case, child `<string>` tags defining each string data value and giving the value a (variable) name. We will get into variables in Chapter 5. The reason this file doesn't require an `xmlns:android` XML naming schema definition at the top of the XML definition is because the attributes (parameters) used inside of the child tags in this file do not preface themselves with something else (such as `app:` or `android:` or `tools:` for instance, which require `xmlns:app`, `xmlns:tools`, or `xmlns:android` repository definition parameters).

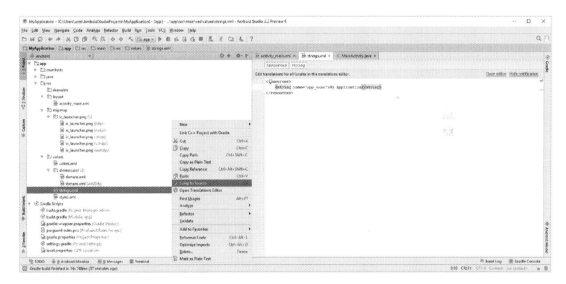

Figure 4-2. Right-click on the strings.xml file located in the app/res/values folder, and select Jump to Source from the menu

Notice in Figure 4-2 and the line of code below the XML markup uses `name="app_name"` and not `android:name="app_name"`. If you needed to use `android:name="app_name"` then you would need the `xmlns:android` XML name schema definition in the top of the definition (resource tag) before you used this parameter naming convention.

The way a `<string>` child tag defines a string (text) variable is that the name parameter is used as the parameter in the first part of the string value XML definition. This defines a string **variable name**, and the actual text data value for a string goes inside of the `<string>`text data`</string>` as you can see in Figure 4-2. The app_name string XML definition would thus be:

`<string name="app_name">My Application</string>`

Next, we will add an `app_message` string constant with the data "Hello World" in it, because we want to collect all the string constants in one place, so we can customize the application text in one place.

XML Constants: Adding New Constants Using XML

Since the "Hello World!" message is "hard-coded" in the `activity-main.xml` UI layout XML definition, I will show you how to change this to a string constant value in the `strings.xml` file that is referenced from the `activity_main.xml` file using the @ character. Why Android Studio did not follow text constant convention, and install this in the `strings.xml` file, I do not know (previous versions of Android did set all of the bootstrap application text constants up in this way). I will simply take this as an opportunity to teach you in a more "hands-on" way how to do this, so you can experience inter-XML file referencing.

Select the entire first `<string>` child tag construct, and either use **CTRL-C** (Copy) and then **CTRL-V** (Paste), or right-click the selection and select **Copy**, and then click in the beginning of the line the `<string>` tag is on, and right-click and select **Paste**. This will give you two identical `<string>` constant constructs, and you can edit the second one to name it app_message with a data value of **Hello World**, as can be seen in Figure 4-3. Notice we are using Hello World without the exclamation point, so we can see the change, as well as when Android Studio renders that change in the **Preview** pane on the right-hand side, which will be visible in Figures 4-4 and 4-5.

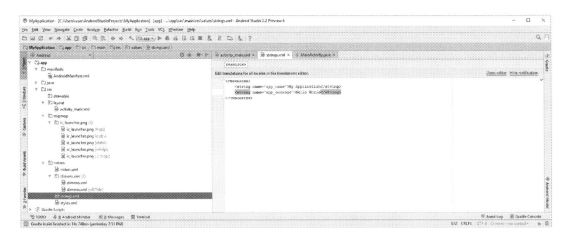

Figure 4-3. *Add a string constant named app_message with the Hello World data value underneath the app_name constant*

Once your `strings.xml` file looks like the following XML markup, click the `activity_main.xml` editing tab.

```
<resources>
    <string name="app_name">My Application</string>
    <string name="app_message">Hello World</string>
</resources>
```

In the `<TextView>` child tag `android:text` parameter value area, remove **Hello World!** and type in `@string`. As you can see in Figure 4-4, Android Studio will give you a drop-down **selector** containing all the current constant values which are currently in the `strings.xml` file in the `app/res/values` folder.

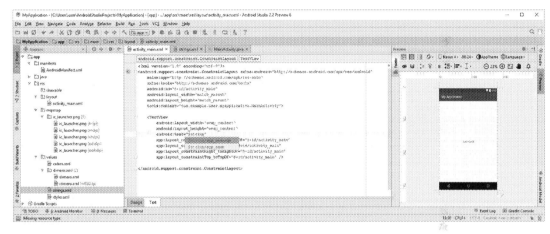

Figure 4-4. *Edit activity_main.xml and change the <TextView> android:text parameter to reference a new @string constant*

Select the `@string/app_message` constant, as seen in Figure 4-4, under the line of markup that you are editing. Notice that Android names the String constant XML definition file `strings.xml` (more than one String is usually in this file) but it references it using `@string` only (no "s" at the end). Also notice that while you are editing this change, the preview on the right shows the previous (hard-coded) text value. Once you select the `app_message` String constant, the preview on the right shows the new Hello World without the exclamation point. This can be seen in Figure 4-5, along with the completed (new) `android:text` value, a reference to your `app_message` constant in the `app/res/values/strings.xml` String constant repository for the Android application. I zoomed in 33% so you could see this better.

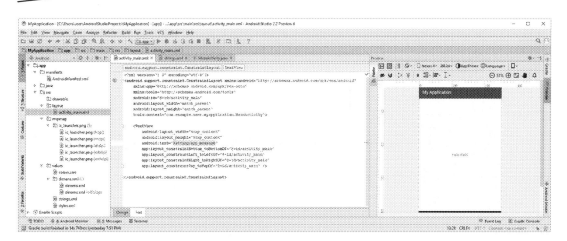

Figure 4-5. *Zoom in 33% in the Preview pane to make sure the new referencing is working with a new Hello World message*

Now, if you wanted to change this text message, you can change it in this `strings.xml` file without touching any of your other XML markup or Java programming logic. Next, let's take a look at the dimensions constants XML definition file located in your `app/res/values/dimens.xml` project hierarchy.

XML Dimensions: Editing Dimensions Using XML

Let's take a look at the `dimens.xml` file in the `app/res/values` folder and see what global application margin spacing has been set up for your Android application by Android Studio. Right-click on your `dimens.xml` file, and select the **Jump to Source** option from the context-sensitive menu.

As you can see in Figure 4-6, there are two `<dimen>` child tags defined inside the parent `<resources>` tag. These are similar to what you just created in your `strings.xml` file, but instead of `<string>` tags, your child tags are `<dimen>` tags. These also use the name= parameter to name the dimension constants, and then set a data value of **16 dp**, or **density pixels**. This is done in exactly the same way that your text string values were set. Here is an example of the XML child tag and parameter format that was used:

```
<resources>
    <dimen name="activity_horizontal_margin">16dp</dimen>
    <dimen name="activity_vertical_margin">16dp</dimen>
</resources>
```

If you wanted to put a little more space between your UI design (or content), and the edges of your Android device hardware, you could edit these values, and use something like 24dp or 32dp. You can try and edit these values and play around with the results of how close to or far away from the edge of the display screen you want your application content to be, to get some practice with using Android Studio. I'll be covering dp (or DP), also known as **device-independent pixels** (DIP) during more advanced chapters (Chapters 6 through 9), covering UI design and graphic design.

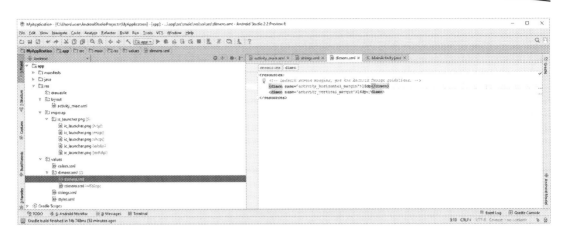

Figure 4-6. *The dimens.xml file is located in the app/res/values folder, and has two <dimen> dimensions constants defined*

Next, we are going to take a look at the second dimensions constants file, which has been defined using an **alternate resource folder** called \res\values-w820dp\ that we will learn about how to locate using the context menu in Android Studio by using the **File Path** command.

Alternate XML Resource: Dimensions for Tablets

As you can see in Figure 4-7, there are two dimens.xml files in the app/res/values folder, one of which has a (w820dp) next to it, telling us that there is an alternate resource folder named /values-w820dp somewhere that has another dimens.xml file in it. If you want to use the same file name for another file, it needs to be in another folder. So, how do we find out where this alternate folder is located? Android Studio has a **File Path** command in its context-sensitive menu (right-click menu) that will show you this.

As you can see in Figure 4-7, I right-clicked and used Jump to Source to open the w820dp\ dimens.xml tab in the editing area, and I also used the File Path command to show me the path to the file, which is shown in a File Path pop-up, seen next to the context menu in Figure 4-7. As you can see the file is located in C:\Users\user\AndroidStudioProjects\ MyApplication\app\src\main\res\values-w820dp, and this is the actual physical address on your hard disk drive, whereas the **Project** folder structure in Android Studio represents a **simplified view** of your Android 7.1.1 application's project hierarchy.

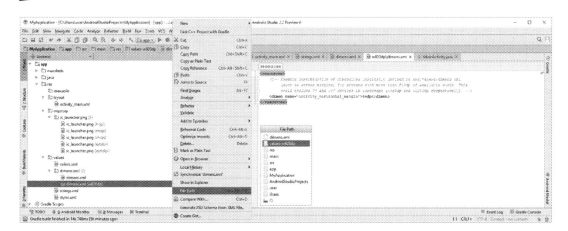

Figure 4-7. The dimens.xml file is located in the app/res/values folder, and has two <dimen> dimensions constants defined

You can use this File Path command on any file in your project pane to see where that file is being stored on your workstation hard disk drive. As you can see in the `res/values-w820dp` alternate folder version of the `dimens.xml file`, tablets with width (w) greater than 820, which would include your 960, 1024, 1280, 1920, 3840, and 4096 pixel devices) would get 64dp of horizontal margin allocated to the Activity screen. The vertical margin dimensions would remain whatever you had set them to be in the `res/values/dimens.xml` file, which sets the baseline or default dimensions, so in this case that would be 16dp (which can also be coded as 16DP, 16dip, or 16DIP, if you prefer). Also notice that on your operating system hard disk drive directory structure is delineated using the **backslash** character, as I did above for the actual location of the `\values-w820dp\dimens.xml` file on my workstation, whereas in Android coding and markup (as well as in the Linux OS) the project folder structure is delineated with a **forward slash** character, as I have been doing in most of this chapter, as in `/app/res/values/dimens.xml` for instance). If you think that this is confusing, I agree, it is, and it is one of the things that you'll just have to get used to, and probably are already, if you use both Linux and Windows.

XML Styles: Editing Styles or Themes Using XML

Whereas text strings and density pixel dimensions are fairly straightforward, Android styles and the Android OS themes they reference, which are actually a collection of style definitions, are a bit more involved and detailed, and hence are more complicated. If you're familiar with websites, e-books and applications created using HTML5 and CSS3, then you are already familiar with the concept of styling something by using a style definition, which is held separate from your Java code and XML content.

Styles and themes, as of Android 5.0 are called "materials," and will be covered in Chapter 6 covering UI design. In short, what a style does is allow you to define, in one central location, how the UI design of your application is going to look, as far as color, spacing, and font characteristics (text typeface, type, and size) are concerned. This approach will allow you to extract the styling of your UI design from the actual content within that design, and from the programming logic behind how that UI design functions.

We're not going to completely cover styles and themes in this chapter, as that more advanced subject matter is better suited for the UI design chapter, but I am going to show you how the `styles.xml` file fits into your overall app structure, and how it sets a default OS theme, so you can make your application use "light" (white or light gray) or "dark" (black or dark gray) operating system user interface themes.

Right-click on your `styles.xml` file, in your `app/res/values` folder, and select the **Jump to Source** option from your context-sensitive menu, so you can take a look at the XML markup in the `styles.xml` file in the central editing pane of Android Studio, as can be seen in Figure 4-8.

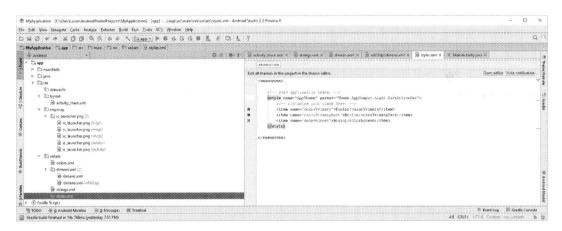

Figure 4-8. *The styles.xml file is located in the app/res/values folder, and has the Theme.AppCompat.Light theme defined*

As you can see, the parent `<style>` container has a name `AppTheme` that will be referenced in your `AndroidManifest.xml` file, as well as a `parent` parameter that is set to the Android OS constant `Theme.AppCompat.Light.DarkActionBar` standard Android theme definition. There is also a Light ActionBar theme as well. Inside the `<style>` tag are child `<item>` tags that override the style settings.

What this does is to set up the `<style>` tag named `AppTheme` to reference the standard or "parent" Android theme, which is simply a collection of all styles and their settings. This is done using the `parent` parameter, which makes the `Light.DarkActionBar` theme the parent of the `AppTheme` style. The `Light.DarkActionBar` and the `Light.LightActionBar` are part of the `Theme.AppCompat` application compatibility library that makes styles and themes work across all versions of Android OS. There may also be a `Dark.DarkActionBar` and a `Dark.LightActionBar` theme included in Android 7.x someday.

As you will see later this `AppTheme` style is referenced as the theme for the Android application in the `AndroidManifest.xml` file, which we will be looking at a bit later in the chapter, and the "chaining" that I talked about earlier between XML definitions would go something like this:

```
Manifest XML theme="@style/AppTheme > AppTheme Style > parent="Theme.AppCompat.Light.
DarkActionBar"
```

As you can see in Figure 4-8 you can change any of the components of Android's Light.DarkActionBar theme inside of your <style> parent tag by using <item> child tags. In the markup below, the primary (light) color, primary dark color, and accent color for Android 7.1.1 OS can be customized by using the <item name="style-constant-name">new data value</item> child tag structure, using references to the colors.xml color constants using the @color/constant-name reference structure.

```
<resources>
   <style name="AppTheme" parent="Theme.AppCompat.Light.DarkActionBar" >
      <item name="colorPrimary">@color/colorPrimary</item>
      <item name="colorPrimaryDark">@color/colorPrimaryDark</item>
      <item name="colorAccent">@color/colorAccent</item>
   </style>
</resources>
```

Next, let's take a look at the colors.xml file that is referenced in these <style> child <item> tags.

XML Colors: Define Application Color Using XML

Right-click on the app/res/values/colors.xml file, and select **Jump to Source** to open it. Figure 4-7 shows that there are three custom colors defined using hexadecimal notation using <color> child tags named colorPrimary, colorAccent and colorPrimaryDark, inside of the parent <resources> tag. This is to define the primary and accent colors for the Android theme you are modifying in the styles.xml file.

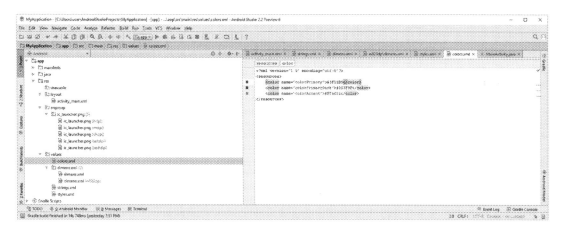

Figure 4-9. *The colors.xml file is located in the app/res/values folder and has three hexadecimal app color constants defined*

Just like the @ symbol is used to preface a reference value, an # (hash or pound sign) is used to preface a hexadecimal value, as is shown in the XML markup below. We will cover this hexadecimal notation in Chapter 9 covering graphics design in Android 7.1.1, so for now, let's just focus on the XML tags.

```
<resources>
    <color name="colorPrimary">#3F51B5</color>
    <color name="colorPrimaryDark">#303F9F</color>
    <color name="colorAccent">#FF4081</color>
</resources>
```

As with the other XML resource constant definitions, a `<resources>` parent tag contains `<color>` child tags. Now that you have taken a look at the file resource XML definition files in your app/res/values folder, and the alternate value folder, let's look at the XML that is used to define your app itself. This is defined inside of the app/manifests/AndroidManifest.xml file.

Configuring an App Using XML: Android Manifest

Open your app/manifests folder (if it is not open already), and right-click on the AndroidManifest.xml file, and select the **Jump to Source** command option from the context-sensitive menu, and open the XML manifest definition file from the central editing area of Android Studio.

The parent tag of the manifest is the `<manifest>` tag, as you may have expected, which references an XML repository for android:parameter names as well as a com.example.user.myapplication package that you created and named back in Chapter 3. This tells Android where your application Java code will be stored, as well as a repository reference for the XML definition syntax used in the manifest file.

As you can see in Figure 4-10, the `<application>` child tag defines your application attributes, and its `<activity>` child tag defines your MainActivity attributes, which you created and named in Chapter 3.

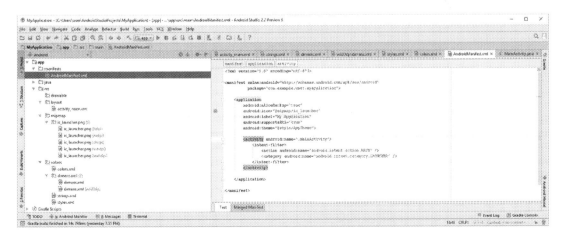

Figure 4-10. The AndroidManifest.xml file defines your application characteristics, theme, assets, activities, and permissions

As you can see in this manifest XML definition, which I will list below, inside of the `<manifest>` parent tag there is an `<application>` child tag that has parameters defining the **theme** in the `styles.xml` file we looked at earlier, the application **label** (title in Actionbar) in the `strings.xml` file we looked at earlier, the application **icon** in the `app/values/mipmap` folder, shown on the left middle in Figure 4-10, opened up to show the PNG32 images used for the application icon, and two switches, both set to "on" or true for `allowBackup` (allows backups) and `supportsRtl` (right to left language support).

```
<?xml version="1.0" encoding="utf-8"?>
<manifest xmlns:android="http://schemas.android.com/apk/res/android"
          package="com.example.user.myapplication">
    <application
        android:allowBackup="true"
        android:icon="@mipmap/ic_launcher"
        android:label="@string/app_name"
        android:supportsRtl="true"
        android:theme="@style/AppTheme">
        <activity android:name=".MainActivity">
            <intent-filter>
                <action android:name="android.intent.action.MAIN" />
                <category android:name="android.intent.category.LAUNCHER" />
            </intent-filter>
        </activity>
    </application>
</manifest>
```

There is also a child `<activity>` tag under the `<application>` parent tag referencing the MainActivity Java class, which uses a **period** character to reference the Java `.class` file. Inside the `<activity>` there is also an `<intent-filter>` child tag, which we will be learning about during Chapter 7. This tells the app to launch the main Activity upon app startup. Next, let's take a look at the Android Studio Visual Design Editor.

UI Design Editor: XML Markup Generation

Since this is an Absolute Beginner title, and Android Studio 2.3 has added a new Visual Design Editor that will generate the XML markup for your UI design automatically, I am going to spend the rest of this chapter showing you how this works, and how you can use it to learn XML, by switching back and forth between the **Design** and **Text** (Secondary Editing) tabs at the bottom of your `activity_main.xml` primary top tab, or any other Activity user interface XML tab. Select the `activity_main.xml` top editing tab, which is seen in Figure 4-11, and then click the **Design** tab at the bottom left of the central editor area in Android Studio. Select your **Button** widget (UI elements are called "widgets" in Android), and drag it onto the visual application design on the right, as shown on the right-hand side in Figure 4-11.

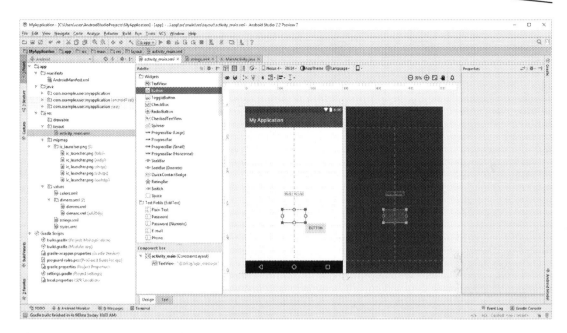

Figure 4-11. *Select the bottom Design tab and drag a new Button UI element onto the current Hello World UI design screen*

As you drag the Button UI element onto the existing visual design, you will see an outline and dashed red lines that will change as you drag the Button around the screen, showing in real time how this UI element will be aligned to other UI elements. Notice I am centering this under your existing TextView UI element, a comfortable distance down the screen. Let's define its properties (parameters) next.

Once you release (drop) your new Button UI element in place, as shown in Figure 4-12, you will get a **Properties** pane on the right side of the Visual Design Editor. Name the Button ID `button_universe`, and the Button text "Upgrade App" using the data fields shown on the far right in Figure 4-12. Once you hit the return key to enter these values they will appear on the Button UI element preview as well.

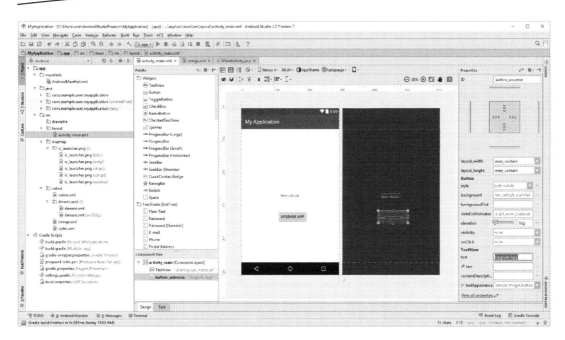

Figure 4-12. *In the Properties pane that appears once you drop the Button in place, provide the Button ID and Button text*

The next UI element we're going to add is the **CheckBox** widget, at the bottom of the screen, which will allow the user to select an alternate "Hello Universe" application message. The CheckBox widget is two widgets under the Button widget, as seen in Figure 4-12 in the **Palette ➤ Widgets** folder on the left-hand side of the Visual Design Editor.

Go ahead and use the same work process that you utilized for the Button UI element placement, and drag the CheckBox widget under the Button widget, and use the dashed red line to center it perfectly with the rest of the user interface design you are creating using Android Studio's Visual Design Editor.

Once you drop the CheckBox into the design, the Properties pane for the UI element will appear, and you can create the **checkBoxEarth** ID (so we can all say Hello Universe to everyone in the Galaxy), and enter the **Hello Universe** text value. This is very similar to what we did for the Button UI element.

Notice that underneath the Palette pane that contains all of the UI Design elements, there is also a Component Tree pane. As you add user interface elements to your design, this pane keeps track of the UI element XML markup child tags that you are going to see inside of the ConstraintLayout parent tag when you switch back over into the XML Text editing tab. We will be doing this soon to show you that Android Studio is indeed writing your XML markup for you, which is really quite cool!

As you can see in Figure 4-13, the CheckBox UI element is now in place and informs the user that if checked, the Hello World message will be upgraded to a Hello Universe message. We will be doing the actual code implementation for this in the next chapter on Java 8 programming in Android 7.1.1.

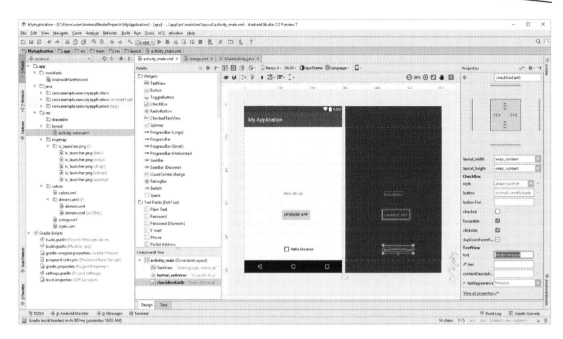

Figure 4-13. *Drag a CheckBox UI element onto the visual design editor and name it checkBoxEarth, with text Hello Universe*

As you can see below adding these two UI elements has added two child tags and seven parameters, including an ID (which is used in Java code to reference UI components) and the text values that you specified in the Properties pane, as is shown in Figure 4-14.

```xml
<?xml version="1.0" encoding="utf-8" ?>
<android.support.constraint.ConstraintLayout xmlns:tools="http://schemas.android.com/tools"
    xmlns:android="http://schemas.android.com/apk/res/android" android:id="@+id/activity_
    main"
    xmlns:app="http://schemas.android.com/apk/res-auto" android:layout_width="match_parent"
    android:layout_height="match_parent" tools:context="com.example.user.myapplication.
    MainActivity">
    <TextView android:text="@string/app_message"
        android:layout_width="match_parent" android:layout_height="match_parent"
        app:layout_constraintBottom_toBottomOf="@+id/activity_main"
        app:layout_constraintBottom_toLeftOf="@+id/activity_main"
        app:layout_constraintBottom_toRightOf="@+id/activity_main"
        app:layout_constraintBottom_toTopOf="@+id/activity_main" />
    <Button android:text="Upgrade App" android:id="@+id/button_universe"
    android:elevation="0dp"
        android:layout_width="wrap_content" android:layout_height="wrap_content"
        android:layout_editor_absoluteY="312dp" android:layout_editor_absoluteX="143dp" />
    <CheckBox android:text="Hello Universe" android:id="@+id/checkBoxEarth"
    android:checked="false"
        android:layout_width="wrap_content" android:layout_height="wrap_content"
        android:layout_editor_absoluteY="453dp" android:layout_editor_absoluteX="150dp" />
</android.support.constraint.ConstraintLayout>
```

As you can see in my above XML markup, how you space out the tags and parameters is flexible as long as you indent properly and can easily ascertain what your XML tags and parameters are doing.

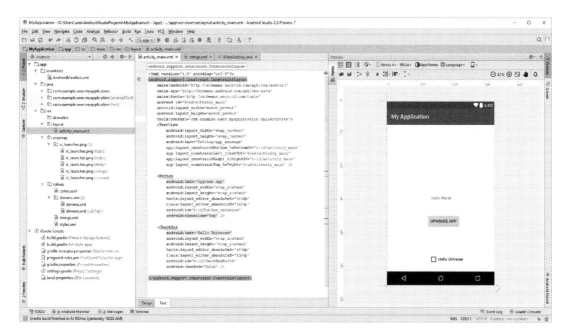

Figure 4-14. *Click the Text tab at the bottom of the activity_main.xml edit tab to look at the new XML tags and parameters*

To follow convention, create `app_button` and `app_checkbox` constants in the `strings.xml` file as seen in Figure 4-15. Next, change your text values, to "`@string/app_button`" and "`@string/app_checkbox`" respectively, in the `<Button>` and `<CheckBox>` `android:text` parameters, as you did for `app_message`.

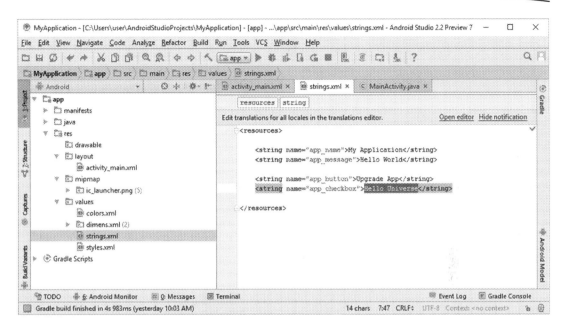

Figure 4-15. Create String constants in strings.xml for Button (app_button) and CheckBox (app_checkbox) UI elements

Next, let's add a friendly image to this design. This is done using the **ImageView**, seen selected in gray in Figure 4-16 in the Palette pane. Notice your @string reference now shows in the Properties pane, shown labeled with a red 1. We will right-click on app/res/drawable and use **File Path** to see where we need to place our SmileyFace.png file. This is labeled with a red 2 in Figure 4-16.

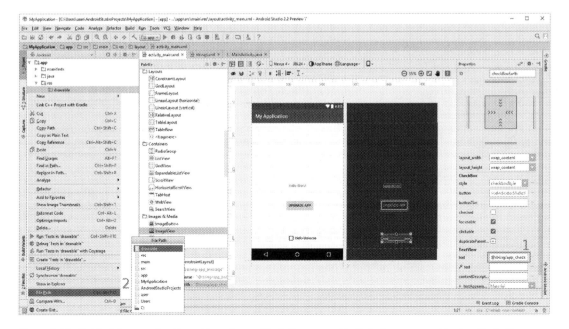

Figure 4-16. Right-click on app/res/drawable and use a File Path command to find where you need to place SmileyFace.png

Use your file management utility to place the SmileyFace.png image into the folder on your hard disk drive indicated by the file path that you got using the File Path command, as is shown in Figure 4-17. In my case it's `C:\Users\user\AndroidStudioProjects\MyApplication\app\src\main\res\drawable`.

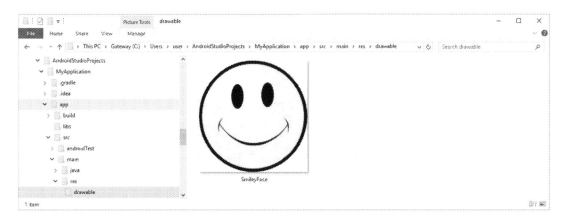

Figure 4-17. *Place the SmileyFace.png file*

As you can see in Figure 4-18, once you copy this PNG file into the correct folder, it will appear in the `drawable` folder, as shown highlighted in the top left. Drag the ImageView into the UI Design and drop it in the top center of the Activity screen, as seen in Figure 4-18 with a red dashed center align guide.

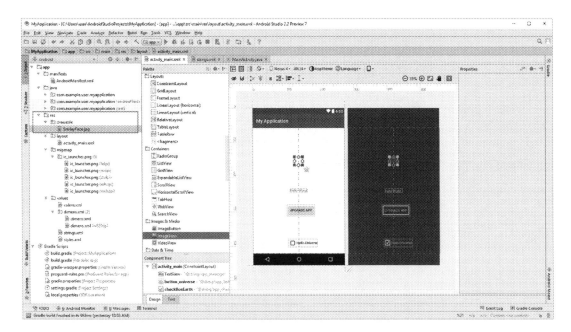

Figure 4-18. *Make sure your drawable is in place and drag the ImageView onto the UI Design and drop it once it is centered*

Once you drop the ImageView, the **Resources** dialog will open and you can select the drawable, as is shown highlighted in blue in Figure 4-19. Click the **OK** button to load the drawable in your ImageView.

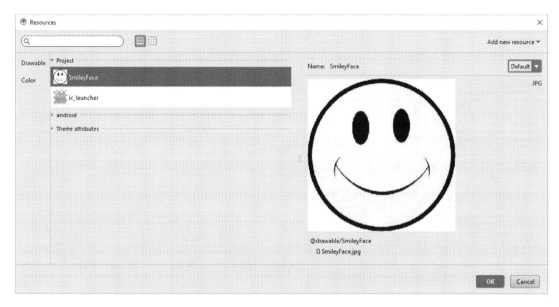

Figure 4-19. *Select the SmileyFace drawable asset and click the OK button to use it in the ImageView*

As you can see in Figure 4-20, the image is bigger than the ImageView you dragged onto the screen, so you will reduce the image size about 50%, and position it so that it fits in the top of the UI Design. I have highlighted the new component tree, as well as the `@drawable/SmileyFace` reference (note you do not need to specify the `.PNG` file extension) shown circled in red in Figure 4-20.

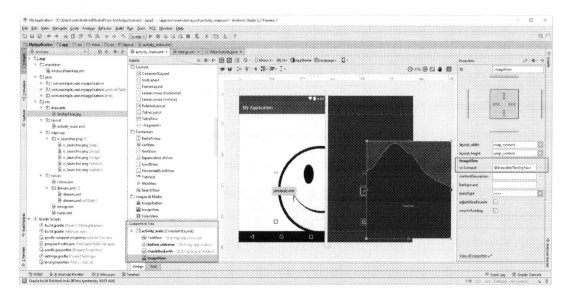

Figure 4-20. *Use the resizing handles on the perimeter of the ImageView to scale the image down 50% so it will fit in the UI*

Drag the lower-right corner (solid) resizing handle for this ImageView, until the `layout_width` and the `layout_height` are set to 220 pixels (DP), which is about half the original image dimension. You can also enter these values directly into the data fields in the Properties pane if you prefer to work that way; the Visual Design Editor is very flexible.

As you will see in Figure 4-21, Android 7.1.1 has a very effective scaling algorithm. We will be covering scaling of imagery in Chapter 9 on graphics design. You may be wondering what the `wrap_content` means in the `layout_width` and `layout_height` data fields in Figure 4-20, and we will be covering this `wrap_content` UI design constant in detail during Chapter 6, so don't worry about what that does or what it means, at least for now. Here's a hint: Think Shrink-Wrap! More on this later.

To position the resized ImageView click in the middle of it, and drag it into position using the centering guidelines, until you have a well-balanced UI design, as is shown in Figure 4-21. We now need to adjust or "tweak" the UI design a bit more to perfect it, for instance, the Hello World text is too small to be read comfortably on a smartphone, so we will need to use a large font instead of a small one.

After we do that, we will take a look at the Text (XML markup) tab once more to see how Android Studio's coding of our UI design for us is progressing (an automated labor force is always nice). I will then show you how to fix any anomalies Android Studio finds in our design, and we'll be ready to get into Java programming in Chapter 5's Java primer. This just keeps getting more and more exciting!

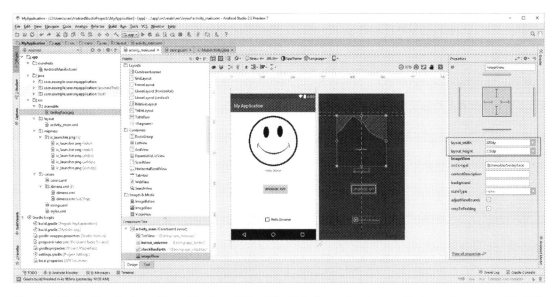

Figure 4-21. *Position the ImageView at the top middle of the UI design, and make sure the image is a square 220x220 pixels*

Select the **TextView** widget in the UI design (in either rendered view or architect view) and drop-down your `textAppearance` constant selector, seen circled in red in Figure 4-22. Select `AppCompatLarge` for your constant, which will give you a nice, large text font size across all versions of the Android OS.

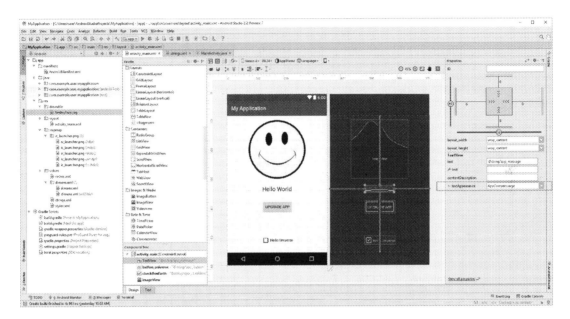

Figure 4-22. *Select the TextView widget, drop-down the textAppearance parameter, and select a AppCompatLarge font size*

Now that we are getting close to a more professional UI design, let's click the **Text** tab at the bottom of the XML editor pane (tab) and look at all of this XML markup Android Studio generated, which is shown in Figure 4-23. There are some problems (red underlined markup) that we need to look into!

My Application
Hello World
UPGRADE APP
Hello Universe

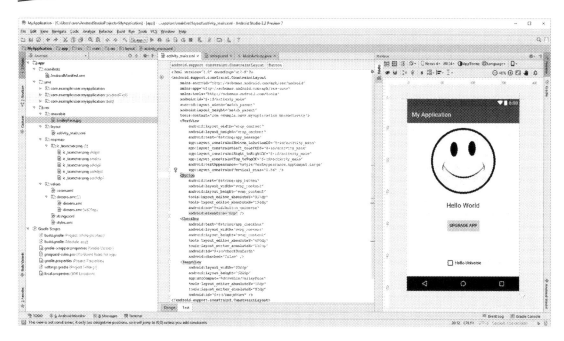

***Figure 4-23.** Android Studio generated two dozen lines of additional XML markup that you did not have to write yourself*

If you place the mouse over the red underlined tag, you will get the pop-up shown in Figure 4-24. This informs you that although the UI layout design (technically called a view in Android, as it comes from the `View` superclass) has design-time positions, it will snap, jump, or collapse to the upper-left corner of the screen (pixel X,Y location 0,0) unless you add constraints. Fortunately, this is easy to do in Visual Design Editor so let's take a look at how you'll do this next. Constraints will remove all of these errors.

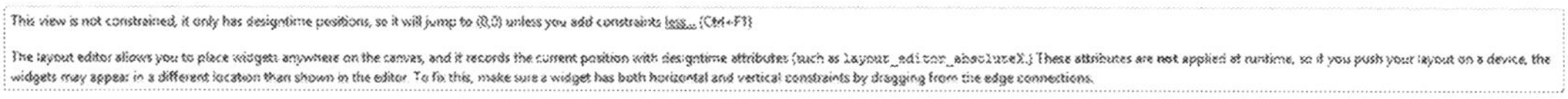

This view is not constrained, it only has designtime positions, so it will jump to (0,0) unless you add constraints less... (Ctrl+F1)
The layout editor allows you to place widgets anywhere on the canvas, and it records the current position with designtime attributes (such as layout_editor_absoluteX.) These attributes are not applied at runtime, so if you push your layout on a device, the widgets may appear in a different location than shown in the editor. To fix this, make sure a widget has both horizontal and vertical constraints by dragging from the edge connections.

***Figure 4-24.** Mouse-over any of the three error highlights (Figure 4-23), and you'll get the following positioning advisement*

To set constraints, you use the edge (middle) handles, which will have a round white circle around them when you mouse-over them. Let's do the Button UI widget first, dragging the left constraint, shown in Figure 4-25 in panes 1 and 2, to the left side of the screen. Release the mouse to create the left constraint, as shown in pane 3, and then drag the right constraint to the right side of the screen, shown in pane 4, which will then re-center the Button widget, which is shown in pane 5. Repeat this process for the top and bottom constraint (middle) handles, and you will get the result that is shown in pane 1 in Figure 4-26, which shows the constraint results (sawtooth constraint lines in place) for all three of the UI widgets that were generating errors in the XML markup shown in Figure 4-23.

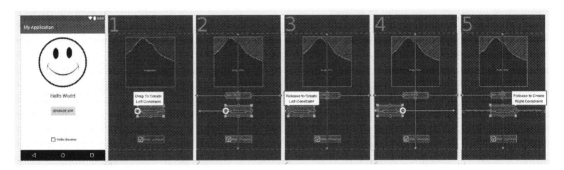

Figure 4-25. Set UI widget positioning constraints using the middle edge handles on each widget and drag to edge of screen

The reason this sawtooth (or accordion) line representation is used, is because when the screen size and (or) shape changes, the position of the UI widget stays the same, while the space on the top, left, bottom, and right will expand or contract, thus making sure the design maintains the same spacing or alignment. You could also think of these alignment constraint lines as being springs, if you prefer.

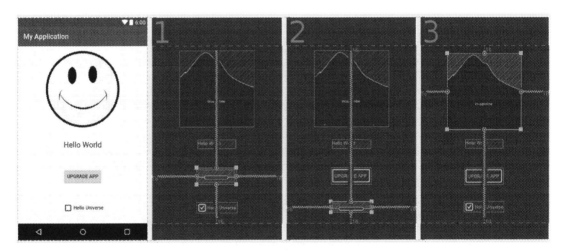

Figure 4-26. UI widget position constraints in place for Button, CheckBox, and ImageView widget so they can conform to the UI

Now if you click on the Text tab at the bottom of your XML editing pane (tab) as shown in Figure 4-27, you will see that your XML markup is error free. There are now app:layout_constraint parameters in all of your three new UI widgets, similar to the ones that were already in the TextView widget that Android Studio had in the UI design in the first place. Since the XML tag parameters use a verbose, detailed parameter naming schema, you can pretty much figure out what each parameter is doing, based on what it is named, which makes working with XML markup that much easier, as long as you understand user interface design terms and concepts. If you don't, take a look at the *Pro Android UI* title from Apress, which covers UI design concepts, UI design prototyping (with Evolus Pencil), and UI layout containers and the XML markup that is needed to create different UI design approaches and scenarios.

Figure 4-27. *Use the Text tab to check the XML markup to make sure all errors are gone and layout_constraint parameters are inserted and correct*

We will be learning more about XML-based user interface design in Chapter 6, but just in case you want to look over the parameter names (which are fairly self-explanatory), I will list the code that the Visual Design Editor created for us (four dozen lines of code that we didn't have to write ourselves) here in case you want to examine how XML defines and places these user interface components on the screen. I can't teach you all of the Android XML in this book in one chapter, so we will be using (and learning) XML markup for the rest of the book, excepting possibly Chapter 5 covering Java.

```
<? xml version="1.0" encoding="utf-8" ?>
<android.support.constraint.ConstraintLayout
    xmlns:android="http://schemas.android.com/apk/res/android"
    xmlns:app="http://schemas.android.com/apk/res-auto"
    xmlns:tools="http://schemas.android.com/tools"
    tools:context="com.example.user.myapplication.MainActivity"
    android:id="@+id/activity_main"
    android:layout_width="match_parent"
    android:layout_height="match_parent" >
    <TextView android:layout_width="wrap_content"
            android:layout_height="wrap_content"
            android:text="@string/app_message"
            app:layout_constraintBottom_toBottomOf="@+id/activity_main"
            app:layout_constraintLeft_toLeftOf="@+id/activity_main"
            app:layout_constraintRight_toRightOf="@+id/activity_main"
            app:layout_constraintTop_toTopOf="@+id/activity_main"
            android:textAppearance="@style/TextAppearance.AppCompat.Large"
            app:layout_constraintVertical_bias="0.56"
```

```xml
                    android:id="@+id/textView2" />
    <Button android:text="@string/app_button"
            android:layout_width="wrap_content"
            android:layout_height="wrap_content"
            android:id="@+id/button_universe"
            android:elevation="0dp"
            android:layout_marginStart="16dp"
            app:layout_constraintLeft_toLeftOf="@+id/activity_main"
            android:layout_marginLeft="16dp"
            android:layout_marginEnd="16dp"
            app:layout_constraintRight_toRightOf="@+id/activity_main"
            android:layout_marginRight="16dp"
            app:layout_constraintTop_toTopOf="@+id/imageView"
            app:layout_constraintBottom_toBottomOf="@+id/activity_main"
            android:layout_marginBottom="16dp"
            app:layout_constraintVertical_bias="0.78" />
    <CheckBox android:text="@string/app_checkbox"
            android:layout_width="wrap_content"
            android:layout_height="wrap_content"
            android:id="@+id/checkBoxEarth"
            android:checked="false"
            android:layout_marginStart="16dp"
            app:layout_constraintLeft_toLeftOf="@+id/activity_main"
            android:layout_marginLeft="16dp"
            android:layout_marginEnd="16dp"
            app:layout_constraintRight_toRightOf="@+id/activity_main"
            android:layout_marginRight="16dp"
            app:layout_constraintBottom_toBottomOf="@+id/activity_main"
            android:layout_marginBottom="16dp"
            android:layout_marginTop="16dp"
            app:layout_constraintTop_toTopOf="@+id/activity_main"
            app:layout_constraintVertical_bias="0.97" />
    <ImageView android:layout_width="220dp"
            android:layout_height="220dp"
            app:srcCompat="@drawable/SmileyFace"
            android:id="@+id/imageView"
            android:layout_marginStart="16dp"
            app:layout_constraintLeft_toLeftOf="@+id/activity_main"
            android:layout_marginLeft="16dp"
            android:layout_marginEnd="16dp"
            app:layout_constraintRight_toRightOf="@+id/activity_main"
            android:layout_marginRight="16dp"
            android:layout_marginTop="16dp"
            app:layout_constraintTop_toTopOf="@+id/activity_main"
            app:layout_constraintBottom_toBottomOf="@+id/activity_main"
            android:layout_marginBottom="16dp"
            app:layout_constraintVertical_bias="0.03" />
</android.support.constraint.ConstraintLayout>
```

Now we are ready to show you how Java can be used to "inflate" the XML definitions (turn them into Java objects) as well as make them interactive and functional so you can make Android applications.

Summary

In this fourth chapter, you learned about the XML markup language, as well as how Android utilizes XML markup to simplify the application development work process, so that non-programmers can get involved. You learned about how XML uses tags and parameters to define XML definition structures, as well as how levels of nesting define parent and child XML tags.

You also learned about XML naming schemas, and how these are defined in the parent tags at the beginning of XML definition files. You looked at some of the types of XML files that are always included in an Android application. These were created by Android Studio in the bootstrap XML files that were generated by the **New Android Application Project** series of dialogs in Chapter 3.

You examined, and in some cases edited, XML files defining String value constants, application styles from Android OS themes, and the Android Manifest, which defines your entire application. You learned how to utilize the @ sign to reference one XML file from inside of another XML file, allowing you to create more complex and organized XML infrastructures, and allowing a modularization similar to what Java offers via objects, classes and packages, which we will be learning about next.

Finally, you learned how to use the Visual Design Editor in Android Studio 2.3, and added a Button, CheckBox, and Imagery to the Hello World UI design, refining the UI design in its entirety and learning how to use the primary components (panes) in the Visual Design Editor. You observed how this can be used to learn XML markup by switching back and forth between the Design and Text tabs at the bottom of the XML editing pane in Android Studio.

In the next chapter, you will learn all about the Java SE programming language by taking an in-depth look at the Android application that you created in Chapter 3, including the Java files in the app/java/ folder. You'll also learn all about Java objects, classes, methods, variables, constants, and interfaces in Chapter 5 for those readers who are really absolute beginners and do not know Java.

Chapter **5**

Introduction to Java: Objects, Methods, Classes, and Interfaces

The programming language used for developing your Android applications is Oracle's **Java SE**, which was created by Sun Microsystems and later acquired by Oracle. As you learned in Chapter 2, Java SE stands for Java Standard Edition, though many programmers shorten this to just "Java." Java is what is called an **object-oriented programming** (or "OOP") language, which you are going to learn all about during this chapter. It is important to note that all of these Java programming concepts, components, and constructs that you will be learning during this Java primer chapter will apply equally well to both the 32-bit Android 4.4.4 OS; as well as to the 64-bit Android 5.0 OS, released in 2014; Android 6.0 released in 2015; Android 7.0, released in the fourth quarter of 2016, and Android 7.1.1, released in the first quarter of 2017.

OOP is based on the programming concept of developing **modular**, self-contained constructs that are called **objects**. These OOP constructs can contain their own attributes and characteristics. In this chapter, you will learn a great deal about the OOP characteristics of Java, and the logic behind using a modular programming approach and OOP techniques to build applications that are easy to share and debug due to an OOP approach. You'll also learn about all of the other Java programming language constructs, like packages and classes, methods and interfaces, loops and arrays, variables and constants, and application programming interfaces (APIs), which tie everything together into one coherent computing ecosystem, such as the 100 Android Java platform APIs discussed in Chapter 2. Together these Java constructs will allow you to create the application's objects and then modify them according to the programming logic that the application will utilize. This creates a user experience for your end users. We will also learn what the bootstrap Java code in your existing application is doing.

© Wallace Jackson 2017

W. Jackson, *Android Apps for Absolute Beginners*, DOI 10.1007/978-1-4842-2268-3_5

The Three Versions, or Editions, of Java

There are two other "editions," or versions of the Java programming language, in addition to the Java SE. These are called **Java EE**, short for Java Enterprise Edition; and **Java ME**, or Java Micro Edition, which was originally used for mobile application development, thus a lot of people incorrectly assume that Java ME stands for Java Mobile Edition. Many mobile phones now use the Android OS, which uses the more powerful Java SE, instead of Java ME, due to much more powerful hardware that is utilized.

Java EE was designed for use on massive computer networks. These types of computing networks are used to run large enterprises, that is, corporations with thousands of active users. This could be termed "server-side" computing. Conversely, Java SE could be termed "client-side" computing, as the Java application, in the case of this book, an Android application, runs on a user's personal computing device, which is termed the "client" in the computer programming industry.

It is important to note Java EE can also be run on smaller installations, as long as they have enough system memory and a couple of processing cores, and this is sometimes done in companies that are developing applications for use on Java EE installations, so that they can work in, and simulate, that type of environment for their testing. Java EE's differentiating feature to Java SE is Java EE features a multi-user, scalable design, whereas Java SE has been designed for use by a single user, on a single computer system, say a home PC or a laptop, or better yet, on an Android device such as an iTV Set, e-book reader, tablet, smartphone, game console, set-top box, auto dashboard, or smartwatch.

Java ME was designed for low-power, embedded systems, to create highly portable computers such as mobile phones. It has fewer features than Java SE, so that it can fit onto a phone without using too much memory and resources to run it. Most mobile flip-phones run Java ME, but Android phones run the more powerful Java SE. Android phones can run Java SE because most have a gigabyte or more of memory, and a 1GHz or faster CPU, so essentially, today's Android devices are Linux computers.

A Foundation of OOP Constructs: An Object

The foundation of OOP is the **object** itself. Everything you create in Java is an object and uses other objects (and data primitive values). Objects in OOP languages are similar to the objects that you see around you every day, except Java objects are virtual, and are not tangible, since computers will use zeroes and ones (binary) to represent things. Just like tangible real-world objects, Java objects have **characteristics**, called **states** or **attributes**, and things that they do, called **behaviors**. One way to think about this distinction is that Java objects are nouns, or things that exist in and of themselves, whereas their behaviors are like verbs, or things that these nouns can do.

As an example of Java objects, let's define a Java object based on a popular real object that we see around us every day in all of our lives: the automobile. Some of the characteristics, or **states**, of the common automobile might be defined as follows:

- Color (candy apple red, for instance)

- Direction or heading (north, south, east, or west)

- Speed (45 miles per hour, for instance)

- Engine type (gas, diesel, biofuel, hydrogen, propane, electric, or hybrid)

- Gear setting (1, 2, 3, 4, 5, 6, or reverse)

- Drivetrain type (2WD or 4WD)

The following are some things that you can do with a car, that is, the car's **behaviors**:

- Accelerate

- Shift gears

- Apply the brakes

- Turn the wheels

- Turn on the stereo

- Use the headlights

- Use the turn signals

You get the idea. Objects can be as complicated as you wish them to be, and Java objects can nest, or contain, other Java objects within their object structure, just like XML. An object hierarchy is like a tree structure, with a main trunk, branches, and sub-branches as you move up (or down) its structure. An example of a hierarchy you use every day would be your multi-level directory, or folder structure, which is on your computer's hard disk drive (refer to Figure 4-17 in Chapter 4 for a visual example). The directories or folders on your hard disk drive can contain other directories or folders, which can in turn contain yet other directories and folders, allowing complex hierarchies of organization to be created. We saw another great example of this in Chapter 3 in Figure 3-8, where your Android `MyApplication` project folder was shown in the Android Studio Project pane, showing project subfolder hierarchies, with an app folder, Java and resource folder, and subfolders for layout, drawable, values, and so on.

Figure 5-1 shows the simple "Anatomy of a Car Object" diagram of the Java object structure, using a car as the example. It shows the characteristics, or **attributes**, of the car, which are central to defining the car object, and around those, behaviors that the car object can perform, and which effect changes on the attributes or states of the car. The states and behaviors serve to define the car to the outside world, just like your application objects will define the states and behaviors regarding the functionality of your Android application for your end users. It's all very logical, as you will see during this chapter.

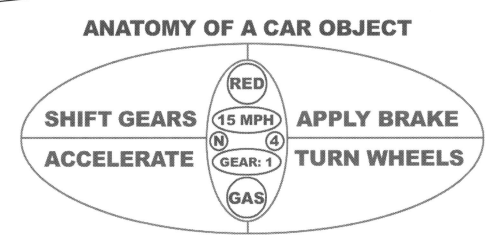

Figure 5-1. A car object showing the car attributes or characteristics (inner oval) and car behaviors (outer oval)

You can do this same hierarchical construction by using Java objects, which can contain subobjects, which can themselves contain further subobjects, and so on and so forth, as needed to create your object hierarchy structure. You will see nested object hierarchies when you are working with Android, because nested objects are very useful for grouping related objects that are used together, but that are used in more than one place, as well as for more than one type of use. After all, one of the goals of modular code in object-oriented programming is to foster effective code reuse.

In other words, some types of objects are also useful to other types of objects in an Android app. You will see examples of this during this book, as we will be covering all of the primary Java-based classes (which as you will soon see, are used to create objects) in the Android 7.1.1 OS during the course of this book.

As an exercise, you should practice identifying different objects in the room or space around you, and then break down their definition or description into various states (variable characteristics, and fixed, or constant, characteristics) as well as behaviors (things that the object can or will do). This is a good exercise to perform, because this is exactly how you'll need to start thinking in order to become more successful in your OOP endeavors using the Java programming language, and even using the XML markup language, for that matter, which you learned about in Chapter 4.

It is important to remember that you can use both Java programming logic, as well as XML markup, to define objects for Android applications, as you learned in the previous chapter, when you learned about object inflation from XML object definitions. You've already defined a `TextView` user interface object, having several characteristics, in Chapter 4, using XML markup, as well as a `Button` UI object and a `CheckBox` UI object. You have also defined an `ImageView` object as well, so you are well on the way to defining hundreds of objects for use in Android 7.1.1 applications over the course of this book.

Some Programming Terms: Variable, Method, and Constant

Next, let's cover some of the technical terminology used in Java. First, objects have data fields to hold **variable** data, **constants** to hold fixed data, and **methods** to define behaviors, as follows:

- Data fields that hold a Java object's states that can change over time are called **variables.** Using the car example, the direction you're driving in, the gear that you're driving in, and the speed you're driving at change in almost real time, and therefore are all variables.

- Data fields that hold an object's states that do not change over time are called **constants**. Using a car example, the candy apple red paint job on the car could be a constant, as is the car's engine type (unless you own a paint and body shop, or are an auto mechanic, that is).

- **Methods** are programming logic or program code routines that operate on, and will change, the object's internal variable data fields. Methods will also allow other Java objects that are external to the object itself to communicate with that object, as long as the method is declared to be public. We will be getting into methods in greater detail a bit later on in the chapter, so I won't get into how exactly they work here.

One of the key concepts of OOP is **data encapsulation**. In Java, data encapsulation is implemented by only allowing a Java object's variable data fields to be modified directly through that same Java object's internal methods. This allows a Java object to be self-sufficient, or encapsulated.

Using the car example, in order to turn the car, you would use the `.turnWheels()` method, shown in Figure 5-1 on the bottom right of the diagram. This method would be comprised of Java programming logic that would correctly position the wheels of the car, ultimately causing it to move in the desired direction. You would not see details of how the object's wheels are turned, because of encapsulation. That detail is left to the private, internal functionality contained (encapsulated) inside the method in the Java object.

> **Note**   Notice the empty parentheses I am using after my method names in the text. These are always used when writing about a method, so that the reader knows that the author is referencing a Java method. Additionally, since method calls are invoked using dot notation, I usually will preface the method names with a dot, further reinforcing that this is a method call, so that you can visualize it. You will see this method naming convention used throughout the rest of this book.

Using data encapsulation, you can individually build and test each object that is part of a larger object construct, without requiring any data to be accessed from other objects, or modules, of an application. External data access can translate into bugs, so encapsulation helps when developing complicated, large-scale applications. Without data encapsulation, developers on your team could simply access any part of your object data and use it however they pleased. This could introduce bugs affecting the methods you have perfected to manipulate your object and to provide your encapsulated solution. So data encapsulation promotes the core concept in OOP of **modularity**. Once an object is created and tested, other objects can use it without worrying about its integrity.

Data encapsulation thus allows **code reuse**, so programmers can develop **libraries** of useful objects, which don't need to be rewritten or retested by other programmers. You can see how this might save developer time and money by structuring only the work that needs to be done and avoiding redundant work processes related to testing multiple code modules in conjunction with one another at the same time. Data encapsulation will also allow developers to hide the data and the internal logic of their Java object, if that is so desired.

In the car object example, the attributes of our car are encapsulated inside of the car object, and can thus be changed only via the methods that surround them in each diagram. For instance, one would use a .shiftGears() method to change the Gears=1 field variable to Gears=2.

Finally, Java objects make **debugging** easier, because you can add or remove them modularly, or isolate them during testing in order to ascertain where bugs are located within the overall code.

Java Constructs: Create Your Own Objects

In the next few sections of this chapter, you will learn about the primary Java programming constructs (or code structures) that developers will create to be able to define their own custom Java objects. These custom objects will have their own characteristics (variables and constants), behaviors (methods), accessibility (access control modifiers), procreation (constructors), and even can have their own rules of engagement (interfaces). They can even have their own home offices (packages).

This is in large part accomplished using the top-level structure in Java, which is called a Java **class**. For this reason, we will start learning about classes first, since all of the other structures in Java are either created (nested) inside of the class, or relate to its usage and implementation in some way. The exception to this is the Java package, which houses, collects, and contains these Java classes. Java 9 will introduce the concept of modules (collections of packages) when it is released in the fourth quarter of 2017.

The Java Class: Java Code Structure Container

In real life, there is seldom just one single type or kind of object. Usually, there is a large number of different object types and variations. For instance, for a car object, there are different manufacturers, sizes, shapes, colors, prices, seating capacities, engine types, fuel types, transmission types, drivetrain types, roof types, carrying capacities, luxury features, sound systems, and so on and so forth.

In Java SE, you write something called a **class** that defines what your object can do (its methods), and what data fields it will possess. Once the class has been coded in Java, you can then create an **instance** of an object that you wish to use, by **referencing** a class definition. In architectural terms, the class is a kind of blueprint as to what the object will be structured like, including what states it will contain (its variables), its other attributes (constants), and the tasks it can perform (the methods that it has).

> **Note**   An **instance** is a concrete object created from the blueprint of the class, with its own states or unique data attributes. For example, you might have a (second) baby blue car instance that is traveling south and is in third gear. (In the example, our first car instance is red, and is traveling north, and is in first gear.)

To illustrate this further, let's construct a basic class for our car object example. To create a car class, you use the **Java keyword** `class`, followed by a **custom name** for the new class you are writing, and then curly brackets, which will eventually contain Java code for a class definition. It looks like this:

```
class Car {
          // Java code definition for the car class will go in here. We will do this next.
}
```

The first thing that you will usually put inside of the class (inside of the curly {} brackets) are the **data fields** (**variables**). These variables will hold the states, or characteristics, of your object that will be created by the class. In this case, you will have six data fields, which will define the car's current gear, current speed, current direction, fuel type, color, and drivetrain (two-wheel drive or four-wheel drive), as was specified in the basic diagram which was shown earlier in Figure 5-1.

To define a variable in Java, you must first declare its **data type**.

- An **integer** or **int** data type declares a variable to be able to hold a whole (non-fractional) number.

- A **String** data type declares the variable to hold a text value.

- A **Boolean** data type declares the variable to hold a **true** or **false** value (I think of this like a switch or a toggle, like a binary on or off state).

The next portion of the variable definition or **declaration** after the data type has been specified is your custom **variable name**, which you will use to refer to that variable later on, within your Java programming logic. If you want to know technically what the Android OS is going to do with these variable declarations, it is essentially going to set aside, or **allocate**, an area in the system hardware (the system memory, to be more precise) to hold this value for your application to access while it is running.

You can also (optionally) set a **default** or a starting data value for your variable. This is done by using the **equal sign** and a starting data value. The variable definition is ended once it reaches, or is terminated with, a **semicolon** character. This is how the Java compiler in Android Studio 2.3, which is reading or **parsing** your Java code, knows that each statement is finished being defined.

> **Note**   Semicolons are used in programming languages to separate each code construct, or definition, from the other code constructs within that same body of code (package, class, method, or interface), which I often refer to as a Java code structure, or Java logic structure.

So, with the six variables from our Anatomy of a Car Object diagram, shown in Figure 5-1, in place, the core Car class definition would initially look something like the following:

```
class Car {
    int speed = 15;
    int gear = 1;
    int drivetrain = 4;
    String direction = "N";
    String color = "Red";
    String fuel = "Gas";
}
```

Remember that since we specified a starting value using the equal sign for all of these variables, that these variables will all contain this default, or starting, data value. These initial data values will be set (in the system memory) as the Car class variable's initial data values upon object creation in system memory.

Notice how the example spaces out the curly braces ({ }) on their own lines, as well as **indenting** certain lines, similar to what you did with your XML markup. This is done as a Java programming **convention**, so that you can visualize the organization of the code constructs that are contained within your Java class structure, inside of those curly braces, more easily and clearly. This would be analogous to having a bird's eye view of your Java code construct.

The Java Method: Java Code Function Definition

The next part of your Java class definition file will contain your **methods**. A Java method will define how your Car object will function; that is, how it will **operate** on the variables that you defined at the top of the class, which hold the Car object's current state of operation.

Method **calls** can invoke a variable (state) change, and methods can also **return** data values to the entity that calls or **invokes** the method, such as data values that have been successfully changed, or even the result of an equation. For instance, there could be a method to calculate driving distance by multiplying speed by driving time, and this method would return this driving distance data value to the Java code that invoked this method.

You will see a bit later on exactly how a Java method is invoked; this is usually accomplished by using something in the Java programming language called **dot notation**. Next, let's take a closer look at how a Java method is **declared** and created inside of your Java class structure.

To declare a Java method that does not return any data values to the calling entity, and that only invokes some sort of state change in the object, you would utilize the Java **void** keyword before the method's name.

> **Note**   In this chapter especially, but also throughout the book, you will be learning about a plethora of Java and Android **keywords**. Keywords are **reserved words** that cannot be used in your own custom code (because that would confuse the compiler, which needs to have everything that is defined be 100% unique, and thus not ambiguous), because each keyword does something specific in Java or Android. As an Android programmer you will need to learn all of the programming language keywords and what they mean (do) and how to implement them properly, which we will be doing throughout the rest of this book.

The `.shiftGears()` method is a good example of using void in a method that triggers something. This type of method would be used to trigger (invoke) a change in the object, such as a shifting in gears, and thus would not need to send any specific data values back to its calling entity.

```
void shiftGears (int newGear) { The Java code which defines the method's functionality }
```

If your method or function returns a data value, then instead of using the void keyword, you would use the **data type** of the data value that needs to be returned, say int or String. As an example, a simple, whole number addition method might return a number data value after finishing its sum calculation, so you would declare a data type using the int keyword.

```
int addTwoNumbers (int x, int y) { int z; x + y = z; return z; }
```

After the data type keyword comes a **name** for the method (say, addTwoNumbers). This is followed by the type of data (in this case, an int) and variable name or names (x and y) in parentheses, which is called the **parameter list**, and then finally the curly braces, which will contain the method's Java code, which will add the two input x and y integers, returning a result held in a z variable to the calling Java code.

The data variable's data type and name, seen within the parameter list, contains the data parameter that will be passed into the method, so the method now has this passed-in data variable to work with inside of the Java code that is defined inside of the method programming logic (inside of its curly braces). This declares the variable for use, so you can use these parameter variables inside the method as you can see in the previous example, where I had only to declare the z variable for use.

> **Note**   The normal method naming convention is to start a method name with a **lowercase letter**, and then to use uppercase letters to begin words embedded within the method name, called **CamelCase** like this `methodNameExample()`. Read more about Java naming conventions at: `http://www.oracle.com/technetwork/java/codeconventions-150003.pdf`.

Some methods, such as those that trigger something, will be called without using any variables, as would be done in a .turnCarEngineOff() method, which would be called in your Java code as follows:

```
carObject.turnCarEngineOff();
```

To call the .shiftGears() method, you would want to pass the desired gear over using the parameter list as an integer data variable, so you would therefore utilize the following **method call** format:

```
carObject.shiftGears(4);
```

This passes over the integer value of 4 using the .shiftGears() method's newGear data variable, which sets this data value as well as passing it into the method. This data value is then utilized in the interior of the .shiftGears() method logic (the part inside the curly braces), where it is finally used to set the object's gear (internal) field to the new gear shift value of 4, or fourth gear. We will be looking at that code construct next. If you want to set up your .shiftGears() method so that it does not require any integer data values, that is, if you wanted to set it up to be a method with no calling parameter, you would need to create a .shiftGearUp() as well as a .shiftGearDown() method. The programming logic inside of these methods would add (or subtract) a value of one from the current gear setting, instead of setting the gear value to the passed-in (desired) gear value. In Java coding, there's always more than one way to skin a car! Or is it, there's always more than one way to shift a cat?

A common reason to use a method without any parameters is to invoke a **state change** in an object that does not depend on any data being passed into the method. In the case of this particular gear shifting example, this would also fix a potential problem of skipped gears, as you would simply code a .shiftGearUp() method and a .shiftGearDown() method, which would upshift and downshift by one gear level each time they were called, rather than change to a gear selected by the driver. If you have ever shifted from first into fifth gear on your car, you know that it does not work very well, and could even cause a stall. This might be a smarter way to code this particular method, and then you would not need to pass a parameter in order to shift gears on your Car object; you would just simply call .shiftGearUp() or .shiftGearDown() whenever any gear shifting for the Car object was needed.

After the method declaration, the method's programming logic procedures are contained inside the curly braces. In this Car class and object definition example, we have four methods, as defined back in Figure 5-1:

- The .shiftGears() method will set the Car object's gear to the gear value that was passed into the .shiftGears() method. You should allow an integer to be passed into this method, to allow "user error," just as you would when you are driving your car in the real world. The Car object's gear attribute is set to the newGear data value, which is passed into the method using the method parameter list area.

```
void shiftGears (int newGear) {
        gear = newGear;
}
```

▒ The .accelerateSpeed() method takes your object's speed state variable and adds your acceleration factor to the speed, which causes your object to accelerate. This is done by taking your object's current speed setting, or state, and adding an acceleration factor to it, and then setting the result of this addition operation back into the original speed variable, so that the object's speed state now contains the new (accelerated) speed value.

```
void accelerateSpeed (int acceleration) {
      speed = speed + acceleration;
}
```

▒ The .applyBrake() method takes the object's speed state variable and subtracts a braking factor from the current speed, which causes the object to decelerate, or to brake. This is done by taking the object's current speed setting, and subtracting the braking factor from it, and then setting the result of the subtraction back to the original speed variable, so that the object's speed state now contains the updated (decelerated) braking value.

```
void applyBrake (int brakingFactor) {
      speed = speed - brakingFactor;
}
```

▒ The .turnWheel() method is straightforward, much like the .shiftGears() method, except that it uses a **string** value of N, S, E, or W to control the direction that the car turns. When .turnWheel("W") is used a car will turn to the left, when .turnWheel("E") is used, the car will turn to the right, given, of course, that the Car object is currently heading to the north, which according to its default direction setting, it is.

```
void turnWheel (String newDirection) {
      direction = newDirection;
}
```

The methods that make the Car object function go inside of the Car class's code body inside of the curly braces, and after the variable declarations. The updated Car class would look like the following:

```
class Car {
    int speed = 15;
    int gear = 1;
    int drivetrain = 4;
    String direction = "N";
    String color = "Red";
    String fuel = "Gas";

    void shiftGears (int newGear) {
        gear = newGear;
    }
```

```
    void accelerateSpeed (int acceleration) {
        speed = speed + acceleration;
    }

    void applyBrake (int brakingFactor) {
        speed = speed - brakingFactor;
    }

    void turnWheel (String newDirection) {
        direction = newDirection;
    }
}
```

This Car class allows us to define a Car object, but only if we include a Car() **constructor method**, which we will be covering in the next section of this chapter.

Constructor Methods: The Java Object Blueprint

If you want to be able to make an object with preset values out of your class definition, then you need to include what is called a **constructor method**. If you don't, Java will create one for you called a default constructor. This method will need to be named the same as the class name, in this case, it would be the Car() constructor method, and should be the first method that is defined inside of the class construct, after the variable (data field) definitions. The constructor method is used to construct an object, configure it, and load it into memory for use. The first thing we will want to do is to make our variable declarations undefined, by removing the equal sign and initial data values, so we can use the constructor to set the variables differently for each object created using the class. If all objects that are created using the class need to have the same starting variables, you can include these in the class instead of the constructor. This is shown in the following Java code:

```
class Car {
    String name;
    int speed;
    int gear;
    int drivetrain;
    String direction;
    String color;
    String fuel;
    public Car (String carName) {
        name = carName;
        speed = 15;
        gear = 1;
        drivetrain = 4;
        direction = "N";
        color = "Red";
        fuel = "Gas";
    }
}
```

As you can see above, a Car() constructor method will set the data values as part of the construction and configuration of the Car object, and thus the Java code for the Car() constructor method contains your data field initialization values, not the Java class itself. As you may have inferred from this, some Java classes are built to create objects, others are built to process logic; the choice is yours regarding how to use the powerful Java programming language.

> **Note**   Later in this section I'll show you how to change this constructor to set more of the variables.

The Java constructor method differs from a regular Java method in a number of distinct ways. First of all, a constructor method does not use any of the data return types, such as void and int, because it is used to create a **Java object**, rather than to perform some function. It does not return nothing (the void keyword) or a number (the int, double, or float keywords), but rather, it returns an object! Indeed, that's why it's called a **constructor** in the first place – because its function is solely to construct or create the new Java object; in this particular case, that would be a basic or generic Car object.

Note that every class that needs to create a Java object will feature a constructor with the same name as the class itself, so a constructor is the one method type whose name can (and will, always) start with a capital letter, which is essentially disobeying the standard Java method naming convention.

Another difference between a constructor and a standard method is constructors must use the **public** access control modifier, and cannot use any non-access-control modifiers, so be sure not to declare your constructor as: static, final, abstract, or synchronized. We will be covering these modifiers a bit later on in this chapter, so stay tuned!

In case you may be wondering how you would modify the previous Car() constructor method example if you wanted to not only name the new Car object using the constructor method, but also wanted to define its speed, direction, and color using that same Car() constructor method call, you would do this by simply creating a longer parameter list for the constructor method call. This revised Car(carName, carSpeed, carDirection, carColor) constructor method code structure would look something like this:

```java
class Car {
    String name;
    int speed;
    int gear;
    int drivetrain;
    String direction;
    String color;
    String fuel;
    public Car (String carName, int carSpeed, String carDirection, String carColor) {
        name = carName;
        speed = carSpeed;
        gear = 1;
        drivetrain = 4;
```

```
        direction = carDirection;
        color = carColor;
        fuel = "Gas";
    }
}
```

It is important to note that this Car() constructor method will not do anything at all until you use it to instantiate an **instance** of the Car object. An instance is just what it sounds like it is; the Android OS will allocate system memory space to hold each particular instance of any Java object created by its class's constructor method.

A constructor method must be called or invoked in conjunction with the Java **new** keyword, which we will cover next. The new keyword creates a new object in a new area of system memory, so it's keyword appropriate!

Next, let's look at how you would create new Car objects in an Android onCreate() method structure.

Instantiating Objects: The Java "new" Keyword

To create an instance of an object, you **instantiate** it. Here's what it would look like if you added this code to the .onCreate() method of your current Android application. This shows the creation of two Car objects, as well as how you would use these Car objects along with the dot notation used to call the methods which would operate upon them. Refer to Figure 3-8 in Chapter 3 to see this bootstrap .onCreate() method code for the Android Hello World (MyApplication) application.

```
protected void onCreate(Bundle savedInstanceState) {
    super.onCreate(savedInstanceState);
    setContentView(R.layout.activity_main);
     // Two forward slashes will allow you to insert comments into your code
    // Create two new Car Objects by using the Car() constructor method
    Car carOne = new Car("carWon", 20, "S", "Blue");
    Car carTwo = new Car("carTwoon", 10, "N", "Green");
 // Invoking three methods on CarOne Car Object through the use of dot notation
    carOne.shiftGears(3);
    carOne.accelerateSpeed(15);
    carOne.turnWheel("E");
 // Invoking three methods on CarTwo Car Object through the use of dot notation
    carTwo.shiftGears(2);
    carTwo.applyBrake(10);
    carTwo.turnWheel("W");
}
```

Upon creation of this Android application, which is what the .onCreate() method is used for, we now have instantiated and configured two Car objects. Note that this code will only work if you have created a Car class in your Android application, so this is for example purposes only. We have done this by using the Car() class constructor and the Car object name, along with the Java new keyword, which creates each new Car object for us, using the following Java code format:

```
Car carOne = new Car("carName", carSpeed, "carDirection", "carColor");
```

The syntax for doing this is very similar to what we used to declare our variables, which are declared with a variable type, variable name, and (optional) variable starting data value. Object instances will be declared similar to this, with an object constructor, object name, and configuration values, like this:

- Define the object type `Car` using the constructor method

- Give a name to our `Car` object (`carOne`) that we can reference in our class and method code constructs

- Set the `carOne` object equal to a new `Car` object definition using four state parameters (a `String carName`, an integer `carSpeed`, a `String carDirection`, a `String carColor`)

It is also important to notice that I have put **comments** in the Java code by using two forward slashes, which tells the Java compiler to "ignore everything else on this line after these, as it is a comment!"

To invoke our methods using our new `Car` objects requires the use of dot notation. Once you have created and named a Java object, you can call methods on it, by using the following code construct:

```
objectName.methodName(parameter list variables);
```

So, to shift into third gear on the `Car` object named `carOne`, we would use this Java code statement:

```
carOne.shiftGears(3);
```

This calls or invokes the `.shiftGears()` method on the `carOne` `Car` object, and passes over the gear parameter, which contains an integer value of 3. This value is then placed into the `newGear` variable, which is then utilized by the `.shiftGears()` method's internal code.

So, as you can see in the final six lines of code in the `public void onCreate()` method, we set the `carOne` `Car` object to third gear, using `.shiftGears(3)`, accelerate it from 15 to 30 mph, by accelerating by a value of 15, using `.accelerateSpeed(15)`, and then turn east by using the `.turnWheel()` method with a String value of `"E"` (the default direction is north, or `"N"`).

Car two (`carTwo`) we shift into second, using `.shiftGears(2)`, then `.applyBrake(10)` to slow it down from 15 to 5 mph, and finally turn the car west, by using a `.turnWheel("W")` method call, all using dot notation. Dot notation connects the Java method call to the Java object, invoking that method on that Java object. Once you understand all of this, you will see it is actually really cool how Java works.

Extend an Object's Structure: Java Inheritance

There is also support in Java for developing different variations on custom objects, in this case, it is a `Car` object. This is done using a technique called **inheritance**. Inheritance is where more specialized `Car` classes (more uniquely defined `Car` objects) can be **subclassed** using the basic `Car` **superclass**. This allows Java developers to develop more organized, modular, inheritance-oriented approaches to designing their Java objects, making them into building blocks, and thus powerful for the construction of an infinite number of future object types. This inheritance process can be seen in Figure 5-2.

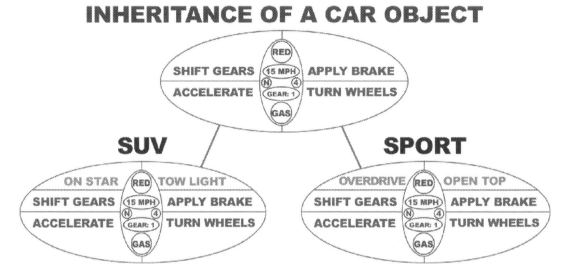

Figure 5-2. Inheritance of the Car Object superclass to create the SUV and the SPORT Car object subclasses

Once a class is used for inheritance by **subclassing** it, it becomes a superclass. Ultimately, there can be only one superclass at the very top of the chain, but there can be an unlimited number of subclasses. All of the subclasses **inherit** the methods and fields from the superclass. If you want to change a superclass's method, you can use the Java keyword @Override before the subclass's method, and your custom method implementation will then be used instead of the superclass method.

The ultimate example of this in Java SE is the java.lang.Object superclass (I call it the masterclass), which is used to create all other classes in Java.

The SUV subclass might have additional .onStarCall() and .turnTowLightOn() methods defined, in addition to inheriting the usual Car object operational (basic car function) methods allowing the Car object to shift gears, accelerate, apply the brakes, and turn the wheels.

Similarly, we might also generate a second subclass, called the Sport class, which would create sport car objects. These might include an .activateOverdrive() method to provide faster gearing, and an .openTop() method to put down the convertible roof.

To create a subclass using a superclass, you **extend** the subclass from the superclass, by using the Java extends keyword inside of the class declaration. The Java class construct would thus look just like this:

```
class Suv extends Car { // Additional New Variable Data Fields, Constants, and Methods Go In
Here. }
```

This extends the Car class so that SUV objects have access to, essentially contain, all of the data fields and methods that the Car object features. This allows the developer to have to focus only on just the new or different data fields and methods that relate to the differentiation of the SUV object from the regular or master Car object definition.

Since classes create objects, given that they have a constructor method, the same hierarchy should be applied at the spawned object level. So logically, the SUV object will be more complex (more data fields and more functionality) than the parent Car object.

To refer to one of the superclass's methods from within the subclass you are coding, you can use the Java super keyword. For example, in the new SUV class, you'll probably want to use the master Car class .applyBrake() method, and then apply some additional functionality to the brakes that will be specific to SUVs. You can call a Car object's .applyBrake() method by using super.applyBrake() in the Java code. The following Java code will add additional functionality to a Car object .applyBrake() method, inside of the SUV class's .applyBrake() method, by using the super keyword to access the Car class's .applyBrake() method, and then adding in additional logic:

```
class SUV extends Car {
    void applyBrake (int brakingFactor) {
        super.applyBrake(brakingFactor);
        speed = speed - brakingFactor;
    }
}
```

This code makes the SUV object's brakes **twice as powerful** as the generic Car object's brakes, which is again something that would have to take place in real life for an SUV to be safe for use. The reason the Java code doubles the SUV braking power is because the SUV object's .applyBrake() method first calls the Car object .applyBrake() method from the Car superclass from inside SUV using super.applyBrake(brakingFactor); line of Java code in the SUV subclass's .applyBrake() method, and then the line of Java code that comes next (again) decreases the speed variable, by applying the brakingFactor a second time, making the brakes twice as powerful, or twice as effective!

Be sure to use good programming practices and refer to documentation for your superclass's fields and methods within each subclass that uses the super keyword to reference superclass programming infrastructures in one way or another. The Java class documentation should let users (developers) of your superclass know which of your superclass fields and methods are public and are available for use, since these do not explicitly appear in the Java code for the subclass, as only incremental code (new and different methods and variables) will appear in the subclass Java code.

Java Interfaces: Defining Class Usage Patterns

In many Java applications, as well as in the Android 7 APIs, Java classes must conform to a certain usage pattern. There is a specialized Java construct called an **interface** that you can **implement**, so that other application developers will know exactly how to utilize your Java classes implementing an interface, as well as which methods are **required** for proper implementation of your Java class. Implementing the Java interface will allow your class to become more conformant regarding those behaviors that your class offers for other programmers to utilize. To implement a Java interface you would use the Java `implements` keyword, as you will see later on during this section.

Interfaces in essence form a **programming contract** between your class and the rest of the development world. For any class implementing a Java interface, the Java compiler can enforce this contract at build time. If a class claims to implement a public interface using the `implements` keyword, all of the methods that are defined by that Java interface definition must be implemented (be present) in the source code for the class that implements that interface before that class will successfully compile.

Interfaces are especially useful when working within a complex Java programming framework such as Android 7.1.1, which is utilized by other developers who build applications based on the Java classes that the Google Android 7.x OS developer team members have written specifically for that purpose. A Java interface can be used like a road map, showing developers how to best implement and utilize the Java 8 code structure that is provided by that Java class within another larger Java program structure. Basically, a Java interface guarantees that all methods in a given class will get implemented together, as an inter-working, interdependent, used-as-a-collective, programming structure, guaranteeing that any individual function needed to implement this functional collective doesn't get inadvertently left out.

This public interface that a class presents to the other developers who are using the Java language and Android platform makes using that class more predictable, and allows developers to safely use that class in their own programming structures and objectives where a class of a particular end-usage pattern is suitable for their implementation.

In other words, a public interface is an implementation road map that will tell your application what functions that class needs to be able to perform, and how to implement it without your application needing to test any of that class's functional capabilities. In case you are wondering, Java 8 (Android) does not allow a private interface; however, the new Java 9 programming language will allow this later on in 2017. When Android will adopt Java 9 is anyone's guess, however.

In Java terms, making a class conform to a usage pattern is done by **implementing** a Java interface. The following is an `ICar` interface, that forces all cars to implement all of the methods that you will be defining within this Java interface.

These methods must each be implemented (exist) even if they are not utilized, that is, no additional or custom code exists inside their curly braces. This also guarantees that the rest of the Java application knows that each `Car` object can perform all of these actions, or behaviors, because implementing the `ICar` interface defines this public interface for all of the `Car` objects that implement the `ICar` interface.

The way that you will implement the `ICar` public interface for the methods in your `Car` class would be as follows:

```java
public interface ICar {
    void shiftGears (int newGear);
    void accelerateSpeed (int acceleration);
    void applyBrake (int brakingFactor);
    void turnWheel (String newDirection);
}
```

So, the Car class that implements this ICar public interface must implement all of these declared methods.

To implement an interface, you need to use the Java implements keyword, as follows, and then define all of the methods exactly as you did before, except that the methods must now be declared using a public **access control modifier in addition to the** void **return data type**. We'll be covering Java modifiers in a future section of this chapter, after we cover the Java package and the concepts of an API.

Here is how a Car class would implement this ICar interface, by using the Java implements keyword:

```
class Car implements ICar {
    int speed = 15;
    int gear = 1;
    int drivetrain = 4;
    String direction = "N";
    String color = "Red";
    String fuel = "Gas  ";

    public void shiftGears (int newGear) {
        gear = newGear;
    }

    public void accelerateSpeed (int acceleration) {
        speed = speed + acceleration;
    }

    public void applyBrake (int brakingFactor) {
        speed = speed - brakingFactor;
    }

    public void turnWheel (String newDirection) {
        direction = newDirection;
    }
}
```

Notice we added the public keyword before the **void** keyword, which allows any other Java class to be able to call or invoke these methods, even if those classes are in a different package (packages are discussed in the next section). After all, this is a **public interface**, and anyone (more accurately, any class) should be able to access it. The Java 8 interface cannot use any of the other Java access control modifier keywords, so it cannot be declared as **private** or **protected**. We'll be learning about these access control modifiers in a future section of this chapter.

It is important to note that only the methods declared in the interface absolutely need to be included. The data fields that I have at the top of the class definition are optional and are in this example to show its parallel to the Car class that we declared earlier without using an interface. There is not much difference other than using the implements keyword, except that implementing an interface tells the compiler to check and make sure that all of the necessary methods that make a Car class complete (work properly) have been included by the developer who is using the class and interface.

Logical Collection of Classes: Using a Package

As you know, each time you define a new project for Android 7.1.1 Android Studio will create a **package** to contain your own custom classes, which you will define as you implement your application's custom functionality. In your `MyApplication` Android 7.1.1 application, which you created back in Chapter 3 using the New Android Project series of dialogs, you named your package `com.example.user.myapplication`. If you remember, that first dialog in the **New Android Studio Project** series of dialogs asked you to specify this package name (refer to Figure 3-2 if you need to refresh your memory).

The Java **package declaration** is the first line of code in any Android application class, or in any Java class in any application for that matter. The package declaration tells Java how to package your application. Recall the first line of code in our Hello World application `MainActivity.java` Activity class, as was shown in Figure 3-8:

```
package com.example.user.myapplication;
```

After the `package` keyword and declaration come the import statements, which import existing Java classes and packages into your declared package. So, a package is not only for your own code that you write yourself, but rather for all code that your application uses, even if it is open source platform code; or even code that has been written by another programmer or company; or, in the case of Android applications, Android API code, which serves up Android 7 OS functionality that is only available within the Android 7.x OS and earlier OS versions.

Basically, a Java package naming strategy is similar to the folder-naming hierarchy on your computer. A package is just a way of organizing (grouping) Java code according to functionality. As an example, Android organizes its classes into over 100 logical packages, which we will routinely import, and use, throughout this book. Each Android API Level contains a vast collection of functional packages that are utilized by developers to access the Android OS feature set. These were shown in Chapter 3 in Figure 3-10 on the left-hand side. We will take a closer look at APIs in the next section of this chapter.

In your Hello World bootstrap application we've been examining over the past couple of chapters, the Android environment needs us to have these following two `import` statements in the `MainActivity.java` file to be able to utilize the Android `AppCompatActivity` and the `Bundle` class:

```
import android.support.v7.app.AppCompatActivity;
import android.os.Bundle;
```

This `import` keyword references that API address where Java code needed to complete each `import` statement is located. Here is a generalization of how an `import` statement follows a path to the class:

```
import platform.functionality.version.classification.classname;
```

The functionality and version portions are not always utilized, as you can see in the above two `import` statements.

The Android `AppCompatActivity` class `import` statement tells the developer the following information about the Android `AppCompatActivity` Java class, as well as telling the compiler where to locate it:

- `android` indicates that this is the Android OS software development platform API

- `support` refers to the backward compatibility support functionality

- `v7` refers to Android OS Version 7.0 and 7.1.1

- `app` refers to the application area of Android component classification

- `AppCompatActivity` refers to the proper name of the class that we intend on using

Thus, the `AppCompatActivity` class, which is the superclass for any Android Activity that you want to be backward compatible across previous Android versions, is found in the `android.support.v7.app` package. This `.app` part says that this package logically contains classes that are necessary for the creation of Android applications, and one of these is the `AppCompatActivity` class, which allows us to create Activity subclasses that work across all Android OS versions. The `Bundle` class, which allows us to bundle together application variables into custom `Bundle` objects, is kept in a different package for OS utilities, as `Bundle` objects can be used in any area of Android, not just in Activity.

The API

You might be wondering if a Java package is the highest level of organization in Java. The answer is actually no; there is one even higher level, which is, as you might well imagine, a collection of these packages themselves! This level is sometimes called the **platform** or the **application programming interface** (API) level. An API for any given programming platform, like Android or Java, is a collection of all of the packages that comprise the totality of that particular computer programming language.

Thus, there is a separate API for Java SE, Java EE, and Java ME, containing all those packages for each specialized platform's implementation, as well as an Android TV, Android Wear 2, and Android Auto API. You are using the core Android (phone and tablet) API in your Hello World application, as can be seen on the right side in Figure 3-2 in Chapter 3.

Android 4.4.4 KitKat API Level 19 was the 19th Android platform to be released, and Android 4.4 "W" API Level 20 was for Android Wear, Android API Level 21 is the first 64-bit version of Android 5, and Android API Level 23 was for Android 6.0. The current Android API Level was 24 for the Android 7.0 API when I started writing this book in 2016, and is currently at API Level 25 for Android 7.1.1. Android 7.1.1 is expected to be released at the same time as this book.

For this reason, if you want to develop applications using any given programming language, you must download and obtain (and eventually learn) the API for that programming language in order to be able to develop any applications using its API, which is simply a collection of all of that language's classes, methods, and interfaces, which have been logically grouped into categorized packages. We essentially will be learning about some of the core classes used in Android 7.x API during the course of this book.

Modifiers: Data Type, Access, Inheritance

Java uses **strategic keywords** prefacing, or in front of, its major constructs, called **modifiers**. Java constructs that can be classified using modifiers include variables, methods, interfaces, and classes. Since we have already looked at data type keyword modifiers in the chapter already, at least the void (signifying no data type used), String (text data type,) and int (integer or whole number data), I will go over the other data type keywords that are used in Java and Android here, and then we will cover the more advanced access and non-access modifiers that are used in the Java programming language.

It is important to note, that even though using a data type keyword in front of your variable name will modify the type of data they are defined to contain, a more precise technical term in Java for this data type keyword is the data type **specifier** keyword. These two terms are often used interchangeably in Java. In the next section, the access control modifiers could be looked at as access control specifiers, as they're specifying a level of access, by prefacing a Java keyword in front of a Java code construct.

Other types of data type specifier keywords used in Java (and therefore, in Android 7) include **float** or floating-point numbers, which have a fractional component, represented using decimal notation, for instance, 1.375, as well as **boolean**, which hold Boolean math states" such as true and false. There are other data types in Java for holding more complicated (longer) numeric representations, such as the **long** and **double** data types, which have 64-bit accuracy, and can accommodate extremely large or extremely small numeric representations. There is also a data type that can hold one single 16-bit Unicode character, called the **char** data type. The **byte** data type can hold one number from an 8-bit range (256, from -128 to +127) of numeric data values, and finally, the **short** data type can hold one number from a 16-bit range (65,536, from -32,768 to +32,767) of numeric data values. Data types are relatively easy to understand in comparison to access or non-access modifiers, which we cover next.

Java Access Modifiers: Four Levels of Access

Java has a number of modifiers that you can place before Java constructs, to define what they are and who can see them. There are two types of Java modifiers: **access control modifiers** and **non-access control modifiers**. In case you are wondering what I mean by **access control**, I am talking about other Java programming constructs outside of a given Java class or package being able to see or reference (utilize) Java assets inside of that class, or even the package that class is contained in.

You can apply access control modifiers to classes, methods, interfaces, constructors, constants, and variables, and include the public, private, and protected Java access modifier keywords. Not using any access control keyword at all also defines the **package protected** level of access control, so let's cover all of these concepts here, in order from the most restrictive (closed) level of access control, to the least restrictive (open) level of access control. Table 5-1 shows four levels of Java access control modifiers in one place. Remember, the last one is no modifier (blank) but is called package protected.

Table 5-1. *Access Control Modifier keywords in the Java programming language and their functionality definition*

Access Control Modifier Keyword	Functionality Definition
private	Access is allowed only within that particular class
protected	Access is allowed to subclasses of that class, as well as to other classes within the same package
public	Access is allowed to all classes, even those that are located outside of your package
package protected (unspecified)	Access is allowed to other classes in that package

As you might imagine, the `private` access modifier is the most restrictive, and, if declared, only allows access to **private variables** and **private methods** from inside of the containing class. It is important to note that classes themselves cannot be declared as private unless they are inside of another class, in which case they are a special case, and are called **private inner classes**. Java interfaces, which we learned earlier, are public interfaces, and therefore also cannot be declared as private, since they are inherently public in their access control. As I have mentioned, this will change in Java 9, as well as in Android when it adopts Java 9.

The next most restrictive access modifier keyword is the `protected` access modifier keyword, which is utilized with Java classes that are intended to be used as superclasses and that need to allow access to their subclasses only, to protected variables, protected methods, as well as protected constructors. Protected access can be viewed as being protected from access by any class outside the inheritance chain, keeping it in the family, if you will. Like a private access modifier, the protected access modifier cannot be applied to any class itself, only to Java code elements inside of the class. Protected access cannot be applied to a Java 8 interface definition, as these are required to be declared using the public access modifier. It also follows that methods or data fields (variables) within a Java interface definition also cannot be declared using a protected access control modifier keyword, as they also must always be declared using a public or an abstract access control modifier. If an access modifier is not explicitly provided for a Java method that is inside a Java interface, it will default to being declared as public.

The next most restrictive access modifier is actually using none of the access control modifiers at all, which is the norm in Java, as we saw when we created our original `Car` class, using the data type declarations of `void`, `int`, or `String` without any `public`, `private`, or `protected` modifier in front of them. Using no access control modifier allows visibility **throughout your entire package**, essentially, inside of your entire application, if you have your entire Android application in one package, as we will be doing in this book, and which Android Studio 2.3 does for you, as you saw during Chapter 3.

The least restrictive access modifier, which removes all access restrictions, is the `public` access control modifier. This allows Java code in other packages to access your Java variables, methods, interfaces, and classes from outside of your package. It's like you are opening the door to your code and saying, "come on in, folks, I'm giving you access to everything." Use this modifier with caution!

It is important not to confuse access control and non-access control modifiers with Java variable data type declarations that are used before variables to declare their data type, and which thus look a lot like a modifier. In fact, modifiers and data type declarations are often utilized right next to each other, like we did in the `public void shiftGears()` method.

Java methods have their own rules regarding inheriting access control modifiers, as the classes that contain methods are later subclassed or enhanced to become more detailed and refined subclasses. For instance, any method that has been declared using a public access in a superclass must also be declared using public access in all subclasses. Similarly, any method that has been declared using protected access in a superclass must either be declared using the protected access, or using public access, in any subclass. It can never be declared using a `private` access control modifier.

A method declared without using an access control modifier is the only scenario where a method can be declared using a private access control modifier in a subclass. It is important to note that a method that has been declared using a private access control modifier keyword is not inherited, because it is private relative to that class within which it is contained, and no others, including any subclasses.

As you can see, although access control modifiers seem fairly simple and straightforward, you have to pay attention to what you are doing with them, especially where inheritance (superclasses and subclasses) is going to be utilized in your Java programming structure and Java package design.

Non-Access Modifiers: Static, Final, and Abstract

There are also modifiers in Java that are not access control modifiers, and not data type declarations. These are called **non-access modifiers** and these are the most complicated ones to understand and to implement in practical usage. There are three modifiers that are frequently used in Java programming that we'll be covering in this section of the chapter: a **static** modifier, a **final** modifier, and an **abstract** modifier. There are also some more advanced modifiers such as **synchronized** or **volatile**, which are used to manage the use of system memory using something called threads. Memory allocation using modifiers is a topic that is largely beyond the scope of an Absolute Beginners Android programming book, although we will cover what a `Thread` class in Android is in Chapter 13.

The static Keyword: Share Variables Between Objects

A `static` modifier keyword when used in conjunction with a variable will create a variable that will exist independently of any object instances created using that class. Static variables will be initialized only one time, at the start of the execution of the application, sometimes called the app launch. The variables that use the `static` modifier keyword will be initialized first, before the initialization of any instance variables. Only one copy of a static variable will exist in system memory regardless of the number of instances of the class that contains that variable are created. Thus, static in Java code means that variable that belongs to the class, and not to the object instances created by that class.

Objects created by that class can share that variable with the class and with each other, so use of static variables can optimize system memory. The opposite of static is **dynamic**, and thus, any variable not declared as static would therefore be dynamically created (created at the time it is instantiated, not ahead of time as when it is declared statically). System memory will be allocated for dynamic variables as each object instance is created by that class constructor method.

To use a variable from the Car class example, if you wanted all Car objects to reference the fuel variable, which is set in the code to "Gas" at the class level, and wanted that fuel variable to belong only to the class, and not to any of the Car objects that will be created using that class, you would declare the fuel variable as follows:

```
static String fuel = "Gas";
```

The static modifier keyword works in much the same way for methods that are declared as static, thus a static modifier would be utilized to create methods that are intended to exist independently of any object instances created using the class. This again fixes the method in place, so it is the only copy of that method that will be used by your class and objects from that class.

A static method can be referenced using the class name and dot notation even without an object instance of the class ever being created. For instance, if you declared the .applyBrake() method to be static, you could reference it using the code statement Car.applyBrake() even without having created a Car object using the new keyword.

Static methods cannot use any **instance variables** of any object instances created using the class in which they are defined, until one of those object instances has been created. Static methods should take all their data values from the incoming parameter list, and then compute something from those parameters, with no reference to variables, which are inherently not static, because they're variable!

So, to re-code your .applyBrake(int brakingFactor) method as static, and reference the class speed variable, you would modify your method to look something like this:

```
public static void applyBrake (int brakingFactor) {
    Car.speed = Car.speed - brakingFactor;
}
```

Notice that the access control modifier comes first, then the non-access modifier, and then finally the return data type declaration comes last in the list. This is the modifier and declaration ordering convention for the Java 8 programming language. Next, let's look at the final modifier, which sometimes gets confused with the static modifier, as the final modifier also means that something cannot be changed, and is thus fixed as well! Java can be confusing in a number of areas, and this happens to be one of them!

The final Keyword: Lock Down Your Java Code

You can define a class using the `final` modifier keyword, and if a class is designated final, it cannot be subclassed. This is usually implemented for reasons of Java security, so tested, mission-critical Java code cannot be modified or changed. You will notice as we get deeper into the Android API and Java that many standard Android Java-based library classes are declared using the `final` modifier keyword. As an example, the `java.lang.System` and `java.lang.String` classes are declared to be `final` so that their functionality cannot be altered.

All methods in a final class are implicitly final methods. Any method declared using the `final` modifier keyword cannot be overridden by subclasses. This is also for security reasons and is used to prevent unexpected behavior resulting from a subclass altering a method that might be crucial to the function or to the consistency of a class's functionality.

You can explicitly initialize a final variable only once. A reference variable that is declared as final can never be reassigned to refer to a different object, if the variable references an object, rather than a data value. If the final variable references an object, the data contained within that object can still be changed, only the reference to the object is fixed, and is said to be final.

Thus, you can change the state of an object referenced by the final variable, but not the reference to the object, which is what is locked or final. With variables, the `final` modifier is often utilized in conjunction with the `static` modifier to make the class variable into what is considered a **constant,** or an immutable fixed variable, for the duration of the class. So this is how you would make your own constant values in your own code.

As an example, the `<string>` constant named `app_name` that you defined using XML in the `strings.xml` file would have to be declared in your application's Java code by using the following single line of Java syntax:

```
public static final String app_name = "Hello Universe";
```

This above constant definition contrasts how using XML to define constants is much simpler than using Java, because Android sets all of your modifiers and puts it all into proper Java syntax for you. Next, let's take a look at the `abstract` modifier keyword, which allows you to create classes that can be subclassed (used for Java logic development), but which not instantiated (used as Java objects in memory).

The abstract Keyword: Designate Class as a Superclass

A class declared using an `abstract` modifier keyword can never be instantiated, or placed into memory as an object and actually utilized in the functionality of an Android (or Java/JavaFX) application. Think of the literary use of the word abstract, which means a summary or a guide to a literary work, but not the literary work itself. Java code designated as abstract is used for a guide or template (superclass) for creating other code that may actually be used as an object, later on down the subclassing line.

If your class is declared as abstract, then the sole purpose for that class is to be **extended**—that is, **subclassed**. If a class contains any methods that have been declared using the `abstract` modifier, then the class should also be declared using the `abstract` modifier. If your class contains any abstract methods, and is not declared as abstract, a compiler error will be **thrown** when you use the **Run ➤ App** work process, which invokes the Java compiler.

An abstract class can, however, contain both abstract methods as well as standard (non-abstract) methods, so the rule is, if you want to put an abstract method inside of a class, make sure that class is declared as abstract as well, or you will get a compiler error. In summary, you cannot have abstract methods inside of a class that is not also declared to be abstract.

A Java interface differs from an abstract class in a couple of key ways. Your abstract class can have instance methods that implement your default or baseline behaviors. A variable declared in a Java interface is final. An abstract class can contain non-final variables. A Java class can implement more than one interface, but may only extend a single abstract class.

Let's take a look at the Java code that Android Studio wrote for you in Chapter 3 and see what it does, and how we can upgrade it.

Analyzing Your MainActivity.java Class

Let's use what we have learned to analyze the Java code for our Hello World application, which is shown in Chapter 3 (Figure 3-8), so I won't waste space with that screenshot here. The Java code shown in the Android Studio `MainActivity.java` editing pane looks like the following:

```
package com.example.user.myapplication;
import android.support.v7.app.AppCompatActivity;
import android.os.Bundle;
public class MainActivity extends AppCompatActivity {
    @Override
    protected void onCreate(Bundle savedInstanceState) {
        super.onCreate(savedInstanceState);
        setContentView(R.layout.activity_main);
    }
}
```

The first line of code uses the Java `package` keyword to declare the `com.example.user.myapplication` package name, which is also declared in the `AndroidManifest.xml` as you saw in Chapter 4. The manifest file defines your application and also ties Google Play to the application, and defines what the application is allowed to do, what hardware device types and Android OS versions the application supports, and defines its included components (Activity, Service, Receiver, Provider, etc.).

The next two lines of code import the `AppCompatActivity` and `Bundle` Android classes into the package, as they will be utilized in the `MainActivity.java` class.

The fourth line of code is the `MainActivity` class declaration. The class extends the `AppCompatActivity` superclass, so we'll take a look at that next, and is designated using the `public` access modifier. One of the superclass methods, `.onCreate()` has been overridden using an `@Override` annotation, so we can replace some of the standard `AppCompatActivity` class Java code with our own application logic, such as the `.setContentView()` method that will be used for inflating your UI layout XML definition, which as you know from Chapter 4 is contained in an `activity_main.xml` file in an `app/res/layout` folder. This Activity subclass is also referenced specifically, using the `AndroidManifest.xml` `<activity>` tag.

The protected void onCreate() method allows access to other classes in your package, and returns no values (void), and simply starts up the Activity screen on the device display, as well as creating the application Main Activity in memory. This is done my calling the superclass onCreate() method using the super.onCreate(savedInstanceState); line of Java code. The savedInstanceState Bundle object contains all of the Activity state values, so that if you leave the Activity, to do something else on your device, and return to your app Activity later, it can restore where the Activity was (its states) correctly. This Bundle object passed into the MainActivity.onCreate(Bundle) method will be passed to Android's AppCompatActivity.onCreate(Bundle) superclass method by using this super.onCreate(Bundle) call.

The next line of code in onCreate() uses the setContentView(Resource) method to inflate your UI design by referencing the /app/res folder using an R, and the app/res/layout folder (R.layout), and finally the activity_main.xml file (file extension not required) using R.layout.activity_main path as the value passed into the method. This renders your design to the screen in the same way that the Visual Design Editor renders it to the Preview pane in Android Studio.

Next, let's learn more about Java by taking a look at one of the Android classes that are used in the Hello World (MyApplication) application. The AppCompatActivity class is the superclass that is used to define the MainActivity class that extends it (see above Java code), and therefore is used as the code template for the MainActivity class. This makes it important for us to review it to see what the MainActivity class is able to do, as it gets its functionality from Android's AppCompatActivity class.

The AppCompatActivity Class: Spans OS Versions

Let's take a look at how you will look at the AppCompatActivity superclass on the Android developer website, to see what methods you can override, and what variables and functions you have available to you. You should familiarize yourself with every Android class you use in this way, so this is a good exercise. Google "Android AppCompatActivity class," and you'll get the following documentation URL:

https://developer.android.com/reference/android/support/v7/app/AppCompatActivity.html

At the top of the class documentation you will see the Java Object (master class) to superclass to subclass hierarchy. Half a dozen classes contain Java code which will affect the AppCompatActivity class, because it's an object, needs to have Context information, is a type of Android Activity with application (backward) compatibility features added. The chain of Java class design is as follows:

```
java.lang.Object
  ↳ android.content.Context
    ↳ android.content.ContextWrapper
      ↳ android.view.ContextThemeWrapper
        ↳ android.app.Activity
          ↳ android.support.v4.app.FragmentActivity
            ↳ android.support.v7.app.AppCompatActivity
```

It also tell you at the top of the class what the access is, and which interfaces which are implemented.

In this case there are three interfaces, `AppCompatCallback`, `TaskStackBuilder`. `SupportParentable`, and `ActionBarDrawerToggle.DelegateProvider`, and the class is public. There is also one known direct subclass, `ActionBarActivity`, the base class for activities that use `ActionBar` features in the V7 support library. Under this information are the inherited constants from the `Activity` and `Context` superclasses, and the inherited data fields (variables) from the `Activity` superclass. There is also one constructor, `AppCompatActivity()` and then a few dozen methods that can be used (overridden) in your class. I don't have the time to go into all of these methods in detail in this Java primer chapter, but you should review them if you plan to use this Activity type extensively or at an advanced level once you become more proficient in Android 7.x application design and programming.

Summary

In this fifth chapter, you learned all about the Java programming language, as well as how the Android platform utilizes Java 8 to facilitate the application development work process. You learned about Java versions used in enterprise, client, and mobile application development, and about OOP. You learned about `java.lang.Object`, which is the foundation of OOP, and about how Java objects define attributes, characteristics, states, and behaviors which allow Java programmers to mimic real-world objects in a virtual software development environment.

You learned about various components of Java 8 programming structures, such as methods, constants, variables, classes, public interfaces, and constructor methods. You learned about the Java concept of inheritance, and how to use the new keyword to instantiate an instance of a Java object by using this constructor method call. You looked at the higher-level Java organization constructs called packages, and how the total collection of packages in a programming language forms the API for the language. We also covered some Java 9 features which are not yet in Android, but which will be in the future.

Next, you looked at some of the data type specifiers and access control modifiers, as well as the more complex non-access modifiers, and after that you were ready to take a closer look at the `MainActivity` Java class, which you created in Chapter 3, to see how its Java code works and integrates with XML.

In Chapter 6, you will start to learn more about Android user interface design using the Android View class, the `ViewGroup` class, and more about XML UI definition tags, parameters, and work processes.

Android User Interface Design: Using Activity, View, and ViewGroup Classes

Now that you've been exposed to the Android 7 operating system and have seen how it works from a high-level view, using XML and Java, and how these are used in Android application development, the next thing we need to do is take a closer look at how Android addresses, or writes things to, a device screen, to display UI and content.

In this new age of touchscreen devices, such as smartphones, tablets, e-book readers, and smartwatches, your display screen has become the center of not only the visual feedback for the application but also for interacting with it. This chapter will cover those classes that allow your Android app to write things to the device display screen, such as your Activity class; core User Interface (UI) classes; and, of course, your Android application primary subject matter, text, audio, video, animation and graphics content.

There are some very important Android superclasses, such as Activity, View, and ViewGroup, which provide a foundation for the subclasses that you will utilize to get your application content and UI onto the display screen. These superclasses are not used directly in your application, but you need to know about them nonetheless.

We will look at **AppCompatActivity** subclasses, which provide support across all Android versions, and can be utilized for organizing your application's functional screens, which ultimately will provide the structure for your end-user's workflow; let's call it the "use-flow" for your Android application.

© Wallace Jackson 2017
W. Jackson, *Android Apps for Absolute Beginners*, DOI 10.1007/978-1-4842-2268-3_6

We will look at **View** subclasses used for creating your application's UI element components, which as you know are known as **widgets** in Android jargon. We'll look at the **ViewGroup** subclasses, used for creating Android UI **layout containers**. Layout containers are used to contain View (subclassed) UI widgets, which make up the body of the UI design, providing the UI layout with its functionality. Since Android Studio now has drag-and-drop UI design functionality, we will use the UI layout compatible with the Application Compatibility (AppCompat) Android 7 backward support (support.v7) library. This is so that I can show you how to develop Android 7.1.1 applications with as little coding and XML markup as possible, leveraging Android Studio 2.3 as thoroughly as possible.

Finally, you will put all of this newfound knowledge to use and will create your first original Hello Universe UI design so that you get some hands-on experience in creating your own UI design. We will create a Hello Universe Galaxy and Smiley Face user interface design for your Hello World bootstrap application.

How Activity, View, and ViewGroup Classes Interrelate

Before we look at the Android Activity, View, and ViewGroup UI superclasses and their more functional subclasses (those classes that you should actually utilize to construct your apps), it is important to understand how these relate to each other, within the user interface design and display context of your Android 7.1.1 application.

The reason I am not including the Menu superclass and its functional subclasses in this chapter is because Android menus are handled separately from UI widget View and UI layout ViewGroup UI design elements. Menus pop up over a screen triggered by a hardware **MENU** button or the ActionBar Overflow menu. For this reason, we are going to cover Menu objects separately, in a future chapter.

As you've learned already, the Android runtime environment (ART) resides on top of a Linux kernel, and talks to the Android 7.1.1 OS, under which your application executes (or runs). Your application defines itself to ART using the AndroidManifest.xml application definition XML file that we looked at in detail, in Chapter 4.

For each functional display screen in an app, which will generally contain some sort of UI design, as well as related app content, your application will define an **Activity subclass**. Your Hello World application currently has one of these Activity subclasses already, as you saw in Chapter 3 in Figure 3-8 with an AppCompatActivity Activity subclass, used in your public class MainActivity extends AppCompatActivity declaration at the top of the class.

Each Activity subclass in your Android application would be required to have an .onCreate() method defined, and this method will in turn be required to contain the setContentView() method call, to load a user interface ViewGroup (layout), and View (widget) UI elements. The setContentView() parameters contain the reference to your Activity subclass's UI layout XML definition. For the MainActivity.java class, this reference is R.layout.activity_main, which is Android shorthand to reference the /res/layout/ activity_main.xml file, as you can see in Figure 3-8, which, after our Java primer during Chapter 5 should be making a whole lot more sense to you!

A **parent tag** in a UI layout XML definition will generally reference a ViewGroup subclass such as the ConstraintLayout class, which in the activity_main.xml file is represented by a <ConstraintLayout> parent tag. The ViewGroup superclass in Android is used to subclass (create) custom layout container classes in Android, which I'll be covering in detail throughout the rest of this book. There are a large number of custom layout container classes in Android, because these UI layout classes provide the foundation of UI design in Android.

Inside of ViewGroup UI layout container parent tags are **child tags** representing **UI elements**, which are called **widgets** in Android. UI widgets are based on Android's View superclass. Each widget, like that <TextView> child tag you used in Chapters 3 and 4, references your Android TextView widget class, which is subclassed using the View superclass. Inside each (View subclass) UI widget child tag, you set **parameters** that **reference** the new media assets for your application, such as **drawables** (images and bitmap animation), **animation** (procedural, tween, or vector animation), **audio** or **video**, scalable vector graphic (SVG) **shapes**, custom UI elements and similar assets.

Thus, getting your app's assets onto the Android device display screen involves putting parameters in child widget tags inside of parent UI layout tags referenced by the Activity subclass that you have declared in the application Android manifest XML file. All of this can be done in Android Studio.

Code is passed over to the ART engine, which then converts all this into machine language, and then passes it over to the Linux kernel, whose job it is to interface the OS software with the hardware, and to render your application's UI design and content to the Android device display screen hardware with pixel-perfect accuracy. Whew! This chain from Android Runtime to app resources looks like this:

```
Android RunTime > Manifest > Activity Subclass > ViewGroup Parent Tag > View Child Tag >
Resources
```

To make this even easier to visualize, I created a diagram, seen in Figure 6-1, which shows layers (and connections) between your application's new media resources, your UI widgets that hold them, UI layouts that hold your UI widgets and resources, and the Activity subclasses that defines and control your UI layout XML definition, by referencing it using your .setContentView() method call. It is important to note that since you can set a background image or animation for the UI layout container, so a ViewGroup can also reference new media resources; thus, the new media resource area of the diagram in Figure 6-1 connects with both View and ViewGroup subclasses.

As you learned in Chapter 3, your Android manifest defines for ART what Activity classes an application contains, as well as what your application is allowed to do; and other information about your application's version history, support, structure, permissions, communications, intents, network access, Google Play access, and so on.

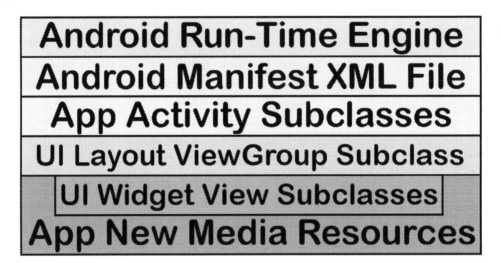

Figure 6-1. Stratification of Android app, from new media resources up to execution

Next, you will take a closer look at the relationship between ViewGroup (layout container) and View (UI widget) superclasses in Android, since the ViewGroup superclass is actually a subclass of the View superclass. It is interesting to remember that a superclass can also be a subclass.

ViewGroup inherits characteristics from View like margin settings, which as you will see, are supported in both layout containers (ViewGroup subclasses) as well as UI widgets (View subclasses), thanks to Java inheritance and how well the Android OS developers have designed and coded the user interface design superclass structures.

The ViewGroup Class: A Known Direct Subclass of View

Even though View widgets are nested inside of ViewGroup layout containers, the ViewGroup superclass is actually subclassed from the View superclass in Android's Java class hierarchy. Starting with the Java Object master class, the inheritance hierarchy is structured as follows:

```
java.lang.Object
  > android.view.View
    > android.view.ViewGroup
```

The reason that the Android OS development team structured the View class hierarchy in this fashion is because View class attributes such as top, bottom, left, and right **margin** attributes (properties, or parameters), should also be available for use in a ViewGroup layout container, as well as in every View UI widget. So, the logical Java structure would be subclassing ViewGroup from View, so that the ViewGroup subclasses inherit all of those same variables, constants, and methods that the View subclasses will include.

If you look at the ViewGroup class documentation page, on the Android developer website, you will see that the ViewGroup class has 18 **known direct subclasses**. Some of the most common UI layouts include your LinearLayout, for horizontal or vertical UI design; GridLayout for grid UI design; Toolbar for UI toolbars; ViewPager for UI page viewing; DrawerLayout and SlidingDrawer for UI in drawers; AbsoluteLayout and FrameLayout for fixed layouts, or fullscreen content; SlidingPaneLayout for sliding UI design; TvView for iTV set UI design; RecyclerView for efficient, long-item list UI design (recycles or optimizes memory use); and several others for specialized UI.

> **Note** A known direct subclass is a subclass that has been created from the class that is being documented on that developer website class reference page. **Known** means it has been officially added to the Android API. If you subclass your own Android class, it would be called an **unknown direct subclass**, because it is unknown to the public Android API. A **known indirect subclass** will represent a subclass of a known direct subclass. It is **indirect** to the class being documented, because it is more than one level away from, and not a direct subclass of the documented class.

There are **55 known indirect subclasses** of this ViewGroup class. These are the subclasses of the 18 known direct subclasses. These are even more highly customized user interface layout container classes, and thus you have around 75 user interface layout containers to choose from. There are a couple that have not yet been added to the developer documentation since they are new in Android 7, including the one we are going to using with the Visual UI Layout Designer tool (ConstraintLayout).

You'll be learning about some of these UI layouts over the course of this book. ViewGroup UI layout subclasses are just as important as View UI widget subclasses; however the ViewGroup class doesn't have as many subclasses as the View class does. If you want to explore the ViewGroup documentation further, it's found at this URL:

http://developer.android.com/reference/android/view/**ViewGroup.html**

We'll be looking at several popular ViewGroup subclasses during the rest of the book. When using ViewGroup subclasses, termed UI layout containers in Android, and View subclasses, termed UI widgets in Android, your View widgets will be contained **inside of** the ViewGroup layout containers. This is why the ViewGroup class is named the way it is, as it **groups** View objects together into a UI layout design, as shown in Figure 6-2. The ViewGroup layout container specifying your user interface design is then referenced inside of, and contained in, your Activity using R.layout.uiName inside of a setContentView() method that loads the UI and content into the display.

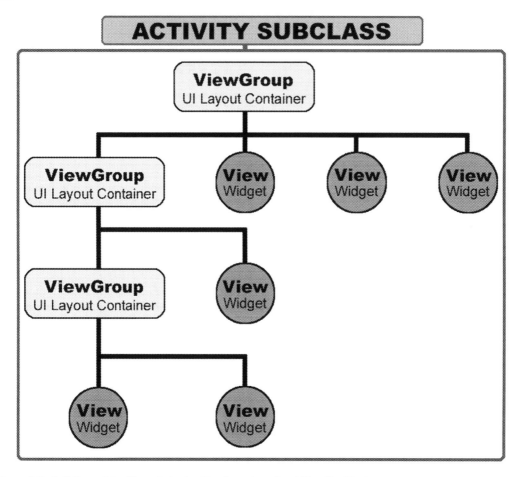

Figure 6-2. Activity contains UI created using ViewGroup layout and View UI widgets

It's important to note that even though a ViewGroup subclass must be used for a parent object in an XML UI layout design, ViewGroup subclass objects might also be nested underneath a parent ViewGroup, such as a LinearLayout UI containing Buttons.

ViewGroup objects are able to be used as both parent and child objects, whereas View widgets are child UI design element objects. Hands-on experience is the best way to show you all of this UI design theory, which we will be doing a bit later on during this chapter as well as during the second half of the book. Before we get into more UI design, let's take a closer look at the Android View superclass.

The View Class: A Foundation of User Interface Design

As you may have surmised from its class name, a View object is designed to hold anything that needs to be viewed in an Android app using the device display screen. Since devices are almost 100% comprised of display screen on their front; this is ostensibly the most important class in Android at least from your visual design and user interface usability standpoint. Since I already showed the class hierarchy in the previous section, this time I will show you the `View` class declaration from the developer documentation (this is always at the very top of the class documentation):

```
public class View
extends Object implements Drawable.Callback, KeyEvent.Callback, AccessibilityEventSource
```

This tells us that `View` can be publicly used by all Android application classes in the API, that it extends the `Object` superclass, and that it implements Java interfaces for graphics (`Drawable.Callback` interface) and interactivity (`KeyEvent.Callback` interface), and supports users with disabilities (`AccessibilityEventSource` interface).

If you look at the `View` class documentation page on Android's developer website, you will see that this `View` class has a dozen known direct subclasses, one of which is the `ViewGroup`. Some of the most common UI widget objects are created using these classes include your `ImageView`, which you have already used in Chapter 4; `TextView`, which Android Studio created for you in Chapter 3; `TextureView` for texture mapping; `SurfaceView` for rendering graphics; `AnalogClock` for creating clocks; `KeyboardView` for creating virtual keyboards; `ProgressBar` for creating progress bars; and several utility classes relating to `View` user interface design.

Because of `ViewGroup`, there are hundreds of known indirect subclasses for `View`, some of which we will be using during this book, but each of which we would not be able to cover even in one book, and especially in an Absolute Beginner Android book – as you can imagine. Even advanced Android users are not familiar with all of these! Many of them are covered in the 2014 Apress title *Pro Android UI*, however.

If you want to take a closer look at what the Android `View` superclass includes, you can see for yourself, by visiting the following URL:

`http://developer.android.com/reference/android/view/View.html`

Whereas `View` subclasses in Android 7 control what you see on the screen, each `Activity` object controls how the Activity that hosts the `View`(s) and `ViewGroup`(s) start, load in memory, stop, and manage the `View` object hierarchy that you will create in the Android Studio Visual Design Editor.

The Activity Class: A User Interface Design Container

As you've seen in Chapter 5, whereas a `View` UI design hierarchy is crafted with XML markup, an `Activity` is crafted using Java, and references that XML UI design definition. The `Activity` fuses the OS theme, as you can see below in the class definition that extends `ContextThemeWrapper`, with your user interface design. It implements Java 8 interfaces for UI inflation, window, keyboard, menu, and components.

```
public class Activity
extends ContextThemeWrapper
implements LayoutInflater.Factory2, Window.Callback, KeyEvent.Callback,
          View.OnCreateContextMenuListener, ComponentCallbacks2
```

This tells us that an Activity inflates (turns XML elements into Java objects) your UI design, handles OS windowing calls, listens for ContextMenu usage, handles Android components, and passes through KeyEvents to user interface elements.

If you look at the Activity class documentation page on the developer website, you will see that this Activity class has 7 known direct subclasses; the AppCompatActivity subclass you are using in your Hello World app is an indirect subclass of the FragmentActivity direct Activity subclass. Some of the most common Activity subclasses besides the indirect subclass AppCompatActivity, which allows your app to be used across all versions of Android currently in the marketplace, include the FragmentActivity, which allows you to assemble UI fragments into one Activity; ListActivity and ExpandableListActivity, which manage lists (i.e., data collections); and AccountAuthenticatorActivity, used for log-in (account authentication) screens. There is also a NativeActivity, declared in the manifest, for use with the Android NDK (Native C++ Development Kit) and an AliasActivity for aliasing Activity classes (also declared using the manifest), both of which are used for advanced Android developer use.

There are five known indirect subclasses for Activity according to the Android documentation, including the AppCompatActivity used with the Visual Design Editor (ConstraintLayout), TabActivity (tabbed UI design), ActionBarActivity (ActionBar UI design), LauncherActivity (launchers of other activities), and PreferenceActivity (preference screen UI design). As you can see, Android offers Activity subclasses that are already customized for most of those application UI tasks you want to do. Android applications will almost always contain more than one Activity (functional screen with its own purpose and a user interface design to accomplish the purpose).

An Activity object in Android contains a single UI focused on a specific task or feature that your application offers to the user. Almost all activities interact with the user, so each Activity object must take care of creating a window, using a call to the Android OS so the user can interact with a UI that is loaded using the setContentView(R.layout. uiDesignName) method call. Activities are usually presented to a user in a fullscreen window. They can be used in floating windows (windows and their styling is called the operating system's UI elements or "Chrome") to simulate a conventional OS, using a theme with a windowIsFloating parameter set.

All activity classes will have a corresponding <activity> declaration in their package Android manifest XML file. You have already seen this in Chapters 3 and 4 in your Android Studio AndroidManifest.xml editing pane. We'll be adding more of these <activity> child tag (and their child tag) entries in the <manifest> parent tag as we add Activity UI design screens to our Hello World application during the first half of the book. You'll be adding Activity UI screens for all apps created during this book, in fact, so be sure to understand the material contained in this chapter.

There is one Activity class method Android classes must implement to get your UI design screen into system memory: the onCreate(Bundle), where you initialize the Activity object and use setContentView() to reference and load your UI design. You can also use six other Activity state methods, including onPause(), onResume(), onStart(), onStop(), onRestart() and onDestroy() to control what your Activity does throughout each of the stages of an Activity object's life cycle. I have outlined these seven life-cycle states in Figure 6-3, and shown how they are logically paired and how they are logically classified in the create, utilize, and destroy phases of the Activity object (constructed using your Activity subclass) in your Android device's system memory. As you can see creating and starting launch the Activity, a pause and resume can be used for a running the Activity, and a stop and destroy end the Activity life cycle. They are logically paired as one might expect from their names.

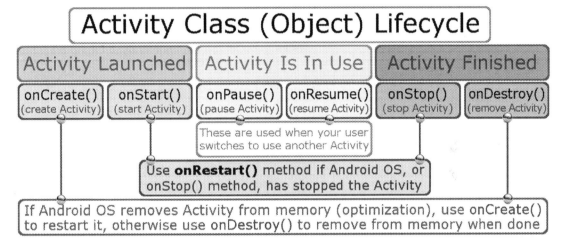

Figure 6-3. The Activity class (object) life cycle spanning creation to destruction

It is important to note that these other six methods do not need to be implemented, unless you wanted to do something other than what the Activity superclass will already do to make your Activity work well with other Android apps installed on the same end-user device. So if in onCreate() you opened up a socket on a media server, in onDestroy() you will want to close that socket so as not to hang your media server. If in onStart() you start streaming data of some kind, in onStop() you may want to stop streaming that data to save bandwidth. You may want to tell your users "Welcome Back" in onResume(), or check what your Activity is doing regarding its given functionality. You might want to resume your data stream onRestart(), for instance.

If you want to take a closer look at what the Activity superclass includes, you can see for yourself, by visiting the following URL:

https://developer.android.com/reference/android/app/**Activity.html**

Next, let's get back into UI Design in Android Studio, using the Design Editor.

Creating UI Design from Scratch

Let's use all of this knowledge you have learned over the past few chapters and implement a new Activity. The first step that we need to take to do this is to do a UI design for the screen that the Activity will display; in this case that would be your Hello Universe screen, which you can select at the bottom of the current Hello World user interface in your main Activity (activity_main.xml). In the last half of this chapter we will learn how to design a user interface design from scratch using your Android Studio Design Editor, which will write your XML for you. Over this chapter, and the next one on interactivity, we will connect these two Java `Activity` classes together using interactivity (Events and Intents). Since this chapter is on user interface design, we will focus on creating your new user interface design XML definition, called `activity_universe.xml`, so we have everything we need for Chapter 7, where we will focus on the Java programming part of creating this new `Activity`.

Let's fire up Android Studio to create a new user interface design XML definition for the new `Activity` we're going to create in Chapter 7. As you will see in Figure 6-4, Android Studio does a **Gradle build** on your current project, when you first start the IDE. If there are any issues, or problems, the Gradle Build Messages window (pane) appears at the bottom. Android requires lowercase letters and numbers to be used in asset file names, so it points out the SmileyFace PNG32 asset uses the capital S, and advises us that "File-based resource names must contain only lowercase a-z, 0-9, or underscore" characters. So, let's fix this now!

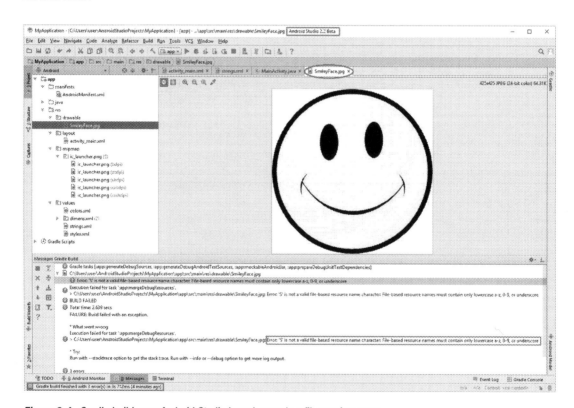

Figure 6-4. Gradle build upon Android Studio launch reveals a file naming error

Find your `SmileyFace.png` file in your `User/AndroidStudioProjects/MyApplication/` folder hierarchy on your hard disk drive, and rename it to `smileyface.png`. Also make sure to change the referencing to this asset file name in your XML UI definition to also be lowercase. This is seen circled in red in Figure 6-5, as well as the **Tools ➤ Android ➤ Sync Project with Gradle Files** command, which will trigger a rebuild so that you can see if you have fixed this particular problem.

Remember if you can't find your project files on your hard disk drive using the operating system file management utility, you can right-click on the `SmileyFace.png` file in your /app/ res/drawable/ folder, and select your **File Path** context-sensitive menu option, which will show you where to go with the file management utility. Once you right-click on that file, and rename it smileyface.png, it will show up in your Android Studio project with the correct name. This can be seen in Figure 6-5 on the left side of the screen. Also shown is the updated markup in the `activity_main.xml`.

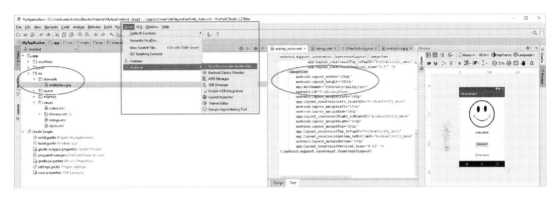

Figure 6-5.   Rename smileyface.png using all lowercase and Sync Project with Gradle

Now we are ready to create the new user interface design for the `Activity` we're going to code in Chapter 7. Let's call this `activity_universe.xml` since we're going to call this new `Activity` class `UniverseActivity.java`. The way you create a new XML UI layout definition is to right-click on your app/res/layout/ project folder, then select **New ➤ Layout resource file** from the context-sensitive menu, seen on the left side of Figure 6-6. This will open the **New Resource File** dialog, shown on the right side of Figure 6-6. Name the XML resource file **activity_universe**, and select a **Root element** class value of **android.support. constraint.ConstraintLayout** as seen highlighted.

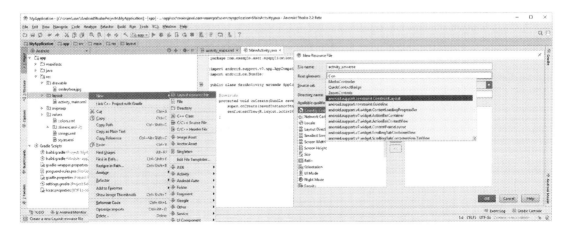

Figure 6-6.   Right-click on app/res/layout and select the New ➤ Layout resource file

Leave the other data fields at their default values and click on the **OK** button. This will create the new `activity_universe.xml` file in the `app/res/layout/` folder, and open it in an editing tab at the top middle of Android Studio. Click on the **Design** tab at the bottom of the XML editing pane to switch into Visual XML UI Design mode, which can be seen in Figure 6-7 with an empty screen design ready for you to create your new design in. We will create a universe UI from scratch to use in the `UniverseActivity` that we will be creating in Chapter 7, to learn about events and Intents, and how these can add interactivity to your Android 7.1.1 applications.

In the Properties panel name the **ID** for the UI design **universe**, as shown on the right of Figure 6-7, and click on the **View all properties** link at the bottom of the pane. Make sure that the Component Tree panel has the ConstraintLayout selected, which is should be, as it's the only layout in use in the user interface design currently!

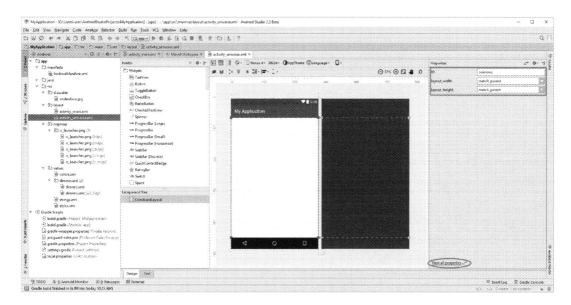

Figure 6-7. *Select your activity_universe.xml editing tab, and the Design mode tab*

The first thing that you want to do is to set a black background color for this universe UI, since a universe is largely black. Mouse-over the background property that actually tells you how to use **#ff000000** to specify a **Black** color background.

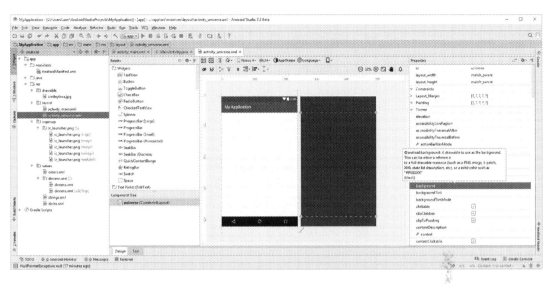

Figure 6-8. Mouse-over the background property to see how to set the color to black

Select the `ImageView` UI widget, shown selected in Figure 6-9, then drag it into the upper-left corner of the UI design, which now has your Black background color. Select a **galaxy.jpg** image from the **Resources** dialog and click the **OK** button.

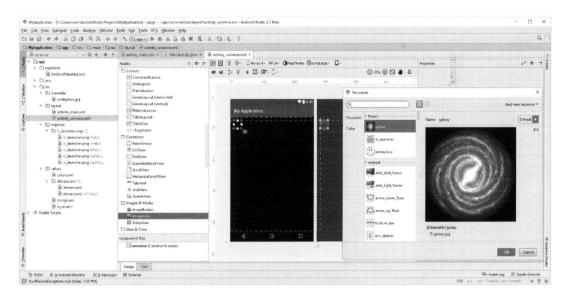

Figure 6-9. Drag an ImageView into the upper-left corner; select a galaxy.jpg image

In the blueprint mode, seen on the right in Figure 6-10, drag your `ImageView` so that it fits into your UI screen. Notice the `@drawable/galaxy` reference.

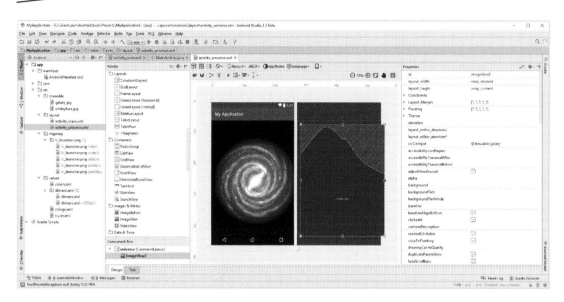

Figure 6-10. *Drag the ImageView into position in the UI screen using blueprint mode*

Next, let's add a CheckBox UI element so that the user can switch back to Hello World mode if they so desire.

Add a CheckBox User Interface Element to your Design

Select the **CheckBox** UI widget, as is shown on the left side of Figure 6-11, and drag it to the bottom-left side of the user interface design underneath the galaxy. Keep the default (suggested) **checkBox ID** and enter "Hello World" in the text field, in the Properties dialog, as shown on the right side in Figure 6-11.

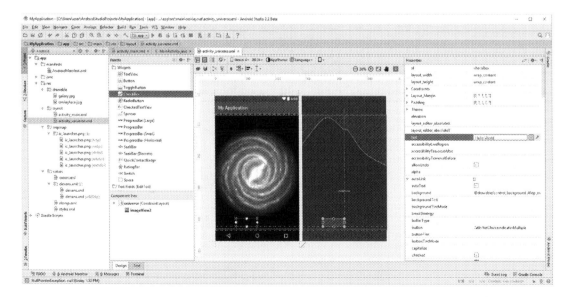

Figure 6-11. *Add and Position a CheckBox UI widget, and set its text to Hello World*

You can see in Figure 6-11 that we have a problem, since the default text color is set to Black and our background is now black to accommodate the Universe design. The checkbox itself is also not showing, as it also uses black in its default color configuration. Let's address this issue first before we move on with our UI design.

The property (or attribute, or parameter if you prefer that term) that controls the color of the checkbox part of the UI element is **buttonTint**, shown at the bottom right portion of Figure 6-12.

The property (or attribute, or parameter if you prefer that term) that controls the color of the checkbox text for the UI element is **textColor**, which you can find if you scroll down the Properties dialog using the scrollbar shown at the top-right corner in Figure 6-12.

After you scroll down to the UI text parameters, which are shown in Figure 6-12 on the left-hand side, click the three dots (called ellipses), on the right of your **textColor** parameter (numbered as 1), and open the Resources dialog and select **white** (numbered as 2). Click the **OK** button (numbered as 3), which should install the white color constant in the property field as @android:color/white. Click your **View fewer properties** link (numbered as 4), and then enter the hexadecimal #ffffffff value for the buttonTint property (numbered as 5) as is shown in Figure 6-12.

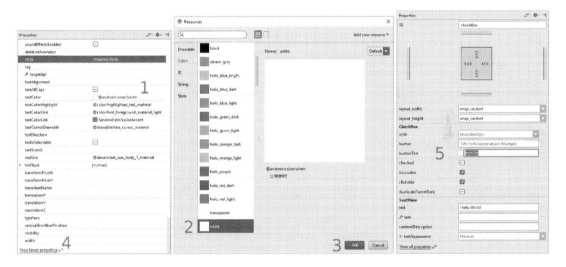

Figure 6-12. Set textColor and buttonTint to white, using a constant or hexadecimal

It's important to note that you could also use the same work process as you did for the textColor property for the buttonTint property if you wish, since the white color constant ultimately installs this hexadecimal value into system memory at the end of the day, so you can use either of these in your specification of color. Next set your constraints, as shown in Figure 6-13, and set **textSize** to **18sp** and specify the **sans typeface**. To better match the Hello World UI design use the **Bold textStyle** as well. All these settings make your CheckBox element significantly more readable.

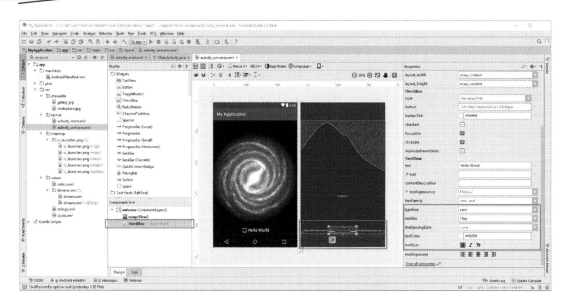

Figure 6-13. Add side and bottom constraints and adjust your textSize and textStyle

Notice that I have constrained the left and right of this CheckBox to the sides of the screen to center it, but only constrained the bottom of the CheckBox to the bottom of the screen, which keeps it at the bottom of the design where we need it. You are not required to implement all of the constraint sides if you don't need to.

Add a TextView User Interface Element for Your Title

Next, select a **TextView** widget, shown selected in blue in Figure 6-14, and drag it into the top center of your UI design. Keep the **textView** suggested (default) ID, and set the text value to "Hello Universe" using **36sp textSize** and set an **#ffffffff textColor** value and a **Bold textStyle** setting as seen in red in Figure 6-14. Set the side constraints to center the TextView heading at the top center of the UI design.

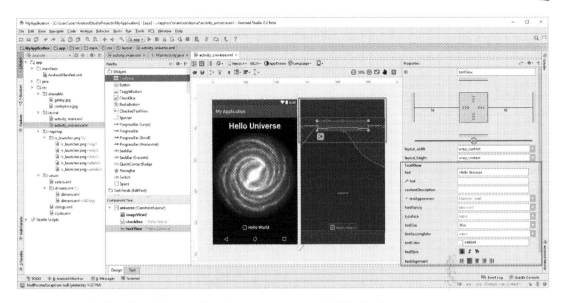

Figure 6-14. Add a TextView widget; configure its parameters as an Activity heading

Next, let's add a UI `Button` widget, so that the end user can return their Hello Universe app back to being just a simple Hello World app again.

Add a Button User Interface Element for Interactivity

Next, select a **Button** widget, seen selected in blue in Figure 6-15, and drag it into the bottom center of your UI design. Keep the **button** suggested ID, and set the text value to "Downgrade App," because when your user clicks it, it will return the user to the Hello World `MainActivity.java` Activity subclass.

Let's use default `textSize`, `textStyle`, and `textColor` values. All you have to do now is to set the side constraints to center the Button and add a bottom constraint that attaches the `Button` to the top of the `CheckBox`, so that these UI elements stay aligned relative to each other. Let's do that next, and then we can see if there are any **errors** that we need to address, and how that's done in the Visual Design Editor.

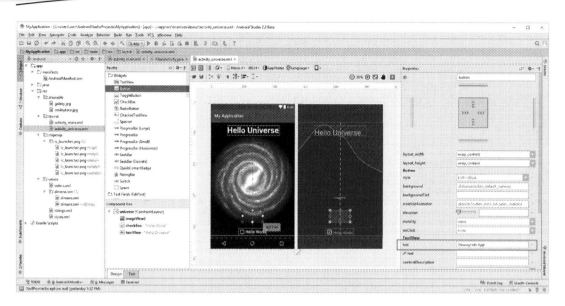

Figure 6-15. *Drag a Button UI widget in the design and center it above the CheckBox*

Set your side constraints to center your Button at the bottom center of your UI design, as shown circled in red in Figure 6-16, and drag the bottom constraint onto your CheckBox widget, to show the constraint system you want to constrain these two UI widgets to each other. Set constraints have a dot in the middle of each circle.

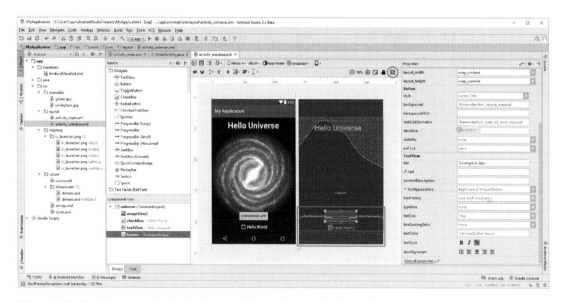

Figure 6-16. *Set side constraints for the Button widget so it centers in the design*

You can see the bottom constraint dot for the `Button` widget has not been set in Figure 6-16, but that it has been set in Figure 6-18 (look for a tiny center dot). Let's take a break from our user interface design creation and see if we can remove some of the errors, which are shown circled in red at the top right in Figure 6-16.

Squashing Bugs (Removing Errors) in the Design Editor

If you click on the red square with a number (of errors) in it, as seen circled in red in Figure 6-16, you will pop up the **Lint Warnings in Layout** dialog, shown in Figure 6-17. This dialog lists errors and warnings, regarding user interface design in the Visual Design Editor; in this case, there are half a dozen issues that we should address.

> **Note**   The Android Studio editors, both Text Editor (Java code and XML markup) and the Visual Design Editor, will give you hints, suggestions, warnings, and errors, using different colored wavy underlines (text editors) and colored squares (design editor). You can mouse-over these and get pop-up helpers or click on them in the Visual Design Editor to get a Lint Warnings in Layout dialog. Android Lint was added in Android Tools API 16 and scans Android project Java code and XML markup in real time to find bugs (errors) and issues (warnings) of varying severity in your Android application project.

The top of the Lint Warnings dialog contains the errors and warnings themselves in red (Error) or black (Warning). Click on any of these, and in the bottom you will get your **Issue Explanation** (right), and **Applies To** (left) UI element description and location, as you can see in Figure 6-17. I left the top constraint for the `TextView` unset, so that I could show you this feature, and how to fix it, which we are going to do next. In fact, let's fix all six of the issues, before we finish this user interface design.

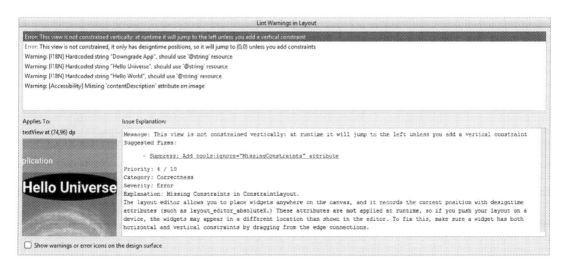

Figure 6-17.   A Lint Warnings in Layout dialog organizes errors and warnings for you

As you can see selected in Figure 6-17, Lint will tell you it needs the vertical (top) constraint, which will bind the UI element to the top of the screen.

To fix this first error, drag the top `TextView` constraint to the top of your UI design screen, until it says "Release to Create Top Constraint," as shown in Figure 6-18.

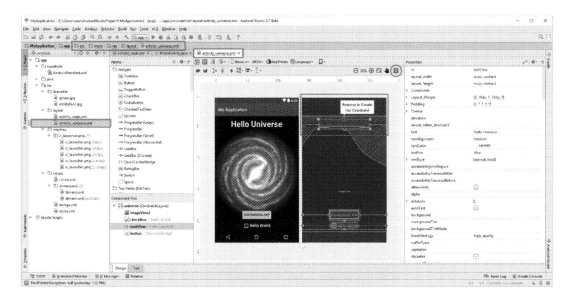

Figure 6-18. *Create TextView top constraint; click error count flag, to show errors*

Also notice that now that you have invoked Lint, the wavy red underlines appear under those files in the project that contains errors. The next error applies to an `ImageView`, and says that it is not constrained, as shown in Figure 6-19. This error is more difficult to solve, because the `ImageView` fills the design, thus you cannot simply pull the constraint markers to each edge to set this widget's constraints.

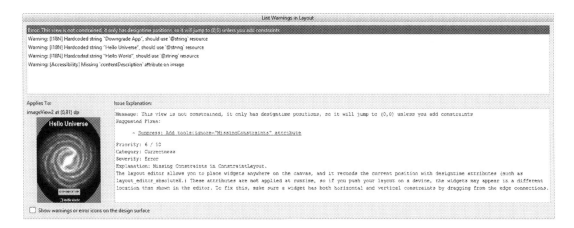

Figure 6-19. *Click second error, to see what it applies to, and is needed to solve it*

Whenever I am looking for a solution I always right-click and check the context-sensitive menu, to see if there is a solution. As you can see in Figure 6-20, this is exactly what I did to find the solution to how to set constraints when there is no room to drag the arrow indicator. I right-clicked inside the hatched area of the `ImageView`, and in the **ConstraintLayout** submenu, I found the solution: the algorithm that will **Infer Constraints** for you in situations such as this one. After clicking this, my error count decreased yet again, and I was ready to deal with the Warnings.

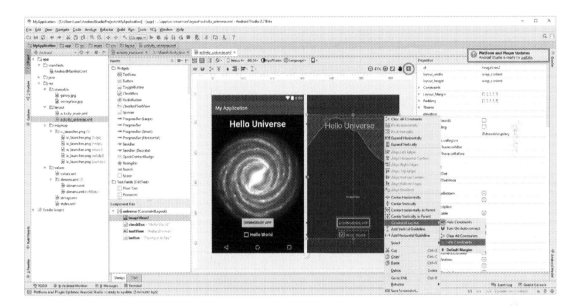

Figure 6-20. Right-click the ImageView and use ConstraintLayout ➤ Infer Constraints

The next three warnings suggest using the `@string/` method of entering text constants in the `strings.xml` file, even though the Hello World app was created by Android Studio using literal (hard-coded in quotes) string constants! I modified the `strings.xml` file to add the new constants, by using this following XML markup:

```
<resources>
    <string name="app_name">My Application</string>
    <string name="app_message">Hello World!</string>
    <string name="app_button">Upgrade App</string>
    <string name="app_checkbox">Hello Universe</string>
    <string name="app_message2">Hello Universe!</string>
    <string name="app_button2">Downgrade App</string>
    <string name="app_checkbox2">Hello World</string>
    <string name="image_desc_world">Hello World Image</string>
    <string name="image_desc_galaxy">Hello Universe Image</string>
</resources>
```

Once you modify the `strings.xml` file accordingly, you can use those three dots, called ellipses, at the end of the text parameter in the Properties pane, to access the **Resources** dialog, seen in Figure 6-21, which will list text (string) resources.

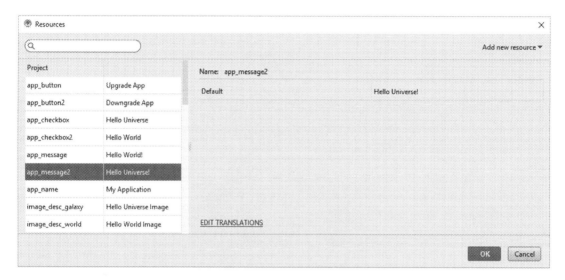

Figure 6-21. *Select the app_message2 string constant for your TextView UI element*

As you can see in Figure 6-22, your `TextView` UI element's text parameter is now referencing an `@string/app_message2` constant and the error count has now gone down.

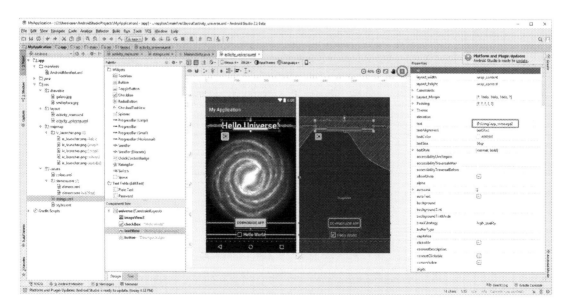

Figure 6-22. *Error count decreased, as TextView text parameter referencing @string/*

Once you have replaced all of the text parameters for your widgets with @string references, there is only one Warning left, regarding using your **contentDescription** parameter to reference text describing the **ImageView** for use by the sight impaired. I added two string constants for this, for both Activity UI designs for Hello World as well as Hello Universe. Figure 6-22 shows this contentDescription referencing in place, and the removal of all errors and warnings, shown in red at the top right of the screenshot.

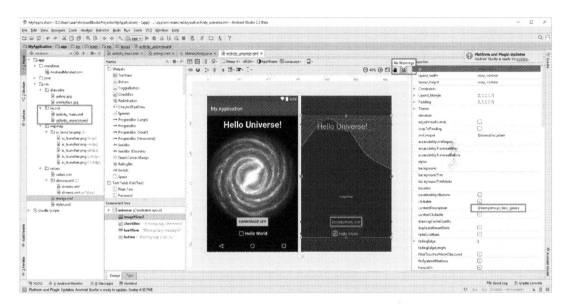

Figure 6-23. Add an @string/image_desc_galaxy contentDescription for your ImageView

As you can see on the left side of Figure 6-23, there are still errors in your XML file, which means you can eliminate errors in your Visual Design Editor, and still have errors or issues in the Text (XML Markup) Editor. Let's take a look at how you eliminate those next. You will be eradicating errors in both Java and XML using Lint throughout the rest of the book. It is important to note this is one of the best ways to learn Android application programming (Java and XML markup) because your IDEA is guiding you as to the latest rules for Android 7.1.1 (and later, as new APIs come out) development.

Eliminate Any Remaining Errors Using the XML Text Editor

Click on your Text (XML Editor) tab, at the bottom of the activity-universe.xml editing tab. The results, before and after the fix, are shown in Figure 6-24. What is causing a problem is the textAlignment parameter, which the Visual Design Editor has set to textStart as it was generating the XML markup for the UI design. Since I want the title to center at the top of the design, I clicked on the Design tab at the bottom of the editing pane, and found the textAlignment parameter, which needs to be changed from textStart to a different (better) setting so that I do not have to add yet another layout gravity parameter.

The fewer parameters you can utilize to achieve your user interface design, the less code your Android application has to process, and less device memory is used.

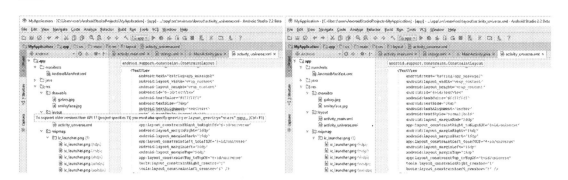

Figure 6-24. *Mouse-over wavy red underline parameter to see what is needed to solve*

Once you find the textAlignment parameter, click on the drop-down selector, and select the **center** option, as can be seen on the right-hand side of Figure 6-25. I then went back into the Text tab and confirmed that the error had been removed from the XML markup, as shown on the right-hand side of Figure 6-25.

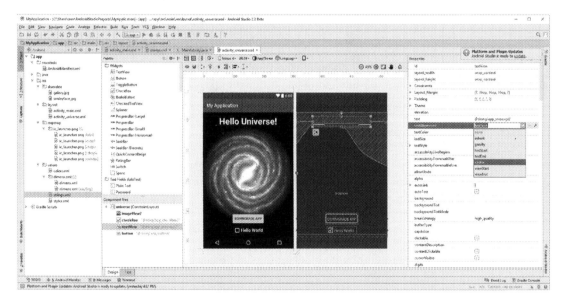

Figure 6-25. *Find the textAlignment parameter, and select a center alignment option*

You can choose to address these errors and warnings at any time; most choose to deal with them as they notice them. I will suggest keeping an eye on the error icon and dealing with them as they pop up, as the more they accumulate the harder they will be to find and fix, especially if any of them are related or reference each other! I saved up a half a dozen of them for this section of the chapter, to show you how to address several of these different issues; and now that we have, I will continue on with the chapter and add more advanced UI design features to the Hello Universe Activity user interface design we're creating in the Visual Design Editor.

Summary

In this chapter, you learned about several important Android superclasses that are used to create Android applications, and get them running on the device display screen. These include the `Activity` class, the `View` class, and the `ViewGroup` class; and the subclasses of these classes, which are actually used to create your Android applications, such as the `AppCompatActivity` class that you've seen in use already.

You already know you do not have to write an `Activity` subclass all by yourself, and as far as `View` and `ViewGroup` subclasses are concerned, Android 7.1.1 has generously written all of these subclasses for you as well. All you have to do is to "include" them in your Android application code, by using an import statement, and of course you have to implement their features correctly, which, as you have seen in this chapter, the new Visual Design Editor will do for the Absolute Beginner as well, as long as you use it correctly. This feature makes Android 7.x development more accessible to all Absolute Beginners!

You learned about the inter-relationships between the `Activity` class, the `View` class, and the `ViewGroup` class, and how these can be used together to get your application UI design and content onto the device display screen. You learned how to create a user interface layout XML definition from scratch in Android Studio using the Visual Design Editor, Lint, and the right-click context-sensitive menu and the New ➤ Layout Resource dialog.

In Chapter 7, you will start to learn about how Android 7.1.1 handles **Events** and uses **Intent** objects, and all about how to make your UI design interactive, by using **Event Handlers** and **Intent objects.**

Making Apps Interactive: Events and Intents

User interface designs are built upon the foundation of the `Activity` superclass as well as the `View` and `ViewGroup` superclass, as you learned in Chapter 6. However, without interactivity in a UI design, the usefulness of what users can accomplish with your Android 7.1.1 applications will be somewhat limited. For this reason, I'm going to cover some more advanced programming concepts, for the absolute beginner at least, including events and intents.

We will look at how **Events** and **Event Listening** work in Android, as well as how **Intent** objects will be utilized to switch between your Activity subclasses. You can use Intent objects to switch between functional UI screens in your Android applications, each of which is defined using one of the Android `Activity` subclasses, which references a `ViewGroup` UI layout container XML definition containing `View` UI widgets that generate the events that your event listeners will handle (process).

Besides covering Android `Intent` objects and event handling capabilities, we will also cover broader concepts, such as **Implicit Intents**, **Explicit Intents,** and **Intent Filters** and how they relate to the Android Manifest and other Android applications. You encountered Intent Filters in Chapter 4, in Figure 4, near the bottom of the screenshot, when we looked over the bootstrap `AndroidManifest.xml` file in detail.

In this chapter, we'll switch between Hello World and Hello Universe Activities using Intent objects. This will allow users to update the application, using `Button` and `CheckBox` widgets along with event handling (i.e., processing) and Intent objects.

Adding interactivity to user interface elements, or widgets, would require that you learn what **Event Listeners** are, and how to implement them. Event Listeners will be used to make UI elements (widgets) interactive. Now that your Constraint Layout UI design is completed, and referenced using your `.onCreate()` and `.setContentView()` methods, we will instantiate `Button` and `CheckBox` objects, and then attach `.onClick()` event listener Java structures to them, so that your user can use them interactively to upgrade the status of your Hello World application, and downgrade it, as well.

© Wallace Jackson 2017
W. Jackson, *Android Apps for Absolute Beginners*, DOI 10.1007/978-1-4842-2268-3_7

About Intent Objects: The Android Intent Class

An `Intent` object is used within the Android 7.x framework as a **messaging construct** that you dispatch to request some sort of **action** from one of your other components within your Android application. Intents can also be used to request actions within someone else's Android application, that is, one which is external to your Android application. There are three primary uses for `Intent` objects in Android:

* Launching `Activity` subclasses
* Starting `Service` subclasses
* Sending messages in your app

As I mentioned, these uses can also be accomplished even using external Android applications. This is done with broadcast receiver classes and methods. We'll cover advanced Intent usage during advanced chapters at the end of the book.

Here's a basic workflow that shows how your `Activity` uses this `Intent` object:

```
Activity > Intent object containing the Start Activity Action > New Activity (will be launched)
--or--
Activity > Intent object containing the Start Service Action > New Service (will be launched)
```

As you have learned, `Activity` subclasses each represent one single user interface design within your application's functionality. You will start each new instance of an `Activity` subclass by passing an `Intent` object over to its `startActivity()` method.

An `Intent` object passed into the **startActivity()** method will contain **action data** that will dictate which one of your application's `Activity` subclasses you wish to start. The `Intent` object also includes a **Context** object that describes the current context for your application. We'll cover the concept of Context within the chapter as well, as it is used often in Android programming.

You will also use the `Intent` object to start **Service** subclasses. We're covering services in Chapter 13. A service is an Android component that can perform operations in the background. These operations usually do not require user interfaces, and can be performed "asynchronously," or out of sync, with the user's normal flow of use of your application and its purpose and objective. An example of a service would be playing a background music track. You can also start a `Service` subclass using an `Intent` object in order to perform a one-time operation, like a file download. This is done by passing the `Intent` object over to your `.startService()` method call. This `Intent` should describe the `Service` subclass to start, as well as any necessary data that is needed for the `Service` to process.

You can also use an `Intent` object to deliver a message broadcast across the Android OS, including anything running on the user's Android device. A **broadcast** in Android is a term for any message that any apps running on the same Android device as your app can potentially receive. Your Android operating system will schedule broadcasts for system events, such as when the system boots up, or when your device is plugged in, or when it is finished charging.

Developers can deliver a broadcast message to other apps by passing `Intent` objects via the `.sendBroadcast()`, the `.sendOrderedBroadcast()`, or the `.sendStickyBroadcast()` method call.

Intent Types: Explicit Intent versus Implicit Intent

There are two types of `Intent` objects you can create and utilize within Android OS: **explicit** `Intent` objects and **implicit** `Intent` objects. The explicit `Intent` object will specifically reference the Android application component to start, by using an application component (`Activity` or `Service`, for instance) name and component type.

An implicit `Intent` object provides a description of the component you want to launch but does not specify which one (name) to utilize. Implicit `Intent` infrastructures are more complicated to set up correctly than explicit `Intents` are, because you have to set up an `Intent` filter object to specify exactly what Android OS should look for, as an exact component (class) name is not specified for launch (loaded into memory and processing). If you think of an `Intent` as something that you wish to do (your intent), there are two types. For example, go out to see the new *Star Wars* film (an explicit intent), or, go out and see any of the newly released films (similar to an Android implicit intent).

Explicit Intents: A Direct Reference to the Component to Launch

When you create an explicit `Intent` object to start your `Activity` subclass or to start a `Service` subclass, the Android operating system will start (place in memory) the component specified in that `Intent` object and schedule it for processing.

In the next section, you will start the `HelloUniverse.class` by using this fully qualified `.class` (compiled) class name. `HelloUniverse.java` is your uncompiled (code) file name. A fully qualified compiled class name should be referenced in your Android Manifest XML definition as `HelloUniverse.class`.

In other words, your Android `Intent` is launching your `.class` **compiled version** of your `Activity` subclass from within your compiled package, designated as .APK, or Android PacKage.

You would typically need to use the explicit `Intent` object to start a component within your own application. This is because you inherently know the class name for your `Activity` subclass or `Service` subclass that you want to launch, and so you can utilize, or **hard code**, that component name in the Android Manifest and Java code.

Implicit Intents: A Description of a Component You Want to Launch

Implicit `Intent` objects do not specify their target application component, but instead declare a general action to perform. This implicit `Intent` approach allows an application component, even from another Android application outside of your own Android app, to handle that `Intent`. The reason that Android also has `Intent` filters and the `IntentFilter` class is to aid with the processing, action determination, and successful handling of these implicit `Intent` objects.

For example, if you wanted to show your app user a location on a map, you could use an implicit `Intent` object to ask, or request, that another map-capable Android application show your application user that specific location on the map that your application is referencing. Implicit `Intents` allow Android apps to work together seamlessly!

When you create an implicit `Intent` object the Android operating system finds an appropriate application component (`Activity`, `Service`, broadcast receiver) to start up, by comparing the contents of your implicit `Intent` object to the `<intent-filter>` definitions declared in the Android Manifest XML file for other apps on the same Android device.

If the implicit `Intent` matches up with one of the `IntentFilter` definitions, the Android operating system will start that component if it's not already running, and delivers your implicit `Intent` object to it for processing. If multiple `IntentFilter` definitions are found to be compatible on the Android device, the Android operating system will display a pop-up dialog, so the user can select which app to use.

It's important to note that every Android user will install different apps, and therefore, different Android devices will invariably exhibit different combinations of installed Android applications. This results in different pop-up dialog selection choices. A good example of this is when you click a URL and an implicit Intent goes out to find apps which have WebKit (browser API) capability. A dialog comes up with an internal browser; Chrome, Firefox, Opera, or whatever browsers you have installed on that particular device. This is what implicit `Intent` objects should be used for: to allow users to control which applications are used with your applications. Let's take a look at `IntentFilter` objects next, to better understand how implicit `Intent` objects work as they need good IntentFilter definitions in order to work optimally.

IntentFilter: Construct an Implicit Intent Definition

Each `IntentFilter` object is an `Intent` processing definition construct, which is defined using the application's Android Manifest XML definition. An `<intent-filter>` construct defines a structure for each type of implicit `Intent` object your Android application's components would like to be able to receive and process. This can be quite powerful, and can also get quite complex as well, as it allows developers to create Android applications that do things (perform tasks) for other Android apps. This effectively opens up an entirely new genre of Android application that Android developers can create so other Android developers can incorporate that service in their applications as well. The leading example of this type of app is Google Maps.

By declaring an `IntentFilter` object for an `Activity` subclass, as Android Studio did for your `MainActivity` class, in your `AndroidManifest.xml` (see Figure 4), you make it possible for other applications to directly start your `MainActivity` `Activity` subclass by using an `Intent` object that evaluates to the **MAIN action** and the **LAUNCHER category**. In this case, the application that will start your `Activity` would be the Android OS application launch screen.

If you do not create `<intent-filter>` XML definitions, constructing `IntentFilter` objects for any of your `Activity` subclasses, then these `Activity` subclasses will be invisible to outside Android applications. This means that they will only be able to be started using an explicit `Intent` object. A good example of this is what we're doing in this chapter with your

HelloUniverse Activity subclass, since we only want your MainActivity class Button object to be able to start this private component of your MyApplication Android 7.1.1 application.

Finally, remember one important rule regarding the use of Intent objects in your Android programming. To ensure that your Android applications are completely secure you will generally want to use an explicit Intent object when starting your Service components (any of your Service subclasses). This also means that you wouldn't want to declare <intent-filter> XML constructs that create IntentFilter objects for your application's Service subclasses, since IntentFilter objects are only utilized with implicit Intent object processing, and aren't needed when utilizing explicit Intent objects. You will need one <intent-filter> definition for Android OS to use for the application launch sequence, as you've seen already in Chapter 4 (see Figure 4-10).

The reason for this security rule is because by using an implicit Intent object to start a background processing Service class, you risk creating a **security hazard** within the Android OS on your end user's device. This is because a developer cannot always ascertain what Service subclass will respond to their implicit Intent object and the end user cannot see which Service is starting on their Android device. This opens up the ability for destructive Services to be created. Do not launch Services using the implicit Intent object approach unless it is absolutely necessary.

Instantiating an Intent Object: Passing App Context

Let's look at the way you'll instantiate, name, and configure an explicit Intent object, named upgradeIntent, which we will use to start the HelloUniverse Activity subclass, which we are going to create as the next step in this work process. This Activity will be similar to your MainActivity, and will use a user interface design created using the Visual Design Editor. You will declare the Intent object for use, provide a name, and "load" the Intent object using an equal sign, while at the same time, within the same Java statement, create your Intent object by using a Java new keyword, configuring the new Intent with the class name that you will be starting.

All of these programming tasks would be accomplished by utilizing the following single line of Java programming logic in Android Studio:

```
Intent upgradeIntent = new Intent( this, HelloUniverse.class );
```

The Intent declares the object type; the upgradeIntent gives the object a name; the equals sign signifies that we are about to instantiate it; the Java new keyword creates an instance of the Intent object in memory; and finally, the parameter list passes over a Context object for our MainActivity Activity subclass, using the Java **this** keyword, as well as the HelloUniverse.class Activity subclass that we want to start, or launch, using an **explicit** Intent object created with this Java statement.

Next, we will go over what the Java this keyword and a Context object do for your Android application, and then we will continue our work process in the section after that, and allow Android Studio to create our **MainActivity.java** class.

Explaining Context: The Android Context Class

The concept of context in Java programming is simple in its definition, and yet is often complex in its implementation. It is something that you would need to know about, regarding what this application context is doing, and why it is needed, to be able to accomplish certain things in Android. This isn't something you will need to manipulate directly, at least not until you become an advanced Android developer.

Android provides a Context class, which by the very nature of a Java class, can construct a Context object, which is used to hold the context for each application component. The context defines how the component fits into the overall application, which is inherently what the word context actually means, so this class and object are aptly named. If you want to take a look at the Context class in greater detail, visit the following Android developer website URL:

https://**developer.android.com**/reference/android/content/**Context**.html

This Context object, which is represented by the Java **this** keyword, essentially passes over a Context object for the MainActivity.class Activity component for your Android application containing detailed **contextual** information, referencing how your MainActivity application component will integrate with other application components to accomplish a cohesive working application, which is properly wired together.

If someone asks you to do something for them you will usually ask them what the context for the task is, so that you know what, why, and how to accomplish the task! The reason for giving a receiving application component this context (clever Java keyword pun intended) is that these Context objects will allow a called application component to see or ascertain what the calling application component is doing, so that it can do the job (task) that it is being asked to do efficiently, effectively, and with proper referencing to the other components that comprise the application.

When the Context object is filled or populated with information regarding the calling application component, this data is combined with the (inherent) knowledge of what the called application component is doing. The result is total application context, which, as we all know from real life, can be defined as the clear, overall view of the entire work process that we are currently involved with.

A Context object is similar to a Bundle object, in that it contains a collection of related application information all bundled together into one complex object and sub-object hierarchy. Bundles tend to contain the states of the application, whereas the Context objects tend to clarify how the application components reference each other, and how they should work together.

> **Note** You've already used a Bundle object to save the current "state bundle" for your MainActivity Activity subclass, with your Bundle object named savedInstanceState in your onCreate() method call. The Bundle class allows you to put together bundles or collections of variables and data, so it is not complex enough to merit its very own section in the book. That said, if you are really into bundling data, you can take a detailed look at the Android Bundle class if you like. It is located at the following Android developer website URL:
>
> https://**developer.android.com**/reference/android/os/**Bundle**.html

Where Android Manifest XML definition files are used to provide some of the **global** information to the Android OS when it goes to launch the application, the Context object provides all of the **local** technical-, systems-, component-, and resource-level information for each of your application's components, in real time (these attributes change) while an application is running.

As I mentioned previously, you only need to know how to pass application component Context objects (often using a Java this keyword) properly in order to be successful in the majority of your Android 7.x application programming, design, and development endeavors, so I am not going to spend too much time delving into Android's public abstract Context class during this Absolute Beginners book. I just thought you might want to understand why this Context object was used so frequently in Java and Android.

Now we can continue on in our work process for creating a second Activity that will be launched using a Button UI element from your MainActivity class. The second HelloUniverse Activity subclass will use the second UI design created in Chapter 6, making it functional with event processing, using UI events and event listeners.

Event Processing: Using Events with Event Listeners

Android uses something called an event to allow the users of your application to interact with your UI design. There are different events for button (or mouse) click, touchscreen usage, and keyboard usage, and your Java code must **handle** these events, by implementing event listener code structures that trap these events as they move from your UI elements through your event handling code structures.

When a user interfaces with their Android device hardware, the user interface elements will generate events, and the Android OS will deliver these events to your Java code for processing. This is done by using event listener Java constructs that take the form of an **event listener method** construct. The most common event listener methods include onClickListener() for MouseClick (supports touchscreen tap as well), onTouchListener() (touchscreen support only), or onKeyListener() (keyboard support). These listener methods listen for (wait for) and then process different kinds of events relating to user interface elements that are accessed by different hardware features on different kinds of Android devices. These include touchscreen devices, like phones and tablets; and keyboard devices, like iTV sets, tablets, and laptops.

Events: Turning Device User Interaction into Events

There are a handful of important events that relate to things like keypresses and mouse clicks, which we need to go over here so you have a comprehensive overview of what is available to you for your user interface design and its interactivity.

The primary events are for keyboard keystrokes (onKey), mouse clicks (onClick), which user interface element is being used (called "focus" or onFocus), touchscreen usage (onTouch) and menu usage (onCreateContextMenu). There is also an onLongClick event, which is the equivalent of a right-mouse button click for touchscreens, where you touch the screen for a longer period of time (called a "Long Click") to pop up (create) the ContextMenu.

Text (onKey) events are used for the text editing field UI element; mouse click events are used for UI elements such as buttons, radio buttons or checkboxes; touch events are used with touchscreen hardware; and focus events are used when moving to the next (or previous) UI element on the user interface design screen (Activity).

Event Listener: Java Methods Process UI Widget Events

An event listener is a Java interface for the View superclass, which as you now know, is used to construct your user interface widgets in Android. These event listeners are termed "callback methods," because they listen for the event, and then execute your application code when they encounter that event. These methods will be called by the Android framework when each View widget to which the listener has been registered (attached) is triggered by your user's interaction with the UI element. This interaction will generate an event (and often, more than one event).

There are a half dozen event listener Java interfaces that are included in the View superclass, and therefore are available to all of the widget subclasses that are created using the View superclass. Since the ViewGroup superclass used to create layout containers is also a subclass of View, these are also available to UI layout container classes as well, since these UI layout contains extend ViewGroup.

The most common of the events, because it works with touchscreen as well as the mouse, trackball, and similar pointer hardware, is the onClick() event. This is used inside of the View.OnClickListener interface. An onClick() event handler is called by the Android OS when a user touches any UI element when using touchscreen, or focuses upon an item with a navigation key, trackball or mouse, by pressing a mouse button, or any device navigation hardware's enter key or by pressing down on the trackball itself.

The next most common event, also because it works with touchscreen and with the mouse, trackball, and similar pointer hardware, is the onLongClick() event. This is inside of the View.OnLongClickListener interface. An onLongClick() handler is called by the Android OS when a user long-touches a UI element when using touchscreen, or right-clicks a trackball or mouse, by pressing the right-mouse button, or the right trackball button.

Another very common event is the onKey() event, which is used with text-related content and user interface elements. It is used with hardware keyboards. This is inside of the View. OnKeyListener interface. This is called when the user is focused on the text element and presses or releases a hardware key on the device or uses a keyboard peripheral with a tablet, laptop, or iTV set hardware device.

There is also an onTouch() event specifically for use with touchscreen devices, and this is in the View.OnTouchListener interface. An onTouch() handler is called when the user performs an action that Android terms a "touch event." This includes a touch, a release, or movements (called gestures) on a touchscreen within the UI element.

If you want to pop up a context-sensitive menu that contains options for the UI element, there is also an onCreateContextMenu() event construct that is used inside of View. OnCreateContextMenuListener. This is called when a context menu is being opened as the result of a long-click, and therefore this event will be fired at the same time as a LongClick event, since a LongClick event would be needed to open the ContextMenu.

Another event that will often get fired at the same time as other events is the onFocusChange() event, which is inside of the View.OnFocusChangeListener interface. An onFocusChange() handler is called when the user navigates into (or exit from) the UI element, using the navigation keys hardware, keyboard tab key, mouse clicks, or the trackball. It is common that other events (key, click, touch, or long-click) should usually accompany an onFocus event for this reason, so there may be scenarios where a number of separate but related events are fired during user interface activity.

These are the six primary (core) events that you will use in Android. There are also six more specialized types of events that I will cover for you here so you will be exposed to all twelve event types in Android. For mouse (or trackball) use, there's an onHover() event handler that has a View.OnHoverListener for when a pointer is over a View (subclass) but not clicked. There is also an onDrag() event handler that uses the View.OnDragListener for when a View (subclass) is being dragged around the screen.

There is a GenericMotion event that uses a View.OnGenericMotionListener used to handle MotionEvents and three events that detect changes in UI layout configuration, including onLayoutChange, onAttachStateChange, and onSystemUiVisibilityChange, each of which have their own associated event listener interfaces. These would contain code for what you want to happen when your UI layout (arrangement) changes, when you attach or detach UI elements, or when the system UI (status bar and action bar) becomes visible (or invisible) or on an orientation change of the hardware device.

Event Handler: Java Methods Process Global Event Type

The term event handler is oftentimes used interchangeably with the term event listener, but there is a difference. The event listener is part of each widget View subclass, and implements the View.OnEventTypeListener interface for each of the UI element (widget) subclasses. This means that the implemented method construct processes a specific type of event, and is doing so for a specific user interface element (widget) type. This means that this event processing code is much more localized to that user interface element's instance, and the type of event that you want to execute your Java code statements for. This approach leaves little room for confusion, from the code design standpoint.

An event handler, on the other hand, forces you to define your event processing code for each event type, irrespective of the widget or layout container that may generate that particular event. For this reason, creating code that handles all occurrences of that particular event is therefore global in nature, as the processing is not part of the widget class definition. Event handlers are thus more complex, and not used as frequently as event listeners, which attach each event type you want to process to a specific UI element. Since this is an Absolute Beginner title, we will focus on mastering event listeners, as these are what you will use most of the time to make your user interface interactive. The way I look at it is the outer method structure "listens" for the event and the inner method structure "handles" the event. So .onClickListener() listens, and onClick() handles.

Creating a Second Activity: The UniverseActivity Class

Now that you know what the Java **this** keyword is, which we will use here to pass over the Context object for your MainActivity.class to your UniverseActivity.class, we can go ahead and pick up where we left off in Chapter 6, and finish programming the application Java logic to process events and leverage explicit Intent objects.

Let's add code that switches from the `MainActivity` to another `Activity` when the user clicks on a `Button` user interface element. This will demonstrate how `Intent` objects and events work together.

The first thing that we'll need to do in Android Studio 2.3 is to create a new `Activity` class. Click on the `app/java/com.example.user.myapplication/` folder, and select the **New ➤ Activity ➤ Empty Activity** menu sequence, as shown selected in blue in Figure 7-1.

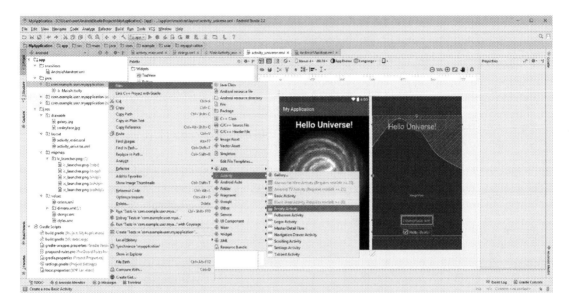

Figure 7-1. *Right-click Java app folder, and select New ➤ Activity ➤ Empty Activity*

In the **Configure New Android Activity** dialog use an **Activity Name** field to name your new Activity **UniverseActivity**. Next, deselect the **Generate Layout File**, shown as number 1, on the right side of Figure 7-2. Notice on the left side of Figure 7-2 that if you leave this selected, Android Studio will create your `activity_universe2` XML UI definition file, since you already create the `activity_universe.xml` Universe Activity UI back in Chapter 6.

Make sure that you check the **Backwards Compatibility (AppCompat)** option so that Android Studio extends the AppCompatActivity superclass, just like Android Studio did when you created your application. This assures that your application will be compatible across all of the earlier versions of Android that are still in use.

Finally, leave the default package name setting in your drop-down selector, as it is set to your current package name already, so there is no need to change this.

Once you are finished setting all of these options, click on the **Finish** button, shown as number 2 in Figure 7-2, and have Android Studio write your Activity Java code for you. Next, you will open up the `UniverseActivity.java` tab in your editing area, so you can click on it, and continue adding to the bootstrap Java code.

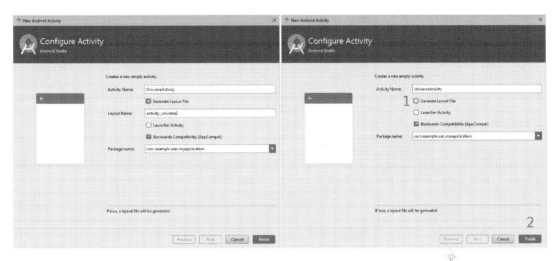

Figure 7-2. Name your Activity UniverseActivity, and deselect Generate Layout File

In the Project navigation pane, right-click your `UniverseActivity` Java file found in the app/
java/com.example.user.myapplication/ folder, and select the **Jump to Source** option from
the context-sensitive menu which appears, seen on the left side in Figure 7-3.

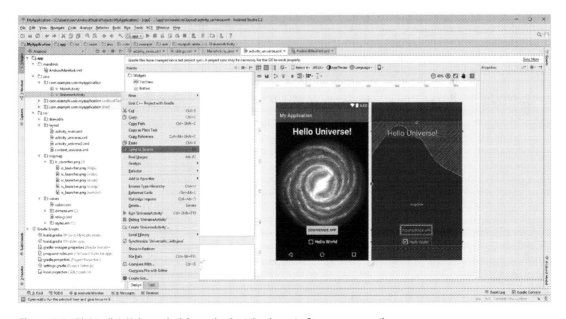

Figure 7-3. Right-click UniverseActivity and select the Jump to Source menu option

This will open a `UniverseActivity.java` editing tab, which can be seen in Figure 7-4. Notice
that since you've changed the project, the Gradle files will eventually need to be put in sync.

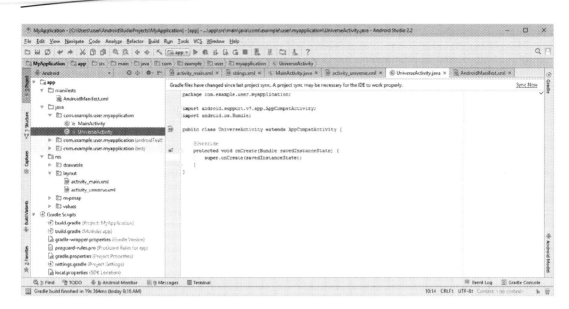

Figure 7-4. Android Studio created the bootstrap empty Activity code infrastructure

As you can see, Android Studio created the AppCompatActivity subclass, named it UniverseActivity, and created an onCreate() method. Next, add your setContentView() method call referencing the /app/res/layout/activity_universe XML as seen in Figure 7-5.

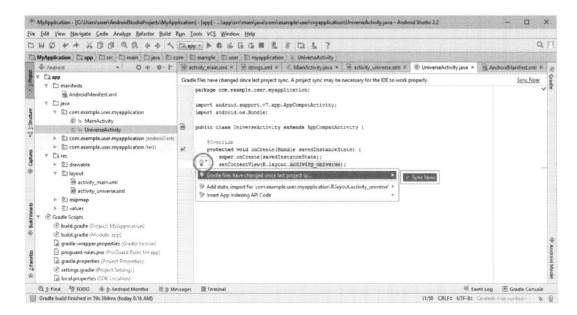

Figure 7-5. Add setContentView( ) method referencing activity_universe, and Sync Now

Also seen in Figure 7-5 is a warning drop-down telling you that you need the sync operation to be performed on your project Gradle files. Select the **Sync Now** option, to have Android Studio do this for you as well. Android Studio 2.3 can do a lot for Absolute Beginners; they just have to follow the proper work process (steps), which I am going to be showing you how to do over the course of this book. As you can see in Figure 7-6, Android Studio even added your `<activity>` tag for `UniverseActivity`.

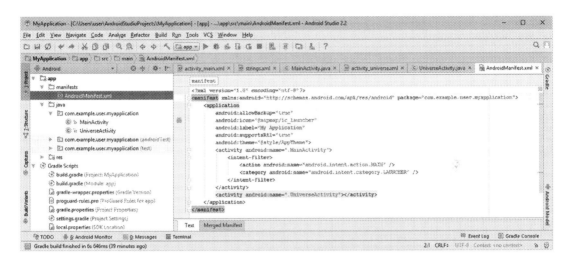

Figure 7-6. Android Studio added a second <activity> declaration in AndroidManifest

Let's click on your `MainActivity.java` editing tab, and add the `Button` object so that we can wire in your UI button, and then add `onClick()` event processing to it. At the top of your class, type the word Button, and then double-click on the **Button android.widget** option in the pop-up dialog to have Android code an `import` statement.

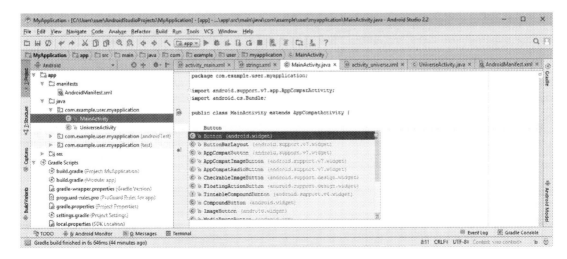

Figure 7-7. Declare Button object top of class; double-click adds import statement

As you can see at the top of Figure 7-8 you now have an **import android.widget.Button** statement that allows you to use the Android Button class. Inside of the onCreate() method, add an instance of the Button object, named **universeButton**. This is done by using the findViewById() method. Reference the button element ID value that was used in your user interface design XML definition, which, following the Android naming conventions we are following, was **button_universe**.

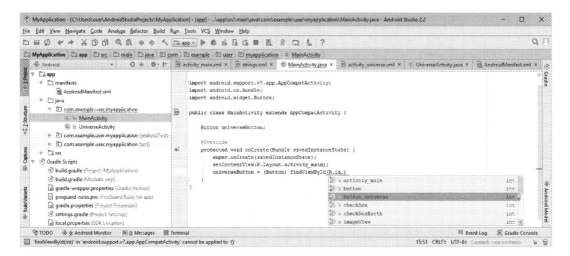

Figure 7-8. In onCreate( ), instantiate universeButton, using findViewById( ) method

After you double-click the button_universe ID (notice it is an integer, or int) in the drop-down, Android Studio will complete the method call. Android Studio will **cast** the findViewById() method as being from the Button class by adding (Button) before the method call. Add a semicolon, as is seen in Figure 7-9, at the end of the Button instantiation statement to complete it. I clicked on universeButton in Android Studio to color its declaration and use.

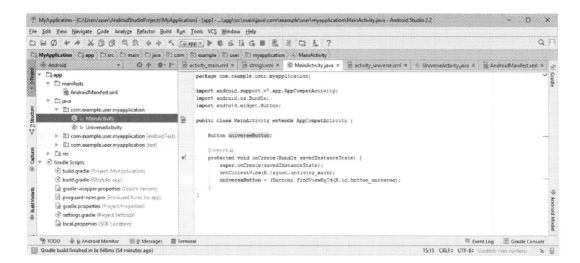

Figure 7-9. The universeButton object is now declared and instantiated (error free)

Notice when you click on an object or variable in Android Studio, it allows you to visually trace where it is being used in your code. Now do the same Button code in your UniverseActivity. java editing tab with the worldButton Button object, as is shown highlighted in Figure 7-10 using **Button worldButton = (Button)findViewById(R.id.button);**. Your UI button elements are now wired from XML to Java and are error free, so we can now move on to add our event listener Java code.

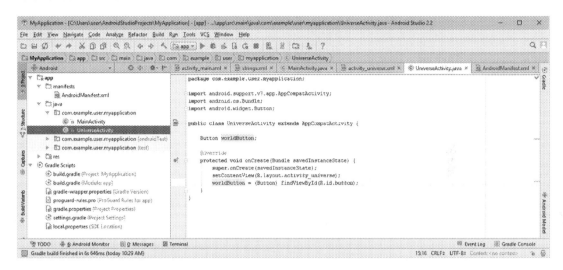

Figure 7-10. Add your worldButton declaration and instantiation to UniverseActivity

Adding Event Listeners to the Activity Button Objects

Now that your Button objects have been declared, and instantiated, they will be used to call methods such as the .setOnClickListener() method that sets the event listener to an implementation of View.OnClickListener that in turn contains your onClick() event processing infrastructure.

Add a line of code under the worldButton instantiation in the onCreate() method in your UniverseActivity.java tab. Hit the period to invoke dot notation, then type **setOn**, as is shown in Figure 7-11. Select the setOnClickListener(OnClickListener l) option from the drop-down, which will highlight it in blue, and double-click on it, which will then tell Android Studio to insert the method into your code structure.

Since we have not declared and instantiated an OnClickListener required for the method, we will be using the Java **new** keyword inside of the .setOnClickListener()'s parameter area, as a short-hand format for creating this event listening construct. The long form way to do this would be to create a public listener class, like this:

```
public class WorldButtonListener implements View.OnClickListener {
    @Override
    public void onClick (View view) {
        // Your Intent processing code to start the Universe Activity would go in here
    }
}
```

This would create a plethora of classes for handling all your UI events, so the shorter, denser, code construct has become the convention for setting up listeners.

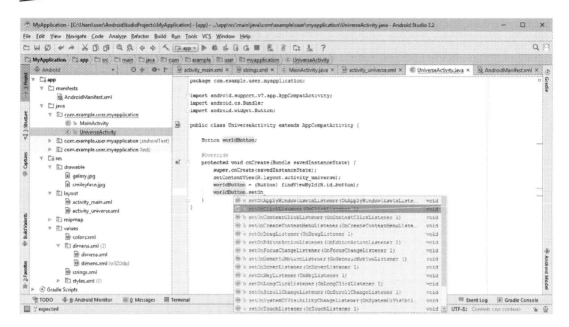

Figure 7-11. Call a .setOnClickListener( ) method off the worldButton Button object

Inside of your `.setOnClickListener()` parameter area, you will instantiate a new `View.OnClickListener` that will contain your `onClick()` event handling construct.

Inside of the method parens, as is shown in Figure 7-12, type **new View.On** and double-click on the **View.OnClickListener (android.view.View) (android.view)** option. This will tell Android Studio 2.3 to insert an empty `View.OnClickListener(){}` Java code construct, inside of which you will soon be writing the Java code for the `public void onClick(){}` event handling infrastructure.

What this is doing in a short-hand or "dense" Java code construct, which is providing you with an instance of the `View` superclass `OnClickListener` interface, which will be used to contain your `onClick()` event handling Java programming logic, which is really where your primary event processing programming logic is going to end up.

Once you double-click the Android Studio Java code writing helper (drop-down), you will have the empty construct `{}` for your code, which will override the `onClick()` method, which is the next step in our event listening and handling work process.

The rest of the code for this construct will be entered inside of the empty `{...}` `View.OnClickListener`, just as you would have done if you had coded an event listener using a `WorldButtonListener` class, as I showed you earlier in this section.

This can be seen in Figure 7-13, if you want to look ahead, and once this Java code structure is completed, you will then have one of your two `Button` click event processing code structures, and you can get some practice duplicating the process again for the `MainActivity.java` class.

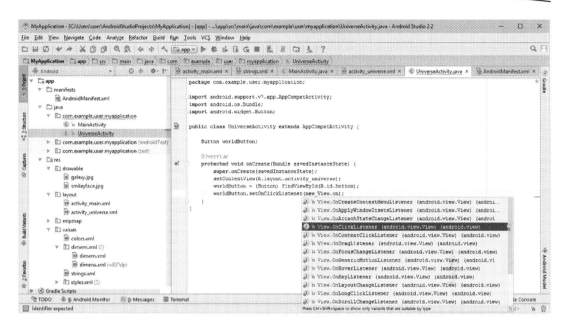

Figure 7-12. Call .setOnClickListener( ) off worldButton and use new keyword in call

Type **@** and select **Override (java.lang)** from the drop-down shown in Figure 7-13.

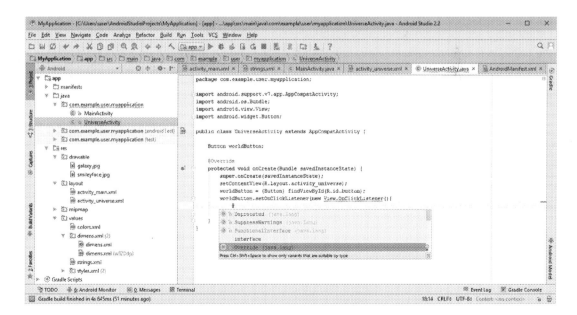

Figure 7-13. Inside OnClickListener() use Java @Override keyword to override method

Next, enter the `onClick()` method declaration as **public void onClick(View view){ }** after the `@Override`, and create another empty method. Notice that I am creating Java code constructs that are initially empty and that are error free as I go along, so that any errors that may arise are isolated, and easier to diagnose and fix. I show this empty `onClick()` code structure, which thus far is error free, in Figure 7-14.

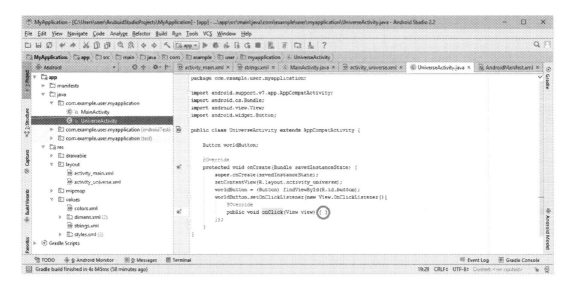

Figure 7-14. *Create public void onClick empty method structure for event processing*

Once you finish typing in your empty `onClick()` event handling method structure, Android Studio might pop up a dialog, advising that your empty Java method structure needs an `import` statement. If it does, click **OK**, as seen in Figure 7-15, and one will be added for you! If Android Studio sees something missing, it will alert you and even add it for you!

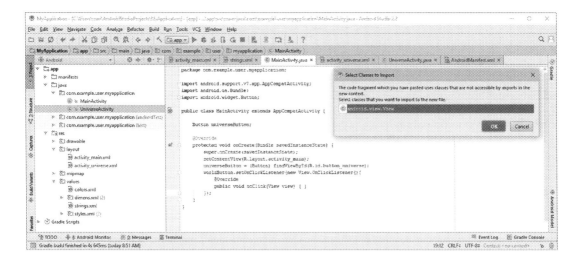

Figure 7-15. *Select android.view.View package for Android Studio to import for you*

Adding Intent Processing to your Event Handling

The first step in adding an `Intent` object is very similar to declaring a `Button` object, in as much as you declare the `Intent` at the top of the class, double-click the pop-up helper to have Android Studio import your `android.content.Intent` class, and then name the `Intent` object, finishing your declaration statement using a semicolon. This process is shown in Figure 7-16; I am naming this `Intent` **worldIntent**.

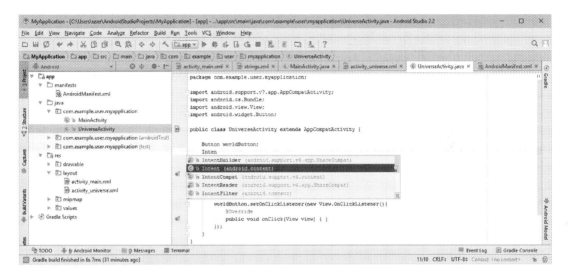

Figure 7-16. Declare an Intent at top of class; double-click adds import statement

Now that you have declared and named your `Intent` object, you will instantiate it inside of your `onClick()` structure using the Java **new** keyword along with the `Intent` class constructor, which takes a `Context` object using the Java `this` keyword and the class that you want to launch, which in the case is your `UniverseActivity` class.

Inside of your `onClick()` construct, type in the **worldIntent** object and then the equals sign. On the right side of your equals sign, utilize the Java **new** keyword to instantiate the `Intent` object using the **Intent(Context, Target)** constructor method.

Once you type in **worldIntent = new Intent(this, Ma)** Android Studio will show you your `MainActivity` (`com.example.user.myapplication`), which you can select and double-click to add it into the Java programming statement (Figure 7-17).

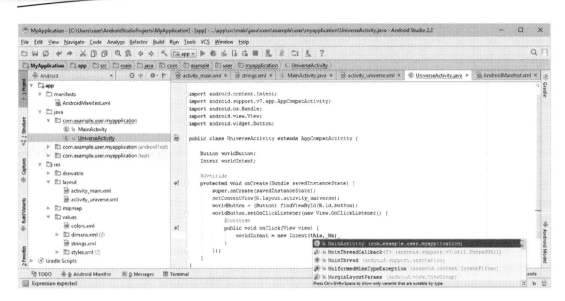

Figure 7-17. *Instantiate Intent inside onClick( ) method, and reference MainActivity*

As you can see in Figure 7-18, Android Studio puts its wavy red error underline under the parameter area, indicating there may be a problem. Mouse-over this so you can see what Android Studio thinks that the problem may be related to (Android could not resolve the Context object passed into the constructor method because it was not for the calling class).

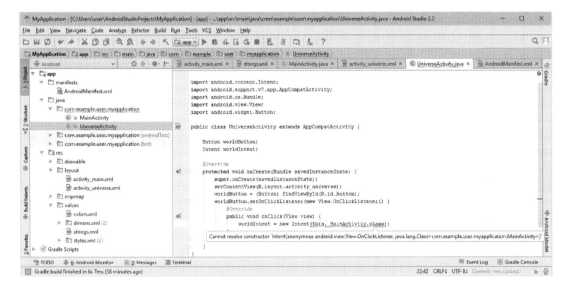

Figure 7-18. *Mouse-over red underline error, to see what the issue is with the code*

Android cannot resolve the Context of android.view.View.OnClickListener because it needs the Context for the UniverseActivity class, so you can fix this error with **dot notation**. Append a UniverseActivity class name before your Context **this** keyword so that the this (Context) becomes the **UniverseActivity.this** (your UniverseActivity class's Context object, rather than your OnClickListener method's context). As you see, in Figure 7-19, this gives you an error-free statement.

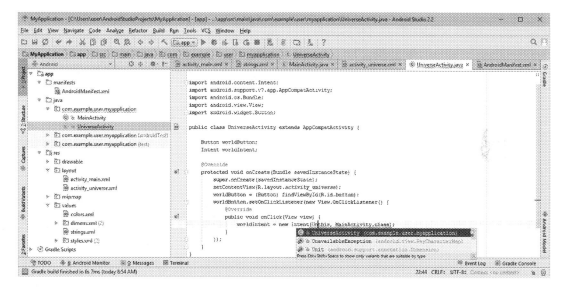

Figure 7-19. Add path for Context object to the UniverseActivity using dot notation

The final step is to add the startActivity() method call. Type startActivity(), as is shown in Figure 7-20, and inside of the parens type "wo" and double-click the **worldIntent** Intent object from the drop-down helper menu to insert it in your code.

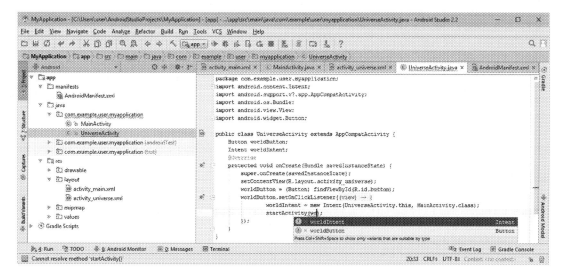

Figure 7-20. Use the startActivity( ) method with your worldIntent to start Activity

This startActivity() method is contained in every Activity subclass. It takes as a parameter the Intent object that you defined using the UniverseActivity Context and the MainActivity.class (which you would like to start). Make sure to also complete this same Java code structure for the MainActivity class (where you want to start the UniverseActivity instead of the MainActivity), which I show on the right side of Figure 7-21, and references UniverseActivity from MainActivity.

Emulating Hardware: Creating an AVD to Test Your App

Before we "Run" and test this application, we need to create an Android Virtual Device (AVD), which is called an emulator, as it emulates real-world hardware devices like smartphones, tablets, iTV sets or smartwatches. Use the **Tools ➤ Android ➤ AVD Manager** menu sequence, seen in Figure 7-21, and let's open the AVD Manager dialogs.

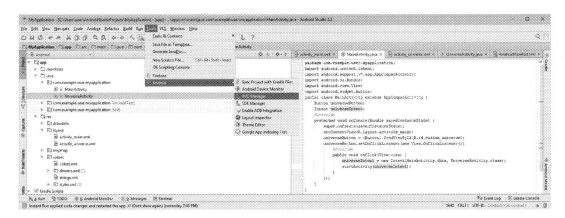

Figure 7-21. *Replicate code in MainActivity; then use Tools ➤ Android ➤ AVD Manager*

Click the **Create Virtual Device** button in the AVD dialog, shown in Figure 7-22.

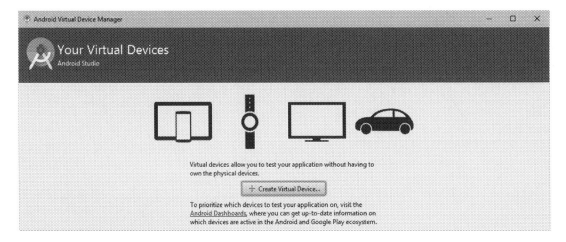

Figure 7-22. *Click on Create Virtual Device, and enter Virtual Device Configuration*

This will bring you to a **Select Hardware** dialog, where you will select the type of hardware device that you would like to emulate for your application testing. We are developing a Phone application, so, leave the default **Phone Category** selected, and select the popular **Nexus 5**, as shown in Figure 7-23. The Nexus 5 has a True HD display, and at about five inches diagonal, is a competitor for the Samsung Note 5.

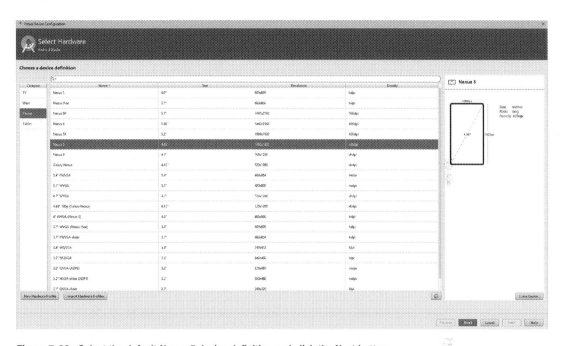

Figure 7-23. Select the default Nexus 5 device definition and click the Next button

If you are using the AMD CPU, you will want to install the ARM System Image, because in the next dialog, you will be selecting either an Intel (x86) or an AMD (ARM) ABI for use as your AVD emulator. An Application Binary Interface (ABI) defines how the machine code for your app will run on your CPU as it executes your AVD emulator. If you want to look ahead and see the System Image dialog, take a look at Figure 7-25.

To install ARM v7a System Image files, you'll use the same **Tools ➤ Android** menu sequence, and select the **SDK Manager** option, which you are quite familiar with, and which can be seen in Figure 7-21 immediately under the AVD Manager in the submenu.

Once the SDK Manager opens, select the **SDK Platforms** tab and select the Android 7.1.1 Nougat API. Select the **Show Package Details** checkbox at the bottom-right corner of the dialog to show what is underneath the API and select all the ARM v7a related entries, as is shown in Figure 7-24.

Next, click on the **Apply** button, and select **OK** in the **Confirm Change** dialog, as is shown on the right side in Figure 7-24. Once you click on the main OK button, at the bottom of the SDK Manager Default Settings dialog, you will get an **SDK Quickfix Installation** dialog, which will then show you what packages are being downloaded or installed, along with a progress bar for each operation, as it is occurring.

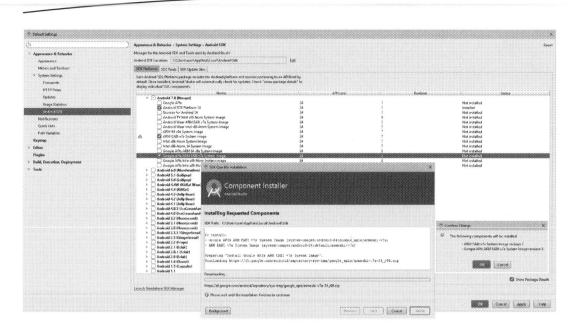

Figure 7-24. If using AMD CPU, install the ARM v7a System Image in your SDK Manager

If you have an AMD CPU, and have installed these ARM v7a system image files for Android (and for Google Play Services if the app needs them), you will then have both Intel (x86) and AMD (ARM v7a) system image options available in AVD Android Virtual Device Configuration dialog's System Image panel, which follows the System Hardware panel shown in Figure 7-23.

If you are using Intel you can skip the step seen in Figure 7-24. I had to make sure all readers could install and use an AVD emulator for application testing, so I had to include that important SDK Manager step for our AMD users so that the next step will work, regardless of what CPU you have decided to develop applications on.

If you're using an Intel system click the **x86** tab, if you're using an AMD click on the **Other Images** tab. I selected the latest Nougat Android 7.0 API Level 24 ABI, which as you can see in Figure 7-25, I have now downloaded in the step shown in the previous Figure 7-24. This is why there's no **Download** link next to the Release Name in the far-left column.

AMD users can now safely ignore the red warning on the right and click the **Next** button to advance to the Verify AVD Configuration dialog, where we will confirm all of the default settings.

After we complete this last step, Android Studio will create your AVD and use it when you run your application, so that we can make sure all of the code is working that we have created (and Android Studio has created for us using the Visual Design Editor and New Android Application series of dialogs).

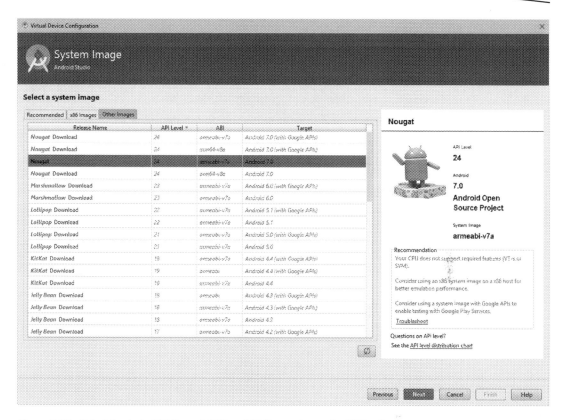

Figure 7-25. Select the Android 7 Nougat API Level 24 System Image for AMD or Intel

To see all of the default settings, which are obviously the ones Android Studio recommends for use with that particular AVD emulator, click Show Advanced Settings, a button on the bottom left of the AVD **Verify Configuration** (fourth) dialog in the series. Once you do this, you can define how everything about an AVD is configured.

As you can see, I have the AVD launch in **Portrait** (vertical) mode, although the AVD has a toolbar that allows you to change this orientation as you are testing the application. We will be using this feature in future chapters of the book.

I leave the **Cameras** as emulated, although if you have webcams installed on your workstation, you can pipe these through the emulator using these drop-down menus.

Leave your **Network Speed** at maximum with no **Latency**, which is best for testing, because there is enough latency on the busy (often overloaded) Google Play Server to make your testing process slow down as it is, no need to add to your wait times.

Leave **Graphics** (GPU) performance optimization set to **automatic** and leave **Multi-Core CPU** capability enabled (selected), which are the default settings. The settings here will allow Android Studio to optimize the most speed out of your AVD emulator.

If you have a high-capacity (memory, hard disk drive, etc.) workstation you can increase the values in the Memory and Storage section of the dialog to make the AVD emulator work faster. I used the defaults to simulate what the AVD would work like for most readers. Finally, I left the **Device Frame** enabled to simulate the Nexus 5. See Figure 7-26.

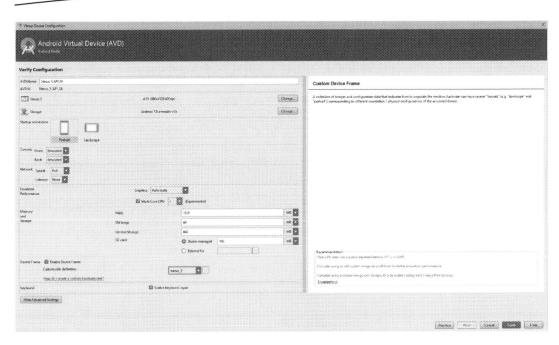

Figure 7-26. *Accept default Portrait orientation, and accept the other AVD defaults*

If you want to see what the device frame looks like, take a look at Figure 7-27 to see that the device frame simply makes your application look like it is running on a smartphone. I left this on, to make screenshots for this book more realistic.

Once you click the **Finish** button, you will get the Your Virtual Devices dialog, with an entry for the Nexus 5 API 24 device. I'm not sure why the Your CPU does not support required features and the ARM CPU/ABI is supported for the AMD CPU, as you will soon see in the next section. Possibly some code should be added in this dialog series to detect if the AMD processor is in use and the ARM v7a ABI System Image has been installed and remove this message from this dialog. Ignore it for now, and no need to "Troubleshoot" (link) a problem that does not actually exist. Let's run the application next, and make sure that it (and the AVD) actually works!

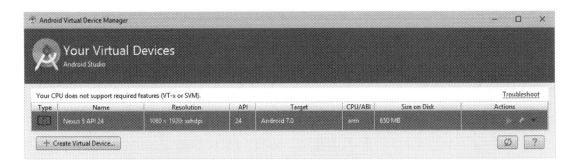

Figure 7-27. *The Nexus 5 API 24 AVD is now shown in the Virtual Device Manager list*

Running the Application: Building the App Using Gradle

Now that you have installed your AVD, you can use your Android Studio **Run** menu, and test your application. As you can see in Figure 7-28, your **Run ➤ Run 'app'** menu sequence is used to test your app the first time. Once you have used Run, make sure that you use the **Run ➤ Stop** menu sequence to stop the executing app in memory, even if you have minimized or even closed the AVD emulator, which is a separate process.

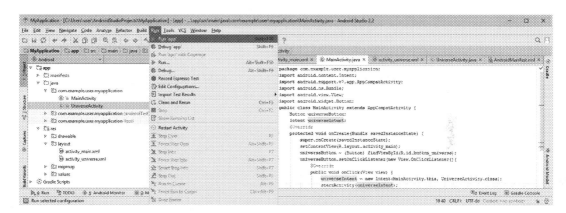

Figure 7-28. Use a Run ➤ Run 'app' menu sequence and test your Java code in the AVD

This will open the **Event Log** pane at the bottom of the Android Studio IDEA, and start telling you what is being done, primarily in the Gradle Build System, to sync and build your application in to an executable format, as is shown in Figure 7-29.

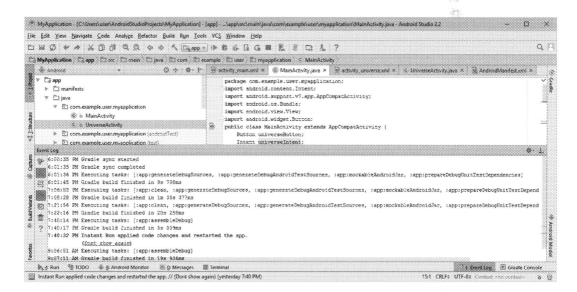

Figure 7-29. Open your Event Log pane to see Gradle events (sync, build, execution)

If there are no errors in the app Java or XML, the AVD emulator, seen in Figure 7-30, will open, execute (run), and display your Android 7 Hello World application.

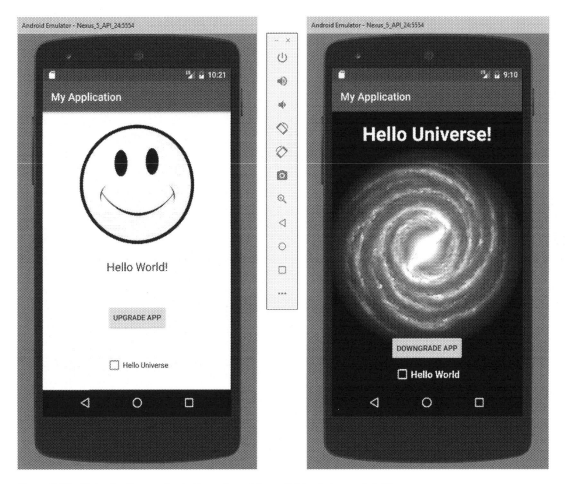

Figure 7-30. MyApplication running in Nexus 5 emulator switching between Activities

Let's test your application, by clicking on the UPGRADE APP button, seen on the left side of Figure 7-30, and make sure your event handling and `Intent` processing opens the Hello Universe activity, shown on the right side of Figure 7-30. To test all of your code, click on the DOWNGRADE APP button next, and make sure your event handling and `Intent` processing opens the Hello World activity (`MainActivity`), shown on the left side of Figure 7-30. Click these buttons back and forth a few times to make sure there are no memory leaks or errors generated, to stress test your app.

Notice the Icon Toolbar (in the center of Figure 7-30) that accompanies the AVD emulator. The top two (tiny) icons will minimize (left) and close (right) your AVD, and the rest are hardware (in this case smartphone) controls including, from top to bottom, Power, Audio, Orientation, Camera, Zoom, as well as the Back, Home, History and Overflow menu buttons found in Android's ActionBar, and on the hardware device.

Congratulations, you have created your first Android 7 application! We will be looking at other user interface design paradigms in the remaining chapters, as well as how to use other types of new media assets, and advanced concepts such as MySQL databases and `Services` (background processing and threads).

Summary

In this seventh chapter, you learned about how to make your Android application interactive. This is done by leveraging `Intent` objects, **events**, **event listeners**, and **event handling**. Intent objects are unique to the Android platform; however, events and event processing can be found in many programming platforms, including Java and JavaFX, HTML5 and JavaScript, and other OOP languages as well.

We spent the first part of the chapter learning some basic concepts regarding the important Android superclasses and Java interfaces that allow these events and Intent objects to be processed, allowing user interface designs to be interactive.

You learned about how to add a **new class** to an application, to create the Hello Universe `Activity` subclass that was used to host the Universe UI design you created in Chapter 6 by using Android Studio 2.3's new Visual Design Editor.

You coded an event listener structure and an `onClick` event listener, which starts a new `Activity`, by using an `Intent` object, configured with the `Activity Context` and the target `Activity` subclass name. You cross-wired the two `Activity` classes together, so you could go back and forth from Hello World to Hello Universe.

Next, you learned how to set up an AVD emulator that you can use to launch and test an application. You did this by using the **AVD Manager** series of dialogs.

Finally, you tested your application using the Android Studio **Run** menu, and saw that your two Hello World `Activity` UI designs work properly and can call each other back and forth without any crashes.

Next, in Chapter 8 you will start to learn about some of the other more popular Android UI design paradigms, such as the navigation drawer UI design, tab-based UI design, and a scrolling UI design.

Android Design Patterns: UI Design Paradigms

Android Studio includes a number of popular user interface design approaches, called "patterns," as pre-coded `Activity` subclasses found in the Create New Project series of dialogs that you used during Chapter 3. Since this is an Absolute Beginner title, we will be leveraging these application design and user experience templates to teach you how to quickly create apps using some of the most popular Android 7 UI approaches. At the same time, I will teach you what the Java code or XML markup is doing for the application, so that you will learn Android 7.1.1 development rapidly and efficiently, while also creating several types of Android applications.

This approach will make some very advanced (and popular) user interface layout designs immediately available to every Absolute Beginner Android Studio developer. This is precisely why I am including this chapter in the book, and only halfway through the book, to accelerate us into professional Android 7.1.1 application development, now that we have covered the basics of what Android is, how to install it, how to create an application, how to design a user interface, how to make a UI interactive, and now how to access popular UI design patterns recently included in Android Studio's "coding and UI design helper" functionality introduced in 2016 in Android Studio 2.2.

To be able to implement advanced Android UI design patterns right out of the gate as Absolute Beginners is a real testament to the quality and reach of Android Studio 2.3, and the advanced nature of the new Android APIs, which are focusing on making code structures, and design patterns, available to developers who might just be Absolute Beginners. Google's marketing motivation regarding this is to get many more developers creating Android 7.1.1 applications, as you probably have already surmised.

One of the ways that I am "refreshing" this *Android Apps for Absolute Beginners* title in its *fourth edition* is the incorporation of many of the changes that have taken place with Android Studio 2.3 and in Android 7.1.1 APIs that are specifically targeted at helping Absolute Beginners. Two of the areas that have had the most change in Android Studio 2.3 and

Android 7 include the area of drag-and-drop user interface design (Visual Design Editor, Chapter 6) and creating new bootstrap applications with the Create New Android Application series of dialogs (Chapter 3). We will be looking at the Create New Application series of dialogs further in this chapter. Three of the most popular UI design pattern Activity application design approaches have been added to this series of dialogs since Android became 64-bit (in Version 5), so I added these to the book, to expose them to Absolute Beginners.

In this chapter, we will be covering Android **design patterns**. These will assist you in making Android applications that conform to what Android users expect from a user experience. We'll also cover several application design approaches provided as `Activity` classes in the Create New Android Application dialogs. These also include, and conform to, the Android design patterns, making for a very synergistic chapter.

Android Design Patterns: Ensuring App Visual Quality

An **Android design pattern** is a work process for, that is, a way of going about, designing Android application user interfaces (UI) and user experiences (UX). These Android applications are hosted in the Google Play marketplace, and therefore Google has an interest in having all their apps conform to a stringent UI design standard.

In the first section of the chapter I will be going over what would be included in these Android design patterns, all of which are targeted at increasing the user experience of Android users so that they're captivated by your Android application.

Besides captivating Android users with your visually exciting Android UI design and content, Google also wants to make sure that you keep your applications simple to use and easy to comprehend. This involves making sure the app is usable even for first-time users, and that users are not overwhelmed by a plethora of choices or by complex tasks, which should be performed in the background whenever possible.

We'll be conforming to, and covering, these Android design patterns throughout the rest of this book. I wanted to have a chapter specifically covering this topic, before we got too far along in the book. Let's start by looking at **material design**.

Material Design: i3D Animated User Experience Designs

Material design is a definition of how visual elements, animated motion, and GUI interactivity should work across all Android devices (smartphone, tablet, iTV set, e-book reader, smartwatch, auto dashboard, game console, etc.) and Android platforms (Android TV, Android Auto, Android Wear 2, Android Glass, etc.). Android now contains material design components that we'll be referencing and using throughout the book, so that you can develop the most professional Android applications as an Absolute Beginner.

Material design is a three-dimensional environment that will allow Android developers to control light, shadowing, and materials, sometimes called **textures** or **shaders** in 3D software packages. This runs in sharp contrast to the "flat design" currently in use in HTML5, iOS, and template-driven systems, such as WordPress and Wix. These 3D features will allow Android application developers and i3D designers to set themselves apart from the crowd, allowing the visual sensation that Google wants to set Android apps far apart from the rest of the marketplace, and continuing to increase their dominant market share.

Each material design object in Android 7 supports an X, Y, and Z dimension, as well as a variable that holds its current Z axis (height) position in the layer stack, which will be used to calculate automated shadowing features and options. Material design support for key lights allows developers to create directional and even animated shadows. Ambient light is also supported to create softer shadows, for realistic 3D effects.

Material design attributes sets Android distinctively apart from flat template-driven 2D design. Material design occupies XYZ coordinates for 3D spaces, allows 3D mutable (morphable) shapes, enables seamless joins with other material design components, allows UI elements and content to split (separate) and heal (join), can move along any axis, and can be created (placed into memory) or destroyed (removed from memory) in real time, and interactively, using Java code within your Android applications.

Some of the new material design components available for 64-bit Android (5-7) apps include new themes, widgets, and layout containers, a visual design editor, and new APIs that allow custom shadowing and animation. We have already covered some of the material design features in this book, such as themes and the visual design editor, and we'll continue to cover the other ones during the course of this book.

Hardware Devices: Code Design Patterns Across Devices

As there are a plethora of consumer electronics hardware genres that will run Android OS, some of which we will cover in this section specifically, it's becoming a challenge to design a UI that can morph between different screen sizes, shapes, and orientations. Android provides tools and capabilities that address this issue directly, and other operating systems, including four HTML5 OSes, are copying these features to deal with running apps, and websites, on hundreds of different devices.

Smartphones, Tablets, Phablets, and e-Book Readers: Core Android API

In the beginning, with Android 1.x, the operating was a mobile operating system used for mobile phones. Android 2.x added tablet support, and 2.3 was used for the popular Amazon Kindle Fire e-book reader. Android 3 added features for phablets, or phone-tablet hybrids. At this point in the Android API, there were no specialized APIs like the ones we will cover later on in this section; those started around Android 4. The "core" Android API, that is, the one that holds the primary features and has been known as "Android OS" since day one is the Android API that is used on smartphones, tablets, e-book readers and now even on laptops and personal computers.

These four devices will require two user interface designs, one for users using their device vertically, or up and down, called "portrait mode," and one for those who prefer using their device horizontally, or widescreen, called "landscape mode." The trend is toward landscape mode due to previously popular devices (laptops and personal computers), as well as the more rapidly growing (in sales figures) device, the iTV set, or interactive television set, hardware device. These only function in widescreen (landscape) mode, allowing better use of screen real estate for working and cinematic entertainment.

These devices used to vary widely in resolution, however, this is changing again, due to iTV technology and content, which exists in three primary HD and UHD resolutions: 1280 by 720 (1280 by 800 devices) 720P Blu-ray, 1920 by 1080 (1920 by 1200) 1080P HD, and 3840 by 2160 (or 4096 by 2160 devices) 2160P UHD. Most popular content is also developed and distributed using these formats, so the trend for all device manufacturers has been to support one of these three resolutions, so that content does not have to be **scaled**, which can take up most of a devices memory and CPU capacity by calculating pixel arrays. Scaling also reduces image quality. A good example of this is the recent 2560 by 1440 resolution, which plays 1280 by 720 Blu-ray content with no reduction in quality, as if scaling is done by 100% (2X) up or down, the visual quality is maintained. If you want to learn more about pixels and scaling, check out the *Digital Image Compositing Fundamentals* title (Apress, 2015).

There are three primary screens used on all these devices: an apps screen that contains all of the launcher icons for the apps on the device; a Home screen, which contains widgets, icons for your favorite apps, folders and the like; and a recent screen, which shows your recently used applications.

The core Android OS has two system bars for OS UI functions, your top-mounted **Status Bar** for system, network, and hardware status indicators; and notifications. For hardware that does not have hardware navigation keys, there is also sometimes a bottom-mounted **Navigation Bar** that provides the **Back** (triangle), **Home** (circle), and **Recent** (square) icons. Developers can also provide their own **Action Bar**, underneath the Status Bar as well as **Navigation Drawers**, which we'll be looking at during this chapter, along with other popular user interface design and content navigation approaches that will enhance usability, overall user experience and Wow-Factor.

Smartwatches and Wearable Technology: The Android Wear 2 API

An Android Wear API, now in its second version, was introduced in Android 4.4W, a special version of Android 4.4.4. Android versions previous to Version 5 were 32-bit, and therefore only able to address 3.24 GB of system memory. Smartwatches are square and therefore have a unique 1:1 aspect ratio (screen shape), and thus will require a third UI design for optimal user interaction and user experience. Initially smartwatch devices had a low resolution of 240 or 320 pixels, later devices supported 400 or 480 pixel screens; and I expect to see 640 or 800 pixel resolution screens out by 2018, or even sooner. High-resolution smartwatches will further enable innovation by new media content developers.

Wearable devices demand a totally different user interface and user experience than phones, tablets or iTV sets, as they have different ergonomics, usage profiles, and hardware specifications. The smaller (in resolution, width, and height) form-factor portends that you use what Google terms the "suggest and demand" design approach, which is why Android 5 introduced card-based UI layouts and widgets, for use with smartwatches.

To suggest, Android uses the "context stream," a list of cards that scrolls in a vertical dimension to show top or home cards, and which can be swiped horizontally, to show additional cards underneath the home (top or title) card. Background images can provide visual context, so users can browse the context stream to see what is going on in their devices, and drill down into only what currently interests them.

For user demands, Android provides the "cue card" that can be opened by saying "OK Google." Swiping up on a cue card will show a list of commands; these can be touched to select, or spoken for use with the smartwatch voice recognition features. Each top or voice command is wired to a different Intent object, which you learned about in Chapter 7. If an implicit Intent object is used, applications that conform to the category and action of this Intent will be listed for preferential selection by the smartwatch user. Intents can trigger the launch of an application, Activity, or an update (or addition) of a context stream card.

Android smartwatches also feature a Home screen that is usually a custom-watch face design, created by using the Android WatchFaces API. If you are interested in the WatchFaces API, check out the *Pro Android Wearables* title (Apress, 2015). There are also status icons in the watch face showing charge, watch modes, and unread card status (count). Watch faces can also show "peek cards," which show a portion of the card at the bottom of the WatchFace design.

Automobile Dashboards: The Android Auto API

Around the same time as the Wear API was introduced, Google also added the **Auto API** to provide a custom Android user interface for automobile dashboards, which are increasingly using digital OLED displays, rather than expensive analog dashboard gauges. This API is designed toward **minimizing driver distraction** by optimizing quick selection of as few salient options as possible displayed prominently on the screen, a design approach that I've been implementing for my international clients for decades now.

When the driver connects their Android device to their auto, they will encounter the Android Auto "Overview screen," which displays widescreen context cards based on the auto location, weather, time, date, and so forth. This screen can also display a user's messages and also supports voice recognition. Touching a headphone icon will give users a list of all Auto apps installed. Auto apps use a standard transport UI that can be customized as needed to add feature icons to the audio playback icon. Android Auto also supports different color themes for day (light) and night (dark).

iTV Sets: The Android TV API

The next customized API that Google released for Android products in the international marketplace targeted the exploding **interactive television set** product currently replacing "dumb TV sets" in all big brand brick and mortar stores, as well as in online retail. **Android TV** competes with HTML5 iTV OSes, including Firefox OS (Panasonic HDTVs), Opera OS (Sony Bravia HDTVs), and Google Chrome OS (ChromeCast).

Most iTV sets use one of two resolutions currently: **True HD** (1920 by 1080P); or **Ultra HD** (3840 by 2160P), which is twice the resolution of True HD on each X/Y axis, or four times the resolution of True HD in total. This much resolution, 2,073,600 pixels (HD) to 8,294,400 pixels (UHD) allows iTV set device screens to span several feet across with high-quality imagery. This gigantic screen size yields by far the best user experience of any Android hardware device type, especially if you have the 24-bit HD Audio piped into your home stereo system and Dolby THX 5.1 speaker system with 24 inch sub-woofers! Interactive Television Sets also can hook into the types of peripherals (game controllers, keyboards, mouse, HD camera, etc.) that can enhance the interaction with the iTV set using USB, Bluetooth, or Wi-Fi connections.

Finally, iTV sets are used in a situation where your users can (and will) focus 100% of their attention on the application being used on their iTV set, as they are in their favorite easy chair, undistracted in the comfort of their bedroom or living room. Compare this to using phones, tablets, or auto dashboards out in public, and you will see a major difference in ergonomics and environment for the iTV set device type.

Again, Android UI design can be customized to fit iTV set ergonomics and iTV end use case scenarios, in order to optimize the end user experience, which should be vastly different than smartphone, smartwatch, dashboard, e-reader, or tablet usage.

The Android TV Home screen is the entry point into the iTV user experience, and offers content search, recommendations, and application launch. Developers can offer cinematic previews or animated overviews of their content in this Home screen area.

Game and iTV applications both have their own separate areas on the Home screen and will be placed in the order that reflect the user's usage and allow easy access to the most often used games and applications. Settings and Wi-Fi networks are also accessible at the bottom of the Home screen.

Interactive Television design guidelines are similar to good UI design for tiny devices such as smartphones, because the iTV set is mounted up on the wall a good distance (10 feet or more) from the user (viewer). A large 16 to 24 pixel font size for text with a sans serif (Arial or Roboto) typeface will be readable by anyone from any distance, and easy-to-select buttons can be quickly accessed via remote or touchscreen without having to figure out how to zoom or scroll around, which should be unnecessary on a screen with that resolution and dimension using good UI design.

Future APIs: Android Glass, Android Home, Android VR, Android Robot

If Google brings Google Glass back, there will be an Android Glass API added to Android Studio, and with all of the VR goggles out there, I expect an Android VR API sometime in the future as well for use with i3D, VR and AR (Augmented Reality). I'd also like to see an Android Home API sometime soon for Home Appliance and Security; and an Android Robot API, for a growing number of Android-powered robots! I already have several Android robots already, for use in my *Pro Android IoT* book, (which is slated to come out in 2018). As long as Android keeps dominating consumer electronics device verticals, these customized APIs should continue to be released.

Pure Android: Application Design Branding Conformance

Android OS powers billions of smartphones, tablets, e-book readers, iTV sets, game consoles, smartglasses, smartwatches, home appliances, home media centers, and new emerging devices that come under the heading of IoT, or Internet of Things. The devices support a wide variety of screen sizes, form factors (shapes, or aspect ratios), and orientation (portrait and widescreen or landscape). This means that developers must properly leverage Android's layout system in their Java 8 code, XML markup, and user interface design. If you optimize your application so that it can morph UI layout design between device types, you can create apps that seamlessly accommodate display screens from smartwatches to smartphones to tablets to laptops to PCs to game consoles to home media centers (often called set-top boxes) iTV sets.

Display Shape, Resolution, and Orientation: User Interfaces That Morph

To do this your user interface design approach must be flexible enough to fit your UI layout design in such a way that optimized the design to use the screen real estate to a wide variety of screen aspect ratios (shapes), heights, and widths.

On larger (usually widescreen) iTV set, laptop and tablet devices, you should take advantage of valuable screen real estate with a user interface that stays out of the way on the top and sides of the screen allowing your content to dominate the view, rather than a logo, banner, or user interface panels. Gone are the landing pages of old, replaced by immediate gratification of content surrounded by a touch-once go anywhere user interface design optimized for touchscreen, not mouse scroll-wheels. How often on your widescreen tablet or iTV set do you go to a blog site where 40% of the screen is used in the center (with 30% on each side unused) where you have to endlessly scroll for miles to find that content needle in the digital haystack?

Android now has hundreds of API features that allow developers to correct this design malady that plagues almost all current content; all you have to do is to design, optimize, implement, and code your user interface to utilize every pixel on every screen optimally to give the user a fast and easily understandable user experience.

To do this is not easy (like drag-and-drop, template-driven CMSes are), as you must provide three or four different sets of digital asset resources for different screen densities (MDPI, HDPI, XHDPI) to ensure that apps look great on all devices.

Designing for multiple screens is an art form that few have sought to master due to the ease of drag-and-drop CMS and templates, which don't make for a unique brand experience, which a "Pure Android" standard requires. The best approach is to work in UHD (4K), designing for the far more popular (and usable) widescreen devices with the larger screen sizes, and then scale down (down-sampling pixels retains quality, while up-sampling pixels reduces quality); then figure out any UI "compromises" you will need to make on smaller screens, portrait smartphones, and square smartwatches.

Backwards Compatibility: Support 32-bit Android Versions and Devices

Android 7 has enhanced the OS backwards compatibility capabilities, which we'll be leveraging in this book, since it is an Absolute Beginner title, and since these features are also tied into the Visual Design Editor, as you have already seen over the course of the first half of the book. This ensures apps work on 32-bit Android 2.37 (Kindle Fire) and Android 4.4.4 devices, which are still in use (phones and tablets).

Confirmation and Acknowledgment: Are We All on the Same Page?!

Part of Pure Android Design involves staying in sync with your users. When your users take part in a user interface interaction in your app, which we covered in Chapter 7, it is a good idea to **confirm** or **acknowledge** that action through text if there are no change to the screen's content (such as loading a new Activity screen).

Confirming involves asking a user to verify that they want to proceed with the action they just invoked using your user interface. In some cases, the confirmation will be presented along a warning dialog and (or) important information related to the result of that action that you feel that they will need to consider.

Acknowledging involves a display of text that lets a user know that the action they just requested be performed has been completed. This removes any uncertainty about background (Service) operations that the operating system may be undertaking to accomplish (complete) that action. In some cases, an acknowledgment is presented along with an option dialog allowing the user to undo (reverse) the performed task.

Communicating to users using confirmation and acknowledgment helps to remove any uncertainty regarding actions that have been undertaken or that are about to be performed by the Android OS have happened. This ensures a good user experience for your users by making them think about what they are doing, preventing them from making mistakes that they otherwise might regret using your (branded) application.

Accessibility: Design Your Apps for the Hearing and the Sight Impaired

Accessibility is defined as the measure of how successfully your product can be utilized by a wide range of people who have disabilities of one type or another. Examples of these would include visual impairment, hearing impairment, color deficiency (commonly called "color blind"), hearing loss, limited manual dexterity, and afflictions which cause symptoms such as these.

Universal accessibility design involves including code that makes your product user interface and user experience easily accessible to all users regardless of their physical capabilities. An Android design pattern should be optimized to be in accordance with universal design principles. Adhering to universal design means you should enabling all of the Android accessibility-related tools and API features, so as to make your application, game, iTV show, e-book, etc. as accessible as possible.

Android includes a number of features that support access for users with visual impairments. These are built into the Android API and do not require drastic visual changes to your app; however, they do require Java code or XML markup to implement in your user experience design patterns. **TalkBack** is a pre-installed screen reader service that is provided by Google. It uses vocal feedback to describe the result of end user actions, like launching an app or Activity, dialogs, and notifications. The Explore by Touch operating system feature works hand in hand with TalkBack, allowing users to touch the device screen and hear what's under your finger (or the cursor) via TalkBack vocal feedback. Android OS accessibility settings allow users to modify the device display, as well as audio options. This includes increasing font sizes, changing the speed at which text is spoken, and similar settings.

The Pure Android design principle, "Users should always know where they are" is key for a successful accessibility user interface design. As users navigate through an application, they need visual feedback as well as a GUI model of where they are, like navigation tabs or 3D UI buttons that show where you are in the content. Users will always benefit from this strong sense of hierarchy and logical content access.

All users benefit from visual, haptic (sense of touch) feedback during their UI navigation. This is aided by 3D, button labels, color, icons, single touch feedback and logically placed UI elements. Low-vision users can benefit from explicit verbal descriptions, large font sizes, large buttons, and large visuals with high contrast. The following are Pure Android Design guidelines that enable effective navigation.

The first objective is to design intuitive, easy-to-use, navigation. You should design well-defined, clear, information or task flow with minimal navigation steps, and minimum navigation levels (called "flat" navigation). Make sure that tasks and information are navigable via user interface design elements that pass focus (which UI element is active or in use is said to have "focus") in a logical, ordered fashion.

A second objective is to use recommended UI element "touch target" sizes. Small buttons or tabs with small text labels will not be usable on small screen displays. **48 DIP** (or Density Independent Pixels) is the Pure Android recommended touch target size for screen UI elements. For some users it might even be appropriate to use a larger touch target. An example of this is educational apps and games where buttons larger than the minimum recommended size are easier to use for children with developing motor skills and disabled people who have manual dexterity challenges.

A third objective is to label your visual UI elements with short, concise text, using a large font size, with a word that sums up a description of that information or function. If you want to use **glyphs** (picture-based navigation icons), be sure to use the contentDescription attribute to label functional UI components that have no visible text. Those components can be buttons, icons, tabs with icons, and icons with state (like stars) information. As you've experienced already in Chapter 6 on Visual Design, developers must use a contentDescription attribute to set the glyph's label.

The Android system-wide font size control is not often considered by developers. Users can enable a system-wide large font size under their OS Settings. Using the default system font size in an application will enable a user's system font size preferences to be used in your application as well. To enable system font size in your app, mark text UI elements and their associated UI layout containers to be measured using SP (scale pixels) instead of DP (Density Pixels) or DIP.

Home Screen Widgets: Miniaturized Applications

Android Widgets are an essential aspect of your home screen customization. They are essentially entire applications that can be viewed at a glance and can contain important data and functionality that is accessible right from the user's home screen. Users can move widgets across their home screen panels, and, if supported, resize them to tailor the amount of information displayed. For example, if you were a pharmaceutical company, you could create a widget that advised customers when to take their dosages throughout the day. Widgets classify as one of these categories:

- **Information widgets** typically display critical information elements in real time, which are important to the user, and which will track how information changes over time. Examples of information widgets are health widgets, weather widgets, clock widgets, games, or sport score trackers. Touch an information widget to launch an associated application, which will open a detail view of the widget information.

- **Collection widgets** specialize in displaying multitude elements of the same type, such as a collection of pictures from a gallery app, a collection of articles from a news app, or a collection of emails/messages from a communication app. Collection widgets typically focus on two use cases: browsing the collection, and opening an element of the collection to its detail view for consumption.

▓ **Control widgets** can be used to display frequently used functions that your user can select right from the home screen without having to open the app first. These are kind of like having a remote control for your app. An example of control widget would be a music app widget that allows your users to play, pause, or select music tracks from outside of the music app itself. While widgets tend to show attributes of the three types described above, many widgets turn out to be **hybrid widgets**, which combine design elements of these different types of widgets.

Swiping Views: More Efficient Content Browsing for Modern Devices

Efficient content navigation is one of the hallmarks of a well-designed digital application. While websites and apps have historically been built in a hierarchical fashion, where many levels of information nesting and scrolling are the norm, there are many instances on most consumer electronics devices where horizontal navigation can "flatten" vertical hierarchies, eliminate vertical scrolling, and make access to related data items faster and more enjoyable. Swiping views to the side allows your users to far more efficiently and effortlessly move from item to item, using simple swipe gestures. This makes browsing (consuming content) a more seamless experience.

We will be creating some user interface design patterns during this chapter that involve swiping gestures that allow easy UI access and content browsing. For instance, you can swipe from tab to tab in a tabbed UI paradigm, which we will be looking at in detail. If your app uses an action bar tab user interface approach, the user will be able to simply swipe to navigate between the different page views.

Now that we have reviewed some of the most important aspects of Pure Android and Android Design Patterns, let's take a look at how we can get Android Studio 2.3 to create a **Sliding UI Drawer** paradigm for use in an Activity that does Sliding Drawer Navigation. After we create and test this bootstrap application, I will show you what the XML markup and the Java 8 code does to create this type of UI, which you can use in your own applications, user interface design and content delivery pipelines. As an Absolute Beginner, this is the fastest way that I can get you up and running using advanced, Pure Android 7.1.1 application design and programming.

Creating a Sliding Drawer: UI Only When Users Need It

First, let's close the current MyApplication Hello Universe project. The way to do this in Android Studio is to use the **File ➤ Close Project** menu sequence, shown on the top left in Figure 8-1.

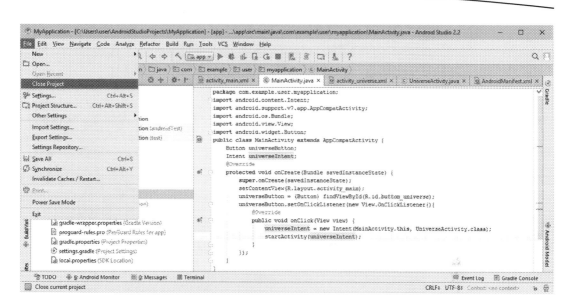

Figure 8-1. *Use File ➤ Close Project to close Hello Universe MyApplication project*

This will close Android Studio and open up the Welcome to Android Studio dialog, which you get when you first install Android Studio 2.3, and which can be seen in Figure 8-2.

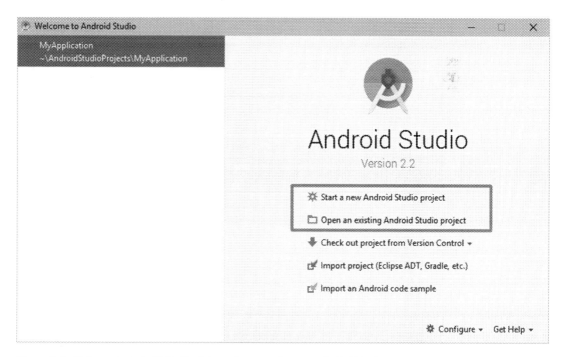

Figure 8-2. *Welcome to Android Studio dialog, where you Start new Android Projects*

There is a difference in this welcome dialog now, as you can see, since we have a project that we have developed, and now closed, but not deleted, which is shown on the top left of the dialog in blue. What this means that we can reopen this project, or any project(s) we have created and closed, at any time. This means that you can work on more than one project at a time.

We will be using this feature during this book, as we reopen and enhance projects we will be creating during the next few chapters, as we add content, special effects, digital imagery (called "Drawables" in Android), digital audio, and animation, among other things, as chapters continue to get more advanced throughout the book. This allows us to focus on Android Design Patterns during this chapter.

During the rest of this chapter we will be exploring a popular user interface design paradigm that Android Studio will code for us using the Start a new Android Studio Project dialog series, which you are about to get some more practice using.

Select the **Start a new Android Studio project** option seen in red in Figure 8-2.

In the New Project dialog, seen on the left in Figure 8-3, name the application **NavDrawerPattern**. Target the core Android **Phone and Tablet** API (Figure 8-3 middle), and use a standard **MainActivity** naming convention for a main activity for this app.

Figure 8-3. *Name app NavDrawerPattern, select Phone & Tablet API, name MainActivity*

Select a **Navigation Drawer Activity** for your UI pattern, as seen in Figure 8-4.

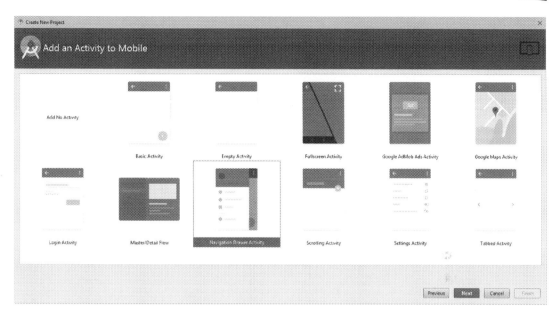

Figure 8-4. *Select the Navigation Drawer Activity for your Android Design Pattern*

Once you click **Finish**, Android Studio 2.3 will open with a `NavDrawerPattern` project already created for you, with the `content_main.xml` file open in an editing tab. For the rest of the section we will dissect how the XML UI definition is set up using four XML files in the `app/res/layout` folder. All of this can be seen in Figure 8-5.

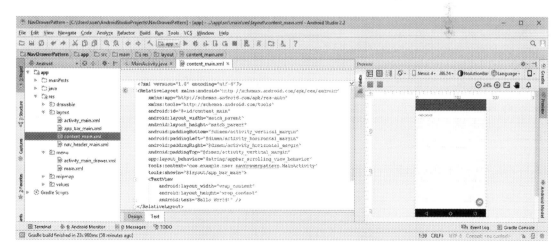

Figure 8-5. *Android Studio opens with NavDrawerPattern project and content_main.xml*

As you might have surmised, `content_main.xml` is where your application content will be displayed, and currently contains the bootstrap Hello World placeholder text, as you can see on the right side of Figure 8-5, in the Android Studio Preview pane.

This content UI layout uses one of Android's legacy layout container classes, the `RelativeLayout` design pattern, which, as you may have guessed, lays out your UI elements relative to each other. This is similar to the `ConstraintLayout` class, but you have to create the XML, whereas `ConstraintLayout` uses the Visual Design Editor.

The `RelativeLayout` (layout container or `ViewGroup`) UI design pattern positions its children (widgets or `View` objects) in relation to each other as well as to the parent `RelativeLayout` container. It was created in Android V1 (API Level 1) using the `ViewGroup` superclass, which is a subclass of the `View` superclass, as you know. If you want to research the **RelativeLayout** class in greater detail, you can do so at the following Android Developer website URL:

https://**developer.android.com**/reference/android/widget/**RelativeLayout**.html

As you can see in the XML markup in the center editing pane in Figure 8-5, the content layout ID is **content_main**, the `layout_width` and `layout_height` scale to fill the screen using a **match_parent** (the parent container's dimensions) constant, the padding references the @ dimens dimension constants in `/app/res/values/dimens.xml`.

At the end of the `RelativeLayout` container parent tag there are two `xmlns:tools` parameters that wire up the content view to the rest of the application. `Context` references the `MainActivity` class and `tools:showIn` tells the content view to locate itself inside (under) the `app_bar_main.xml` UI definition, which we will be looking at after we look at the primary `activity_main.xml` top-level UI definition XML file.

Next, let's take a look at the `activity_main.xml` top-level UI definition that is called from the `MainActivity.java` class `onCreate()` method, as is standard operating procedure in Android application development. Right-click on `activity_main.xml`, and select the **Jump to Source** menu option to open this XML file in its own editing tab.

As you can see in Figure 8-6, this is the user interface definition that wires most of the XML files in the `res/layout` and `res/menu` folders to create a navigation drawer, shown in the **Preview** area, on the right side of the Android Studio IDEA.

The UI definition uses a `DrawerLayout` class for the parent layout container and uses an `<include>` child class to include the `app_bar_main` navigation bar, which you know contains the content view as well. Over this slides a navigation drawer, which uses the `NavigationView` class to define the sliding UI drawer layout definition, as you can see in Figure 8-6, highlighted in red. The NavigationView child tag uses an `app:headerLayout` to reference a `nav_header_main.xml` file and the `app:menu` attribute to reference the `activity_main_drawer.xml` menu hierarchy definition as shown by red lines drawn between the XML editor onto the Project hierarchy pane, in Figure 8-6.

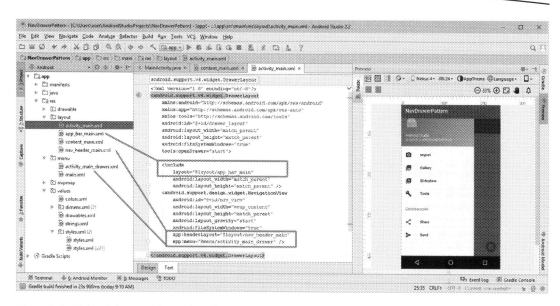

Figure 8-6. Right-click on activity_main.xml to Jump to Source to view DrawerLayout

This child `NavigationView` class is part of the `support.design` library's `widget` package, and is a subclass of the `FrameLayout` class, which provides fixed UI layout design containers. This class was designed to be used to provide developers with a standard **navigation menu** for their application. This `NavigationView` will typically be nested inside of a `DrawerLayout`, so the drawer slides out with a menu of options in it. This menu's selection options can be created using an XML menu resource file as we will see later on during this section. If you want to investigate this class further, you can visit the `NavigationView` page at the following developer URL:

https://**developer.android.com**/reference/android/**support**/**design**/
widget/**NavigationView**.html

The parent `DrawerLayout` class is part of the **support.v4** library's `widget` package, as you see highlighted in blue at the top of Figure 8-6, and as a layout container, is created (subclassed) using the `ViewGroup` superclass. The **DrawerLayout** serves as the top-level container, in this case, that is a UI drawer, to contain UI elements. This class was designed to allow developers to relatively easily create interactive "sliding drawers" that can be pulled out from one (left or primary) or even from both (left and right) sides (also called "edges") of the display screen.

Drawer position and direction are specified using a **layout_gravity** attribute set in child views, in this case, `NavigationView`. This attribute constant will define which side of the user interface design you want the drawer to open from. This will be left or right, unless you are supporting multi-directional language (left to right as well as right to left), in which case you will use start or end. You should only define one drawer for each vertical edge of your UI. If your layout configures more than one drawer per side, an exception (an error) will be "thrown" at runtime.

As you can see in Figure 8-6, you specify, using an `<include>`, the **app_bar_main** layout as a first child, setting width and height to **match_parent** using no layout_gravity. Next, add drawers as child views after the content view, and set the `layout_gravity` to left or `start`. Drawers commonly use `match_parent` for height with a fixed width; in this case, we use `wrap_content`, so that the drawer conforms to the menu content.

As per the Pure Android design pattern guidelines, any drawer positioned to the left (or start) would always contain content for navigating around the application. Any drawer positioned to the right (or end) would always contain actions to take on the content in the content view. This preserves the Pure Android navigation to the left, actions to the right, design pattern present in the `ActionBar` and applications. If you want to research the `DrawerLayout` class further, visit the following URL:

`https://`**developer.android.com**`/reference/android/`**support**`/`**v4**`/widget/`**DrawerLayout**`.html`

Let's drill down further into the UI design and take a look at the `app_bar_main.xml` file referenced in the `<include>` child tag in the `<DrawerLayout>` parent tag. **Include** is used to reference and nest a UI design component. Right-click the `app_bar_main.xml` file and select **Jump to Source** to open the tab seen in Figure 8-7.

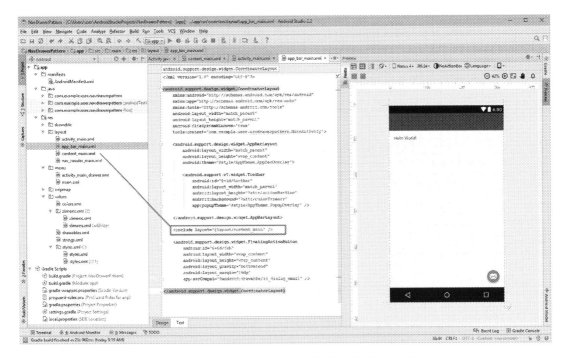

Figure 8-7. *Right-click app_bar_main.xml; Jump to Source and view CoordinatorLayout*

As you can see, this UI design component uses `CoordinatorLayout`, and references `content_main.xml` using another child `<include>` tag, as shown in red. Above the content view is an `<AppBarLayout>` layout container child tag containing a `<Toolbar>` widget as its child tag. Below the content view is a `<FloatingActionButton>` widget.

Android's `CoordinatorLayout` class is part of the Android support design library and widget package as you see highlighted in blue at the top of Figure 8-7, and as a UI layout container, is created using the `ViewGroup` superclass. A **CoordinatorLayout** is similar to a `FrameLayout`, and can be used to create fixed, top-level application user interface design such as a navigation bar over a content view, as Android Studio is doing here. It is used as a layout container to coordinate interactions between one or more child views, in this case, this includes a Toolbar, a FloatingActionButton, and the content view. To learn more about the `CoordinatorLayout`, visit this URL:

`https://`**`developer.android.com`**`/reference/android/`**`support`**`/`**`design`**`/`
`widget/`**`CoordinatorLayout`**`.html`

A `Toolbar` layout container is also a `ViewGroup` subclass, added in Android 5 API Level 21 to provide a standard toolbar for use in application content or UI design. The `Toolbar` design element is a generic `ActionBar` for use with application layouts. Whereas the Android `ActionBar` is part of an `Activity` that is controlled by the Android framework, the `Toolbar` is controlled by the developer and can be located at any (nesting) level of your UI design view hierarchy. An application can even designate this Toolbar to serve as the `ActionBar` for your `Activity`. This is done by using the `.setActionBar()` method call or the `.setSupportActionBar()` method call.

From left (or start, for bidirectional text language support) to right (or end) a `Toolbar` UI element can contain a number of different types of nested UI elements. The most common, located on the left, would be a navigation button, which can be seen as a three-bar icon in the `Toolbar` for the app on the left side in Figure 8-12 in the AVD. Notice that your Android Studio Preview does not include this, as it is passed through from the OS to the `Toolbar` using the `.setSupportActionBar()` method call. Navigation elements supported include the **Up arrow**, navigation **menu** icon, **close** icon, **collapse** icon, **finished** icon, or another icon of the application developer's choice. This button should be used to access navigation destinations within `Toolbar` UI layout container. The navigation button icon will be vertically aligned with, and scaled relative to, the Toolbar height attribute.

You can include a brand (sometimes called a "logo") image for your application, and this will come next in the `Toolbar`. This will be vertically aligned with, and scaled relative to, the `Toolbar height` attribute, and can be as wide as you like. I recommend a 2:1 or 3:1 aspect ratio, so you don't take up too much of your `Toolbar`.

Next comes a title, and (optionally) a subtitle. A title should be an indicator of the `Toolbar`'s current position in the navigation hierarchy and content contained there. A subtitle, if present, should indicate any additional information about the current content. After the title you can optionally add one or two UI elements such as icons, if you have room, based on your logo and title size. The application can also dynamically add views to the `Toolbar`. They will appear at this center position within a Toolbar. If your `Toolbar.LayoutParams` attribute for a UI element indicates a `Gravity` value of `CENTER_HORIZONTAL` that view will attempt to center in available space that remains in the `Toolbar`, after all the other elements have been measured.

The Action Menu, in this case the **Settings** menu item, will pin to the right (or end) of the Toolbar. This is shown in Figure 8-13 as three dots on the right side of the `Toolbar`. This offers important or typical actions along with an overflow menu for additional actions. Action buttons are vertically aligned with the Toolbar height. If you want to delve further into the Toolbar class, visit this URL:

https://**developer.android.com**/reference/android/widget/**Toolbar**.html

The FloatingActionButton class does not involve the ViewGroup class and is thus a UI widget and not a UI layout container. It's created using the ImageButton class, which is in turn created using the ImageView class (a direct View subclass itself).

Floating action buttons are often used to expose actions (UI options) you wish to prioritize for your users. In this case, this is e-mail access, as you can see in Figure 8-7. These are earmarked using a circular icon, floating (using shadows) above the UI surface. These floating action buttons come in two sizes, default and mini. The size can be controlled with the fabSize (Floating Action Button Size) attribute, but most developers will use the Pure Android design constants provided.

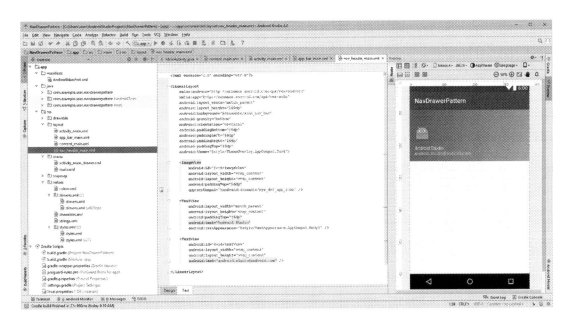

Figure 8-8. Right-click on nav_header_main.xml; Jump to Source to view LinearLayout

Because this class descends from ImageView, it inherits the .setImageDrawable() method, so you will be able to control the drawable (graphic) which is used in the Button using a .setImageDrawable(Drawable drawable) method call. The background color for this FloatingActionButton is preset to utilize your OS theme colorAccent attribute. If you wish to change the color, you can specify a different color using the .setBackgroundTintList(ColorS tateList) method call.

Whereas the app_bar_main.xml UI definition contains the AppBarLayout container, which contains the Toolbar, includes the content_main.xml UI definition and finally a FloatingActionButton, the nav_header_main.xml UI definition, shown in Figure 8-8, is referenced with a NavigationView layout container in the top-level activity_main XML UI definition. This combines it with the navigation menu, which we will be looking at next. This main navigation header design uses another "legacy" Android layout container from API Level 1 called a **LinearLayout**, which is used to create a horizontal or vertical (in this case) orientation collection of UI design elements.

The LinearLayout container, seen in Figure 8-8, contains ImageView and TextView UI elements (View widgets) just like the Hello Universe application you designed in Chapter 6, so you already know what these widgets do for your UI design. The result of this design can be seen in the Android Studio Preview pane (on the right side).

Creating Menu Structures for a UI Design: The Android Menu Interface

In Android, most of the heavy lifting to create and implement a menu is done by Android OS, making this perfect for an Absolute Beginner title, so we'll cover it here in Chapter 8. Developers design their Menu objects using XML menu definition files, contained in the app/res/menu folder, as seen on the left in blue in Figure 8-9.

Android supports several important types of menus, each of which have different features. **Context menus** are like right-click context-sensitive menus in popular OS platforms, and in Android these do not support key shortcuts and visual icons. The long-click on any UI or layout element is used to access these context menus (using a touchscreen) if a right-mouse button is not available to the user.

Options menus are provided in the OS **chrome** (remember chrome is perimeter OS-provided UI functions and decoration), as shown in Figure 8-13. Icon menus don't support item check marks, and can only display the "condensed" (shortened) title for each menu item.

Expanded options menus become available if six or more menu items are visible. These can be accessed via a 'More' item in the icon menu and don't show item icons. Pure Android design principles also recommend against using item check marks so the menu stays compact for the user. However, you can use them, if they are necessary.

Menus can also feature **submenus**. Submenus do not support icons for menu items and do not allow nested submenu structures, to try to keep Pure Android menuing as simple as possible for the users.

Android provides the Menu interface for managing the **MenuItem** objects contained in a **Menu** object. By default, every Activity supports an options menu of actions or options. You can add items to this menu and handle clicks on your additions. The easiest way of adding menu items is by "inflating" an XML file into the menu via the **MenuInflater** method. The easiest way of attaching Java code to clicks is via onOptionsItemSelected(MenuItem) and onContextItemSelected(MenuItem) method calls.

The important thing for you to learn regarding menu design in Android is how to create the parent <menu> XML structure with child <group> and <item> substructures. This can be seen in the **activity_main_drawer.xml** file, which is seen in Figure 8-9.

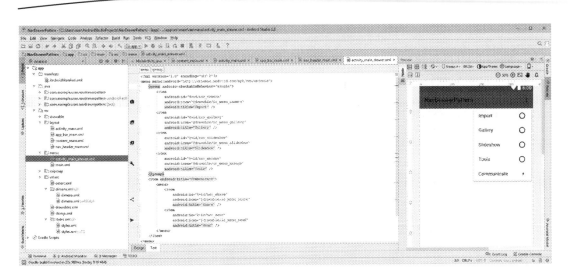

Figure 8-9. *Right-click activity_ main _drawer.xml and Jump to Source and view Menu*

To view the `activity_main_drawer` Menu object XML definition, right-click on the XML file and select **Jump to Source**. As you can see, there is a parent `<menu>` object, which contains a child `<group>` object that contains four `<item>` MenuItem objects. These MenuItem objects each contain an ID, `icon` (drawable) and `title` (text) values, which provide Import, Gallery, Slideshow, and Tools menu options, in a sliding navigation drawer. The drawables are kept in the `app/res/drawable` folder and can be seen in Figure 8-14, if you want to see the actual files that are referenced.

After the main menu group, there is an `<item>` tag used as a **menu header**, using only an `android:title` attribute (or parameter if you prefer that term). Since it is not a MenuItem that will generate click events, it does not need an `android:id` attribute because the object will not be referenced in your Java code; it is simply decorative. There is a child `<menu>` tag under this `<item>` tag, which creates your submenu structure, under which are your child `<item>` tags, defining submenu items. Submenus are thus created using child `<menu>` objects under a parent `<menu>` object. There are two submenu items created using `<item>` tags for share and send functions.

Finally, let's right-click on the other application **main.xml** definition file and select **Jump to Source** and take a look at the **Settings** menu item available using the **overflow** (three vertical dots in the ActionBar) menu, as shown in Figure 8-10. The main.xml holds the top-level menu for the application, and uses the same design process of a parent `<menu>` tag and child `<item>` tags; in this case, the settings for the application are all that we need in the menu, at least for the moment. We could add a **Help** menu item, for instance, to explain how this application should be used.

Figure 8-10. Open the menu.xml application menu; preview your Settings menu (right)

Now that we've taken a look at how the XML UI design definitions have been put together, let's take a high-level view of how this all wires together, to cement how this all works together in your mind, and then we'll run the application in the AVD and see how it works. Then we'll look at the Android Manifest XML definition, and finally at how the Java 8 code works.

Visualizing the UI Design: High-Level View of XML and Classes Used

Let's visualize the complex layout using a diagram, which can be seen in Figure 8-11, since there is a lot of nesting (at least three levels of nested XML definitions) and Java classes used within all of these XML definitions. As an Absolute Beginner, you should always do this, either in your head or on paper (or using GIMP, as I did), to make sure that you comprehend exactly what's going on in Android to create a design pattern, using Android's View (widget) and ViewGroup (layout container) classes. As you become a more advanced Android developer, you'll need to do this less and less.

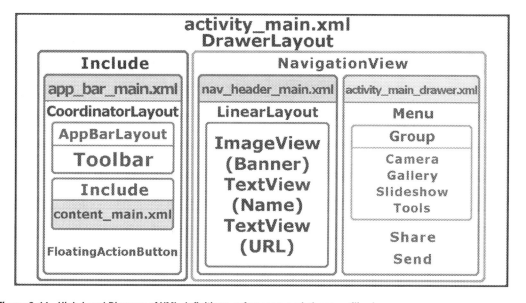

Figure 8-11. High-Level Diagram of XML definitions, references, and classes utilized

As you can see the top-level `activity_main.xml` UI design pattern definition has the `DrawerLayout` class as its parent tag, and as the parent class, from a UI design perspective. As you can see in the right side of Figure 8-13, when the options menu (the three horizontal bar icon) is clicked, the sliding drawer will cover the other major UI components (`ActionBar`, or `AppBar`, and main content view), and contains the navigation header and drawer menu system, seen on the right portion of Figure 8-11.

The `app_bar_main.xml` second-level definition, seen on the left, handles the `AppBarLayout`, which contains the `Toolbar`, using the `CoordinatorLayout` to combine this `AppBar` with the `FloatingActionButton`, and uses an `Include` to tie in the third-level `content_main.xml` definition, which contains your content for each screen referenced using the Menu's `MenuItems`. This is also contained in this top-level `DrawerLayout`.

The `nav_header_main.xml` is contained in a `NavigationView` in the `DrawerLayout`, and uses `LinearLayout` to build a header bar for the sliding drawer using an `Image` (`ImageView`) and `Text` UI elements. Also contained in this `NavigationView` is your `activity_main_drawer.xml` Menu object definition, with four `MenuItem` objects in one group and two `MenuItems` at the end of the Menu definition that are not in a group.

Previewing the UI Design in the Nexus 5 AVD: Rendering the UI Design

Let's use your Nexus 5 AVD, and preview the design in an Android device, so you can see the menu icon in the `app_bar_main.xml`, which is provided by the Android OS menu system but which is not (as yet) supported in the Android Studio Preview pane. Use the **Run ➤ Run 'app'** menu sequence, and launch the AVD, as shown in Figure 8-12. Select the Nexus 5 and click the **OK** button. After the AVD loads into memory the app will launch in the emulator, which you can see in Figure 8-13. Click the menu icon, to make sure a UI drawer slides onto the screen, seen on the right, in Figure 8-13.

Figure 8-12. Use the Run menu to run the app, which will initialize the Nexus 5 AVD

Click on menu items to make sure they do nothing, for now. The menu will close.

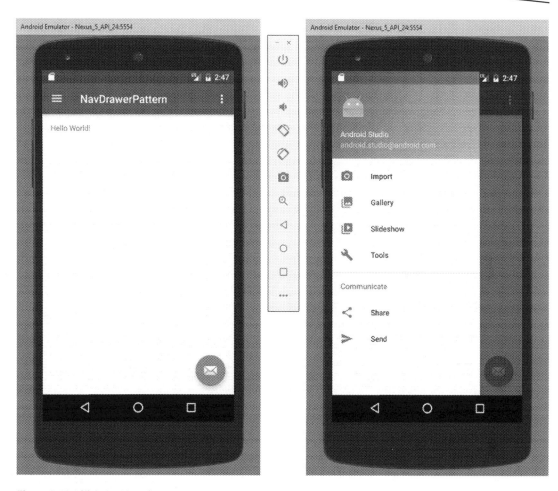

Figure 8-13. Click the Menu icon at the top left and test the sliding nav drawer

Now that we have tested (and analyzed) the Android Studio code, let's take a quick look at the Android manifest, and then dive into the Java code, which is the most complex part of the Android application created by Android Studio for you.

Application Configuration XML: The AndroidManifest.xml

All of this functionality does not require any special Android manifest XML definition permissions, and only a couple of new settings, which we will go over in this section, to reinforce your knowledge of working with the Android manifest XML.

As you can see in Figure 8-14, highlighted in green, Android Studio has set the android:label attribute, for both the <application> and the <activity> section, to label the app NavDrawerPattern.

There is a new attribute (parameter) called `android:supportsRtl` that turns on the bidirectional screen language display (LTR or RTL for some non-ASCII languages), which is highlighted in yellow in Figure 8-14. This is why we are using `start` instead of left and end instead of right in the UI design XML definitions in this chapter, and since this is an application-wide setting it is in the `<application>` tag, along with the `android:theme`, `android:icon` and `android:allowBackup` parameters, which you are already familiar with, from the first application we created earlier.

Also, notice that in the `<activity>` tag we set the `NoActionBar` application theme since we have provided our own decorative `ActionBar` in this user interface design. In the next section, you will see how to make the `AppBarLayout` and its `Toolbar` into the `ActionBar` for this UI design pattern using Java methods of the `Activity` superclass, allowing us to use the `NoActionBar` theme to remove the Android OS `ActionBar`, which would be redundant (and confusing to the user) since the UI design provides one of its own, with features customized to the sliding drawer UI pattern.

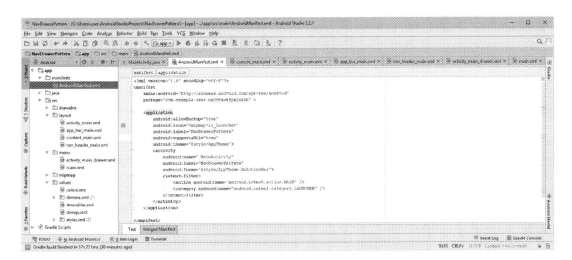

Figure 8-14. Right-click AndroidManifest.xml, and Jump to Source to preview the XML

Next, let's get a bit more advanced, and take a look at what the Java code is doing for this admittedly more advanced sliding drawer Android application design pattern, while at the same time learning more about the Android classes involved in making this main activity reference the UI design XML, and making it interactive.

Application Programming Logic: Looking at the Android API Java Code

Finally, let's get a bit complicated (for the Absolute Beginner, at least), and take a look at the `MainActivity.java` code generated by Android Studio. Click on the `MainActivity.java` editing tab, shown selected on the left in Figure 8-15, and look at five methods that comprise this public class, which extends `AppCompatActivity`, which we covered in detail earlier in the book, in Chapter 6, and which implements a `NavigationView.OnNavigationItemSelectedListener` Java interface. Let's start with the smaller (shorter) methods, which deal with menu processing and UI navigation, and then cover the two larger (longer) methods that deal with the event processing (onNavigationItemSelected) and creating the objects for the application in system memory (onCreate). All this code is needed to make the sliding UI fully functional.

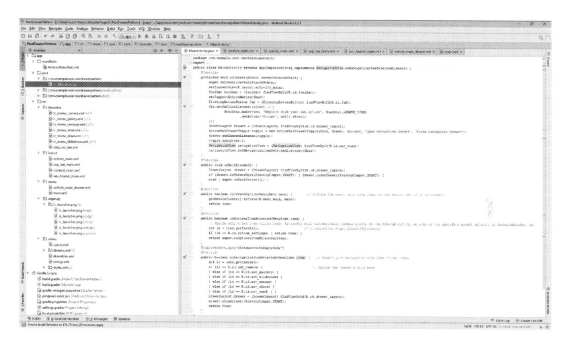

Figure 8-15. Click on the MainActivity.java editing tab to look at the five methods

The public Boolean onCreateOptionsMenu(Menu menu) method creates the options menu in system memory by inflating (turning XML definitions into Java objects) an XML menu definition, called main.xml, in your app/res/menu/ directory, by using the getMenuInflater().inflate() method, and returns a true value to the calling method, signifying the menu is inflated into memory. Your method Java code looks like this:

```
@Override
public boolean onCreateOptionsMenu(Menu menu) {
    getMenuInflater().inflate(R.menu.main, menu);
    return true;
}
```

Although used with a Menu object, onCreateOptionsMenu(Menu menu) is a part of the Activity superclass, and therefore its subclass. This is where you'll initialize the contents of your Activity's options menu, using a MenuInflater object using a **method chain**. The getMenuInflater() method chains to (calls) the .inflate() method, which takes the XML Menu object definition and loads it into the Menu object named menu. After this has been done, the onCreateOptionsMenu() method returns true, to signify successful inflation of the Menu object named menu, passed into the method.

Although also used with the Menu class, onOptionsItemSelected(MenuItem item) is also a part of the Activity superclass, and therefore its subclasses. This is where you process your menu item selections in your Activity's options menu, by using the .getItemId() method from the Adapter class (object) that is used to process **lists**.

This method takes a MenuItem object named item passed into the method, and then calls the .getItemId() off of that item MenuItem object, and places that integer value into an id variable, which is then processed using an if-then-else loop, to determine which MenuItem has been selected by the user. In this case, if the "Settings" MenuItem has been selected the method will return a true value. Finally, the method calls the superclass method with the same name, for further processing, using super.onOptionsItemSelected(item), using the following Java code method structure:

```
@Override
public boolean onOptionsItemSelected(MenuItem item) {
    int id = item.getItemId();
    if (id == R.id.action_settings) { return true; }
    return super.onOptionsItemSelected(item);
}
```

The onBackPressed() is also a part of the Activity superclass, and therefore each of its subclasses. This is where you define what is to be done when the **Back** button is used in the Android OS or the Android device hardware. In this case, this will close the sliding drawer UI, if it is open, or pass the onBackPressed() up to the superclass for further processing using the **super** keyword, if the sliding drawer UI is closed. The Java 8 code will look something like this:

```
@Override
public void onBackPressed() {
    DrawerLayout drawer = (DrawerLayout)findViewById(R.id.drawer_layout);
    if (drawer.isDrawerOpen(GravityCompat.START) { drawer.closeDrawer(GravityCompat.START); }
    else { super.onBackPressed(); }
}
```

What this does is to instantiate a DrawerLayout object (named drawer), and call the .isDrawerOpen() method, to see if the sliding drawer is open on the screen. If it is, the .closeDrawer() method is called to close the drawer. The **GravityCompat** class (a backwards compatibility gravity constants helper class defining constants) is used with the **START** constant we have been using for our bidirectional interface design (supports RTL and LTR text and user interface design). If the drawer is not open, then the else part of the statement passes the onBackPressed() method call up to the superclass for processing, using super.onBackPressed().

The onNavigationItemSelected() method also takes in a MenuItem object named item as its input and processes it, however, this menu is the one inside of the drawer, not in the Activity menu, which has only one Settings option. This menu is accessed through a NavigationView parent, as you saw earlier in the XML definition.

Our Activity subclass definition implements a NavigationView Java interface for the onNavigationItemSelectedListener, using the following class declaration code:

```
public class MainActivity extends    AppCompatActivity
                          implements NavigationView.OonNavigationItemSelectedListener { code
                          body }
```

The next method that we need to examine is onNavigationItemSelected(MenuItem). This is in the body of our class code due to the **implements** keyword, which wires in the NavigationView.onNavigationItemSelectedListener interface, and therefore requires that we override this method with one of our own, which processes MenuItem selections. Since this is an "empty method body" for now, while we get the bootstrap infrastructure code working, we need to add the **@SupressWarnings** statement, telling the Android Studio compiler that our application UI doing nothing is not an error, and that we know what we are doing, so it can suppress the errors regarding this.

```
@SupressWarnings("StatementWithEmptyBody")
@Override
public boolean onNavigationItemSelected(MenuItem item) {
    int      id = item.getItemId();
    if      (id == R.id.nav_camera)    { // Camera Logic Here    }
    else if (id == R.id.nav_gallery)   { // Gallery Logic Here   }
    else if (id == R.id.nav_slideshow) { // Slideshow Logic Here }
    else if (id == R.id.nav_manage)    { // Manage Logic Here     }
    else if (id == R.id.nav_share)     { // Share Logic Here      }
    else if (id == R.id.nav_send)      { // Send Logic Here       }
    DrawerLayout drawer = (DrawerLayout)findViewById(R.id.drawer_layout);
    drawer.closeDrawer(GravityCompat.START);
    return true;
}
```

The actual onNavigationItemSelected() method takes in a MenuItem object, names it **item**, inside of the parameter area of the method, and processes it within the body of the method and returns a Boolean result (true if the processing completed).

Inside the method an **id** integer variable is created and assigned to the item ID value using a .getItemId() method call. The majority of the method body is a 6-line if-else-if evaluation loop that ascertains which MenuItem has been clicked by using XML ID values referenced by using the R.id.name method used by Android to reference XML-defined application UI objects.

After the if-else-if processing, a DrawerLayout object is instantiated, and the .closeDrawer() method is called with the GravityCompat.START constant to show which direction the drawer should slide shut. When you tested this application, you saw that selecting any of the menu options automatically closes this sliding UI drawer.

Let's split the onCreate() into logical sections to examine it object by object to see how the sliding drawer UI is inserted to memory and controlled by the events queue (CPU). The first two lines of onCreate() are standard fare in Android, and set up the object's instance states in a Bundle passed up to the Activity class onCreate() using the super keyword, and wire the ContentView object to your top-level UI definition, activity_main, which we analyzed during the first two-thirds of this chapter. After that Android instantiates a Toolbar object named toolbar and wire it up to the <toolbar> definition seen in the middle of Figure 8-7, by using an android:id parameter, inside of a findViewById(Resource) method call. The next line sets support for that Toolbar object named toolbar to serve as the ActionBar object for the Activity. The code for this Activity creation and Toolbar instantiation looks like the following:

```
@Override
public void onCreate(Bundle savedInstanceState) {
    super.onCreate(savedInstanceState);
    setContentView(R.layout.activity_main);
    Toolbar toolbar = (Toolbar)findViewById(R.id.toolbar);
    setSupportActionBar(toolbar);
```

The next section of code instantiates the FloatingActionButton object and names it **fab**, referencing the UI widget's XML definition in app_bar_main.xml using the ID parameter. Then it uses the fab object to call the .setOnClickListener() method and sets up an onClick() event handler structure, which you learned about in Chapter 7.

```
FloatingActionButton fab = (FloatingActionButton)findViewById(R.id.fab);
fab.setOnCLickListener(new View.OnClickListener() {
    @Override
    public void onClick(View view) {
        Snackbar.make(view, "Replace with your own action", Snackbar.LENGTH_LONG)
                .setAction("Action", null)
                .show();
    }
});
```

Inside of the onClick() event handler Android Studio 2.3 creates a **Snackbar** object, using the Snackbar.make() method call, and chains a .setAction() and .show() method call to this creating a Snackbar.make().setAction().show()code chain. The .make() method takes in the onClick() method's view object, the message, and the Snackbar.LENGTH_LONG constant, which defines the length of time to display the message. The .setAction() method allows users to interact with a Snackbar, and allows you to specify the button name value, in this case "Action" and the action to execute, for this empty bootstrap application this is currently null (do nothing).

Android Snackbar is a fairly new class, which is used to display brief messages on the lower portion of the screen to update users as to what is happening with the processing of your application logic for the current action or operation. Snackbars appear above all the other UI elements on the screen. One Snackbar can be displayed at a time, and will automatically disappear, after the specified length of time, or after user interaction elsewhere on the screen. Snackbars may be swiped off-screen.

The next section of code instantiates a DrawerLayout object and names it drawer and references the DrawerLayout ID of drawer_layout, in the activity_main.xml file. Then an ActionBarDrawerToggle object is instantiated and named toggle, using a Java **new** keyword and the ActionBarDrawerToggle() constructor method, which takes Context (this), DrawerLayout and Toolbar objects, as well as content description strings to be used by users who may have physical impairment, such as blindness, for instance.

```
DrawerLayout drawer = (DrawerLayout)findViewById(R.id.drawer_layout);
ActionBarDrawerToggle toggle = new ActionBarDrawerToggle( this, drawer, toolbar,
                                                "Open navigation drawer",
                                                "Close navigation drawer" );

drawer.setDrawerListener(toggle);  // Deprecated Method!
toggle.syncState();
```

The ActionBarDrawerToggle class provides an object that will wire together the functionality of this DrawerLayout sliding drawer UI design pattern and the Android ActionBar functions, which have been replaced with a custom Toolbar in this design.

The .setDrawerListener(toggle) method call off the drawer object wires the DrawerLayout object to the toggle ActionBarDrawerToggle object. You will notice that this method is deprecated (lined-out in Android Studio) which means that it is scheduled for removal from the API. We will look at the solution to this in the next section. The final line of code calls the .syncState() method off the toggle object. This synchronizes the toggle indicator with the state of your DrawerLayout.

The last two lines of Java code instantiates a NavigationView object, and names it navigationView and uses the nav_view ID in the activity_main.xml UI definition file to inflate the NavigationView object, configuring it with the specified XML parameters, which can be seen in Figure 8-6. Notice that you do not always have to use an .inflate() method to configure (inflate) a Java object with XML specified parameters in Android. Finally, the .setN avigationItemSelectedListener(Context) method call is used to attach an event listener to the NavigationView object.

```
NavigationView navigationView = (NavigationView)findViewById(R.id.nav_view);
navigationView.setNavigationItemSelectedListener(this);
```

Finally, let's take a look at how you would deal with recently deprecated code, so that you know the work process regarding how to research this scenario using the search engine of your choice (since I am a Google Android and Chrome developer, I'd logically select Google for this task).

Deprecated Java Code: Researching Replacement APIs

The last thing I want to show you in this chapter, since Android Studio coded a deprecated method that was lined-out in the editing pane, which to me is not optimal, is how to research what to do if the Google Android OS Development Team takes away one of your API calls that you are utilizing for your application. The fastest way to find a solution is to use a **keyword pair** "API-component deprecated," in this case, this would put **setdrawerlistener deprecated** in your search bar, as is shown at the top of Figure 8-16. As you can see in the search result, you'll often find the solution to the problem in the short description of the search listing, in this case, "Use addDrawerListener() instead" as shown at the bottom of Figure 8-16.

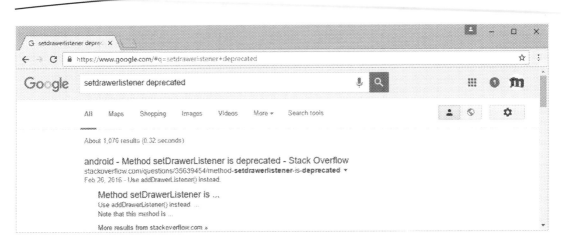

Figure 8-16. *Search for information with search term "setdrawerlistener deprecated"*

It can often be that easy, and luckily, it is here, since this is an Absolute Beginner title! So, let's try this simple solution, and see if it works. Click on the MainActivity. java editing tab and change the onCreate() method's fourteenth line of code, drawer. setDrawerListener(toggle); to be drawer.addDrawerListener(toggle); as can be seen highlighted in light blue and yellow near the bottom of Figure 8-17. No wavy red error highlights appear, so the next step is to use a **Run ➤ Run 'app'** menu sequence and test the application in the Nexus AVD emulator to see if it works the same way.

Figure 8-17. *Replace the .setDrawerListener(toggle) with .addDrawerListener(toggle)*

I will forgo another screenshot that would be a duplicate of Figure 8-13, as the application works in exactly the same way as it did with the deprecated method call. Congratulations, you have now created a second more advanced user interface design pattern, which we can enhance during the second half of the book with new media assets and special effects as we learn about advanced Android API components.

Summary

In this eighth chapter, you learned about Android design patterns, as well as implementing a sliding drawer user interface, which conforms to the sliding/swiping UI design pattern, as well as the concept of optimizing screen real estate, so the user has the best experience possible.

We covered Android design patterns, including material design; hardware device characteristics; specialized APIs; future APIs, for emerging market verticals; and Pure Android concepts, such as accessibility, compatibility, confirmation, acknowledgment, widgets, swiping, and sliding view designs.

Next we looked at another popular Android design pattern and learned how to have Android Studio create this design pattern for us, using the Create New Android Application series of dialogs. We analyzed the XML markup, user interface design, and Java programming logic to learn new Android API components and design concepts.

We learned how to diagnose and solve deprecated API components, even if these are introduced by Android Studio, and how to correct and test these upgrades and get a clean, functional application.

Next, in Chapter 9, you'll learn about digital imaging concepts, and how to use digital image assets in Android applications, like NinePatch assets and multi-state ImageButton user interface elements. We're going to start getting more advanced from this point on out in the book, so you will no longer be an Absolute Beginner!

Android Graphic Design: Making UI Designs Visual

In the first half of this book, I tried to stay as much "inside" of Android Studio, the Android API, and Android OS as much as possible, so that we can get the IDEA to either code or help us design as much of an application as possible. This approach still gives you a good "head start" on the core classes, methods, and design concepts that an Android 7 developer should have knowledge of, and eventually mastery of. I am trying to give you the global overview of what the main components are in Android currently, and how everything in Android OS fits together.

In the second half of the book, which will show you how to incorporate new media elements into your app's UI design, such as digital imagery, digital audio, digital video, and 2D animation, we will venture "outside" of the core Android development tools, allowing you to use open software packages outside of Android Studio that are commonly used by application developers for new media content development. In this chapter, we'll cover digital imagery.

We will utilize GIMP 2.8 in this chapter, to explore the graphics concepts for this chapter and get some hands-on experience in applying image compositing concepts and techniques we will be discovering during the course of the chapter. There is no way I can cover all of the graphics concepts and topics I would like to in one single chapter, at least not using less than a hundred pages! If you want to dive into digital imaging specifically, check out the *Digital Image Compositing Fundamentals* (2015) title or the *Android Studio New Media Fundamentals* (2015) title, both of which are currently available on the http://www.apress.com website (search under my author name of Wallace Jackson).

We will be covering several of the core Android classes that are used to implement graphic design elements, such as `ImageButton`, `ImageView` (which we have already covered in Chapter 6), and `NinePatch`. During this chapter, you will utilize these three Android graphics classes to **skin** the Sliding Drawer UI layout container design. **Skinning** the UI design using graphics elements will enhance the visual aspects of this UI design, and increase its interest to the end user, as well as increasing its perceived level of professionalism. First, we will go over some foundational digital imaging concepts, so that this material makes more sense to you.

© Wallace Jackson 2017
W. Jackson, *Android Apps for Absolute Beginners*, DOI 10.1007/978-1-4842-2268-3_9

Imaging Concepts, Formats, and Techniques

The first thing that we need to do is to get a knowledge foundation regarding the concepts, formats, and terms that we are going to use during the rest of this book regarding working with digital images. This area is most commonly called graphic design, although I am going to approach it from a more professional "digital imaging" or "image compositing" standpoint. As you already know, Android terms graphic design elements **drawables**.

The concepts, formats, techniques, and terminology that I cover in this chapter will also apply to animation and digital video new media assets, as both of these are based on digital imagery in one way or another, so we will be able to build on the knowledge base created in this chapter in future chapters, which I am trying to do in each and every chapter in this book, so your knowledge of Android 7.1.1 development increases exponentially, and in a logical fashion.

First, we will cover the **pixel**, the foundational element of the digital image; and then the concept of **resolution**, or the size of the digital image; and then the concept of **aspect ratio**, or the shape of the digital image. Once we are done with the second dimension (2D) aspects, we will go into the third dimension (3D) and look at how the colors of each pixel are created, using red, green, and blue (RGB) **layers** of color, and then at how transparency is defined within an image using a fourth **alpha** layer that contains transparency values. After that, we'll get into more advanced digital imaging concepts, like **compositing** and pixel **blending**, and take a look at how all this knowledge is used when using digital image formats and their **codecs** to compress digital image assets.

The Foundation of Digital Images: The Pixel

Digital imagery is made up of two-dimensional (2D) arrays (grids) containing **pixels**. The industry term pixel is a conjugation of two words: **pictures** (commonly called **pix**) and **elements** (shortened, to be simply **els**). The number of pixels in a digital image asset should be expressed using a term called **resolution**. This is the number of pixels in both the width (denoted using a **W,** or an **X** for the **x-axis**) and the height (denoted using an **H,** or a **Y** for the y-axis) image dimensions. The resolution of an image asset is usually expressed using two (X and Y) numbers with an "x" in the middle, such as **800x480**, or using the word "by," such as **800 by 480 pixels**.

To find the total number of pixels that are in a 2D image, simply multiply the width pixels by the height pixels. For instance, an HDTV resolution 1920 by 1080 image will contain 2,073,600 pixels, over 2 million pixels, also referred to as two **megapixels**. The more pixels that are in an image, the higher its resolution. Just like with digital cameras, which range from 3 megapixel smartphone cameras to 75 megapixel DSLRs, the more pixels that are in the digital image grid or array, the higher quality level the image will have.

Android supports everything from **low-resolution**, 320 or 480 pixel display screens for Android smartwatches, or entry-level flip-phones and small screen phones; to **medium-resolution**, 854 by 480 pixel display screens for mini-tablets and smartphones; to **high-resolution**, 1280 by 720 pixel display screens, for HD smartphones and medium tablets; to **extra-high-resolution**, 1920 by 1080 pixel display screens for large tablets and iTV sets, to the recent **super-high-resolution**, 2560 by 1440 phones (such as Samsung's Galaxy S5), and finally, new ultra-high-resolution, 4096 by 2160 (known as "4K") pixel display screens for tablets, smartphones, and 4K iTV sets.

The Shape of a Digital Image: The Aspect Ratio

A slightly more complicated aspect (no pun intended) of image resolution would be the image's **aspect ratio**, a concept which also applies to Android device (hardware) display screens. Aspect ratio is the **ratio of width to height** or **W:H**, or, if you like to think in terms of an x-axis and y-axis, it would be X:Y. The aspect ratio will define the shape of an image or display screen; that is, how square or rectangular (popularly called widescreen) the image or the display screen might be. A tall rectangular display is popularly termed a portrait display.

A 1:1 aspect ratio display screen (or digital image) is perfectly square, like a smartwatch screen. It is important to note that it is the ratio between these two numbers that defines the shape of the image or screen and not these numbers themselves. That is why it is called the aspect **ratio**, although it is often called the "aspect" for short.

Many Android display screens these days use an HDTV widescreen aspect ratio, which is **16:9**. However, some use a less wide, or taller, **16:10** (or 8:5, if you prefer) aspect ratio. Even wider screens will also surely appear on the market soon, so look for **16:8** (or 2:1, if you prefer) ultra-wide screens, which will have the 2160 by 1080 resolution, and instead of being taller than 16:9 aspect ratio screens will be shorter than 16:9 screens.

An image aspect ratio is usually expressed as the smallest set or pair of numbers that can be achieved on either side of the aspect ratio colon. If you paid attention in high school, when you were learning all about lowest (or least) common denominators, then this aspect ratio mathematics should be fairly easy to understand and to calculate.

I usually do this mathematical matriculation (say this five times rapidly, to make what we are about to do seem easier) by continuing to divide each side by **two**. Taking the fairly odd-ball 1280 by 1024 (called SXGA in the display industry) resolution as our example, half of 1280:1024 is 640:512, and half of that would be 320:256, half of that is 160:128, and half of that again is 80:64, half of that is 40:32, half of that is 20:16, half of that is 10:8, half of that is 5:4, so an SXGA screen will be said to utilize a **5:4** aspect ratio.

All of the above ratios are the same aspect ratio, and all are valid. So if you want to take the really easy way out, replace the "x" in your image resolution with a colon and you have an aspect ratio for the image, although distilling it down to its lowest format, as we've done here, is far more useful to visualize the shape.

Original PC screens used a squarer **4:3** aspect ratio, and early **3:2** aspect ratio CRT "cathode ray tube" TV sets were nearly square. Smartwatch aspect ratios are square, at 320x320, 400x400, 480x480 or 1:1 aspect ratio. HD and UHD iTV sets use a 16:9 widescreen aspect ratio. The closer the numbers on either side of the colon are to each other in size, the more square an image or a screen will be.

A 2:1 aspect is a widescreen display, and a 3:1 aspect display would be downright **panoramic**! The current market trend is certainly toward wider screens and higher resolution displays; however, Android smartwatches could change this trend back toward square aspect ratios, which are certainly useful in a wide variety of applications.

Coloring Your Digital Images: RGB Color Theory

So now you understand digital image pixels, and how they're arranged using 2D rectangular arrays, at a specific aspect ratio that defines their rectangular shape. The next logical aspect (again, no pun intended) to look into, is how each of those pixels assign their color values. Color values for pixels are defined by the amount of three colors, **red**, **green**, and **blue** (hence the term **RGB**), which are present in varying amounts in each pixel.

Android (as well as other device) display screens utilize **additive color**, which is where the wavelengths of light for each RGB color plane are summed together. Additive color can be used by consumer electronics devices to create literally billions of different color values, and is used in popular LED displays used in iTVs, smartphones, laptops, e-readers, and tablets. Additive color is the opposite of **subtractive color**, which is utilized in printers.

To show the difference, under a subtractive color model, mixing a red color with a green (using inks) will yield a purple color, whereas in an additive color model, mixing a red color with a green color (using light) will yield a yellow color. Subtractive color models are limited in the spectrum of color that they can produce, whereas the additive color model can produce every color under the rainbow (or, I should say, every color in the universe!).

The amount, or numbers, of red, green, and blue "shades" or intensities of light that you have available to mix together will determine the total amount of colors that you will be able to reproduce. In today's digital device hardware capabilities, we can produce **eight bits** (8-bit) or **256 levels** of light intensity for each red, green, and blue (RGB) color. Some of the newer devices are supporting **ten bits** (10-bit) or **1024 levels** of light intensity.

We can generate these color values for each pixel individually, so every pixel in your image can have 256 levels (or 1024 levels) of color intensity variation for each of the red, green, and blue values. This will therefore use one byte (8-bits) of data per red, green, and blue color, unless you are using 10-bit color. A byte uses an 8-bit data value, which allows it to represent the color intensity level from a minimum of zero (off, no color contributed, or black, if all the RGB planes are using this value) to a maximum of 255 (on, maximum color contributed, or white, if all RGB planes are using this value).

The Number of Colors in a Digital Image: Color Depth

The amount of data that is used to represent the amount or number of colors in a digital image is referred to as the **color depth** of an image. It's important to note that in digital images less than 8 bits can be used to represent the amount of color in an image when using an **indexed color** model that uses a color palette instead of RGB. There are several common color depth levels used in the digital imaging industry. I'll outline the most common ones here, along with the digital image file formats used with each color depth in the Android 7 OS. The lowest color depth exists using **8-bit indexed color** digital image format. The indexed color image has a maximum of 256 total color values per pixel, and would use the GIF and PNG8 image formats to contain this indexed color type of digital image data. An indexed color image does not have three RGB color planes, so it is generally three times smaller than "True Color" RGB imagery. Instead of three RGB color planes, indexed color uses a **palette**, which is a data array containing up to 256 color values, used to represent all of the colors in the indexed image.

A medium color depth image, which is not natively supported in Android, but which I will discuss here, for continuity of learning, will feature the **16-bit** "High Color" color depth. A high color depth image will contain **65,536** colors. This would be calculated as 256 times 256 (8-bit and 8-bit is 16-bit), and is supported using TARGA (TGA), Tagged Image File Format (TIFF), and the Windows BMP digital image file format.

A 24-bit truecolor color depth image will feature the full 8-bit color data values for each RGB color plate (color plane) and will be capable of displaying more than 16.7 million potential colors per pixel. This is calculated as 256 times 256 times 256 (8-bit red and 8-bit green and 8-bit blue is 24-bit RGB), and equals **16,777,216** colors. Android file formats that are capable of supporting 24-bit color include JPEG (using the .jpg file extension), PNG24 **and** PNG32 (using a .png extension), and WebP (using a .webp extension), which stands for WebPhoto.

Using 24-bit color depth will give you the highest digital image quality level, which is why Android 7.1.1 prefers the use of the PNG24 or the JPEG image file format. Since PNG24 is **lossless**, which means that it loses no quality (and none of the original image's data) during the compression process, it has the highest quality compression, and the lowest original image data loss, along with the highest quality color depth. This is a reason why PNG24 and PNG32 are the preferred digital image formats to use, as far as Android OS is concerned, because the usage of Portable Network Graphics ultimately produces the highest quality visual result for an Android application.

It is important to note that there are higher color depth images out there, as we discussed with 30-bit color, or "Deep Color," images. These are also called **HDRI**, or **High Dynamic Range Images**, which use 30-bit, 36-bit, 48-bit, and even 64-bit color depth (if there is an alpha channel). The hope is that the Android 7.1.1 OS (and device hardware) will move to support these extremely high quality digital image color depth standards, which are now currently being utilized for advanced i3D console games, as well as in the new Samsung SUHD 4K iTV Set.

A 30-bit deep color depth image will feature a full 10-bit color data value for each RGB color plate (color plane), and will be capable of displaying **1,073,741,824** potential colors per image pixel. This is calculated as 1024 times 1024 times 1024 (10-bit and 10-bit and 10-bit is 30-bit). High Efficiency Video Coding (HEVC) which Android now supports, allows a color depth of 8-bits to 10-bits per color plane. The second version of HEVC will feature five profiles, which allow for a bit depth of 8-bits to 16-bits per sample, or 48-bit color digital video assets.

Representing Colors in Android: Hexadecimal Notation

Now that you know what color depth is, and that colors are represented as a combination of three different red, green, and blue (RGB) color channels within any given image, we need to look at how as Android 7.x, Java 8, and JavaFX 8 (now part of Java) programmers, we are going to represent these three RGB color channel values inside of our Android applications. This knowledge will allow us to create any single one of these 16,777,216 colors, and even add alpha channel transparency values, which we will be covering in the next section of this chapter.

It is important to note that in the Android OS, color is not only used in digital images, commonly called **bitmap** images, but also in **2D illustration,** which is commonly referred to using **shapes** or **vector** SVG imagery, as well as in **color settings**, such as the background color value utilized in your Android 7 Theme specifications, or for your textColor values, for instance, that define what color your text UI elements will be.

In Android, different levels of RGB color intensity are represented as data values using **hexadecimal notation**. Hexadecimal notation is based on the original **Base-16** computer notation used decades ago to represent 16 bits of data value. Unlike Base-10, which counts from zero through 9, Base-16 counts from zero through F, where F would represent a Base-10 value of 15 (remember that counting from zero through 15 gives you 16 data values).

To tell the Android OS that we are giving it a hexadecimal value, we preface these Base-16 values with a **pound sign** like this: #FFFFFF. Because each slot in this 24-bit hexadecimal representation represents one Base-16 value, to get the 256 values we need for each RGB color will take **2** of these slots, as 16 times 16 equals 256. Thus, for a 24-bit image, you would need **6** slots after the pound sign, and for a 32-bit image, we would need **8** slots after the pound sign. We will be covering what these 32-bit type of digital images are, and what they are used for, during the next section of this chapter, when we look at alpha channels.

These hexadecimal data slots represent the RGB values in the following format: #RRGGBB. Thus, for the color white, all red, green, and blue channels in this hexadecimal color data value representation are at the maximum luminosity of fully on, or FF, which would be 16 times 16, or a full 256 data value for each RGB color channel. For this reason, the value #FFFFFF would represent the whitest white that is possible on a given device screen.

> **Note**   As you can see, I'm giving you all of the different industry terminology (color channel, color plane, color plate) that you will find currently being used in the graphics industry. All of these terms can be used interchangeably.

When you **additively sum** all of the RGB colors together, you will get white light. As I have mentioned before, the color yellow is represented by the red and green channels being on, and the blue channel being off, thus the hexadecimal notation representation for the color yellow would be #FFFF00, where both red and green channel slots are on, using FF for a color intensity (level) value of 256, and the blue channel slots are fully off, using 00.

As I mentioned earlier in this section, there is also a 32-bit image color depth whose data values are represented using the **ARGB** color channel model, where the **A** stands for **alpha,** which is short for **alpha channel**. We'll be going over the concept of **image alpha** and alpha channels in detail during the next section of the chapter, and we will also cover the related concept of **pixel blending**.

The hexadecimal notation data slots for an ARGB color channel model data values will hold data in the following format: #AARRGGBB. Thus, to represent the fully opaque color white, all alpha, red, green, and blue channels in this hexadecimal color data value representation would be at a maximum luminosity (as well as opacity), and the alpha channel fully opaque, as represented by an FF value, so its hexadecimal value would be #FFFFFFFF.

A **100% transparent** alpha channel is represented by the alpha channel slots being set to **zero**; thus, a fully transparent image pixel could be #00FFFFFF, or #00000000. It is important to notice that if an image alpha channel is set to be fully transparent, then each pixel's color value (represented by the last six hexadecimal data slot values) does not even matter, and thus you could put any color value into these last six data slots.

Image Compositing Transparency: Alpha Channels

In this section of the chapter, we will take a look at how digital images are composited together, which is a process known as **image compositing**, which is usually done by a professional who is called a digital image **compositor**. Digital image compositing is a process of blending together more than one layer of digital imagery in order to obtain a resulting image. A composite image on a display screen will appear as if it is one single image, when, in fact, it is actually a collection (a "layer stack") of several seamlessly composited digital image layers.

To be able to accomplish seamless image compositing using layers, the images used in each layer other than the bottom-most background or "backplate" layer need to have **alpha channel** (transparency) values associated with each pixel in the image contained within that layer. We can utilize this alpha value for each pixel in the image to precisely control the **blending** of that pixel with other pixels in the same overall image composite coordinate or location, that is, pixels on other layers above and below that particular image layer using the same pixel coordinates.

It is because of this stacked layer paradigm that I refer to this compositing as 3D, as the layers are stacked into place along, or using, the **Z-axis**, and can be said to have a particular **Z-order or Z-depth**. Don't get this confused with 3D modeling software, such as Silo or Blender, as the end result of your digital image compositing (layer) stack is still a resulting 2D digital image asset, and not a 3D geometric model asset.

Like the other RGB channels, the alpha channel also has **256 levels of transparency** that are represented via the first two slots in the hexadecimal representation for the ARGB data value, which as you have seen has eight slots (for 32-bits) of data, rather than the 6 slots used to represent a 24-bit image. A 24-bit image could thus be thought of as being a 32-bit image with no alpha channel data.

If you think about it, if there is no alpha channel data, why waste another 8 bits of data storage, especially if that alpha channel is filled with #FF alpha values, representing fully opaque pixel transparency values. The uncompressed 32-bit image with an alpha channel filled with #FF values has 25% more data than a 24-bit image with no alpha channel, and yet it would yield the same exact visual result. So don't use a 32-bit image unless you need to use transparency values for the pixels in that image (for multi-layered digital image compositing purposes).

Therefore, to summarize, 24-bit imagery has no alpha channel, and isn't going to be used for image compositing, unless it is the bottom backplate in the compositing layer stack. A 32-bit image is always going to be used as a compositing layer, on top of something else which will need the ability to show through via transparency values defined in the image alpha channel. These transparency values may vary from pixel location to pixel location, in order to allow compositors to create special effects and apply image enhancing treatments, such as anti-aliasing, which we will be discussing later.

How does having an alpha channel and using digital image compositing factor into my Android graphics design pipeline, you might be wondering? Your primary advantage here is the ability to split what looks like one single image into a number of component layers. A reason for doing this may be to apply Java code to individual layer elements in order to control various parts of a 2D image that you would not be otherwise able to individually control, were the image simply one single 24-bit image. A single image can be transformed as a whole, or as a pixel array, but not on a per-subject (per pixel area) basis, as it could be if each image element were on its own layer, and thus a separate element in memory, which could later be controlled by using your Java program logic. The Apress *Pro Android Graphics* title covers this in detail.

Algorithmic Image Compositing: Blending Modes

There is another even more powerful aspect of image compositing called **blending modes.** Any of you familiar with Photoshop or GIMP know that you can set each layer in your image composite to use a different blending mode. Blending modes are **algorithms** that specify how the pixels that are contained within a layer are blended (mathematically) with the previous layers (underneath that layer). These pixel blending algorithms will take into account the transparency level. By combining blending modes and transparency, you can achieve virtually any digital image compositing result, or special effect, that you are trying to achieve. Since there are entire books written on using blending modes, and the effects that you can create, I won't get into this too much here.

Interestingly, blending modes can be implemented in the Android OS, by using the Android PorterDuff class. This is a real tribute to, and an indicator of, the 2D power that lies in the Android 7.1.1 software development APIs. The PorterDuff class gives developers many of the powerful blending modes that Photoshop (or GIMP 2.10) affords to digital imaging artisans. The PorterDuff class essentially allows Android apps to implement powerful image compositing features similar to GIMP or Photoshop. The major difference, of course, is that you can control the blending modes interactively, using custom Java programming logic, which is the exciting part for Android 7.1.1 developers. The *Pro Android Graphics* (2014) title from Apress covers how to implement PorterDuff blending modes inside a complete digital image compositing pipeline, if you are interested in diving into this advanced graphics compositing and blending area of Android 7.1.1 in greater detail.

Masking Digital Imagery: Using Alpha Channels

One of the most popular uses of the alpha channel is to **mask** out an area of a digital image. This is usually done in order to create a layer that can be utilized in the digital image compositing **layer stack**. Masking is the process of extracting subject matter, essentially cutting that subject matter right out of the image, by placing it (pasting it) onto its own transparent layer. I will show you how this can be done in GIMP a bit later.

The masking process yields a part of your image on its own layer. The masked subject will be **isolated** from the rest of the source image, but because of layer transparency, will look like it is still in the final image composite. The advantage to this is that now you can do things to that subject matter, in GIMP, or later on in Android 7.1.1, and not have those operations, whatever they may be (rotate, tint, distort, fade and so forth) affect the rest of that image. If you save one of these transparency layers that has subject matter on it in GIMP or Photoshop the transparency layer will be converted into an alpha channel.

The masking work process allows you to put image elements (subject material) to use inside of other images, or in an animation, or to use in a special effects application like Fusion. Digital imaging software (Photoshop, GIMP, Painter, Fusion, or Corel Draw) has many tools and features that are specifically there for use in masking images for use in image compositing. You can't really do effective image compositing without creating a mask, so this is an important area to master for graphic designers and Android 7.1.1 application developers alike.

You can mask automatically, using blue screen or green screen backdrops, and computer software that can automatically extract those exact color values, in order to create a mask using an alpha channel. You can also mask manually, by hand, using a digital imaging software package such as GIMP, and its wide array of pixel selection tools.

The most important consideration in the masking process is getting smooth but crisp edges around your masked object, so that when you drop it in a layer over a background image, it looks as though it had been photographed there in the first place. The key to this is a proper selection work process, using digital image software selection tools (and there are a half-dozen of these in GIMP 2.10) in the proper way. Using the optimal work process is the key to "pulling a clean image mask" (more cool graphics industry terms for you to throw around, to make you appear savvy and professional). The *Digital Image Compositing Fundamentals* (2015) book from Apress covers this work process in more detail, if you happen to be interested in this area of digital imaging, and *VFX Fundamentals* covers this using Fusion 8.

For instance, if there are areas of uniform color around the subject matter you wish to mask, maybe you shot it using a blue screen or green screen, you can use the **magic wand tool** along with a **threshold setting** to select everything except the object, and then **invert** that **selection set**, in order to obtain a selection set containing the object. Other selection tools contain complex algorithms which can look at color changes between pixels, which can be very useful for **edge detection**, which you can use in other types of selection work processes. The edge detection selection tool will allow you to drag your cursor along the edge of the object that you wish to mask, while the edge detecting selection tool's algorithm lays down a precise, pixel-perfect placement of the selection edge, ultimately creating or "pulling" that object's mask for you. You can also use spline tools to create your Bezier outline, and then convert that outline into a selection set. This approach is covered in the *VFX Fundamentals* (2016) title from Apress.

Smoothing Edges: The Concept of Anti-Aliasing

Anti-aliasing is a digital imaging technique that is implemented using an algorithm, where two adjacent colors in an image that share an edge between two color areas are blended together along that edge. This will make that edge **appear** to be smoother (crisper, or more razor sharp) when the image is zoomed out; that is, when the pixels are not individually visible. What anti-aliasing does is it tricks your eyes into seeing a smoother edge, to eliminate what is commonly termed "the jaggies" due to a jagged appearance along the edges in the imagery.

Anti-aliasing provides impressive results, and does so by using only a very few (usually seven or eight) averaged color values of the pixels that lie along the edge that needs to be made smoother. By averaged, I mean some colors, or spectrum of colors, that are a portion of the way between the two colors that are intersecting at the jagged edge in an image, which you can see along the right-hand side in Figure 9-1.

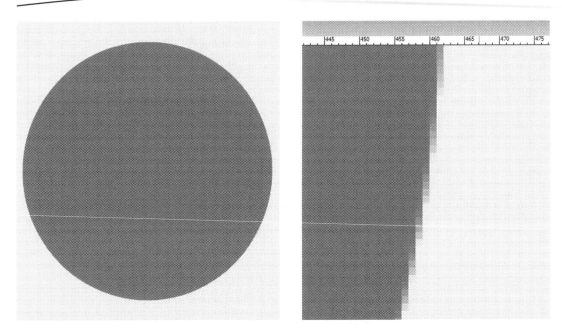

Figure 9-1. *A red circle on a yellow background (left) and a zoomed-in view (right) showing the anti-aliasing*

I created a basic example of anti-aliasing to show you visually exactly what I mean. In Figure 9-1, you will see that I created a (seemingly) smooth red circle against a yellow background. I then zoomed into the edge of that circle, and I grabbed a screenshot. I placed this alongside of the zoomed-out circle to show these anti-aliasing (orange) values of a color between (that is, made using) the red and yellow color values that border each other along the edge of the circle. If you are looking at black and white, you will see all of this anti-aliasing using grayscale. Luckily for alpha channels, anti-aliasing works just as well in grayscale as it does using color values.

The best way to get good anti-aliasing is to use a proper image masking work process, and using the proper settings for any given selection tool that you might be using. One of the other tricks to implementing your own anti-aliasing is to use a **Gaussian Blur** tool with a very low blur value (0.15 to 0.35) on the (transparency) layer containing the object that has the jagged edges. This will provide the same effect seen in Figure 9-1, and not only that, it will "blur" the transparency values for the alpha channel (mask) itself as well, allowing you to anti-alias that image object with any background imagery you may be attempting to seamlessly composite it against.

Optimizing Digital Images: Compress and Dither

There are a number of technical factors that affect digital image compression, which is the process of using a **codec**, which is short for **CO**der-**DEC**oder. A codec is also an algorithm that looks at image data and finds a way to save it in a file using significantly less data. A codec's **encoder** essentially finds data patterns in an image, and then turns these data patterns into a form of data that the **decoder** part of the same codec can reconstruct the original image from, many times with zero loss of image quality. There are strategies that you can use to get a better quality image compression result, which will result in a smaller file size, along with higher image quality. Images with a small file size, and a high level of quality can be said to have a "highly optimized data footprint."

Let's start out by discussing all of the digital image attributes that affect the image data footprint the most, and later we can examine how each of these aspects will contribute to the data footprint optimization for any given digital image. Interestingly, the order of aspects that are important to data footprint optimization are similar to the order of the digital imaging concepts that we have covered thus far during this chapter.

The most critical contributor to the resulting image file size (that is, the data footprint) is the number of pixels, or the resolution of the digital image. This is logical because each of these pixels needs to be stored, along with the color values for each of these pixel's (ARGB) color and alpha channels. Thus, the smaller you can make the image resolution, while still having the image still look detailed, the smaller the resulting file size will be. This is because there is less data overall that will need to be compressed by the codec's data encoding algorithm.

You can calculate raw, uncompressed image data footprint using the formula:

Width times Height times Color Channels

Recall that for 24-bit RGB images, there are three (RGB) color channels, and there are four (ARGB) color channels for a 32-bit image. Thus, any uncompressed, true color (24-bit) VGA image will have **640 times 480 times 3**, equaling **921,600** bytes of original uncompressed data. If you divide 921,600 by **1024** (the number of bytes in a kilobyte), this will give you the number of kilobytes (K or KB) that are in a raw VGA image, and that number is an even **900KB**. Since deep color imagery uses 16-bits per color channel, simply double this amount of data used.

As you can see, image color depth is therefore the next most critical contributor to a data footprint of an image, because the number of pixels in that image is multiplied by **1** (8-bit) or **2** (16-bit) or **3** (24-bit) or **4** (32-bit) or **6** (48-bit) or **8** (64-bit) color and alpha data channels. Both GIMP and Photoshop have color channel palettes just like they have layer palettes. Both channels and layers are represented in the same way in these digital imaging software packages, as composited layers along a Z-axis, in a given Z-order. For color channels, this Z-order goes R-G-B.

Compact pixel color data (one channel) is one of the reasons indexed color (8-bit) images are still being widely used today, usually via the PNG8 image format, which features a superior lossless compression algorithm to the one that the outdated CompuServe GIF format utilizes. Lossless compression algorithms such as PNG lose zero image data (quality). A lossy compression algorithm, such as JPEG, will throw away original image data, and therefore, some of your image's quality, to achieve more data compression at the expense of the visual quality.

Using Indexed Color Imagery: Dithering Pixels

Indexed color images can simulate truecolor images, if the colors that are used to create the image do not vary widely. Indexed color images use 8-bit data to define the image colors, using a palette of 256 optimally selected colors, rather than 3 RGB color channels. Depending on how many colors are used in the image, using only 256 colors to represent an image can cause an effect called **banding**, where the transfer between adjoining colors is not smooth. Indexed color image codecs have an option to correct for this visually called **dithering**. Dithering is the process of creating dot patterns along the edges of two adjoining colors in an image. This tricks your eye into thinking there is a third color being used besides these two colors, when, in fact, there is not.

Dithering gives you a maximum perceptual amount of colors of 65,536 colors, (256 times 256), but only if each of those 256 colors borders on each of the other 256 colors; otherwise, this would be less than 65,536 perceived colors. You can see the potential there for creating a plethora of additional colors, and you will be amazed at the result an indexed color image can achieve in some scenarios (that is, with certain images). Let's take a true color 3D image, such as the one shown in Figure 9-2, and save it as an indexed color image to show you the dithering effect. We will take a look at this dithering effect on the driver's side rear fender on the Audi racecar 3D image, as it contains a smooth gradient of gray color.

Figure 9-2. Truecolor source image using up to 16,777,216 colors that we are going to optimize to 5-bit PNG5

I set the Photoshop Save For Web and Devices dialog's codec to encode a **PNG8** image, shown in Figure 9-3, using **5-bit** color (**32** colors), so that you can see this dithering effect. As you can see, the dot patterns are made between adjacent colors, in this case this is shades of gray, to create a perception that there are additional gray colors beyond the 32 total colors (5-bit data) that are being used to create the PNG5 indexed color image asset.

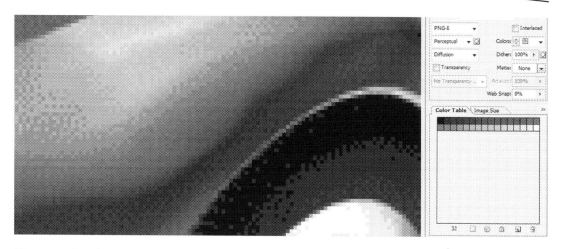

Figure 9-3. The dithering effect in an indexed color image with compression set to 32 colors (5-bit color)

It is interesting to note that there is this option to use less than 256 colors when compressing your 8-bit indexed color image. This is usually done to reduce the data footprint even further. For instance, an image that can attain good results using 32 colors would actually be a 5-bit image, and thus is PNG5, even though the general format is termed PNG8, or Indexed PNG. The **Colors:** "spinner" value selector is where you set this number of colors, and you can set any number from 2 (1-bit color, or on or off, or black and white) up to 256 colors (8-bits data).

Also, notice that you can set a **percentage** of dithering to use. I usually select either the 0% or 100% setting, but you could fine-tune your dithering effect anywhere in between those two extreme values. You can also choose a **dithering algorithm** type; I use diffusion dithering, as it will yield a smoother gradient effect along an irregularly shaped gradient, such as the one that you see in Figure 9-3, on the Audi racecar fender.

Dithering, as you might well imagine, will add data patterns to an image that are more difficult for the codec's algorithm to compress. Because of this dithering should increase your data footprint by a few percentage points. Be sure to check the resulting file size with, and without, dithering applied, to make sure the dithering provides improved visual results, and to see if the dithering adds any "data weight" to the resulting file size (data footprint).

The final concept that we have learned about so far that can increase the data footprint of the image is the alpha channel, as adding an alpha channel will add another 8-bit (or 16-bit for deep color imagery) color data channel containing pixel transparency data values to the image being compressed. If you need an alpha channel to define transparency, in order to support future compositing needs with that image, there is not much of a choice but to include this alpha channel data. Just make sure not to use a 32-bit image format to contain a 24-bit image with an empty (completely opaque, and not defining any transparency) alpha channel.

It is interesting to note that many alpha channels that are used to mask objects in an image will compress very well. This is because alpha channels contain large areas of white (opaque) or black (transparent), with very little gray value in the pixels along edges between the two colors to anti-alias the mask. These gray values in an alpha channel are essentially the anti-aliasing values, and as you now know, are used to provide visually smooth edge transitions between the masked object and the imagery that will be used behind it. Large areas of the same color will yield the best compression as the codec can essentially say "this entire area is white, and this entire area is black," rather than "this pixel is this color, and that pixel is that color," and so on.

Alpha channels can also provide real-time anti-aliasing for applications that utilize compositing. The reason for this is because in an alpha channel image mask, the 8-bit transparency gradient is defined using a white to black spectrum (gradient) that defines the alpha channel transparency. So these gray values along the edges of each object in the mask are essentially averaging, or blending, the color of the (RGB) subject object (the image that carries the mask with it) with color in the target background image. This essentially provides a real-time anti-aliasing for the image element (object) on your transparency layer with any background imagery that might be placed behind the masked image that carries its own transparency (and anti-aliasing) data via PNG32 format.

Android Image Formats: Lossless versus Lossy

Android supports several popular digital image file formats, some of which have been around for decades, and which are also available in other popular open source content development platforms, such as HTML5 and JavaFX.

These range from the decades-old CompuServe GIF (Graphic Information Format) and the Joint Photographic Experts Group (JPEG) formats, to the more recent PNG (Portable Network Graphics) and WebP (Web Photo) formats. I will cover these in order of origin, from the older (and less desirable) GIF, to the newer WebP format. WebP support has recently been added to the Opera and Chrome HTML5 browsers.

CompuServe GIF is fully supported by the Android OS; however, it's not recommended for general use. GIF is a lossless digital image file format, as it does not throw away any image data to achieve its better compression result. This is because this GIF compression algorithm (codec) is not as refined (effective) as PNG, and it only supports indexed color, which we covered earlier in the chapter. That said, if all your image assets are already created, and they use the GIF format, you will still be able to use them without any problems (other than the resulting quality to file size ratio) in an Android app. Android 7.x does not yet support the Animated GIF (aGIF) format.

The next oldest digital image file format that Android supports is the JPEG format, which uses the truecolor color depth, instead of an indexed color depth. JPEG is a lossy digital image file format, because it throws away the original image data in order to be able to achieve the smaller file size. The file sizes achieved by using this JPEG algorithm can be an order of magnitude (10X) smaller than the original raw uncompressed image data.

It is important to note that the original (often referred to by using the term **raw**) uncompressed image data is unrecoverable after compression by the JPEG codec's encoder has taken place. For this reason, you will want to make sure you have saved your original uncompressed image file before you compress the image through the JPEG compression algorithm.

If you zoom into a JPEG image after compression, you will see discolored areas that clearly were not present in the original image. These "degraded" areas in the JPEG image data are termed **compression artifacts** in the digital imaging industry, and compression artifacts only occur when you utilize lossy image compression. This is the primary reason why the JPEG file format is not the most highly recommended digital image format for use in Android, as the Pure Android approach we covered in Chapter 8 seeks to provide a pristine visual result.

The most recommended image format for use in Android application development is called PNG, or Portable Network Graphic, file format. PNG is always pronounced **Ping** in the digital image industry. PNG has both an indexed color version, called PNG8, or PNG5 if you only need to use 32 colors as we saw earlier in the chapter; and a truecolor version, called PNG24, and a truecolor with alpha channel version, called PNG32.

The PNG8, PNG24, and PNG32 numbering extensions I am using represent the bit depth of color support, so a truecolor PNG that has an alpha channel would technically be referred to as a PNG32. Similarly, a PNG using 16 colors would be said to be a PNG4, a PNG using 64 colors could be referred to as a PNG6, and a PNG using 128 colors could be referred to as a PNG7, and so forth. The reason PNG is the recommended format for use with Android is because it uses lossless compression, and yields high image quality along with a very decent (respectable) compression efficiency.

The most recent image format was added to Android when Google acquired ON2 and is called the WebP image format. The format is supported under Android 2.3.7 for image read, or playback support, and in Android 4.0 or later for image write, or file saving support. Image write support in Android, in case you might be wondering, would be used with the Android device camera, so that your users can save (write) images to their SD card or to the "cloud" via remote web server. WebP is a static image version of the WebM video file format, which is also known in the industry as the ON2 VP8/VP9 codec, which was acquired by Google, and released as open source.

Creating Android NinePatchDrawable Assets

This section of the chapter will outline how to create the **NinePatch** graphic using the Android **Draw 9-patch** tool, which used to be a DOS command prompt based tool (in the previous three editions of this book), but is now integrated into Android Studio 2.3. NinePatchDrawable objects are unique to Android, although there is some movement to add this intelligent-tiling digital image format to the HTML5 and JavaFX standards as well.

A NinePatch image uses the PNG image format, and is designed to be able to tile efficiently and asymmetrically in either the X or the Y image dimension, or in both dimensions at the same time. This allows NinePatch images to be able to morph to fit different size and shape UI widgets and/or display screens, if used as a border element.

You will need a source PNG image with which to create your NinePatchDrawable object. I have provided a PNG32 (truecolor with alpha channel) digital image asset, which you'll find in the project assets repository for the book, called ninepatchframe. The reason I am using an alpha channel to define transparency in the center area of the 9-patch that we're about to create is so that any image layers (intended composites) that are behind the image asset inside Android will composite perfectly with the 9-patch image asset in the image compositing stack, which we will be implementing using XML UI layout design definition markup, later on in this chapter.

Installing the Draw 9-Patch Source PNG32 Image

Let's get started by copying the **ninepatchframe.png** source image that we are going to use with the Draw 9-patch editor in Android Studio into your project folder hierarchy, in the tools subfolder. Open your operating system file navigation utility, for Windows this is the Explorer. Download the ZIP file containing the assets for this book from the software repository on Apress.com and copy the ninepatchframe PNG32 file to your project AndroidStudioProjects/ NavDrawerPattern/app/src/main/res/drawable folder, as shown in Figure 9-4.

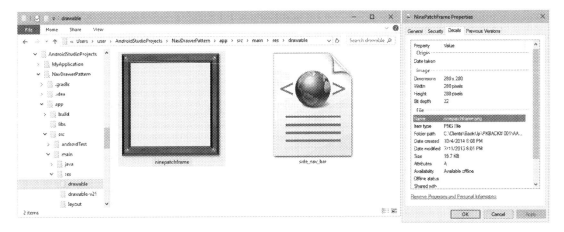

Figure 9-4. *Copy the ninepatchframe.png source file into the NavDrawerPattern/app/src/main/res/drawable folder*

Once you launch Android Studio, as can be seen in Figure 9-5, you'll see the ninepatchframe. png source file in the /app/res/drawable project folder. Right-click on the ninepatchframe. png file and select the **Create 9-Patch file** menu option. This will bring up the **Save As .9.png** dialog shown on the right side of Figure 9-5 where you select the same app/src/main/res/ drawable folder path that you did in Figure 9-4 to save your NinePatch asset in.

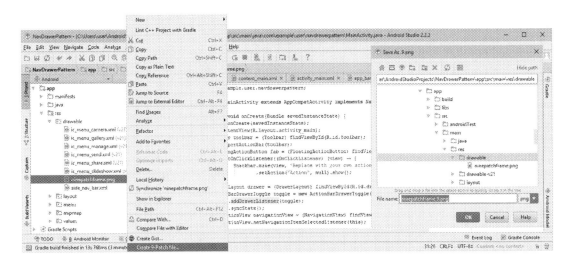

Figure 9-5. *Right-click on the ninepatchframe.png file and select Create 9-Patch file, and save in drawable folder*

Creating a NinePatch asset does not open it for editing. Right-click the ninepatchframe.9.png file created by the steps in Figure 9-5, and use a **Jump to Source** option, to open it in a 9-Patch Editor tab, as is seen in Figure 9-6.

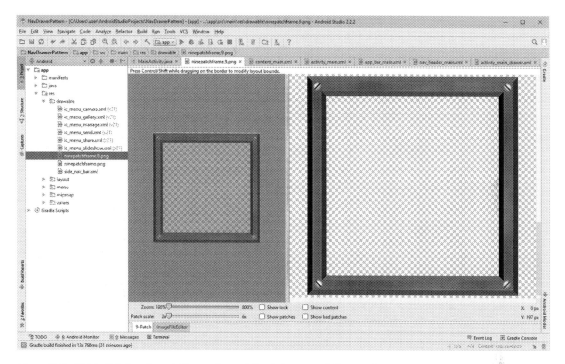

Figure 9-6. Right-click the ninepatchframe.9.png 9-Patch image, and Jump to Source to open the 9-Patch Editor

Exploring Android Studio's 9-Patch Editor

Make sure that the **ninepatchframe.9.png** tab is selected at the top of the IDE, as well as the 9-Patch tab at the bottom, as seen in Figure 9-7. The left gray pane is the NinePatchDrawable asset **editing pane**, where you will create your one-pixel wide black lines which allow you to define "9 patches." These patches will tell the NinePatch class (the 9-Patch engine) in Android what the scalable areas are for this NinePatchDrawable asset are, as well as defining where the center (called the padding area for a 9-Patch asset) content area will be.

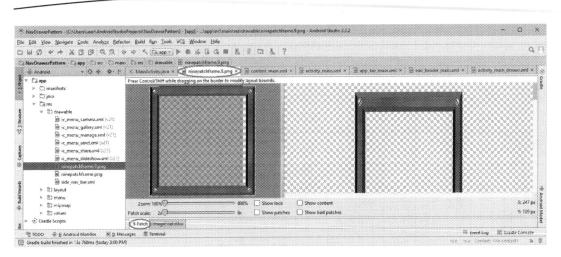

Figure 9-7. *Draw out a horizontal patch using the top one-pixel black line segment to define an active X-axis area*

The right pane is the result of the `NinePatchDrawable` asset configuration shown using a preview pane, as you can see on the right side in Figure 9-7, where you can see what the resulting `NinePatchDrawable` asset will look like when it is scaled according to the one-pixel black border line definitions that you are about to learn how to define using the left editing pane of the Android Studio **9-Patch Editor**. As you can see, currently the 9-Patch definition is incorrect, and skews part of the tiling effect, warping the screws, and the top (and bottom) frame.

Defining the NinePatchDrawable Asset's Scalable Areas

To define how your `NinePatchDrawable` asset will scale along the X-axis dimension, click in the top, one-pixel transparent perimeter area, starting on the right side, after the corner screw, as shown in Figure 9-7, and drag toward the left corner screw. This will draw out a one-pixel black line, which will define your X-axis scalable patch. Once you draw in the rough approximation of what you want, you can fine-tune the line using one pixel, light gray lines that extend into the medium gray surrounding areas (these are difficult to see in the current 9-Patch UI color schema). If you place the mouse-over these gray lines the cursor will change into a double arrow, and you can then click and drag the grayed-out area, until it fits pixel perfectly with the transparency area in the center of the `ninepatchframe` PNG32 source image, which you are using to create the `NinePatchDrawable` asset.

You can also right-click (or if you use macOS, hold the Shift key, and click) to erase any previously drawn lines. As you can see in the preview pane on the right side of Figure 9-8, you are now getting a visual result that is more in line for what we are going for, as the `NinePatchDrawable` asset is not distorted.

Next, let's use one of the more colorful 9-Patch Editor options, the **Show patches** checkbox option. As you can see circled in red at the bottom of Figure 9-8, this is located at the very bottom of the 9-Patch editing pane. This option is there so that you can visualize your 9-patch X or Y settings using different colors. Look for the empty checkbox next to this Show patches option, and select it, and turn this feature on. As you can see in Figure 9-8, this option will provide coloration for your selection areas, by using a combination of purple and green colors. This will make it more clear to you during your editing process which areas of an image asset are being affected by the patch definitions that you are implementing, by drawing in these one-pixel black perimeter lines.

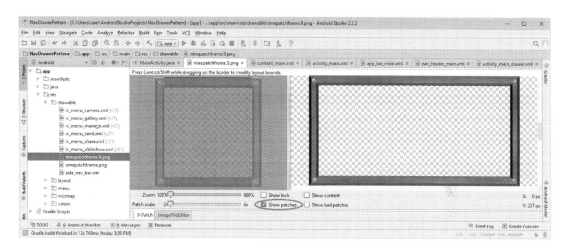

Figure 9-8. *Turn on the Show patches check box option; finished drawing of the top one-pixel black line segment*

As you can see in Figure 9-8, a number of other useful controls exist at the bottom of the 9-Patch editing pane. These include a **Zoom** slider, which we will be using later to fine-tune all of our control lines, which will allow you to adjust the zoom level of your source graphic in the editing area from 1X up to 8X. The other slider at the bottom is the **Patch scale** slider, which will allow you to adjust the preview scaling of your NinePatchDrawable asset, from 2X (200%) to 6X (600%), which is being shown in the preview area, on the right side of the display.

The **Show lock** option check box will allow you to visualize the non-drawable areas of the NinePatchDrawable when you mouse-over them. The **Show content** option checkbox, which you will be using later on, highlights your content area in the preview pane image, where blue areas will show the region in which any Android View subclass (widget or layout container) content will be allowed to composite (to display, or to show through your transparency from other z-order layers in your user interface compositing stack) with your NinePatchDrawable.

Finally, at the top of the editing area, there is a **Show bad patches** button, which will add a red border around patch areas which might (emphasis on "might") produce scaling artifacts when the 9-Patch graphic is scaled. Visual excellence for scaled 9-Patch images can be achieved if you strive to eliminate all bad patches in your NinePatchDrawable design, however, depending on the pixel colors used, artifacts may not be an issue (visible).

Now it is time to draw in our left one-pixel border to define the Y-axis scaling behavior, as shown in Figure 9-9. As you can see in Figure 9-9, I did not draw this one-pixel black border line all the way down the left side. I did this so that you could visualize how well this Show patches option works. This option will allow us to visualize exactly what we are doing right down to the pixel level, as you can see in Figure 9-9, when you look at the color areas and how they blend with the transparency checkerboard pattern and the source image asset. This precision is necessary if you want to define a pixel-perfect 9-patch image asset for use in your NinePatchDrawable object.

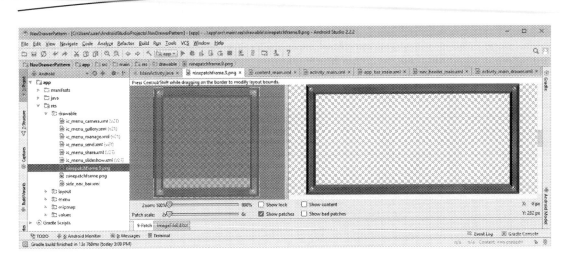

Figure 9-9. *Draw down a vertical Y patch using the left one-pixel black line segment to define a Y-axis patch area*

Figure 9-10 now shows your `NinePatchDrawable` PNG32 image asset with both the top, as well as the left, one-pixel (border) black line definitions in place. As you can now visualize, thanks to the **Show patches** option, we have now defined our static areas, shown as clear (no coloration), which will not scale, and our scalable areas, shown using the green overlay. The Show patches option has allowed us to do this with surgical pixel precision.

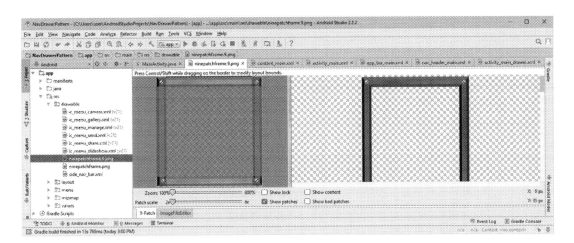

Figure 9-10. *Both your horizontal and vertical patch one-pixel black line segments now define active axis areas*

Also notice in Figure 9-10 in the right-hand preview of the 9-Patch Editor that the `NinePatchDrawable` PNG32 image asset's patch scale definition is now giving you a professional scaling result. If you grab that scrollbar on the right side of the preview area of the screen, and pull it up or down, you will see that the NinePatch algorithm is now scaling in the portrait as well as in the landscape container shape, with perfect visual results. This is what NinePatch technology is for, after all, to provide asynchronous scaling regardless of the aspect ratio (shape) of a container that is holding the NinePatch asset, so that you don't have to "lock" aspect ratio, to prevent distortion.

Defining the NinePatchDrawable Asset's Padding Areas

Now that you have defined the **scalable areas** for your NinePatchDrawable image asset, it is time to define the **padding areas** for a NinePatchDrawable image asset. This is accomplished by using the one-pixel black border lines on the **right** and **bottom** of the editing pane. As you can see in Figure 9-11, I have drawn in, on the right-hand side, the one-pixel black border line segment that is necessary to define the Y image dimension for our center (padding) area for the NinePatchDrawable image asset. The center area, in the case of this PNG32 asset, contains an alpha channel value of #00000000, or 100% transparency, which you could also define, as you now well know, using any other color value, such as white, or #00FFFFFF, and the editor will still display it using a checkerboard pattern, which those of you who use GIMP 2.8.20 or 2.10 know represents transparent pixel values.

Also notice in Figure 9-11 that I have also drawn in a second, one-pixel black border line segment at the bottom of the image. I am doing this in order to define the X dimension for the center padding area, which will define where content or other (composited) assets for our user interface design will display in the NinePatchDrawable image asset. If I didn't have transparency in this graphic, image assets behind it (on a lower z-order layer) would not show through, so this transparent area further increases the flexibility of using this 9-Patch asset for your Android UI compositing purposes. Due to the padding, images on top of this image would draw inside the NinePatch image. So if the NinePatch had a white interior, and you used it in the background container, the image in the source UI plate would respect the interior padding area, drawing on top of it (background is behind source or foreground).

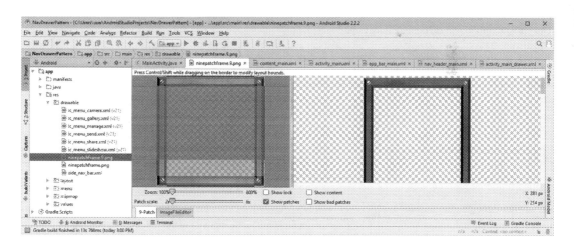

Figure 9-11. *Defining the interior padding areas, using the one-pixel black line segments on the right and bottom*

Notice the muted colors in Figures 9-11 and 9-12, which are used to show different layers of the scalable versus padding area definitions. The padding definitions use a gray overlay on a green or purple (or pink, if you prefer) scalable area definition. As you can see on the right side, the NinePatchDrawable scaling result is giving us an exceptionally professional result, regardless of the source image's orientation or dimensions, which the 9-patch image asset is being scaled into. Notice in Figure 9-12 that I'm pulling the right side one-pixel black border line segment up, showing the light gray patch adjust guides, and how you can adjust padding parameters precisely.

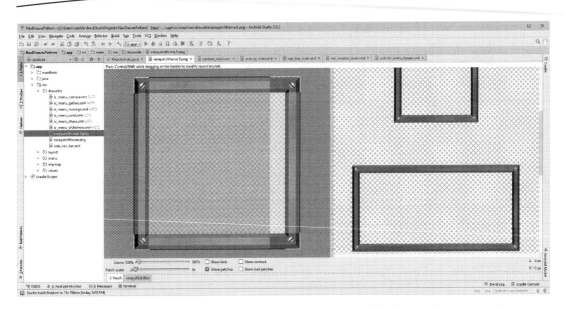

Figure 9-12. Adjust Padding area via the bottom one-pixel black line segment (showing patch adjust guide)

Figure 9-13 shows a finished NinePatch image asset definition, with both a scaling set of border line segments, as well as a padding set of border line segments. We've utilized patch definition guides on four sides of a PNG. It's important to note that if you place the mouse in the left editing pane over any section of a 9-Patch definition, and then hold it there, a tool-tip pop-up will appear giving you the precise pixel patch coordinates for your final NinePatchDrawable component definitions, which you may want to know about for your XML markup or Java 8 code.

In our case, this will show that you have utilized 256 pixels minus 26 pixels, or 230 pixels of our total 280-pixel image dimension, for our center scalable area. Note that 256 is a numeric value that scales quite well, because it is a "power of 2" data value (2, 4, 8, 16, 32, 64, 128, 256, 512, 1024). This means that you have used 25 pixels, or half of the 50 remaining pixels, for the actual image assets (bars and screws) that will be scaled. The reason this isn't 26 pixels is because the NinePatchDrawable image format uses one-pixel borders to define its patches.

This also means that the fixed areas of this 9-Patch, in this case, it is a corner of the frame with a standard screw in it (to hold the frame in place, of course, or so it appears), will each be exactly 25 pixels square in size. These corner areas of the NinePatchDrawable will not be distorted in either the X or Y dimension, although these may be uniformly scaled as needed. There are enough corner pixels (more than two dozen) to be able to scale up, if it is used on high pixel density (resolution) screens, and to have the detail to appear photo realistic if scaled down.

As you can see in Figure 9-13, on the right-hand side of your 9-Patch Editor preview pane, our scaling picture frame graphic looks extremely crisp, and quite realistic. If you scroll the preview pane, this holds across all of the scaling orientation previews. The reason that the interior of the NinePatchDrawable asset is blue is because I have selected the Show content (area definition, that is, padding) checkbox, as shown in red in Figure 9-13.

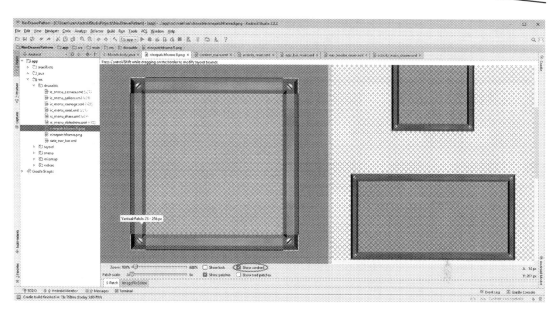

Figure 9-13. *Final patch definition using the Show Content checkbox to fine-tune how the padding fits the content*

Using Your NinePatchDrawable Asset in Android

Android Studio will automatically save your NinePatchDrawable image assets as you work on them, saving any modifications to the new asset that has the required .9.png file name extension, which is required by Android OS when using NinePatchDrawable assets. If you want to "force" a save, use a **File ➤ Save All** menu sequence.

When Android detects this type of PNG file in your app/res/drawable folder, it automatically loads it, using the NinePatch class algorithm, and converts it into a NinePatchDrawable image asset once it is referenced in your XML markup. A NinePatchDrawable can be utilized within any Android class that supports using an Android drawable asset. In UI design this is referenced using either a source (android:src) image plate or the background image plate (android:background) parameter. Classes (widgets and layout containers) that are logical for the use of NinePatchDrawable objects include ImageButton, ImageView, View widgets, and ViewGroup subclasses.

Now that you've created a NinePatchDrawable asset, let's go into the XML markup for your NavDrawerPattern project that you started creating in the previous chapter, and we'll see how a NinePatchDrawable is installed. After that we will get into using external digital image editing software (GIMP) with Android Studio, and create the digital image assets needed for the multi-state ImageButton widget. I will then show you how to modify the code to change the static image button in your NavDrawerPattern project into a dynamic multi-state UI button.

Using NinePatchDrawable Assets in an App

Let's fire up Android Studio 2.3 and implement the new NinePatchDrawable asset you just created. As you can see at the bottom of Figure 9-14, an error has appeared in a **Messages** pane in Android Studio, which informs us that duplicate resources have been detected. Since we just added these PNG files, this tells us and .png and .9.png image assets might be being considered to be the same asset, if they have the same file name. This is fine with us, as we want to use a NinePatchDrawable rather than a BitmapDrawable, because it has unique asymmetric scaling superpowers!

Let's ignore this for now, since we are going to investigate what is causing this, and add an android:background parameter to the UI layout container parent <RelativeLayout> tag, as seen highlighted at the top of Figure 9-14. If you type in "android:bac" you'll get a pop-up helper with all of the background related parameters. Double-click on the one that says background to insert (add) the parameter in your parent layout container specification.

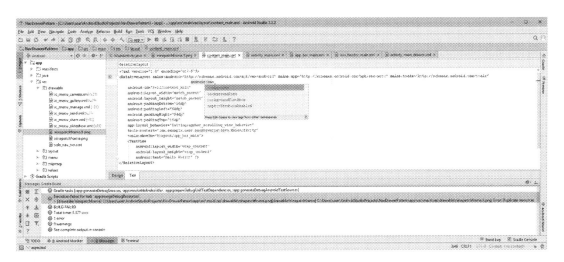

Figure 9-14. Add the android:background parameter to your content_main.xml's parent <RelativeLayout> tag

Just to make sure that Android Studio (Android SDK and API) considers both of these files to be the same, let's start to type the @Drawable referencing path inside of the quotation marks in the android:background parameter we have just added, and see what Android Studio brings up in the pop-up helper dialog. If it shows two of these ninepatchframe assets, we'll know Android Studio can tell the difference between these two files; if not, it will tell us that a .9.png and .png are considered to be the same if they have identical file name prefixes.

As you can see in Figure 9-15, there's only one ninepatchframe asset on the list of drawable assets, so you need to delete the ninepatchframe.png file, which is easy to do in Android Studio, using the context-sensitive menu. Double-click on the @drawable/ninepatchframe reference to insert it as an android:background reference value.

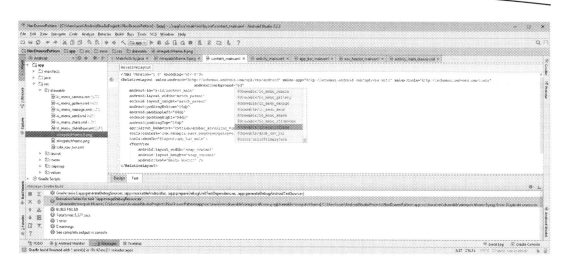

Figure 9-15. *Reference a ninepatchframe NinePatchDrawable asset inside of the parameter value, using quotes*

Next, right-click on the `ninepatchframe.png` file in the Android Studio project pane, and select the **Delete** option shown numbered as 1 in red in Figure 9-16. When the **Safe Delete** dialog opens, shown numbered as 2 in red in Figure 9-16, leave both options selected and click **OK**. When the **Usages Detected** dialog appears, shown numbered as 3 in red in Figure 9-16 click on the **Delete Anyway** button since Android Studio can't differentiate between the `.9.png` and the `.png` files, and therefore, in fact, the `ninepatchframe.png` version is safe to delete.

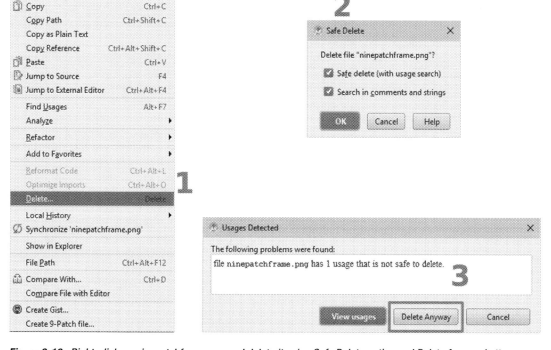

Figure 9-16. *Right-click on ninepatchframe.png and delete it using Safe Delete option and Delete Anyway button*

As you can see in Figure 9-17, `ninepatchframe.png` is now gone and there are no wavy red error underline markings in Android Studio, so we have cured the problem. Use the Run ➤ Run 'app' menu sequence to launch the AVD and test the application to make sure there are no gradle, compile, or runtime errors, and to preview how the `NinePatchDrawable` asset scales to fit the UI design. As you can see at the bottom of Figure 9-17, there are no errors in the build, the load into the AVD, or in the launch of the application in the Nexus AVD emulator.

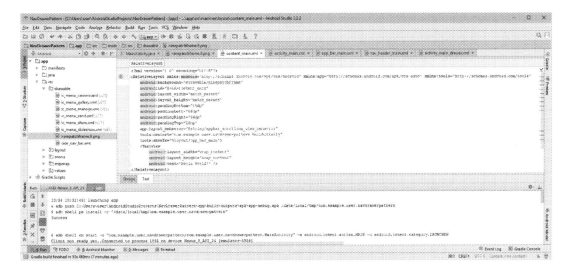

Figure 9-17. Review completed error-free content_main.xml, and use Run ➤ Run 'app' and see no runtime errors

As you can see in Figure 9-18, the `ninepatchframe.9.png` asset scales to fit the content view layout container perfectly, with no scaling or stretching artifacts, and a visually professional looking end result.

Click on the Menu (three vertical bars) icon and side the drawer out over the content view to make sure the app is working, and to see how your `NinePatchDrawable` asset looks with the tinting that dims out the content view.

Notice that we will either have to add some padding to the `RelativeLayout`, or to the `TextView`, and to the `ImageButton` UI element in order to nudge them back inside of the `NinePatchDrawable` image frame, which we will do during the next section of the chapter when we upgrade the `ImageButton` element to use multi-state imagery with 3D components to add some pizzazz to the current application.

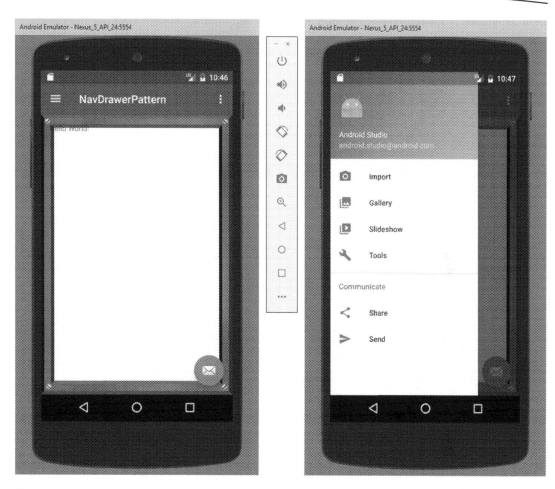

Figure 9-18. Run the app, and make sure the NinePatchDrawable is in the background of content_view UI layout

Next, let's create different density PNG32 image assets for use in upgrading the e–mail button to be multi-state.

Creating Multi-state PNG32 Image Assets

Since we are going to look at the ImageButton class next as well as how to create multi-state (mouse-out or un-clicked, mouse-over or hovered, mouse-down or clicked UI button use-states) UI elements, let's take a quick look at how to create digital image assets using GIMP and how to save them as XXHDPI, XHDPI, HDPI, and MPDI assets for use with 4K, 2K, Blu-ray, and 1K screen resolution devices. Since this is the chapter on image design and implementation this is important for Pure Android design patterns to make an app look professional.

Let's find a better envelope graphic online. Google "free commercial use artwork" and locate pixabay.com, as shown in Figure 9-19, and enter the word "envelope" in the search bar and then click the magnifying glass icon.

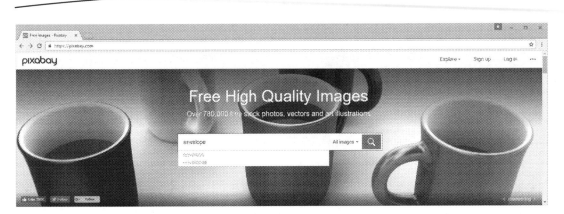

Figure 9-19. Find the www.pixabay.com *free high quality images website and enter "envelope" in the search bar*

Click on the envelope graphics you want to use, and download the native or **original** (print) resolution that they were created in, as is shown on the right side of Figure 9-20 in green. Click the **Download** button to download.

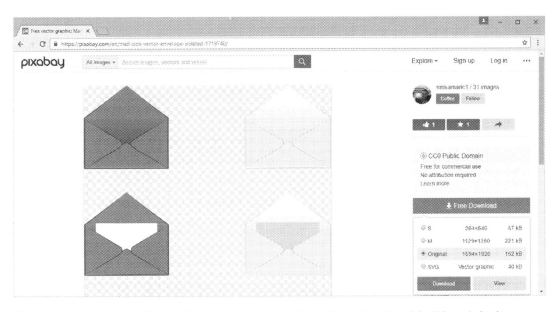

Figure 9-20. Select a professional looking set of envelope graphics and download the original hi-resolution image

If you want to use the ones I extracted from the above file, visit the book repository and download the PNG files that start with the word envelope and are centered in a 500-pixel square file that fits the ButtonDecoration.png file that we are going to use in GIMP to create image composites for the various ImageButton states. Also, if you have now downloaded and installed either GIMP 2.8.20 (used here) or GIMP 2.10 do so now, and launch it.

Use the **File ➤ Open as Layers** menu sequence to open EnvelopeClosed.png (PNG32 file) into its own layer in GIMP, as shown in Figure 9-21. The checkerboard pattern represents transparent areas (the alpha channel data).

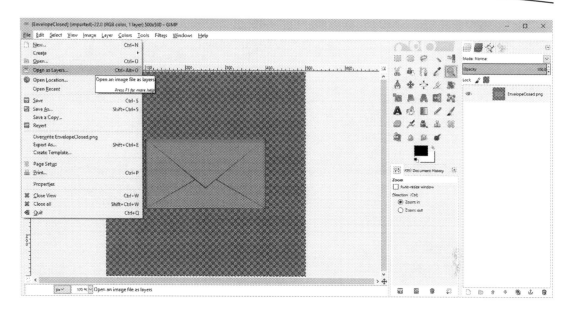

Figure 9-21. Use the File ➤ Open as Layers menu sequence, and import EnvelopeClosed.png into its own layer

Use the **File ➤ Open as Layers** command a second time to import the `ButtonBorder.png` file into the layer that is above `EnvelopeClosed.png`, as shown in the Layers palette shown in the center of Figure 9-22. Use the **File ➤ Export As** menu sequence to access the **Export Image** dialog shown on the right side in Figure 9-22, and name the file `envelopeclosed.png` and use it as an XXHDPI 500-pixel digital image, for use with the IMAX (4K by 4K) or UHD iTV Set (4K by 2K) resolution.

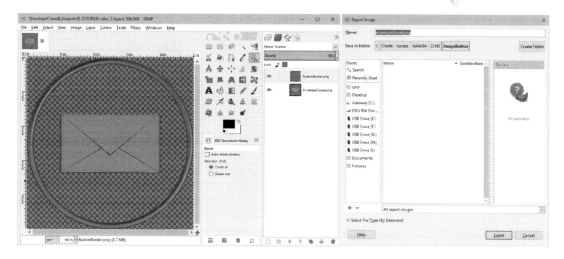

Figure 9-22. Use File ➤ Open as Layers to import ButtonBorder.png into a layer and export as envelopeclosed

Next, click on the EnvelopeClosed.png layer to select it in blue, as shown in the left half of Figure 9-23, so that when you import (open) the next graphic it goes underneath the topmost ButtonBorder.png layer, as can be seen on the right half of Figure 9-23. Use the **File ➤ Open as Layer** to open the EnvelopeOpened.png file and place it into its own layer. Then select the ButtonBorder.png layer, seen in blue on the right, and use the **Colors ➤ Hue-Saturation** menu sequence, and shift the Hue value **-20 degrees** to a bright cyan color, as shown in the Preview area on the right half of Figure 9-23. In this way the hoop will brighten on mouse-over (hover) and the envelope will magically open, connoting the "open mail" function for the ImageButton. Use the **File ➤ Export As** menu sequence to open the Export Image dialog, as shown on the right side in Figure 9-24, and name this PNG32 file envelopeopened.png.

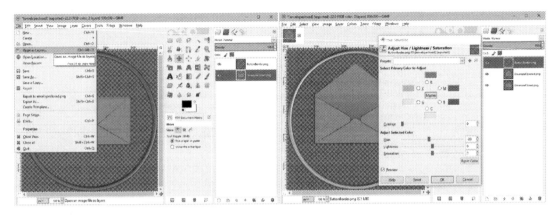

Figure 9-23. *Select the EnvelopeClosed layer, and use Open as Layers to add the EnvelopeOpened layer on top*

Follow the same work process and select the EnvelopeOpened.png layer and import the EnvelopeFilled.png into its own layer, as can be seen on the left side of Figure 9-24. Use the **Colors ➤ Hue-Saturation** dialog to shift the UI hoop border decoration to a gold color, to offset the blue envelope color, and use the **File ➤ Export As** menu sequence to open the Export Image dialog, as shown on the right side in Figure 9-24, and name this PNG32 file envelopefilled.png. I'm saving my ImageButton files in an AA4AB4/CH09/ImageButton folder, as you can see.

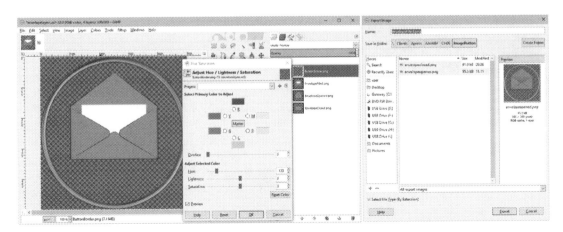

Figure 9-24. *Use Open as Layer to import EnvelopeFilled.png into a layer and shift the ButtonBorder.png to gold*

The next step in creating multi-state image assets for an Android application is to save multiple resolution DPI versions to fit the Android XXHDPI, XHDPI, HDPI and MDPI constants used to define screen density and resolution. I'll use the original 500 pixels for Ultra High (4K) XXHDPI, 250 pixels for Extra High (2K) XHDPI and 125 pixels for High (Blu-ray 1280) HDPI and we'll even create a Medium (1024 and 854 resolution) MDPI asset for older (or less expensive) low-resolution phones and tablets. Let's use the **Image ➤ Scale Image** menu sequence to open the **Scale Image** dialog, seen in Figure 9-25, and down sample the image pixels 100%, to **250** pixels, and then use the **File ➤ Export As** work process, and export (save) the file as envelopefilledxhdpi.png.

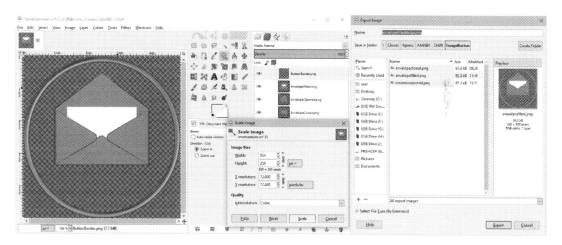

Figure 9-25. Use Image ➤ Scale to create 250-pixel XHDPI version and File ➤ Export to save envelopefilledxhdpi

Once you have saved the XHDPI asset, use the **Edit ➤ Undo Scale Image** to return to the 500-pixel version, so that when you scale to 125 pixels the algorithm has the original (and more) data to resample so it can obtain the best result. Then use the Scale Image dialog and Export Image dialog to create and save envelopefilledhdpi.png.

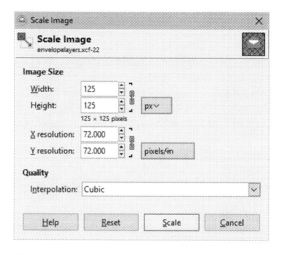
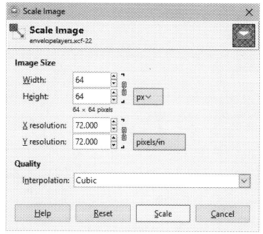

Figure 9-26. Create HDPI 125 pixel and MDPI 64 pixel resolution versions, for use with Blu-ray and 1K and lower

Perform the same work process (Undo, Sample to 64 pixels, Export/Save) and create a envelopefilledmdpi.png asset. Then you will have all four assets done for the envelopefilled ImageButton state. Repeat this process for the other two envelopeclosed and envelopeopened multi-state buttons to create image states for all resolution devices. The Scale Image dialog settings can be seen in Figure 9-26 for the last two button state resolutions.

The ImageButton Class: Multi-state Button

Android's ImageButton class is a direct subclass of the ImageView class, which is itself a subclass of the View superclass, which, as you learned in Chapter 6, is a subclass of the java.lang.Object master class. It is primarily utilized to create UI widgets and layout containers (via the ViewGroup superclass). The Android class hierarchy for the ImageButton class would thus be structured as follows:

```
java.lang.Object
  > android.view.View
    > android.widget.ImageView
      > android.widget.ImageButton
```

The ImageButton class, like its parent class ImageView, is stored in a separate Android package for UI widgets, which is called the android.widget package. This is because the ImageButton is an often-used UI widget which can be leveraged to create custom button UI widgets which can be skinned using Android drawable objects. We're looking at this class in this chapter not only because it is used frequently by Android developers, but also because it is the parent class (superclass) used to create the FloatingActionButton used in NavDrawerPattern, so anything we can do with an ImageButton should also apply to the FloatingActionButton class.

The ImageButton class is extremely powerful, as Android drawable objects can be BitmapDrawable (images), NinePatchDrawable (asymmetric tiling imagery), AnimationDrawable (animation), ShapeDrawable (vector illustrations) or any other Android drawable subclass. I wish I could cover all the Android drawable subclasses in this book; however, if you wanted to explore Android drawables further, you'll want to check out the Apress *Pro Android Graphics* (2013) title.

The ImageButton UI widget would be used when developers need to create a custom button UI element, which will display the button using an image instead of using a standard text label on a square gray background, as the standard UI Button widget should do. We have already implemented both Button and ImageButton elements in previous chapters that covered user interface layout design classes, including the LinearLayout, RelativeLayout, CoordinatorLayout, and DrawerLayout.

Just like the Android Button class UI widget, an ImageButton UI widget can be pressed, using a click or a touch event by the user, and can have button focus characteristics defined as well by implementing multi-state images, such as hovered (over but not pressed), and the default (not pressed and not hovered, that is, not used yet) state.

If you don't utilize any of its custom parameters, your ImageButton widget should have a visual appearance of a standard Android Button UI object with a gray button background that changes color to blue when the button is pressed. The real power of the ImageButton class comes when you use it with alpha channel capable images, in conjunction with multiple image states, both of which you will be learning about in detail during this chapter.

The ImageButton UI widget can define up to four different ImageButton states that are defined using XML markup, which we will be doing a bit later on in this chapter. We will cover these ImageButton states in detail in the next section of this chapter, after I cover a couple of the key XML parameters and Java methods here in this section on the ImageButton class member methods and features.

The **default image** for your ImageButton, or in our case FloatingActionButton, UI widget, which will define its **normal state**, can be defined statically using the app:srcCompat XML parameter in a <FloatingActionButton> child tag inside of a CoordinatorLayout XML layout container UI definition, as you did for your DrawerLayout in Chapter 8.

You can also define a default image for the FloatingActionButton UI widget, which will define its normal state, **dynamically** (at runtime) in your Java code. You'll implement this by using the .setImageResource() method. Static definition would be defined as setting an ImageButton state in advance, that is, before execution of your application, using XML markup. Dynamic definition on the other hand occurs during an application execution, in real-time, if you will, by using Java programming logic. Most Absolute Beginners will use a static definition.

For this reason, I will be using XML to define our UI designs, which the Android OS prefers that we do, for this book. If you use the app:srcCompat parameter to reference Drawable assets, this will put the Drawable asset on your FloatingActionButton, as you saw in Chapter 8. Now we are going to enhance this UI design.

It is important to note developers can use both the android:background parameter, which allows a background image plate, or layer, to be added to the ImageButton element, as well as the android:src parameter, or, in the case of appCompat the app:srcCompat parameter, which allows you to install a foreground image plate (layer). This enables you to perform image compositing inside of any ImageButton UI element (or subclass) itself.

If you do this, you will want to use alpha channels in your images, as we have been, and will be, doing in this chapter. This is why I have been getting into alpha channels so deeply during this chapter, as they will allow you far greater flexibility inside of your Android graphic design pipeline.

The reason that you would want to define both a foreground image plate and a background image plate at the same time, in the same UI element, would be so that you could take advantage of the power of digital image compositing that Android affords you by allowing multiple image plates (parameters that support drawable objects). This would give you two image layers (24-bit backplate and one 32-bit compositing layer) and at least one text layer, very similar to what you could do in GIMP, but within a single Android UI element.

You can extend this amount of compositing layers in your UI design by using your parent layout container and nested layout containers to also do the same thing, as long as you use alpha channels creatively, which is again why I went into this in such detail at the beginning of this chapter.

For instance, if you also set the `FloatingActionButton` background color value to transparent (#00000000), you can composite it with a background image in your `CoordinatorLayout` container. This holds true for any other UI elements you position behind the `FloatingActionButton`, as well as containers (like `NavigationView`) which are nested inside of other layout containers (such as the `DrawerLayout` class), such as we've done in the current `NavDrawerPattern` application we are working with during this chapter and the previous one. Next, let's look at the `ImageButton` states, which work with hardware pointers (mouse, trackball, etc.) as well as touchscreens to a more limited extent.

The States: Normal, Pressed, Focused, Hovered

An `ImageButton` object allows you to define a custom image asset for each of the **states** for your UI buttons. States include **normal** (the default or not in use), **pressed** (a user touching, or pressing down on, device click selection hardware), **focused** (recently touched and released, or recently clicked and released) and **hovered** (a user is over an `ImageButton` with the mouse or navigation keys, but has not touched it, or clicked on it, as yet).

The hovered state was added recently in Android 4, API Level 14, possibly in anticipation of using the Android OS for the Google Chromebook product, which now runs Android applications natively, or in anticipation of an Amazon Fire iTV set or nVidia Shield iTV set product, or other 2K or 4K iTV sets, which come with a mouse, a keyboard, and one or more game controllers. I've summarized the four currently supported `ImageButton` states as of Android 4.4.4, the last 32-bit Android OS, along with their mouse event programming equivalents, that would be used on non-touchscreen devices, in Table 9-1.

Table 9-1. The Android ImageButton Class Primary Image Asset State Constants and Mouse Usage Equivalents

ImageButton State	**Description of Button State along with its Mouse Event Equivalent**
NORMAL	Default `ImageButton` state when not in use. Equivalent: **Mouse Out**
PRESSED	`ImageButton` state when touched or clicked. Equivalent: **Mouse Down**
FOCUSED	`ImageButton` state when touched and released. Equivalent: **Mouse Up**
HOVERED (API 14)	`ImageButton` state if focused (not touched) Equivalent: **Mouse Over**

`ImageButton` UI elements are time consuming to create, because you will want to create a unique digital image asset for each `ImageButton` state. Different images will visually indicate to a user a different `ImageButton` state. The reason this can be difficult is not because of the XML markup that is involved, but rather due to extensive digital imaging work that you will need to do for each button, across several `ImageButton` states and across several different resolution densities, as you have seen earlier in this chapter, when we created the minimum 12 image assets for NORMAL, PRESSED and HOVERED in the four most common resolution densities (4K, 2K, Blu-ray, and 1K or 854 pixel).

After learning the lengthy work process for creating the dozen digital image assets you will need to create your XML structures that will implement these multi-state ImageButton UI elements we can then move on to learn the standard work process for defining each ImageButton state. This is done by using an XML drawable asset, in the form of an **image selector** definition file, which lives in your root /res/drawable folder. This file will use the parent <selector> tag with child <item> tags. The <item> tags will define each of your ImageButton's states, using digital image asset references. Once this XML definition is set up, Android will handle changing the image state for you based on what the end user is doing with the device hardware.

Creating Android Multi-state ImageButtons

The standard work process to define an Android multi-state ImageButton UI element is to utilize an **XML Drawable definition** file, which will use a <selector> parent tag and be located in the /res/drawable folder.

This file will have a parent <selector> tag and child <item> tags that define each of your ImageButton states, using custom PNG digital image asset references. Once an XML definition is set up, Android OS will select the correct image asset to utilize. It will do this based upon hardware device resolution, and the ImageButton state that is needed (normal, pressed, focused, or hovered) at the time.

First we need to set up the res/drawable alternate folders that will hold the XXHDPI down to MDPI assets we created earlier, which we will do now, so that you see the correct files displayed in Android Studio once we launch it and begin to create the fab_state.xml file, which will define the various image button visuals (states).

Right-click on the /app/res folder, and select the **New Directory** context-sensitive menu option. This will open the New Directory dialog that is seen in Figure 9-27. Name your first **alternate** app/res/drawable folder drawable-xxhdpi, and then click on the **OK** button, and create it. Repeat this work process three more times, and create alternate drawable directories that are named drawable-xhdpi, drawable-hdpi, and drawable-mdpi.

Figure 9-27. Right-click the /res folder and create a new directory named drawable-xxhdpi

You may notice that as you create these alternate folders that they do not show up under the /app/res/ directory. This is because the Project pane is set to "Android" perspective, that is, how the Android OS "sees" the project resources. This can be seen at the top left of the Android Studio Project pane in a drop-down selector, which has a downward facing arrow on the right side, which you can click to access the drop-down menu item list, as can be seen in Figure 9-28 in the top left portion of the screenshot.

Select the "Package" perspective, which is shown selected in blue in Figure 9-28. This will show you the actual directory and subdirectory path infrastructure that is being used for your project. This can also be seen in the User/user/AndroidStudioProjects folder hierarchy on your hard disk drive, which can be seen in Figure 9-29 on the left side of the screenshot. If you are the inquisitive type, you can take some time now to try some of the other options, and see what the other eight perspective views will show you regarding your Android Studio project.

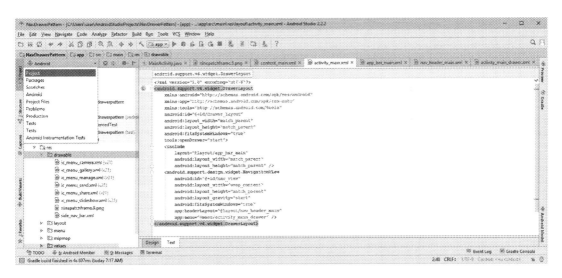

Figure 9-28. *Select the Project perspective from your Project navigation pane drop-down menu item selector*

Next, let's open your operating system file management utility, and select the XXHDPI PNG files (hold down a CTRL key modifier to group-select non-contiguous files), as shown in Figure 9-29, and drag (and drop) them in the /res/drawable-xxhdpi folder. If you want to copy (instead of move) the files, you can hold down the CTRL key before you drop the files into the folder, which is also shown on the left side in the middle of Figure 9-29.

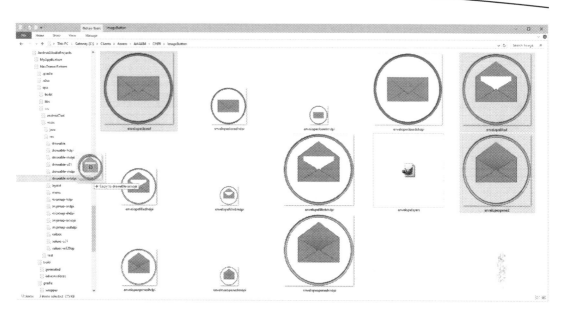

Figure 9-29. *Select each of the three matching resolution density versions, and drag them into their correct folder*

Figure 9-30 shows resolution density specific files, in resolution density specific folders, in **Project** perspective.

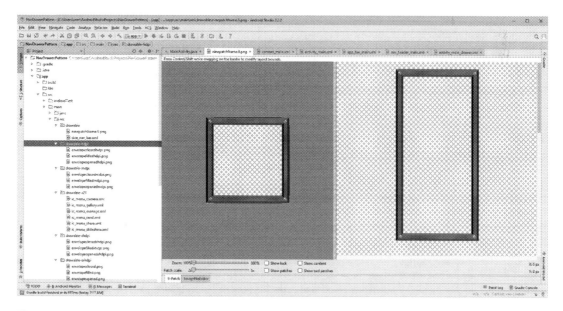

Figure 9-30. *The density specific PNG files are now in density specific alternate folders in the Project perspective*

Right-click on the res/drawable folder as seen in Figure 9-31 and select **New ➤ Drawable resource file**. In the **New Drawable Resource File** dialog name the file fab_state, and keep the default <selector> root (parent) tag.

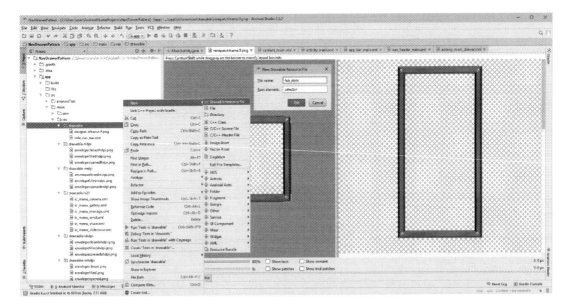

Figure 9-31. *Right-click on the /res/drawable folder and select New Drawable resource file, and name it fab_state*

Android Studio will open up the fab_state.xml definition file in your editing area with the <xml> and <selector> tags in place, and ready to add child <item> tags, which hold the state definitions and drawable asset references.

The order of the state definitions inside of the <selector> parent selection container is important. This is because these states will be evaluated in the order that they are encountered in the XML drawable definition file. This is why your normal image asset that has the default normal state (that is, no state defined) must be referenced last, because it will only be displayed after android:state_hovered, android:state_pressed, and android:state_focused states are evaluated by the Android operating system. Read it like this: Any hovering? No. Anything Pressed? No. Does it have Focus? No. Then display the normal (unpressed, unclicked, not focused) default state graphic.

The <selector> XML state definition parent tag will allow you to implement a **selection set**, much like the Java switch-case or if-then-else statements. A selector will allow the Android OS to select among several different ImageButton, or its FloatingActionButton subclass, drawable assets based on the set of android:state parameters that will define your ImageButton states. There are dozens of these state parameters, which you will see in your Android Studio pop-up helper, when you type the <item> tags inside the <selector>, which we'll be doing next.

The child <item> tags inside of the parent <selector> tag will implement the android:state parameters, as well as referencing the image assets, using the android:drawable parameter. This is shown in the fab_state.xml tab in Android Studio in Figure 9-32, and utilizes the following XML markup, with pressed and focused using the same graphic:

```
<? xml version="1.0" encoding="utf-8" ?>
<selector xmlns:android=http://schemas.android.com/apk/res/android>
        <item android:state_hovered="true" android:drawable="@drawable/envelopeopened" />
        <item android:state_pressed="true" android:drawable="@drawable/envelopefilled" />
        <item android:state_focused="true" android:drawable="@drawable/envelopefilled" />
        <item android:drawable="@drawable/envelopeclosed" />
</selector>
```

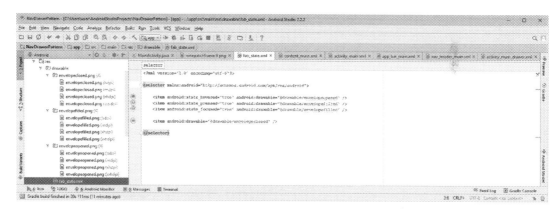

Figure 9-32. Enter the four <item> child tags inside of the parent <selector> tag defining your multi-state imagery

To get some practice, try using envelopeopened for both hovered and pressed so that you can see all three states when you test the XML (and app) in the AVD emulator, since the emulator simulates a touchscreen and doesn't support the hover state. With that drawable set up, the envelope will open on mouse-down and fill on mouse-up.

You may have noticed when you typed in the @drawable part of the <item> tags that a lot of envelope assets came up in the helper, and we really want only the three asset names to come up, even though we have a dozen different resolution density versions of those PNG32 files. What you need to do is to go into your file manager software (seen in Figure 9-29) and remove the density part of the filename for all of these (dozen) assets. The result of this can be seen in Figure 9-33, on the left side of the screen, in your Project pane. The reason we can now use the same file name for different resolution density image assets is because they are now "sequestered" away from each other, using different directory (folder) names, so we can use the same names and not have the files replace each other or get a naming error from the operating system regarding duplicate file names, because the folder name is part of the file name's path. To select between different screen densities at runtime using the different alternate drawable folder names, the actual file names inside of these folders must be exactly the same.

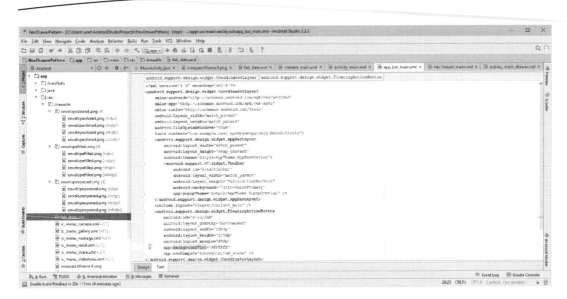

Figure 9-33. Add an app:backgroundTint parameter to remove a pink background, and tweak the button spacing

All you have left to do to upgrade the FloatingActionButton XML is add the app:backgroundTint="#FFFFFF" parameter, to remove the pink background color, upgrade your android:layout_margin to **40DP**, to push in your button corner spacing, upgrade your layout_width and layout_height parameters to use the value of **120DP**, and change the app:srcCompat parameter to reference the @drawable/fab_state value, all of which can be seen in Figure 9-33 at the bottom left in the Android Studio app_bar_main.xml editing pane (see yellow highlight bar).

It's important to note that not all of these interactive ImageButton states work in every AVD emulator, so if you want to test the focused or hovered states, be sure to use an Android hardware device that supports these to test your multi-state XML markup. The reason I taught you the most extensive and complete work process, all four state across all four resolution densities that would apply to 99% of the devices out there, is so you know how to do this in case you want your application to span every possible hardware device type and configuration. If one of these states is not supported on a given hardware device, the Android OS will simply not access that image asset that is attached to that android:state parameter. To play it safe, implement all these states in all densities!

Figure 9-34 shows the envelope closed and envelope filled button states, and the SlidingDrawer is still working.

Figure 9-34. Test the multi-state FloatingActionButton and SlidingDrawer layout in the Nexus 5 AVD emulator

Summary

In this ninth chapter, you learned all about 2D graphic design concepts and principles, as well as about Android drawables and supported image formats, including a NinePatch image format, used to create a type of drawable in Android called a NinePatchDrawable. You learned how to create NinePatchDrawable assets using Android Studio's **Draw 9-patch** Editor and then implemented this NinePatch asset inside your SlidingDrawer UI design.

Next, you learned about the Android ImageButton class and used GIMP to create all of your assets, 12 of them in total, needed to implement 4 different resolution density **multi-state** ImageButton elements, each having 4 UI states. You learned quite a bit about the proper way to utilize GIMP for streamlined digital image editing and compositing, and got a lot of practice creating image assets for ImageButton interactive states (which animate a button based on interaction) across 4 resolution densities, spanning smartwatches through 4K iTV sets. You also learned how to implement multi-state ImageButtons and NinePatchDrawables all by using XML markup.

Next, in Chapter 10, you will learn how to create animation in Android, including animation theory, concepts; how to create a wide spectrum of resolution density animation assets, as well as how to create frame animation assets for use with Android's ImageView class; and how to make them work within your SlidingDrawer layout.

Android Animation: Image and Procedural Animation

In the previous chapter on graphic design, I covered two-dimensional (2D) concepts, such as pixels, resolution, and aspect ratios, as well as three-dimensional (3D) concepts, such as layers, color channels, and their z-order. In this chapter, we are going to take all of that knowledge into the fourth dimension (4D), which is **time**, and discover how to implement animation concepts, including **motion** and **frame rates**. We are again going to build upon all of these fundamental graphics design concepts you learned about in the previous chapter, because you can also apply all of these foundational digital imaging concepts to animation. Thus we will be taking static (motionless) graphics concepts from the previous chapter, and turning them into **motion graphics**, which can look even more realistic because it looks like the subject matter is moving (animated), and therefore achieves even more realism.

You can use image animation to create an illusion of motion, using **cels** or **frames**. You will be learning about all of these concepts, terminology, and techniques during this chapter, which you will use to create animation. During this chapter, we will take a look at exactly how to set up frame-based image animation for your Android app using an XML animation definition containing a parent `<animation-list>` tag as an image animation frames container. An `<animation-list>` parent tag allows you to add individual frames of an animation as child `<item>` elements. This allows you to create XML-based frame animation definitions you can use as multimedia assets.

I will be covering more of the core Android classes that are used to implement graphic design elements, such as `ImageView`, and Android classes that are used to implement motion graphics, by using frame animation as well as procedural animation, `AnimationDrawable` (frame animation), and `Animation` **(procedural animation)**. During this chapter we'll utilize these Android animation and drawable classes to animate the `SlidingDrawer` UI layout container content. We will install an `ImageView` UI widget underneath your `content_layout` to hold an animation. We will also take a look at how to add procedural animation to your frame animation so that you can scale, rotate, and move your frame-based animation, creating powerful hybrid animation using only XML markup. We'll also look at how you can animate (interpolate, actually) Android OS and UI settings to achieve cool effects.

© Wallace Jackson 2017
W. Jackson, *Android Apps for Absolute Beginners*, DOI 10.1007/978-1-4842-2268-3_10

Frame Animation: Concepts and Techniques

The first thing that we will always need to do is to get our knowledge foundation regarding frame animation concepts, formats, and terminology, since we're going to use these during the rest of this chapter, in conjunction with working with Android animation. This new media is commonly called image animation, bitmap animation, or 2D animation, and I'm going to cover 2D **vector** animation, also known as **procedural** animation or **tween** animation, later on during this chapter, as it can be used in conjunction with 2D bitmap image frame animation.

Frame Animation: Cels, Frames, and Terminology

Frame-based animation could be termed cel-based animation, because of the original 2D animation created by Walt Disney. Disney animators drew on what at the time were called **cels**, in order to represent each individual movement in their cartoon animation. Interestingly, original cels from these 2D animation projects are now **framed**, and sold to collectors for thousands of dollars. Thus there are both physical and conceptual connections between these two animation industry terms, **frame animation** and **cel animation**. Later on, with the advent of feature films, the term "frame" replaced the term "cel." This was because the analog film projectors that were used to display 24 frames per second used frames of film. These frames of film were displayed using one or more reels containing film frames, which would create the illusion of motion when light was projected through the moving frames using film projectors in a theater projection room behind an audience.

The technical term for frame-based image animation is **raster animation**, as the frames, or cels, are made up of collections of pixels. Pixel-based imagery is commonly known in the industry as **raster imagery**. Raster images are also commonly called **bitmaps** because they are a map (array) of bits (pixels). In fact, there is the bitmap (.BMP) file format that was originally used in Microsoft Windows, and is now supported for use under Android OS. Raster animation is also frequently called bitmap animation within the multimedia production industry. We'll utilize these various animation industry terms interchangeably throughout this chapter, so that you will get used to using all of these different, but accurate, terms to refer to your frame-based 2D animation, which can also be called raster animation, bitmap animation, frame animation, cel animation, 2D animation, and image animation.

Android Image Format: PNG, GIF, JPG, WebP, BMP

Android supports the same open source digital image file formats that you use for 2D imagery in the Android application for use within the frame-based animation assets. If you think about it, this is logical as 2D animation is defined using individual 2D digital image frames as the foundation for 4D motion. The significance of this is that you can use indexed color images if you want to create 8-bit frame animation, using PNG8 or GIF formats. You can use truecolor image formats to create your 24-bit, or 32-bit, frame animation. You will do this by using PNG24, PNG32, WebP or JPEG digital image file format. Just as with image file formats Android prefers PNG over GIF, WebP, or JPEG when used in frame-based animation. This is due to a superior lossless image quality.

Android OS support for several mainstream digital image file formats gives us an impressive amount of latitude to be able to optimize the frame animation's data footprint. Because of Android's support for the PNG32 format, you will also be able to implement an image compositing work process in your frame animation endeavors. You can do this using 8-bit alpha channel transparency capabilities in the PNG32 format on a frame-by-frame basis.

Optimizing Frames: Color Depth and Frame Count

In frame animation, there are three primary ways to optimize your animation data in order to achieve a smaller data footprint. You can reduce the resolution of each frame, you can reduce the color depth used to define each frame, and you can reduce the number of frames utilized to create an illusion of motion in the animation. Since we should provide at least three different resolution density targets to support Android, we will focus on optimizing color depth and total number of frames as much as possible first, for practical purposes. You're going to want to provide frame resolution spanning from at least 120 pixels for MDPI through 240 pixels for HDPI to 480 pixels for XHDPI. As you will see during this chapter, you do have the option to provide fewer resolution density targets and have Android down sample the others. The hope is that Android will scale your assets down (term: down sample) rather than scaling assets up (term: up sample) as the quality results are better.

Since we have a choice between using a lossless PNG32 (which as you now know is a truecolor PNG with a full 8-bit alpha channel) and an indexed color PNG8, which is many times smaller (per each frame), we will use this lossless PNG8 for animated elements that do not need to be composited (compositing requires a PNG32 8-bit alpha channel). We use ImageView elements layers to implement a compositing pipeline by using a background plate for static graphics and a source (foreground plate) for the animation.

It is interesting to note that there is an advanced way around this compositing challenge, which is to use a white or a black background color for a PNG8 animation using no alpha channel and then composite with the Android PorterDuff class. This is because using certain PorterDuff **blending modes**, you can make white or black values become transparent, using blending algorithms rather than alpha channels. Alpha channels are more efficient (but have a heavy data footprint, especially when used across multiple frames in an animation) because they are static (that is, predefined), whereas using a dynamic algorithm at runtime will use valuable CPU processor cycles (system hardware resources). This PorterDuff image blending algorithm class is covered in great detail in the *Pro Android Graphics* (Apress, 2013) title, which I wrote before writing this Absolute Beginners title.

If you are not going to have to composite your animation over other graphics or UI elements, or are compositing using blending algorithms with Android's PorterDuff class, you can also consider a JPEG format, to get a much smaller per-frame data footprint. As you know, a JPEG codec does this by throwing away some image data, and thus throws away some of the original image quality. It's important to note that using JPEG for animation could increase image artifacts in each frame of an animation. If you apply too much image compression on each frame, this will cause **motion artifacts**. When you animate JPEG artifacts, it causes the effect commonly termed in the industry as "dot crawl" or "pixel crawl." With JPEG animation, not only do you have artifacts, but because the medium is animated, and the artifacts are on different pixels on each frame, it's like they are waving their hands in the air and saying: "Here I am, I'm an important artifact!" This does not lend itself to a great user experience if the JPEG frames are poorly optimized, and this is contrary to the Pure Android design principles we covered.

Just as you can optimize a 2D animation by using the indexed (8-bit) color depth, you can also optimize the 2D animation by using fewer frames to create the illusion of motion. As you will see in the next chapter on digital video, the same concepts hold true for bitmap animation as with digital video: fewer frames to store will yield a smaller data footprint, which ultimately should translate into a smaller Android application (or .APK) file size.

Also, the smaller the number of frames that will be used to achieve realistic motion, the fewer frames will have to be defined in your frame animation XML definition markup. It's also important to note that at runtime, fewer frames will require less processing power in order to play your frame animation, and less memory resources to hold the frames in, before they are displayed on the device display screen. In fact, we get professional results in this chapter by using only a few frames of animation for your ImageView UI's 3D animation new media assets.

Data footprint optimization becomes more important as the number of frame animations that are included in the application increases. New media applications such as games and e-books tend to have several frame animations running at any given time inside of the application Activity screen. Thus you need to consider processing power and system memory as valuable resources! Animation assets require careful optimization, so that the application does not use up your user's Android hardware device memory and CPU resources while your app is being used.

Animation Resolution: Pixels Add to File Size!

The number of pixels in each animation frame (the frame resolution for your image animation) is of tantamount importance for optimization of an image animation asset data footprint. Review the raw image data mathematics that we covered back in Chapter 9, and apply this to each frame in your animation, so that you can calculate the exact raw data system memory footprint you will need to hold all of the frames in your image animation.

Just like you did with your static digital image button assets, you will need to provide several resolution density-specific raster animation image target resolutions so you can span every popular Android device screen density. For this reason, if you can make an animation a few dozen pixels smaller for each dimension, without affecting its visual quality, this adds up to memory savings across the different power-of-2 down sample density versions.

It is important to make sure to trim any unutilized pixels within your animation, so that the animated elements come as close (one pixel away) to touching the edges of your image container as possible. You will see that I've done this in all the animation frame assets we will be using in this chapter, so you'll be able to see what I mean.

Similar to what you learned about digital imagery in Chapter 9, Android will automatically handle the decisions regarding which of the 2D frame animation pixel densities to implement for each device screen that the OS is running on. Our largest 480 by 480 pixel resolution frame animation asset is for the XHDPI resolution density, and I will create a 240 by 240 pixel version for HDPI, as well as a 120 by 120 pixel version to use for MDPI.

The reason that I'm not creating an XXHDPI resolution version on the high end (4K iTV) is because the XHDPI animation frames can be scaled up if needed for those devices, which represent 5% of the device market, and on the low end (240 pixel flip-phone or smartwatch), the MDPI animation frames can be scaled down if needed for those devices, which also represent about a 5% market share among all the current Android hardware devices.

Frame Animation: Using AnimationDrawable

Android's `AnimationDrawable` class is used to create frame animation drawable objects, using digital image assets. This object holds a list of drawable assets that define the frames of the animation. The object also has data fields that hold playback parameters such as frame rate (speed) and looping parameters.

Android's `AnimationDrawable` class is part of the `android.graphics` package, as you might imagine, and is kept with all of the other types of drawable objects in Android, using the `android.graphics.drawable` sub-package.

The class hierarchy starts with the `java.lang.Object` class. This is subclassed to create a `Drawable` class, which is subclassed to create the `DrawableContainer` class, which is subclassed to create this `AnimationDrawable` class. The Java class hierarchy for the `AnimationDrawable` class would therefore look like the following:

```
java.lang.Object
  > android.graphics.drawable.Drawable
    > android.graphics.drawable.DrawableContainer
      > android.graphics.drawable.AnimationDrawable
```

The reason that this `DrawableContainer` class is between `Drawable` and `AnimationDrawable` is because it was logical to create the `DrawableContainer` class for what you might consider "multi-drawables," or drawables with **more than one** state, level, layer, frame, or other such drawable asset element. Examples of these `ContainerDrawable` subclasses include a `StateListDrawable`, used to create your **multi-state** ImageButton, a `LevelListDrawable`, used for **level indicators**, such as the signal level meter for your smartphone, and this `AnimationDrawable`.

The simplest way to create one of these frame animation drawable assets is to define the animation frames using an XML file, which will be stored in your `NavDrawerPattern` project's `res/drawable` folder. We will be creating three image animations during this chapter, using `AnimationDrawable` and `Animation` classes, after we discuss how the `AnimationDrawable` and `Animation` classes function. After we create the `AnimationDrawable` object(s), we will set them up with images, using the `ImageView` object. Later on in the chapter, when we write your Java code for the `SlidingDrawer`, we'll call the `.start()` method to start an `AnimationDrawable` object playback cycle.

The XML animation definition construct that you are going to be specifying later in the chapter gets inflated by your Java code, and becomes the `AnimationDrawable` object. This object contains all information regarding your frame animation asset, including each actual animation frame's image asset reference, as well as playback (duration) and looping (direction) settings.

After an `AnimationDrawable` object has been instantiated and inflated, you can trigger it using a `.start()` method from within your application's Java code. This is usually done from the inside of your event handler, such as the one that we will be adding to the `ImageButton` UI elements later in the chapter. You would use an event handler if you wanted the frame animation to be triggered (started) interactively.

You can also call the .start() method from the inside of your AppCompatActivity subclass onCreate() method, if the animation is intended to simply run on your Activity startup screen somewhere, once the Activity is created. This can be done for content decoration where looping animation adds realism to elements such as barber poles.

If you want to research more detailed information regarding the Android AnimationDrawable class, you should investigate the more technical details for this class on the Android Developer website using the following URL:

```
https://developer.android.com/reference/android/graphics/drawable/
AnimationDrawable.html
```

Now that we have gone over the AnimationDrawable class basics, let's take a look at how to use XML markup to create the frame animation definition file, which will live in the Android Studio project res/drawable folder.

Creating Frame Animation: XML Frame Definition

The way that frame animation is defined in Android is by using an XML definition file containing markup that defines an **animation list** filled with **frame items**. This XML file should be stored in your /app/res/drawable/ folder, which you created in Chapter 9, and which holds your Android drawable asset XML definitions, such as multi-state (StateListDrawable) ImageButton elements, NinePatchDrawable asymmetrically-scalable digital image assets, and soon your AnimationDrawable digital image frame animation assets.

In case you are wondering why this XML file is kept in your /res/drawable folder, and not in a /res/anim folder, this is because there are two types of animation in Android.

- Frame animation uses the /drawable resource folder hierarchy to hold AnimationDrawable XML definitions, and alternate image assets in / drawable-dpi subfolders.

- Procedural animation, which we'll be covering later on in this chapter, uses the /res/anim project folder along with the Android Animation class to create (procedural) Animation objects.

The frame animation XML file will specify the individual frames in your AnimationDrawable object definition. Essentially the XML definition file is an AnimationDrawable object constructor using a <animation-list> parent tag and <item> child tags. A frame animation XML construct essentially creates the AnimationDrawable object, which contains references to numbered frames (image files). The image file references represent your individual frames for a raster animation. A procedural (also known as vector) animation XML file on the other hand, won't specify any frames, but will instead specify algorithmic, or procedural, transformations, that when **interpolated**, will create the illusion of motion. We will be covering this type of animation a little bit later on in this chapter.

The <animation-list> Tag: Your Image Frames Container

Your frame-based animation assets will be created by using an `<animation-list>` XML parent tag along with its playback and visibility configuration parameters. The primary configuration parameter that you will be using is an `android:oneshot` parameter. A `oneshot` parameter controls whether animation playback loops continuously (using the `oneshot="false"` setting), or if it will be configured to play just one single time (using the `oneshot="true"` setting). One-single-time playback is usually used with an event handling setup, because you want the animation to play one time whenever it is clicked. The continuous playback method, on the other hand, is usually set up with a `.start()` method call inside of an `onCreate()` method, so that your animated design element continues playing (all the time, forever), somewhere on that `Activity`'s display screen.

Later on you'll reference the XML file that contains this `<animation-list>` parent tag, and its child tags, by using its first name (that is, the first part of the filename) without the extension, just like you did with your multi-state `ImageButton` definition, in the previous chapter. We will create a frame animation XML definition file that uses an `anim_logo.xml` file name, but which references this file in XML markup and Java code as: anim_logo. Once this `<animation-list>` is defined using XML, you'll be able to reference the frame-based animation that you have defined from any of your UI design or content containers across your entire application.

Finally, there is the `android:visibility` parameter, which you can utilize if you are going to control the visibility of your `AnimationDrawable` object within your Java code. You can use this parameter to set the **initial visibility** setting, which is usually going to be "true" or visible, until a user clicks it, or some other code function hides it.

As you will see later, there is also a way to auto-start your animation using XML, so that you do not have to use any ID parameter, which is generally used to provide a way for Java 8 code to reference your XML tag construct. This approach allows you to avoid declaring, instantiating, and referencing the Java `AnimationDrawable` object!

The <item> Tag: How to Add the Image Animation Frames

The `<animation-list>` tag will always be the parent tag, because it is designed to contain `<item>` tags, which will always be the child tags. The item tag is used to define the frames in your `<animation-list>` tag, with one `<item>` tag for each animation frame. There are two parameters utilized inside of an `<item>` tag: the `android:drawable` file name referencing parameter; and the `android:duration` parameter, which specifies a frame display duration integer value, using milliseconds. A millisecond is one-thousandth of a second, so one second of frame duration would use the 1000 integer value. All these `<item>` tags exist inside of the parent `<animation-list>` container, in the order in which they are to be displayed. Essentially you are loading the animation frames into a data array in system memory, using an `AnimationDrawable` object that will control and play these frames to create motion.

The math for calculating this duration value, which is ultimately going to represent the animation's **frame rate**, which is usually specified in **frames per second**, or **FPS**, is the number of seconds you want the animation to last times 1000, divided by the number of frames that you have in your animation. So if you want the logo to rotate once every second, and you have 9 frames to create the smooth illusion of motion (40 degrees of rotation per frame), then **1 times 1000 divided by 9** gives you **111.111**, so you would use an android:duration="111" parameter for each <item> tag. If you want a slower 2-second rotation, you would use a **222** value, a 3-second rotation would be 3000 divided by 9 or a value of **333**, and so forth. Using XML markup will make it easier to experiment with these data values, until you get the exact animation motion you are looking for.

Next, you will create the XML animation definition file with Android Studio, using a very similar work process to what you did in the previous chapter, in order to create the XML for the multi-state ImageButton UI element. After we create the logo_anim.xml file we will create the XML markup; transfer nine frames for the seamlessly looping 3D animated logo; add an ImageView widget to the content_main.xml definition to hold the animation; reference the logo_anim.xml in the content_main.xml definition; write the Java code to declare, instantiate, and wire up the ImageView and AnimationDrawable objects needed in memory to play back the animation; and test the animation in the Nexus 5 AVD emulator. We have a lot of XML and Java work to do, so let's get started!

Creating Frame Animation in XML and Java

Let's go through the process of creating your AnimationDrawable XML definition file, coding image animation frames using XML, installing the image frames, coding the Java objects, and testing the image animation itself.

Create the XML Frame Animation Definition File

In Android Studio, right-click the /app/res/drawable folder in your NavDrawerPattern app, and select the **New ➤ XML ➤ Layout XML File** menu sequence. Once Android Studio adds a New ➤ XML ➤ Drawable XML File option, you will use that, but for now, Android Studio is only auto-creating files for /res/layout and /res/value subfolders, so we will have to use what we have available to us. Figure 10-1 shows you the above-described work process. Frankly, Android Studio should also have a New ➤ XML ➤ Anim XML File for the /res/anim folder, as you'll soon see when we create vector animation in the next section of this chapter on procedural (vector) animation.

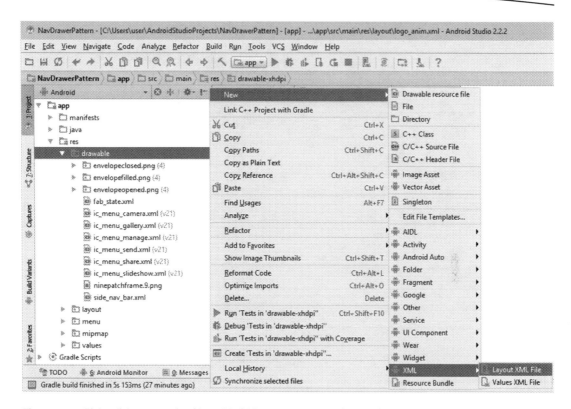

Figure 10-1. *Right-click your app/res/drawable folder, and select: New ➤ XML ➤ Layout XML File menu sequence*

In your **New Android Component** dialog, shown in Figure 10-2, configure your file name as logo_anim, and enter your animation-list parent tag (Root Tag), and then click the **Finish** button, and create this new XML file.

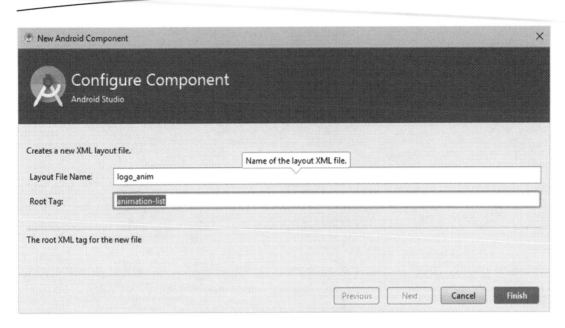

Figure 10-2. Use the New Android Component dialog to name file logo_anim, and set parent tag to animation-list

Since there is no New ➤ XML ➤ Drawable XML File option (yet), we'll have to remove the two android:layout parameters, shown encircled in red in the middle of Figure 10-3. Also shown on the left encircled in red is your /app/res/layout folder, which contains the logo_anim.xml file which needs to be moved to the app/res/drawable folder by using a cut and paste operation inside Android Studio. The first step in this operation is to right-click on the logo_anim.xml file and select the "Cut" menu option, which will remove (gray out) the file from layout.

Figure 10-3. To change XML to an animation list, remove the layout parameters, and cut and paste into drawable

The second step, seen in Figure 10-4, is to right-click on the /app/res/drawable folder, and select **Paste** from the context-sensitive menu options. This will bring up the **Move** dialog, where you specify the drawable folder.

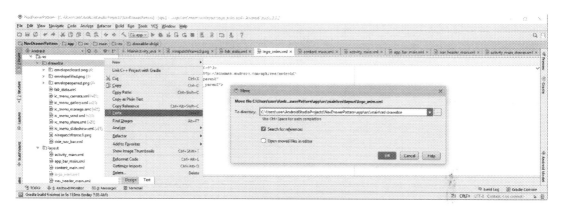

Figure 10-4. Right-click on the drawable folder and select Paste and enter the drawable folder in the Move dialog

Notice that where you locate the logo_anim.xml file doesn't change anything regarding the open logo_anim.xml editing tab, which can be seen in Figures 10-3 and 10-4, as well as in 10-5 with the animation-list XML markup. Your frame animation XML definition markup will look like the following, once you remove the android:layout parameters, add an android:oneshot parameter, and add the nine child <item> tags specifying the image frames:

```
<?xml version="1.0" encoding="utf-8"?>
<animation-list
    xmlns:android="http://schemas.android.com/apk/res/android"
    android:oneshot="false" >
    <item android:drawable="@drawable/logoanim_0" android:duration="111" />
    <item android:drawable="@drawable/logoanim_1" android:duration="111" />
    <item android:drawable="@drawable/logoanim_2" android:duration="111" />
    <item android:drawable="@drawable/logoanim_3" android:duration="111" />
    <item android:drawable="@drawable/logoanim_4" android:duration="111" />
    <item android:drawable="@drawable/logoanim_5" android:duration="111" />
    <item android:drawable="@drawable/logoanim_6" android:duration="111" />
    <item android:drawable="@drawable/logoanim_7" android:duration="111" />
    <item android:drawable="@drawable/logoanim_8" android:duration="111" />
</animation-list>
```

Notice that the screenshot in Figure 10-5 shows the slower two-second spin rate, using the duration value of 222 milliseconds, while the XML markup above shows the faster one-second spin rate, using a duration value of 111 milliseconds.

You can play around with this frame duration (frame rate) value to achieve the spin rate that gives you the most realism for the 3D logo animation. I like to get it to spin as slowly as I can, without detecting any jerkiness in the rotation motion.

Also notice in Figure 10-5 that the @drawable/logoanim_n references to the PNG8 image animation frames are highlighted in red in Android Studio. This tells us that there is something that will cause an error, and we know what that is, since we have not installed the 240 by 160 pixel XHDPI resolution density assets in the appropriate /app/res/drawable-xhdpi folder, which we'll be doing next, to get rid of these red error highlights in the markup.

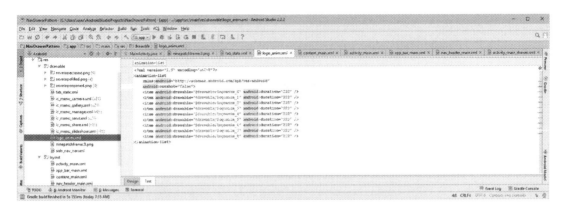

Figure 10-5. Create a logo_anim.xml frame animation definition using numbered files

Copy the nine PNG8 animation frames (logoanim_0 through logoanim_8) from the book assets repository to the AndroidStudioProjects/NavDrawerPattern/app/src/main/res/drawable-xhdpi folder with an operating system file management utility. In my case, this was the Windows Explorer utility, as is shown in Figure 10-6.

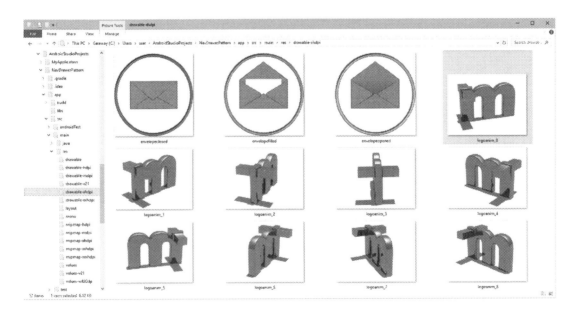

Figure 10-6. Use the operating system's file management utility to copy the image frames to /res/drawable-xhdpi

If you want to get some practice with that GIMP resolution density work process you learned in Chapter 9, you can down sample this XHDPI into HDPI 120 by 80 and MDPI 60 by 40 assets. The reason I am not doing this is because these are 8-bit (indexed) images, and it would be better to have Android 7.1.1 try and use these XHDPI 240 pixel images, if possible, and use the Android 7.1.1 OS down sampling algorithms to reduce the image pixels only if necessary. The 64-bit Android OS has improved the sampling algorithms considerably over the ones in 32-bit versions.

Figure 10-7 shows the `logoanim_n.png` (xhdpi) files in the `/app/res/drawable` folder in the Project pane on the far left, and the error-free image animation frame definition markup on the right.

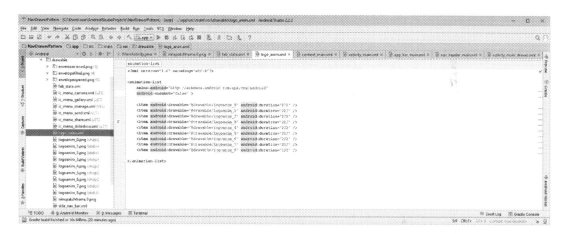

Figure 10-7. *Once PNG files are in res/drawable-xhdpi, they will show up in the IDE and markup will be error free*

The next thing that you need to do is reference this animation definition file inside of the `content_main.xml` file. To do this you need to add an `ImageView` to hold the image animation, so click on the `content_main.xml` tab in the Android Studio IDE and click the Design (Editor) tab at the bottom left and drag an `ImageView` element out of the Images & Media subpalette into the center of the UI design as shown in Figure 10-8. Enter a background (plate) reference to `@drawable/logo_anim` to wire the `ImageView` to the `AnimationDrawable` definition, and add a `contentDescription` parameter data value of **Logo Animation** to provide aural feedback for the impaired, and leave the default **imageView2** ID, as can be seen in the Properties panel on the far-right side of Figure 10-8.

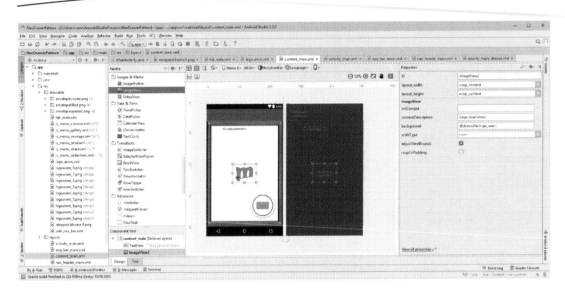

Figure 10-8. Test UI design in Galaxy Nexus AVD (left), and add a 38 DIP left margin parameter to center (right)

Let's also click on the TextView in the Design Editor and enter "3D Logo Animation" to replace Hello World and add "Logo Animation" to the contentDescription data field for the disabled (impaired). The final XML, as shown in Figure 10-9, for your new ImageView UI widget child tag markup should look like the following:

```
<ImageView
    android:layout_width="wrap_content"
    android:layout_height="wrap_content"
    android:background="@drawable/logo_anim"
    android:id="@+id/imageView2"
    android:layout_centerVertical="true"
    android:layout_centerHorizontal="true"
    android:adjustViewBounds="true"
    android:contentDescription="Logo Animation" />
```

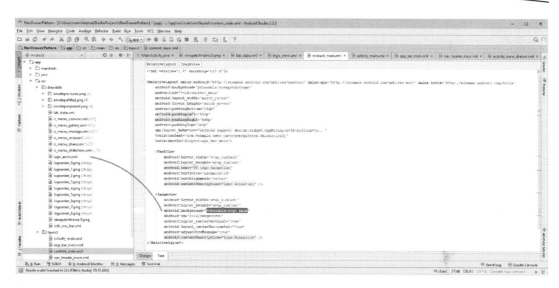

Figure 10-9. Click the XML Text tab and view the XML tags and parameters generated by the XML Design Editor

Notice in Figure 10-9 that Android Studio highlights your new parameters that it added using the Visual Design Editor (seen in Figure 10-8), as well as key parameters which reference assets or assist the impaired or disabled users. We will be tweaking these parameters as we continue to create our animated content_main UI definition, over the course of this chapter covering the different types of animation available to Android 7 developers.

I also drew a red arc showing the connection between /src/drawable/logo_anim.xml and the android:background parameter. This parameter references a logo_anim.xml AnimationDrawable image frame asset XML definition.

Now that you have created an XML definition for an AnimationDrawable object and updated content_main.xml to reference this image animation's frame sequence in the background plate of an ImageView, let's go into your Java code using the MainActivity.java tab, so that you can declare, construct, instantiate, and inflate the objects that will be needed to hold these object definitions in system memory so they can be processed. In this case, processing involves blitting (animating) image frames at your specified millisecond intervals, to create motion.

Create ImageView and AnimationDrawable Objects

Now we have to use Java to create (instantiate) objects in memory to hold your ImageView receptacle, and your AnimationDrawable frame animation engine. As you've seen before, an object can be declared, instantiated, and inflated using a single Java statement. For an ImageView object, this looks like the following Java statement:

```
ImageView imageView2 = (ImageView) findViewById( R.id.imageView2 );
```

Type in ImageView, which will display in red, as there is no import statement yet. Mouse-over this error, until the **android.widget.ImageView? (import)** pop-up appears and then use **Alt+Enter** to have Android Studio write an import statement for you. Name the ImageView **imageView2** and use an equal operator to use an ImageView findViewById(R.id.imageView2) method to inflate the ImageView using the parameters defined in the XML. Note that if you type R.id. in the findViewById() method parameter area, Android Studio will provide you with a list of all of the android:id parameters you have defined across all of your XML object definition files, as you can see in the bottom-middle portion of Figure 10-10. Select, and double-click on, **imageView2** to insert it.

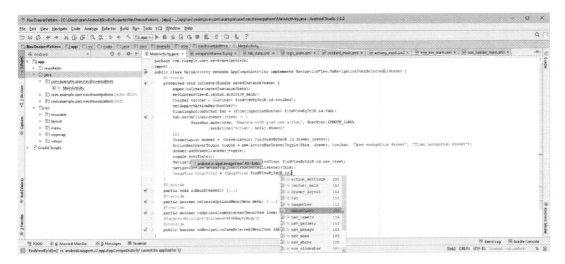

Figure 10-10. Declare and instantiate an ImageView object named imageView2, and inflate it using findViewById

The next thing we have to do is to create (instantiate) an AnimationDrawable object in system memory that will hold your image animation frames, as well as the AnimationDrawable frame animation engine. As we did with the ImageView object, we will declare, instantiate and inflate the AnimationDrawable object using a single Java statement. For the AnimationDrawable object, this should look like the following Java programming statement:

AnimationDrawable **imageAnimation** = (AnimationDrawable) **imageView2.getBackground**();

To inflate your AnimationDrawable object, as well as wiring it up to your ImageView object, you call the .getBackground() method off the imageView2 ImageView object, which loads the logo_anim.xml image frames definition that's referenced by using android:background="@drawable/logo_anim"" in the content_main.xml.

This AnimationDrawable object preparation can be seen highlighted in pale yellow in Figure 10-11, along with a second Java statement, which starts the image animation frames sequence displaying at around 5 FPS (222ms) using a .start() method call off the imageAnimation AnimationDrawable object, or: imageAnimation.start().

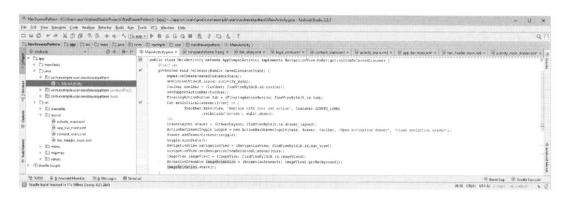

Figure 10-11. *Add the AnimationDrawable object instantiation, and start image animation using a .start( ) method*

Use the **Run** feature (or **Clean and Run**) to test the image animation in the AVD. As you'll see in Figure 10-12 the animation is running, due to the android:oneshot="false" parameter, and the UI elements still work well.

Figure 10-12. *Test your image animation, multistate button, and menu system*

Next, let's take a look at how to set up the other type of animation, vector or procedural animation, in Android.

Android Tween Animation: Vector Concepts

The patron saint of 2D animation, Walt Disney, is also responsible for the animation term **tween** since cels were "tweened," which is short for "in-betweened," by his apprentice animators. Senior animators would create the primary key movement frames called **key frames** and the junior animators would then create the tweens.

Tweening is now done **algorithmically** for you by the Android OS, using something that's called **interpolation.** Interpolation algorithms are provided by the Android **Animation** class, which we will be learning all about after we get up-to-speed on all of our tween animation (or vector or procedural animation) concepts and terminology. One of the cool things that was added in 64-bit Android (5.0 and later) were additional interpolation algorithms.

The procedural animation attributes are types of vector attributes that can be interpolated, or more accurately, which can be transformed by using mathematical interpolation, which you learned about in high school. They include **alpha** (transparency), which you've already learned about to some extent; as well as **translation**, which is the 2D industry term for movement, **scale**, which is the industry term for size; and finally, **rotation**, which is the industry term describing which direction something is facing.

Each of these concepts (rotate, scale, translate, and alpha) has an XML tag and class in Android, so let's cover these new vector animation concepts next. In case you might be wondering, a vector is a ray that is traced out in two or three dimensions, starting at one point and shooting out through another point (a line, basically). Vector graphics allow us to define shapes algorithmically, rather than using arrays of pixels (bitmaps). If you want to dive into SVG and vector graphics in depth, see the popular *Digital Illustration Fundamentals* (Apress, 2015) title.

Procedural Concepts: Rotate, Scale, Translate

Let's start out by learning about some of the concepts involved in vector imaging and vector animation. First of all, there are two primary types of vector platforms: 2D (two-dimensional, flat) vector graphics, like we find in Illustrator or Inkscape; and 3D (three-dimensional, volumetric) vector graphics, like we find in 3D modeling software such as NewTek Lightwave, open source Blender, or Autodesk 3D Studio MAX. Concepts that we cover in this section of the chapter apply to both 2D and 3D imagery and animation; however, we will be only covering the basic 2D vector animation implementations for this Absolute Beginners title.

The 2D vector that uses x and y coordinates is used in 2D, and 3D vectors, which use x, y, and z coordinates, are used in 3D. Both 2D and 3D animation involve core concepts of translation (movement), rotation (direction), and scale (size). There is a z concept in 2D animation, but it is not a z-axis, but rather a z-order. Z-order in 2D is akin to layers in digital imaging as we've already discussed earlier during the book. Z-order involves what layer order each 2D (flat) layer is in, and whether it is front of, or behind, other 2D layers, making z-order the number that orders the layers in a 2D composite. This z-order number defines what is in front of, and what is behind, any given 2D layer. Changing this z-order numeric value in real time using your Java programming logic can create flip-book types of special effects, and is a technique often utilized in 2D game programming.

Translation in 2D involves movement along an x or y axis and is the most basic of the three transformations you can achieve in 2D animation. Translation is defined by a **starting point** for a movement; an **amount** or distance for that movement in pixels or percentages; and a **direction** of movement, along either an x or y axis (horizontal or vertical movement), or along some relative combination of both x and y axis values (diagonal movement).

Rotation in 2D involves rotation around any given x,y **pivot point** coordinate. The amount of rotation is defined using **degrees**, **direction** (positive/clockwise, or negative/counter-clockwise) of the rotation, and the pivot point (center) **location** of the rotation. Since there are **360** degrees in a full circle, rotational mathematics involves this 360 number specifically, like FPS calculations involve the number 1000 (number of milliseconds in a second).

Scale in 2D involves a size for a given shape, and is defined by a **decimal number** relative to the current size of the shape. For instance, a **0.5 scale** would be **half** of the current size, or 50%, and a **2.0 scale,** or 200%, would be **twice** the current size of that shape. Like translation, scaling has an x and a y component. If the values are the same, this scaling can be said to be **uniform scaling**; if they're not the same, the scaling would be said to be **non-uniform** scaling.

To draw a parallel to something that you have learned about previously, uniform scaling maintains aspect ratio, and non-uniform scaling skews or distorts (that is, changes) the aspect ratio. Therefore, non-uniform scaling is most often used for animation special effects, such as making a ball squash when it bounces off the ground.

Interestingly, you can also define a **pivot point** for your scaling operation, which allows **skewed scaling**, where the placement of the pivot point can influence your scaling operation. For irregular shapes, this can give a more precise level of scaling control over a resulting shape-warping special effect for a scaling operation. Given that sometimes the 2D shapes being scaled contain bitmap images (patterns and textures), you can obtain some very interesting results using a pivot point placement that is not at the exact center point of the vector shape being scaled. The industry term for putting digital imagery in a 2D shape or on a 3D object is called **texture mapping**.

Procedural Data Values: Ranges and Pivot Point

In order to be able to interpolate, we need to specify more than one single numeric value, because interpolation (tweening) involves creating new **interim values** between starting and ending values. So, information learned in the previous sections (interpolation) will be applied to information found in this section (ranges), and then in the next section we'll cover alpha blending and more complex procedural animation parameters that are available to control animation start time offsets, loop type characteristics, and how many times your animation will loop.

To have any procedural animation, you will always need to specify a **range** using a starting value, called a **From** value, and an ending value called a **To** value.

Like a value range, a pivot point will also require two values to establish. However, unlike a value range, which utilizes a From and To value, a pivot point uses a two-dimensional location on your display screen, and uses the **x** and **y** coordinates, just like pixels do, to define where the pivot point is to be placed within that 2D plane" A plane in 2D is like a sheet of paper, or like a layer in compositing, and is an "infinitely flat" with only 2D (x and y dimensions) surface (no volume). By infinitely flat, I mean that there is no z dimension (depth) to a 2D plane.

Pivot points are also used extensively in 3D animation, where setting the pivot point requires three (x, y, and z) data coordinates in order to be properly specified in 3D space. In this book, we are only covering 2D, as that is the best starting point to use for Absolute Beginners. As you get more advanced you can add 3D to your repertoire. Let's take a look at a fourth type of procedural transform, **alpha blending**; then we will look at advanced parameters.

Procedural Animation Compositing: Alpha Values

There is one other attribute that can be animated procedurally in Android, but it is not a transformation. Alpha blending is much more akin to a compositing feature; in fact, it is a crucial part of compositing. If you transform an object, the object changes physically in some way, moving it to a different location (translation), changing its size (scaling), or what direction it is facing or how it is **oriented** (rotated).

Alpha blending an object with its background to create procedural animation is done by specifying a change in the object alpha (transparency) value, with zero being transparent and one being opaque. This is usually termed as a **fade-in** or a **fade-out** in the content production industry, and technically is image compositing. In Android, alpha blending is included with a procedural animation toolset, because alpha values are logical attributes to animate, especially if you are creating an animated children's ghost story, or a sci-fi transporter beam special effect, or something similar.

You can finely control the Alpha attribute of an object you are animating procedurally by using alpha parameter with **floating-point** values, and you can use an AnimationSet class to seamlessly combine alpha (transparency) blending with movement, scale, or rotation transformations.

Like most of the other procedural animation attributes, alpha blending amounts are specified using real (floating-point, or float) numbers, between 0.0 (transparent) and 1.0 (visible). The exception to this is pivot points, which you specify using a percentage, such as 50%; and degrees, which you specify using degrees in decimal numbers (also called real, floating point, or float) using values between 0.0 and 360 degrees.

It is important to note that using more than one decimal place (precision position) is allowed when using real or float values. Thus if you wanted your object to be precisely one-third visible, you would use 0.3333 or, for three-quarters visible, you could simply specify 0.75 as the starting or ending value for your object's alpha value.

You'll set alpha starting and ending values by using the fromAlpha and the toAlpha parameters. So, to fade-out any object, you would set fromAlpha to 1.0, and toAlpha to 0.0, in order to achieve that fade-out special effect.

To combine multiple different types of procedural animation parameters together, you should create a **set** for the animation transformation parameters. Using a procedural **animation set** will allow you to group transforms and compositing together in a logical and organized fashion. This enables us to create very complex procedural animation.

We'll be covering how to create procedural animation sets using the Android `AnimationSet` class (and object) in detail a bit later on during the chapter. First, let's take a look at procedural animation timing and looping values.

Procedural Timing: Using Duration and Offsets

You might be wondering how you set the timing that is used between all of these different range data values. You actually have done this already for your frame animation using the `android:duration` parameter, which sets the duration for displaying one single frame. In procedural animation, duration sets the timing value for the entire range, and will also to some extent define how many interpolated data values are created by the Android OS during that range duration, as well as the duration of each of the segments between each interpolated value.

It is important to remember that the Android `Animation` classes decide this value based on the device processing power, and what those algorithms (the procedural animation "engine") calculates will provide the most optimal, that is, the smoothest, visual results, given the current processing power to applications in use ratio, or trade-off.

The duration for any given procedural animation range is set using the duration parameter, which, like it does in frame animation, also takes an integer value in milliseconds. It's interesting to note that programming languages such as Java, JavaFX, and JavaScript will utilize these millisecond values for all of their timing functions and operations.

It is also important to point out here that 64-bit Android OSes (5, 6, and 7) can provide even finer timing granularity, by using **nanoseconds**, or "nanos," which allow a billion time slices per second, instead of a thousand! That being said, you can still also use milliseconds, which are more reasonable to use for both image and vector animation. This capability was primarily added to support high frame rate (60 FPS) i3D game development, so that things could be synchronized with seamless perceptual precision to the game player.

If you wanted the fade-out we discussed in the previous section to take four seconds, the XML parameter would be `android:duration="4000"` since 4000 milliseconds equals 4 seconds. If you wanted alpha fade-outs to take (or "span") 4.352 seconds, you would use a millisecond value of 4352, and thus you have a one-thousandth of a second "granularity," which is the level of precision, available for your procedural animation timing accuracy.

Each transformation (or alpha blend) range that you define has its own separate duration settings, allowing for a great deal of precision in the XML markup definition of the composite procedural animation special effect that you are trying to achieve.

There is one other important timing-related parameter, which allows you to delay when the specified range will start playback. This is called an animation **offset**, and it is controlled using the `startOffset` parameter data value.

Say that you wanted to delay the start of your four second fade-out by four seconds. All that you would have to do is to add the `android:startOffset="4000"` to your `<alpha>` parent tag, which we will be using for real, a bit later on during this chapter, and this four-second timing delay control would then be implemented.

The `startOffset` parameter is especially useful when utilized in conjunction with animation loops, which we are going to be covering next. The reason for this is that when used with looping animation scenarios, a `startOffset` parameter will allow you to define a pause during animated element loop cycles.

Let's take a look at loops next along with different parameters, which are also called attributes or characteristics, for controlling looping procedural animation. As you'll soon see, the definitions for these procedural animation composites can become quite complex, using `AnimationSet` objects and deeply nested XML constructs.

Procedural Loops: RepeatCount and RepeatMode

Like frame animation, procedural animation can play once, and then stop, or can play continuously in a loop, either forever (an infinite loop, which is acceptable for animation) or for a specified (integer) number of times.

There are two parameters that control looping, one which controls whether the animation will loop or not, and another which controls the direction in which the animation will loop back and forth. The procedural animation parameter that controls the number of times an animation, or component part of an animation set, will loop is called the **repeatCount** parameter. This parameter will require a whole number (integer) data value.

If you leave this `repeatCount` parameter out of (that is, unspecified in) the procedural animation definition, then an animation will play once and then stop. This means the default setting is `android:repeatCount="1"` for this parameter. The exception to using an integer value for this parameter is an **infinite** constant. If you want to have an animation loop forever, you would want to use an `android:repeatCount="infinite"` parameter setting.

In case you're wondering, the value that the constant `infinite` defines is **-1**, so an `android:repeatCount="-1"` parameter definition works just as well. The parameter that defines what style of looping is used is the `repeatMode` parameter, which you can set to one of two predefined constants. The most common of these two is `restart`, which will cause an animation to loop seamlessly, unless you've defined the `startOffset` parameter. In case you're wondering, the value that a `restart` constant defines is **1**, so `android:repeatMode="1"` works too.

The other **repeatMode** of animation looping is the `reverse` mode, which is also called **pong animation**, as it causes the animation to reverse at the end of its range, and run backward, until it reaches the beginning again, at which time it will run forward. Back and forth, ad infinitum, like the video game **Pong**! In case you're wondering, the value that a `reverse` constant defines is **2**, so `android:repeatMode="2"` will also work.

These parameters may seem simple on their own, but when combined in structures using an `AnimationSet` class, which we'll take a look at later, or by nesting parent and child tags, these parameters can quickly become quite complicated in combination with each other. Don't underestimate the power of these parameters when they are put together by a savvy developer, in the right XML structure. Next, let's take a look at the Android `Animation` class and its subclasses that implement tween animation, and then implement procedural animation using XML.

Android Animation Class: Tween Animation

The `Animation` class is used to create tween animations of `View` objects in Android. This is via the interpolation of data values, within constructs of predefined transform types. This will create frames of procedural animation, with Android deciding how many frames are needed to create a smooth animation result. The `Animation` class is part of the `android.view` package, and is kept with the other `Animation` classes, subclasses, and methods, using the **android.view.animation** package. This is quite different from the image (bitmap or raster) frame animation type, which uses the `ImageView` and `AnimationDrawable` objects, and the frame animation engine is kept in the `android.graphics.drawable` package. This is centered around graphic design and drawables rather than `View` UI.

The `Animation` class hierarchy starts with the `java.lang.Object` master object, which is then subclassed, to create the `Animation` class. The Java class hierarchy for the `Animation` class would therefore look like the following:

```
java.lang.Object
    > android.view.animation.Animation
```

It is interesting to note that any class that is subclassed from `java.lang.Object` is essentially "scratch coded" in the sense that the class is created from nothing, other than the `Object` infrastructure, so, in this case, the Android `Animation` engine was created using only the procedural animation objectives of Android's development team.

The `Animation` class was then used to create the subclasses, which are actually used via the XML tags, which we will learn how to implement a bit later on during this chapter. There is one subclass for each of the four types of tween animation you learned about in the previous section, including the `AlphaAnimation`, `RotateAnimation`, `ScaleAnimation`, and `TranslateAnimation` classes. There is also the `AnimationSet` class, which can be used to create groupings of more complicated tween animation transforms, called, you guessed it: animation sets.

Since we have already covered all of the XML parameters that can be used with the Android `Animation` class, and therefore with any of its subclasses, in previous sections of this chapter, let's jump right into some hands-on XML markup, and create your `/res/anim` folder, and procedural animation assets to put inside of that folder that takes a `View` widget, and applies some procedural animation transforms to it to vector animate it, so that you'll start to learn about how to create tween animation in Android.

After you create the tween animation we'll create a **hybrid animation** using both the frame (`AnimationDrawable` class) and tween (`Animation` class) animation engines together, for the ultimate in Android animation power!

Creating Tween Animation Using XML Markup

The simplest way to create one of these tween animation assets is to define your procedural animation using an XML file. This will be stored in the NavDrawerPattern project /res/anim folder. We'll create this folder before we create an Animation object XML definition that will live inside of that folder. The work process is similar to what you did previously to create a /res/drawable folder and your AnimationDrawable XML asset definition.

Since we're creating three different types of animation during this chapter (raster, vector, and hybrid) using both an AnimationDrawable object and an Animation object, we will create our second logo animation by scaling the AnimationDrawable object to give that animation the appearance that it is coming in out of the distance.

This will show you how to combine vector and raster animation in Android to create more advanced animation effects, which will show you how to create what I call "hybrid" animation in Android. After that, I'll show you how to use tween animation to create more advanced vector animation effects that can be used on UI widgets.

After you create a /res/anim folder and XML file containing procedural animation parameters, we will get back into Java coding and wire up the ImageView UI element to the vector animation so I can show you how to set up and trigger both frame animation and tween animation at the same time. After that we'll look at how to combine rotate and translate transforms along with the scale transform using the AnimationSet parent container. By the end of this chapter, you will have a nice overview of the Android bitmap and vector animation engine classes.

Create an /anim Folder: Tween Animation Assets

Right-click on the NavDrawerPattern project app/res folder, and select the **New ➤ Directory** menu sequence, as shown in Figure 10-13. In the **New Directory** dialog name the folder **anim** and click the **OK** button to create the new folder. This adds a sixth type of Android asset (procedural, vector, or tween animation), a motion graphics asset, to your hierarchy, which already includes static graphic assets (/res/drawable), UI design assets (/res/layout), menu design assets (/res/menu), application icons (/res/mipmap), and constant values (/res/values).

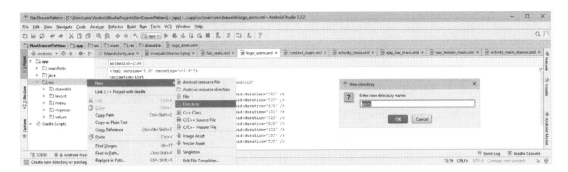

Figure 10-13. Right-click on the project app/res folder, and create an app/res/anim folder under the app/res folder

Once you have a /res/anim folder in place, seen in Figure 10-14 on the left, right-click on that folder and select the **New ➤ Animation resource file** menu sequence, to open the **New Resource File** dialog shown on the right side of Figure 10-14. Since you right-clicked on the /res/anim folder, Android Studio will automatically set the **Directory Name** field to **anim**. All you need to do is to name this file tween_anim, and leave the other default settings as they are. Once you click **OK**, Android Studio will open your empty bootstrap tween_anim.xml file.

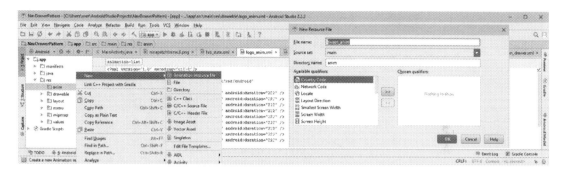

Figure 10-14. *Right-click on anim folder and use New ➤ Animation resource file to name the XML file tween_anim*

Since we talked about the primary parameters earlier in the chapter, we will get down to business, and configure the scale transform so we can bring our rotating logo in out of distance to increase the animation realism.

Android ScaleAnimation Class: Animated Scaling

The Android public class named ScaleAnimation extends the Animation primary procedural animation engine class and focuses on scaling animation, which changes the size of the object that you want to animate. The class hierarchy for the Android ScaleAnimation class looks like the following:

```
java.lang.Object
    > android.view.animation.Animation
        > android.view.animation.ScaleAnimation
```

The ScaleAnimation object constructed using this class, and generally specified using a <scale> tag, in an XML definition file, creates animation that will animate, or more accurately, interpolate, the scale of an object. You can specify the point to use for the center of this scaling operation using a pivotX and pivotY parameters, along with a percentage, in our case this will be the exact center of the object, or pivotX=50% and pivotY=50%. Let's get right into creating the XML markup for this scale operation, inside of the tween_anim.xml you just created.

The Scale Transform: Configuration Parameters

Let's go through the process of having Android Studio help us code a child `<scale>` animation construct, inside of the `AnimationSet <set>` parent tag. Inside of the parent `<set>` tag type a < left-facing chevron and select and double-click on the scale vector animation child tag, as shown in Figure 10-15. Notice that when you resize the IDEA window that there is a control on the right to access the open tabs, four in this case, that you cannot see, using a drop-down (arrow) menu with the number of "overflow" tabs that are contained within the drop-down.

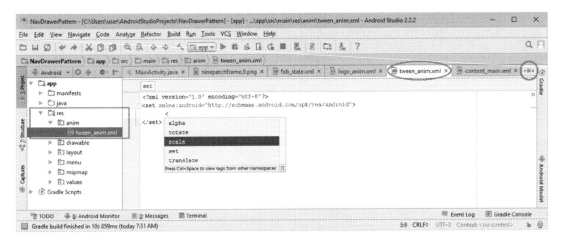

Figure 10-15. Type a left-facing chevron inside of your parent <set> tag, and double-click on the scale animation

To add parameters, type a space after the `<scale` tag and select one of the six available parameters for this tag, in our case, this would be `android:pivotX`, and then double-click on it, and insert it, as can be seen in Figure 10-16.

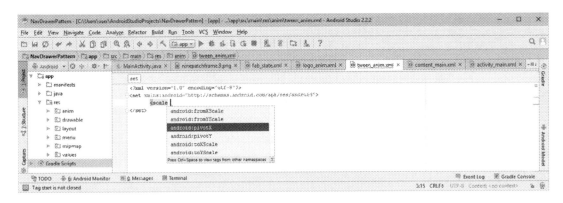

Figure 10-16. After the <scale opening tag, type a space and select and double-click on android:pivotX to insert it

Now that you have defined your perfectly centered pivot point by using the android:pivotX and android:pivotY configuration parameters using a 50% value, you'll need to reference the starting scale range in both the X and Y dimension using the fromXScale and fromYScaled configuration parameters. Add a line of markup after the pivot parameters, and then type an "a" to bring up a helper drop-down, and select and double-click on the fromXScale parameter, as can be seen selected in yellow and blue in Figure 10-17. Set your fromScale data values for both the X and Y dimensions to zero using the "0.0" floating-point number. Now all you have to set is the toScale X and Y range.

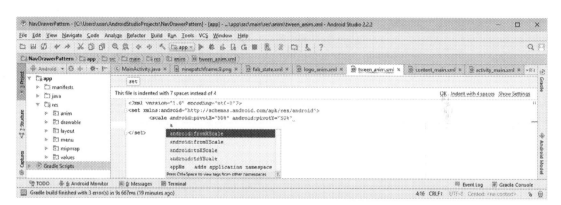

Figure 10-17. After the pivot parameter, type an "a" and select and double-click on android:fromXScale to insert it

Add another line of markup, after your fromScale parameters, and then type an "a" to bring up the helper drop-down. Select and double-click on the toXScale parameter, and specify a 100% full scale, using a "1.0" floating-point number. Notice that for this parameter, the 0.0 equates to 0% and the 1.0 equates to 100%.

Then hit a space (spacebar) character, and select and double-click on the toYScale parameter, as can be seen selected in yellow and blue in Figure 10-18. Also notice in Figures 10-17 and 10-18 that Android Studio has put a yellow warning header on the top of the XML markup editing pane that advises you that the markup is indented with 7 spaces, instead of using the standard 4 spaces. This is because I wanted to show all of the code and the pop-up helper drop-downs unhindered by one another, and so I had to space the markup out a bit more!

After I was done with the screenshots, I selected the "Indent with 4 spaces" link (option). The number of spaces you use to indent your code for readability purposes will not affect the efficacy or execution of that code, either in Java or in XML editing for your Android applications, so do whatever you feel the most comfortable with!

Figure 10-18. After the fromScale parameters type an "a," select and double-click on android:toYScale to insert it

The XML markup for the six initial transform definition parameters are shown in Figure 10-18, and should look like the following child `<scale>` tag (and its scaling parameters, attributes, or characteristics) XML markup:

```
<scale xmlns:android="http://schemas.android.com/apk/res/android"
       android:pivotX="50%" android:pivotY="50%"
       android:fromXScale="0.0" android:fromYScale="0.0"
       android:toXScale="1.0" android:toYScale="1.0"  />
```

Next, let's learn a bit more about the parent `<set>` AnimationSet class, and then add more parameters to the AnimationSet, so that we can specify and control the vector animation duration, loop type, offset, and more.

Android AnimationSet Class: Transform Grouping

The Android public class named AnimationSet extends the Animation primary procedural animation engine class and focuses on grouping animation, which allows you to apply group hierarchies to procedural animation to allow more complex animation by combining the four types of procedural animation (scale, rotate, move, alpha). The class hierarchy for the Android AnimationSet class looks like the following:

```
java.lang.Object
   > android.view.animation.Animation
     > android.view.animation.AnimationSet
```

The AnimationSet object is constructed using this class, and generally specified using a `<set>` tag, in an XML definition file, creates animation hierarchies that will contain constructs of the four vector animation types as well as other AnimationSet constructs, allowing you to deeply nest the different types of procedural animation relative to each other to create any desired animation result imaginable. Let's get right into creating the XML markup for this AnimationSet operation, which forms the foundation of the tween_anim.xml you have created.

To the `Animation` class the `AnimationSet` is used to construct a group of `Animation` subclasses that are designed to be played together, either serially, or in parallel, or in more complex animation constructs, both. Visually, the transformation of each individual animation will be composed together into one single more complex transformation.

If an `AnimationSet` parent grouping specifies any properties (parameters) that its children also specify, for example, duration, the values of the parent `AnimationSet` will override the same values set in the children (tags). The way `AnimationSet` inherits behavior from the `Animation` engine is different based upon each parameter. Some of the `Animation` parameters applied to `AnimationSet` affect the `AnimationSet` as a whole, while others will be "pushed down" into its children, while others will be completely ignored.

The `duration`, `repeatMode`, `fillBefore` or `fillAfter` properties, when specified for an `AnimationSet` object, will be pushed down to all of its children animation transformation types. The `fillBefore` and `fillAfter` parameters control whether the initial value of the animation is applied before its start time (`fillBefore`) and whether the animation's ending values persists after it has transformed (`fillAfter`). These are for more advanced applications, and therefore will not be delved into in this book, but you are welcome to dive into them on the developer site.

The `repeatCount` and `fillEnabled`, which switches on or off the `fillBefore` and `fillAfter` parameters, will be completely ignored if specified for the parent `AnimationSet`, as they are inherently used at the transform level. The `startOffset` or `shareInterpolator` parameters on the other hand only apply to an `AnimationSet` as a whole. The `shareInterpolator` tells children of an `AnimationSet` whether to share (if set to "true') the `AnimationSet` Interpolator parameter, or if `AnimationSet` defines `shareInterpolator="false"`, to put different Interpolator values into each of the child transforms, to achieve a far more advanced vector animation effect. Let's get right into it!

AnimationSet Container: Groups and Subgroups

Let's go into the `tween_anim.xml` tab and add some of the commonly used parameters into the parent `<set>` tag. If you add a space before the end (right-facing) chevron of the `AnimationSet` parent `<set>` tag, you will get the drop-down helper selector where you can select and double-click on the `android:duration` parameter to add it, as is shown in Figure 10-19. Set duration to 5000 milliseconds to make the animating logo come into view slowly.

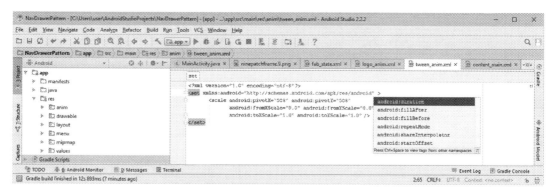

Figure 10-19. Add a space before the closing ➤ chevron of the parent <set> tag, and select a duration parameter

Next, add the repeatMode parameter set to "reverse" and the sharedInterpolator parameter set to "true" so that all of the transforms we will be adding later use the default LinearInterpolator. Add a small 100 millisecond startOffset so that the animation takes a little while to appear in the distance to add more realism. These parameters are shown inside of the parent <set> tag in the middle of Figure 10-20, and configure the animation.

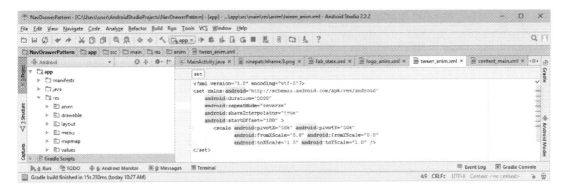

Figure 10-20. *Add repeatMode, startOffset and ShareInterpolator parameters to your parent AnimationSet <set>*

Since your <ImageView> UI element already has an ID value in your XML markup and has been instantiated in the Java code, all you have to add is the Java code in your MainActivity.java file that will wire the tween animation to the ImageView in order to scale it into view (out of the distance), to create this hybrid animation, which is frame animating the background image assets, and vector animating your ImageView container itself!

Java Code: Tying Two Animation Types Together

Since you are going to use the ImageView object inside of your event handler for the FloatingActionButton, to trigger the logo animation to emerge from the distance (scale), let's declare your ImageView object at the top of your MainActivity class, as is seen highlighted in yellow in Figure 10-21. Also declare an Animation object and name it tweenAnimation, as we will be instantiating that next, underneath your AnimationDrawable Java code.

Figure 10-21. *Declare an ImageView object named imageView2, and Animation object named tweenAnimation*

Make sure to remove the ImageView from the beginning of your ImageView findViewById object instantiation statement (after the two NavigationView statements), or you'll get a red wavy error highlight in Android Studio.

Next, instantiate the tweenAnimation Animation object after the imageAnimation.start() method call, as seen in Figure 10-22, so that Android will instantiate this object when your application's MainActivity starts. Reference your tween_anim.xml XML definition using a .loadAnimation() method called on the AnimationUtils class, as shown highlighted in yellow in Figure 10-22. The AnimationUtils class defines common utilities for working with vector (procedural) animation, such as loading Animation objects, loading Interpolator objects, and polling these objects so you can ascertain their current time (progress into the animation's duration) using milliseconds.

Figure 10-22. Instantiate the animImageView inside of the onCreate() method using the findViewById( ) method

The next thing that you will need to do is to wire the Animation object to the ImageView object. This is done by calling the .startAnimation() method off of the imageView2 object and passing the tweenAnimation object over in the parameter area of the method call, like this:

```
imageView2.startAnimation(tweenAnimation);
```

We will do this inside of the OnClickListener() event handling code for your FloatingActionButton, instead of posting a text message about inserting your own code. As you can see, highlighted in Figure 10-23, this makes your event handling routine simpler, and gives you control over triggering the vector animation, so you can test your code.

Figure 10-23. Declare an Animation object and name it tweenAnimation at the top of your MainActivity.java file

Speaking of testing the `Animation` code, let's do that now using the **Run ➤ Run 'app'** or **Run ➤ Clean and Rerun 'app'** menu sequences. When you click the `FloatingActionButton`, which we have "borrowed" here to control the test of our vector animation, and to keep it separate from our raster (`AnimationDrawable`) animation, the animating logo comes in from the distance, as can be as seen in the left-hand AVD emulator preview seen in Figure 10-24.

Figure 10-24. Test the vector animation by clicking on the the FloatingActionButton

Finally, we need to look at `Animation` **interpolator** constants, so that you can create complex motion curves for your image (raster) or tween (vector) animation constructs. In this case, we are building a hybrid animation that uses both the `Animation` (engine) classes and the `AnimationDrawable` (engine) class together for special effects.

Complex Animation: Android Interpolators

Let's get more complex and add some motion curves, called Interpolator constants in Android, to enhance the realism of the way that the animated objects (we will be animating the `TextView` as well) fade-in and scale up. This will allow me to show you how `shareInterpolator` works and teach you about Android's Interpolator engine and how to incorporate two different types of motion curves in the complex `Animation` transform subgroupings.

Creating Complex Animation Using XML Markup

Let's add a second `<alpha>` (transparency) transform child tag to the parent `<set>` tag, since the primary purpose of an `AnimationSet` is to group transforms together, to make them run as one seamless transform. It is important to note that you can use one transform inside of a `<set>` without any issues or errors, as you have just seen in the previous section.

Add a carriage return (a new line of markup or newline character) and type in **<alpha** to open an `<alpha>` tag and hit the spacebar to bring up the pop-up helper and select and double-click on the `fromAlpha` parameter to insert it in your code, which is shown in Figure 10-25 highlighted in blue.

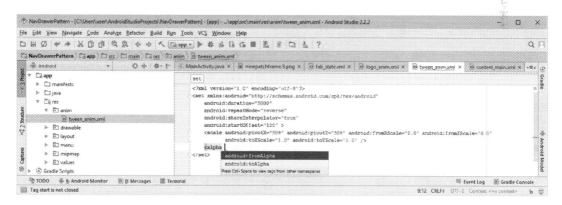

Figure 10-25. Add an <alpha opening tag, and hit the spacebar to bring up the parameter pop-up helper selector

Set fromAlpha to a data value of **0.0**, or 0% opacity. Repeat this work process and add your toAlpha parameter, and set it to a data value of **1.0** or 100% opacity, as shown in Figure 10-26. The resulting `<alpha>` tag and parameters should look like this:

```
<set android:parameters are in here >
    <scale android:parameters are in here />
    <alpha android:fromAlpha="0.0" android:toAlpha="1.0" />
</set>
```

Figure 10-26. Add a toAlpha parameter set to a data value of 1.0, and add a closing tag to the alpha child object

Next, let's add another level of complexity to a compound (multiple transforms) vector animation definition, by adding motion control curves. A motion control curve is a mathematical or algorithmic definition regarding how the animation frame rate should be transformed in real time, changing how the vector transform will be applied over time. This is done by using an Android Interpolator interface, which is part of the view.animation package.

Android Interpolator Interface: Motion Curves

The Android public Interpolator interface implements the Android public TimeInterpolator interface, which defines the rate of change over time for an animation. This allows animations to have nonlinear motion, such as acceleration and deceleration, for instance. The Interpolator interface therefore also defines your rate of change for Android procedural animation. This will allow the four basic animation effects (alpha, scale, translate or move, and rotate) to be accelerated, decelerated, cycled, bounced, anticipated, overshot, or made to follow a predefined vector path.

The Interpolator interface is kept in the **android.view.animation** package, and has fourteen known indirect subclasses, including: AccelerateDecelerateInterpolator, AccelerateInterpolator, AnticipateInterpolator, AnticipateOvershootInterpolator, BaseInterpolator, BounceInterpolator, CycleInterpolator, PathInterpolator, DecelerateInterpolator, FastOutLinearInInterpolator, FastOutSlowInInterpolator, LinearInterpolator, LinearOutSlowInInterpolator and OvershootInterpolator.

Next, inside your parent <set> tag, type a space after your <scale> child tag's
android:toYScale parameter, and type android:interpolator="@android:anim" This will bring
up a pop-up helper containing the Interpolator constants, which is seen in Figure 10-27. The
XML markup for the <scale> tag should look like the following:

```
<set android:parameters are in here >
    <scale android:pivotX="50%" android:pivotX="50%" android:fromXScale="0.0"
android:toXScale="1.0"
        android:fromYScale="0.0" android:toYScale="1.0"
        android:interpolator="@android:anim/overshoot_interpolator" />
    <alpha android:fromAlpha="0.0" android:toAlpha="1.0" />
</set>
```

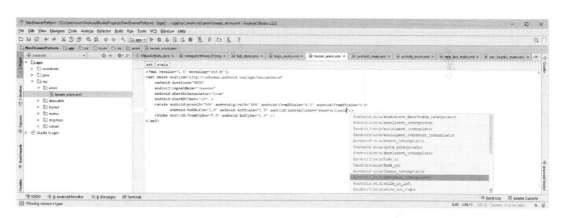

Figure 10-27. Add an android:interpolator parameter, set it to @android:anim, and select /overshoot_interpolator

Let's follow the same work process, and add a different motion curve interpolator to your
<alpha> child tag, to create a more complex animation. Since we are using more than one
Interpolator constant, the first thing that we will need to do is to set android:shareInterpo
lator="false" in the parent <set> AnimationSet tag as shown in red in Figure 10-28. Next,
add a space after the android:toAlpha parameter in the <alpha> child tag, and then, add an
android:interpolator="@android:anim/accelerate_decelerate_interpolator" parameter,
seen in Figure 10-28. The XML markup after the second Interpolator has been added should
look like the following:

```
<set android:parameters are in here >
    <scale android:pivotX="50%" android:pivotX="50%" android:fromXScale="0.0"
android:toXScale="1.0"
        android:fromYScale="0.0" android:toYScale="1.0"
        android:interpolator="@android:anim/overshoot_interpolator" />
    <alpha android:interpolator="@android:anim/accelerate_decelerate_interpolator"
        android:fromAlpha="0.0" android:toAlpha="1.0" />
</set>
```

Figure 10-28. *Change shareInterpolator to false; add the accelerate_decelerate_interpolator to your <alpha> tag*

Now we are ready to instantiate the TextView object in the MainActivity.java code (tab) so that I can show you that your procedural animation assets can be attached to more than one widget, including text or button widgets, as well as widgets that use graphics, images, video, and SVG (scalable vector graphic) assets. This will also give you more practice in how to set up procedural animation assets to work with UI widgets and event handlers.

Java Code: Two Widgets Use the Tween Animation

To implement this new more complex animation set on the TextView at the top of the main content UI design in content_main.xml, and the first thing you need to do is add an android:id="@+id/textView" parameter in the <TextView> child tag so that this TextView object can be declared at the top of the MainActivity.java class, and instantiated at the bottom of the onCreate() method, and animated within your OnClickListener() event handling structure. Declare a TextView object named textView at the top of the class under the ImageView and Animation objects, then instantiate the TextView in onCreate() using:

```
textView = (TextView)findViewById(R.id.textView);
```

In the OnClickListener add the following statement, seen in Figure 10-29:

```
textView.startAnimation(tweenAnimation);
```

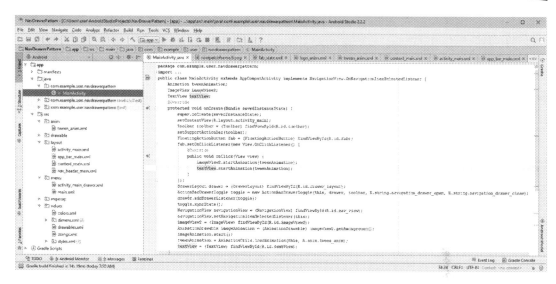

Figure 10-29. Declare, Instantiate, and call Animation off the TextView object to wire a TextView to the Animation

To see the TextView and ImageView with the new Fade+Scale vector animation applied, use your Run ➤ Run 'app' or Run ➤ Clean and Rerun 'app' menu sequence. When you click the FloatingActionButton that we "borrowed" to control the test of our vector animations, to keep it separate from our raster (AnimationDrawable) animation, the animating logo comes in from the distance, and fades into view, and the TextView also scales and fades into view, using a different timing (motion through time curve) than the scaling timing. Try different parameters on your own time, and see how they affect the animation result, to get some experience with procedural animation.

Procedural Animation or Frame Animation?

Finally, I wanted to discuss some of those higher-level theories, principles, concepts, and trade-offs, which will serve to differentiate the image-based frame animation AnimationDrawable approach from the mathematics-based procedural animation (vector or tween) Animation approach.

Image (frame or raster) animation will tend to be more **memory-intensive** than it is processor-intensive. This is because each frame that is going to be placed on the display screen would need to be loaded into memory, so that these frames can later be used in your application. Displaying these images from system memory in a View is fairly straightforward, and does not require any complex calculations, so the processing overhead is low, as it only involves moving each frame's image asset from system memory over to the Android device display screen.

Frame animation would give you more creative control outside of Android OS, because you can use production software, including 3D, digital imaging, digital video, digital illustration, special effects, particle systems, fluid dynamics, morphing, digital painting and the like, to manipulate all your pixels into exactly the animation effect that you are looking to achieve. I have a half-dozen new media fundamentals titles from Apress, including the *Android Studio New Media Fundamentals* (2016) title, which covers how to produce these multimedia assets.

Since Android does not yet include all of these advanced multimedia production tools, using a frame animation will allow you to leverage powerful production tools, some of which we will be using within this book, during the digital imaging, digital video, and digital audio chapters, outside of the Android development environment. You can then bring the results into your Android application using the image, video, audio, SVG, and 3D assets. For image animation this would include image bitmaps defined as frames within an `AnimationDrawable` object.

Procedural animation tends to be more processing intensive because it involves numeric value interpolation, as well as the application of interpolator "motion curves" to the resulting interim data values. Additionally, if sets and subsets are utilized to create a complex animation structure, there can be a great deal more data processing involved, as well as the memory space that would be required to hold the plethora of settings, ranges, pivots, interpolation values, and similar animation processing data that will be needed by the `Animation` engine classes.

Procedural animation gives you more control inside of Android 7.1.1. This is because you are doing everything that controls your animation by using Java code and XML markup, and your animation data can be made to interact within the Java programming logic. This is because Java code and data, and even your UI element widgets, can be crafted to interface with the procedural animation in real time, allowing animation to be made interactive, whereas frame animation at least by itself, is not interactive. Frame animation by itself is a more linear medium, like digital video, where frames are played sequentially in order to achieve the motion graphics end result.

Since you can apply procedural animation to just about any `View` object in Android, including your text, UI widgets, images, video, and frame animation, if you set things up correctly, such as using image compositing techniques to their best end result, you can achieve some impressive interactivity by using frame animation, audio, and digital video in conjunction with procedural animation, as you have already seen during this chapter.

If you are combining image animation with procedural animation, as we did during this chapter, you will have a load on both processor and memory resources, so you must try and optimize what you are doing, so that you don't use up too much of the system resources needed to run the rest of your application code and UI. This is why we touched upon the topic of data footprint optimization in Chapter 9, and why we're learning about the same type of optimization principles here. We will also touch upon data footprint optimization in the digital video chapter (11) and the digital audio chapter (12) for exactly the same reason; if you run out of memory, your application stops working, and may even take down the rest of the Android user's phone, tablet, or iTV set.

The Animator Class: Parameter Animation

There is one other animation engine class (besides `Animation` and `AnimationDrawable`) in Android which I did not cover in this chapter, as it is not vector or raster animation of a new media asset, but rather a way to animate **attribute changes** for any Android class, which can also be done using Java programming loops.

Developers can use this Android `Animator` class as a predefined (pre-coded) shortcut to animating object properties inside of Android that would usually be animated (interpolated or changed over time) by using Java programming structures to accomplish smooth iteration of object attributes using the same mathematics that is already defined for you using this `Animator` class.

If you wanted to research this on your own, you can visit the following Android Developer website URL, if this area is of interest for your application development requirements:

`http://developer.android.com/reference/android/animation/`**`Animator`**`.html`

Since Chapters 10 through 12 cover advanced new media assets (animation, digital video and digital audio) in detail, I have opted to focus on image (animation), vector animation, digital audio, and digital video specifically.

Summary

In this chapter, you learned all about **2D animation** concepts and principles, expanding on the 2D graphics concepts and principles that you learned about in the Chapter 9, into the **fourth dimension** of **time**. Changing images over time is the foundation for both 2D animation as well as digital video media. We will be covering digital video in the next chapter, as a logical follow-on to subject material you learned in this chapter.

You learned about Android's `AnimationDrawable` object and frame-based animation and the supported digital image formats (PNG) utilized for animation frames. You learned about how to define frame animation, as well as how to implement it inside of your `DrawerLayout` UI design from Chapter 8, using the Android `ImageView` class, which is used to hold Android `Drawable` objects, such as images and frame animation XML definitions.

Next, you learned about the Android `Animation` class, used to implement the other major type of animation in Android, known as tween animation, procedural animation, or vector animation. Tween animation uses XML tags and parameters to create animation, using **alpha** blending, **scaling**, **rotation**, and **translation** (movement).

You learned how to define procedural animation, as well as how to implement it in your `DrawerLayout` design from Chapter 8, using the `ImageView` class and `Animation` class. You declared and instantiated these objects in your `MainActivity.java` `AppCompatActivity` subclass in order to be able to "wire up" your procedural animation settings data to the `AnimationDrawable` 3D logo image animation created during the first section of the chapter.

You also added an event listener to your multistate `FloatingActionButton`, which you enhanced in the previous chapter. You created **hybrid** animation, which used both frame animation and procedural animation, to achieve the ultimate 2D animation special effects. You learned how to build even more complex animation, by using the `AnimationSet` class and Interpolator interface and constants, and how to attach these to both text and image UI elements, so that you can achieve the same special effects you can in DVE, SFX, or Titling animation software.

Finally, we discussed trade-offs between frame animation's use of **system memory** and procedural animation's use of **CPU processing cycles**. I also pointed out a third Animator class that animates Android class attributes (or parameters, as I like to call them), which we did not cover, as that class is not technically new media 2D or 3D animation at all, and is not in the `AnimationDrawable` (raster) or `Animation` engine (vector) animation classes.

In Chapter 11, you will learn all about digital video in Android including foundational digital video theory and concepts, what digital video file formats are best to use in Android, how to create digital video assets for use with Android's `FrameLayout` container class, and how to use the Android `VideoView` class and widget. You'll also learn how that class works with the Android `MediaPlayer` class, the Android `Uri` class, and the Android `MediaController` class. Chapter 11 will be just as advanced as this chapter, if not more so, as video is complex.

Digital Video: Streaming Video, MediaPlayer, and MediaController Classes

In the previous chapter covering 2D Animation, we implemented motion graphics in Android and digital image file formats such as PNG or JPEG in conjunction with XML constructs to create frame-based animation, as well as using procedural (tween or vector) animation to rotate, scale, move, and fade UI elements.

There is another way that you can play a series of frames in Android, called **digital video**. Digital video assets are especially well-suited for situations when you have hundreds or even thousands of frames, and cannot easily handle them all using an Android `AnimationDrawable` class. Additionally, digital video can be **streamed** over a network connection, which 2D animation assets cannot, and so new media can be external to your application.

In this chapter, we are going to take all of the newfound knowledge that you gained in Chapter 10 regarding the fourth dimension of **time**, as well as concepts that you learned about such as frames and frame rates, and we will again expand upon that knowledge with new concepts such as **bitrates** and new digital video codec (file format) support in Android, including the popular MPEG-4 and WebM digital video formats that are also the formats that are used in HTML5 and JavaFX 8.

We will be covering several frequently utilized Android classes you can use to implement video graphics design elements, such as a `VideoView` UI widget, a fullscreen UI layout container great for use with video, and three media-related Android classes that you can utilize to implement a digital video (or digital audio) transport UI, control and playback, including `MediaPlayer` (media playback), `Uri` and `MediaController` **(transport controls)**. During the chapter we'll use these digital video-related classes to create a digital video playback Activity. We'll create a 3D flythrough with Terragen 4, and learn how to optimize digital video using Sorenson Squeeze Desktop Pro 11.

© Wallace Jackson 2017
W. Jackson, *Android Apps for Absolute Beginners*, DOI 10.1007/978-1-4842-2268-3_11

Creating a Video App: FullscreenActivity

The first thing we need to do is to see if there is one of the dozen pure Android design patterns in Android Studio that is attuned to, or suits, digital video playback applications. Fortunately there is, and this gives us a chance to dive into yet another (a third so far) of the application development bootstrap templates that the New Android Studio Project series of dialogs offers to all the Android 7.x application development Absolute Beginners.

Go into Android Studio 2.3 and the currently open NavDrawerPattern project and use the **File ➤ Close Project** menu option to close the project and open the Android Studio master dialog, as shown in Figure 11-1. As you can see on the left side of the dialog, your two existing projects are easily accessible at any time you wish to continue working on them. Since we are going to start a new digital video project, so that you can explore some of the other pure Android design pattern application templates that build a full working Android application for you, click on the **Start a new Android Studio project** option, which can be seen in the middle right of Figure 11-1, highlighted in red.

Figure 11-1. Use File ➤ Close Project on NavDrawerPattern, and then select Start a new Android Studio project

In your **Configure your new project** dialog, name your application **DigitalVideoMedia**, and accept the other default settings and leave **Include C++ Support** unchecked, as is shown in the first pane in Figure 11-2. Click **Next** and accept the default settings in the **Select the form factors your app will run on** dialog seen in the middle of Figure 11-2.

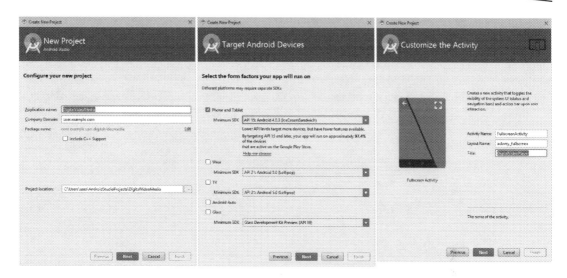

Figure 11-2. *The Configure Your New Project, Select the Form Factors, and Customize the Activity dialogs*

Click **Next** from the **Select Form Factors** dialog, and select the **Fullscreen Activity**, shown selected in blue in Figure 11-3, and click the **Next** button. In the final **Customize the Activity** dialog, seen on the far right in Figure 11-2, title the Activity **DigitalVideoPlayer**, and leave the default Activity and Layout names as suggested by Android Studio as **FullscreenActivity** and **activity_fullscreen**, and again click on the **Finish** button.

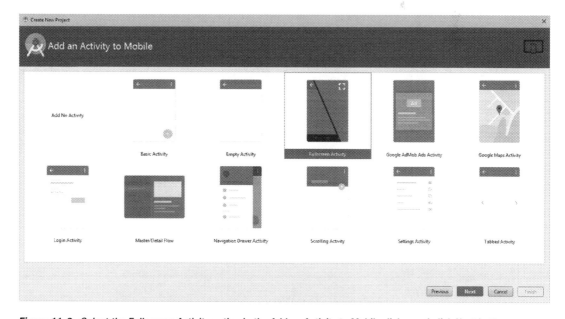

Figure 11-3. *Select the Fullscreen Activity option in the Add an Activity to Mobile dialog and click Next button*

This will create a DigitalVideoMedia project and FullscreenActivity in Android Studio as shown in Figure 11-4. Take a look at the XML UI design hierarchy to ascertain how it works like you did in Chapter 6.

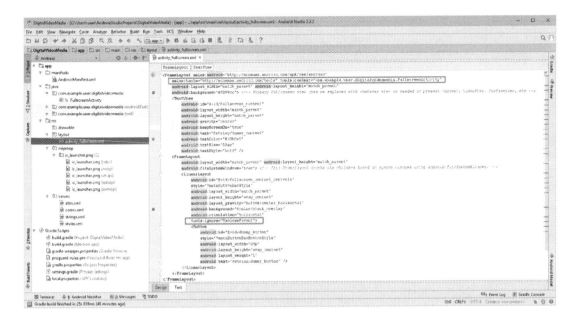

Figure 11-4. Take a look at the activity_fullscreen.xml UI XML file to ascertain how the tag hierarchy is set up

Next, let's test the bootstrap code that Android Studio has created for us to make sure that it works. Be sure to use your AVD often at each stage of development to make sure your application works after each major code addition, even the initial bootstrap code, to make sure none of the API that underlies the code has changed.

Use the **Run ➤ Run 'app'** menu sequence to execute the DigitalVideoMedia application in the Android emulator, as is shown in Figure 11-5. I show the initial startup screen on the far left, the fullscreen mode with dummy content in the middle pane, and the UI overlay mode (non-fullscreen content) on the far right.

Figure 11-5. Test the DigitalVideoMedia project with Run ➤ Run 'app' to see how the FullscreenActivity works

Let's take an in-depth look at Android's Framelayout class, which provides a foundation for this design pattern.

The FrameLayout Class: Framing DV Content

The Android FrameLayout class is the most basic layout container class, as it provides simple frame layout for content. Often this content involves fullscreen digital video, which is why I waited until this chapter to cover the FrameLayout class in detail. A FrameLayout is often utilized to contain one single UI widget that contains some sort of new media content such as digital video or animation. An example of a complex UI widget that would be perfect to use in conjunction with this FrameLayout container would be the VideoView widget. The VideoView widget (class), which we'll go over in detail later on this chapter, is designed to contain an MPEG-4 or WebM digital video asset. We will be covering how to create a digital video asset from scratch, and how to optimize it.

The FrameLayout class is a **public** class that extends the ViewGroup superclass, which as you know is a master blueprint class that is used to create Android layout container subclasses. The FrameLayout class hierarchy, which starts with the Java language Object master class, would look like the following Java class hierarchy:

```
java.lang.Object
  > android.view.View
    > android.view.ViewGroup
      > android.widget.FrameLayout
```

The FrameLayout class was designed by Android OS developers to specify the area on the display screen that is intended to display one single item. This is why it is named using the term "frame," as typically a frame holds a single image. For this reason, you should design a FrameLayout UI to hold one or two child widgets. Because the FrameLayout class does not have a lot of methods defined that allow a lot of layout positioning attributes (or parameters), it's most basic of the Android layout classes. This also makes the class quite memory efficient!

If you try to use multiple child UI widgets inside of your parent FrameLayout container, you will find that it can be difficult to position multiple design elements accurately in a way that is scalable across different screen sizes, shapes, and orientations. This is due to the lack of advanced layout positioning attributes.

What happens if you attempt to use FrameLayout containers to organize multiple UI elements is that you would see a high occurrence of UI elements overlapping each other. This is not the professional result that you should be seeking for your pure Android design patterns. There are better layout containers, some of which you have seen already in this book, like the (horizontal or vertical) LinearLayout, RelativeLayout, and the GridLayout.

The only way to control positioning of your child UI widgets within the parent FrameLayout UI container is by assigning a layout gravity parameter for each child widget. This is done using the **android:layout_gravity** parameter inside of each UI widget's child tag in your FrameLayout XML user interface definition file, which you have seen in lines 9 and 23 in Figure 11-4. Here the TextView uses android:layout_gravity="center" and the LinearLayout container uses the android:layout_gravity="bottom|center_horizontal" to place a UI Button at the bottom of the non-fullscreen UI design. We will be learning all about the FrameLayout class during this section, as well as its nested classes, which provide FrameLayout parameters, during the next section.

This layout_gravity design parameter does not allow developers to do the pixel-precise positioning, or relative positioning, that is possible using the other more advanced (and less memory-efficient) layout container classes. The FrameLayout class essentially allows Android to do all of your UI design positioning, so that you can scale your UI design to fit all the different Android device screen sizes and orientations, usually in fullscreen mode, which is the optimal mode for use with digital video assets. This gravity parameter for the FrameLayout class is provided by a nested class called FrameLayout.LayoutParams. We'll be covering this nested class in the next section of this chapter. It's identical to the gravity parameter that is used in other ViewGroup layout container classes. I am going to cover layout gravity in detail in this chapter, because it is an important UI design concept.

> **Note**   Nested classes are attached to the parent class in Java using dot notation, so the
> FrameLayout nested LayoutParams class would be FrameLayout.LayoutParams.

Since it is a basic UI layout class, you can also utilize the FrameLayout class as a superclass, for the purpose of creating more specialized UI-related classes. Any class that you create by subclassing the FrameLayout class would be termed a **direct subclass** of the FrameLayout class. If added to the Android API, it becomes a known direct subclass; otherwise if it remains private (with you), it would be termed an (unknown) direct subclass.

Some of the **known direct subclasses** of FrameLayout, that is, FrameLayout subclasses that have already been coded for you, would include: DatePicker, TabHost, MediaController, CalendarView, ScrollView, TimePicker, ViewAnimator, HorizontalScrollView, GestureOverlayView, and the AppWidgetHostView class.

FrameLayout also has several **known indirect subclasses**. These are part of the Android API and are subclasses of the above known direct subclasses. Indirect subclasses include: TextSwitcher, ViewFlipper, ImageSwitcher, FragmentTabHost, and the ViewSwitcher class. Next, let's take a look at the FrameLayout.LayoutParams class.

FrameLayout.LayoutParams Nested Class: Gravity

The FrameLayout.LayoutParams class is a nested class that subclasses the ViewGroup. MarginLayoutParams nested class, which, in turn, subclasses (extends) the ViewGroup. LayoutParams nested class, which was coded originally in order to create layout parameters for all ViewGroup subclasses. Android layout parameter, or LayoutParams, nested classes are what provide the layout parameters for your UI designs, which are usually created via XML, as you have seen throughout the course of this book. The Android Java class hierarchy would therefore be structured in the following fashion:

```
java.lang.Object
  > android.view.ViewGroup.LayoutParams
    > android.view.ViewGroup.MarginLayoutParams
      > android.widget.FrameLayout.LayoutParams
```

FrameLayout.LayoutParams inherits all ViewGroup.LayoutParams as well as ViewGroup. MarginLayoutParams (margin parameters), and then the class adds the layout_gravity parameter and its constants, which we're going to cover in detail in this section, since these constants are specifically intended to be used with the FrameLayout UI container that we're going to be using for the digital video playback engine we are creating in this chapter.

MarginLayoutParams was created between FrameLayout.LayoutParams and ViewGroup. LayoutParams to leverage the modularity of Java class design. This splits the margin layout parameters out from LayoutParams, so that if you do not need to include margin support in a layout container, you can subclass LayoutParams rather than MarginLayoutParams. A nested class is usually a helper class, containing constants or parameters to be used with that nesting class.

The most often used gravity constant with the FrameLayout container is fill, as one usually wants content or UI elements, such as the VideoView, to be scaled up to fit the frame (display) if they are smaller (pixel dimension) than the device screen. Your second most often used constant would be **center**, which is similar to fill, but does not scale (upsample) the content; rather it centers the content or the UI element (the child widget) in the display.

There are also constants provided to fill or center your UI widget, or any nested UI layout container, in only the horizontal (X-axis) or the vertical (Y-axis) dimensions. These would be the fill_vertical or fill_horizontal, and the center_vertical or center_horizontal constants. These constants, shown in Table 11-1 along with the other 14 constants, will allow you to fine-tune how Android will position your UI widget inside of your FrameLayout UI container. It is important to note that using fill_vertical or fill_horizontal may well change the content aspect ratio, which may distort that content in an undesirable way, especially if that content has human subjects in it.

There are some more advanced constants, such as `clip_horizontal` and `clip_vertical`, which are conceptually a bit more challenging, as these will "clip" (that is, remove a portion of) your UI element or content, in either the horizontal (X-axis) or the vertical (Y-axis). In digital imaging, this operation is termed "cropping," and instead of scaling your content (or UI design) to fit any given screen dimensions, these clipping constants will instead remove parts of your content or design, in order to make it fit the new screen size and dimensions. This prevents often unwanted aspect ratio distortion, by removing fringe pixels, rather than distorting the asset using assymetric scaling.

Table 11-1. The android:layout_gravity constants defined by nested class FrameLayout.LayoutParams

Gravity Constant	The function that is specified by using this Gravity Constant
top	Aligns UI element to or at the **TOP** of a FrameLayout container
bottom	Aligns UI element to or at the **BOTTOM** of a FrameLayout container
left	Aligns UI element to or at the **LEFT** of a FrameLayout container
right	Aligns UI element to or at the **RIGHT** of a FrameLayout container
center_vertical	Centers the UI element (or UI layout container) vertically
center_horizontal	Centers the UI element (or UI layout container) horizontally
center	Aligns UI element to or at the **CENTER** of a FrameLayout container
fill_vertical	Scales UI element (or layout container) to fill Frame vertically
fill_horizontal	Scale UI element (or layout container) to fill Frame horizontally
fill	Scales UI element to **FILL** the FrameLayout container
clip_vertical	Clips the top and bottom edges of the UI element for FrameLayout
clip_horizontal	Clips the left and right edges of the UI element for FrameLayout
start	Aligns UI element to or at the **START** of the FrameLayout container
end	Aligns UI element to or at the **END** of the FrameLayout container

Finally, you can use `start` and `end` constants to implement both **RTL** (Right To Left) and **LTR** (Left To Right) directional UI layouts. These would replace your left and right constants (for LTR), or right and left constants (for RTL). If you are developing for end users that use RTL languages, and you need your UI designs to be able to **mirror** this type of RTL language design scenario, use the start and end constants, instead of left and right.

The RTL and LTR layout constants were added in Android 4.2 to allow design support for languages that are read starting on the right side of the screen, and moving toward the left side of the screen. Android 7 OS will automatically reverse the value of the start and end constants, depending on whether a RTL or LTR screen direction is being used by the user (that is, depending upon the language setting).

Often these gravity constants will be used in a FrameLayout when there is more than one child widget (multiple UI widgets, or nested ViewGroup layout containers). This is similar to the way you should use the top, bottom, left, and right constants to pin UI widgets or layout containers around the sides of the FrameLayout (display). Again, be sure to not use too many child UI elements within your FrameLayout, and use gravity parameters to position them so that they do not overlay, even when screen dimensions, size, and shape change across Android devices such as smartphones, tablets and iTV sets.

It is important to remember that gravity is used for **generalized positioning**, not for precise positioning, like the parameters that you find in the RelativeLayout class, for instance, which can provide UI designs that are precise and at the same time are also scalable to different screen sizes and shapes in a much more advanced fashion.

Before we can recode our current fullscreen UI design, shown in Figure 11-4, into a digital video playback UI design pattern, we should get up to speed on the particulars of the VideoView UI widget and the lifestyle stages of a digital video asset and its playback parameters.

The VideoView Class: A VideoPlayer Widget

Before we get into all of the Java 8 code and how it interfaces to the XML markup to implement a video player inside of the FrameLayout container that Android Studio has installed in the DigitalVideoMedia Android application, I want to get into the **VideoView** class in detail, so that you have the foundational knowledge about how all of these classes work. After that we will be able to implement this knowledge and finish up the XML UI design definition that will feature a FrameLayout that contains a VideoView. After that, we'll take some time to learn about digital video concepts as they relate to Android 7 OS, and create video using the Terragen 4 virtual world creation software package along with Sorenson Squeeze, a video encoding suite. At the end of the chapter we will learn about the MediaPlayer and MediaController classes, and finish up with the Java 8 programming.

Android's VideoView widget class is a direct subclass of the SurfaceView class, which is a direct subclass of the Android View class, which is a direct subclass of the java.lang.Object master class. Android's VideoView class hierarchy would therefore be structured as follows:

```
java.lang.Object
  > android.view.View
    > android.view.SurfaceView
      > android.widget.VideoView
```

The SurfaceView superclass (a View subclass) is similar to the FrameLayout (ViewGroup subclass) in as much as it is intended to provide a class for creating View widgets that are used for one sole purpose: playing content on their surface. In the case of a VideoView subclass, this would be playing digital video content on the surface of the View object, as is clearly evident in the naming of this digital video playback optimized class.

The Android VideoView class is stored in the **android.widget** package, making the VideoView a user interface element, which we know is called a UI widget in Android OS. For this reason, your **import statement** for using a VideoView class in an Android application would reference android.widget.VideoView as its package path.

This VideoView class is a public class, and has two dozen method calls and callbacks that one might think of as actually being part of the Android MediaPlayer class, which we'll be covering in a future section of the chapter.

You can access these MediaPlayer functions (method calls) via the VideoView class. Thus, ultimately, you will utilize these two classes as inexorably bound together. You'll see how these two key Android classes intertwine as we progress through this chapter, especially when we get into Java program logic a bit later on in the chapter. It is rare that a UI design class will integrate with a media playback engine in Android, so this is a special case.

We will take a closer look here at some of the more useful video playback control method calls, so that you are familiar with them, in case you need to implement any of the extended digital video features in your own video playback applications. In the next section, you will also need to review your Android VideoView digital video **playback lifecycle**, so that you will know exactly how all of the various video playback **states** all fit together.

The basic VideoView method calls include .pause(), .resume(), .stop(), .start(), .suspend(), and .stopPlayback(). There's also a .setVideoURI() and a .setMediaController() method call, as well as a .setVideoPath() method call which accomplishes much of the same end result as the .setVideoURI() method call using a different parameter.

There are four .get() method calls for polling or getting information about digital video assets. They include .getDuration(), .getCurrentPosition(), .getBufferPercentage() and .getAudioSessionId() as well as an .isPlaying() method call, so that you can see if the digital video asset is playing back at the current time.

There are also three .can() method calls that ascertain what actions the VideoView can (or cannot) do, regarding the MediaPlayer object. These include: .canPause(), .canSeekBackward(), and .canSeekForward() method calls.

There are also all of the standard **event handling** method calls, that will be **inherited** from the Android View superclass. These include the .onTouchEvent(), onKeyDown(), and onTrackballEvent() method calls, among all of the other event handlers. The event handler that is usually used with the VideoView, for instance, to bring up the MediaController transport UI control panel, is the onTouchEvent() event listener.

Finally, there are specialized method calls, such as .resolveAdjustedSize(), or .onInitializeAccessibilityEvent(), which are included to allow developers to implement **accessibility standards** if needed for their video playback.

The VideoView Lifecycle: Video Playback Stages

Before you start working with the Android digital video-related classes, learn about digital video concepts, and create custom 3D digital video assets, you'll need to understand the different stages which a digital video asset goes through in Android. Playing digital video may seem simple from an end user's perspective. A **Play**, **Pause**, **Rewind** and **Stop** function will provide basic video transport control. All these are involved in the overall video playback process, which is sometimes referred to as the video playback **lifecycle**.

There are some other under-the-hood stages that allow Android to load the video asset into memory, or to set parameters for playback, and similar system-level, behind-the-scenes considerations. These unseen digital video lifecycle stages will allow developers to have the flexibility to create an optimized digital video user experience, and these will serve to provide Android developers with a much wider variety of playback options.

When you implement a VideoView widget, you are also instantiating a MediaPlayer object, even though you do not have to write any XML markup, or even write any Java code, to create the MediaPlayer object! MediaPlayer objects are essentially video playback engines, and will play digital video assets associated with the VideoView UI element. This is done using a URI object, and a video asset reference, which the URI object contains.

The digital video codec (stands for: COder-DECoder) algorithm references the digital video asset using the URI, places it into memory and then decodes it, placing the result in the FrameLayout, using the VideoView. We will cover URI and MediaPlayer classes later on in this chapter. The video playback states are shown in Table 11-2.

Table 11-2. Video Playback States, and how these affect the Android MediaPlayer object and its video playback

Digital Video Playback State	What is happening with the MediaPlayer object (digital video playback stages)
Idle State	MediaPlayer object is **instantiated** and ready for configuration
Initialized State	MediaPlayer object is **initialized** with data path, using a **URI**
Prepared State	MediaPlayer object is **configured**, or "prepared," for playback
Started State	MediaPlayer object is **started** and is decoding the video stream
Paused State	MediaPlayer object is **paused** and stops decoding video frames
Stopped State	MediaPlayer object is **stopped** and stops decoding video frames
Playback Completed	MediaPlayer object is **finished** decoding the video data stream
Ended State	MediaPlayer object is **ended** and **removed from system memory**

I'll go through these eight states in the logical order in which they are used, as well as in the order in which they are listed in Table 11-2.

1. When the MediaPlayer object is first instantiated it will not actually be doing any active video playback. A MediaPlayer object would therefore initially be in what is termed the **Idle** state, much like a car idles when it is not in gear and engaged.

2. Once you load your MediaPlayer object with the digital video data reference, using your URI object, using the Uri.parse() method call or the .setDataSource() method call, a MediaPlayer object will enter what is termed its **Initialized** state. There is also an interim state, between the Initialized MediaPlayer object state, and the **Started** MediaPlayer object state, which is called the **Prepared** MediaPlayer object state.

3. The Prepared state is accessed using the `MediaPlayer.`
    `OnPreparedListener`, which is a nested class that we will be learning
    about in the `MediaPlayer` sections of this chapter, and which we will
    be using a bit later on inside of your `DigitalVideoMedia` application
    Java code in the `MainActivity.java` `AppCompatActivity` subclass,
    which we will recode to play a video asset.

4. Once the `MediaPlayer` object has been initialized, and is loaded with
    video data, it is usually **prepared** (that is, configured, using various
    playback option settings). After this is done, a `MediaPlayer` object
    can then be **started**, which means the digital video asset frames will
    start being decoded out of system memory, using the codec, and
    placed into the `VideoView`, inside of the `FrameLayout`, which can (and
    will) go fullscreen to allow optimal playback quality.

5. Once started, and the video is playing, it can be **stopped** by using a
    `.stop()` method call, or **paused** by using the `.pause()` method call.
    These three video states, started (play), stopped (stop), and paused
    (pause) should be the most familiar to all users of digital video, as
    they are represented by three primary buttons that are found on the
    video transport bar. In the Android OS, the digital video transport bar
    is provided using the `MediaController` class, as you will soon see.

6. The final `MediaPlayer` object digital video playback state is called a
    playback completed state. When a `MediaPlayer` object reaches this
    state it signifies that the video asset has stopped playing, and has
    reached the **EOF** (End Of File) marker inside of your video asset. You
    will bypass this playback completed state if you have invoked the
    `.setLooping(true)` method call and looping on (true) boolean flag.
    This would be called off of the `MediaPlayer` object. In this use case,
    your digital video will continue to loop seamlessly forever until you
    specifically call the `.stop()` method to stop it.

> **Note**   There are also `.start()` and `.reset()` method calls available for the `MediaPlayer`
> object, which will start and reset a `MediaPlayer` object at any time, based on the needs of the
> Java 8 program logic. If you call the `.start()` method, your digital video asset would enter the
> started state; conversely, if you call the `.stop()` method, your digital video playback will be
> stopped. Methods will do to your video asset what their method names suggest that they will do.

7. Finally, there is the `.release()` method call, which invokes an **ended**
    state for a `MediaPlayer` object. This will terminate your `MediaPlayer`
    object, which means that the Android OS will completely remove it
    from the Android device's system memory, allowing room for users to
    run other apps on their Android devices.

As you will see in the MediaPlayer sections of this chapter, there are other nested classes that will also allow you to do things such as listen for errors, such as MediaPlayer. OnErrorListener, as well as for other states of the MediaPlayer, such as when it reaches the Playback Completed state (MediaPlayer.OnCompletionListener).

First, you will need to create your <VideoView> widget inside of your parent <FrameLayout> as that is the next logical step in implementing video inside of your DigitalVideoMedia application. We will do this in the next section, and then we can get into some foundational information regarding digital video assets and formats, and show you how exactly you would create digital video content using open source software packages, and how to optimize it for Android devices using something like DaVinci Resolve, EditShare Lightworks or Sorenson Squeeze Desktop Pro.

Once we get through all of that foundational digital video information, we can review the MediaPlayer class and all of its related classes, and then get into some Java coding to implement digital video setup and playback!

Create a VideoView Layout Design with your XML

Let's change the DigitalVideoMedia bootstrap FullscreenActivity application, which Android Studio 2.3 generated for us, and which works well, as we saw in Figure 11-5, into a digital video playback application. The first thing that we need to do is to change the placeholder <TextView> tag into a <VideoView> tag, as is seen in Figure 11-6, and remove any related parameters that do not apply (android:text parameters) or which will be covered up by the fullscreen video (android:background). Android will still put a default background color in place, and this will not be seen, but a custom background color is no longer needed, and we are optimizing system memory here by removing objects and attributes that would have taken memory locations to store and process later on.

Figure 11-6. Change the opening <TextView child tag into a <VideoView child tag and delete unused parameters

I optimized the remaining code for screen space, as you'll see in Figure 11-7, and optimized the `strings.xml` file.

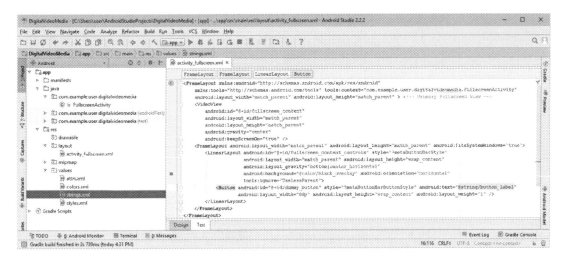

Figure 11-7. Condense the XML; change the <Button> android:text parameter to reference @string/button_label

I removed the text constant for the dummy text, and changed the dummy_button text to "Swap Video" and then I changed the name of that <string> attribute to be button_label, as you can see referenced in Figure 11-7 in the lower-right corner, highlighted in your <Button> child tag, as well as in the `strings.xml` file seen in Figure 11-8.

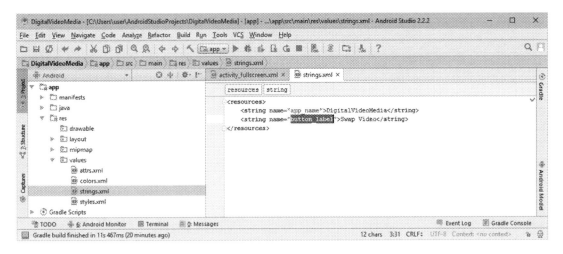

Figure 11-8. Edit the strings.xml file to remove the dummy text, and create a button_label named "Swap Video"

Note that Android Studio uses different colors (blue, green, yellow, and orange in this case) to highlight the nesting hierarchy, and shows the nesting hierarchy at the top of the XML markup editing pane as well using these same color values. The reason I did not change the ID parameter of `dummy_button` is because that is referenced in the Java code as an `R.id. dummy_button`. We will update that later on, when we change our Java code into what we want this application to do for us. The reason I left the `<LinearLayout>` background constant (`black_overlay`) is because it has an alpha value, as you can see in Figure 11-5. Let's take a break from Android Studio 2.3, and get up to speed on concepts in digital video media.

Digital Video Concepts: Bitrates and Codecs

Like the 2D animation we learned about in the previous chapter, digital video extends digital imaging into 4D, the fourth dimension of time, by using something called frames in the digital video (and film) industry. Video is therefore comprised of an ordered sequence of frames that are displayed rapidly over time. The difference from animation, at least in real-world use, inside of Android, is that digital video usually has a fairly massive number of frames (up to 30 for every second of video playback), which require a different asset optimization approach.

The optimization concept using frames in a digital video is very similar to the one regarding pixels in an image (the resolution of the digital image), because video frames increase data footprint with each frame used, as will the number of pixels in each frame. In digital video, not only does the frame's (image) resolution greatly impact file size, but so does the number of frames that the codec has to look at to encode. This is commonly referred to as FPS or the "frame rate." Standard industry video uses 30 frames per second, but you can use less if you want!

Since digital video is made up of a collection of thousands of digital image frames, the concept of digital video frame rate, expressed as frames per second, or more commonly referred to as FPS, is also very important when it comes to digital video data footprint optimization. This is because with video optimization, lowering a frames per second value the codec looks at encoding will lower the total amount of data encoded, which lowers file size.

In Chapter 8, we learned that if we multiply the number of pixels in the image by its number of color channels, we'll get the raw data footprint for the image. With digital video, we will now multiply that number again using the number of frames per second at which our digital video is set to play back, and again by the number of total seconds that represent the duration of a video "clip" being encoded into a digital video asset file. You can see why having a digital video codec that can compress this raw data footprint down is extremely important.

You'll be amazed (later on in this chapter) at some of the digital video data compression ratios that the MPEG-4 video file format can achieve, once you understand exactly how to optimize the digital video compression work process by using the correct bitrate, frame rate, and frame resolution for your digital video content. We will also get into the concept of bitrates, as well as video optimization, during the next few sections of the chapter. In this next section, let's review the different open source digital video codecs that the Android 7.1.1 OS currently supports. These can also be used in Java9, JavaFX, HTML5 or other platforms, so this will be of significant interest for the developers out there that want to use their digital video assets across all of those popular open source platforms.

Digital Video in Android: MPEG4 H.264 and WebM

Android supports both MPEG-4 H.264 (MPEG stands for: Motion Picture Experts Group) as well as the ON2 VP8 or VP9 formats, which were acquired by Google from ON2 Technologies, and distributed under a WebM moniker, and then released into the open source environment. These open source formats are quite optimal from a content production standpoint, as video content that a developer produces and optimizes could then be used both in HTML5 engines, such as HTML5 apps, browsers, and devices, as well as in JavaFX and in Android OS. This open source digital video format cross-platform support thus affords us content developers with a "produce once, deliver everywhere" production scenario. This will reduce content development cost, thus increasing your revenues, as long as this "economy of scale in content development" is taken advantage of by app developers.

Since Android devices these days have displays that are using a medium (1280x720) to high (HD 1920x1080) resolution, or even UHD 3840x2160 resolution, if you are going to use MPEG-4 file format, you should utilize the MPEG4 H.264 AVC format, which is currently the digital video format most often used in the world today, for Android and HTML5 apps, as well as on the Internet and Business and Government formats, such as PDF. This MPEG-4 H.264 AVC (Advanced Video Coding) digital video file format is supported across all Android OS versions for video playback, and under Android 3.0 (and later versions) for video recording. It is important to note that recording video is only supported if the Android device hardware has video camera capabilities.

If you're a video content producer, you will find that the MPEG4 H.264 format has the best compression result, especially if you're using one of the more advanced encoding suites like the Sorenson Squeeze Desktop Pro 11 software, which we will be using to optimize our 3D planet-fly-over video asset later on during this chapter.

File extension support for MPEG-4 video files includes a .3GP (MPEG-4 SP which stands for "Standard Play") and a .MP4 (MPEG-4 H.264 AVC). I suggested using the latter (.MP4 AVC), as that is what I use for HTML5 apps, and MP4 is more common to stream in AVC format. Either type of file should work just fine in Android apps, depending on what Android OS versions (1.5, 2.3, 3, 4.4, 5, 6, 7) you are targeting delivery of your app to.

A more recent digital video format that Android supports is called the WebM (VP8, VP9) digital video format. The format provides great quality results with a small data footprint. This is a reason why Google acquired ON2, the company that developed the VP codec. VP is used in OGG Theora (VP3), JavaFX 8 (VP6), and Android 7.1.1 (VP8 and VP9). We'll learn about codecs later on in this chapter. WebM video playback was first **natively supported** in Android 2.3. The term **native support** is used with code (in this case, it is a codec) that has become natively a part of the operating system software, which means it is included with the rest of the operating system and API.

WebM also supports something called **video streaming**, which you will also be learning about in a later section of the chapter. WebM video streaming playback capability is supported only if your users have Android version 4.0 and later. For this reason, I would recommend using WebM only for **captive** video assets, as Android 2.3 through 4.4 supports non-streaming WebM codec use. If you're only delivering to later version Android devices you can use WebM, to deliver across all Android devices and versions, use MPEG-4. In case you're wondering, captive video is video that is not streamed, meaning video assets are captive inside of the /res/raw folder. Use an MPEG4 H.264 AVC if you are only going to be streaming video, as all of the Android versions, including Android 7.x, support that codec, both for captive video playback, as well as for streaming video playback.

Digital Video Compression: Bitrate and Streams

Let's start out covering the primary resolutions used in commercial video. Before HDTV, or High Definition TV, came along, video was usually called SD, or Standard Definition, and used a standard vertical resolution of 480 pixels. High Definition (called HD) video comes in two resolutions, 1280x720, which I call "Pseudo HD" and a higher resolution 1920x1080, which the industry calls "True HD." There's also a new "Ultra HD" (UHD) resolution, which is 3840x2160. All use a 16:9 widescreen aspect ratio, and are used not only in film, television, and iTV sets, but also in smartphones (Razor HD was 1280 by 720) and tablets (Kindle Fire HD is 1920x1200).

This 1920x1200 resolution is, by the way, a less wide, or taller, 16:10 pixel aspect ratio, and is becoming more common as a widescreen device aspect ratio, as is a 16:8 (or 2:1) aspect ratio, with 2160x1080 screens out now. There is even a 2560x1440 resolution screen on the Samsung Galaxy S5 smartphone. Why this resolution, you may be wondering? Power of Two (even) up sampling of the most common 1280x720 digital video content will provide the best viewing results. Multiply 1280 by 2 and 720 by 2 and see what resulting screen resolution you come up with.

There is also 16:10 Pseudo HD resolution, which features 1280 by 800 pixels. In fact, this is a common laptop, netbook, and mini-tablet resolution. I would not at all be surprised to see the 16:8 1280 by 640 screen offered at some point in time as well. Generally, most content developers try to match their video content resolution to the resolution (and thus, the aspect ratio as well) of each Android device upon which the video asset will be viewed.

Regardless of the resolution you use for the digital video content, your application can access videos in a couple different ways. The way I do it, because I'm a data optimization guru, is captive to the application. This means the data is inside of (captive to) the Android application APK file itself, inside the /res/raw data resource folder.

The other way to access video inside your Android app is by using a **remote video data server**. In this case, the video is **streamed** from this remote server, over the Internet, and into your user's Android device as the video is playing back, in "real time." Let's hope that your video server does not crash, lose power, get hacked, or get too many playback requests (that is, lots of data traffic), as these scenarios are some of the downsides of streaming.

Video streaming is inherently more complicated than simply playing back captive video data. This is because an Android device is communicating in real time with a remote data server, receiving video data packets, decoding the data packets as the video plays, and writing the frames to the Android hardware display. Video streaming is supported via WebM format on Android 4 and later devices, or using MPEG4 across all Android OS versions.

The last concept that we need to cover in this section is the concept of **bitrate**. Bitrate is a key setting used in the video compression process, as you will see when we utilize Sorenson Squeeze Pro, later on in the chapter. Bitrates represent the **target bandwidth**, or data pipe size, which is able to accommodate a certain number of data bits streaming through it every second. Bitrates must also take into consideration CPU processing power for any given Android phone, making video data optimization even more important to video playback quality.

This is because once bits travel through the data pipe, they also need to be processed and displayed on the device screen. In fact, captive video assets that are included in Android application APK files only need optimization for processing power. This is because if you're using captive video files, there is no data pipe for the video asset to travel through, and no data transfer overhead. Therefore, bitrates for digital video assets need to be optimized not only for bandwidth, but also in anticipation of variances in CPU capability. We'll look at data footprint optimization next.

In general, the smaller the video data file size you are able to achieve, the faster the data will travel through any data pipe, the easier it will be to decode the data using the codec and the CPU, and the smaller the APK file size will be, for obvious reasons. Single-core CPUs in devices such as smartwatches may not be able to decode high-resolution, high bitrate digital video assets without "dropping" frames. This is a playback quality issue, so make sure to thoroughly optimize lower bitrate video assets if you plan to target older (or cheap) devices, so they have fewer bits (smaller file sizes) to process, which uses less memory overhead and therefore fewer CPU cycles.

Digital Video Optimization: Codec and Settings

Digital Video is compressed using a software utility called a **codec**, which stands for **COde-DECode**. There are two opposing sides to each video codec; one will **encode** the video data (for captive or streaming), and the other will **decode** this video data (captive video or streamed video). A video decoder will be part of a platform (Java 9, JavaFX 8, Android 7.x, or HTML5), or an HTML5 browser, across all operating systems. The decoder side of the codec will always be optimized for **speed**, as smoothness of video playback is a key issue, and the encoder side will be optimized **to reduce data footprint** for the digital video asset that it is generating, which can also boost playback speed. For this reason, an encoding process may take a long time, depending on how many cores your workstation contains. Most digital video content production workstations should support 6, 8, 12, 16 or 20 processor cores (threads).

Codecs (on the encoder side) are like **plug-ins**, in the sense that they can be installed into different digital video editing software packages, in order to enable them to encode different digital video asset file formats. Since the Android OS supports H.263, H.264 or H.265 MPEG-4 formats, and ON2 VP8/VP9 WebM formats for video, you need to make sure that you are using one of the codecs that encodes video data into these digital video file formats.

More than one software manufacturer makes MPEG encoding software, so there will be different MPEG codecs (encoder software) that will yield different (better or worse) results, as far as encoding speed and file size goes. The professional solution I recommend you secure if you wish to produce professional video is called Sorenson Squeeze, which is currently at Sorenson Squeeze Desktop Pro version 11. Squeeze has a professional-level version, which I will be using in this book, which costs less than $750, and whose value is significantly in excess of that suggested list price amount.

There is also an open source solution called EditShare LightWorks **12.6** that is scheduled to natively support output using MPEG-4 and WebM VP9 codecs sometime in 2018. So for now, I will have to use Squeeze Pro 11 for this book, until the codec support for Android 7.1.1, Java 9 and HTML5 is added to EditShare LightWorks 14. DaVinci Resolve 12.5.4 may also soon add this support as well, as it is now free.

When optimizing for digital video data file size using encoder settings, there are a number of important settings that directly affect the data footprint. I'll cover these in the order in which they affect file size, from the most impact to the least impact, so you know which parameters to "tweak" or adjust in order to obtain the best result.

As in digital image compression, the resolution, or number of pixels, in each frame of video, is the best place to start your data optimizion work process. If you are targeting 1280x720 or 1920x1080 smartphones, tablets, iTV Sets, or auto you don't need to use 3840x2160 resolution to get great visual results from the digital video assets.

With high-density (termed high **dot pitch**) displays (XHDPI and XXHDPI) currently common in the Android market, you can scale 1280 video up 33% and it will look reasonably good. The exception to this might be iTV apps for GoogleTV, which has a medium (or even low) dot pitch, due to large 50 to 70 inch screen sizes. In this use case, if you are developing applications for iTV sets, you'll want to use "True HD," 1920x1080 resolution.

The next level of optimization will come in the **number of frames** used for each second of video, called **FPS**, assuming the actual seconds contained in the video itself cannot be shortened by editing. This is known as your frame rate, and instead of setting the video standard 30 FPS frame rate, consider using a film standard frame rate of 24 FPS, or the multimedia standard frame rate of 20 FPS.

You may even be able to use a low 15 FPS frame rate, depending upon your content. Note that 15 FPS is half as much data as 30 FPS, a 100% reduction in data going to the encoder. For some video content this may playback (look) the same as 30 FPS content. The only reliable way to test how low you can get the frame rate before you start to affect video playback quality is to set, encode, and review with these standard video framerate settings. This would be done during your content optimization (final original or raw video asset encoding) work process.

The next most optimal setting to tweak (experiment with settings for) in obtaining a smaller data footprint will be the bitrate that you set for a codec to try and achieve. Bitrate settings equate to an amount of compression applied, and thus sets the visual quality for video data. It is important to note that you could simply use 30 FPS, HD 1920x1080 video and specify a low bitrate ceiling. If you do this, your results might not look as good as if you first experimented with lower frame rates and resolutions while using the higher (quality) bitrate settings. The only way to find out what any give codec (encoder algorithm) will do is to experiment with the settings and look at the resulting filesize, playback speed, and visual quality for the resulting asset using an Android decoder.

The next most effective setting in obtaining a small data footprint is the number of **keyframes**. The codec uses your keyframe settings to know when to sample the digital video. Video codecs apply compression by looking at a frame, and then encoding only the changes, or offsets, over the next few frames, so that it does not have to encode every single frame in your video data stream. This is why a talking-head video will encode better than a video where every pixel moves on every frame, such as video with fast panning or rapid zooming, for instance.

The keyframe setting in the encoder will force the codec to take a fresh frame sample of a video data asset every so often. There is usually an **auto** setting for keyframes; this allows the codec to decide how many keyframes to sample. There is also a **manual** setting that allows you to specify a keyframe sampling every so often, usually a certain number of times per second, or a certain number of times over the duration of the video (total frames). The more keyframes the codec needs to sample (and store in the file) the larger the resulting file size will be.

The next most effective setting in obtaining a small data footprint is the quality or sharpness setting, which is usually implemented using some sort of slider or spinner user interface element. Sharpness controls the amount of blur that a codec will apply to the video pixels before compression. A 100% quality doesn't apply algorithms (pixel processing on any frames); as you reduce this percentage, the amount of algorithmic processing increases.

In case you are wondering how this blur trick works, so that you can apply it yourself in GIMP during your own digital image optimization work process, applying a slight blur to your still image or video, which is usually not desirable, can allow for better lossy compression, such as that found in JPEG and MPEG, or WebP and WebM.

The reason for this is that a sharp transition in a raster image, such as the sharp edges between colors, are more difficult for the codec to encode optimally (that is, using less data). More precisely (no pun intended), sharp or abrupt transitions in color will take more data to reproduce than soft transitions will. This does not hold true in vector images (SVG, AI, EPS or PDF) as the edges between strokes and fills are rendered and then anti-aliased.

I would recommend keeping the quality or sharpness slider between an 80% and 100% quality setting, and try to get your data footprint reduction using many of the other variables (data footprint optimization approaches), which we have discussed in this section of the chapter.

Ultimately, there are a significant number of different variables that you'll need to fine-tune in order to achieve the best data footprint optimization for each particular video data asset. Each video asset will be different (mathematically) to the codec, as each video asset is a different array or collection of pixel color data.

For this reason, there is no "standard" collection of settings you can develop to achieve any given result. Your experience tweaking various settings will eventually allow you to get a better feel, over time, as to the settings you need to change as far as all the parameters go, to get your desired result with different types of uncompressed video source assets.

Next, lets create some digital video content using Terragen 4.0, which came out recently, is a professional-level production software package from Planetside Software, which also happens to have a free version and a very affordable professional version as well. I highly recommend this software, which, like Blackmagic Fusion, has a visual programming paradigm that makes advanced production easier and more visual, like Android Studio's new Visual Design Editor.

Creating Digital Video Content: Terragen4

The next thing that you need to learn is how to create digital video content that you can use to show the various concepts that you just learned about in the previous sections of this chapter. I'm going to use Terragen 4.0, a world creation 3D animation software package from Planetside Software, because it is not only an impressive 3D software package, but is also a professional-level 3D production software package. Fortunately, there is the free version as well as a paid Pro version, which I suggest that you purchase if you are serious about having all the top production tools in your quiver. Go to the website, at Planetside.co.uk, and download the latest version of Terragen 4. After you download and install the software, you'll follow the following steps:

1. Launch Terragen 4, using your shortcut icon, and you will see the startup screen, as shown in Figure 11-9. You can see exactly what this 3D software is capable of by viewing this startup screen, as these clouds were not photographed, but instead created using Terragen algorithms!

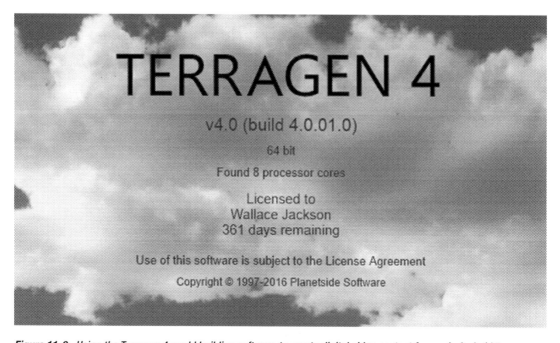

Figure 11-9. Using the Terragen 4 world building software to create digital video content for use in Android 7.x

2.   First, you will open a basic seamless looping camera fly-over of a basic world that you will find in this book assets folder called looping0rbit_v03.tgd (tgd is TerraGen Data). Use a **File ➤ Open** menu sequence to open it in the software, the result of which can be is seen in Figure 11-10. Use an **Edit ➤ Preferences** menu sequence and in the **File Saving** section select the BMP format and numbered animation file output path, in my case this was C:\Terragen4.

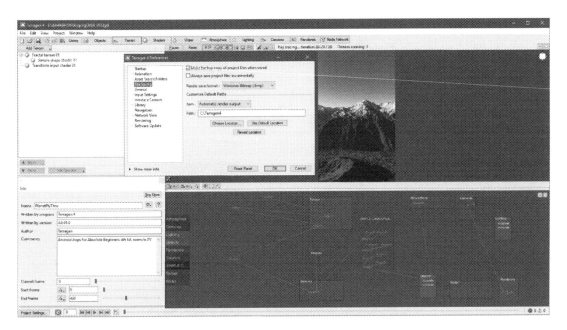

Figure 11-10. Start Terragen3 and use File ➤ Open menu sequence to open loopingOrbit_v03

3.   In the top of the **Add Renderer** tab which is seen on the left in Figure 11-11, and is accessed using the **Renderers** button, shown circled in red, set an **image width** of **1080** pixels, and an **image height** of **1920** pixels. This is your Nexus 5 AVD resolution. This **True HD** resolution will have enough pixels to be able to scale up (to UHD) or down (to Blu-ray) with good visual results. Leave all the other render settings at their default settings. If you just wanted to render one frame, you could use the **Render Image** button, which is in the middle of this dialog, but this will not create a **sequence of frames**, which you will need to create **motion video** data. The **Render All To Disk** will also not create a sequence of numbered files, although it seems like it would. At the bottom of this tab you'll see seven tabs that control **advanced settings**.

4. Click on the seventh (right-most) tab, which is labeled **Sequence/ Output** to set the output file specifications as well as the image sequence settings. Enter your **project files directory** in the **Output image filename** field, as seen in Figure 11-11. Mine is C:\Terragen4 as you can see.

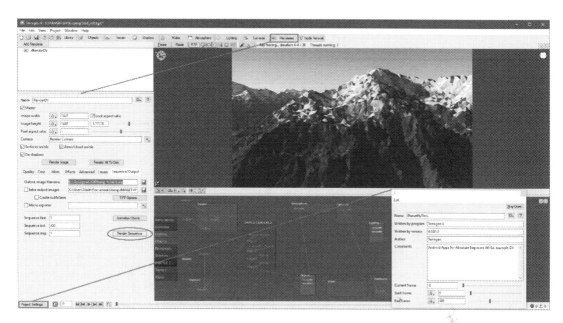

Figure 11-11. Use Project Settings and Renderers buttons to open option dialogs, then Render Sequence button

5. Make sure that your **Sequence first** field is set to a data value of **1**, and set the value of **400** in the **Sequence last** data field. Set **Sequence step** to **1 frame** for a smoother camera movement.

6. Once you have set all of your parameters for the render, click the **Render Sequence** button at the bottom of the Sequence/Output tab. This will instruct Terragen to generate 400 frames of custom digital video fly-over for you. Since Terragen outputs numbered files, instead of .AVI format that most NLE software requires, unless you are using Squeeze 11, which will read in numbered files, you will need to use a software utility called VirtualDub to create an AVI file.

Figure 11-12 shows one of the frames of the rendering sequence, which took 4 days on my 64-bit OctaCore PC.

Figure 11-12. *Make sure render output window shows Frame number and total render time*

Next, let's take a look at how to turn these rendered frames into a digital video asset, using Sorenson Squeeze Desktop Pro 11, and take a look at some of the settings we discussed in the data footprint optimization section.

Digital Video Compression: Sorenson Squeeze 11

Next, we're going to use Sorenson Squeeze Desktop 11 to compress the digital video asset. One of the reasons I utilized Terragen 4 was to create completely uncompressed source video with zero compression artifacts, so that you can see what a codec can do with clean data, as video camera data tends to be somewhat chaotic from the codec's perspective of pixel data values. 3D software tends to output adjacent pixel values that relate in some way or another to each other, whereas a camera CCD will simply output what it sees in real life, which tends to be more chaotic, unless you are filming the night sky (or a clear blue sky), in which pixels will closely relate to each other in both location and color. Also, many video cameras pre-compress data using Motion JPEG or even MPEG to fit more minutes on a cartridge, so if you want less chaos (less compression artifacts) using a camera, you should use Firewire, capturing full frame uncompressed (raw) video data to your hard disk drive, instead of going through the on-camera MPEG or Motion JPEG codec and onto a captive digital video cartridge inside of the camera.

The other reason I am using Sorenson Squeeze Desktop is because it is the most professional video compression solution, has affordable $199 (Lite), $549 (Standard), and $749 (Professional) price points, and has support for every platform (as you'll see in Figure 11-14) that you will ever want to optimize digital video for. There is also a 30-day trial version that you can use to follow along with this work process on the SorensonMedia website, and I recommend purchasing one of the non-expiring versions for your digital media production workstation, as this is currently the industry standard for digital media data footprint optimization.

Let's take a look at the work process for optimizing a Terragen 4 flythrough, using Sorenson Squeeze Desktop.

1. Install Sorenson Squeeze Desktop Pro 11, and launch it. Use **File ➤ Import Image Sequence**, shown numbered as 1, in Figure 11-13, and open your **Select image sequence to open** dialog. Select the **Terragen4** folder (or wherever your files are stored) shown as number 2, and select the first file in the import image sequence shown as number 3. Finally, click the **Open** button, shown as number 4, and set a **25** FPS frame rate, shown as number 5. I used 25 FPS as it is an even multiple of 400, giving us a clean full 16 seconds of looping video. To invoke the import into Sorenson Squeeze Desktop 11, click the **OK** button, shown as number 6 in Figure 11-13.

Figure 11-13. A six-step work process for importing a sequence of image frames to be used as a digital video clip

2. If you're using a digital video file such as an uncompressed AVI (Microsoft) or MOV (Apple) format file, click on the **Import File** icon, seen in Figure 11-14, on the upper left. Notice that the Squeeze software has left mounted panels for holding **codec Formats**, **Favorites settings**, and **Workflow** options, as well as a top previewing area and a bottom timeline area, which we will be using to apply codec presets to the image sequence, seen selected in light blue. This is done by dragging a codec on top of the video source, and dropping it on top of it. This shows Squeeze that you want to apply that codec to a source video (in this case, an image sequence).

Figure 11-14. The Squeeze Desktop 11 user interface panel (left), source preview (top), and timeline (bottom)

3.   Next, let's take a look at how you can edit existing codecs, to see what their default settings are, and how you can then create (and rename and add) new codecs that are customized to your projects. Open the **MPEG-4 (mp4)** codec section in your Squeeze **Presets** tab, as shown selected in blue, on the left in Figure 11-14. Find the **HEVC_3300Kbps_1080p** preset, shown selected in blue in Figure 11-15, and right-click on it and select the **Edit** option from a context sensitive menu that appears. This will open a **Presets** dialog for that codec settings collection, as shown in the middle of Figure 11-15. An **MPEG-4 H.265** (technically an MPEG-H codec) is a High-Efficiency Video Codec (hence HEVC) which was recently added to 64-bit Android OSes, so I am taking a look at it here first. It uses the **x265** codec, as shown in Figure 11-15, a single-pass, variable bitrate (VBR) encoding method (algorithm), and the target 3Mbps (**3068** Kbps) quality level, **Auto Key Frame on Scene Change** selected, to allow the codec to insert key frames (algorithmically). These are the settings you'll adjust to get the best data footprint.

Figure 11-15. Right-click on HEVC 1080 codec, and use Edit to open the codec Presets dialog for codec settings

4. Click **OK** to close the HEVC codec, since we're going to use a more widely supported AVC, or Advanced Video Codec, for this exercise. This is so that we can span earlier versions of the Android OS that don't contain an HEVC codec but which represent a significant percentage of the Android devices out there. If you are producing Android TV apps, you will want to use HEVC codec to get a better quality HD/UHD result, since Android TV was recently released.

5. Let's create an **Android_1080p** MPEG-4 H.264 AVC preset by selecting an Apple_TV preset and reconfiguring it for our use in Android (versions 1.6 through 7.x support decoding AVC). Right-click on the Apple_TV_1080p codec seen in Figure 11-16, and right-click on it and use the **Edit** command to open it in the Presets editing dialog. Select the MainConcepts codec, as I know it works well from my previous books on Android, or the Sorenson codec, which is a new addition to this software. In fact, you might try both with identical settings to see which gives you a better data footprint to get some practice using this software package! I set 2-Pass VBR (slower but better compression) as the Method and 2Mbps (2000 Kbps) as the Data Rate Target and used Constrain Maximum Data Rate to make sure the codec did not exceed this. I also renamed the **Preset Name** to **Android_1080p**, and the **Preset Desc** to **For Android OS supports 1080p resolution**, as you can see at the top of the dialog in Figure 11-16. It is also interesting to note that Apple does not call their Apple_TV product iTV (like iPad, iPhone) as iTV is the "public domain" term for interactive TV (or intelligent TV, or Internet TV, if you prefer). Smart TV is trademarked by Samsung. Connected TV is also privately trademarked.

6. To create the compressed video file, click on the **OK** button in the Presets dialog to create the Android_1080p preset, and drag it out of the Formats (Presets) tab and drop it on the source (numbered image files). To start the compression process, click the **Squeeze It!** button at the bottom-right corner of Squeeze Desktop. If your HEVC 1080 codec is still attached to the video source, right-click on that entry in the timeline view, and delete it using the context sensitive menu, before you apply the Android_1080p codec preset that you have just created.

Figure 11-16. Create an Android_1080p codec, by editing an AppleTV codec and selecting MainConcept's codec

As you will see the HEVC codec gives you a 6.75MB file and the AVC codec gives you a 4MB file, because of the high 2MB compression setting. The HEVC file will have much better quality and could be used for Android TV, whereas we'll use the AVC file across Android devices as well as across all Android OS revisions as well. Now we are ready to create the /res/raw folder to hold the video asset and continue with our Java programming.

Creating a Digital Video Folder: Raw Resources

Go back into Android Studio, and right-click on your `DigitalVideoMedia` project's **/app/res** folder, and select the **New ➤ Android resource directory** menu sequence, shown on the left side of Figure 11-17 to create a resource subfolder for already optimized digital video (as well as digital audio) assets. Android will not attempt to double compress (which would reduce the visual quality) and assets in this folder, which is what this **/res/raw** folder is used for. I use this folder quite a bit, as it allows me to control optimization for files contained in the .APK file.

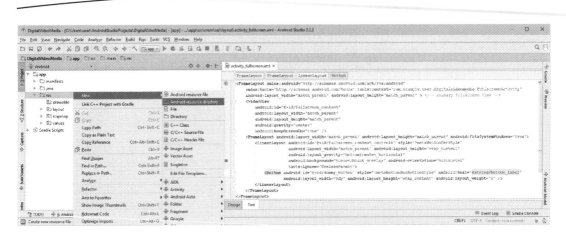

Figure 11-17. *Right-click on the project /res folder and use the New ➤ Android resource directory menu sequence*

In the **New Resource Directory** dialog, in your **Resource type** drop-down selector, select the **raw** option, as is seen in Figure 11-18 in blue, and make sure the **Directory name** is **raw**, and then click the **OK** button to create the app/res/raw/ folder. Now all you have to do is install the digital video asset in this folder using your explorer file management utility, and we'll be able to move on to finish all the Java 8 code to implement the digital video.

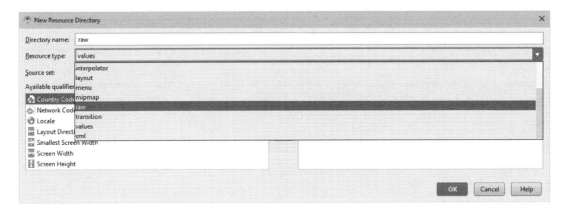

Figure 11-18. *Select a raw resource type in the second drop-down selector in a New Resources Directory dialog*

Open your OS file management utility, for Windows 10 this is the Windows Explorer, and find the digital video asset, in my case this was C:\Terragen4\1080temp.001_Android_1080p.m4v, and right-click on it, and select the **Copy** option. Then find your AndroidStudioProjects\DigitalVideoMedia folder, in my case, this was located at C:\Users\user\AndroidStudioProjects\DigitalVideoMedia\app\scrc\main\res\raw, as shown at the top of Figure 11-19, and right-click on the folder (or in the empty area to the right), and select the **Paste** option.

Since Android OS will look for an .MP4 file, you will also need to rename your file generated by Squeeze 11 to be `flythru3d.mp4`. Right-click on your file and select the **Rename** menu item from the context sensitive menu, and replace the Squeeze generated `.m4v` filename with a custom `flythru3d.mp4` file name you'll use in Android.

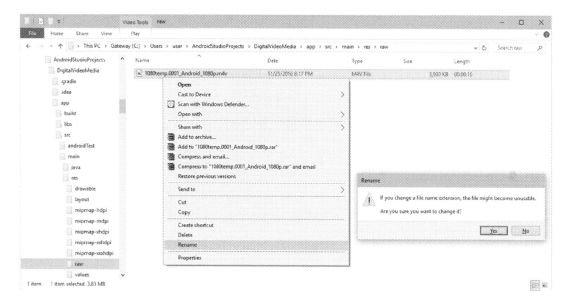

Figure 11-19. *Place the MPEG-4 file you created in the project /res/raw folder, and rename it to be flythru3d.mp4*

Before we get back into Java coding, let's take an in-depth look at how digital video assets are referenced using a URI in Android OS, as well as how that `Uri` object is parsed, and passed into your `VideoView`'s `MediaPlayer`.

The Uri Class: Referencing the Video Data

URI is an abbreviation for Uniform Resource Identifier. Uniform because it is standardized, Resource because it references a data path to some data (content) that applications will operate on and utilize. It is an Identifier because it identifies where to go and load the data, which is also known as the content's **data path**.

The Android `Uri` class only capitalizes the U, the industry term capitalizes all three (URI) letters in the term. A URI has four parts. The first is a URI **schema** such as `HTTP://`. Next comes an **authority**, like `apress.com`. Next comes the **data path**, such as `/data/video`. Finally comes a **data object** itself in its file format such as `asset.mp4`.

A `Uri` object in Android contains a reference to a data path that will be used to access raw or specialized data, of one type or another. One example of data would be a SQLite database, or in this case, the digital video asset. Other examples might include your website's URL, or similar types of content which the application might use.

Android's Uri class is a direct subclass of the java.lang.Object class, and therefore, was created specifically for holding URI references. Just so that you don't get confused when you look at current Android 7.1.1 developer's site documentation, note that the java.net.Uri class exists alongside the android.net.Uri class. However, I suggest that you use the Android-specific version of the Uri class, since it is optimized for use within the Android 7.1.1 OS. The Uri class is a **public abstract** class, and has over three dozen methods that allow developers to work with Uri objects (and data path references).

Since this is an Absolute Beginner's book, we will not be getting into this Uri class at a great level of depth, but you're welcome to research it yourself, on the Android developer website. The Android Uri class hierarchy is structured as follows:

```
java.lang.Object
  > android.net.Uri
```

The Android Uri class is kept in the android.net package, making it a tool for accessing data across a **network**. For this reason, the import statement for using the Uri class inside of your Android application would reference a package path of android.net.Uri, as you will see in the next section.

The Android Uri class allows developers to create Uri objects which provide what is termed an **immutable** URI reference. Immutable objects and variables **cannot be changed** (think "mutate," or something that has been changed, usually with undesirable results), and you certainly do not want something critical like your URI reference to change. In Android, you make objects immutable by placing them into system memory for use, and you'll need to do this for your URI data path reference, by using Android's Uri class, and its Uri.parse() method.

Your Uri object reference includes a URI specifier, as well as a data path reference, which is the component of the URI that follows the '://'. The Uri class will take care of the process of building and parsing the Uri object, which will then reference data in a manner that will conform to the popular RFC 2396 technical specification.

To optimize the Android operating system and application performance, a Uri class performs a minimal amount of data path validation. What this means is that Uri methods aren't specifically defined for handling invalid data input, so you will need to define your own data validation. This means the Uri class is very forgiving in the face of an invalid input specification. It also means that if data is invalid, your user may not get the result you desire!

This means that as a developer you have to be very careful about what you are doing, as Uri objects could return garbage data rather than throw an exception, unless you specify otherwise in the Java code. Thus, error trapping and data path validation are left up to the developer to create, inside their code. This is why URI is an advanced area, which we are only covering at an introductory level, so that you will be able to load the digital video data.

Next, we will create your Uri object as well as creating your VideoView object, so we will be able to access our digital video asset. Let's do that next, and after that we can get into the MediaPlayer class and its related classes.

The Uri.parse() Method: Loading Your VideoView

Next, let's declare the Uri and VideoView objects at the top of the FullscreenActivity class, so that we can later instantiate them inside of the onCreate() method to set up the MediaPlayer engine, so we can play digital video.

1. Declare a VideoView object at the top of the FullscreenActivity class naming it videoHolder, as is shown in Figure 11-20. To have Android Studio create the import statement for you, use the **Alt+Enter** shortcut to instruct Android Studio to write the code. The two Java statements that you'll be coding at the top of the FullscreenActivity class should look like the following:

```
public class FullscreenActivity extends AppCompatActivity {
VideoView videoHolder;
Uri videoAssetUri;
                    // The rest of your class goes in here }
```

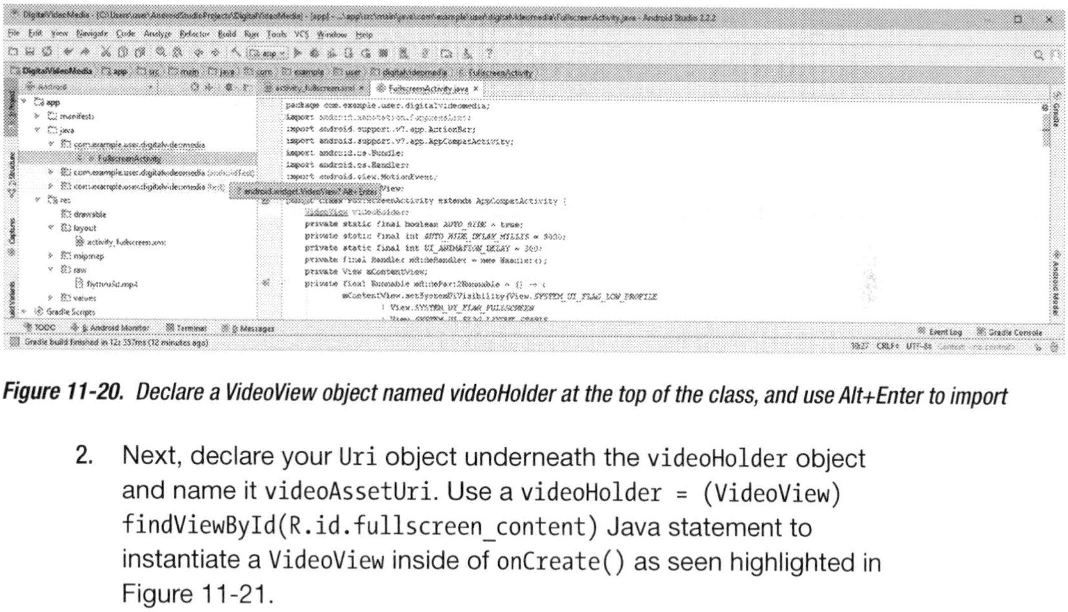

Figure 11-20. Declare a VideoView object named videoHolder at the top of the class, and use Alt+Enter to import

2. Next, declare your Uri object underneath the videoHolder object and name it videoAssetUri. Use a videoHolder = (VideoView) findViewById(R.id.fullscreen_content) Java statement to instantiate a VideoView inside of onCreate() as seen highlighted in Figure 11-21.

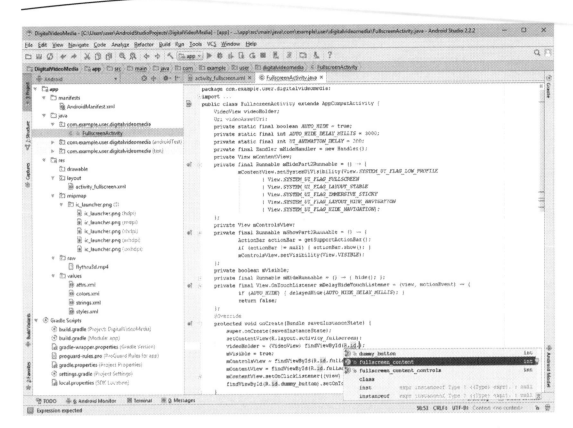

Figure 11-21. *Declare a VideoView object named videoHolder at the top of the class, and use Alt+Enter to import*

Once you've instantiated the VideoView, you will then instantiate the Uri object by setting it equal to the result of a Uri.parse() method call. This is done by using the following Java statement, shown being created in Figure 11-22, using the Android Studio helper drop-down selector that comes up once a videoAsset.Uri = Uri. (portion) of the Java statement has been typed into the onCreate() method, after the VideoView instantiation:

```
videoAssetUri = Uri.parse( "android.resource://" + getPackageName() + "/" + R.raw.flythru3d );
```

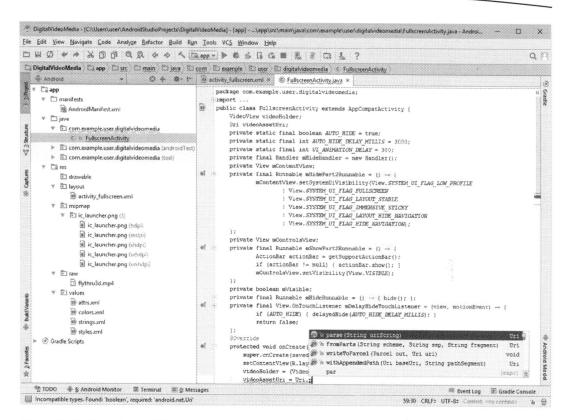

Figure 11-22. Use a New ➤ Folder menu sequence to create a /res/raw folder, then copy the fly-over asset into it

This Java statement sets the videoAssetUri (Uri) object to the result of the Uri.parse() method call. Inside this method call is a **concatenation operation** that uses a + operator, which is used in Java to concatenate things together. What this concatenation inside of the Uri.parse() method parameter area does is create the URI path to the video data asset by concatenating the android.resource:// with the package name and then the resource path. The resulting URI, shown below as equated by this concatenation, provides Android OS with the full path that starts with the Android resource area down to the package name, and finally down to your digital video asset:

android.resource://com.example.user.digitalvideomedia/R.raw.flythru3d.mp4

Figure 11-23 shows the latter part of Android Studio creating this Java code statement for you, which it will do regarding the Uri.parse(), getPackage() and R.raw.flythru3d portions of this Java Uri object instantiation.

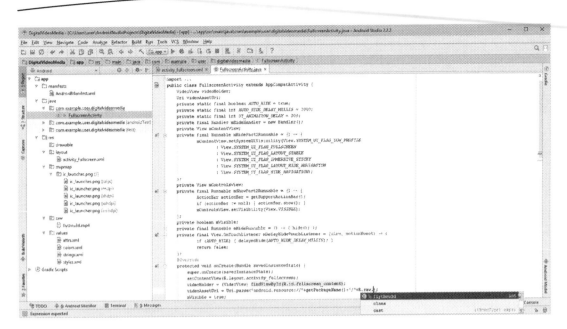

Figure 11-23.   Load the videoAssetUri object using the Uri.parse( ) method, and the data path to /res/raw/flythru3d

Now that your `videoAssetUri` `Uri` object is loaded with the correct URI data path reference, you can "wire" this `videoAssetUri` (`Uri`) object to the `videoHolder` (`VideoView`) object using the `.setVideoURI()` method call, using the compact line of Java code shown in Figure 11-24, which looks like the following Java statement:

```
videoHolder.setVideoURI(videoAssetUri);
```

This Java statement uses the `setVideoURI` called off of the `videoHolder` `VideoView` to install the `videoAssetUri` object containing the URI reference to the digital video asset that needs to be played.

The only line of Java code that we have not yet put into place is the call to the `.start()` method, which we will make off of your `videoHolder` `VideoView` object. Since you have loaded with a URI for `/res/raw/flythru3d.mp4`, you now have a digital video asset that can be played, and so you can call the `.start()` method. Make sure that you call the `.start()` method **after** you have wired all of the other components and new media assets together!

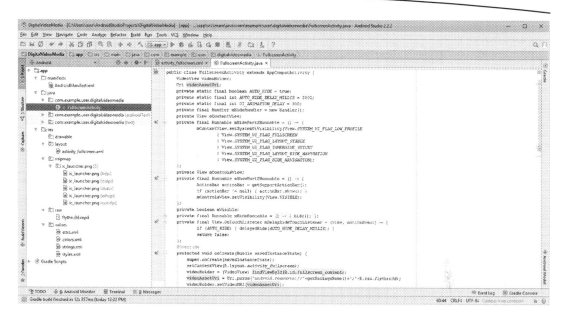

Figure 11-24. *Configure videoHolder VideoView object to reference the videoAssetUri object with .setVideoURI( )*

A call to this `.start()` method off of the `videoPlayer` VideoView object is done using the following simple line of Java code (more of a Java statement, actually) which is seen in Figure 11-25:

```
videoHolder.start();
```

As you can see in Figure 11-25, you have implemented digital video playback in your Java code in a half-dozen lines of Java code, not including two new import statements, which brings the total new lines of code to eight.

If you want to use **Run ➤ Run 'app'** to run the application, you can if you wish, and as seen in Figure 11-30, the digital video asset does indeed play fullscreen, which is our objective in this chapter, to do a fullscreen video playback application!

As you can see in Figure 11-30, we will also be adding a media control transport using the `MediaController` class (and object) after we learn more about the `MediaPlayer` class and the `MediaController` class.

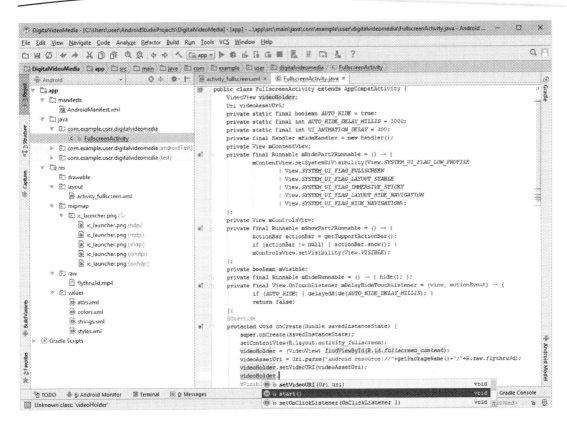

Figure 11-25. Add the videoHolder.start( ) method call to finish implementation of a VideoView and start playback

Let's take a look at two of Android's media playback related classes before we continue with more Java coding.

Android MediaPlayer: VideoPlayback Engine

The MediaPlayer class is a direct subclass of the java.lang.Object master class. As you know, this indicates that this Android MediaPlayer class was designed specifically for the purpose of providing MediaPlayer objects. A MediaPlayer object is a part of your VideoView widget, and you will learn how to make the MediaPlayer object visible inside your Java code in a future section of this chapter. The MediaPlayer class hierarchy looks like this:

```
java.lang.Object
  > android.media.MediaPlayer
```

The MediaPlayer class belongs to the android.media package. The import statement for using the MediaPlayer class in an app would reference the android.media.MediaPlayer. This MediaPlayer class is a **public** class, and features **nine nested classes**. Eight of the nested classes offer **callbacks** for determining information regarding operation of MediaPlayer's video playback engine. We'll be using one of these in a future section of the chapter.

The ninth nested class, the `MediaPlayer.TrackInfo` nested class, is utilized to return video, audio, or subtitle track metadata information. The `MediaPlayer` nested class callback that we'll be implementing later on in the chapter is the `MediaPlayer.OnPreparedListener`, which allows us to configure a `MediaPlayer` object before the digital video asset playback starts for the first time.

Other often-used callbacks include your `MediaPlayer.OnErrorListener`, which responds to (that is, handles) error messages relating to a digital video asset or a network connection, `MediaPlayer.OnCompletionListener`, which you can use to trigger Java programming structures once your video asset playback cycle has completed, `MediaPlayer.OnSeekCompletedListener`, which is called when a digital video **seek operation** has completed, and a `MediaPlayer.OnBufferingUpdateListener`, which is called in order to obtain data buffering status for a video asset that is being streamed over a network.

There are also a couple of less-often-utilized nested classes, such as the `MediaPlayer.OnTimedTextListener`, used when video **timed text** becomes available for display, and the `MediaPlayer.OnInfoListener`, used when **information** or **warnings** regarding video media being used become available for display. These nested class callbacks are not used that often, at least not to my knowledge, but they are available to you if you need them for specialized digital video implementation scenarios within your Android applications.

Android MediaController: A VideoTransport

The `MediaController` class is a direct subclass of the `android.widget.FrameLayout` class. As you know, this is a `ViewGroup` layout container class, and a `FrameLayout` is a static layout, in this case used to create a fixed video transport UI element. A `MediaTansport` object is used to provide a video transport control set, which is a collection of Play, Pause, Stop, and Rewind buttons, along with a Shuttle slider and current time readouts. You will learn how to "wire" (connect or reference) a `MediaController` object up to your `VideoView` object in the next section of this chapter. The `MediaController` class hierarchy should look like the following Java class hierarchy:

```
java.lang.Object
  > android.view.View
    > android.view.ViewGroup
      > android.widget.FrameLayout
        > android.widget.MediaController
```

Android's `MediaController` class belongs to your `android.widget` package. The `import` statement for using the `MediaController` class in an app would reference the `android.widget.MediaController`. The `MediaController` class is a **public** class, and features one nested class: `MediaController.MediaPlayerControl`. This class is the public static interface that contains eleven methods used to control a media player using the `MediaController` class. These include `seekTo()`, `isPlaying()`, `getCurrentPosition()`, `getAudioSessionId()`, `getDuration()`, `getBufferPercentage()`, `canSeekForward()`, `canSeekBackward()`, `canPause()`, `pause()` and `start()`.

A MediaController at the highest level (other than Object) is a View object containing the transport controls for a MediaPlayer object that it is wired to via the VideoView which accesses that MediaPlayer object. Typically, a video playback transport UI will contain buttons such as play, pause, rewind, fast forward, go to start, and a progress bar and current position. The MediaController class takes care of the synchronizing of the UI controls with the state of the MediaPlayer (object) being used by the VideoView (object) inside your fullscreen layout.

The way to use this class, as you will see in the next section of this chapter, is to instantiate it programmatically. The MediaController object will then create a default set of controls using its FrameLayout superclass and place these in a window floating above your application.

Specifically, the controls will float above the view that is specified by the developer using the setAnchorView() method call, in most cases this will be the VideoView which is hosting your digital video asset and playing it using the MediaPlayer object that the VideoView utilizes to play back that new media asset.

The video transport window will appear when the (in this case, fullscreen) video is touched or clicked, and will disappear if left unused for video control for three seconds. It will then reappear again when the user touches the anchor view; in our case this is a VideoView inside a FullscreenActivity, which means anywhere on the screen.

Add a Video Transport UI Using MediaController

Next, let's implement your MediaController UI transport controller, the UI buttons used to control your video.

1. Once you declare a Java MediaController videoTransport; statement at the top of your FullscreenActivity subclass, and hit the Alt+Enter to have Android Studio write your import android. widget.MediaController statement you'll be able to instantiate and construct your new MediaController object inside of your onCreate() method. The next step is to use a new keyword in conjunction with the MediaController(this) constructor method with the passed parameter containing your standard Java Context object, which in this case is passed using the Java keyword **this.** This code will construct a MediaController object named videoTransport using the following Java programming construct, which can be seen in Figure 11-26:

    ```
    videoTransport = new MediaController(this);
    ```

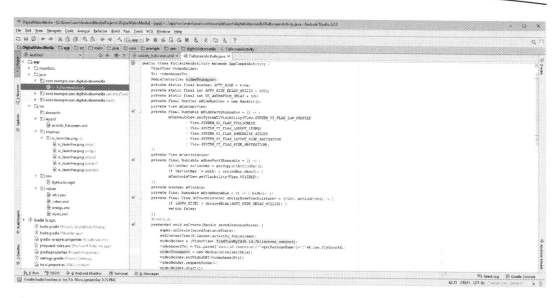

Figure 11-26. Declare a MediaController named videoTransport, and construct your new MediaController( ) object

Notice in both Figures 11-26 and 11-27 that I've clicked on the videoTransport MediaController object in the Java code, which tells Android Studio to highlight the (purple colored) tracking of the instantiation. I did this in the next screenshot to show both your videoTransport MediaController object declaration and instantiation, as well as the object usage for the videoTransport MediaController object. This is an effective technique to track an object's use through your Java logic. The next thing you'll need to do is to wire the VideoView object to the MediaController object, such that they know each other are there, and so they will work together seamlessly.

In pseudo-code speak, we need to tell the MediaController object that it is controlling the VideoView, and tell the VideoView to use the MediaController object to control its new media asset (in this case, digital video). This cross-wiring of the two objects will take two lines of Java code, which, after they are in place, will give your user the ability to click (or touch) the digital video content and bring up the MediaPlayer transport UI element. This MediaController, or the MediaPlayer transport, whichever way you want to look at it, will always work, regardless of whether you have your digital video asset set up to loop, or to only play once.

1. As you can see in Figure 11-27, we will first use the .setAnchorView() method call, off of the videoTransport object, to wire the videoTransport and the videoHolder objects together. This tells the videoTransport object: "the videoHolder VideoView object is your anchor View.

2. Then we will use a .setMediaController() method call off of the
    videoHolder object, to wire the videoHolder and the videoTransport
    objects together. This will tell the videoHolder object "use the
    videoTransport MediaController object as the MediaController for
    this VideoView object named videoHolder." These two lines of Java
    logic should look like the following:

```
videoTransport.setAnchorView(videoHolder);
videoHolder.setMediaController(videoTransport);
```

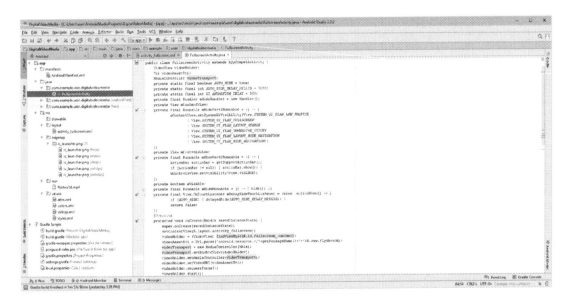

Figure 11-27. Wire the videoTransport and videoHolder together with .setAnchorView( ) and .setMediaController( )

Use the **Run ➤ Run 'app'** menu sequence and launch your Nexus 5 AVD, as seen in
Figure 11-28, and rotate the device 90 degrees by using the rotate icon on the AVD icon
control bar, shown on the right, circled in red.

Figure 11-28. Use Run ➤ Run 'app' and test your fullscreen VideoView, MediaPlayer and MediaController

Once the digital video starts playing, even if it is set to loop, which I will be showing you how to do in the next section of this chapter, you can click on the screen at any time, and bring up the video media transport controls. After a few seconds, these transport UI controls will fade away, if they are not being actively used to start, stop, pause, rewind (reset), or shuttle the digital video asset's frames. Also notice in Figure 11-28 that the current time (00:14) and the duration (00:16) are also shown in the transport bar user interface element (MediaController).

Congratulations, you've essentially mastered the basics of digital video playback for your Android applications development thus far during the chapter, doing everything from learning the fundamentals of digital video asset concepts and creation to optimization and encoding digital video assets, to coding a FullscreenActivity for video playback. Soon we will add looping capabilities and streaming video playback support for your users to use.

Pretty comprehensive, for just one single chapter! If you wanted to venture more deeply into this subject, look for my titles **Pro Android Graphics** (Apress, 2014) and *Pro Android UI* (Apress, 2014) that delve deeper into this subject area, and combine it with more advanced graphic design and user interface design topics.

Now, let's continue with Java programming, and expose a MediaPlayer object using OnPreparedListener. This will allow you to set your digital video asset to loop continuously. Fortunately you learned about event listeners early on in the book, in Chapter 7, so that I could cover more advanced callbacks, such as this one, during the second half of the book.

Loop Digital Video: Using OnPrepareListener

Now we are going to implement one of the most-used nested interfaces from the MediaPlayer class, MediaPlayer.OnPreparedListener, which will allow you to configure the videoHolder VideoView digital video asset to loop seamlessly. You'll do this by calling a .setOnPreparedListener() method off of your videoHolder object. Inside of that Java programming construct, you will then utilize a new keyword to create an OnPreparedListener implementation. Inside of that construct will live the onPrepared() event listener. This will be accomplished via the following initial Java statement that creates an empty event listening structure:

```
videoHolder.setOnPreparedListener(new MediaPlayer.OnPreparedListener(){empty onPrepared()
method });
```

As you can see in Figure 11-29, as you type in the videoHolder.setOnPreparedListener() method call, off of your videoPlayer VideoView object, as you type in the .setOn part of the statement, Android Studio will figure out what you are trying to do, and will pop up the VideoView event listener helper dialog, shown at the bottom-right corner of the partial screenshot.

It is important to notice that I am calling the .setOnPreparedListener() method before I call the .start() method, because I don't want to start the video before I prepare (configure) it for use! Remember, the order of Java programming statements is extremely important, and putting method calls in the wrong order would generate unintended results!

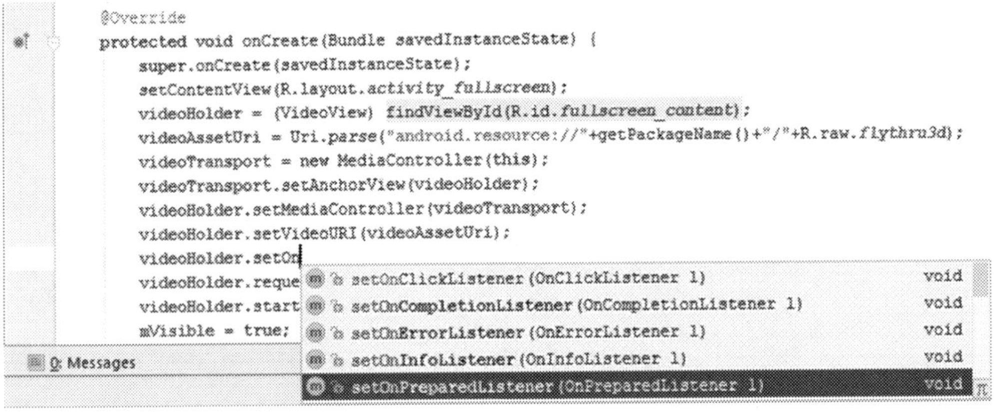

```
@Override
protected void onCreate(Bundle savedInstanceState) {
    super.onCreate(savedInstanceState);
    setContentView(R.layout.activity_fullscreen);
    videoHolder = (VideoView) findViewById(R.id.fullscreen_content);
    videoAssetUri = Uri.parse("android.resource://"+getPackageName()+"/"+R.raw.flythru3d);
    videoTransport = new MediaController(this);
    videoTransport.setAnchorView(videoHolder);
    videoHolder.setMediaController(videoTransport);
    videoHolder.setVideoURI(videoAssetUri);
    videoHolder.setOn
    videoHolder.reque  ⊕ ⓢ setOnClickListener(OnClickListener l)                    void
    videoHolder.start  ⊕ ⓢ setOnCompletionListener(OnCompletionListener l)          void
    mVisible = true;   ⊕ ⓢ setOnErrorListener(OnErrorListener l)                    void
 ▓ Q: Messages         ⊕ ⓢ setOnInfoListener(OnInfoListener l)                      void
                       ⊕ ⓢ setOnPreparedListener(OnPreparedListener l)             void
```

Figure 11-29. Type videoPlayer.setOn, and select setOnPreparedListener(OnPreparedListener l) option

Inside videoHolder.setOnPreparedListener, type new MediaPlayer and a period and Android Studio will pop up your MediaPlayer nested class callback helper dialog. As you will see, this dialog contains all nine of the nested class callbacks that you learned about in the earlier Android MediaPlayer section of this chapter. Select the first MediaPlayer. OnPreparedListener anonymous inner type option and double-click on it, which will insert it into your Java code structure.

Not only does it insert the OnPreparedListener() structure, but it also will add in an unimplemented onPrepared() method structure, which you usually have to do via another mouse-over operation. All you will have to do now is to add those operations that you want to happen during this video preparation phase of the video asset. In this case, that would be to set the setLooping() method's parameter to be true, so that your video will loop forever.

Next, all you have to do is to add the .setLooping() method call and parameter to the public void onPrepared() method that is inside of the OnPreparedListener() structure, called off a MediaPlayer object named videoPlayer, which Android Studio has created for you. This is done using the following Java logic, shown in Figure 11-30:

```
videoHolder.setOnPreparedListener(new MediaPlayer.OnPreparedListener() {
    @Override
    public void onPrepared(MediaPlayer videoPlayer) {
        videoPlayer.setLooping(true);
    }
});
```

As you can see in Figure 11-30, the code is error free and ready to test using a **Run ➤ Run 'app'** menu sequence. The digital video asset now both loops and fills your screen, and (not in a screenshot; it should look like Figure 11-28) you can now watch the 3D planet flythrough digital video asset loop seamlessly on the screen. You have implemented looping digital video in an application using only 15 lines of Java code, not counting three import statements that Android Studio wrote for you, which brings the total to a dozen and a half. The Java statement count is so low because again, Android has written the majority of the code for you using the classes we learned about during this chapter (MediaPlayer, MediaController, Uri, VideoView, FullscreenActivity, FrameLayout).

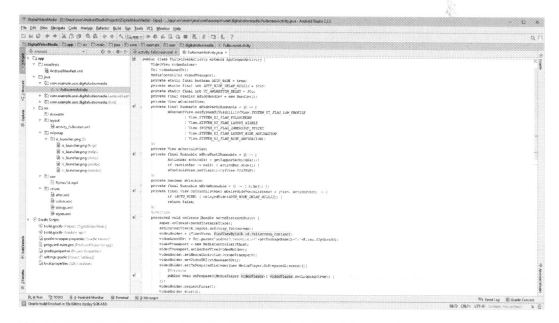

Figure 11-30. Adding the onPrepared( ) method to our new MediaPlayer.OnPreparedListener( ) callback structure

Next, I am going to show you how to modify your current Java code to stream video, instead of using a captive video asset in Android. All that you have to do is change your Uri object to reference the HTTP:// instead of an android.resource:// in the URI datapath referencing string. I already have a pag800x480landscape.mp4 version and a pag480x800portrait.mp4 version of the flythrough on one of my servers at HTTP://www.e-bookclub.com/ that you can use to test the code, so let's get started and stream digital video to an Android FullscreenActivity.

Streaming Digital Video: Using HTTP URL in URI

Since Android handles all of the logistics regarding streaming video from the Internet into the hardware device, all we as developers really have to do is to provide the correct HTTP:// URL, or Uniform Resource Locator, in the place of the android.resource://com.example. user.digitalvideomedia/R.raw.flythru3d URI reference, which we have been using thus far in the chapter. Fortunately, an HTTP URL can also be used in the Uri object.

Do this by replacing the android.resource://com.example.user.digitalvideomedia/R.raw. flythru3d URI path with an HTTP://www.e-bookclub.com/pag480x800portrait.mp4 reference to an external server, using this code:

```
VideoAssetUri = Uri.parse( "HTTP://www.e-bookclub.com/pag480x800portrait.mp4" );
```

As you can see in Figure 11-31, the Uri.parse() method call will accommodate this HTTP:// URL reference, as easily as an android.resource:// URI reference. This makes it easy for us to switch our URI path references from captive video to streaming video. Notice the HTTP URL is contained in quotes, and includes the file extension, which will tell Android which codec family is utilized. This is needed as it is now "outside" of the Android OS.

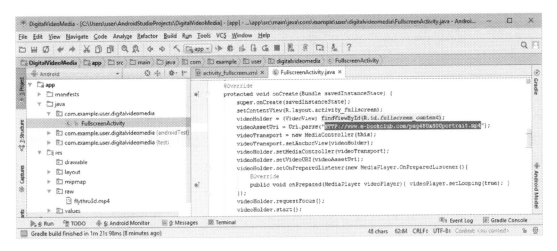

Figure 11-31. Streaming digital video into your Android application using an HTTP URL in the Uri.parse( ) method

Test the streaming video using **Run ➤ Run 'app'**, and watch the video stream! It is important to note that once the video streams over the network the first time, the asset's data will loop out of the system memory thereafter.

Summary

In this chapter, you learned all digital video concepts, formats, codecs, principles, creation, optimization, and coding for Android, expanding on 2D animation concepts, formats, and principles you learned in Chapter 10. You learned about Android's FrameLayout UI layout container class, and the FrameLayout.LayoutParams nested class along with the concept of layout **gravity** and how to position UI elements inside of a FrameLayout container. This FrameLayout superclass was used to create the VideoView widget used to contain your video, and to play it back using the MediaPlayer engine, and eventually, the MediaController transport UI element.

You created a FullscreenActivity class and modified its FrameLayout UI XML definition file, so that you had a foundation for adding digital video functionality. After doing that, you learned about the VideoView class and the video lifecycle stages and then you added a VideoView to the FrameLayout. You learned about the Android Uri class and its Uri.parse() method, used to implement the address or path to your digital video asset.

You learned about the foundational concepts of digital video encoding and optimization, including frame rates, bitrates, codecs, resolution, quality (blur), and how these all work together to allow you to optimize the digital video asset's data footprint. After that, you learned how to use Terragen 4 and Squeeze 11 to create a 3D planet-fly over video asset and optimize that asset from image frames into MPEG-4 format, taking data that was over 2310MB and turning it into a usable 4MB digital video asset. Amazing compression technology.

You learned about the Android MediaPlayer class and its nine nested classes, most used for callbacks allowing you to control the user's digital video experience. You learned about how the VideoView uses the MediaPlayer internally, as well as how to expose it for use in your Java code.

You implemented a MediaController object named videoTransport and then wired it up to your videoHolder VideoView by using the .setAnchorView() and the .setMediaController() method calls.

You added an OnPreparedListener event listener to your videoHolder VideoView object and then used a .setLooping(true) method call to tell the video asset to loop forever. Then you learned how to alter a URI so that you were **streaming video**, instead of using **captive video**. You have learned a plethora of core Android information, tricks, classes, methods, callbacks, and techniques relating to digital video!

Next, in Chapter 12, you'll learn about digital audio in Android, including foundational digital audio theory and concepts, what digital audio file formats are optimal to use in Android, and how to create digital audio assets for use with the Android SoundPool audio sequencing class.

Chapter 12

Chapter 12

Digital Audio: Sequencing Audio Using SoundPool

In the previous chapter on digital video, we covered the `Uri`, `MediaPlayer`, and `MediaController` classes, which you can also use with digital audio, which we are going to cover in this chapter. Since these classes are used in the same exact way with digital audio assets, I am going to show you how to use the Android `SoundPool` audio sequencing class in this chapter, so I can cover as many of Android's new media classes as possible in this book.

If you want to play long-form digital audio, such as songs, albums, or audio books, you would use the Android `MediaPlayer` class along with the Android `MediaController` and URI classes, using the **SeekBar** widget, instead of the `VideoView`. You can also loop long-form audio for background music without using the `SeekBar` widget, as you will see in Chapter 13 when we do just that using the Service class.

If you want to play short-form digital audio however, such as sound effects for your games or your UI elements, for use as aural (that is, audible) feedback, you would use the Android **SoundPool** class. The `SoundPool` "engine" is actually more versatile than the `MediaPlayer` class, when it comes to controlling digital audio assets. `SoundPool` is a powerful **digital audio sequencing** engine, basically allowing you to **composite audio** in the same way that you use layers in digital image compositing to composite imagery. `SoundPool` is a complex and versatile digital audio class, which Android 7.x continues to improve, and I wanted to cover some of Android's more powerful classes during the course of this book.

Digital audio is a bit different from digital imagery and digital video as you can't see it; you have to rely on your ears. Instead of using waves of light, as color does, digital audio uses waves of sound, and as such, the technical fundamentals are completely different. If you are new to digital audio, part of this chapter will cover the theory and the concepts behind digital audio, as well as the plethora of digital audio codecs, that is, digital audio file formats, which are supported in Android 7.1.1, as well as what each of them will be used for inside of an Android application.

© Wallace Jackson 2017
W. Jackson, *Android Apps for Absolute Beginners*, DOI 10.1007/978-1-4842-2268-3_12

In this chapter, we'll utilize Android's SoundPool digital audio sequencing class to add amazing sound effects to ImageButton UI elements in the ScrollingActivity design pattern. We will do this to add aural feedback for your users. We'll learn how to implement this SoundPool engine correctly in your Android applications, as this is no easy task. Digital audio sequencing and synthesis is an advanced topic indeed, but a key part of an Android app, and something I will cover even though this is an Absolute Beginners title.

Audio Waves: History, Concepts, and Theory

For Android 7 developers to use digital audio assets wisely and optimally, they would need to know the basic foundation of both analog audio and digital audio—where they came from, why they do what they do, and how to correctly "harness" them. I felt that this chapter would not be complete without an in-depth discussion of analog and digital audio.

Foundation of Analog Audio: Sound Waves of Air

Those of you who are "audiophiles" already know that sound is created by sound waves pulsing through the air. This is the reason you see sub-woofers with massive 18- to 30-inch cones rapidly pushing out thunderous sound waves into audiences containing thousands of screaming fans at rock concerts. Before the digital audio industry existed, the analog audio industry was one of the major consumer electronics forces. In fact, it still is today, with sound waves being created with complex analog electronics products, featuring capacitors, resistors, oscillators, crystals, vacuum tubes, circuit boards, speaker cones, cardiod microphones, and similar advanced high-quality analog audio technologies.

As mentioned, digital audio is quite complex, and part of this complexity comes from the need to bridge analog audio technology and digital audio technology together. Analog audio is usually generated using speaker cones of different sizes, manufactured using resilient membranes made out of one space-age material or another. The speakers generate sound waves by vibrating, or pulsing, them into existence. Our ears receive this analog audio in exactly the opposite fashion, by catching and receiving pulses of air, or vibrations with different wavelengths, and then turning them back into "data" that our brains can process. This is how we "hear" sound waves, and our brains interpret different audio sound wave frequencies as different notes, words, sounds, or tones.

Sound waves generate various tones depending on the **frequency** of a sound wave. A wide or infrequent (long) wave produces a lower (bass) tone, whereas a more frequent (short) wavelength produces a higher (treble) tone. It is interesting to note that different frequencies of light produce different colors, so there is a close correlation between analog sound (audio) and analog light (color), which also carries through to digital content production.

The volume of a sound wave will be predicated on the **amplitude**, or height, of that sound wave. The frequency of the sound waves equates to how closely together waves are spaced, along the X-axis. The amplitude equates to how tall the waves are as measured along the Y-axis. Sound waves can be shaped uniquely, allowing them to "carry" different sound effects. A baseline type of sound wave is called a **sine wave**, which you learned about in high school math, with your sine, cosine, and tangent math functions. Those of you who are familiar with audio synthesis are aware that there are other types of sound waves, utilized in sound design, such as the **saw wave**, which looks like the edge of a saw (hence its name), and the **pulse wave**, which is shaped by using right angles, resulting in immediate on and off sounds, which translate into pulses.

Even randomized waveforms, such as noise, are used in sound design to obtain "edgy" sound results. As you may have ascertained, using previous knowledge regarding data footprint optimization, the more "chaos," or "noise," that is present in your sound waves, the harder they will be to compress for a codec, resulting in a larger digital audio file size for that particular sound. The next section takes a closer look at how an analog audio sound wave is turned into digital audio data, by using a process called sampling. The "sampler" is the core audio sample production tool for sound designers and music synthesis.

Digital Audio: Samples, Resolution, and Frequency

The process of turning analog audio (sound waves) into digital audio data is called *sampling*. If you work in the music industry, you have probably heard about a type of keyboard (or rack-mount audio equipment) called a *sampler*. Sampling is the process of slicing an audio wave into segments, so that you can store the shape of that wave as digital audio data using a digital audio codec format. This turns an infinitely accurate analog sound wave into a discreet amount of digital data, that is, into zeroes and ones. The more zeroes and ones that are used, the more accurate the reproduction of that infinitely accurate (original) analog sound wave. Sample accuracy determines how many zeroes and ones will be used to reproduce the analog sound wave, which is also the data footprint, so I will get into that discussion next, so that you know how to optimize your Android digital audio assets.

Each digital segment of a sampled audio sound wave is called a **sample**, because it samples that sound wave at that exact point in time. The **precision** of a sample is determined by how much data is used to define each wave slice's height. Just like with digital imaging, this precision is termed the resolution, or more accurately (no pun intended), the **sample resolution**. Sample resolution in digital audio is usually defined with 8-bit, 12-bit, 16-bit, 24-bit, or 32-bit resolution samples. Today's HD audio uses 24-bit audio samples, and uncompressed audio usually uses 32-bit.

In digital imaging as well as digital video, resolution is quantified using a number of colors, and in digital audio, the resolution is quantified in how many bits of data are used to define each of the audio samples taken. Just like in digital imaging (more color yields better quality), a higher sample resolution yields better sound reproduction. The only difference between the two is that digital audio supports the **12-bit** sample resolution. Higher sampling resolution— using more data to reproduce a given sound wave sample—will yield higher audio playback quality, at the expense of a larger data footprint. This is the reason that 16-bit audio, termed "CD-quality" audio, sounds better than 8-bit audio, just like true color imagery will always look better than indexed color imagery.

In digital audio there is now a 24-bit audio sampling, which is known as "HD audio" in the consumer electronics industry. HD digital audio broadcast radio uses the 24-bit sample resolution, so each audio sample, or slice of a sound wave, contains 16,777,216 different potential units of sample resolution, like 24-bit color allows 16.8M potential colors. Most new Android devices now support HD audio, such as the smartphones you'll see advertised featuring "HD quality" audio, and more recently, HD and UHD iTV sets. This means they have 24-bit audio hardware, 24-bit capable audio decoder chips in their circuitry.

Beside a digital audio sample resolution, there is also a digital audio **sampling frequency**. This is how many of these samples at a particular sample resolution are taken during one second of sample duration. In digital image editing, the sampling frequency would be analogous to the number of pixels that are contained within an image. More pixels in an image would equate to an analog image being sampled more frequently, just as a higher audio sample frequency would equate to a sound wave being sampled more frequently, yielding a better reproduction.

Sampling frequency can also be called the **sampling rate**. You are probably familiar with the term CD-quality audio, which is defined as using a 16-bit sample resolution and a 44.1kHz sampling rate. This is taking 44,100 samples, each of which contains 16-bits of sample resolution, yielding 65,536 bits of audio data in each sample. Let's do some math, and find out how many bits of data are available to provide one second of "uncompressed" digital audio data. This is calculated by multiplying the 65,536 sample resolution by the 44,100 sample frequency. This gives you a maximum potential value of 2,890,137,600 bits to represent one second of CD quality audio.

Divide this by 8 to get 361,267,200 bytes, and by 1,024 to get 352,800 kilobytes, and by 1,024 again to get 344 megabytes. Not every CD quality 16-bit sample will use all of these potential data bits, however, thus your original raw, uncompressed audio samples will be much smaller than this, usually only a few dozen megabytes. So, to figure out raw data in an audio file, you would multiply the sampling bit-rate by the sampling frequency by the number of seconds in that audio snippet. You can see that it can potentially be a huge number! Audio codecs are great at optimizing this sampled data down to an amazingly small data footprint, with little audible loss in quality.

In a visual medium, optimization is achieved using color depth and pixels. With digital video, this also includes frames. In the aural medium, optimization is controlled via sample resolution in combination with the **sampling rate**. Common sample rates in the digital audio industry include 8kHz, 22kHz, 32kHz, 44.1kHz, 48kHz, 96kHz, 192kHz, and even 384kHz. Lower sampling rates, such as 8kHz, 22.5kHz, and 32kHz, are optimal for sampling any "voice-based" digital audio, such as a movie dialog or e-book narration track, for instance. Higher audio sample rates are more appropriate for music and other sound effects, such as rumbling thunder, which require a high dynamic range (high fidelity). High sample rates are best for game or movie theater (THX) sound quality.

Digital Attributes: HD, Stream, and Bitrate

As mentioned, the industry "baseline" for superior audio quality is known as CD-quality audio, and it is defined using the 16-bit data sample resolution at a 44.1kHz data sample frequency. This was used to produce audio CD products way back in the 20th century, and it is still used as a minimum quality standard today. There's also the more recent HD audio standard, which uses a 24-bit data sample at a 48kHz or 96kHz sample frequency. This is used today in HD radio as well as HD audio-compatible Android devices, such as Hi-Fi HD audio smartphones and iTV sets.

If you are going to use HD audio in your Android applications, you need to make sure that your target users will own the HD audio-compatible hardware that will be required to utilize a higher level of audio fidelity. Just like with digital video data, digital audio data can either be captive within the application, with data files in the **/raw** folder, or digital audio can be streamed with remote data servers. Similar to digital video, the upside to streaming digital audio data is that it can reduce the data footprint of an application just as streamed digital video data can. The downside is reliability. Many of the same concepts apply equally well to digital audio and digital video.

Streaming audio will shrink the size of your application's data footprint, because you do not have to include all of that heavy new media digital audio data inside of your .APK files, so if you are planning on coding a digital Jukebox application, you may want to consider streaming the digital audio data. Otherwise, try to optimize your digital audio data so you can include it inside the .APK file. This way, the digital audio will always be available.

The downside to streaming digital audio is that if your user's connection (or your audio server) goes down, your digital audio file may not be available for your users to play and listen to! The reliability and availability of your digital audio data is a key factor to be considered on the other side of this streaming audio versus captive digital audio data trade-off. The same trade-offs that are discussed in this book for digital video assets could also be applied to digital audio assets. Just like with digital video, one of the primary concepts regarding streaming your digital audio is the **bitrate** of that digital audio data. As you learned in Chapter 11, this bitrate will be defined during your compression process. As with digital video, digital audio files that need to support lower bitrate settings are going to have more compression applied to the data, which will result in a lower digital audio quality level.

Android Digital Audio: Digital Audio Formats

There are considerably more digital audio codecs in Android than there are digital video codecs, as there are only two video codecs—MPEG-4 and WebM. Android audio support includes .MP3 (MPEG-3) files, WAVE (PCM, or Pulse Code Modulated) .WAV files, .MP4 (or .M4A) MPEG-4 audio, OGG Vorbis (.OGG) audio files, Matroska (.MKS) audio files, FLAC (.FLAC) or Free Lossless Audio Codec audio files, and even MIDI (.MID, .MXMF, and .XMF) Musical Instrument Digital Interface files, which technically are not digital audio. Let me explain what MIDI is first, since it is not a format that we are going to be using in the digital audio application we will be creating next.

MIDI stands for Musical Instrument Digital Interface, and it is one of the very first ways that digital audio and computers could work together, dating all the way back to ancient times (the 1980s). The very first computer to feature integrated MIDI data port hardware was Atari's ST1040. This computer allowed me to plug a keyboard synthesizer, at the time, it was my Yamaha TX-802 and Roland D50, into that MIDI port. MIDI allowed me to play and record performance data into the computer using the MIDI data format, along with an audio software genre called a MIDI sequencer, and MIDI Sequencing software called Final Track, created by Charles Faris.

A MIDI file contains zero audio sample data, it only contains **performance** data. When this performance data is played back into the synthesizer, using the MIDI hardware (cable and ports), the synthesizer generates the audio tones using this MIDI performance data. MIDI would record which keys on the synth or sampler keyboard were pressed, when they were pressed, keypress duration, how hard it was pressed (after-touch), and similar nuances. When MIDI files are played back through a synthesizer, the synth replicates the exact performance of the performer or composer, even though that person is no longer playing that performance track; the computer is now playing that performance data exactly the way that it was originally performed.

The way that MIDI data was used in MIDI sequencing software is that you can play an instrument track, record it as MIDI data, and the sequencer will then play it back for you, while you play another instrument track right alongside of it. This enables digital songwriters to assemble complex musical arrangements using the computer, instead of hiring a studio full of musicians. You can download open source MIDI software called Rosegarden at rosegardenmusic.com; it not only contains a full MIDI sequencer, but also contains a music notation (scoring) program as well. Rosegarden was originally for Linux OS, but is currently being ported to the Windows OS.

Android supports playback of MIDI files, but doesn't implement a MIDI class, although SoundPool can be used as a sequencer. It would not be an easy task to code a MIDI sequencer for Android although some on the coding forums have been talking about it. For that reason, it is beyond the scope of this book; I mention it here, only to educate you as to the history and scope of digital audio. MIDI played an important role early on in the evolution of digital audio, and is still part of digital audio today, especially if you are a songwriter or a sound designer.

The most common digital audio format supported by Android is the popular MPEG-3, or MP3, digital audio file format. Most of you are familiar with MP3 digital audio files, due to music download websites, such as Napster. Most people collect songs in this format to use on popular MP3 players and via CD-ROM- or DVD-ROM-based music collections. The reason the MP3 digital audio file format is popular is because it has a good compression-to-quality ratio and because the codec needed to play the audio back can be found almost anywhere, even in the Android OS. MP3 is an acceptable format to use in Android applications, as long as you get the highest quality level possible out of the codec, by using an optimal encoding work process, and original (raw) audio data input.

It is important to note that MP3 is a lossy audio file format, like JPEG is for imagery, where some of the audio data (and thus, quality) is thrown away during the compression process, and cannot be recovered. Android does have a lossless audio compression codec, called FLAC. This stands for Free Lossless Audio Codec. FLAC is an open source audio codec whose support is widespread, primarily due to the free nature of the software decoder.

FLAC is also very fast, so the decoder is highly optimized for speed, it supports 24-bit HD audio, and there are no patent concerns for using it. This is a great audio codec to use if you need very high-quality audio within a reasonable data footprint. FLAC supports a wide range of sample resolutions, from 4-bits per sample up to 32-bits. It also supports a wide range of sampling frequencies from 1Hz to 65,535kHz (65kHz), in 1Hz increments so it is extremely flexible. From an audio playback hardware standpoint, I would suggest using the 16-bit sample resolution and either a 44.1kHz or 48kHz sample frequency. FLAC is supported in Android 3.1 and later, so, if your users are using modern Android devices, you should be able to safely utilize the FLAC codec. Therefore, it is possible to use completely lossless new media assets for your Android applications, by using PNG24, PNG32, and FLAC as long as you are targeting Android Version 3.1 and later OS revisions, which you probably will be.

Another open source digital audio codec supported by Android is the **OGG Vorbis** codec, another lossy audio codec from the Xiph.Org Foundation. The Vorbis codec data is most often held in an .OGG data file container, and thus Vorbis is commonly called OGG Vorbis digital audio data format. The OGG Vorbis supports sampling rates from 8kHz up to 192kHz, and supports up to 255 discrete channels of digital audio (as you now know, this represents 8-bits worth of audio channels). OGG Vorbis is supported across every version of the Android OS. Vorbis is quickly approaching the quality of HE-AAC and WMA (Windows Media Audio) Professional, and is superior in quality to MP3, MPEG-4 AAC-LC and WMA. It uses a lossy format, so the FLAC codec is superior to OGG Vorbis, as it contains all of the original digital audio sample data (and as such, it is therefore lossless).

Android supports the popular **MPEG-4** AAC (Advanced Audio Coding) codecs, including AAC-LC, HE-AAC and AAC-ELD. These can all be contained in MPEG-4 containers (.3gp, .mp4, and .m4a) or file extensions, and most of them can be played back across all versions of Android. The one exception to this is AAC-ELD, which is supported only after Android 4.1. ELD stands for Enhanced Low Delay, and this codec is intended for usage in a real-time, two-way communications application, such as a digital walkie-talkie or Dick Tracy smartwatch.

The simplest and most widely used AAC codec is **AAC-LC**, or Low Complexity codec. It should be sufficient for most digital audio encoding applications. The AAC-LC should yield a higher quality result, at a lower data footprint than an MP3 format. The next most complicated AAC codec is the **HE-AAC** or High Efficiency AAC codec. Its codec supports sampling rates from 8kHz to 48kHz and both Stereo and Dolby 5.1 channel encoding. Android supports decoding both the v1 and v2 levels of this codec, and Android will also encode audio, using this HE-AAC v1 codec after Android Version 4.1. Use AAC-LC codec to support earlier versions of Android.

For encoding speech that usually features a different type of sound wave than music there are two other **AMR** or **Adaptive Multi-Rate** audio codecs. They are highly efficient for encoding things like speech or short-burst sound effects that do not need high-quality reproduction (such as a bomb blast sound effect). There is also the AMR-WB (Adaptive Multi-Rate Wide-Band) standard in Android, which supports nine discrete settings from 6.6 to 23.85kbps audio bitrates, sampled at 16kHz. This is a high enough sample rate where voice is concerned. This is the codec to use for a narrator track, if you are creating interactive e-book applications, for instance.

There is also the AMR-NB (Adaptive Multi-Rate Narrow-Band) standard in Android OS, which supports eight discrete settings, from 4.75 to 12.2kbps audio bitrates sampled. This can be an adequate sample rate if the data going into the codec is high quality, or if the resulting audio sample does not require a high level of quality due to the noisy nature of the content (such as a bomb blast).

Finally there is **PCM** (**Pulse Code Modulated**) audio, commonly known as the **WAVE** or .WAV audio format. Many of you are familiar with this lossless digital audio format, as it is the original audio format used with the Windows operating system. It is lossless because there is no compression applied whatsoever! PCM audio is commonly used for CD-ROM content, as well as for telephony applications. This is because WAVE audio is an uncompressed digital audio format, and therefore has no CPU-intensive decompression algorithms applied to the data stream. Thus, decoding overhead the data is not an issue for the telephony equipment or for CD players.

For this reason, when you start compressing digital audio assets into the various file formats, you can use PCM as a "baseline" file format. You probably won't put it into an APK file, however, because there are other formats (such as FLAC and MPEG-4 AAC) that will give you the same quality, using an order of magnitude less data. Ultimately, the only real way to find out which audio formats supported by Android have the best digital audio codec result for any given audio data instance is to actually encode your digital audio in the primary codecs that you know are well supported and efficient. We will be looking at how that is done as well during this chapter.

Digital Audio Optimization: Device Compatible

Optimizing your digital audio assets for playback across the widest range of Android devices in the marketplace is easier than optimizing your digital video or digital imagery (and thus animation) across Android devices. This is because there is a much wider disparity of screen resolutions and display aspect ratios than there is a disparity of digital audio playback hardware support across Android devices, except for some Android hardware devices that feature 24-bit (HD) audio playback hardware compatibility. This is because your ears cannot perceive the same quality difference in audio that your eyes can, with digital imagery, animation, or digital video. Generally, there are three primary "sweet spots" of digital audio support, across all Android devices, which you should target.

Lower-fidelity audio, such as narration tracks, or short sound effects, can use a 22kHZ or 32kHz sampling rate, with 8-bit, 12-bit, or 16-bit sampling resolution. Your high-quality audio targets include CD-quality audio, also known as 16-bit data sampling at 44.1kHz and HD-quality audio will be at the other end of this high-end audio spectrum, using a 24-bit data sampling resolution and a 48kHz audio data sampling rate. There is an unnamed "somewhere in the middle" specification, which uses 16-bit data sampling at a 48kHz sampling rate. Ultimately, however, it comes down to the quality-to-file-size results that emerge from your digital audio data footprint optimization process, which can yield some amazing results.

Thus, the initial process for optimizing your digital audio assets across all of the Android devices is going to be to sample 32-bit assets at 44.1kHz or 48kHz, and then optimize (compress) them, using different audio formats supported in Android. Once that process has been completed, you'll then see which digital audio assets provide the highest quality digital audio playback in conjunction with the lowest possible data footprint. You'll do this using the latest version of the open source Audacity 2.1 digital audio editing and engineering software package. This software package is freely available at `www.audacityteam.org`, and will be accessible to all readers, no matter which OS platforms they prefer, whether it be Windows, macOS, Ubuntu, Fedora, RedHat or SUSE Linux.

Audio Sequencing: Concepts and Principles

As you now know, the earliest forms of digital audio sequencing actually utilized MIDI. MIDI sequencers such as the Rosegarden for Linux (and soon Windows) software are still popular and allow performance sequencing. This is where a composer plays each instrumental part into a computer using a synthesizer to play an instrument sample, say a guitar, bass, drum, or piano sample, and then the computer plays back this performance data later on, while the composer accompanies the computer-replayed version of that performance.

Eventually, MIDI sequencing software added digital audio capabilities alongside MIDI playback capabilities, as increased computer processing power, as well as specialized digital audio adapters, such as Creative Labs X-Fi, became available to consumers at affordable prices. It turns out that this concept of audio sequencing is applied equally well to digital audio samples that are manipulated directly by a computer, as long as this computer is powerful enough. The Linux **Qtractor** software package combines MIDI and Audio Sampling, and the **Ardour** software for Linux is a DAW, or Digital Audio Workstation, which focus primarily on digital audio sampling. In fact, my Ubuntu 17.04 Linux workstation has Ardour, Qtractor, Audacity, and Rosegarden all installed on it right now!

Computers—in this case, Linux-based Android devices—keep getting more and more powerful, and all feature four or eight processor cores, and one, two, or even four billion bytes of system memory. This means Android devices today can hold several digital audio samples in memory, and thus memory optimization is an issue with Android SoundPool, as you will soon see. I wanted to cover SoundPool, an advanced audio sequencing engine class in Android, during the book, even though the book is technically supposed to be for "Absolute Beginners." The reason for this is because if you want to utilize digital audio assets in your application, especially using samples or short audio snippets, rather than playing back long-form audio or songs, SoundPool is the way to go.

Audio Synthesis: Concepts and Principles

Some of the very first MIDI keyboards were digital audio samplers. These played back digital audio samples, prerecorded (sampled) by digital audio sample design professionals such as Frank Serafine, using a range of sample resolutions and sample frequencies. You learned about samples in a previous section, so what you are going to focus on here is how those samples are taken to the next level using **audio synthesis** (via algorithmic processing). Synthesizers can also apply these algorithms to raw waveforms, such as sine, saw, or pulse waves.

Synthesizers take digital audio—whether it's a generated wave, borne out of an oscillator on a circuit board in a consumer electronics device, or a more complex sampled waveform, such as a sample of a plucked instrument string—and apply algorithmic processing to the waveform to create a different tonality, sound, or special effect. We're all familiar with the synthesized instruments in popular music today; these virtual instruments are created solely by using math and programming code! One of the foundational mathematical manipulations that can be applied to audio waveforms within the digital audio domain is called **pitch-shifting**. This was a core technology that made keyboard samplers viable, as one sample could be used up and down the keyboard, simply by shifting its pitch! Pitch-shifting algorithms can take a sound wave up or down an octave (or even a small fraction of an octave, which is commonly known as a pitch) to create a usable range for that sample, much as though you were playing it up and down the keys of an electronic piano, a sampler keyboard, or a synthesizer keyboard.

As you learned previously, the tone of a waveform can be determined by the frequency of that waveform itself, so it becomes a fairly straightforward mathematical computation to be able to accurately shift that pitch (wave) up an octave by shortening that wavelength by cutting it in half, or shift the pitch down an octave by doubling that wavelength. Any fraction between these two extremes changes the pitch of the audio sample, which is how you would get different notes along a keyboard using a single waveform. You can even create fractions between "known" pitches (common notes such as A, B, D, E, F, and G), which can be used to create "micro-tonal" music. Digital audio synthesis is amazing and the Android SoundPool class we'll be using later supports these features.

SoundPool can perform pitch-shifting on your digital audio samples, which is why you are learning about these concepts in the first part of this chapter. SoundPool has impressive audio engineering capabilities and probably will add even more features in future versions of the Android OS. You'll need to understand these digital audio synthesis concepts in order to leverage what SoundPool can do for your application effectively and optimally. If you need the SoundPool engine, you'll know how to use it correctly, as it can use a lot of the system memory. After this chapter, you'll understand why you need to optimize audio data in this way to get SoundPool to work well.

Another core audio synthesis mathematical manipulation is the **combination**, or **compositing**, of digital audio waveforms. This will allow the playback of two or more sounds at the same time, using a single oscillator, or using the speaker hardware. Just as with digital imaging, 2D animation or digital video compositing, this will involve adding two or more different sample data values to arrive at the final data value. Today's Android audio hardware features impressive multi-channel support and will probably have a capability for playing stereo (two channels) or quadrophonic (four channels) quality audio (effects, music, vocal tracks, and so on) with the audio hardware that is inside of any given consumer electronics device (iTV set, tablet, e-reader, smartphone, etc.).

But what if you want to combine six or eight tracks of digital audio in real-time, like an audio sequencer can? This is why SoundPool is important to master, because it provides you with a digital audio sequencing engine right inside your Android application. The Android SoundPool audio sequencing and synthesis engine is a very complex class, as you might well imagine. To make it work properly, you need to load it with the most highly optimized samples possible. This class is in Android to stay, and its code will continue to be debugged, refined, and improved, so if your Android app is going to be audio-centric, you need to master it. This chapter gets you up to speed on how to best use SoundPool, as well as what it can accomplish for your apps.

Raw Audio Data Optimization: Memory Footprint

What is important, if you are going to attempt the real-time audio compositing of six or eight audio samples, is that each of these samples is well optimized. This makes what you'll learn about digital audio data optimization extremely relevant, especially when it comes to using SoundPool. For instance, if you don't really need HD (24-bit sample resolution) audio, in order to get your quality target, you should use CD-quality 16-bit audio, or even 12-bit audio, as you will save valuable memory, and get the same result. If you get the same audio quality using the 32kHz sample rate instead of the 48kHz sample rate, you are using 50% less sample (system) memory! For voiceover or sound effects audio these memory savings are there for the taking, as often you can sample a bomb or laser blast effectively using only 8-bit resolution with an 8kHz sample rate. You often won't be able to detect much aural difference between 16-bit 48kHz stereo audio and the lower bitrate mono audio, as you will see in later on in this chapter, when we dive deeper into the data footprint optimization concepts and techniques.

If you don't absolutely need stereo samples, and can mix them down into mono samples, you will save 100% in memory. Combine this with lowering bitrate for the sample frequency and bit depth for the sample resolution, and you can get an even greater digital audio data footprint optimization result with the same level of quality, at least from the end user's perspective, oftentimes using a hundred times less data in many circumstances. It's important to remember that your end users don't hear the "before" (uncompressed) and the "after" (compressed) audio samples like you do. As long as they sound similar, you are good to go!

The other significant variable you can optimize is the length (in time) of the sample. Reducing sample durations by removing silent or unnecessary audio data can result in a reduction in raw audio data that has been sampled in the first place. This kind of data savings can add up the more digital audio samples that you are using.

I just showed you three different levels (sample resolution, stereo vs. mono, and sample duration) of audio data reduction. You can think of this as system memory usage once the digital audio data has been decompressed by the Android OS into the device's memory. This is before you get into file size optimization using the encoders.

Codec optimization will affect your application's .APK file size, but when the audio sample needs to play back inside your app, this audio sample still needs to be re-created in (decompressed into) system memory, before it can be triggered by the SoundPool engine.

Therefore there are really two stages to audio optimization. The first is what you do to a raw audio wave sample prior to encoding, relating to the sample resolution, sample frequency, sample duration, and mono versus stereo sample playback. The second is what you do when you export to various codecs, using settings to ascertain how much APK file size they can save your application as captive digital audio assets.

Digital Audio Synthesis and Sequencing Caveats

Just like with digital imaging, animation, and digital video, optimizing your digital audio assets is important for two completely different, but related, reasons. With digital audio samples, especially in regard to using Android SoundPool, you must consider the amount of system memory needed to hold each sample once they have been decompressed by a codec, and placed into the raw, uncompressed state, inside of the Android device's memory. The second reason that well-optimized audio is important is the CPU processing part of the equation. It is pretty obvious that with less audio (duration, resolution, frequency, and the number of stereo/mono tracks) to process, even if that is just sending the audio data to the audio playback hardware, there are less CPU cycles being used.

Therefore, if you can get the same basic audio quality result with a lower sample resolution (fewer bits per slice of audio) or lower sample frequency (fewer slices of audio waveform each second), or fewer data tracks (mono, or one audio track instead of stereo, or two audio tracks), and shorter playback duration, you will be saving both your Android operating system's memory resources, and your user's Android CPU processing power resources.

The reason I'm going into all of this audio sample optimization information in such great detail in this chapter is because Android's SoundPool class will often get a bad rap, because the raw audio sample sizes that developers load into SoundPool are too data heavy. The SoundPool engine gets blamed for sluggish performance and slow playback response times due to this, rather than the developer's lacking a data footprint optimization skill set. I am making sure that this does not happen here, and that you have the best chance for success using SoundPool.

Raw audio data optimization thus becomes more and more important, at least where SoundPool is concerned, as the number of digital audio samples that you require increases. This is again true for both system memory use as well as system processing cycle usage considerations, because as you add in samples both of these resources are utilized more and more. Don't forget that there are other things the application might be processing, such as user interface event handling, digital imagery, animation, digital video, 3D rendering, Internet access, and so on.

Another reason providing highly optimized digital audio samples is so important when using a SoundPool class is because there is currently a one megabyte limit on digital audio sample data when using a SoundPool engine. Although the limit might be increased in future Android API revisions of this digital audio sequencing class, it's still always best practice to optimize any digital audio assets effectively and efficiently. Therefore, digital audio synthesis and sequencing using SoundPool in the Android application is a balancing act, both within the device that you are testing it on at the moment, as well as across all devices that your application will ever be run on.

If a given hardware platform (smartphone, tablet, e-book reader, iTV set, auto dashboard, or smartwatch) can't handle playing a given audio data load, then it will simply not play a given sample. As time goes on, this would happen less and less due to better code and faster device processor and memory hardware. As you have learned thus far, digital audio synthesis, sequencing, and compositing are heavily predicated on the speed of a processor, the number of processor cores available, and the amount of system memory that is available to hold all of the digital audio samples that will be needed, in their uncompressed (raw or PCM) data format.

The bottom line is that you need to be extremely smart about how you are doing things with SoundPool. This is not as much about how you write your code, although that is certainly important, but more about how you set up your audio samples, so that they use less memory, and can be leveraged further in the application. The common mistake many Android developers make regarding SoundPool is trying to use it more like a sequencer than like an audio synthesizer. Developers focus on SoundPool's ability to load multiple audio assets in memory, but do not leverage its processing capability for creating new waveforms, by using a few waveforms and pitch-shifting.

Here's a good example of sequencer versus synthesis (optimization) use. SoundPool allows pitch-shifting across two full octaves, from a setting of 0.5 or down one full octave (half of your original sample waveform) up to 2.0 or up one full octave (twice of your original waveform's width). Remember that the waveform height equates to amplitude, commonly referred to as volume, and waveform width equates to pitch (tone, or octave). Developers tend not to use this pitch-shifting feature, but instead, use different samples to achieve different notes. This fills up memory rapidly and the end result is an app works less and less well, especially across the older devices. The correct way to use SoundPool is to take your samples: say one string pluck from a guitar, one horn blow from a saxophone, one piano key strike, and three different drum samples, and using only six short mono 48kHz 16-bit high-quality samples, make a basic synthesizer that has all four basic jazz instruments using the pitch-shifting.

Using this basic synthesizer setup, your users would be able to play instruments up and down two full octaves. This application would use less than a megabyte of memory to hold these 16-bit 48kHz uncompressed samples. If you used a high-quality microphone for the sampling process you would be amazed at the high-quality results that you can obtain these days using a 16-bit 48kHz Mono sampling format. If you wanted to save memory, you could also use a mono 16-bit 44.1kHz CD-quality audio, or mono 16-bit 32kHz audio with similarly acceptable results. I hope I've covered enough digital audio sampling and synthesis concepts in the first part of this chapter to give you some real insight as to how to optimize your digital audio assets for use with the SoundPool engine!

Audacity 2: Creating Digital Audio Assets

In this section of the chapter, you will learn how to use the open source audio engineering software Audacity, currently at version 2.1.2. First, we will make sure that Audacity and all of its plug-ins and codecs are installed that are available for free so that you have the audio software that will make your audio editing environment both professional and powerful. Then we'll learn how to use this software to optimize digital audio assets in some of the Android-supported digital audio codecs (formats), including some that are from the open source domain.

Audacity 2.1.2: Installing Software and Codecs

First, you need to download and install Audacity 2.1.2, as well as to add in some plug-ins, which will greatly enhance the feature set of the software. You'll need to download and add the popular codecs that are supported in Android. Visit the audacityteam.org website seen in Figure 12-1, download Audacity, and then install it.

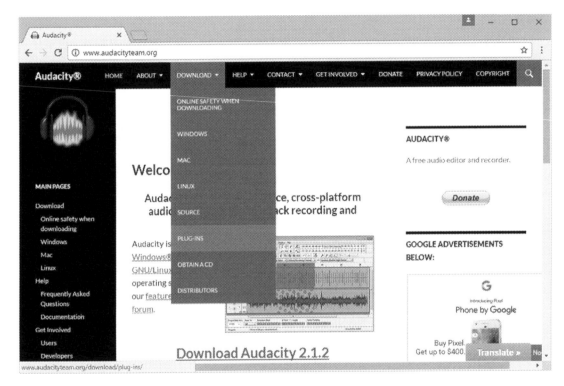

Figure 12-1. Visit audacityteam.org and download Audacity and LADSPA, LAME, FFMPEG and Nyquist plug-ins

Use the **Download ➤ Plug-ins** menu sequence, also seen in Figure 12-1, and download and install the LADSPA, LAME, FFMPEG, and Nyquist plug-ins.

Algorithms that add features and codecs to Audacity 2 are kept in the Plug-Ins folder, so adding features to this software package is as easy as exiting the software (if it is running), copying a file or files into this folder, and restarting the software again. Figure 12-2 shows the Audacity\Plug-Ins folder, with 122 plug-in files installed.

Figure 12-2. The 122 plug-in files after the full installation of Audacity 2.1.2 with LADSPA, LAME, and FFMPEG

The LADSPA installation process alone will have added around a hundred plug-in files to this folder, as shown in Figure 12-2. To install the LADSPA plug-ins, locate and click on the LADSPA plug-ins 0.4.15 link, which is found in the Plug-Ins section of the Audacity site, shown in Figure 12-1, and download the .EXE file. Do the same for the FFMPEG and LAME encoders.

When these downloads finish, launch the file and select the language you are using (I chose English) and click the **Next** button to go through the dialog series for each collection of plug-in algorithms. Be sure to accept the license agreement and use the suggested default destination location suggested. Once you proceed through the installation dialogs, you can click on the **Finish** button, exiting the install process.

Audacity supports other plug-ins, such as Steinberg (Cubase) VST and Nyquist that can add many other digital audio editing, waveform analysis, and sound synthesis algorithms (capabilities) to your Audacity installation. I feel the more power the better, so I suggest getting every plug-in that is currently available for Audacity, but, then again, multimedia production is my hobby, so I don't look at it as work; so have some fun with Audacity!

To check and see if everything you need to perform basic digital audio editing for Android is installed, use your control panel in your OS and go to the (installed) programs and features utility, which is shown in Figure 12-3. I have circled in red the entries on my system showing that these effects plug-ins and audio codecs have all been installed successfully.

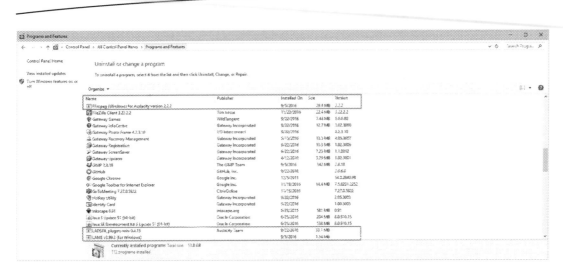

Figure 12-3. LADSPA Setup series of dialogs; Welcome, License Agreement, and Destination Location

Next, let's get some audio samples for your Android digital audio application. I'll include a short section on free digital audio sample searches next, so that we can find some free uncompressed PCM samples to use during the rest of this chapter.

Free Audio: Locate DigitalAudioSequencer Audio

To find some free-for-commercial-use audio samples, I'm going to use the Google Search Engine, and type in a query for something like **Free PCM Audio Samples**, **Free Digital Audio Samples**, **Free PCM Audio Files**, or **Free Digital Audio Files**, and similar Google search term combinations. It's important to note that each of these Google searches will turn up different results, due to keywords used in each of the different websites that offer these digital audio assets. Be advised that many of the paid audio sample websites will put the word "free" in their websites (as an SEO tactic), so that they will come up on these types of free PCM audio sample searches. To find word combinations, use the plus symbol, such as: **Free+Digital+Audio+Files**, for instance. This will tell the search engine that you want to find sites where these words are located adjacent (next) to each other.

There are dozens of good free audio sample websites, all of which will fit the bill for your needs, so be sure and investigate these further when you have some spare time. Make sure that the ones that you use for your Android application development are free for commercial use, do not require any royalty payments, and do not have any copyright (usage) restrictions. What you want to look for is high-quality, uncompressed PCM (.wav file format) samples, using 16-bit or better (24-bit or 32-bit) sample resolution, with a 32 kHz, 44.1 kHz, or 48 kHz sample frequency (sample rates). Note that if you use MP3 files (which most of these sites also offer), they will already have been compressed, and be ready for use, but you will not have any control over the data footprint optimization process. This is because much of the original audio sample data will already have been thrown away during the compression process, and you do not want to compress any kind of data that is already (lossy) compressed!

I decided to use the `freewavesamples.com` website, which features some animal sounds (samples) that we can use for an educational app where kids can click on the picture of the animal and hear the sound that they make. I show the website in Figure 12-4; go there and find the animal sounds section and download your animal sounds.

Figure 12-4. The Free Wave Samples website offers animal sounds you can use for your educational application

I'm going to download animal sounds for a cat, shown in Figure 12-5, dog, monkey, lion, horse, and bird. To go to the download page and link, use the 1 attachment link in the sample description area for each animal. Notice that these samples are each 16-bit, 44,100 Hz, CD quality, stereo format, PCM so we can practice some data footprint optimization techniques to see how significantly system memory can be optimized for the Android 7.1.1 SoundPool digital audio engine.

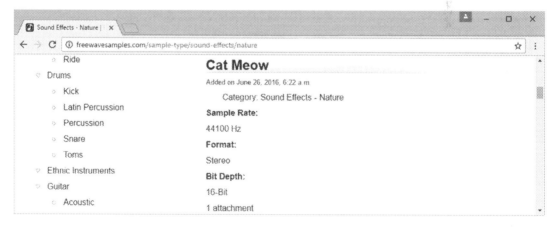

Figure 12-5. Locate the cat, dog, lion, horse, monkey, and bird samples; click the 1 attachment link and download

Now that you have seven uncompressed samples (I downloaded both bird samples), you can listen to them and see which animal sounds you want to use for your `DigitalAudioSampler` application. That is the first step in the digital audio assets optimization process, to decide which samples you must absolutely use in your application. The next steps, which we'll cover after this, are to see what minimum sample rate is needed to retain sample quality, to see if stereo samples are needed, or if mono samples can be used, and compress using the two most widely used, and Android, JavaFX 8 and HTML5 supported, MPEG-4 AAC and OGG Vorbis codecs using a maximum quality setting. I will go through the work process for this in the next section of the chapter, using Audacity 2.1.2, as that software is open source, free for commercial use, and available on Windows, OSX, and all Linux distros.

Digital Audio Optimization: Concepts and Formats

Let's launch Audacity 2.1.2 by clicking its Quick Launch icon on your Taskbar, and use the **File ➤ Open** menu command sequence to open the `Galloping-Horse.wav` file. This is the one with the heaviest data footprint. The first time you open (or more accurately import) an audio file in Audacity, you will get a warning dialog. I selected the **Make a copy of the files before editing (safer)** radio button option, then I selected the **Don't warn again and always use my choice above** check box, and then I clicked the **OK** button to load the initial sample, which can be seen in Figure 12-6 in Audacity 2.1.2 for Windows 10.

Using these audio file import settings, and using a copy of the file, instead of the actual file itself, is called **non-destructive audio editing** and this is a common practice in the digital audio editing and special effects industry. The reason for using non-destructive audio editing practices is because if you mess up in your audio sweetening and special effects application and damage the audio data, you can always go back to square one by going back to loading the original audio data.

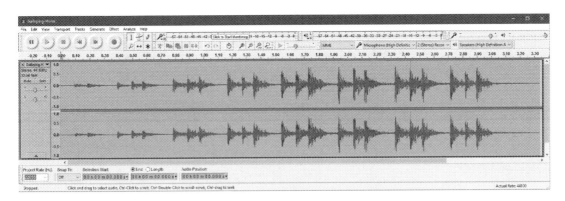

Figure 12-6. Use the Project Rate (Hz) drop-down selector to set your down-sample from 44100 Hz to 22050 Hz

Once the Galloping-Horse.wav sample data is loaded into Audacity, you'll see a screen with an audio transport control, including pause, play, stop, back, forward, and record, as well as editing tools and level meters that show green, yellow, and red signal peak indicators, showing when the audio is playing. There are microphone and speaker selector drop-downs, where you can set which hardware you wish to utilize with Audacity as well.

In the Project Rate (Hz) drop-down selector at the lower-left corner of Audacity, select a 22,050 Hz sample rate, as this is a 100% reduction in data used, and a 2X down-sampling of data, which will provide the best results, just like the concept we use for digital imagery and digital video scaling. As I mentioned, many of the concepts apply equally well to digital audio, digital imaging, and digital video. A 4X down-sample, to 11,025 Hz, would also be an optimal down-sample to make, but might remove too much audio quality (clarity). Try it and see, to get a feel for the Audacity software. The 22,050 Hz setting is shown highlighted in Figure 12-6 on the lower left.

Use the **File ➤ Export Audio** menu sequence, and access the Export Audio dialog, as shown in Figure 12-7, and export the file as Galloping-Horse-22050Hz.wav using the **WAV (Microsoft) signed 16-bit PCM** option.

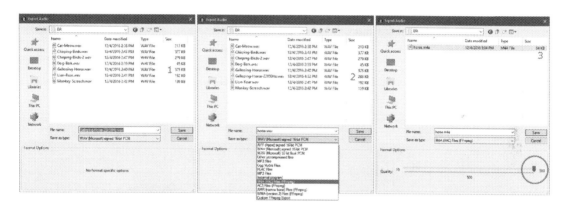

Figure 12-7. Use the Export Audio dialog to export different versions of each audio asset using different codecs

As you can see in Figure 12-7 numbered 1 and 2, the data footprint has decreased 100% from 575KB to 288KB, and you heard using the green Play icon in the transport. For both 44,100 Hz and 22,050 Hz settings, the result is virtually identical in sound fidelity. A bit later, we will reduce this data another 100% (or 4X total reduction) by making the Stereo sample into a Mono sample, which is fine for animal noises for a game or child's application.

This 288KB Stereo sample represents how much system memory will be needed to hold a Stereo Horse sample. Let's save the Stereo sample as an MPEG-4 AAC file, to see how much data the MPEG-4 AAC codec can take out and still give us a high (the 500 setting shown circled in red at the bottom right of Figure 12-7) quality result so that the APK size is even smaller. Remember the decompressed Stereo sample will still use 288KB of system memory, which is why I saved out a 22050Hz Wave file, to get a "baseline" for other codec compression ratios.

Use the same **File ➤ Export** Audio menu sequence, and name the file "horse," using **lowercase letters** (required by Android), and select the **M4A (AAC) Files (FFmpeg)** option from the Save as type selector, shown in blue in the third panel in Figure 12-7. This will generate an 84KB horse.m4a file, shown in Figure 12-7 as number 3.

I have just created a Stereo MPEG-4 AAC file for the application that takes only 84KB to store of the original 44,100 HZ 575KB file (a 685% data footprint reduction) and a 343% data footprint reduction on the 22,050 Hz PCM file. Next, let's reduce memory data footprint another 100% by making the Stereo sample a Mono sample.

To take the uncompressed audio data needed by memory to a mere 144KB for our largest animal sound sample, we will open the Galloping-Horse-22050Hz.wav file and use the Audacity **Tracks ➤ Stereo Track to Mono** (track) menu sequence, which is shown selected in light blue at the top left in Figure 12-8.

What this does is to invoke an algorithm in Audacity, which merges the stereo channel data formerly held in two tracks into one track, which reduces the amount of data going into the codec (or PCM encoder) by 100% (half).

This should give us another reduction in data footprint, this time from 288KB to 144KB, which is a 432KB data reduction from the 575KB original sample, which represents a more than 75% reduction in system memory use, which means we should be able to get these 2MB of animal sound samples into less than half a megabyte of Android system memory overhead. This is exactly what we will need to do to get the SoundPool engine (class) to perform as expected. Next, let's use the open source OGG Vorbis codec to compress this new mono sample.

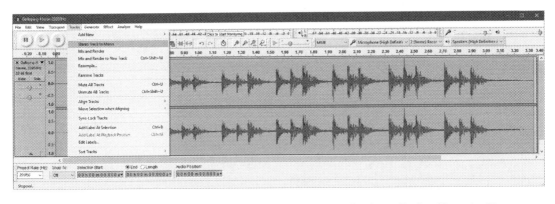

Figure 12-8. Open the 22050Hz version of each sample, and use the Tracks ➤ Stereo Track to Mono algorithm

As you can see on the left in Figure 12-9, I saved out another PCM sample for this Mono track I just created, as Galloping-Horse-22050Hz-mono.wav to see if it was 144KB, which it was. I then used **File ➤ Export Audio** and saved out a horsemono.ogg asset, this time, using another high-quality audio codec supported by Android, OGG Vorbis. This impressive codec is supported in Android, JavaFX, and HTML5, and is 100% open source, whereas the MPEG-4 patents do not completely expire until 2027. It gives us a 43KB data footprint in the .APK file with a full quality-level setting of 10 (100%), which is a 335% reduction in data footprint (that is, 144KB / 43KB).

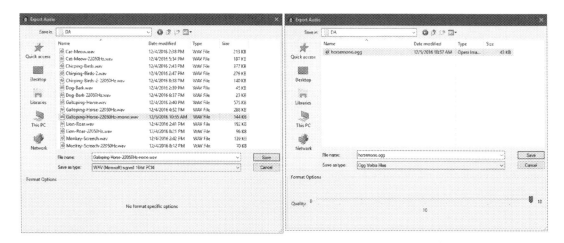

Figure 12-9. Save out mono Wave file to see the 4X data reduction and then as OGG Vorbis for a 14X reduction

As you can see, the OGG file is about half as big as the M4A file, so their compression is similar at maximum quality, given that we are compressing a Mono track here (half of stereo data). We will have a half dozen stereo M4A files, and a half dozen mono OGG files, for use in our application. If we use stereo files, we will be using 721KB of system memory. If we use mono files, we will be using 361KB of system memory. The stereo M4A files total 219KB of APK storage space. The mono OGG files total 116KB of APK storage space, using 100% quality settings no less. So, as you can see, these two codecs (and Audacity 2) are nothing short of phenomenal.

Given that the original samples total 1.4MB, this represents a significant data footprint optimization result, with little to no loss of aural quality, as is seen in Figure 12-10. Even before compression with the two most popular high-quality codecs (MPEG4 and OGG Vorbis are still being improved today), we got a 400% memory footprint reduction using a lower sample rate and a mono track with good-quality animal sound effects. You can see each sample's data go down by half along the left side files (PCM Wave), and applying codecs at full quality takes a data footprint down to 8 to 84K. The stereo M4A files achieve a 640% compression (1400 / 219), and the mono OGG files achieve a 1200% compression (1400 / 116), again with no audible decrease in quality.

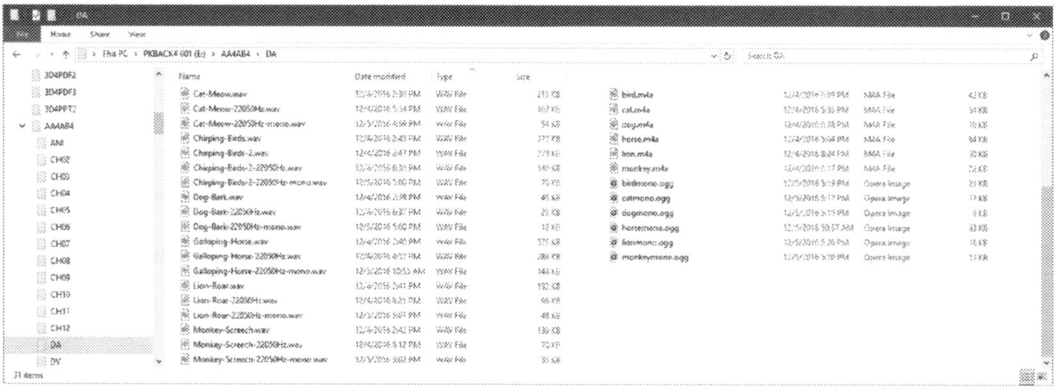

Figure 12-10. Compare data footprint savings for your baseline PCM files with your compressed files in Explorer

Remember, your users cannot hear the before and after sample comparison, only the final result, so as long as it is effective audio for the application, get the most memory and storage data footprint optimization that you can!

You may have noticed that in Audacity, once you click on the Export Audio dialog's **Save** button for any codec, an **Edit Metadata** dialog will appear. This dialog will offer data fields containing text values for Artist Name, Track Title, Album Title, Track Number, Year, Genre, and Comments. Since our application doesn't require any audio metadata, I am leaving these fields blank for now, so that we can get an accurate read on what the precise file size is; that is, the size of a file containing only the audio data. If you're wondering if Android can read, and therefore support audio metadata, if you do want to put this data into audio files, the answer is a resounding yes.

Android has a MediaMetadataRetriever class, which developers can utilize for this very specific purpose. If, for some reason, your audio application needs to leverage audio media metadata, you can use an **Edit Metadata** dialog, which will show itself every single time you save any type of audio file format in Audacity 2, along with the Android MediaMetadataRetriever class, which you can research and learn about at the following URL:

http://**developer.android.com/reference**/android/**media/MediaMetadataRetriever.html**

You should really spend some time with Audacity experimenting with data compression using some of the other Android 7 supported formats, such as AMR (for voice) and FLAC (for lossless HD audio). The MP3 codec has been improved upon by the MPEG-4 AAC codec, so unless you are using audio assets someone else has already compressed, you will want to use open source OGG or FLAC, or something from the MPEG4 family of codecs. Next let's create a ScrollingActivity class for this chapter's application and then we'll take a look at SoundPool.

DigitalAudioSequencer: ScrollingActivity

As you know, I am trying to use all of the primary Android design patterns that Android Studio will code for you automatically, to show you how these can be used to create Android applications quickly, and without a ton of experience. We've already covered basic, fullscreen, and navigation drawer Activity subclasses, so now we're going to explore the ScrollingActivity subclass of AppCompatActivity, which, as you know, allows the Android application to work across all versions of Android OS. Pretty powerful development for an Absolute Beginner!

Use the **File ➤ Close Project** menu sequence to close the DigitalVideoMedia project, and select the **Create New Project** option from the Android Studio primary dialog that appears, and enter your Create New Project series of dialogs that are shown in Figure 12-11. Name the application **DigitalAudioSequencer** and accept the other defaults in the first dialog, seen on the far left, and also accept the defaults in the Target Android Devices dialog seen in the middle of Figure 12-11. We will be coding the SoundPool to work across all versions of Android OS, and setting the API (15) to Android 4 better gives us coverage of close to 98% of Android hardware devices out there.

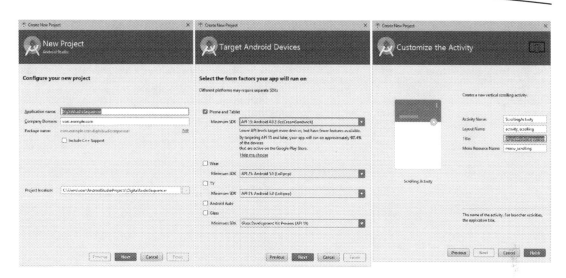

Figure 12-11. Create your Digital Audio Sequencer project by using the Create New Project series of dialogs

Next, select the ScrollingActivity Android design pattern shown selected in blue in Figure 12-12, and click the **Next** button, to advance to the **Customize Activity** dialog, shown on the far right in Figure 12-11. Change your application Title to **DigitalAudioSequencer** and leave the Android Activity, Layout ,and Menu Resource Naming at their default Android component and resource naming convention settings.

As you'll see in Figure 12-13, Android Studio will also create a content_scrolling.xml user interface definition file, which will eventually hold your scrolling content. For this application, this will be a series of animal image assets, which your target users, in this case, young children, will be able to tap, or click on, and hear the animal sounds that they make, courtesy of the Android SoundPool digital audio sequencing engine.

Click on the **Finish** button, shown on the bottom right in Figure 12-11, and create your digital audio sequencer project, so that we can take a look at the bootstrap (Android Studio 2.3 generated) code, and see what it does, next.

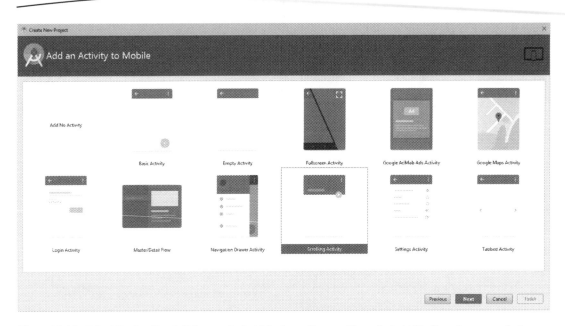

Figure 12-12. Select the ScrollingActivity pure Android design pattern and have Android Studio code your project

As you can see in Figure 12-13, your ScrollingActivity subclass of AppCompatActivity has all of the familiar components, which we have already covered during the book. This will allow us to focus on some new coding structures during this chapter, including creating your own custom method; using if-else structures to detect the user's Android OS version; and how to instantiate, load, and play back SoundPool engine digital audio samples.

I opened the import statements, so that you can see what Android classes we are starting out with, including the core Bundle, View, Menu, MenuItem, Toolbar and AppCompatActivity classes, which are used in most of these pure Android design patterns that you can have Android Studio code for you.

We will be removing the FloatingActionButton and Snackbar class import statements, as we will be modifying this ScrollingActivity to provide scrolling animal imagery that users can use to trigger animal-related audio samples. We will be adding import statements for the digital audio-related classes we will be learning about during this chapter, including SoundPool, AudioManager, AudioAttributes, and Build, as well as the ImageView class used to hold the digital image assets. Build is an object builder class that we will use to build SoundPool and AudioAttributes objects.

We will remove the FloatingActionButton functionality, and replace the Snackbar functionality with triggers of SoundPool digital audio samples inside of the View.OnClickListener() structures. We'll also create a custom method to instantiate (initialize) the SoundPool engine, and configure it for use, and load it with audio samples.

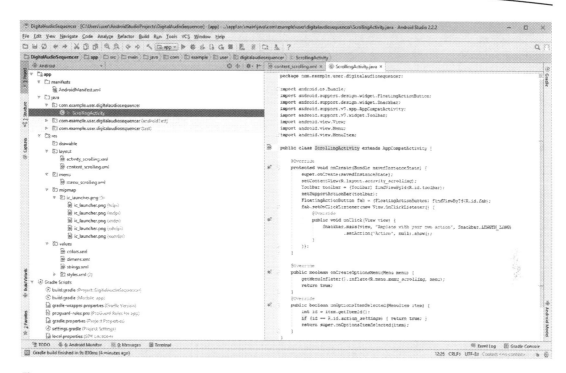

Figure 12-13. *The bootstrap ScrollingActivity class has the basic Android Toolbar, Menu, and Activity features*

The first thing that we are going to modify is in the top-level `activity_scrolling.xml` user interface definition file, so right-click on the **app/res/layout/activity_scrolling.xml** file in the Android ➤ Project pane, shown on the left side of Figure 12-13, and select the **Jump To Source** context menu option. This will open the XML markup in a tab for editing, which can be seen in Figure 12-14.

Delete the `FloatingActionButton` child UI element, at the bottom of this top-level UI definition, underneath the `<include>` child element that references the `content_activity.xml` UI definition that contains the Nested Scroll View. The XML markup to delete is shown at the bottom of Figure 12-14, highlighted in red.

Now we are ready to add our `ImageView` content to the `content_scrolling.xml` file. We will be replacing the `<TextView>` child UI element with a `<LinearLayout>` element full of `<ImageView>` child elements. The reason we have to use the `LinearLayout` is because the `NestedScrollView` parent element must have only a single child UI element defined.

The only other thing that we have to do so that the `<ImageView>` UI elements have something to reference is to go onto the Internet and get some free online image assets to use inside of the `<ImageView>` UI elements. I am obviously going to use animal imagery to go along with those six animal sounds digital audio samples we found online.

Once we download, optimize, and install these in the `app/res/drawable` folder, we will be ready to code!

Figure 12-14. *Delete the FloatingActionButton widget so we just have a scrolling container for our animal images*

Next, go to Pexels.com (Figure 12-15) and get animal images (I chose dog, cat, lion, bird, horse, and monkey) to use in the app.

Figure 12-15. *Go to pexels.com, and search for "animals" and find dog, cat, lion, bird, horse, and monkey images*

I made all of the images the same iTV HDTV resolution and 16:9 aspect ratio and saved them in the book repository as JPEG images (50% to 75% quality). I also created MDPI 480 by 720 versions, and saved them as PNG files, as can be seen in Figure 12-16, and copied these into the /app/res/drawable folder for the project. If you like you can get some practice with GIMP 2.8.20 and create HDPI versions by down-sampling the HDTV resolution versions by 100% to 960 by 540. To use all DPI versions, you create an app/res/drawable-hdpi and /app/res/drawable-xhdpi folder in Android Studio 2.3 (by right-clicking on /app/res and using **New ➤ Android resource folder**), and copy the JPEG originals into the XHDPI folder and the 960 by 540 versions (can be JPEG or PNG) into the HDPI folder. Make sure all of these files are using only the animal name, in all lowercase letters, as shown in Figure 12-16.

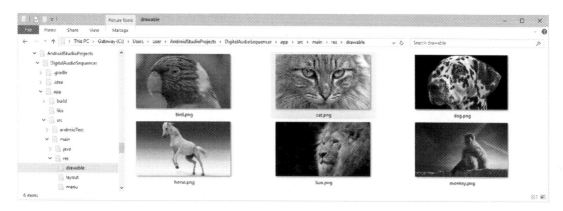

Figure 12-16. Copy the 480 by 270 PNG24 images into the DigitalAudioSequencer project's /res/drawable folder

Replace the <TextView> UI element in the content_scrolling.xml tab with the <LinearLayout> UI layout container, which will contain the six <ImageView> UI elements. Set the orientation to vertical and the layout parameters to match the dimensions of the parent NestedScrollView layout container using the match_parent constant. To match the blue color value in the Toolbar, use the android:background="@color/colorPrimary" attribute, as is shown in the following XML markup, also seen in its finished state in Figure 12-17:

```
<LinearLayout xmlns:android="http://schemas.android.com/apk/res/android"
              android:orientation="vertical" android:layout_width="match_parent"
              android:layout_height="match_parent" android:background="@color/colorPrimary" >
    <ImageView android:id="@+id/bird" android:src="@drawable/bird"
               android:layout_width="match_parent" android:layout_height="wrap_content" />
</LinearLayout>
```

For the <ImageView> child tag elements, you can do one as shown above, and then copy and paste it five more times, then change the animal names so that you have all six animals with their own ImageView display pane in the scrolling view. Notice that I use the match_parent constant to span the scrolling view container's width, but wrap_content in the height (Y) dimension in order to maintain the 16:9 aspect ratio for the imagery. If you used match_parent on both layout parameters, your imagery would expand to fill the container and there would be no blue bars between the images, and the images themselves look distorted and unnatural (especially the horse). If you like, you can try this and see for yourself the difference (see Figure 12-19 for the correct image aspect ratio) just to get a feel for what wrap_content versus match_parent will do, regarding X-axis and Y-axis image scaling.

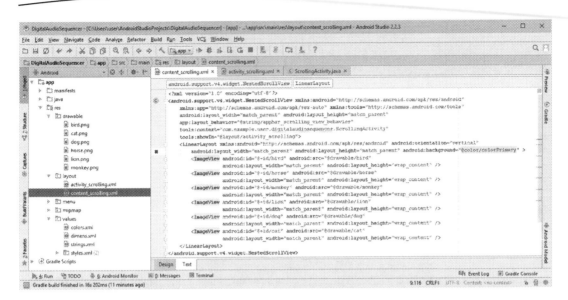

Figure 12-17. *Create a <LinearLayout> and child <ImageLayout> elements inside a <NestedScrollView> parent*

Remove the `FloatingActionButton` class import statement in the `ScrollingActivity.java` tab seen in Figure 12-18, add an `import android.widget.ImageView;` statement, and change the `FloatingActionButton` instantiation to an `ImageView` instantiation. Call the `.setOnClickListener()` off the `ImageView` object, instead of the `fab` object.

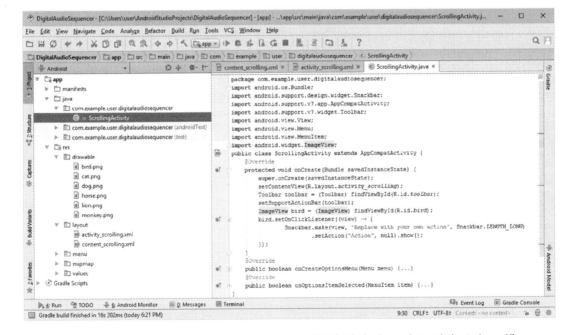

Figure 12-18. *Remove FloatingActionButton import, and change FloatingActionButton instantiation to ImageView*

This essentially uses the FloatingActionButton instantiation and event handling structure, and steals it for use with the ImageView, using the following Java 8 code that replaces the previous FloatingActionButton fab code:

```
import android.widget.ImageView;
...
ImageView bird = (ImageView) findViewById(R.id.bird);
bird.setOnClickListener( new View.OnClickListener() {
    @Override
    public void onClick(View view) {
      // Event Handling: Currently is Snackbar code. Will Be: SoundPool.
play(sampleIdAnimalName);
    }
});
```

Later, we will replace the SnackBar code with SoundPool code, and then copy and paste this structure five more times, to create programming structures for all six ImageViews. Let's use the **Run ➤ Run 'app'** menu sequence and make sure that the code replacement works and that the NestedScrollView now shows six animal images. As you can see in Figure 12-19, this application is starting to look really great! Scroll through all six to test your app. Now all we have to do is to create a custom method setting up and configuring your SoundPool digital audio sequencing engine.

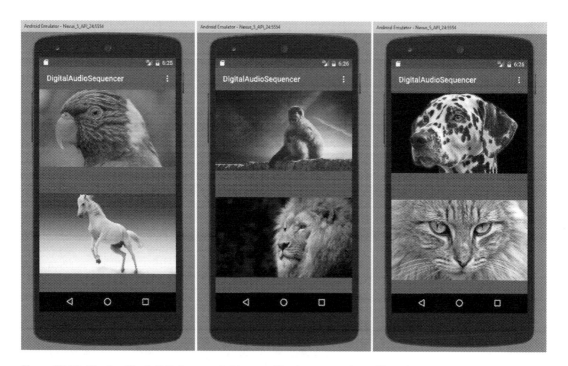

Figure 12-19. The ScrollingActivity is converted to a scrolling image repository, filled with beautiful animal images

Now we are ready to start learning about SoundPool, and Android's digital audio-related classes and methods.

Android SoundPool: Digital Audio Engine

The Android SoundPool class is a direct subclass of the java.lang.Object master class. It's important to note that SoundPool is not a subclass of the Android MediaPlayer class, as one might be liable to assume. However, like the MediaPlayer class, it is part of the android. media package, and thus, the complete path to the class (as used in an import statement) would be android.media.SoundPool. The Java class hierarchy looks like the following:

```
java.lang.Object
  > android.media.SoundPool
```

Since SoundPool is a direct subclass of java.lang.Object, we can infer that it is its own, "scratch-coded" digital audio sequencing engine creation. It is also important to note that you can use a SoundPool object and MediaPlayer objects at the same time, if you need to. In fact, there are distinct applications for both of these audio playback classes. You should use MediaPlayer for "long-format" audio (and video) data, such as albums, songs, audio books, TV shows, or movies. SoundPool is best used for "short-form" audio snippets, especially when they need to be played in rapid succession and (or) combined together, such as in a 2D or 3D game, e-book, iTV show, Android Wear Watch Faces, Android Auto application, or any gamified application.

You can load your SoundPool collection of samples into system memory from one of two places. The first, and most common, would be from inside of the APK file, which I call **captive** new media assets, in which case, they would live in the **app/res/raw** project folder, as they did for your DigitalVideoMedia application in Chapter 11. The second place you can load samples from is an SD Card or similar storage location. This is what one would term the Android 7.1.1 OS file system.

The SoundPool uses the Android MediaPlayer Service to decode an audio asset into memory. We'll be covering Android Service classes in the next chapter in this book (are you starting to see the logical progression here?). It does this using uncompressed 16-bit PCM mono or stereo audio. This is the main reason that I've been teaching you the work process that optimizes digital audio using a 16-bit sampling resolution, because if you use 8-bit audio, Android up-samples it to 16-bit, and you end up with wasted data, which could have been spent on better quality.

This means that you should optimize your sample frequency, but not your sample resolution (use 16-bit). Don't use stereo audio unless you absolutely need to. It is very important to conform your optimization work process to how SoundPool works to get optimal results across the largest number of consumer electronics devices. The 48 kHz is the best sample frequency to use if you can, with the 44.1 kHz coming in second, and 32 kHz coming in third. To optimize, keep a sample short and mono, and use a modern codec, such as MPEG4 AAC, OGG, or FLAC, to retain the most quality, and still get a reasonable amount of data compression for your APK file. You can calculate system memory requirements by using the original PCM uncompressed digital audio file size as your baseline.

When the SoundPool object is constructed in Java 8, as you will be doing later on during this chapter, a developer will set a maxStreams parameter using an integer value. This parameter will predetermine how many audio streams you can composite, or render, at the same time. This parameter sets aside system memory that can be used for digital audio. In our application, we'll set this to six, but you could use less, as a user will play only one sample at a time for this particular application.

Setting the maximum number of streams parameter to as small a number as possible is a good standard practice. This is because doing so will help to minimize CPU cycles used for processing audio samples, and will reduce any likelihood that the SoundPool audio mixing will impact other areas of your application performance. Thus, you could use maxStreams as low as 1 or 2 for the application we are coding as there are only one or two image occurrences per screen, as you can see in Figure 12-19.

The SoundPool engine will track the number of active (playing) audio streams (samples), to make sure that it does not exceed the maxStreams setting. If a maximum number of audio streams is ever exceeded, SoundPool will **abort** a previously playing stream. It will do this based on a **sample priority** value that you can specify. I simply specified 1 through 6, as it is unlikely that the user will scroll and click that rapidly for this application. If SoundPool finds two or more audio samples playing that have an equal sample priority value, it will make the decision regarding which sample to stop playing based upon **sample age**, which means the sample that has been playing the longest is the one that's terminated (playback stopped). I like to call this the **Logan's Run** principle!

Priority level values are evaluated from low to high numeric values. This means that higher (large) numbers will represent the higher priority levels. Priority is evaluated when a call to the SoundPool .play() method causes the number of active streams to exceed the maxStreams value, which is set when a SoundPool object is instantiated. In the case where the sample priority for the new stream is lower than all the active streams, the new sound will not play, and the .play() function will return a streamID of **zero** (nothing played). For this reason, be sure your application's Java 8 code keeps track of exactly what is going on with your audio sample priority-level settings, if you're doing something like a game that needs dynamic, real-time audio sample playback decisions to be made.

Samples are looped in SoundPool by setting any non-zero looping value. The exception to this is that a value of **-1** will cause samples to loop **forever**, and under this circumstance, the application code must make a call to the SoundPool .stop() method to stop the looping sample. So a non-zero integer value will cause a sample to repeat itself that specified number of times; thus, a value of 7 will cause your sample to play back a total of 8 times, as computers start counting using the number 0 instead of 1. For instance with the horse sample, you could remove some of the "dead space" (silence) before and after the hoof beats so that you could extend this sound effect by using a numeric value greater than 1, which would cause a longer hoof beats playback. The reason I did not do this is because the public domain sample applied the Doppler Effect to the sample, causing the hoof beats to fade into the distance. Get some practice with SoundPool, and try this for yourself, as a variation on what we are doing here.

You can change each sample playback rate using SoundPool, which as mentioned makes this class into an audio synthesis tool. A sample playback rate equal to 1.0 will cause your sample to play back at its original frequency. A sample playback rate of 2.0 will cause the sample to be played at twice its original frequency, which will shift it up a full octave higher, if it is a musical instrument note. Similarly, a sample playback rate set to 0.5 will cause SoundPool to play the sample at half of its original frequency. This will sound like it is playing an octave lower. The sample playback rate range of SoundPool is currently limited to 0.5 to 2.0; however, this could be upgraded in a future API revision to, say, 0.25 to 4, which would give us developers a five-octave sample playback range.

Now it is time to learn how to implement a SoundPool object, and learn about a couple of other Android digital audio utility classes that are used in conjunction with SoundPool. As you can see, I'm trying to cover as many powerful Android classes in this book as is humanly possible, especially those new media classes that allow you to set your applications apart from the rest of the applications in the Google Play application marketplace.

Add SoundPool Engine to DigitalAudioSequencer

Now it's time to get into Java programming in the ScrollingActivity.java AppCompatActivity class, and add the SoundPool engine so that you can add different animal sounds to match your six ImageView UI elements. Open Android Studio and open **ScrollingActivity.java** in an editing tab, and declare a **SoundPool** object at the top of your class. Name it **animalSamples** using the following object declaration statement, seen at the top of Figure 12-20:

```
SoundPool animalSamples;
```

Once you type in SoundPool if you double-click on the SoundPool (android.media. SoundPool) pop-up Android Studio will also write the import statement for SoundPool for you.

Add a space after the onCreate() by using the newline character (the return key on the keyboard) and type in **void**, and then select the **public void setAnimalSamples** option, to have Android Studio create a new method infrastructure for you as seen at the bottom of Figure 12-20. Note that because you added an animalSamples SoundPool object, that Android Studio 2.3 suggests a method that will allow you to set up (configure) this SoundPool object.

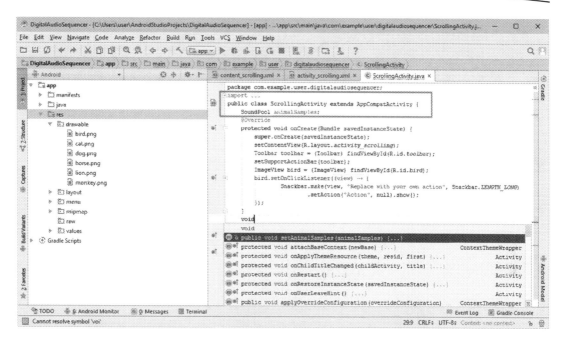

Figure 12-20. Add a SoundPool object named animalSamples and then a method named setupAnimalSamples( )

Edit the **setAnimalSamples()** method name that Android Studio 2.3 created for you to instead be **setupAnimalSamples()** as that more accurately represents what the method is going to be doing. Inside of the method body, create an `if`-`else` conditional logic construct that will use **SoundPool.Builder()** if Android OS is at version 5 or later. As you create this code, be sure to use **Alt+Enter** to have Android Studio 2.3 add an **import os.Build;** statement for you.

This will be accomplished using the following top-level pseudo-code (with some real code) programming structure:

```
public void setupAnimalSamples() {
    if (Build.VERSION.SDK_INT >= Build.VERSION_CODES.LOLLIPOP){ SoundPool.Builder()
    method call }
    else { SoundPool() constructor method  }
```

Inside the if(Build.VERSION.SDK_INT >= Build.VERSION_CODES.LOLLIPOP){...} part of the conditional logic construct, instantiate your animalSamples SoundPool object, using the SoundPool.Builder() approach, as is shown in Figure 12-21, and chain a .setMaxStreams() method call and finally a .build() method call, like this:

```
public void setupAnimalSamples() {
    if (Build.VERSION.SDK_INT >= Build.VERSION_CODES.LOLLIPOP) {
        animalSamples = new SoundPool.Builder().setMaxStreams(6).build(); }
```

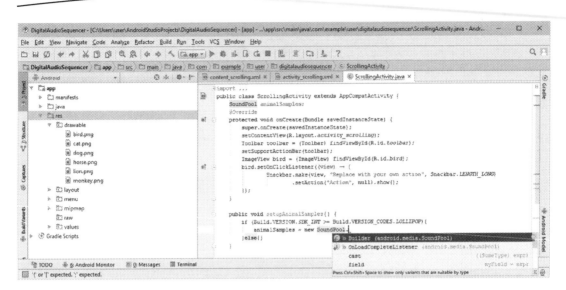

Figure 12-21. Type animalSamples = new SoundPool, and select the Builder class to import and insert into code

In the else {...} section, use the deprecated SoundPool constructor method, seen in Figure 12-22, to instantiate the animalSamples SoundPool object using the deprecated constructor.

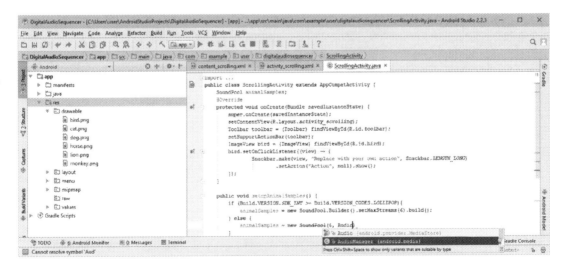

Figure 12-22. Instantiate animalSamples in the else section using a new SoundPool( ) deprecated constructor call

As you can see highlighted in Figure 12-22, this constructor method call is deprecated and therefore is lined-out in Android Studio, which I find unnerving, as it's like Android Studio is saying "you can't use this" when in fact you can use it, especially if you are developing for 32-bit (Pre Android 5) Android devices. When you write this code, be sure to have Android Studio code the `import android.media.AudioManager` statement for you.

```
animalSamples = new SoundPool(this, AudioManager.STREAM_MUSIC, 0);
```

The parameters include the Java `this` keyword, an `AudioManager` stream type, and the sample rate conversion quality level (zero being 100%, this is currently unimplemented but portends more SoundPool development as a synthesizer, which is great for developers). If you type in the AudioManager class and a period, a pop-up dialog in Android Studio 2.3 will list all of the constants currently available to you using this class.

The `AudioManager` class provides access to audio volume and phone ringer mode controls (as constants) for the Android 7.1.1 OS. Take some time and go over these constants, and see what types of digital audio attributes for the Android OS that you as a developer are allowed to control. The 90 constants are located at the following URL:

`https://developer.android.com/reference/android/media/AudioManager.html`

The AudioManager constant we'll be using is the **STREAM_MUSIC** constant, used for music or sound effects in Android applications using the `MediaPlayer` audio (and video) playback engine, which is why the constant is using the word "stream" as many developers choose to stream their audio and video content from an external data server. I prefer to optimize the content and have it in an APK file, so that I do not require an external server or that the end-user must be on-line in order to use the app.

The `setupAnimalSamples()` method, and its core `if-else` structure, which is used to decide if the deprecated constructor method (used prior to API 21 Lollipop), or the new `SoundPool.Builder()` class, is now error-free, and performs the `SoundPool` engine initialization function that will be used to create the `SoundPool` object. The Java 8 code that creates this initial method structure should at this point look like the following Java statements, which can be seen error free and highlighted in Figure 12-23:

```
public void setupAnimalSamples() {
    if (Build.VERSION.SDK_INT >= Build.VERSION_CODES.LOLLIPOP) {
        animalSamples = new SoundPool.Builder().setMaxStreams(6).build();
    } else {
        animalSamples = new SoundPool(6, AudioManager.STREAM_MUSIC, 0);
    }
    // Sample loading statements will be added here using animalSamples.load() method calls
}
```

We will be adding some initialization (sample loading) Java statements after this `if-else` construct a bit later on, after we learn about the new `AudioAttributes`, but at this point, the method is now usable for instantiation of the `SoundPool` object, so we can now add it to our `onCreate()` method without generating any red error highlighting.

To make this setupAnimalSamples() method active in the ScrollingActivity class, we will need to add a method call invoking it inside of the onCreate() method, after the super. onCreate() and setContentView() method calls. This is the "organizational equivalent" of putting the code in setupAnimalSamples() directly inside onCreate(). Add in this **setupAnimalSamples();** method call, inside of your onCreate() method after the super. onCreate() and after the setContentView() method calls, by using the following Java statement, as shown highlighted in red in the middle of Figure 12-23:

```
setupAnimalSamples();
```

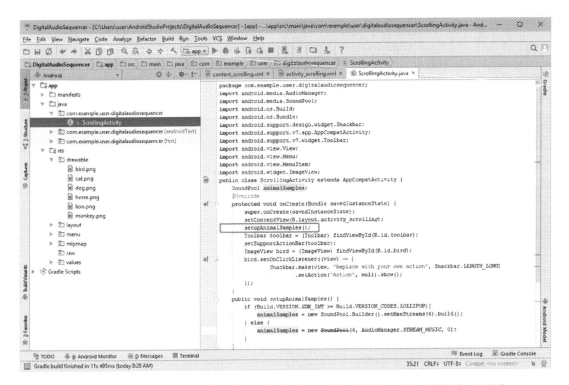

Figure 12-23. *Call setupAnimalSamples( ) in onCreate( ) to implement the basic SoundPool object instantiations*

Let's take a break from coding, and learn about AudioAttributes so that we can configure the SoundPool object.

Android AudioAttributes: Configuring SoundPool

The Android public final class AudioAttributes extends the Java Object class and also implements the Parcelable interface. The AudioAttributes Java class hierarchy therefore would look like the following:

```
java.lang.Object
  > android.media.AudioAttributes
```

This AudioAttributes class was added in Android OS API 21 (Lollipop) to encapsulate a collection of attributes that describe information about the audio stream, for use with the new SoundPool.Builder() object instantiation approach. This AudioAttributes object replaces the AudioManager class stream type constants (for instance, the STREAM_MUSIC or STREAM_ALARM constants) previously used for defining behavior for audio playback.

Attributes will allow the developer to specify more information than is conveyed in the stream type by allowing the application to define how it is using digital audio, that is, why you're playing that sound, and what purposes that sound is being used for. This is achieved using audio "usage" and "content type" information attributes.

Examples of audio usage constants include **USAGE_MEDIA**, which we will be using, and USAGE_ALARM. These two constants are the closest thing AudioAttributes has to AudioManager stream type constants. Usage information is more detailed than stream type information, allowing certain platforms or routing policies to use the information for refining hardware volume and routing decisions. Usage is important information to supply in your AudioAttributes object, and it is strongly recommended by Google to build any object instance with this information supplied, as we will be doing in the next section of the chapter.

The content type attribute, on the other hand, involves what type of audio content you are going to be playing. The content type attribute expresses the general category for your digital audio content. This audio information is optional, but I'm going to use it, so I can show you how to be thorough in your digital audio implementation.

There are five primary content types, as you will see in Figure 12-26, for instance, CONTENT_TYPE_MOVIE would be specified for a movie streaming service, CONTENT_TYPE_MUSIC for music playback applications, CONTENT_TYPE_SONIFICATION for sounds used to accompany UI design elements or app content (this is what we're going to be using for animal sounds that accompany animal imagery), CONTENT_TYPE_SPEECH should be specified for vocal tracks, and CONTENT_TYPE_UNKNOWN for anything else. This digital audio information can be used by an audio framework to selectively configure audio post-processing code structures.

AudioAttributes can be used with Android audio classes other than SoundPool as well. For example, one of the AudioTrack class constructors, AudioTrack(AudioAttributes, AudioFormat, int, int, int) will allow you to configure your MediaPlayer using the .setAudioAttributes(AudioAttributes) method call, or to configure a Notification with audio. An AudioAttributes instance is built using a AudioAttributes.Builder() builder class, which we will be using in the next section of this chapter. In fact, let's dive in and get our hands dirty now, configuring our SoundPool engine object by using AudioAttributes and AudioAttributes.Builder().

Configuring a SoundPool Using AudioAttributes

At the top of your `ScrollingActivity.java` class, add in the `AudioAttributes` object declaration, underneath your `animalSamples` `SoundPool` object declaration. If you type in the `AudioAttributes` and then double-click on the pop-up helper that shows the class and package information, Android Studio will code the `import` statement for you, as is shown in Figure 12-24. The Java object declaration statement should look like the following code:

```
AudioAttributes sampleAttributes;
```

Next, we have to instantiate the `sampleAttributes` `AudioAttributes` object inside of the `if` statement which is in the `setupAnimalSamples()` method. Since this class was introduced in API 21 it uses the `Builder` nested class, just like the new `SoundPool` class `Builder` also used in API 21 and later, we will put this instantiation in the `if` portion of the conditional statement, as is shown in Figure 12-24. Your new Java code should look like this:

```
public void setupAnimalSamples() {
    if (Build.VERSION.SDK_INT >= Build.VERSION_CODES.LOLLIPOP) {
        sampleAttributes = new AudioAttributes.Builder().build();
        animalSamples = new SoundPool.Builder().setMaxStreams(6).build();
    } else { ... }
```

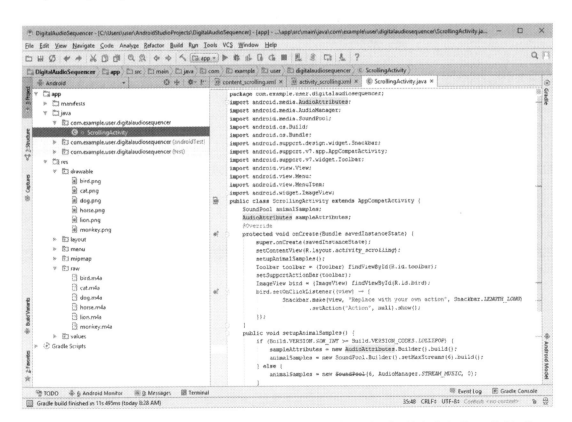

Figure 12-24. Add AudioAttributes object named sampleAttributes and instantiate it with AudioAttributes.Builder( )

This code will build an empty AudioAttributes object named sampleAttributes that will eventually be wired into the SoundPool object using, you guessed it, the .setAudioAttribu tes(sampleAttributes) method call off of the SoundPool.Builder object instantiation chain (this is in Figure 12-27, if you wanted to look ahead).

To add configuration parameters (AudioAttributes class constants) for the USAGE and CONTENT_TYPE attributes we discussed in the previous section, you will insert the .setUsage() and .setContentType() method calls in the method call chain prior to the final .build() method call.

Let's configure the AudioAttributes USAGE attribute (or characteristic, or parameter, or setting if you prefer) first, since that is more important to set, according to the Android developer website documentation. This would be done using the following AudioAttributes. Builder() Java statement, as shown highlighted in Figure 12-25:

```
public void setupAnimalSamples() {
  if (Build.VERSION.SDK_INT >= Build.VERSION_CODES.LOLLIPOP) {
    sampleAttributes = new AudioAttributes.Builder().setUsage(AudioAttributes.USAGE_GAME).
    build();
    animalSamples = new SoundPool.Builder().setMaxStreams(6).build();
  } else { ... }
```

Notice in Figure 12-25 that you can have Android Studio provide you pop-up selectors with Android classes, in this case, AudioAttributes, and constants, in this case, you would use USAGE_GAME (faster response), or even USAGE_MEDIA if you prefer, or even USAGE_UNKNOWN. If you were coding an animal sounds alarm app, you could select USAGE_ALARM. All of these usage constants are shown in a light blue drop-down selector, in Figure 12-25.

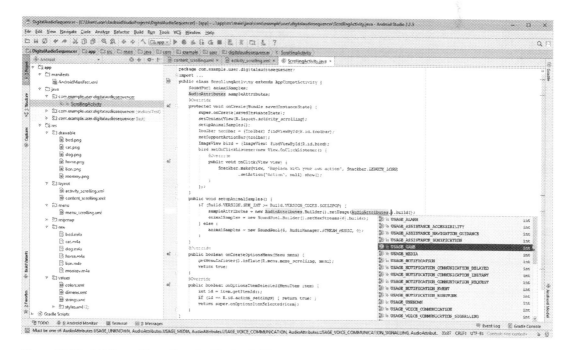

Figure 12-25. Add the .setUsage( ) method in the .Builder( ) method chain, and specify a USAGE_GAME constant

Next, let's add another method call to .setContentType(CONTENT_TYPE) into the builder method chain, which specifies **CONTENT_TYPE_SONIFICATION**. Sonification is exactly what it sounds like it is: it is adding samples or sound effects to visual things, such as user interface elements (Button, ImageButton, or ImageView) to **sonify** them. Since this is precisely what we are doing in this application, this is the content type constant that we'll utilize.

The Java programming constructs for adding yet another method call to this growing method chain necessitates that we use a different code indentation (formatting) approach. The code, shown in Figure 12-26, looks like this:

```java
public void setupAnimalSamples() {
    if (Build.VERSION.SDK_INT >= Build.VERSION_CODES.LOLLIPOP)  {
        sampleAttributes =
        new AudioAttributes.Builder()
                          .setUsage(AudioAttributes.USAGE_GAME)
                          .setContentType(AudioAttributes.CONTENT_TYPE_SONIFICATION)
                          .build();
        animalSamples = new SoundPool.Builder().setMaxStreams(6).build();
    } else { ... }
```

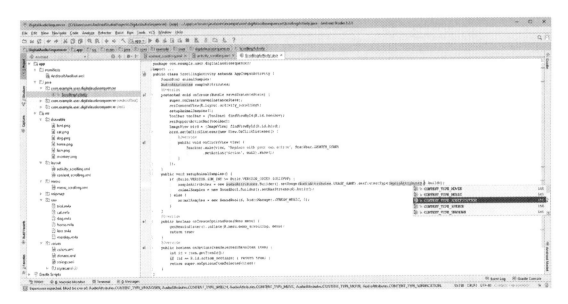

Figure 12-26. Add .setContentType() method into method chain, and specify CONTENT_TYPE_SONIFICATION

To wire the `AudioAttributes` object into the `SoundPool` object, you use the
`.setAudioAttributes()` method from the `SoundPool` class and pass over the
`AudioAttributes` object as its sole parameter. This would be done using the following line of
Java 8 code, as is shown highlighted in pale yellow in Figure 12-27:

```
animalSamples=new SoundPool.Builder().setMaxStreams(6).setAudioAttributes(sampleAt
tributes).build();
```

Make sure that this method call is inserted in your `SoundPool.Builder` chain either before
or after your `.setMaxStreams()` method call, and before the final `.build()` method call that
actually builds a `SoundPool` object.

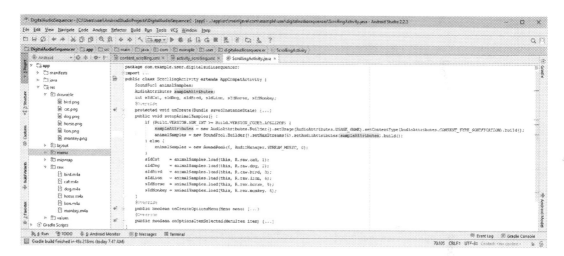

Figure 12-27. *Wire AudioAttributes object to SoundPool object with .setAudioAttributes and add soundId integers*

Now that you have declared, instantiated, and wired together your `SoundPool` and
`AudioAttributes` objects in `setupAnimalSamples()` you can initialize the `SoundPool` object,
by using the `.load()` method to load your six animal sound samples, and assigning them
into their own sample identification numbers (integers). Before you write this code be sure
that you have copied the six animal sample assets you optimized earlier into the `/res/raw/`
folder, as you learned how to do (and create), in the previous chapter on digital video.

Declare six integer `sId` (sample identification) variables, named for each animal, using the
following compound Java code statement, which can be seen at the top of Figure 12-27,
located under the two object declarations:

```
int sIdCat, sIdDog, sIdBird, sIdLion, sIdHorse, sIdMonkey;
```

After the conditional `if-else` statement in the first part of the `setupAnimalSamples()` method that instantiates and configures your SoundPool digital audio engine based on Android version 7.1.1 (Nougat), you will add six Java statements that use the SoundPool `.load()` method to load the digital audio asset data from the `/app/res/raw` folder into the SoundPool, assigning a priority and passing the application Context object by using the Java `this` keyword. The result of this operation is assigned to a sample ID integer value, which you will later use with the SoundPool `.play()` method call, inside of the `onClick()` event handler constructs, which used to contain SnackBar calls to display messages at the bottom of the device screen. The completed `setupAnimalSamples()` method can be seen below, and is also shown in Figure 12-27:

```java
public void setupAnimalSamples() {
    if (Build.VERSION.SDK_INT >= Build.VERSION_CODES.LOLLIPOP) {
        sampleAttributes =
        new AudioAttributes.Builder()
                        .setUsage(AudioAttributes.USAGE_GAME)
                        .setContentType(AudioAttributes.CONTENT_TYPE_SONIFICATION)
                        .build();
        animalSamples =
        new SoundPool.Builder()
                    .setMaxStreams(6)
                    .setAudioAttributes(sampleAttributes)
                    .build();
    } else {
        animalSamples = new SoundPool(6, AudioManager.STREAM_MUSIC, 0);
    }
    sIdCat    = animalSamples.load(this, R.raw.cat,    1);
    sIdDog    = animalSamples.load(this, R.raw.dog,    2);
    sIdBird   = animalSamples.load(this, R.raw.bird,   3);
    sIdLion   = animalSamples.load(this, R.raw.lion,   4);
    sIdHorse  = animalSamples.load(this, R.raw.horse,  5);
    sIdMonkey = animalSamples.load(this, R.raw.monkey, 6);
}
```

We are now ready to replace the Snackbar code in the `onClick()` event handler, which we morphed earlier in the chapter into an ImageView named bird, with `.play()` method calls off of an `animalSamples` SoundPool object, as you can see being created in Android Studio in Figure 12-28. Inside of the `bird.setOnClickListener()` event listening construct, type the object name `animalSamples`, hit a **period** key, and select the `play(int soundId, float leftVolume, float rightVolume, int priority, int loop, float rate)` pop-up menu option.

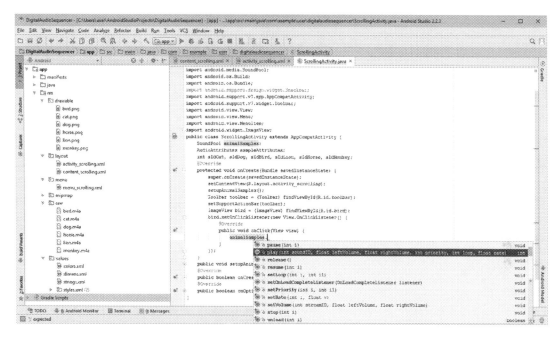

Figure 12-28. Inside the onClick( ) event handler type the animalSamples object and select the .play( ) method call

After you type the period and double-click on the play() SoundPool method call option, Android Studio will add it for you, which is shown on the left half of Figure 12-29. Type an "s" inside the parameter area and select your sIdBird integer sample ID for the play action for the bird ImageView onClick() event handler. Type a comma, a space, and then Android Studio will pop up a parameter list balloon helper, which is shown on the right half of Figure 12-29. I used 100% (1.0f, or float) for leftVolume and rightVolume, 1 (integer) for priority, 0 (integer) for loop and no change (1.0f, or float) for the sample rate pitch-shifter, which implements audio wave synthesis.

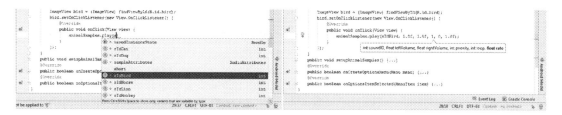

Figure 12-29. Use Android Studio to guide you through all the configuration parameters of the .play( ) method call

Make sure you use the f (float) after decimal numbers like 1.0, otherwise Android Studio will give you an error, thinking that you are using the Java double variable data value. Also make sure integers do not use any decimal, and use correct **float** data value as the SoundPool engine seems to have problems "casting" number types (from integer 1 to float 1.0, for instance). I was getting runtime errors, using .play(sIdBird, 1, 1, 1, 0, 1), and when I then implemented the more precise float number format specifications, the application worked perfectly.

Now we are ready to copy and paste the ImageView related Java constructs for the bird, which we created using the SnackBar construct that Android Studio originally created for us. First make sure to run the application and click on the bird and make sure it chirps, as a great work process for an Absolute Beginner is to make sure that the app works after any material change or addition of new Java 8 programming logic, classes, methods, interfaces, constants, asset references, or variables. The same goes for new XML markup as well.

Now select the four lines of code starting with ImageView bird, right-click on the selection and click copy, and add a line of code under the construct and right-click in it and select paste. You can also use **CTRL-C** (Copy) and then **CTRL-V** (Paste) **twice**. The first CTRL-V replaces the selection, and the second CTRL-V adds the second (copied) construct, which you will then replace the word bird (or Bird) with horse (or Horse), as is shown in Figure 12-30. On the next iteration of copy, paste, and replace, you can copy both constructs and paste both constructs (twice, which is thrice if you are using the CRTL-V method) and easily create all six event listening (outer) plus event handling (inner) structures.

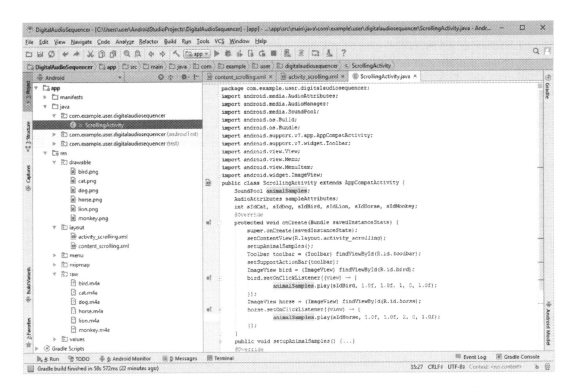

Figure 12-30. Copy and paste ImageView bird statement and event listener structure to create ImageView horse

Make sure that all of your ImageView names, digital image asset reference names, .setOnClickListener() calls off the ImageView object name, and sample ID integer data value names are all the same for each of the six Java constructs that you are duplicating. This is shown in the Java 8 code below using bold text. This code is also shown along with all of the other Java statements that are in the onCreate() method in Figure 12-31.

```java
ImageView bird = (ImageView) findViewById(R.id.bird);
bird.setOnClickListener(new View.OnClickListener() {
        @Override
        public void onClick(View view) {
            animalSamples.play(sIdBird, 1.0f, 1.0f, 1, 0, 1.0f);
        }
});
ImageView horse = (ImageView) findViewById(R.id.horse);
horse.setOnClickListener(new View.OnClickListener() {
        @Override
        public void onClick(View view) {
            animalSamples.play(sIdHorse, 1.0f, 1.0f, 1, 0, 1.0f);
        }
});
ImageView monkey = (ImageView) findViewById(R.id.monkey);
monkey.setOnClickListener(new View.OnClickListener() {
        @Override
        public void onClick(View view) {
            animalSamples.play(sIdMonkey, 1.0f, 1.0f, 1, 0, 1.0f);
        }
});
ImageView lion = (ImageView) findViewById(R.id.lion);
lion.setOnClickListener(new View.OnClickListener() {
        @Override
        public void onClick(View view) {
            animalSamples.play(sIdLion, 1.0f, 1.0f, 1, 0, 1.0f);
        }
});
ImageView dog = (ImageView) findViewById(R.id.dog);
dog.setOnClickListener(new View.OnClickListener() {
        @Override
        public void onClick(View view) {
            animalSamples.play(sIdDog, 1.0f, 1.0f, 1, 0, 1.0f);
        }
});
ImageView cat = (ImageView) findViewById(R.id.cat);
cat.setOnClickListener(new View.OnClickListener() {
        @Override
        public void onClick(View view) {
            animalSamples.play(sIdCat, 1.0f, 1.0f, 1, 0, 1.0f);
        }
});
```

A completed onCreate() method is seen in Figure 12-31, and implements the creation of the application's functionality using less than three dozen lines of code, including declarations at the top of your class. The method that you wrote was around a dozen lines of code, and including imports, you have added (or modified), nearly 50 lines of code (not including XML UI), allowing you to create a learning app for children using Android Studio's scrolling design pattern.

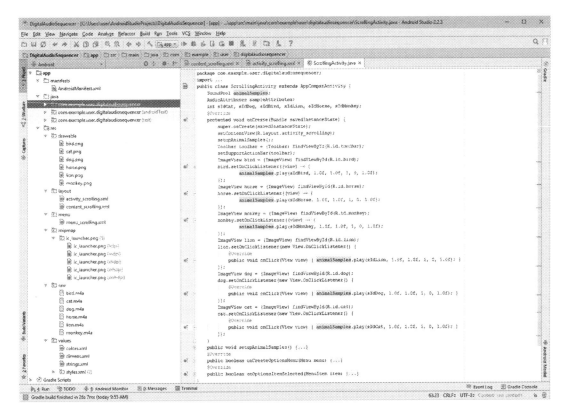

Figure 12-31. *Copy and paste all six animal ImageView instantiation and event listening and handling constructs*

Notice that Android Studio automatically implements the Java lambda expression format for the event listener constructs, shown in Figure 12-31, in the first three of your animal audio processing constructs. This is a coding shortcut that removes the (new View. OnClickListener) and replaces this part of the structure with the view object and an arrow and then replaces the { @Override public void onClick(View view) } inner structure with your (inner) event handling structure's programming logic, which greatly simplifies the event listening and event handling structure. In this case, this is animalSamples.play(sIdAnimal, 1.0f, 1.0f, 1, 0, 1.0f).

As you can see, implementing SoundPool is not so complex that an Absolute Beginner cannot understand it and harness its power, but it does require a decent understanding of digital audio concepts, optimization techniques, and the SoundPool class (engine), which is much more complex than what I have exposed you to here. I wanted to show you how to get it working and that it can indeed work in many applications even at a rudimentary level. If digital audio interests you there is a *Digital Audio Editing Fundamentals* (2015) title available from Apress.

There is a ton of fundamental digital audio effects (panning) and synthesis (pitch-shifting) that you can tap into using the left and right audio level (leftVolume, rightVolume) and sample rate settings. You can also loop audio (loop = -1 for infinite looping), or prioritize memory holding audio effects for your custom game engine design. Just remember, the less memory your samples use (the better optimized they are), the better SoundPool works.

This class also has some code optimization of its own to implement still, and probably a few bugs left to fix, so you may get some Gradle runtime warnings regarding audio playback speed, AudioAttributes, AudioManager (constants) used, and the like. If you get these, simply Google the error message and SoundPool and Android, in the same keyword string, and go to StackOverFlow, and see how other developers are solving the same problem. For instance I got an AUDIO_OUTPUT_FLAG_FAST denied by client, possibly because I set USAGE_GAME. The audio still worked perfectly, at least in an AVD emulator (which is the client in this case).

If you are going to use the more powerful multimedia engines in Android OS 7.1.1 and JavaFX8, such as SoundPool, MediaPlayer, PorterDuff, SVGPath, Vulkan, OpenGL ES, and i3D rendering, and the SQLite databases, some complexity and ongoing development bugs are to be expected as these advanced features are still being added, debugged, and hopefully, perfected.

Summary

In this chapter, you learned all about analog and digital audio concepts and techniques that will allow you to create digital audio applications for the Android 7.x OS, Android Wear, Android TV, and Android Auto platforms. I covered analog and digital audio concepts such as MIDI, waves, sample rate, frequency, PCM, codecs, and how to use PCM format as a baseline, and how to optimize it using sample frequency and stereo versus mono tracks, and how codecs can further reduce your APK file size with little audible loss of perceptible quality to end users.

You learned about how to use Audacity 2.1.2 to optimize digital audio samples that you found on the free audio sample website on the Internet. You learned how to create yet another of Android Studio's pure android design pattern templates, ScrollingActivity, and how to customize it for use as a children's animal learning application. You went onto the Internet and found free-for-commercial-use PCM audio samples at CD quality as well as matching images in HD quality to use in creating a young (age 2–6) children's educational application.

You learned about the Android SoundPool digital audio sequencing engine class, and how it allows you to add multiple audio samples to your Android application, so that you can add digital audio sequencing capabilities to your application. You learned about the various ins and outs of the SoundPool digital audio sequencing and synthesis engine, as well as about all of its caveats and considerations regarding how it works. You also learned about the related AudioManager and AudioAttributes classes, which contain constants that are used to configure the audio-related capabilities of your Android OS, Android TV, Wear, and Auto applications.

You added ImageView tags in your content_scrolling.xml user interface definition and declared and instantiated them in the ScrollingActivity.java code using existing code that Android Studio created for you and added event listening and handling for SoundPool.play(), replacing SnackBar. You created a setupAnimalSamples() method and added digital audio sound effects to each of the ImageView UI elements to teach kids sounds animals make.

Next, in Chapter 13, you'll learn all about **Service** classes in Android, which you actually got some exposure to in this chapter when you implemented the AudioManager object. An instance of this AudioManager object can be obtained using a call to Context.getSystemService(Context.AUDIO_SERVICE) (an Android Service). The next chapter is thus a logical extension to what you learned in this chapter, as well as previous chapters where a Service was used. As you can see, I'm trying to cover things in the most logical, optimal fashion.

Chapter 13

Android Services and Threads: Background Processing

In Chapter 12 on digital audio, you utilized the Android `AudioManager` class, which is a subclass of the Android `Service` class. In Chapter 11, you also learned about the Android `FullscreenActivity`, which has both threads (runnable) and Service features, which we will cover during this chapter. Also in this chapter, we will take a good look at the Android `Service` classes and related processing concepts, such as **processes** and **threads**.

Developers use the Android `Service` class and subclasses to perform background **asynchronous** operations. "Asynchronous" means that these operations, or more accurately, your Java code structures that utilize Service and thread classes, can "go off on their own" and process data streams or perform complex computation, 100% in the background, undetected by your application's user. Background Service asynchronous operations can do this without having to synchronize with an application user interface design, which is probably busy controlling how your application's content (its subject matter and objective) is being presented to your application's users.

Examples of using Android `Service` subclasses include the playback of long-form digital video and audio, using the `MediaPlayer` class, while your user is using other areas of the application, talking to servers, or databases, in the background, downloading data, managing file input-output streams, streaming new media content (digital video streams or digital audio streams), handling networking (SMTP and HTTP) protocol transactions, handling payment gateway transactions, real-time processing of GPS data, and similarly complex computational or data-processing tasks. The user would also be doing other things using their devices, such as answering phone calls. This chapter looks at the Android

Service class and all of the various characteristics of Android `Service` classes. We'll look at how their features, functions, settings, constants, and characteristics are declared in your Android application. Declaring a Service for usage is done in your `AndroidManifest.xml` file, by using the **<service>** tag.

This is one of the most complex topics in Android OS, and is not generally touched upon by Absolute Beginners; however, to cover Android development thoroughly, I had to include it, thus, these last two chapters will be somewhat advanced. This is because this topic involves advanced concepts like binding, synchronization, processes, processor cycles, threads, access control, permissions, and similarly advanced OS layer (under the hood at a core OS kernel level) topics, as these are all accomplished using the Linux Kernel (the lowest operating system layer) for the Android 7.1.1 OS. We looked at these different levels of the Android OS back in Chapter 3, so you can refer to Figure 3-1 if you need another "refresher" view of this Android OS and application hierarchy.

Tasks that are delegated to an Android Service also tend to be very processor intensive, so keep your end user's battery life in mind if you are going to develop processing-intensive applications. As you might guess, your two primary power drains on the Android battery are prolonged CPU processing and display screen backlight usage for long periods of time. Services are generally utilized when you need to handle things that need to be running in the background of an app, in parallel with Android user's real-time usage of your application, but not directly synchronized with (connected with) your end user's real-time usage of your application's user interface design.

Tasks that are delegated to Android's `Service` class are not typically tied to user interface and user experience tasks. This is because forcing concurrent (synchronized) processing might cause that user interface task, which is ultimately a user experience task, to become stilted or jerky. Overloading a processor ultimately will cause stilted playback, and will not portray a smooth user interface response, and will therefore not result in a positive user experience.

Android's Service Class: Characteristics

In Android, a Service can be defined as an application component that can perform CPU processor-intensive functions in the **background**. The Service is provided without the need for any user interface design, or any Activity display screen front end. A Service does not require any user interaction in order to accomplish its processing tasks. As you might imagine, like anything else, an Android `Service` object is created using the class in Android named, you guessed it, `Service`, in the Android app package (so, you import `android.app.Service`).

The Android application starts a `Service` object by using an **Intent** object, and the `Service` object will continue to process in the background, even if the Android device owner switches over to a different Android application to do something else, for instance, answering phone calls, replying to incoming email, or accepting social media connection requests. Any Android application component can **bind** to a started `Service` object and then later interact with it. Components can also perform **interprocess communication**, which you may have heard referred to as simply IPC. We will be taking a closer look at processes and threads in the next section of the chapter, after the overview of the Android `Service` class and primary `Service` object attributes.

Binding is an advanced programming concept, that involves establishing a real-time connection between two separate application component processes. Once bound, the processes will alert each other whenever something has changed in the other one. An alerted process can then check, and see if an update needs to be made based on that change. If you are a game programmer, you will commonly define a bind between the scoreboard UI design and your game scoring logic engine, for instance, so your scoreboard numeric read-out will change in real time, as the game is being played. You'll bind a Service so that your application can follow progress regarding tasks.

An Android Service usually will take one of two forms—either "bound" or "started." Let's start with the started Service, as it is the most common. An Android Service becomes started when an application component, such as an `Activity`, specifically starts it by using a method call. This is done by calling the `.startService()` method.

Once it has started, a Service can run in the background indefinitely, even in a scenario where a component that started the Service gets subsequently destroyed, that is, removed from system memory. This can be done by either the application program logic, or by the Android OS if it becomes necessary for the overall function of the device. A started Service performs a single operation and does not return a result to the calling entity, much like a void method performs its task without returning anything to the object calling the method. For example, a started Service might download (or upload) data files over your network. When your started Service operation is completed, the Service object should automatically stop itself. This helps optimize Android operating system resources, such as device CPU processing cycles and system memory usage, which should always be conserved.

A bound Service is created when an Android application component binds to a Service. This is accomplished by calling a `.bindService()` method. The bound Service offers a **client-server** interface that allows components to interact with the bound Service. Just like with a client-server relationship, you can send requests, get results, and you can even do all of this across (between) different processes, using interprocess communication (IPC). A bound Service remain in system memory as long as other Android application components are still bound to it. Multiple application components can bind to a bound Service at the same time. When all of these application components unbind from the Service, that Service is destroyed: that is, removed from the device's system memory.

We will take a look at both of these types of Service formats, as well as a **hybrid** approach, where your Service can work in both of these ways, and at the same time. What this means is that you can start your Service, so that it is a started Service and can run indefinitely, and later allow it to be bound. Whether the Android Service is specified as started or bound is determined by whether you have implemented a couple of the more often used Service class **callback methods**. For instance, the `Service` class `.onStartCommand()` method will allow components to start a Service, and the `.onBind()` method will allow components to bind to that Service.

Starting in 64-bit Android OSes (5.0 and later versions) there is also a **scheduled** Service. A Service can be scheduled when an object created with the Android JobScheduler class launches the Service. You can use this JobScheduler class by registering jobs, and specifying their requirements for network access and execution timing. The Android OS will then optimally schedule these jobs for execution, at the most optimal time. This JobScheduler class provides methods that allow developers to specify the Service execution parameters. The JobScheduler class and a scheduled Service is more advanced than the basic Service, but I wanted to cover scheduled Service classes here, so that you know it is an option, for more advanced Service scheduling, once you become a more advanced Android application developer, that is.

Regardless of whether your application's Service is started, bound, hybrid (both started and bound), or scheduled, it is possible that other application components can utilize that Service, even from a separate application, if you allow it. This is similar to the way that any of your application components can start (launch) an Activity subclass, by starting it using an Intent object, even if that Activity is not a part of your package. We covered using Intent objects way back in Chapter 7. You will see how Android apps use Intent objects to start a Service subclass, which we will create during this chapter named AmbientAudioService. This class will use a background service to play background ambient audio with Android's MediaPlayer component.

Controlling Your Service: Privacy and Priority

Service subclasses will run at a higher **priority** than inactive Activity subclasses whose UI is not active or being viewed on the device. Because of this fact, it is far less likely that the Android operating system will terminate a Service class than it will an Activity class. If your Activity subclass is **active**, or currently in use by your user on their display screen, it will obviously possess the highest priority, as the assumption is that the user is currently and actively using it to interface (hence the term "user interface") with the application, and therefore with the Android hardware device.

It is important to note that you can declare your Service as **private** using your Android manifest XML file. This will **block access** to your Service subclass from other external Android applications. This is usually a good idea for security reasons, which I also discuss in the chapter. Android developers will often do this as a programming or development best practice, unless other Android applications will absolutely need to use their Service.

A Service subclass, as a default, always runs inside the primary thread of the host application's primary process. This is often called a UI thread, as it runs the UI. Services that run inside of this primary application process are often termed local Services. You will be reading about processes and threads in the next section of the chapter.

A common misconception among Android programmers is that Android Service subclasses always run on their own separate threads. This is certainly possible, if you configure your Service subclass in that way. The Service does not, in fact, by default create its own thread, and thus won't run in a separate thread, unless you specify that.

What this means is that if your Service is going to do any CPU-intensive work (such as decoding streaming data in real time) or blocking operations (such as real-time network access over busy network protocols), you should create a new thread within your Service in order to do that type of processing so UI performance is not affected.

It is important to note that you may not need to use another thread for your Service class apart from the thread it is on (using already); for instance, in the example in this chapter we play a music file using the MediaPlayer in a Service without needing to spawn another thread. The only way to determine if this is needed is to first try using a Service class for your background processing, and then, if it affects user experience, consider using a thread.

Processes or Threads: Foundational Information

When one of your Android application components, such as the MainActivity class, starts, and your application does not have any other components currently running, the Android operating system will launch a new **process** for your application using the Linux kernel. This single thread of execution is commonly called the **UI thread**. A process can generate or launch (I often use the popular industry term **spawn**) more than one thread. There is a **Thread** class (and therefore, a Thread object can be created) for the Android OS. As a rule, all of your Android application components will run inside of this same initial process and thread. This is generally termed the main thread, the primary thread, or the UI thread. If one of your Android application components starts, and Android sees that a primary process already exists for your application, due to the fact that another component from your application already exists, the new component will also be started within that same application process and thread.

To start your own thread, you must do so specifically within your Java code by creating a Thread object. You can also have different components in your application run in separate processes, and you can create additional threads for any process. This is what is usually done with Android Service subclasses. The Service process for Android is created using XML markup, unlike the Thread object, which is created using Java.

You will be taking a look at creating a <service> using XML, during the next section of the chapter. Creating a Thread object, and how to do this, and when to do so, is currently beyond the scope of this Absolute Beginner title. There are entire books written on the subject of multi-process programming, threads, binding, and similar topics for professional Android developers; however, those are on the other end of the spectrum from this book.

The default functionality in the Android OS is all of your Android application components will run in the same process used to launch your application. Most of the bootstrap Android applications will not need to change this behavior, and should not interfere with this default application launching and running functionality, unless there is a very compelling functional reason (which would be too advanced to cover in this book title) for doing so.

For advanced applications (which we are not going to be covering in this book), I will cover this concept here, to be thorough regarding Android OS and its processes. If you happen to find yourself in development situations where you absolutely need to control which Android process/thread a certain application component belongs to, and functions in, you can specify your own custom processes in your application's `AndroidManifest.xml` file. The core difference is threads run in a shared memory space, whereas processes run in their own memory space.

Let's take a look at how to spawn a process using the `android:process` parameter inside of the four major areas of Android. These four major functional areas each implemented by using a superclass, include the Activity, the Service, the broadcast receiver (communication messages), and the content provider (database storage). These use the Android OS `<activity>`, the `<service>`, the `<receiver>`, and the `<provider>` parent tags, respectively.

Spawn a Process: android:process XML Parameter

The `AndroidManifest.xml` application component tags for each major type of application component, whether it is an `Activity` `<activity>` tag, a Service `<service>` tag, a broadcast receiver `<receiver>` tag, or the content provider `<provider>` tag, can include the optional `android:process` parameter. This parameter will allow you to control the process that a component will run inside of (or under, if you prefer to visualize it that way).

An `android:process` parameter should be utilized to specify the process under which the application component needs to run. You can set up this process parameter in such a way that each of the application's components run inside its own process, or you can "mix and match" components and processes in such a way that some of your application components will share a given process, while others will not share that process and would even have their own process (memory space) altogether.

If you want to get really complex, you could set these `android:process` parameters so that components from different Android applications can execute together inside the same Android process (memory space). This can only be accomplished when those particular applications share the same **Linux user ID**, and which are signed with the same certificates. This topic is also too complex for this book; I mention it here just so that you know about it, in case you wish to research it further.

It is interesting to note that the global **<application>** tag in the Android manifest XML file will also accept an **android:process** parameter. Using the `android:process` parameter inside of your `<application>` tag will set the default process value for your application, which would then be applied to all of your application's components, which are located inside of the XML application component definition (nested) hierarchy. Of course, this would not include those application components that then utilize their own `android:process` parameter. In this situation, the application component child tag that utilized the `android:process` parameter to specify a different process for that particular application component would override the global or default process that you set as the process for your application to use via the `android:process` parameter inside the `<application>` tag. If you want all your components, except for one or two, to share the same custom process, define that process in your `<application>` tag and then override it selectively using one of the component child tags with `android:process`.

It is important to note that the Android OS has the option to shut down any of your processes at any given time. This is so that it can efficiently manage your user's system hardware resources (memory and processing cycles). This could be important when system memory is running low or if the memory used by your process is required by other processes that have a higher priority level, or are receiving more usage (attention) from the end user.

Application components running inside of a process that gets terminated by Android are subsequently destroyed (which means they're removed from memory). Not to worry, as any of these processes can be restarted again, at a later time, for any of the application components that still require that something be accomplished for or by a user. In fact, that is exactly why the savedInstanceState Bundle object that you are now familiar with is often utilized.

When deciding which process to kill, the Android OS weighs their **relative importance** to a user. For example, Android more readily shuts down processes that are hosting Activity subclasses that are no longer visible on the screen, as compared to a process hosting a visible Activity that is being used. This decision regarding whether or not to terminate a process depends on the **state** of the components running in that process. The rules Android uses to decide which process to terminate are important to understand, so, let's dive deeper into this topic next.

The Process Life Cycle: Keeping a Process Alive

Android 7.1.1 OS will try to keep your application processes in its system memory for as long as it can. However, it sometimes needs to destroy some older processes running in the OS. This is done in order to reclaim the system memory resources for newer or higher priority processes. After all, so many Android devices ship with only 2 or, at most, 4 gigabytes of main system memory; this may change in 2018 with iTV sets featuring the nVidia Tegra Parker chipset and 8 or more gigabytes of memory. Android system memory can fill up fairly quickly, as users simultaneously play games, launch apps, read e-books, stream music, and place (and receive) phone calls.

Even when iTV set devices start to ship with 8 gigabytes of main memory, you will still have memory management issues, and using processes and threads provide the tools for optimizing these memory management issues, so it is important that you understand how processes are handled in Android. In case you are wondering, a 32-bit OS will only address 3.24 MB of system memory, so Pre-Android 5 devices only have 1 to 3 megabytes! The 64-bit version of Android (5, 5.1, 6, 7, 7.1.1 and later) is based upon 64-bit Linux and 64-bit Java, and has no memory limitation.

The way that the Android OS determines which of its processes to keep, and which of its processes to terminate, is via a **priority hierarchy**. Android will place each running process into this priority hierarchy, which is based on each of the components running in the **process queue**, as well as the current status (running, idle, or stopped) of those application components. The way that Android removes processes from this process priority hierarchy, which is ultimately how memory is cleared, and reallocated, for any Android device, is that the process with the lowest priority (or least importance) is terminated first. Then the next lowest priority process is terminated, then the next lowest, until system resources that are needed for a higher priority process have been recovered for use.

There are **five** process priority levels in this priority hierarchy. Once you know what these are, you will see how practical the process priority hierarchy is, and you'll have an overview of how **Service** subclasses (background processing) or **Activity** subclasses (user interfaces) fit into this process priority schema. Let's get into this now, before we take a look at how to implement a Service using XML markup and Java code.

This process (threading) information is quite important to understand for any Android developer at any level, from Absolute Beginner through an Expert Professional, even if you don't implement custom processes in your Android 7 applications. The five process priority levels are summarized in Table 13-1 for your quick reference.

Table 13-1. Android's five process priority levels, and what type of priority characteristics they exhibit regarding an app

Process Priority	Characteristics
Foreground process	The primary process that is currently actively processing your User Interface and Content
Visible process	A secondary process that will still have an effect regarding what is visible on the screen
Service process	A started process that contains a background processing service that is currently processing
Background process	A process containing an activity that is not currently visible on the device screen
Empty process	A process that does not currently hold any active application components whatsoever

Let's take a look at each of these in greater detail, so you better understand what these priority levels represent.

Foreground Process

The highest priority process level is called the **foreground process**. This is the primary process that is currently running (actively processing), and that is required for the application task that the user is currently engaging in.

A process will be considered a foreground process if it contains an activity (user interface) that a user is actively interfacing with, or if it hosts a service which is bound to that activity that the user is interfacing with. Note that an activity (subclass) in Android OS in an Activity, and that a service (subclass) in Android OS is a Service.

A process will also be considered to be a foreground process if it is actively processing a Service subclass that is running in the foreground, which means that the Service object generated by your subclass implementation has already called the .startForeground() method.

If the `Service` object is currently executing one of the `.onCreate()`, `.onDestroy()`, or `.onStart()` Service life cycle callbacks, which you will be learning about during this chapter, or is broadcasting a `BroadcastReceiver` object that is calling its `.onReceive()` method, it will be given a top foreground process priority-level status in Android.

In an optimal Android operating system scenario, only a few foreground processes will be running at any given time. This is not common as Android device users tend to invoke several different applications and functions at the same time, which is why devices such as smartphones often become hot and lose their power charge rapidly. Regardless of proper use (or overuse), Android processes will be terminated only as a last resort, if the system memory gets scarce, and the Android OS cannot continue to run optimally.

Visible Process

The next highest priority process level is a **visible process**. This is a process that doesn't contain any foreground process components, but that can still affect what the users are seeing on their displays. A process is deemed to be visible if it contains an activity that is not in the foreground, but that is still visible to the user display screen. An example of this would be an activity whose `.onPause()` method has been invoked. Another example would be a foreground process activity that starts a dialog that permits another activity to be seen in the background.

A process that contains a Service subclass that has been bound to a visible process would also be able to get visible process priority. A visible process is considered to be almost as important as a foreground process. Thus a visible process is not terminated, unless that is absolutely required to keep all foreground processes running in the Android OS memory space. Visible and foreground processes are thus extremely similar in the Android OS.

Service Process

The middle priority process level in the five levels is a **Service process**. This is a process that contains a Service that has been started with the `.startService()` method call, but that Android has not classified in either of the two higher-process priority-level categories. The `Service` class processes, because they have no user interface screen, and are running asynchronously in the background, are not directly tied to anything that a user sees on a display, or interacts with. They are important to Android apps development, which is why I cover them in this chapter.

Since a Service is still performing a task that the end user wants to complete, such as playing an album of music in the background, or downloading a file over their network, Android will keep a process that contains a Service object active, unless there is not enough memory to support them along with foreground and visible processes.

Background Process

The second lowest priority process level is the **background process**. This is a process that contains an `Activity` subclass that is not currently visible to the end user. An example of this is when the `Activity` subclass `.onStop()` method has been called. Note that a background process by its very nature should not affect the user experience.

Since a background process has no detectible impact on user experience, Android will terminate these whenever it becomes necessary to recover system memory for any higher priority-level process (foreground, visible, or Service). If there are several background processes running, Android keeps background processes in something called the **LRU** (Least Recently Used) list. This list guarantees that a process containing the Activity most recently utilized by the user is the last process to be terminated.

Note that `Activity` subclasses that implement their life cycle methods correctly, and save their current states using the `savedInstanceState Bundle` object, will not have any discernible effect on user experience due to termination. This is because when a user navigates back to their UI screen for that Activity, a process will again be started for it, and your `Activity` subclass will restore all of its visible states. This is done by reloading your `savedInstanceState Bundle` object.

Empty Process

The lowest priority process level is the **empty process**. This is a process that does not hold any currently active application components. If you are wondering why these empty processes would be kept in system memory at all, the **strategic reason** to keep the empty process alive is for **memory caching** optimization, which improves the startup time the next time a component, most probably an `Activity`, needs to be loaded (run) inside the process.

The Android operating system will terminate these empty processes once system memory is full in an attempt to balance the overall system memory resources between the various process caches, and with its underlying Linux OS kernel memory caches, which are at such a low level that Android 7.1.1 developers cannot directly access them.

Increases in the Priority-Level Ranking

It is important to notice that process priority-level rank might be increased because another process is dependent on a process. Any Android process that is currently servicing another process cannot be ranked lower than the process that it's servicing. This is a very logical ranking behavior, if you think about it for a minute.

Let's say your content provider (which is a database or data store, which we will be covering in more detail in the next Chapter 14) that is contained in Process 01 is busy providing content to a user interface `Activity` in Process 02, or a `Service` object in Process 01 is bound to an application component in Process 02. In these scenarios, Process 01 will always be considered by Android OS to be as important as Process 02. This is logical because the two processes are acting together as one unified user experience, and thus should be ranked equally.

The next section takes a bird's-eye view at **threads**, which are even lower level than processes, and can be utilized within a process (but only implemented using Java 8 code) to schedule processor-intensive or user interface tasks. This is very advanced information, and only included in this book so that you have a comprehensive overview of this "under the hood" programming topic. It is not expected that, as an Android 7.1.1 Absolute Beginner, you will write Java 8 code that controls thread execution.

Thread Caveats: Don't Interfere with UI Thread

After Android launches your application, using the `AndroidManifest.xml` file, the operating system will spawn a thread of execution. This main thread is in charge of dispatching and managing system-level and application-level events, which you learned about during Chapter 7. The events take place between the operating system and your app, such as an incoming phone call, as well as between your user interface widget event handlers and your application Java 8 logic, like clicks on an animal image to trigger audio.

The main thread also controls drawing graphics, playing video, audio, or animation assets to an `Activity` display screen, so it's doing a lot of processing. This is a reason you might need to spawn your own thread, if something you want to do with your Android application might overload the heavy workload that is on the main (primary) thread. Unless (or until) you spawn your second thread, the main thread will be running your entire application.

The main or primary thread is also often referred to as the **UI thread**, or user interface thread. This is because it's the thread inside of which the application components interact with components in the Android UI toolkit. The Android UI toolkit includes all the components, as classes, contained in the `android.widget` as well as the `android.view` packages, which you learned about during Chapters 6 through 9. All of these Android UI toolkit components will run inside of, or under, this main process, and are handled (managed) inside of this UI thread.

For this reason methods that respond to event handling callbacks, such as the `.onKeyDown()` event handler used to report keyboard hardware interaction, or one of the life-cycle callback methods, such as the `.start()` method or the `.pause()` method, will always run inside the UI thread. This UI thread is contained within the main process for your Android 7.1.1 application. When the application dispatches intensive processing in response to user interface interactions, a single thread model can result in a slow user experience performance. This is why you must learn how to utilize threads properly, if you are going to do advanced Android application development in the future.

The reason for this is obvious. If extensive processing is happening in your UI thread, performing long-winded operations, such as network access, complex calculations, or SQLite database queries, this will block some portion of the user interface response processing. These more complex operations will reduce the amount of processing cycles that are available to the UI, and will essentially block the UI-related events from being smoothly, that is, quickly, processed. When application UI threads become blocked, UI events cannot be dispatched for handling, and this includes drawing graphics, playing samples, and animating elements to the display screen. From a user experience standpoint, an application may appear to hang, which is not desirable and is not at all professional.

It is important to note that if your application blocks the UI thread for more than a few seconds (more than five seconds, actually) the user will be shown a dialog containing an undesirable (from a user experience standpoint) "**Application is Not Responding**" dialog (developers often abbreviate this, and call it the "**A N R**"dialog). It is important to note that the Android 7.x UI toolkit is not currently what is known as **thread-safe**. For this reason, you should not at any time manipulate your application's user interface elements from inside a worker thread.

A **worker thread** is any non-UI thread, and is also commonly referred to as the **background thread**. In other words, it is a thread that you have spawned using your application's Java code. This would be done in order to off-load intensive, worker bee background processing, so that your UI will continue to function smoothly.

Just remember, the first rule of Android thread processing is that you must do all manipulation to your user interface elements from the inside of the UI thread, which is the application's main, or primary, thread.

The second key rule is more general, and it is simply to not block the UI thread at any time for any reason. This is why you are able to create worker threads, in case you need to do something that may block the UI thread. By block, I mean to stop a UI thread from smoothly processing the application UI functions and content rendering.

Should Android Apps Use Services or Threads?

An Android Service is an application component that can run in the background, even when your users are not interacting with the application. If you need to perform work outside of your main UI thread, but only while the user is interacting with the application user interface, that is when you should create an Android Thread object within that class in your application. This is commonly used for more advanced applications, such as 3D games.

This would be done by instantiating a **HandlerThread** or an **AsyncTask** object. If you declare a Thread object in your class, you do not have to go to the trouble of declaring an entire Android Service subclass in the manifest. If you look at it using the "static versus dynamic" standpoint, which I have been teaching you over the course of this book, you are implementing a thread dynamically, in Java 8 code, whereas you implement a Service statically, using XML markup to declare it before use in your Android manifest XML file, so Android can optimize it!

Let's say that you wanted to stream some music from a music Service while your Activity is running. What you do is create a Thread object using the .onCreate() method, start it running using the .onStart() method, and stop it by using the .onStop() method. As mentioned, you will probably want to utilize a more refined Android Thread subclass, such as the AsyncTask or HandlerThread class, instead of using a more general Thread class, which is generally used as a superclass in order to create more application-friendly thread-related subclasses.

So when would you use Service subclasses over spawning Thread objects in existing classes, you might wonder? If you remember from the previous section, Android processes containing a Service subclass will be prioritized higher than processes that utilize a background processing activity (Thread object). For this reason, if your apps are going to undertake extensive processing, access, or streaming operations, then you'll want to start a Service component subclass for that operation, rather than simply create a Thread subclass object like an AsyncTask.

This is an especially relevant consideration if your background process is going to outlast your Activity screen. As an example, an Activity that is uploading a video that you created using the Android Camera class to a web server would want to utilize the Service subclass methodology to perform this upload. This is so that this upload process will continue in the background and finish uploading even if the user leaves that video capture Activity.

Thus, the primary reason that you will want to use a Service subclass over a Thread object, is because using the Service component will guarantee that your processing operation will have at least the Service process priority level, regardless of what happens to your Activity subclass. If you use the Thread subclass approach, your application could drop below the Service process priority-level based upon your end user's usage or interaction, because with that approach, your Activity subclass only contains a Thread subclass and not a Service subclass.

Next, you will learn how to write a Service subclass, and how to call it, using an Intent object. You will do this using the ScrollingActivity Activity subclass that you created in Chapter 12. You will implement the Android Service class life cycle by creating an ambient background audio player background Service component named **AmbientAudioService. java**.

This will be a Service subclass that will extend the Service class, by utilizing the Java **extends** keyword inside of the class declaration. You will code the main Service class life cycle methods in your Java code, including onCreate(), onStart(), and onDestroy() methods. You will leverage an Android Intent object in one of these in order to start a background Service, which will play background audio for that DigitalAudioSequencer Android application project you created in Chapter 12.

Finally, you will also look at how to add the <service> tag to the AndroidManifest.xml file, and you'll test your background audio Service subclass inside of your Nexus 5 AVD emulator. This will show you how to mix audio using SoundPool (Chapter 12), MediaPlayer (Chapter 11), and Service (Chapter 13) Android superclasses.

As you can see, you are learning more advanced topics and techniques as this book progresses, as I am attempting to take you from an Absolute Beginner, to someone who is familiar with how Android works, what Android Studio can do, and how advanced you can become during your journey from Absolute Beginner to a working Android developer. To do this, I must cover some topics beyond the Absolute Beginner experience level.

Creating a Service: AmbientAudioService

Let's take a look at how you can direct Android Studio to code a Service class for you, using the Android Studio 2.3 IDE, along with the proper work process, which can be seen in Figure 13-1.

1. Open your **DigitalAudioSequencer** project in Android Studio 2.3 and right-click on your Project pane's /app/java/com.example. user.digitalaudiosequencer/ folder, since that is where you want this **AmbientAudioService.java** file, which you are having Android Studio create, located.

2. Next, select the **New ➤ Service ➤ Service** menu sequence, as shown on the left-hand side of Figure 13-1.

3. This menu selection will open up the **New Android Component – Configure Component** dialog, which is shown in Figure 13-1 on the right-hand side.

4. Name your Service subclass **AmbientAudioService** and select the **Enabled** check box, below the **Class Name** field, and deselect the **Exported** check box, as only this DigitalAudioSequencer project will be using this Service subclass.

5. Finally, click the **Finish** button, which will tell Android Studio to generate the code for you, and open up a tab in Android Studio named AmbientAudioActivity.java with bootstrap code. We will be learning more about the characteristics of the Service by examining the code and then modifying it to fit our particular ambient audio background application for that code.

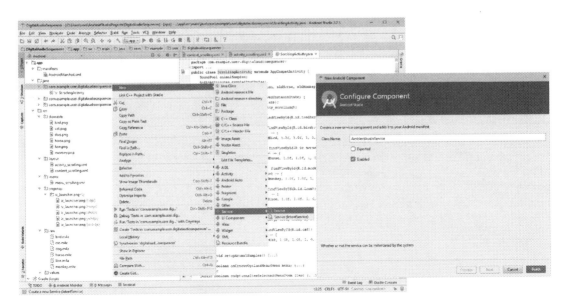

Figure 13-1. Use New ➤ Service ➤ Service menu sequence, and name class AmbientAudioService in Configure Component

6. Take a look at the `AmbientAudioService` class Java code, shown in Figure 13-2, which we will be adding functionality to during the remainder of the chapter, after we take a closer look at some of the involved Service class details regarding the Android Service-related classes.

7. First look at the **import** statements to ascertain what Android classes are utilized to make this Service subclass work. The first is the `Service` superclass that this class is based upon, so obviously we need those methods, constants, and so on which are in the **android. app** package. The second in the `Intent` class, so that we can use `Intent` objects to trigger the Service. The third is the `IBinder` class, so that if you need to create a bound Service, you can create `iBinder` objects to use with the `public IBinder onBind(Intent intent)` method structure, which is also provided for you in this bootstrap class, in case you want to utilize it.

8. After the `import` statements we have the class declaration as public and extending `Service` using the `public class AmbientAudioService extends Service` Java statement.

9. After the class declaration, Android Studio has written an (empty) required constructor method using this empty Java method declaration and body:

```
public AmbientAudioService() {...}
```

10. As you can see, Android Studio has given you a code infrastructure for everything you might need to implement a basic `Service` subclass, which is a great head start for an Absolute Beginner. We will be adding objects and methods to this class to implement a `MediaPlayer` that can be played as a background Service.

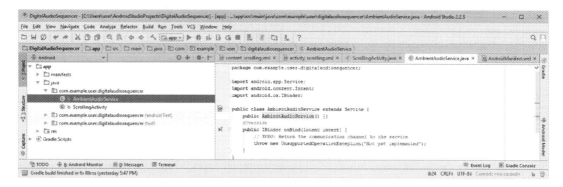

Figure 13-2. Android Studio creates your bootstrap AmbientAudioService subclass using the Android Service superclass

Next, let's take a look at how your Android manifest needs to be set up for a Service class, and any Service subclass that you utilize or create, such as the one we will be creating during the rest of this chapter, to function.

Configuring AndroidManifest to add a <service>

Whenever you add an Android Activity, Service, content provider, or broadcast receiver component into your Android application, you need to declare it for use inside of your Android manifest XML file, which is utilized to define, configure, secure, permission, optimize, specify (hardware device support in the Google Play store), and launch the Android application.

We will take a look at this as it relates to Service, using the <service> tag, next, and see if Android Studio 2.3 added the correct markup to the AndroidManifest.xml. Right-click on your **AndroidManifest.xml** file, which is inside of the project's **/app/manifests/** folder, and select **Jump to Source**. Inside of the <application> tag, there should be a child <service> tag after the first <activity> tag and before closing </application> and </manifest> tags.

The <service> tag Android Studio inserted should implement the android:name=". AmbientAudioService" parameter, which allows Android OS to wire up the Service subclass that will utilize the Service object. Based on your dialog selections, Android Studio also included an android:enabled="true"and an android:exported="false"parameter, to keep your Service private, as a standard security measure, unless you're creating a Service for other apps to use. The <service> tag should look like the following markup:

```
<service
    android:name=".AmbientAudioService"
    android:enabled="true"
    android:exported="false" >
</service>
```

The Android Studio modified AndroidManifest.xml file Service markup is shown highlighted in orange and blue at the bottom of Figure 13-3.

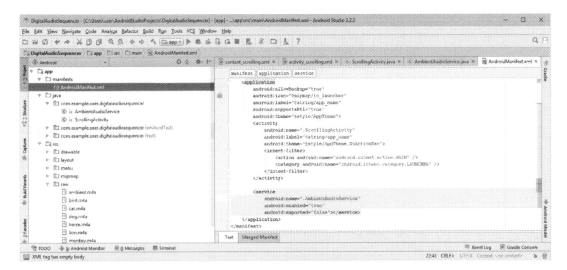

Figure 13-3. Open AndroidManifest.xml file to see how Android Studio added a <service> tag under the <application> tag

Next, let's take a closer look at the Android Service class, and see what we are allowed to add to the basic Service class Java code that is seen in Figure 13-2 to create a MediaPlayer background digital audio player Service subclass, using our bootstrap AmbientAudioService class Android Studio just created.

Service: Background Processing Services

The public abstract class Service extends the ContextWrapper class and implements the ComponentCallbacks2 interface. This is the base class for all Service subclasses. Service has 33 known direct subclasses, which you can use directly, or you can subclass Service and code your own, as we are going to do. Its class hierarchy looks like the following:

```
java.lang.Object
  > android.content.Context
    > android.content.ContextWrapper
      > android.app.Service
```

We will use a simple but popular example of how to use a MediaPlayer inside of a Service to play a one megabyte one minute MPEG4 audio in a seamless loop, just to give you an idea regarding how a Service works.

Configure AmbientAudioService: Play Audio

Let's go into your bootstrap AmbientAudioService.java class, which Android Studio has written for you, and customize it to play a short ambient background audio loop using the Android MediaPlayer class and a one megabyte, highly optimized, MPEG-4 digital audio asset. I am doing this here as a follow-on to Chapter 12, using the same project, to show you how to provide looped long-form background audio for the animal samples.

1. Declare a MediaPlayer object at the top of your AmbientAudioService class, right after the class declaration, as is shown in Figure 13-4. If you type "MediaP" you will get a pop-up helper, where you can double-click on the **MediaPlayer (android.media)** option. Android Studio will then add this object declaration for you, and will additionally write your import android.media.MediaPlayer; statement, which can be seen at the top of Figure 13-5.

2. Name this MediaPlayer object ambientAudioPlayer, and finish off the Java declaration using a semi-colon. You can see the finished MediaPlayer ambientAudioPlayer; declaration in Figure 13-6.

Figure 13-4. *Declare a MediaPlayer object at the top of the AmbientAudioService class, and name it ambientAudioPlayer*

3. The next step is to add an onCreate() method structure where you will instantiate your MediaPlayer object. Add a line of code under the AmbientAudioService() constructor method that Android Studio created for you, and type "on," and in the pop-up helper drop-down menu double-click the public void onCreate() {} option, to insert it into the body of your class. Android Studio will code a bootstrap onCreate() method for the class which should look like the following Java code structure:

```
public void onCreate() {
        super.onCreate();
}
```

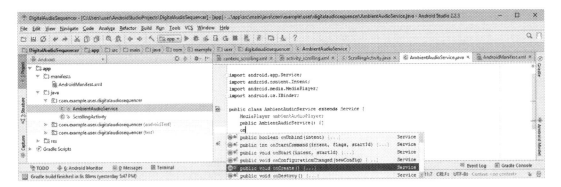

Figure 13-5. *Add a line below the AmbientAudioService() constructor, type "on," and select the public void onCreate() method*

4. Add a line of code underneath the `super.onCreate();` superclass method call and type the word "ambient," and then double-click on the **ambientAudioPlayer MediaPlayer** option to insert the `MediaPlayer` object, so that you can instantiate it using an equals sign and the `.create()` method.

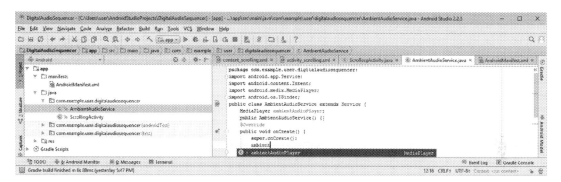

Figure 13-6. *add an ambientAudioPlayer MediaPlayer object after the super.onCreate( ) method in an onCreate( ) method*

5. After you add the equals sign, then type "Me," so that Android Studio's pop-up coding helper drop-down menu will appear. Notice that there is an option on the list to code the entire object plus the method call (including dot notation) needed to instantiate the `MediaPlayer` object.

6. Select your **MediaPlayer.create(Context context, int resId) (android.media)** option, as shown in Figure 13-7, and double-click on this, to tell Android Studio 2.3 to write this instantiation Java code structure for you. You will use the Java **this** keyword to pass the current class's `Context` object, and the `/app/res/raw` resource ID path to the `ambient.m4a` file, using **R.raw.ambient** for the second method parameter. This will instantiate the `MediaPlayer`, and then all you have to do next is to configure the `MediaPlayer` object, and we can move on to create some of the other class methods for starting the `MediaPlayer`, stopping the `MediaPlayer`, and destroying (removing from system memory) the `MediaPlayer` object when the application is done being used.

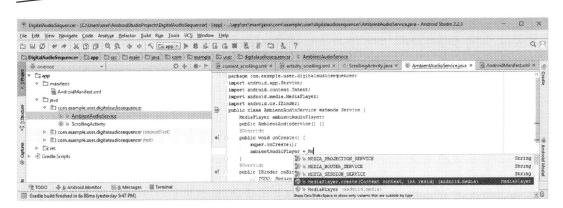

Figure 13-7. Select the MediaPlayer.create(Context context, int resid) (android.media) option, to code the instantiation

7. Copy the **ambient.m4a** audio asset into the DigitalAudioSequencer project **app/res/raw/** folder from the book repository. I omit the figure here, as you've seen how to do this in some previous chapters. The asset will show up in Android Studio 2.3, as shown on the left side of Figure 13-8.

8. Once the audio asset is visible to Android Studio, you will be ready to reference the digital audio asset in your **MediaPlayer(Context, ResourceID)** code construct. Add the Java **this** keyword and resource path to the .create() method, and then add a **.setLooping()** method, and set it to a Boolean value of **true** to configure the MediaPlayer to loop the background audio. The Java method structure should look like the following once you are finished configuring it:

```
@Override
public void onCreate() {
    super.onCreate();
    ambientAudioPlayer = MediaPlayer.create(this, R.raw.ambient);
    ambientAudioPlayer.setLooping(true);
}
```

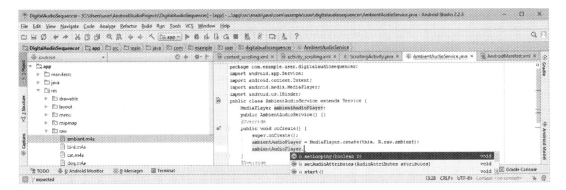

Figure 13-8. Add the ambientAudioPlayer.setLooping(true) method call to complete your onCreate( ) method structure

9. The contents of your onStartCommand() method, which we'll add here next, will be called when you use the startService() method call in the onCreate() method of your MainActivity. This will amount to adding a MediaPlayer.start() method call inside of the onStartCommand() method. Add a line of code under your onCreate() method construct, and again type "on," and select the public int onStartCommand(intent, flags, startId) {...} option, and then double-click on it, and have Android Studio 2.3 code it inside of the AmbientAudioService class, as is shown in Figure 13-9.

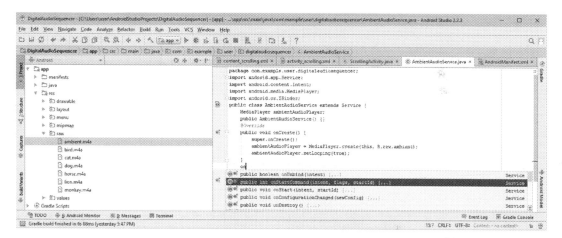

Figure 13-9. Add a line of text, type "on," and select the Service class onStartCommand(intent, flags, startId) method call

10. Android studio will code your onStartCommand() method, which is shown in Figure 13-10, including a **return super.onStartCommand(intent, flags, startId)** statement up to the superclass, passing up all of the parameters coming into this method call. Add your ambientAudioPlayer object, and then hit the period key, and select a **void start()** method call option. Do this **before** your return statement, as any code after the return will not be executed.

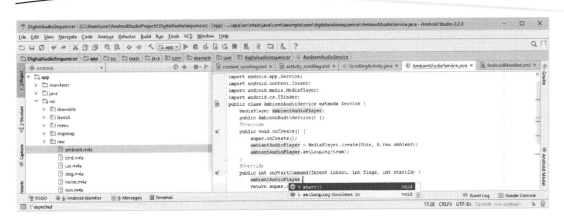

Figure 13-10. Add an ambientAudioPlayer object before the return statement, type a period, and select a start( ) method

11. Once you're done adding the `ambientAudioPlayer` code statement,
the method looks like this:

```
@Override
public int onStartCommand(Intent intent, int flags, int startId) {
    ambientAudioPlayer.start();
    return super.onStartCommand(intent, flags, startId);
}
```

12. Next, add in a line of code after the `onStartCommand()` method, and
type "on," as shown in Figure 13-11, and have Android Studio code
the body of a **public void onDestroy() {...}** method for you.

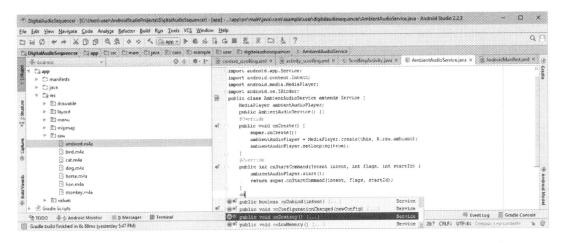

*Figure 13-11. Add a line of text, type "on," and select the public void onDestroy( ) method call from the Service
superclass*

13. The first statement in the onDestroy() method should stop the MediaPlayer from playing your ambient audio loop, using the **ambientAudioPlayer.stop()** method call, shown in Figure 13-12.

14. The second statement in the onDestroy() method should remove the MediaPlayer object from the system memory using the **ambientAudioPlayer.release()** method, which releases system memory for other Android operating systems or application purposes.

15. Make sure that the **super.onDestroy();** method call is last, as you want the MediaPlayer object to stop and release before you want the Service object to stop and release itself, which is done using the .onDestroy() method call. Your completed code will look like the following:

```
@Override
public void onDestroy() {
    ambientAudioPlayer.stop();
    ambientAudioPlayer.release();
    super.onDestroy();
}
```

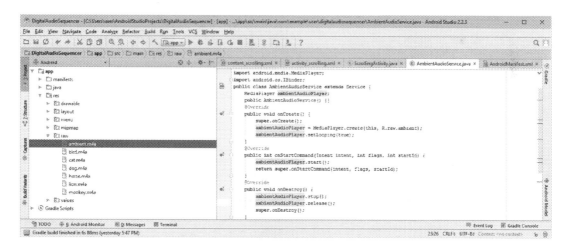

Figure 13-12. Before the super.onDestroy( ) method call add a MediaPlayer object .stop( ) and .release( ) method calls

You have now coded your first `Service` subclass, which is shown in its finished form in Figure 13-13. It has `onCreate()`, `onStartCommand()`, and `onDestroy()` methods that create, start, and stop/remove the `MediaPlayer` object from system memory based on the same three life cycle stages of the `Service` object itself. Pretty cool.

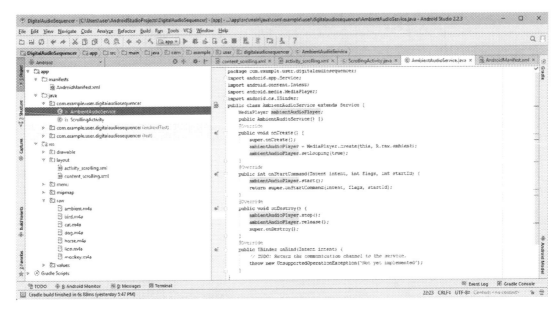

Figure 13-13. *The completed AmbientAudioService class, customized to implement the basic MediaPlayer functionality*

Next, let's take a look at the **ScrollingActivity** class and see exactly what Java code we need to add to that class in the `onCreate()` method, in order to start this Service, and have it play background ambient audio for this Android application.

Starting a Service: Using .startService( )

Now that you have created your `AmbientAudioService` `Service` subclass, and declared it for use in your Android manifest XML file, you are ready to start it by using the `.startService()` method that you learned about earlier in the chapter. This is done using an Intent object, in a very similar fashion to starting up an `Activity`, which you have done already, so this should be familiar to you. Let's get right into the Java 8 programming part of your scrolling `Activity` class, which will contain a `startService()` method call, as the very last step in your `onCreate()` method.

1.   Click the `ScrollingActivity.java` tab and add a line of code at the end of the `onCreate()` method as you want to start the `AmbientAudioService` Service subclass (object) right before you launch your application. Type in "star" as seen in Figure 13-14, and select the **startService(Intent service) ComponentName** option from the drop-down helper menu.

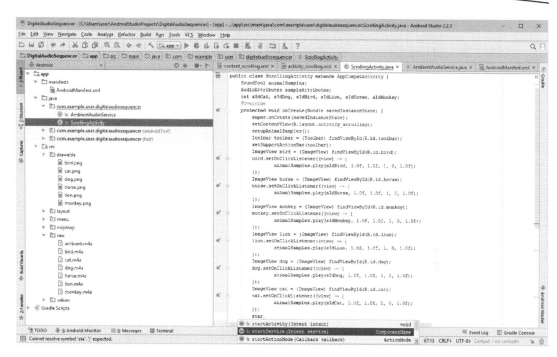

Figure 13-14. At the bottom of the onCreate() method add a line of code, type star, and double-click on the startService()

2. Inside of the `startService()` method parameter area, we are going to nest another Java construct by typing the Java **new** keyword, and then **Intent** (or type "In" and select `Intent`, in your helper drop-down).

3. Inside of your `Intent()` constructor method parameter area, type the Java **this** keyword, to pass the `ScrollingActivity` class `Context` object, and then a comma, and then the name of a `Service` subclass that you want to start, which, in this case, will be the **AmbientAudioService.class**. Your Java `startService()` method call statement, once it is fully completed, is shown in Figure 13-15, and should look like the following Java code:

```
startService(new Intent(this, AmbientAudioService.class));
```

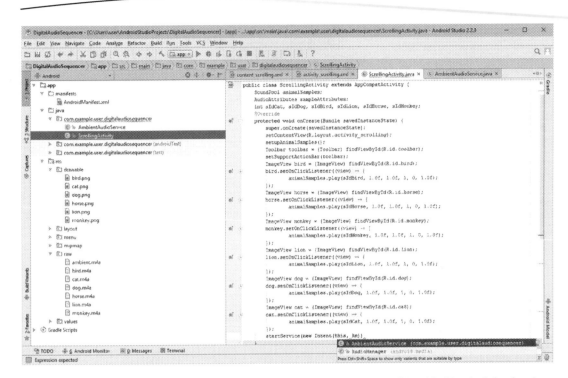

Figure 13-15. *Inside startService() instantiate a new Intent object passing Context (this) and AmbientAudioService.class*

4.   Now you are ready to use the **Run ➤ Run 'app'** menu sequence and test the code in the Nexus 5 AVD. The application now calls the Service, as shown highlighted in pale yellow and blue in Figure 13-16, and plays background music behind the animal samples, which mix perfectly with the ambient audio track in the background when they are triggered via SoundPool. I'll forego the screenshots as the application looks the same as it did in Chapter 12.

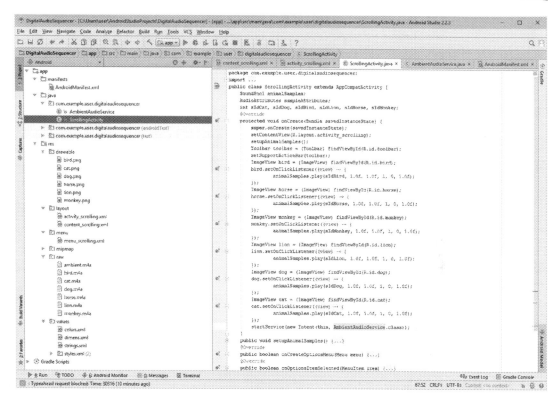

Figure 13-16. The completed ScrollingActivity.java class code with the startService( ) at the end of the onCreate( ) method

You now have a high-level overview of background processing in Android, and have created a `Service` subclass.

Summary

In this chapter, you learned about the Android Service component subclasses as well as about processing concepts, principles, prioritization, and optimization. You learned about Thread objects, and how these threads differ from Service components. You learned all about different types of Android Services, including started Services, bound Services, and a hybrid between these two types, as well as about scheduled Services, characteristics of Services, caveats about using Services, and when to utilize a `Service` subclass versus using a `Thread` class based object.

You learned about processes as well, and how to spawn your own process in your Android manifest XML file. You learned how to assign different application components to their own process (shared memory), by using the `android:process` parameter inside of your parent `<application>` tag or its child component tags, such as `<activity>`, `<service>`, `<provider>`, or `<receiver>`.

You created your own `Service` subclass called `AmbientAudioService` to start a `MediaPlayer` object (and stop it on exit) so that you could play ambient background audio effects while your `SoundPool` effects are being triggered by your users. Then you wrote Java code that called the `Service` subclass from the `ScrollingActivity` subclass using the `startService()` method.

In Chapter14, you will learn all about content provider classes in Android, which is an advanced area that includes **SQLite** database technology. I saved the most complicated chapter for last. As you can see, I am as always trying to cover things in the most logical, optimal fashion, as you progress through this journey to learn Android.

Chapter 14

Android Content Providers: Datastore Concepts

This chapter takes a look at how Android stores data and provides content to an application, using what the Android 7.1.1 (and earlier) OS "jargon" calls a **content provider**. This chapter covers how to share the provided content, as well as how to access, modify, update, and delete the data that these content providers provide. You will also take a look at some of the content providers for contact management that come installed as a part of Android 7.1.1 OS itself.

The topics have become significantly more advanced as you have progressed from one chapter to the next over the course of this book, and this chapter is no different. Data structure access is significantly more complex than event handling, multimedia content, or even UI design. This is because it involves SQLite **database design**, and therefore, you need to know how any given database is designed, in order to be able to access its database structure correctly.

For this reason, I am going to provide you with the foundational basics of database design during this chapter, as I have often done for other core topics for which deep knowledge is needed for Android 7.x development, such as user interface design, digital imaging, 2D animation, digital video, digital audio, services, threads, and processes.

Content provider (database) usage in Android 7.1.1 also involves requesting security permissions for the application, for different types of content provider (database) access, such as "read" and "write" access. As you're probably surmising by now, since you have been paying close attention during this book, this is accomplished using your Android Manifest XML application definition file, by adding in the appropriate Android **<permission>** child tags.

This chapter begins with a high-level overview of exactly what Android content providers are, as well as what they can do for your Android 7.1.1 applications and your end users. After that, you will learn some foundational information regarding database theory, and learn about a SQLite database API used in Android OS. Then you will take a look at the various database structures provided with the Android OS, which you can use with your contact management and new media endeavors, since they have already been created and installed in the Android OS. After that, you will create a `ContactManager Activity` subclass, which will allow you to learn the basics of how data is accessed.

Overview of Android Content Providers: Sharable Data

The term "content provider" is unique to Android OS development. It means nothing more than a **datastore** of data values, and is primarily found in the form of SQLite databases, which are an integral part of the Android OS. You can use the content provider SQLite databases that are provided as an integrated part of the Android OS, or you can create your own content provider databases for your application if you want, although that topic is too advanced for this Absolute Beginner's book. If you want to look for books that are dedicated solely to the topic of Android SQLite database design, go to `www.apress.com` and enter "Android SQLite" in the search field at the top.

An Android content provider provides you with access to **sharable** data structures, commonly called *databases*, which the Android OS has chosen to use for their sharable data structures because databases have the most high-level features, which unfortunately also makes them much more complicated, hence this final (advanced) chapter. The general high-level procedure for utilizing a database management system (DBMS) is as follows:

1. Get **permission** to **read** from a given database. If you wish to modify your database's content, you will also need to get permission to **write** to your database.

2. **Query** (search for and find) the data in the database management system (SQLite) using the "**key**," which, in Android, uses the **_ID** data field. You will be learning about fields very soon.

3. **Access** (read into memory) the data in the database management system (SQLite) once you have located it using the query and **_ID** key. The SQL and SQLite DBMS is open source (free).

4. **Modify** (over-write, append to, or delete) the data in your database management system (SQLite) once you have located it, read it, and ascertained that your data needs updating.

When accessing data, you might read the data, write to the data (change the values of the existing data), append (add) new data onto the database structure, or delete existing data, based on the type of permission and level of security permission that has been established for your application in the Android manifest XML file. Data can be in Android internal (operating system) memory; in an internal (Android API) SQLite database; or in an external Android device storage location, such as an SD card, or even on an external database server, which would be remote to Android OS as well as being remote to the Android device hardware (and require network connection).

Database Fundamentals: Concepts and Terms

A **database management system**, or **DBMS**, is a data storage system that I like to call an "engine" as it is actually a collection of algorithms at its core, which can store data over long periods of time (depending on the storage hardware medium) so that it can be accessed, read, and updated. This capability is quite desirable for a software development platform like Android. If you have never been exposed to database technology, this section covers the database fundamentals. Popular database software packages that you may be familiar with include Oracle, Microsoft Access or Claris FileMaker Pro. The company that is currently developing FileMaker is known as FileMaker, Inc.

As you know, there is a complete open source DBMS API inside of Android OS called **SQLite**, which is actually something called a **Relational DBMS**, or an **RDBMS**. An RDBMS is based on **relationships** that can be drawn between data that is arranged using tables. These **data tables** support **rows** of data and **columns** of data. This is similar to a spreadsheet program like Excel, except that data in a relational database is not usually visible all at the same time, like data in a spreadsheet. It is important to note that you can generate reports using a database that can achieve the same result, if you want to (once you learn about all of the programming that is involved).

Each database table **column** contains a similar type and classification of data within any given database record structure, and this column is generally called a **database field**. This means that, conversely, each **row** in your database table represents one entire **database record**. Generally, when you are writing your database records, you will write one entire row or record of data when you first add that record, usually using a form in the front-end (user interface) application allowing users to interact with the database engine itself. On the other hand, when you search a database for information, you will generally be looking through just one of the data table's columns, a collection of one type or classification of data field, for a specific piece of data or information.

Database columns (fields) can contain many different data types, such as numbers, text, or even references to data stored somewhere else, outside of the database structure itself, such as an image file on a hard disk drive. It is important to note that each data field needs to contain the same exact data type as the other data fields in that same column, as you can see in Figure 14-1. Each row is a database record, and a database record will usually contain all sorts of different data types across the different data table columns.

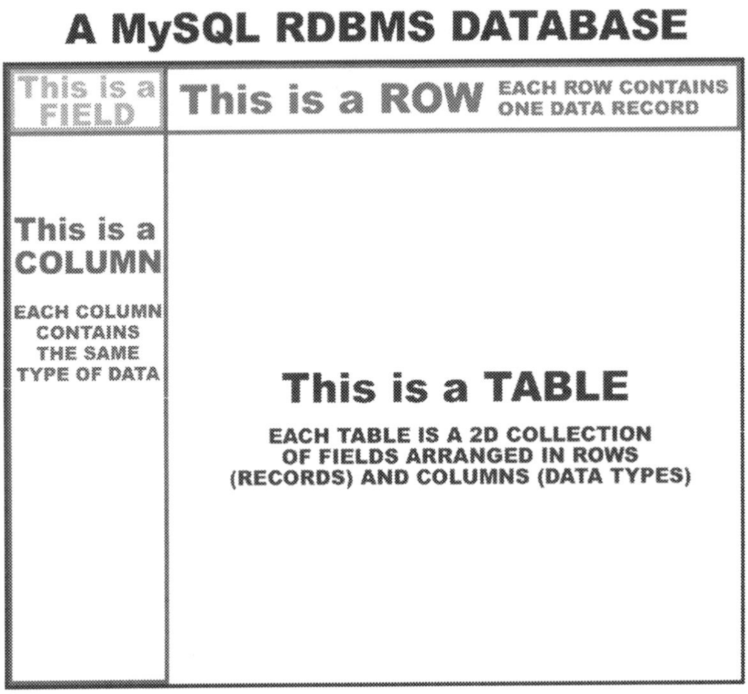

A MySQL RDBMS DATABASE

This is a FIELD	This is a ROW EACH ROW CONTAINS ONE DATA RECORD
This is a COLUMN EACH COLUMN CONTAINS THE SAME TYPE OF DATA	**This is a TABLE** EACH TABLE IS A 2D COLLECTION OF FIELDS ARRANGED IN ROWS (RECORDS) AND COLUMNS (DATA TYPES)

Figure 14-1. Basic overview of an RDBMS database (SQLite)

The classifications of data fields that Android SQLite data records contain usually spans names (text), numbers (int), and references (addresses) to things such as e-mails, websites, social media profiles, passwords, and so on.

> **Caution**   Once the record structure and data fields that define your DBMS record structure have been set up, make sure not to change this record structure later on, if you are designing your own database. This is because currently loaded records (the data field organization) may not fit into the new database structure definition correctly. It is best to design your database structures **up-front**. The database design process is especially critical to the success of your DBMS project over time.

One of the most popular database programming languages in the world is called **SQL**, which stands for **Structured Query Language**. You will be learning about SQL, as used in SQLite API, later on in the chapter.

The **structured** part comes from the structured tabular format of a relational database, and the **query** part comes from the fact that these tables of data are designed to be efficiently searched through, using a specific data value. The **language** part comes from the fact that SQL has evolved over time into a database programming language, which is quite complex and involved. In fact, I would speculate that there are almost as many books regarding SQL, DBMS, and RDBMS topics as there are on Java 8 programming for the Android OS.

If you have a massive amount of data fields (columns) in the database table, you will probably want to optimize your database using more than one table of data. In real-world database design, the theory of which is largely beyond the scope of this introductory book, you will want to have more than one database table for search and access performance, as well as for organizational reasons. In fact, the Android OS uses more than one database table for its end-user information storage and access, as you will soon see, later in the chapter when you get into the Contacts database table structure. This is quite complex, spanning quite a large number of database tables.

The way to create multiple database tables that act together as one, massive, unified database is to have a **unique key** (unique index) for each record in each of the tables. That way, information for a single data record can span more than one database table, by using this unique key. In Android OS, this key is called an **ID** and is always designated using the system database constant _ID in Android's SQLite databases. For instance, if the key, or _ID value, is 154, your e-mail information and phone information could be contained in two different data tables, but stored under that same key (index) value, and therefore will always be accurately associated with the correct Android user account even though the associated data will most likely span across multiple DBMS tables.

SQLite: An Open Source Database Engine

As you know, the SQL in SQLite stands for Structured Query Language. The "Lite" part denotes that this is a lightweight version of an RDBMS, intended for embedded use in consumer electronics devices, and not a full-blown DBMS, as would be used on an advanced computer system such as a LAMP (Linux, Apache, MySQL, PHP) database server. It's also interesting to note that SQLite is included in WebKit HTML5 browsers. All you really need to know about SQLite API is that it is part of the Android OS, and that you can use it for data storage.

> **Note**   If you want to research SQLite a bit more on your own, which would be a great idea, if your Android application needs to leverage SQLite databases extensively, SQLite has its own website! This website is kept up to date on a regular basis. You can check it out at: **http://www.SQLite.org**

There's a full SQLite API package included with the Android OS that contains all of the DBMS functions needed to work with SQLite. These are contained in a series of classes and methods in the **android.database.sqlite** package. All that you have to do is learn how to use them properly, which is not at all a simple task, given that this SQLite database structure complexity has evolved during over the 25 versions of Android (7.1.1 API Level 25). I'll introduce you to the basics during this chapter, so this book provides coverage of all the key Android component types.

SQLite is designed specifically for embedded systems use (similar to JavaME's memory footprint), and as such, it has only a quarter megabyte (256KB) of total memory footprint. This memory space is utilized to host relational database engine implementation. SQLite supports a minimum (standard) set of relational database functions and features, including the most common SQL syntax keywords; basic database operations like read, write, and append; and prepared statements. These features are enough to provide robust Android OS database support.

SQLite supports three different data types: TEXT, which is known as the String value in Java, INTEGER, which is known as the long value in Java, and REAL, which is known as the double value in Java. When working in SQLite, all other programming data types must be converted (also referred to as "cast" in Java 8) into one of these SQL compatible data types, before entering them into any database data field.

It is important to note that SQLite doesn't validate any of the data types that may be written into its data fields (table columns) as being one of the required data types. This means that you can write an INTEGER value into a TEXT (String defined) data column, and vice versa, so you will always need to pay close attention to exactly what you are doing with SQLite for this reason. If you don't validate what you are doing using your Java code, you may get a wrong data type result written into one of your SQLite database fields.

To use SQLite in Android, you construct your SQLite statements for creating and (or) updating your database, which will then be managed by Android OS. When your app creates a database, the database structure will be kept in a specialized Android directory, which will always utilize the following Android OS database path address:

DATA/data/**YOUR_APPLICATION_NAME_HERE**/databases/**YOUR_DATABASE_FILE_NAME_HERE**

Next, you will take a look at the many different types of predefined content providers that come standard with the Android OS. You will also be looking at how these are accessed within the Android 7 operating system and its **android.content** package. You will also be looking at the content provider and content resolver classes and methods used in Android to access its internal database structures that are actually a part of the Android OS.

There are a plethora of Android database structures for all of the different functional areas in the OS. This is why you are getting up to speed on this in the next section, because as you learned in the first part of the chapter, the first step in using any SQLite DBMS is familiarizing yourself with, and completely understanding, its database structure.

Android's Built-In SQLite DBMS Content Providers

A significant number of SQLite-based database structures are "hard-coded" into the Android OS, so that users of Android devices can handle things that they expect from a phone, iTV set, e-reader, smartwatch, or tablet. These include contact directories, address books, calendars, camera picture storage, digital video storage, music albums (digital audio storage), phone books, and so forth.

The most extensive of the SQLite database structures is the **Contacts** database, which contains many different tables (essentially acting as sub-databases, or sister databases, if you like) containing personal information, such as contact names, phone numbers, e-mails, preferences, social media settings, and so forth. These structures are very complex, and since this book is focused on programming for Absolute Beginners, and not database theory, you will be working with the primary contact name database, to keep it more about Java programming and Android content providers, rather than about database structure and theory.

The base-level interfaces of the android.provider package allow you to access those data structures that define the setup and personalization of each user's Android device hardware. Obviously, the data in each of these data structures will be completely different for each user's smartphone, smartwatch, tablet, phablet, e-reader, iTV Set, or automobile dashboard.

Android 1.5 Contacts Database Contact Provider

Table 14-1 lists the now deprecated Contacts database interfaces for Android 1.5, 1.6, or 2.0, which can be found on the Android Developer site. Deprecated, in this case, means that this **Contacts** database has been replaced with a more modern **ContactsContract** database structure. However, the Contacts database structure is still valid, and will work just fine for those users who are still using Android OS versions 1.5, 1.6, or 2.0. The Contacts DBMS structure, shown in Table 14-1, was redone from scratch, starting in Android OS Version 2.1.

Table 14-1. Original Android Contacts database and its data table interfaces to be used for Android 1.5, 1.6, or 2.0 support

Database.Table	Content Description of what is Held in this Database Table Structure
Contacts.OrganizationColumns	Organization
Contacts.GroupsColumns	Groups
Contacts.PeopleColumns	People
Contacts.PhonesColumns	Phone numbers
Contacts.PhotosColumns	Contact photographs
Contacts.PresenceColumns	IM presences
Contacts.SettingsColumns	Phone settings
Contacts.ContactMethodsColumns	Contact methods
Contacts.ExtensionsColumns	Phone extensions

As mentioned, if you browse the current Android Developer website documentation, you will find that these interfaces listed in Table 14-1 are all described as being **deprecated**. The reason that these are called interfaces is because they define how and where you are going to interface with the data, using the format **database.table**, so a table that has people in it is referenced using **Contacts.PeopleColumns**, as you can see in Table 14-1, row 3. You will be taking a look at how these structures have increased in complexity later in the chapter.

Deprecated Database Structures: Software Upgrades

Deprecated is a programming term that means that classes, methods, constants, interfaces, and even database structures have been **replaced** by other more modern programming or data structures. This usually happens during the release of newer versions of a programming language (such as Java 8) or a new Android API version such as the recent Android 7.1.1.

These newer structures replace the older structures, and are usually more robust (fewer bugs), or more complex (more features), but sometimes they will only differ in how they are implemented. In the case of a database, they sometimes differ in regards to how the data fields are distributed amongst the database tables that contain them.

This deprecation is exactly what has happened with the Contacts database interfaces between Android versions 1.x (1.0, 1.1, 1.5, and 1.6) and 2.0, and Android versions 2.1, 3.x, 4.x, 5.x, 6.0, and 7.x. So database interfaces that work on Android 1.x and 2.0 phones are different than the ones that work in Android 2.1 through 7.1.1 phones. The newer versions use more advanced, feature-rich database structures. If you're going to support 1.x or 2.0 phones, you'll use database interfaces listed in Table 14-1. This book uses the Android suggested application support default settings of API Level 15 (Android 4) through API Level 25 (Android 7.1.1), so you need to use a more advanced database structure that replaces the original database structure used prior to Android 2.1 (Level 7).

The good news is that deprecated does not mean disabled. In this case, it more accurately means, "not suggested for general use, unless you need to support pre-2.1 OS versions for your Android users." So, if you need to support Android 1.5, 1.6, and 2.0 phones, you can use the interfaces listed in Table 14-1. Note that inside Android Studio, deprecated structures and method calls are **lined out** in the Java code, to show the developer that they are deprecated. As you know, this can be a bit unnerving, since most devices these days are 2.3.7 through 7.1-compatible, so I suggest you take Android's "advice" and develop for API Levels 15 through 25, or later. This is suggested in the **New Android Application Project** series of dialogs, which you have already encountered several times over the course of this book.

You will not be able to access data from newer database tables until you add support for the 2.1 through 7.1.1 SQL DBMS structures in your code. You can do this by detecting which OS your user is using, and having code sections that deal with each (1.x through 2.0, versus Android 2.1 through 7.1.1) database access structure differently, using different ContentProvider and ContentResolver Java code structures.

> **Note**   If you want to be able to access every new feature, you can always have your Java code detect which version of Android a device is using, and then use custom code that delivers your optimal application functionality for each specific Android OS version.

Deprecation is a common programming situation that developers need to get used to. Hence, I am covering it during this book as needed, so that as an Absolute Beginner, you can learn all about deprecation now, and not be blind-sided by this advanced programming and application development concept later on down the line.

With Android 7.x OS, deprecation is especially prevalent, as different OS versions will feature different support for the hardware features that manufacturers frequently add to their new smartphones, iTV sets, smartwatches, e-book readers, tablets, game consoles, automobile dashboards, and the like. These usually require new APIs, or changes to the existing Android APIs, in order to support these new hardware features.

For instance, Android 1.5 was initially designed for use on smartphones. Android added touchscreen gestures in Android version 1.6, and camera support in version 2.0. Next, tablets and e-readers came along, and Android 3.0 added feature support for large screen consumer electronics devices such as computers, tablets, or iTV sets.

Later, iTV sets came out in huge volumes, and so Android version 4.0 added more iTV set support, and the TVDPI constant for 1280 by 720p resolutions was added to the API. Next, Android game consoles, such as the nVidia Shield, came out, and faster screen refresh (60 FPS) was added to Android 4.1. Likewise, faster touchscreen refresh (60 FPS) was added to Android 4.2, which focused on enhancing its i3D gaming capabilities.

Recently, smartwatches and smartglasses have become popular, and so the faster Bluetooth 4.0 standard support was added into Android 4.3 and 4.4. Android 5.0 featured new health API additions that allow physical fitness hardware to be utilized with the Android OS, as well as Bluetooth 4.1. Android 6.0 featured new Android TV and Android Auto API additions, as well as Bluetooth 4.2, with Bluetooth 4.3 in Android 7.0, along with the Vulkan i3D rendering engine, and Java 8 support. And so the version enhancements will go on and on, driven by the Android hardware manufacturers, and end users' demands for increased performance. Manufacturers number in the hundreds internationally, because Android is an "open" operating system platform.

Note   Over time Android version functionality gets more and more difficult to keep track of. Indeed Android already has over two dozen different OS versions (API Levels) that your code should work across. Keeping track of all these current programming constructs, database structures, and logic mazes is enough of a challenge for most, without another layer on top, that involves remembering which Java constructs and interfaces work, or do not work, with any given OS version. This is one of the primary reasons that Android application programmers are so well-compensated financially.

Table 14-2 lists some of the content providers that are compatible with the new Android versions (2.1 through 7.1.1) and that are used for manipulating contact information. A vastly different content provider database structure approach solidified in API Level 8 and beyond may well be the primary reason that the defaults in the **New** Android Application Project dialog suggests (that is, defaults to) API Level 15 through 25 support.

All of these Contact related database tables replace the deprecated versions listed in Table 14-1. If you want to look into these data tables in greater detail, detailed descriptions of these are available from the Android developer site at this link:

https://**developer.android.com**/reference/android/**provider**/**package-summary**.html

As you can see in Table 14-2, the ContactsContract database table structure is an order of magnitude more complex than the simple Contacts database table structure that was used prior to Android 2.1. With this complexity comes power and flexibility, but at the cost of more complex Java code needed to implement these databases and their features inside your Android applications. This is a complex topic for the Absolute Beginner.

Table 14-2. ContactsContract database tables in the Android provider package, along with the types of data they contain

Database.Table Interface	Database Table Contents
ContactsContract.BaseSyncColumns	Generic columns used by sync adapters
ContactsContract.CommonDataKinds.BaseTypes	All type of datatypes supported
ContactsContract.CommonDataKinds.CommonColumns	Common columns across specific types
ContactsContract.ContactNameColumns	Contact name and contact name metadata columns in the RawContacts database
ContactsContract.ContactOptionsColumns	Columns of ContactsContract. Contacts that track the user preference for, or interaction with, the contact
ContactsContract.ContactsColumns	Columns of ContactsContract.Contacts refer to intrinsic contact properties
ContactsContract.ContactStatusColumns	Data used for contact's status info
ContactsContract.DataColumns	Columns (joined) from the data table
ContactsContract.DataColumnsWithJoins	Combines all Join Columns returned by ContactsContract.Data table queries
ContactsContract.DataUsageStatColumns	Columns in the Data_Usage_Stat table
ContactsContract.DeletedContactsColumns	Deleted Contacts Data
ContactsContract.DisplayNameSources	DataType used to produce display name
ContactsContract.FullNameStyle	Constant for combining into full name
ContactsContract.GroupsColumns	Data used for contact's grouping info
ContactsContract.PhoneLookupColumns	Data used for contact's phone lookups
ContactsContract.PhoneticNameStyle	Constants for pronunciation of a name
ContactsContract.PresenceColumns	Additional datalink back to **_ID** entry
ContactsContract.RawContactsColumns	Data used for the RawContact database
ContactsContract.SettingsColumns	Data used for contact's OS settings
ContactsContract.StatusColumns	Data used for social status updates
ContactsContract.SyncColumns	Sync Information across accounts

Next let's take a look at the `MediaStore` and `CalendarContract` databases and their tables, and then you will get into how to use the Uri object you learned about earlier in the book, using your `content://` content provider URI.

The Android MediaStore Content Providers

The other collections of content providers that you may find important for new media content within the Android OS are the MediaStore content providers. These are listed in Table 14-3.

Table 14-3. The Android MediaStore Content Providers

Database.Table Interface	Database Table Contents
MediaStore.Audio.AlbumColumns	Album information
MediaStore.Audio.ArtistColumns	Artist information
MediaStore.Audio.AudioColumns	Audio information
MediaStore.Audio.GenresColumns	Audio genre information
MediaStore.Audio.PlaylistsColumns	Audio playlist information
MediaStore.Files.FileColumns	Fields for master table for media files
MediaStore.Images.ImageColumns	Digital images
MediaStore.Video.VideoColumns	Digital video
MediaStore.MediaColumns	Generic media storage

Later in this chapter, you will look at how to declare content providers for use, access them, read them, modify them, and append to them. First, let's take a look at one more often-used Android OS database, the **CalendarContract** database, and then you will look at how to use **Uri** objects to reference Android content providers.

The Android CalendarContract Content Providers

The CalendarContract databases include eleven calendar-related databases, each supporting various calendar functions, including events, attendees, alerts, reminders, and other similar calendar-related data support functions.

The reason that the Android operating system provides pre-built support, via its **android. provider** package, for your Android calendar database access is because it would be logical for applications that access these calendar features to be able to add customized, new capabilities to the existing Android calendar feature set.

Table 14-4 shows the CalendarContract content provider interfaces, as well as the different types of calendar functional data they access, and which they will allow you to reference directly using a content provider.

Table 14-4. CalendarContract databases in the Android provider package, and the type of data that they contain

Database.Table Interface	Database Table Contents
CalendarContract.AttendeesColumns	Columns (joined) from attendees database
CalendarContract.CalendarAlertsColumns	Data used for calendar alerts function
CalendarContract.CalendarCacheColumns	Data used for calendar cache function
CalendarContract.CalendarColumns	Calendar columns that other URIs can query
CalendarContract.CalendarSyncColumns	Generic columns for use by sync adapters
CalendarContract.ColorsColumns	Data used for calendar colors function
CalendarContract.EventDaysColumns	Data used for calendar event day function
CalendarContract.EventsColumns	Columns (joined) from the events database
CalendarContract.ExtendedPropertiesColumns	Data Used in Calendar Extended Properties
CalendarContract.RemindersColumns	Data used for calendar reminders function
CalendarContract.SyncColumns	Sync info columns used by other databases

Next, you will take a look at how the **content://** area in Android OS is used to access these database structures using a content provider URI. Fortunately, you are already comfortable with Uri objects, so you have a head start. After we take a look at how content:// URIs are used with SQLite databases in Android OS, we will create yet another pure Android design pattern Activity in Android Studio 2.3 to get you more experience with the bootstrap apps that Android Studio will code for you and then get into how to code access and updates to basic contact data records such as those contained in the ContactContracts SQL DBMS structure held in the android.provider package that we learned the basics about during this section of the chapter.

Referencing the Content Provider: Using a Content URI

If you want to be able to tell the Android OS what content provider you want to access, it is important that you understand the concept of the **Content URI**. You have used Uri objects before, so you are very familiar with the function they play in accurately referencing data (content) pathways in Android apps. Content providers have a specialized path format. Just like the Internet's HyperText Transfer Protocol has a special format, HTTP://, Android content also has a special format that is very similar (and thus easy to remember), which is: content://.

The complete URI for an Android content provider contained in your URI object will follow this data path format:

```
content://Authority/Path/ID
```

Consider in the following (hypothetical) ContactManager Apress Contact database content URI:

```
content://com.example.user.contactmanager/apress/androidapps/12345
```

In this imaginary URI, `com.example.user.contactmanager` is the Data Authority, `apress/androidapps/` represents the Data Path, and finally, the `12345` represents the _ID key for the actual Data Record that is being accessed by the URI path (using an Android `Uri` object).

A Content URI will always contain four necessary parts: The **schema** to use, in this case, `content://` as well as a **data authority**, an (optional) **data path** to the data, and the **_ID** of the data record that you want to access. The schema for content providers is always the word `content`. A colon and a double forward slash (`://`) always appear in the front of your URI reference, and separates the data schema from the data authority.

The next part of the URI is known as the **data authority** for the content provider. As you might have expected, the authority for each content provider must be **unique**. An authority naming convention usually follows your Java package naming convention. Most organizations choose to use the backward dot-com domain name of their organization, plus a data qualifier for each content provider. Thus, the previous example would assume that you own the **example.com** domain name, which, of course, you do not, as it is owned by IANA.

Since the Android developer documentation recommends that you utilize the fully qualified class name of your `ContentProvider` subclass, you might then name your `ContentProvider` subclass `ContactManager.java` if you were following this example Content URI. I am going to use the `ContactManager.java Activity` subclass name in the next section, to follow the Java class naming convention used throughout this book.

The third part of the URI standard is the **data path** to the data. Although it is optional, it is a fairly standard practice for organizational purposes. You would not usually put your data in the root folder of a server where it would get lost; instead, you would place it in an **Apress** folder, using subfolders for each of the literary database **tables**. In this example, one subfolder would be a table named **androidapps**.

The content provider for the Android `MediaStore` (which you looked at in the previous section of the chapter) database, for example, will utilize different path names to make sure that the audio, image, and video files are kept in separate data type (and data table) locations. By using different path names, one single content provider can accommodate many different types of data that are in some way related, such as the different new media content types, for example, kept in the `MediaStore` content provider in the different data tables. For unrelated data types, it is standard programming practice that you would want to utilize a different content provider subclass, as well as a different data authority (and data path, for that matter) for each database.

The last URI reference specification component is the **ID**, which, as you may have surmised, needs to be unique and numeric. This ID, or **_ID** in Android, is utilized whenever you want to access one single database record.

So, as you can see, the URI reference specification progresses from the most general or high-level (**content://**) specification, through the authority (server name), down through the pathway (folder hierarchy) to the database (directory path), and ultimately, to the data record itself (_ID).

Since you are using the default OS support range suggested in the New Android Application Project of API Level 15 (4.0) through API Level 25 (7.1.1), you will use the more modern (that is, not deprecated) content provider for this Android content provider example, which you will be creating during the rest of this chapter.

Let's get started by creating your new Basic Activity subclass of AppCompatActivity (this will be named MainActivity.java by Android Studio 2.3), since we have already explored the Empty Activity, Navigation Drawer Activity, Fullscreen Activity and Scrolling Activity during other chapters. We'll call this **Basic Activity** project the **SQLiteProvider** project. For your UI design layout, we will take a closer look at Android's **RelativeLayout** container class, since it is one of the most popular UI layout containers prior to the CoordinatorLayout introduced with the new Visual Design Editor (and can be used inside a CoordinatorLayout, as you will soon see), and this is a great fit for use with SQLite database tables.

Creating a Basic Activity: The SQLiteProvider Project

Let's create a new Android Studio project using an Android design pattern (Basic Activity) that we have not used thus far, called SQLiteProvider, so that we can take a close look at at least half of these primary app Activity patterns (notice that some are for helper-activity use, such as login, settings, ads, and maps) during this book.

1. Go into your DigitalAudioSequencer project, and use the **File ➤ Close Project** menu sequence, and close the current project, which will open the Android Studio 2.3 start (launch) menu.

2. Select the **Start a new Android Studio project** option. Notice on the left that you already have created four different apps, using four of the most popular pure Android design patterns.

3. In the **Application Name** field name the Application (and Project) **SQLiteProvider**, as is shown in the left panel in Figure 14-1, and leave the other options at their default (or automatic) settings, then click the **Next** button, and proceed to the **Select the form factors your app will run on** dialog.

4. Select the default **Phone and Tablet** option, shown in the middle of Figure 14-2, to create the standard Android application type (rather than using the Wear, Auto, iTV, or Glass APIs), and then hit the **Next** button. Notice I scrolled the drop-down menu, to show that it does not even offer Pre-API 8 options, so everyone will most likely be using the API 7 and later DBMS structures, which is what my examples will use during the rest of this chapter. That said, I'll show you in a future section how to manually set minimum and target API levels in the Android Manifest XML definition, in case you ever wanted to develop for Android 1.5 through 2.2.

5. Select the **Basic Activity** Android design pattern seen on the left side of Figure 14-3, and click **Next**. We've now covered five of seven Android design patterns that Android Studio will create for you!

6. Name the **Title** SQLiteProvider, and leave the rest of the default Android naming conventions the same, as shown on the far right panel in Figure 14-2. Click the **Finish** button to have Android Studio 2.3 create your bootstrap project, which we will look at in the next section of this chapter.

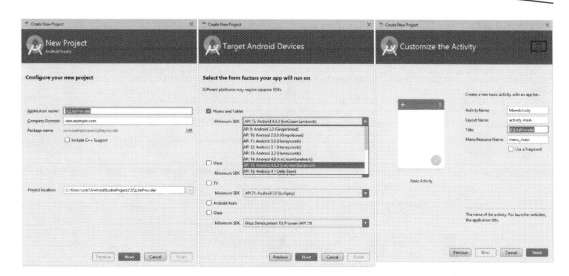

Figure 14-2. Configure your SQLiteProvider project for API 15 through 25 by using the New Android Project series of dialogs

Once you become an advanced Android developer, be sure and check out the other two (Tabbed and Master-Detail Flow) design patterns, seen in Figure 14-3, which utilize a more advanced **Fragments** UI design approach. Fragments are a bit too advanced for an Absolute Beginner's title.

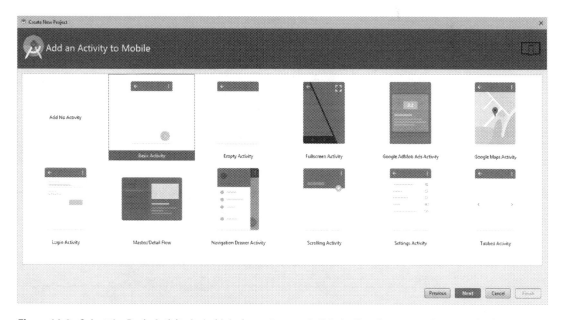

Figure 14-3. Select the Basic Activity Android design pattern, and click the Next button, to advance to the Customize dialog

Examining and Testing Your SQLiteProvider Bootstrap

Let's take a quick look at how this Android application is set up before we start modifying it, as the best approach for an Absolute Beginner is to make incremental modifications to an already working Android application. Click on the **MainActivity.java** tab, shown selected in Figure 14-4, and open the import section, by clicking the plus (+) icon on the left. As you can see, we are using the Bundle, View, and AppCompatActivity now used in most all Android 7.x and later appluications, as well as several user interface design classes we have learned about during the book, including the Snackbar, Toolbar, FloatingActionButton, Menu, and MenuItem classes. Since the database code I am about to embark on in this chapter is complex, I wanted to use an Android design pattern which would reinforce what you've learned thus far in the book, and then build upon that knowledge with new Android provider classes.

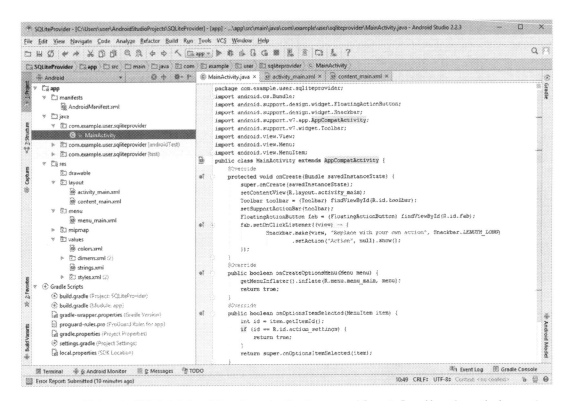

Figure 14-4. Click on the MainActivity.java tab, and examine the classes used (imported), and how the methods are set up

You should be familiar with all of the Java code in Figure 14-4, since we have used and gone over it in previous chapters, which is why I chose this **Basic Activity** design pattern, so that we could cover other subjects and classes in this chapter. Next, let's right-click the activity_main.xml file in the /app/res/layout folder, and use **Jump to Source** to open it in a tab, as seen in Figure 14-5. This top-level UI design should also be familiar, as it is almost identical to the one you learned about back in Chapter 8 (see Figure 8-11), except it references the **content_main** layout.

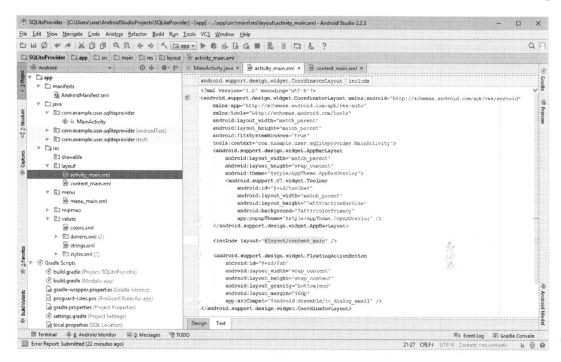

Figure 14-5. *Open the activity_main.xml tab and examine the top-level CoordinatorLayout and AppBarLayout UI structures*

Next, click on the **content_main.xml** tab, the contents of which can be seen in Figure 14-6, and take a look at the basic Hello World TextView content, inside a RelativeLayout user interface layout container. The RelativeLayout is one of the oldest layout containers in Android, and one of the most popular, along with the FrameLayout, GridLayout and the LinearLayout containers.

Since RelativeLayout is so popular, I thought we'd take a deeper look at it during this chapter, along with a deeper configuration of the Android manifest XML definition file, while we learned about Android SQLite database management systems and content providers. I'm trying to pack as much basic information about the voluminous Android OS into this Absolute Beginner's title as possible.

Let's start with the easy <TextView> child tag which uses wrap_content layout configuration constants and uses the hard coded android:text="Hello World" parameter to configure TextView content. Get some practice using Android constants now, and add a Hello World constant to your strings.xml file and then reference it using **@string/hw**.

The parent <RelativeLayout> layout container tag is far more complex in its parameter configuration, as you can see at the top of Figure 14-6. It uses a **content_main** ID, so it can be referenced from the activity_main.xml file's <include> child tag. It uses **match_parent** layout configuration parameters, so it fills the parent layout container, and uses four padding parameters to reference the /app/res/values/dimens XML definitions for app dimensions. It defines a **scrolling_view_behavior** using the **app:layout_behavior** parameter, defines Context as the MainActivity class, and specifies that it will be shown in the activity_main layout container definition.

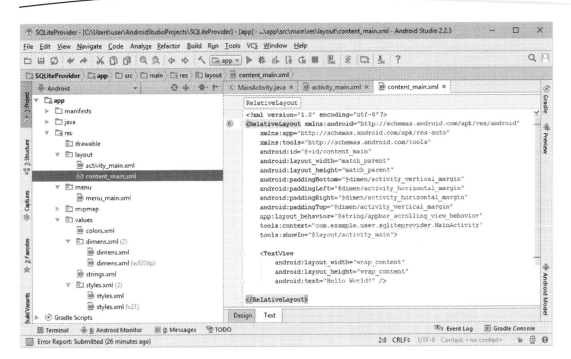

Figure 14-6. *Click the content_main.xml tab, and examine the top-level RelativeLayout, and its UI configuration parameters*

We will be adding to this RelativeLayout UI design during the chapter to add more TextView UI elements as well as other UI elements that will allow us to create a front end for this Activity that will allow us to interface with the ContactsContract SQLite DBMS that is part of the Android 7.1.1 OS.

Before we start modifying the Android manifest XML definition for this project in the next section of the chapter, to add SDK support specifications and SQLite DBMS permissions specifications, let's test the bootstrap code that Android Studio 2.3 created for us to make sure it works, before we start transforming it into a DBMS application.

Use the **Run ➤ Run 'app'** menu sequence to start the Nexus 5 AVD, and launch the SQLiteProvider application, which can be seen in the left-hand side of Figure 14-7, and is thus working well enough to launch in the emulator. Therefore all we have to do now is to test the code concerning the user interface elements (the OptionsMenu and the FloatingActionButton on the upper right and lower right, respectively).

Click the OptionsMenu (three vertical dots) and make sure the Settings option appears, as can be seen in the right side of Figure 14-7. Then click the FloatingActionButton and make sure that the SnackBar appears at the bottom of the screen. This is also shown on the right side of Figure 14-7 (I consolidated screenshots into one Figure). So now you again have a functional (empty) application and user interface ready to use to create your SQLite ContactsContract database management application. Now all we have to do is configure your Android manifest XML definition with database access permissions, and use your AVD's Contacts app to create dummy test data to use to make sure our database code we will be writing after that is actually working properly. This is a complex topic; there are a lot of steps (and classes) to cover, meaning this will be a long (final) chapter.

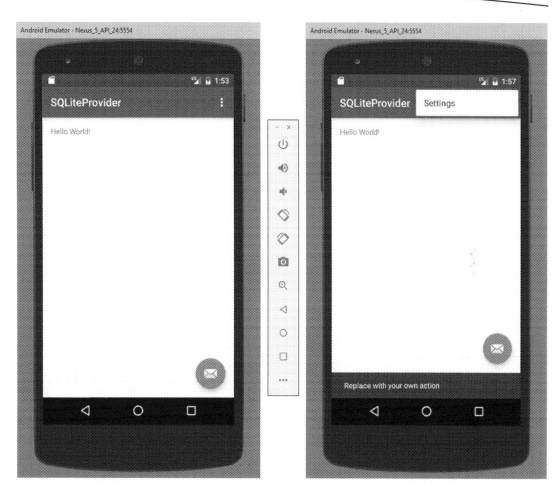

Figure 14-7. Use the Run ➤ Run 'app' menu sequence to test all of the features of the bootstrap app's user interface design

Next, let's take a look at how to use the `<uses-sdk>` and `<uses-permission>` child tags inside of the `<manifest>` tag.

Configuring the Manifest: Uses SDK and Permissions

Open the `/app/manifests/` folder, and right-click on the `AndroidManifest.xml` file, and choose **Jump to Source** to open it in a new tab. Add a line of markup under the parent `<manifest>` opening tag and type **<uses** to get the pop-up helper, and select the **uses-sdk** option, as is shown in Figure 14-8. Once you double-click on this option, Android Studio 2.3 will add this child **<uses-sdk>** tag into your parent `<manifest>` container, and you can then hit the space bar to get your next pop-up helper parameter configuration drop-down menu, where you can select minimum or target API level configuration parameters. This allows you to explicitly define Android OS API level (device software) support.

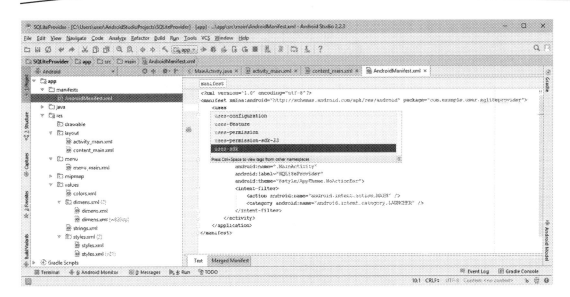

Figure 14-8. *Enter a line of markup after the opening parent <manifest> tag, and type <uses and double-click on uses-sdk*

Select, and double-click on, the `android:minSdkVersion` parameter in the pop-up helper drop-down menu, shown in Figure 14-9, to insert a **Minimum SDK Version** parameter. Set it to a value of **15** (Android 4), and then follow the same work process to set the **Target SDK Version** to a value of **24** (Android 7.0) inside of this `<uses-sdk>` tag.

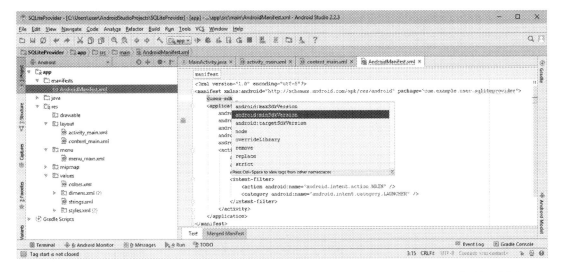

Figure 14-9. *Select the android:minSdkVersion parameter from your drop-down helper menu, and double-click it to insert it*

Now your `<uses-sdk>` manifest configuration is in place, as shown highlighted in yellow in the top in Figure 14-10 and we are ready to do the same work process, only with the `<uses-permission>` child tag. Type `<uses` and select `uses-permission` and hit the space bar and

then type `android:name` (or select it from the helper) and then in the parameter value helper drop-down menu find the `android.permission.READ_CONTACTS` constant from the `Manifest.Permission` nested class. This is also shown in Figure 14-10. The documentation containing all of these constants can be found on the Android Developer website, if you are interested, by following this URL:

https://developer.android.com/reference/android/Manifest.permission.html

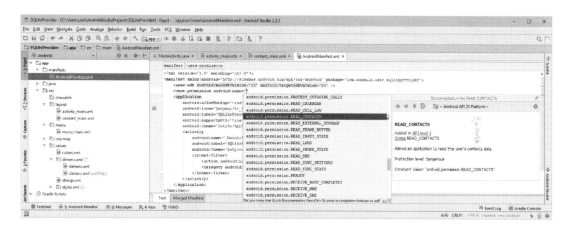

Figure 14-10. *Use the parameter constant value drop-down helper to insert the READ_CONTACT permission in the manifest*

Now that you have your permission to `READ` the `CONTACTS` database, follow the same exact work process and add the permission to `WRITE` to the `CONTACTS` database. This is done by adding a second `<uses-permission>` child tag to the `<manifest>` section of your `AndroidManifest.xml` definition file, as is shown in Figure 14-11.

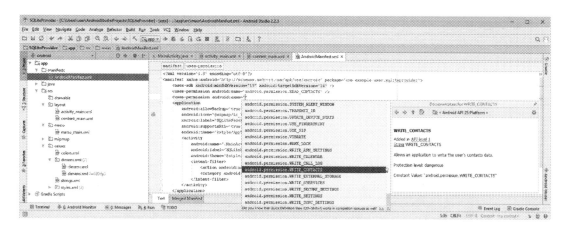

Figure 14-11. *Use the parameter constant value drop-down helper to insert a WRITE_CONTACT permission in the manifest*

Notice in Figures 14-10 and 14-11 that you do not have to have the developer information page for the Android `Manifest.permission` nested class (see previous link) open to ascertain what all of these permission constants do, although reviewing these is a great way to see what you will be allowed to do in your Android applications. This is because the **pop-up permissions constants helper** has a secondary (pale yellow) pop-up helper that you can use to see what each of these constants are, and what they are used for, as well as how dangerous it is considered for an Android developer to utilize it.

As you can see in Figure 14-12, you have now added child tags (objects) to your manifest that define what device support your Android application will provide, which Google Play Store will use to define which device users will be able to see your application in the store. The uses-permissions (child) objects will be used to define what SQLite operations the application will be able to perform on the `ContactsContract` Android database.

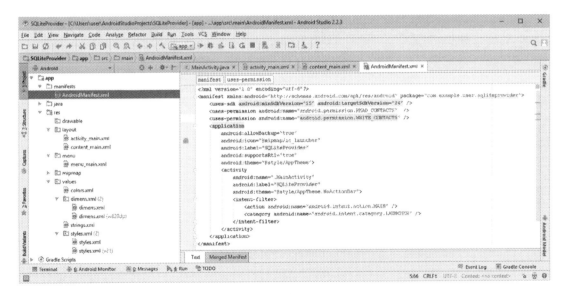

Figure 14-12. The finished <manifest> child <uses-sdk> and <uses-permission> tags configure how your app can be utilized

Next, we need to create some dummy test data, to use with this app. We can use your Nexus 5 AVD to do this.

Creating Your Dummy Contact Database Using an AVD

When your AVD launches, you may have noticed that it appears to be a fully functional Android device, and for the most part, it really is! Touch the circle icon at the bottom of the AVD emulator to switch from your app test (seen in Figure 14-7) to get the main device screen, shown on the left side of Figure 14-13. Click the apps icon, shown circled in red, and then launch the Contacts app, shown circled in red in the center of Figure 14-13. This will launch the Contacts app, shown on the far right in Figure 14-13, where you can click the **Add Contact** icon in the lower-right corner (a plus + next to a person). Do that now, as you need to add a few contacts to work with after we start writing code that will display, add to, edit and remove these contacts from the SQLite database management system (API) in Android OS.

Figure 14-13. The Nexus 5 AVD simulates a real-world Android Smartphone, including all OS UI functions and standard apps

The first screen that you will see the first time that you try and add a new contact is the "Your new contact won't be backed up. Add an account that backs up contacts on-line?" screen, which can be seen on the far left in Figure 14-14. Select the **KEEP LOCAL** option, which is the Button user interface element on the left, shown circled in red. This will write the Contacts database to your AVD emulator, so that it can be accessed by the app you are going to code during this chapter.

The next screen, seen in the middle of Figure 14-14, is the Add new contact screen. Notice that it indicates that it is "Saving to: Phone-only (unsynced contact)" on the top left of the form, shown circled in red. Click in the Name field and enter a faux (dummy) name data value.

As you can see in the far right side of Figure 14-14, I decided to use some popular Star Trek characters, including Mister Spock, Captain James Tiberius Kirk, and Nyota Uhura. I entered **Mister Spock** in the **Name** field, which uses a symbol that looks like a person (head and shoulders) and the Android onscreen keyboard also appeared, just as it would on a real-world smartphone.

When I was finished, I clicked on the seafoam green add contact icon, shown circled in red at the bottom-right corner of the third screen, seen in the far right pane in Figure 14-14.

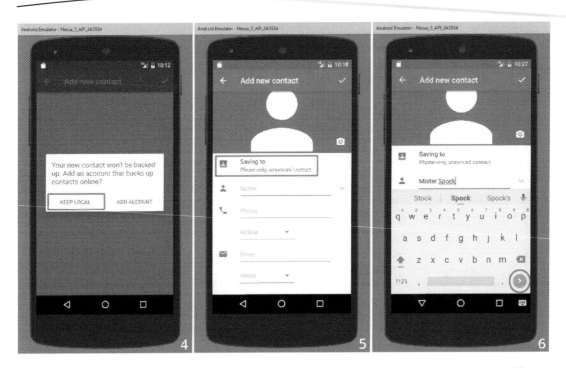

Figure 14-14. *Keep contacts local to your AVD, and start creating the first contact by adding the contact name Mister Spock*

This entered the Name of the first Contact record, and I was then ready to add a phone number and an e-mail address, which we will proceed to do next.

The next data field we can add dummy data in is the **Phone Number** field, which uses a phone handset symbol. Enter a fake phone number, I used 1 234-567-8910, and click the seafoam green enter (done, proceed to next field) button, shown circled in red in the lower right-hand corner of the left-hand pane in Figure 14-15.

To remove the onscreen keyboard and see the rest of the data field inputs, I clicked on the keyboard icon shown circled in red in the left-hand pane in Figure 14-15, underneath the enter and proceed to next data field entry button. This should toggle off (remove) the onscreen (virtual) keyboard, so we can see the lower data fields.

As you can see in the middle pane of Figure 14-15, the first time that you toggle an AVD virtual keyboard off, you will get the **Change keyboard** dialog. This dialog provides you with a slider switch, which if you drag it to the left position, will allow you to choose to use your physical workstation keyboard with the emulator, instead of the current setting, which sets a virtual keyboard function to "keep it on the screen while physical keyboard is active."

After you toggle the virtual keyboard left (off) you will be able to see the rest of the form, which can be seen in the right hand pane in Figure 14-15. Enter an e-mail address in the **E-mail Address** field, shown using an envelope symbol. I used the made-up **spock@ vulcan.planet** e-mail address, as you can see at the bottom of Figure 14-15.

Once you have entered the Contact Name, Phone Number and E-mail Address data, as can be seen in the right hand pane of Figure 14-15, you will have enough data to work with during this chapter. Use Check Mark (Done) icon at the top right of the screen, shown circled in red, to enter this data record, and to advance to the next step.

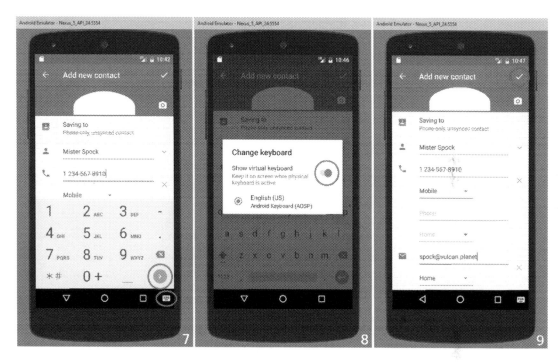

Figure 14-15. *Enter the phone number and e-mail address data fields, and turn off your on-screen virtual keyboard function*

Once you click on the Check Mark button to enter the data record into the ContactsContract database you are creating, you will get a series of screens prompting you to set a series of permissions for the ContactsContract SQLite database structure you are about to create by entering its first data record. This will only happen the first time you add a data record to a new SQLite database structure.

The first screen, shown in the left pane in Figure 14-16, asks "Allow Contacts to access this device's location?" As this is an AVD and there is most likely no GPS hardware on the motherboard, I selected the **DENY** button option, since we are focusing just on the ContactsContract SQLite database and its data during this chapter.

The second screen, shown in the middle pane in Figure 14-16, asks "Allow Contacts to access your calendar?" As we are not dealing with the CalendarContract database (see Table 14-4) during the remainder of the chapter, I selected the **DENY** button option, since we are focusing primarily on the ContactsContract SQLite database and its data during the remainder of the chapter.

The third screen, shown in the right pane in Figure 14-16, asks "Allow Contacts to send and view SMS messages?" As this is an AVD and there is most likely no 4G LTE cellular network hardware on the motherboard, I selected the **DENY** button option, since we are focusing only on the `ContactsContract` SQLite database and its data during this chapter, and not on SMS messaging APIs, which are too advanced for an Absolute Beginners title. After you finish with these three screens, you should see your newly created Mister Spock contact in your AVD smartphone emulator.

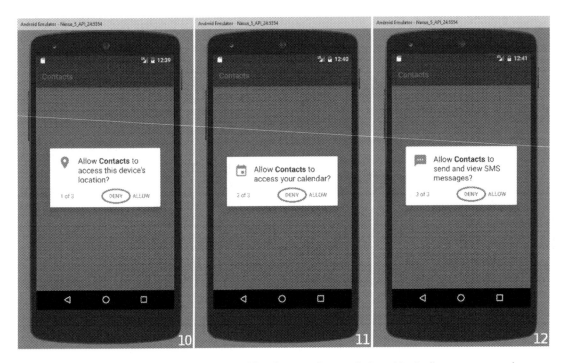

Figure 14-16. Select the DENY option for the three Allow Contacts Screens that would actually come up on real smartphones

Figure 14-17 shows the completed (first) contact data entry, in the far left pane in red, as it would look on a smartphone when it was actually in use, such as when you were making a phone call to that contact. Now you need to add a couple more data sample contacts, Jim Kirk and Nyota Uhura, and we'll be ready to start coding.

To do this you need to retrace the nine primary steps that are shown in Figures 14-13 through 14-15. The way to get back to this position in the emulator is to use the circle icon at the bottom of the Android OS UI, shown circled in red in Figure 14-17 in the bottom of the left pane.

This will allow you to again access the apps icon and then click on the Contacts icon. When you do this you will get the Contacts application start screen, shown in the middle pane in Figure 14-17, where you will now see the Mister Spock contact you have added listed inside of the application.

Use the Add Contact icon at the bottom-right corner of the application as you did before, and bring up the screens that you used to enter contact data in Figure 14-14 and 14-15. Enter a Jim Tiberius Kirk record using a false phone number and e-mail, and a Nyota Uhura record using a false phone number and e-mail.

Once you are finished the Contacts entry screen will have all three contacts, which is shown on the far-right pane in Figure 14-17.

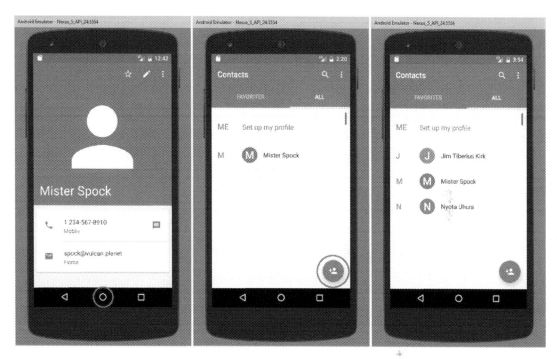

Figure 14-17. After a completed contact record is displayed, do an Add Contact work process twice more to create 3 records

Next, you're going to learn about Android's RelativeLayout class, so you can create the SQLiteProvider UI design.

RelativeLayout: Create Morphing User Interface Design

The Android **RelativeLayout** class is a good layout container ViewGroup subclass to learn about in this chapter, as a database data entry UI uses a **data entry form** UI layout, and that's what the RelativeLayout class is optimized to provide. The RelativeLayout class is most likely going to be used for applications that need to create user interface layouts that can **morph** between different screen sizes and shapes. As such, it is a logical fit for use with databases, and a great UI layout container class to learn about in this chapter, as it is frequently used, and covered in all of my Android books.

The RelativeLayout class is subclassed from the ViewGroup class, which you have already read about, so you will use the layout container to create a data entry form and user interface buttons to trigger the database access functions. You will use Button UI elements as UI widgets inside of the relative UI layout container, so that users can click on these Button UI elements to be able to invoke changes to the database based upon the UI elements.

The RelativeLayout class is a public class that extends ViewGroup, so its Java class hierarchy is as follows:

```
java.lang.Object
  > android.view.View
    > android.view.ViewGroup
      > android.widget.RelativeLayout
```

A RelativeLayout is a fantastic layout container (class) to use in designing a user interface because it can optimize memory usage by eliminating the need to nest multiple UI layout objects (ViewGroup subclasses). This will keep your layout hierarchy "flat," with no deep nesting of objects, which improves memory usage and processing performance. If you find yourself using nested LinearLayout containers to create a user interface design, you'll be able to replace them with one RelativeLayout container, after you learn the material in this section of the chapter.

A RelativeLayout is a ViewGroup subclass that displays child View subclass UI widgets using relative position algorithms. The position of each widget contained inside the parent <RelativeLayout> is specified using a relative positioning algorithm (parameter) specifying sibling elements in the parent layout container or the parent layout container itself. The nested **LayoutParams** class contains constants that implement **algorithms** that will scale and position widgets into positions relative to the parent RelativeLayout container (such as aligned to the bottom, left, right, or center) or to neighboring widgets as the size and shape of the Android device display changes. This allows the same UI design to be used on a smartphone, iTV set, auto dashboard, e-book reader, or tablet.

RelativeLayout lets child widgets specify their position relative to the parent latout container or to each other by specifying the ID of the widget (or layout) that they wish to position relatively to. So you can align two elements by right border, or make one below another, have both centered in the screen, or have one centered to the left of the other, and so forth. By default, all child views are drawn at the top left of the layout, so you must define the position of each view using the layout parameters available from the **RelativeLayout. LayoutParams** nested class. If you want to investigate this class on your own, you can see it at the following Android Developer website URL:

https://**developer.android.com**/reference/android/widget/**RelativeLayout. LayoutParams**.html

Creating Your RelativeLayout UI for MainActivity

Right-click the **strings.xml** file in the **/app/res/values/** folder and **Jump to Source**. First, let's add three <string> constants to serve as Button UI element labels. I added these after the app_name and before the action_settings constants, as shown in Figure 14-18. These will give us buttons to add, edit, and display your Contact database.

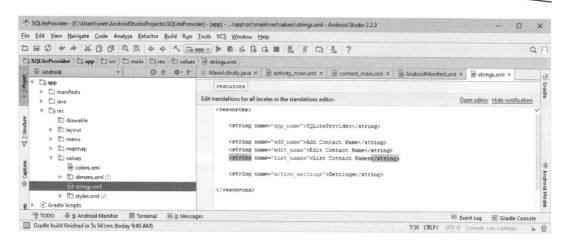

Figure 14-18. Add three <string> constants to strings.xml for use in labeling database read and write operation buttons

Change the "Hello World" text value to be "Contact Name Operations" to label your database access buttons. Add a line of code after the `TextView` and type a left-chevron, as is shown in Figure 14-19, and select the `Button` widget to add that user interface design element to your design underneath the text title for your user interface.

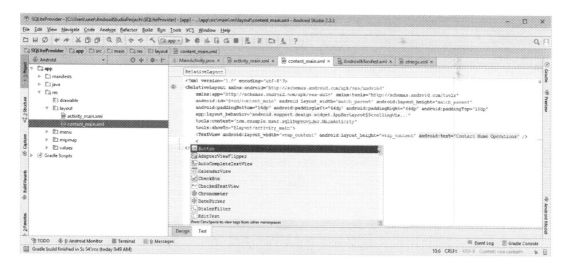

Figure 14-19. Add a line of code after the TextView, type a left-chevron, and select the Button widget from the helper menu

As you can see in Figure 14-20, this will code a `Button` child tag, along with the required layout width and height parameters, which you'll be prompted to select constant values for. Buttons usually use **wrap_content**, so I used this constant for both. I also added an **android:id** parameter set to `@+id/addContact` to allow me to access the `Button` in Java code and an **android:text** parameter set to `@string/add_name`, to add the text label to the `Button`.

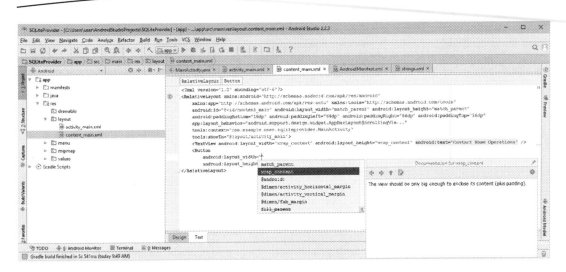

Figure 14-20. *Use the Graphical Layout Editor tab to preview the TableLayout filled with Button UI elements*

Add an `android:id="@+id/screenTitle"` parameter to the TextView so that you can position UI elements relative to it. To implement your RelativeLayout positioning between the first Button element and the TextView element (title), type in **android:layout_below** and select the **@id/screenTitle** option, seen selected in the menu in Figure 14-21.

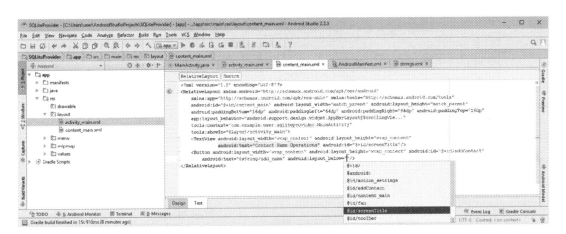

Figure 14-21. *Wire the Button UI element's relative position to the TextView using android:layout_below="@id/screenTitle"*

You now have your UI screen title `<TextView>` and Add Contact Name `<Button>` UI elements in place and referencing each other using the **Layout_Below** algorithm, as shown in the completed code in Figure 14-22. This means if you right align your title, the button will align under it on the right. If you center the screen title, which we will be doing later on, the UI button, as well as anything aligned to it, will follow it. As you will see, RelativeLayout algorithm chains (connections) can be powerful, but will take some getting used to (practice using parameters). I added an **android:layout_centerVertical="true"** to center the button. Notice the `layout_below` will take priority.

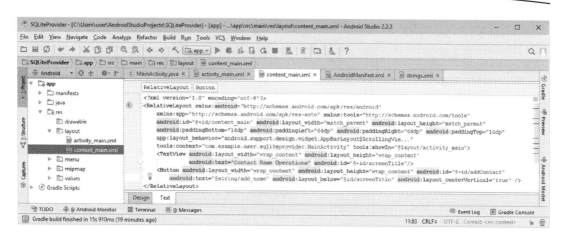

Figure 14-22. Referencing a TextView UI element's master position for a Button UI element subordinate (below) positioning

In this chapter I decided to code the XML markup by hand, to be more advanced than in Chapter 6, where you used the Visual Design Editor to create your markup. You can use the Design Editor tab, shown selected at the bottom of Figure 14-23, to preview what your XML markup is going to be doing. This is especially useful when you are developing RelativeLayout UI container designs, to see what any given chain of inter-connected positioning algorithms referencing your UI widget's relative positioning is going to produce visually on the screen.

Figure 14-23. Use the Design tab to access the Visual Design Editor to preview your hand coded XML

Copy and paste the Button element underneath itself to create a second Button element as seen in Figure 14-24.

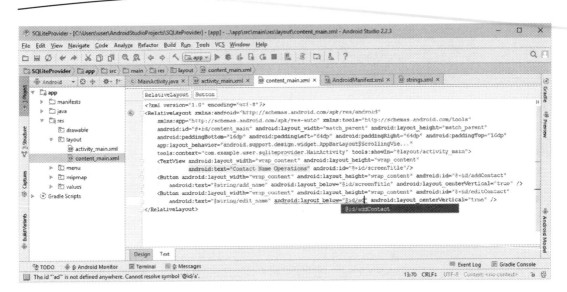

Figure 14-24. Create a second Button from the first, and position it relative to the first with layout_below via addContact ID

Change your second Button ID to **editContact**, change android:layout_below to reference **@id/addContact**, and change android:text to reference **@string/edit_name**. Copy and paste the second UI Button underneath itself, and create a third Button element, as seen in Figure 14-25. Change your third Button ID parameter to be **listContact**, change your android:layout_below parameter to reference **@id/editContact** and change your android:text parameter to reference **@string/list_names**.

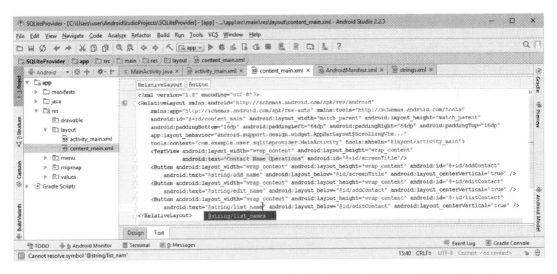

Figure 14-25. Create a third Button from the second, and position it relatively, using layout_below referencing editContact

Again, click on the **Design** tab, at the bottom of the content_main.xml editing pane, and preview the relative positioning results, which can be seen in Figure 14-26. As you can see, each UI element lines up below each other, as specified in each UI widget's XML markup parameters. The blueprint view shows your entire hierarchy, as well as the classes used, assigned names, widget rendering locations, and pixel dimensions and boundaries.

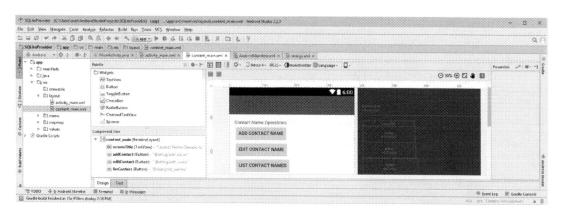

Figure 14-26. Use the Design tab to access the Android Studio Visual Design Editor, and check your relative UI positioning

To demonstrate the power and flexibility of your RelativeLayout positioning hierarchy, let's add an **android:layout_centerInParent** parameter in the TextView UI element, and set its value to **true**. This will center the title in the Activity screen, and RelativeLayout algorithms in the Button tags will then align the buttons underneath it. As you'll see in Figure 14-27, I had Android Studio write this markup for me. Notice the algorithms are named (lower case then camel case) the same way that Java methods are named, telling you that these positioning algorithms are actually implemented as (and eventually calling) custom relative positioning algorithm Java methods.

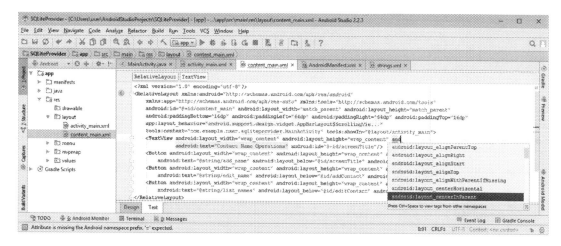

Figure 14-27. Add an android:layout_centerInParent parameter into the TextView UI element, and set its data value to true

To make the screen title more prominent, I also added the **android:textAllCaps** parameter, using the drop-down helper menu in Android Studio 2.3, as seen in Figure 14-28, and set the data value of that parameter equal to **true**.

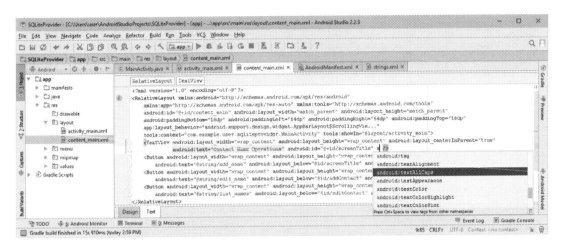

Figure 14-28. Add the android:textAllCaps parameter into the TextView UI element, and set its Boolean data value to "true"

Finally, to center the Buttons in the middle of the screen, underneath the now prominent title, change the **android:layout_centerVertical="true"** parameter inside each of the Button UI elements to instead be an **android:layout_centerHorizontal="true"** parameter, as shown highlighted in cornstarch blue in Figure 14-29.

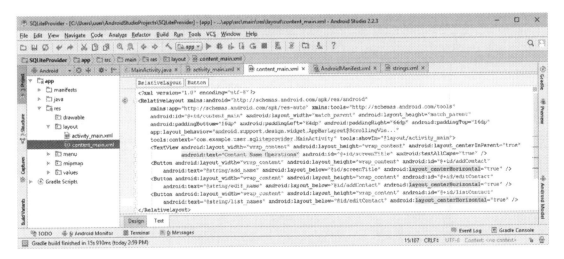

Figure 14-29. Change android:layout_centerVertical="true" Button parameters to android:layout_centerHorizontal="true"

The final XML markup for the contents of your bootstrap content_main.xml RelativeLayout should look like this:

```xml
<?xml version="1.0" encoding="utf-8"?>
<RelativeLayout xmlns:android="http://schemas.android.com/apk/res/android"
  xmlns:app="http://schemas.android.com/apk/res-auto" xmlns:tools="http://schemas.android.
com/tools"
  android:id="@+id/content_main"
  android:layout_width="match_parent" android:layout_height="match_parent"
  android:paddingBottom="@dimen/activity_vertical_margin"
  android:paddingLeft="@dimen/activity_horizontal_margin"
  android:paddingRight="@dimen/activity_horizontal_margin"
  android:paddingTop="@dimen/activity_vertical_margin"
  app:layout_behavior="@string/appbar_scrolling_view_behavior"
  tools:context="com.example.user.sqliteprovider.MainActivity"
  tools:showIn="@layout/activity_main" >
  <TextView android:layout_width="wrap_content" android:layout_height="wrap_content"
          android:layout_centerInParent="true" android:text="Contact Name Operations"
          android:id="@+id/screenTitle" android:textAllCaps="true" />
  <Button android:layout_width="wrap_content" android:layout_height="wrap_content"
          android:id="@+id/addContact" android:text="@string/add_name"
          android:layout_below="@id/screenTitle" android:layout_centerHorizontal="true" />
  <Button android:layout_width="wrap_content" android:layout_height="wrap_content"
          android:id="@+id/editContact" android:text="@string/edit_name"
          android:layout_below="@id/addContact" android:layout_centerHorizontal="true" />
  <Button android:layout_width="wrap_content" android:layout_height="wrap_content"
          android:id="@+id/listContact" android:text="@string/list_names"
          android:layout_below="@id/editContact" android:layout_centerHorizontal="true" />
</RelativeLayout>
```

Use the **Design** tab at the bottom of the XML editor pane to switch to Visual Design Editor mode, and preview the revised design, which now centers nicely, and uses the bottom half of your Activity screen, seen in Figure 14-30.

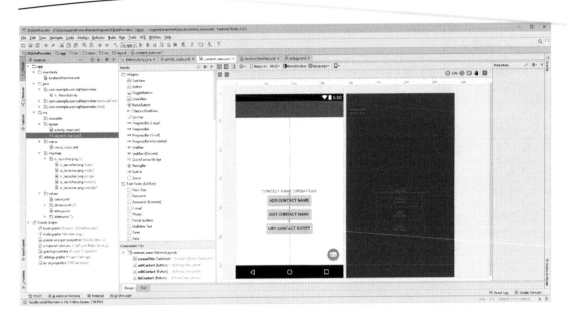

Figure 14-30. *Use the Design tab to access the Android Studio Visual Design Editor, and preview your revised user interface*

Let's use the **Run ➤ Run 'app'** menu sequence, and make sure our UI design looks the same in the AVD emulator as it does in the Visual Design Editor. As you can see in Figure 14-31, the UI design looks good, and I also included a screenshot of the next step (on the right-hand side) where we'll remove the `FloatingActionButton`, and use its Java code for the first `Button` user interface element, which we will then replicate twice more. After that, we will place the database code in the event listener and handler constructs so we can access the database.

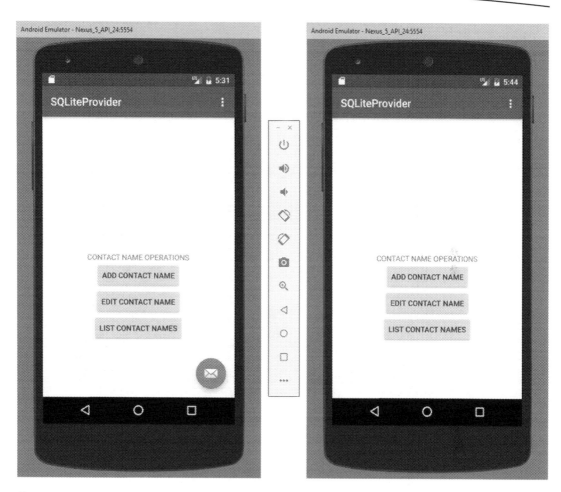

Figure 14-31. Use the Run ➤ Run 'app' menu sequence and test the RelativeLayout user interface design in the Nexus 5 AVD

Next, let's remove the FloatingActionButton from the bottom right of the user interface. We will be using the Java code for the FAB to create one of our Button objects, and then copy and pasting it twice more to create the other two Button event handling structures, adding database access code to the Snackbar code.

Remove the Floating Action Button widget from the bottom of the CoordinatorLayout (Figure 14-5), as is shown in Figure 14-32, by selecting that tag's block of markup, and then hitting the **delete** key on your keyboard.

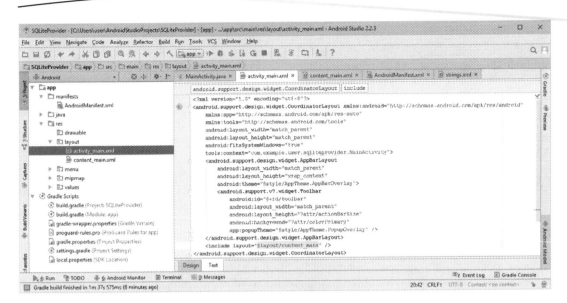

Figure 14-32. *Remove the <FloatingActionButton> child tag and its parameters, by block selecting it and using a delete key*

Next, change the `FloatingActionButton` code to instead reference the `Button` class, change **fab** to **add**, and reference the **addContact** `Button` ID, as shown highlighted in Figure 14-33. Delete the `import` statement for the `FloatingActionButton` class, and use Alt+Enter to have Android Studio write a `Button` class import for you, or add an **import android.widget. Button;** statement at the bottom of your `import` statements block, as shown at the top of Figure 14-33 highlighted in light blue. The reason this is highlighted is because I clicked on one of the `Button` class usage instances in the instantiation statement in order to track the class usage, from import through instantiation through implementation.

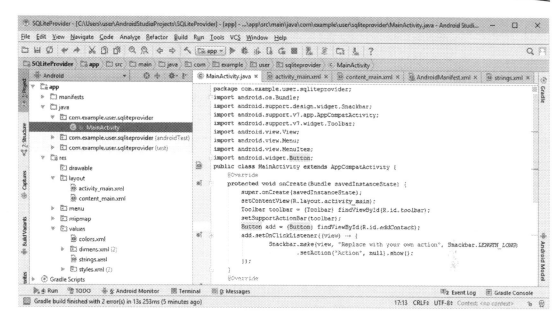

Figure 14-33. *Replace the FloatingActionButton fab code with Button add code referencing an addContact Button definition*

Don't forget to call your `.onClickListener()` off of this new add `Button` object. Your new code should look like this:

```
import android.widget.Button;
public class MainActivity extends AppCompatActivity {
    @Override
    protected void onCreate(Bundle savedInstanceState) {
        super.onCreate(savedInstanceState);
        setContentView(R.layout.activity_main);
        Toolbar toolbar = (Toolbar) findViewById(R.id.toolbar);
        setSupportActionBar(toolbar);
        Button add = (Button) findViewById(R.id.addContact);
        add.setOnClickListener(new View.OnClickListener()   {
            @Override
            public void onClick(View view) {
                Snackbar.make(view, "Replace with your own action", Snackbar.LENGTH_LONG)
                        .setAction("Action", null).show();
            }
        });
    }
```

Now you have enough infrastructure in place to start writing the Java logic that will access your SQLite database.

Transform the MainActivity Class for Database Access

As you know by now, the first step in the process of transforming the `MainActivity.java` `Activity` subclass is to declare and instantiate your UI `Button` objects. These are contained inside of a parent `RelativeLayout` container, which you have already defined using XML markup inside the `content_main.xml` file in the `/app/res/layout` folder. Copy the add `Button` structure underneath itself twice and change add to edit and list as shown in the following Java code, which is also shown in Figure 14-34:

```java
Button add = (Button) findViewById(R.id.addContact);
add.setOnClickListener(new View.OnClickListener()   {
    @Override
    public void onClick(View view) {
        Snackbar.make(view, "Adding to Contact Database", Snackbar.LENGTH_LONG)
                .setAction("Action", null).show(); }
});
Button edit = (Button) findViewById(R.id.editContact);
edit.setOnClickListener(new View.OnClickListener()   {
    @Override
    public void onClick(View view) {
        Snackbar.make(view, "Editing the Contact Database", Snackbar.LENGTH_LONG)
                .setAction("Action", null).show(); }
});
Button list = (Button) findViewById(R.id.listContact);
list.setOnClickListener(new View.OnClickListener()   {
    @Override
    public void onClick(View view) {
        Snackbar.make(view, "Listing the Contact Database", Snackbar.LENGTH_LONG)
                .setAction("Action", null).show(); }
});
```

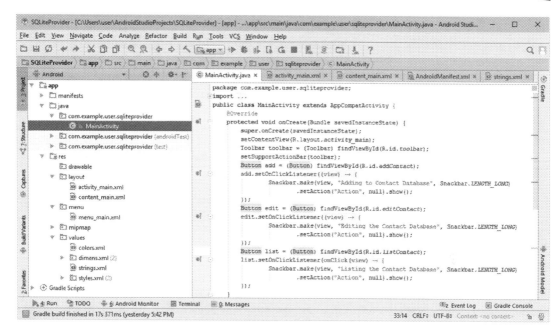

Figure 14-34. Copy and paste your add Button instantiation and event listening/handling structure underneath itself (twice)

Now it is time to get into the most difficult sections of this chapter—the Java code necessary to implement the **ContentProvider** and **ContentResolver** objects, which are needed to access database structures in Android OS.

Creating Your Custom .listContacts() Database Access Method

Since resolving a content provider in Android takes more than one or two lines of code, in fact it, will involve a do while type of loop to read through the database records one by one, you should add a method call in the list Button object's event handler to a listContacts() method, which we will be coding next. Let's add the method call inside of the list Button object's onClick() event handler, right after the Snackbar "Listing the Contact Database" message creation method chain Java code, as can be seen in Figure 14-35. Once you type in the **listContacts();** line of code, Android Studio will give you a lightbulb with an exclamation point in it on the left margin for that line of code. Use the drop-down menu arrow to open the options and select the **Create method 'listContacts'** option, and when the second **Choose Target Class** drop-down menu appears, choose the **MainActivity (com.example.user.sqliteprovider)** option, since you want the method coded in the MainActivity.

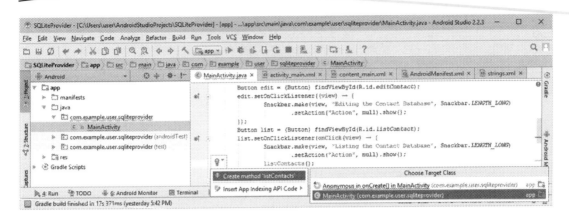

Figure 14-35. Add a listContacts( ) method call, and select the Create method 'listContacts' and MainActivity menu options

This drop-down menu sequence will instruct Android Studio to code an empty Java method body for you to use to code your `listContacts()` database access method. Once you do this the red code error highlighting will disappear, because a method can now be called. As you can see in Figure 14-36, Android Studio writes the **private void** listContacts(){...} empty method bootstrap programming structure for you, at the end of the `onCreate()` method. You'll be adding the database access Java code to the body of this method to list contacts.

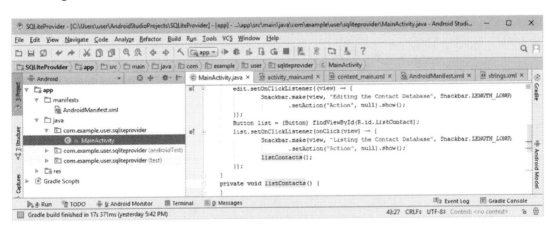

Figure 14-36. A bootstrap private void listContacts( ) method created by Android Studio inserted after the onCreate method

The first step will be to declare and instantiate a **Cursor** object named **nameCursor** and load it with the database content you are going to list by using the **getContentResolver(). query()** method call chain. A `Cursor` object is used to traverse database records looking for the data that you are trying to locate. To create and configure this `Cursor` database searching engine, use the following line of Java code, which is shown in Figure 14-37, along with a series of several pop-up helper dialogs that contain methods and URIs that you will require:

```
Cursor nameCursor =
        getContentResolver().query(ContactsContract.Contacts.CONTENT_URI, null, null, null, null);
```

As you can see in Figure 14-37, once you type the ContactsContract.Contacts (database. table) reference in the .query() method parameter list, and then press the **period** key, a list of possible URIs will then appear. Find the **CONTENT_URI** option, and select it, by double-clicking it to insert that **URI** into your method call parameter. This will create the first ContactsContract.Contacts.CONTENT_URI parameter for your method parameter list.

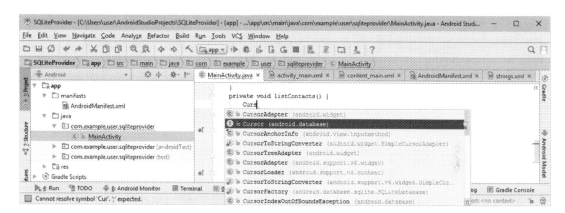

Figure 14-37. Declare Cursor object named nameCursor and instantiate it using getContentResolver( ).query( ) method chain

Remember that you will need to mouse-over the error highlighting for the Cursor object, and trigger the code to **Import 'Cursor' (android.database)** to have Android Studio 2.3 code the import for the Cursor class to use, or simply use Alt+Enter. After the Cursor object is declared and imported, add a space and name it nameCursor, and then use the equals operator to load the Cursor object with the results of the getContentResolver().query() operation. Type "getCon" and select and double-click on the **getContentResolver( ) ContentResolver** class option, as shown in the Android Studio pop-up Java coding helper, seen in blue on the right side of Figure 14-38.

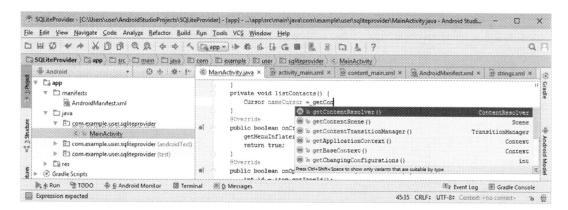

Figure 14-38. Use the ContentResolver class's getContentResolver( ) method to load the Cursor object with your query data

Next, type a period after the **Cursor nameCursor = getContentResolver** portion of the statement, and select the **query(Uri uri, String[] projection, String selection, String[] selectionArgs, String sortOrder)** method (shown as being from the Cursor class), as is shown, selected in blue, on the right side of Figure 14-39.

Notice that the four parameter options for the getContentResolver().query() method call have been specified for you in the drop-down helper menu, on the left portion, and the class (Cursor) that the method is contained in, on the right portion. The parameter list with object or variable types and suggested name is provided to show you what valid data values go in each of these positions in order for the method call to be valid, even if this is a "null" value, which is used to serve as an unused parameter indicator (that is, no data value is provided, or "none").

Since this chapter does not cover advanced SQL database concepts, such as projection, selection arguments, sorting order and selection, you are going to be using null values in these optional database query parameters, as can be seen in the completed and error-free line of code, which can seen in Figure 14-42, if you look ahead.

Figure 14-39. *Type a period and select query(Uri, String[] projection, String selection, String[] selectionArg, String sortOrder)*

Inside of the query() method parameter area type "Contac" and select the **ContactsContract (android.provider)** option, from the Android Studio pop-up helper drop-down menu, as is shown selected in blue in Figure 14-40.

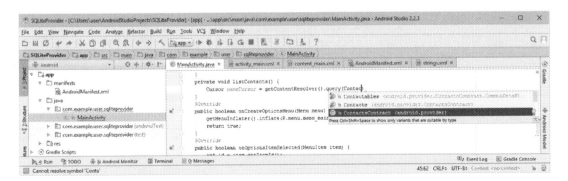

Figure 14-40. *Type in "Contac" and select the ContactsContract (android.provider) option from the drop-down helper menu*

Next, hit the period key and select Contacts from the drop-down helper menu, and then hit the period again and select the CONTENT_URI constant from the drop-down helper menu, as is shown in blue in Figure 14-41. This finishes the first Uri uri parameter requirement and all you have to do is to add the null, null, null, null parameters.

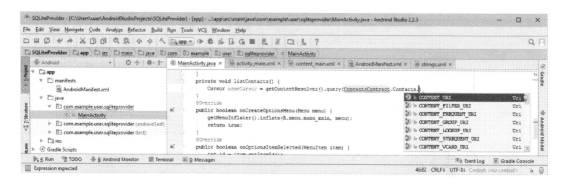

Figure 14-41. Hit a period key and select Contacts from the drop-down, then hit the period again and select CONTENT_URI

Next, add a comma and four **null** parameters (no parameter specified), and you will have your completed Cursor declaration, instantiation and configuration Java statement, as is shown error free in Figure 14-42.

Figure 14-42. Add a comma and four null parameters (no parameter specied), and you have a completed Cursor statement

It is now time to create a do-while loop construct, which will read through the Cursor object loaded using the **ContentResolver** object. In the Android OS, a do-while loop begins with the keyword **while** and then specifies something to evaluate to determine how long to process the statements inside of the do-while loop. In this case, that will be whether your Cursor object, which is used to **traverse** or read through the database content, has reached the end of the database. This happens when the Cursor object reaches the last (final) record in the database, and cannot read another record, much like reaching the EOF (End Of File) character when reading a file. In pseudo-code, the do-while loop structure, which you're going to write next, equates to the following logic:

```
While (there's another record to moveToNext to, and therefore to be able to read, perform
this)   {
   Create String object to hold Contact Name Data; place the name data from a database
   Column into it;
   Use Android Toast and a makeText() method to write this value to the display using a long
   duration;
}
```

Add a line of code after the Cursor code and type a Java **while** keyword and opening parenthesis. Start to type the nameCursor object, and select, and double-click, the nameCursor Cursor object option seen in Figure 14-43.

Figure 14-43. Type while and parenthesis, then type the nameCursor object, and double-click the nameCursor Cursor option

Next, type a **period** and select the Boolean **moveToNext()** method from the drop-down helper menu, as shown in Figure 14-44. This will complete the **nameCursor.moveToNext()** evaluation statement in the while loop condition.

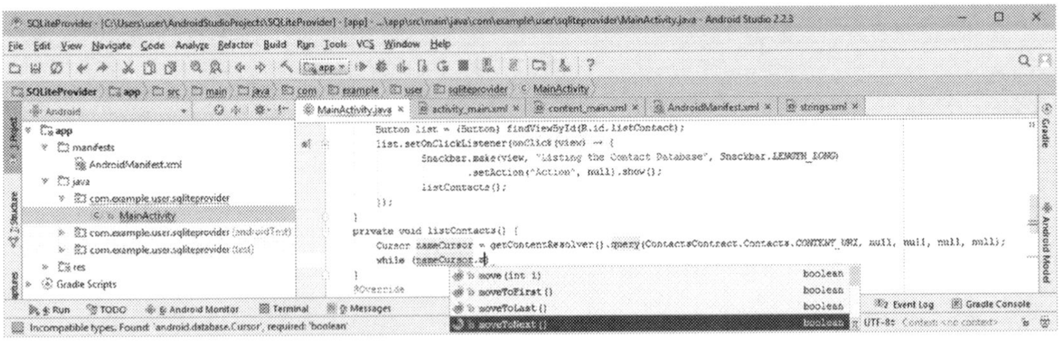

Figure 14-44. Type a period character, and then select the Boolean moveToNext( ) method from the drop-down helper menu

Inside of the while() loop, we will create a String object named contactName, and set it equal to the result of the nameCursor.getString() method call. This will load the contactName String object using the nameCursor Cursor object, which will be accessed using dot notation and the .getString() method. The getString() parameter area will contain a nested Java statement construct that will call the .getColumnIndex() method off of the nameCursor Cursor object. Inside of the .getColumnIndex() method parameter area will be your reference to the **DISPLAY_NAME_PRIMARY** constant using the ContactsContract. Contact reference path. The full Java statement we will be creating would therefore look like the following, and will be constructed using the Android Studio code helper (coding assistant) work process, shown in Figures 14-45 through 14-47:

```
String contactName =
    nameCursor.getString(nameCursor.getColumnIndex(ContactsContract.Contact.DISPLAY_NAME_
    PRIMARY));
```

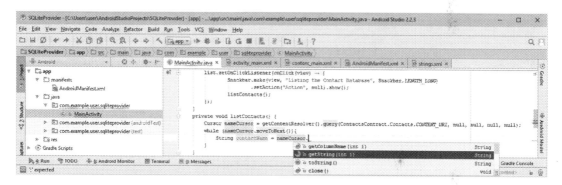

Figure 14-45. Create a String object named contactName; set it equal to the result of the nameCursor.getString(int) method

Inside the .getString() parameter area, enter the nameCursor Cursor object, and hit the period key. In the pop-up helper menu that appears, select the getColumnIndex(String s) integer method as shown in blue in Figure 14-46.

Figure 14-46. Inside the .getString( ) parameter area, enter nameCursor, and hit the period key, and select getColumnIndex( )

Inside the getColumnIndex() parameter area select the **ContactsContract.Contacts. DISPLAY_NAME_PRIMARY**.

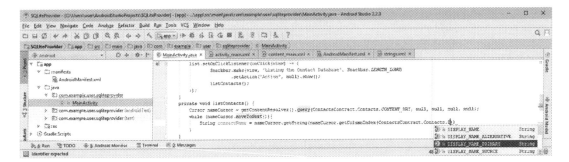

Figure 14-47. *Inside the getColumnIndex( ) parameter area select the ContactsContract.Contacts.DISPLAY_NAME_ PRIMARY*

The second statement will use the Android **Toast** class, similar to the SnackBar class, to broadcast each name as it is read to the screen. Type the letters "Toa" and select the **Toast (Create a new Toast)** option in the pop-up helper menu, as is shown in blue in Figure 14-48. This will create the entire Toast.makeToast().show() method chain, instead of a single Toast object, which you would get if you select the other Toast (android.widget) option.

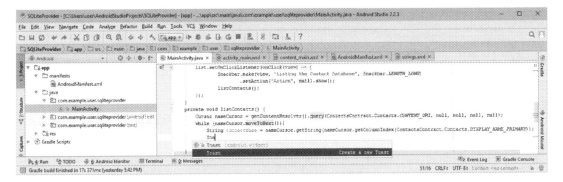

Figure 14-48. *Type the letters "Toa" and then select the Toast (Create a new Toast) option seen in the pop-up helper menu*

Once Android Studio writes the Toast Java code structure for you, as shown highlighted in Figure 14-49, you will need to add the Context object (this) as the first parameter, the String (contactName) as the second parameter, a display time length as the third parameter using the **Toast.LENGTH_SHORT** constant to the .makeText() method called off of the Toast object. Then you chain a .show() method call to the end of the .makeText() method call, to complete the complex Java statement structure. This is also shown completed, in Figure 14-50.

```
Toast.makeText(this, contactName, Toast.LENGTH_SHORT).show();
```

Figure 14-49. *The Toast messaging construct takes a Context object, a String object, and a Toast.LENGTH_SHORT constant*

If you want to research the Toast class (object) further, visit the following Android 7.1.1 developer website URL:

https://**developer.android.com**/reference/android/widget/**Toast**.html

The final code for the listContacts() method can be seen in Figure 14-50.

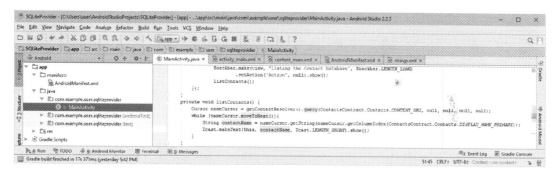

Figure 14-50. *The final Java code structure for the private void listContacts( ) method*

Next, let's take a look at how to do SQLite DBMS write operations, by using the Android ContentValues class.

Writing to a Database: Using the ContentValues Object

Now you are ready to go to the next level of database access and **write** new data values into your Contacts database.

This is more complex, as well as more advanced, because the WRITE operation can change the database, and is thus termed a **destructive** database operation in the database industry. Conversely, a database READ operation is inherently **non-destructive**, as the data is only read, and the SQLite database will not be changed.

In this section of the chapter, you are going to create another custom method for your MainActivity Activity subclass, this time to write new Star Trek officers to the Contacts database, which you are accessing here as an example of how to work with Android ContentProvider, ContentResolver and ContentValues objects.

This chapter is getting a bit long, so I am not going to include a summary of these classes here, however, if this SQLite database management is an area of interest to you, you can get the foundational information regarding these core Android SQLite database management classes by using these Android developer website URLs:

https://**developer.android.com**/reference/android/content/**ContentProvider**.html

https://**developer.android.com**/reference/android/content/**ContentResolver**.html

https://**developer.android.com**/reference/android/content/**ContentValues**.html

Just like you did in the previous section, add an **.addContact()** method call in the add Button's onClick() event handler method structure inside of your add.setOnClickListener() event listener Java code construct.

This will force Android Studio to create your bootstrap **private void** addContact() method structure for you, if you use the **Alt+Enter** keyboard shortcut, that is.

As shown in Figure 14-51, after you add the addContact(); line of Java code, you will select the "**Create method 'addContact'** option in the red exclamation point (error) drop-down in the left margin by the code statement, and then select the second MainActivity (com.example.user.sqliteprovider) class and package to specify at what level you want this method structure to be coded for you, which would be at the same level as all of the other methods which are currently coded in your MainActivity class in your SQLiteProvider application. As you'll see in Figure 14-52, Android Studio again codes your new method structure for you, right after the onCreate() method.

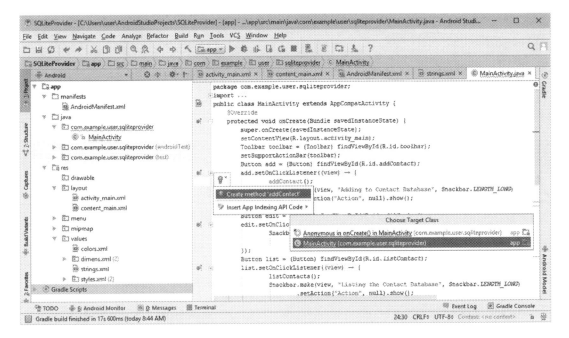

Figure 14-51. *Add an addContact( ) method call in the add Button OnClickListener( ) and have Android Studio code it for you*

In the addContact() method, declare a **ContentValues** object named **newContact**, add an equals operator, and then use the Java **new** keyword to instantiate the object, using the **ContentValues()** constructor method, as can be seen highlighted in Figure 14-52. To get rid of that red ContentValues error highlighting indicating no import statement, use the **Alt+Enter** keystroke combination to import android.content.ContentValues seen in the pop-up.

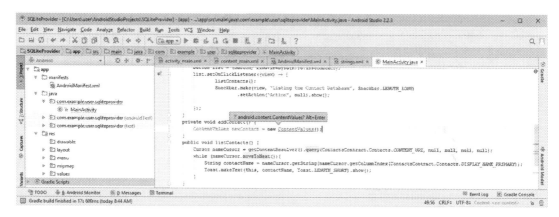

Figure 14-52. Declare a ContentValues object named newContact, instantiate it using new ContentValues( ); use Alt+Enter

Add a second line of code in the addContact() method and type the **newContact ContentValues** object and then a period character, which will open a pop-up helper where you can select the **put(String key, String value) void** option, as shown selected in blue, at the bottom of Figure 14-53. This calls a .put() method off the newContact ContentValues object, allowing you to write a data value in the ContactsContract.RawContacts database table.

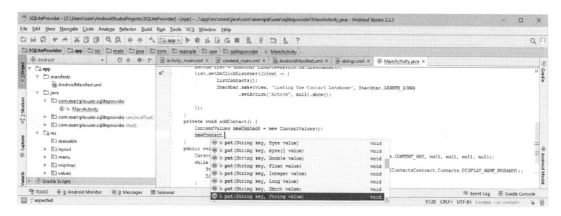

Figure 14-53. Call a void .put(String key, String value) method off of the newContact ContentValues object, to load a DBMS

For the **String key** parameter, type in the **ContactsContract.RawContacts** database table we are using, and type a period character, which will open the pop-up helper, where you can select the **ACCOUNT_NAME** data field, as is seen in Figure 14-54 highlighted in blue.

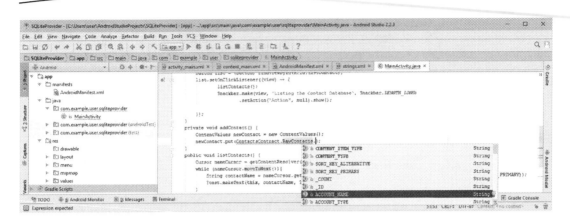

Figure 14-54. Add the ContactsContract.RawContacts database table, then hit a period and select an ACCOUNT_NAME field

Add a String object named **newName** to the addContact() method parameter list, shown highlighted in blue in Figure 14-55, and then reference this newName String object in the .put() method call's second String value parameter. This will put a new name passed into the addContact() method into the **RawContacts** database table, by referencing it inside of your newContact.put(ContactsContract.RawContacts.ACCOUNT_NAME, newName); ContentValues.put() database data loading (WRITE) Java statement, as shown highlighted in Figure 14-55.

Since you added an newName **String** parameter to the addContact method, to pass the new name into the RawContacts database table ACCOUNT_NAME data field, let's also add a new name (using quotes) into your addContact(String newName) method call, as is shown at the top of Figure 14-55 in quotes, using a green color.

I decided to use addContact("Leonard McCoy"); for my addContact() method call. Leonard McCoy was the Chief Medical Officer on the Starship Enterprise, and was commonly known as "Bones" to the crew and to Star Trek fans. Now we are ready to add some more advanced Java statements involving Uris, ContentUris, and ContentResolvers, which will populate other RawContacts data fields, and then utilize these Uri, ContentUri and ContentResolver objects to move data around between this web of database tables and data fields. You are now beginning to see why working with complex database structures is an advanced endeavor in and of itself, Java coding aside. Your understanding of the DBMS structure must be as advanced as your Java programming skills!

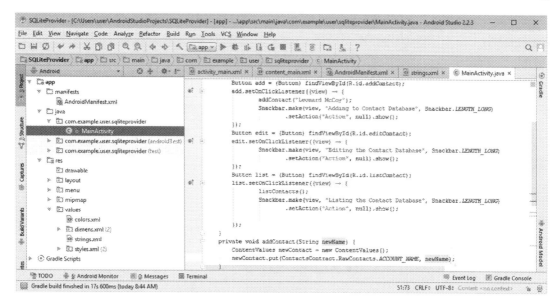

Figure 14-55. Add a newName String to .put( ) call and addContact( ) parameter String; add "Leonard McCoy" to method call

Copy the `.put()` method call that loads the `ContactsContract.RawContacts.ACCOUNT_NAME` table with the `newName String` passed into the method, and paste this underneath itself. Change **ACCOUNT_NAME** to **ACCOUNT_TYPE** in order to put the name into this data field. You could also classify your Account (Contact) Name with a classification using this field if you wanted to classify contacts in some fashion.

Next, create a **Uri** object, name it **newUri**, and load it using a **getContentResolver().insert()** method chain, as is shown in Figure 14-56, highlighted in pale yellow. Insert a `newContact` `ContentValues` object into the `ContactsContract.RawContacts` database table using the **CONTENT_URI** data field constant.

The Java statement for this insert operation should look like the following code:

```
Uri newUri = getContentResolver().insert(ContactsContract.RawContacts.CONTENT_URI, newContact);
```

Now we can use this `Uri` object to create a **ContentUri** object to write the `Contact` name date into the data table!

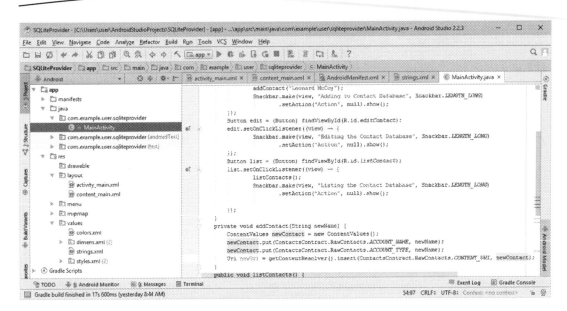

Figure 14-56. Instantiate a Uri object named newUri and then use the getContentResolver( ).insert( ) method chain to load it

What you just accomplished, in a nutshell, was to create a newContent ContentValues object to hold your content values, loading that object with your passed in newName name String data, using the .put() method calls, and loading these content values into the ContactsContract database RawContacts table by using the getContentResolver().insert() method call to place this value into the newUri Uri object. You are about to convert this Uri object data representation into a different type of (long) data value using the ContentUris class .parseId(Uri) method call. Seems like a lot of matriculation to go through to write a value to a data field, doesn't it? I can't say I disagree, but this is how this is done using Android SQLite API classes, methods, and constants.

Now that you have a URI loaded with Uri data for the ContactsContract.RawContacts. CONTENT_URI regarding the newContact ContentValues object, declare a **long** variable named **rawContactsId**, and load it with the result (using the equals evaluator) of the ContentUris class's .parseId() method call, which contains the newUri Uri object as its sole parameter.

Finally, clear the newContact ContentValues object, by calling the .clear() method off of it. This will empty all of the data that you just loaded it with in the previous (first three lines of Java) code, and will thereby clear it for its next use (during the next four lines of Java code). Your Java code should look like the following structure, which can be seen error free in Figure 14-57:

```
protected void addContact(String newName) {
    ContentValues newContact = new ContentValues();
    newContact.put(ContactsContract.RawContacts.ACCOUNT_NAME, newName);
    newContact.put(ContactsContract.RawContacts.ACCOUNT_TYPE, newName);
    Uri newUri = getContentResolver().insert(ContactsContract.RawContacts.CONTENT_URI,
    newContact);
```

```
long rawContactsId = ContentUris.parseId(newUri);
newContact.clear();
}
```

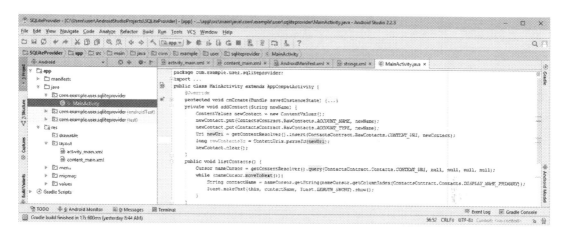

Figure 14-57. Create a long variable named rawContactsId, and set it equal to the result of ContentUris.parseId(newUri)

Next, you are going to use the **rawContactsId** long data value to put this new name data into the ContactsContract.RawContacts database Data table using the **RAW_CONTACT_ID** key (_ID) constant. You will again use the ContentValues.put() method, called off of your newContact ContentValues object, as shown in Figure 14-58. Now the rawContactsId for the new contact name you passed into the addContact() method is loaded in the ContentValues object. Next, we need to add the **MIMETYPE** into the ContentValues object as well.

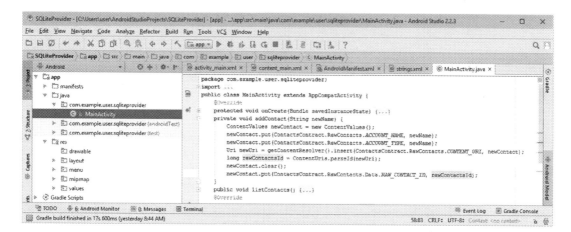

Figure 14-58. Call the .clear( ) method and then the .put( ) method off of a newContact object to clear and load it with the ID

Use another .put() method call to load the ContactsContract.RawContacts.Data.MIMETYPE data field with the ContactsContract.CommonDataKinds.StructureName.CONTENT_ITEM_TYPE MIME type, as is shown in Figure 14-59, using a pale yellow highlight. Adding these classes and constants using the Android Studio pop-up helper drop-down menus will import all of the necessary classes and packages for use with your application.

Figure 14-59. Add another .put( ) method call loading a CONTENT_ITEM_TYPE data constant into the MIMETYPE Data table

Next, you will use a third .put() method call again to place the **DISPLAY_NAME** data field information for the new contact name into the **ContactsContract.CommonDataKinds. StructureName** database tables. You select the DISPLAY_NAME constant, as shown in blue in Figure 14-60, after you type a period after the **StructuredName** table in the Android Studio pop-up helper drop-down menu selector.

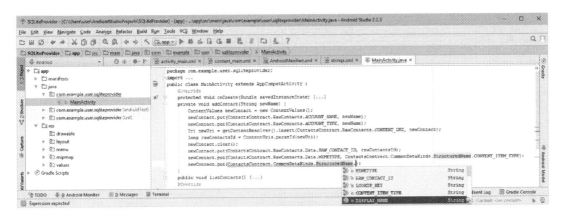

Figure 14-60. Add a .put( ) method call to write the newName String to the StructuredName.DISPLAY_NAME database field

The Java code is highlighted in Figure 14-61.

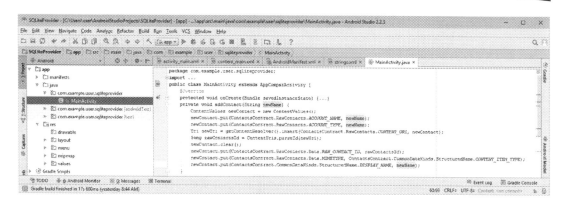

Figure 14-61. Track the newName String object usage from method parameter to three of the ContentValues.put( ) methods

Once the (same) `newContact ContentValues` object has once again been fully loaded for use, you will again use the `getContentResolver().insert()` method call chain to insert this `newContact ContentValues` object into the **ContractsContract.Data** database table using the `CONTENT_URI` data field using the following Java statement:

```
getContentResolver().insert(ContactsContract.Data.CONTENT_URI, newContact);
```

The final Java code for the entire `addContact(String newName)` method should look like the following:

```java
protected void addContact(String newName) {
   ContentValues newContact = new ContentValues();
   newContact.put(ContactsContract.RawContacts.ACCOUNT_NAME, newName);
   newContact.put(ContactsContract.RawContacts.ACCOUNT_TYPE, newName);
   Uri newUri = getContentResolver().insert(ContactsContract.RawContacts.CONTENT_URI,
   newContact);
   long rawContactsId = ContentUris.parseId(newUri);
   newContact.clear();
   newContact.put(ContactsContract.RawContacts.Data.RAW_CONTACT_ID, rawContactsId);
   newContact.put(ContactsContract.RawContacts.Data.MIMETYPE,
               ContactsContract.CommonDataKinds.StructuredName.CONTENT_ITEM_TYPE);
   newContact.put(ContactsContract.CommonDataKinds.StructuredName.DISPLAY_NAME, newName);
   getContentResolver().insert(ContactsContract.Data.CONTENT_URI, newContact);
}
```

The code is shown in Figure 14-62, error free, and is ready to test in the Nexus 5 AVD emulator. You have written a database `WRITE` method using less than a dozen lines of Java code! Congratulations!

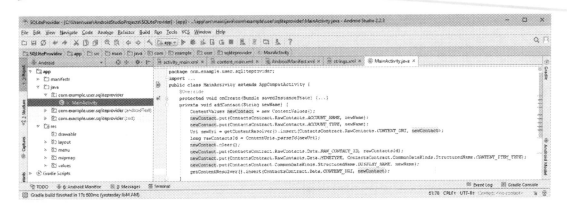

Figure 14-62. *Finalize the work process by using getContentResolver( ).insert( ) method chain to insert the new Contact name*

Now use the **Run ➤ Run 'app'** menu sequence and launch the Nexus 5 AVD and test the application.

Summary

In this chapter, you learned about Android content provider databases as well as about **database** concepts, principles, processes, and optimization. You learned about ContentProvider, ContentResolver, Uri, ContentUris and ContentValues objects, and how to use the getContentResolver(),.query(), and .insert() method calls.

You learned all about different types of databases that come with Android, including Contacts, ContactsContract, CalendarContract, and MediaStore, among others. You learned about CONTENT_URI and about what makes up a URI data path reference.

You created your own database access Activity subclass called MainActivity to read from and write to the ContactsContract database in Android. You learned about the RelativeLayout container class and how easy it is to use to make resizable layouts using just a few lines of XML markup.

You created the infrastructure for your MainActivity class and created your listContacts() database READ method and addContacts() database WRITE method. You used these methods inside of your Button object event listener and handler structures to read and write to the ContactsContract database table structures which come with the Android OS. I hope you have enjoyed your journey from Absolute Beginner to Android Developer!

Index

© Wallace Jackson 2017
W. Jackson, *Android Apps for Absolute Beginners*, DOI 10.1007/978-1-4842-2268-3

▓ C

H

I

Get the eBook for only $4.99!

Why limit yourself?

Now you can take the weightless companion with you wherever you go and access your content on your PC, phone, tablet, or reader.

Since you've purchased this print book, we are happy to offer you the eBook for just $4.99.

Convenient and fully searchable, the PDF version enables you to easily find and copy code—or perform examples by quickly toggling between instructions and applications.

To learn more, go to http://www.apress.com/us/shop/companion or contact support@apress.com.